A World History of Political Thought

To Fumie

A World History of Political Thought

J. Babb
University of Newcastle, UK

Edward Elgar
PUBLISHING

Cheltenham, UK • Northampton, MA, USA

© J. Babb 2018

Cover photograph: © J. Babb (concept) and Dean Chapman (photographer).

All rights reserved. No part of this publication may be reproduced, stored in a retrieval system or transmitted in any form or by any means, electronic, mechanical or photocopying, recording, or otherwise without the prior permission of the publisher.

Published by
Edward Elgar Publishing Limited
The Lypiatts
15 Lansdown Road
Cheltenham
Glos GL50 2JA
UK

Edward Elgar Publishing, Inc.
William Pratt House
9 Dewey Court
Northampton
Massachusetts 01060
USA

A catalogue record for this book
is available from the British Library

Library of Congress Control Number: 2017960007

Printed on elemental chlorine free (ECF)
recycled paper containing 30% Post-Consumer Waste

ISBN 978 1 78643 552 1 (cased)
ISBN 978 1 78643 554 5 (paperback)
ISBN 978 1 78643 553 8 (eBook)

Typeset by Servis Filmsetting Ltd, Stockport, Cheshire
Printed and bound in the USA

Contents

Preface	vi
1 The methodology of comparative history of political thought	1

PART I COMPARATIVE STUDIES

2 The foundational thinkers (600–400 BC)	25
3 The first "schools" of political thought (400–250 BC)	48
4 Political thought of the first empires (250 BC–200 AD)	73
5 Metaphysics, "religion" and the decline of empires (200–500)	98
6 The integration of "religion" and political thought (500–1000)	122
7 Late "medieval" political thought (1000–1300)	149
8 Renaissance and revival (1300–1540)	175

PART II THE INTERDEPENDENCE OF MODERNITIES

9 Popular religious revolt and state building (1450–1670)	203
10 Enlightenment and historicism (1670–1790)	230
11 Revolution, romanticism and reform (1760–1860)	256
12 Imperialism and liberalism (1820–1920)	284
13 Social unrest and the rise of the left (1810–1930)	310
14 Ultra-nationalism, fascism and philosophy (1880–1950)	330
15 Anti-colonialism and neo-liberalism (1920–1980)	356
16 Shifting foundations and return to origins (1980–2015)	373
Bibliography	395
Glossary of concepts	429
Glossary of names	473
Index	511

Preface

The main aim of this book is to identify the key political thinkers throughout world history. I have particularly tried to find and examine those that have had influence, substance and relevance. There is an implicit assumption in most histories of political thought that only Western political thought deserves to be given depth of treatment due to its greater value in some unspecified sense. However, there are certainly non-Western thinkers who should command more attention and Western thinkers who would benefit from being examined in world historical context. At the same time, it does not make sense if thinkers are treated as if they are all the same and of equal merit. The point is that one must make a case for the quality of any thinker and not merely base it on where and when the thinker was active.

It will also constitute a major achievement if this book can make anyone who refers to the "History of Political Thought" but only includes the West feel that they have misled their audience. That is, all histories of political thought focused on the West should be called a "History of Western Political Thought." In a similar way, book editors should be embarrassed when they commission one or two token chapters that cover aspects of the non-West when Western thought is covered in much more detail. This book demonstrates that a more balanced history of political thought can be written.

By adopting a chronological approach, it is not surprising that this book puts an emphasis on historicizing political thought to demonstrate that it cannot be easily isolated from the political context in which it is created and subsequently used. Following from this, there is a need to be sensitive to the history of the text, that is, how it was created, and subsequently adapted and interpreted. This is particularly important for early texts. Even though there is a robust literature on the Buddha's *Dialogues* and the *Analects* of Confucius, it is not uncommon for scholars to ignore the best scholarship and attribute ideas to these thinkers that they are unlikely to have held. Even later texts, such as Dong Zhongshu's *The Luxuriant Dew of the Spring and Autumn Annals* (春秋繁露), can require one confront these issues. When considering such texts, I will try to make my choices explicit in using or avoiding key sections.

This is "A" World History of Political Thought because there are many possible histories that could be written. The chapters in this book have been organized into roughly contemporaneous periods and certain themes have been teased out of the material to provide some coherence to the discussion. My main aim was to develop a vehicle to present the main thinkers and ideas in world political thought in a narrative form to tell the story of political thought as world political thought in its simplest outlines. It is important to have a narrative structure to this type of project. Many different narratives can be woven from the same raw material though not all narratives are equally valid or thought-provoking.

I hope the reader finds the way I have incorporated a wide range of material coherent enough to be useful in making sense of the variety of forms of political thought in world history. In many cases, I have been forced to rely on conventional interpretation to present a "potted" version of the political thought of most thinkers for the sake of simplicity and readability but here and there original evidence and scholarship should be apparent. Although the book can serve as a quick introduction to the thought of all the main thinkers presented, the goal is primarily to put the thinkers in global perspective and not serve as an introduction to each of the thinkers in detail. It is hoped that it will inspire others to pursue the comparisons and issues raised in more depth than was possible here.

For me personally, this is the book I would have liked to have had when I was starting to think about and teach the history of world political thought so, in many ways, this is meant to be a beginning rather than an end. Not everyone will agree with how I have presented the material in detail but it is meant to spur others to look at the potential of treating political thought as world history and not one divided into unrelated civilizations where the West is *primus inter pares*. There is already a trend in academia toward world history and comparative political thought but nothing on this scale has been attempted as far as I am aware. I know this is a ridiculously ambitious project but hopefully one that is a helpful starting point for a larger dialogue on how to study political thought in a worldwide context.

OVERVIEW OF THE BOOK STRUCTURE

The first chapter sets out the methodology used. It is fairly technical and may be skipped by anyone interested only in the history. The methodological discussion seeks to review and improve the practice of comparative political thought. It is based on my guidance to students in order to aid their writing of research papers on comparative political thought.

The main body of the book is in two parts. In the first part, the civilizations are relatively separate. There is some historical interaction between India, the Middle East and Europe, and between India and East Asia but it is usually slow and fitful. The initial discussion of world political thought begins with a relatively simple portrayal of three foundational thinkers. Then the development of the ideas of these early thinkers by their followers and opponents demonstrates the complexity of early theories of political thought everywhere. There is a lull as political ideas were stretched unreasonably to fit the demands of large empires and, then, heavy and sophisticated metaphysical apparatus were added to provide substance and legitimacy for the rulers who sought to take advantage of these political philosophies. This section devotes considerable space to so-called medieval political thought, usually skipped in histories of this kind in the West, often due to the bias of the Western Enlightenment and its more recent secularist legacy, but also because of the relative lack of political thought in the West in this period. Nonetheless, the medieval period everywhere is essential to an understanding of the basic metaphysics of political thought in the different civilizations. The influences of the metaphysical assumptions of this period still linger so must be highlighted.

In the second part, differences between the discourse of different civilizations begin to erode as thought becomes more global. Distinctions between civilizations are still important but increasingly the interpenetration of ideas means that comparison is fraught with difficulty. It becomes more of a challenge to discern what is independent similarity and what is diffusion and learning from others. The other problem is that the rise of the West economically and geo-politically inflates Western thinkers' sense of superiority and puts the rest of the world in a position where it has to defend or adapt older ideas, whether as reactionary ideology or hybrid philosophies. The West and non-West are so self-colonized with Western ideas that decolonization is difficult. Yet, there is some value in looking back at the history of political thought and reviewing how we have arrived at the point we are now. Postmodernism or post-structuralism, feminism and fundamentalism are all examined as contemporary phenomenon with historical relevance. This book omits a discussion of important theories of multiculturalism, cosmopolitanism and post-colonialism because this literature is so intimately related to the approach inherent in this book, no short review theories would suffice. Nonetheless, these approaches and all aspects of contemporary political thought are essential background for how one can read the history of political thought because interpretation depends on context.

There are two glossaries at the end of the book to provide additional background to thinkers and definitions of key concepts. It is hoped that readers will find these glossaries useful when further information is needed on the background of individuals or meaning of ideas.

Finally, the bibliography is split between primary sources, with an emphasis on English language translations, and secondary sources, to provide some academic support for the interpretations given though only a small proportion of the relevant literature could be cited.

USE OF ORIGINAL LANGUAGE SCRIPTS

The names of individuals and most place names and key concepts are given in their original language as well as in English transliteration. This is done for the sake of clarity. For some languages, the systems of transliteration into Western European alphabet varies or has changed over time. In order to make sure that the reader who knows the language can instantly recognize the individual or concept being discussed, the original language script is crucial. It is particularly important in the case of concepts so that the meaning is not taken over by the translation and the presence of the original script is an aid in making the term stand for its own set of meanings rather than the English equivalent. It is also essential because often different words have the same transliteration in English, particularly some terms in classical Chinese, and rather than use superscript numbers to identify the differences, it is better to put the terms in the original language so there is no ambiguity. For purposes of further research, variant readings and transliterations are given in the glossaries at the end of this book.

ACKNOWLEDGMENTS

I have benefited from the encouragement of and interaction with many colleagues, students and others over the time I have been working on this project. This includes but is not limited to Steven Kennedy, David Walker, Thom Brooks, Anthony Black, Rory Cox, Naomi Standen, Valentina Feklyunina, Una McGahern, Jemima Repo and Ikbal Nasreddine. Of course, none should be held responsible for any errors and omissions, which are entirely my own.

BAND-MAID surprisingly kept me sane during especially challenging periods when I was writing this book but, as always, Fumie has supported and put up with me in ways that are impossible for anyone to even begin to imagine (don't try) and it is to her that I dedicate this book.

1. The methodology of comparative history of political thought

Comparative political thought can benefit from a more methodologically informed approach. There is a growing literature on comparative political thought including its methodology, but discussion of method is still in its infancy. This chapter outlines the methodological approach that underpins this history. It is not comprehensive nor is it applied consistently but it is an attempt to lay out the type of issues raised by this type of study in a fairly thoughtful and systematic way.

First, I set out certain basic methodological principles used in this work. I note that it is usually better to compare two thinkers and though not necessarily from the same time period, in the case of this book, I have been compelled to focus on many thinkers who are roughly contemporaries based on loose periodization. The next task in comparison is to consider what it is that is comparable so a comparison can be made. This also raises issues about language, which is not uncommon in the study of the history of political thought, but this book takes language much more seriously across a number of languages. Next, I highlight the importance of metaphysics, that is, the assumptions about the way the universe works that underlie the ethical and political relationships posited by key thinkers. Metaphysics is often ignored or explained away by studies of political thinkers but it is central to understanding political thought, even in contemporary thinkers. This sets the background to this work.

The main contributions to the methodology of the comparative political thought in the rest of this chapter are fourfold. The first is to insist that once any similarities have been explored, it is essential then to point out the inevitable differences that remain because it is a mistake to leave any comparison to rest on what might be superficial similarities. The second is the attempt to steer a middle course between historicism and universalism by using the notion of a productive unresolved dialectic between historical context and universal concepts. The third is the development of the principle of charity that raises it from a mere rhetorical device to methodological tool. The final contribution is to establish criteria for validity in the assessment of texts.

At the end of the chapter, I provide a brief outline of the type of questions pursued and why it is necessary to look at certain subjects more or less consistently across the chapters in order to produce a work that is a true world history of political thought.

BASIC METHODOLOGICAL PRINCIPLES

The first methodological consideration is scope. Primarily, the focus should be on individual thinkers because it provides the most concrete basis for comparison. It is true that in many cases one must compare two or more schools of thought rather than individual thinkers within these schools. Yet, the notion of schools of thought is problematic. It is only used when there is no alternative given the need to avoid too much complexity and try to produce a concise and readable account. Largely, however, the focus is on individual thinkers.

The number of cases to be compared also requires consideration. It is best to compare only two thinkers at a time, which provides for more clarity, coherence and depth. Where it is necessary to expand the number of comparators to be more fully comprehensive, the discussion is more complex and care must be taken to make sure that clarity and coherence is not lost as a result.

If a comparison is to be made, then another key consideration is a justification of the comparison. It is easier, of course, if others have said that they are similar because then one can simply cite the relevant studies and arguments. Where there is no obvious basis for comparison in the literature then some rationale must be made for comparison of thinkers, even if it is just to contrast the two.

In each case, there is a need to select topics for comparison. Within the range of topics raised by each thinker, there will always be a few key areas that are most relevant. First of all, the focus needs to be on the ones for which the thinker is most famous as noted by others in the academic literature and more broadly if necessary. Therefore, it is necessary to summarize the overall arguments of each thinker at the start of the discussion. In many cases, the overview will seem too brief but the value of comparison is not in the depth devoted to any individual thinker's ideas alone but in comparison with others.

Where possible I have compared thinkers and systematically on the same ideas or topics whether or not these ideas are shared. For example, if one thinker is deeply religious and another is not, I tried to be sure to explore the role of religion in both because it may be that religion plays an important role in general so ignoring it in one might overemphasize it in the other. In short, it is best to compare thinkers on the same topics consistently. Nonetheless, I have tried to highlight areas which are not the most obvious and attractive aspects of the thinkers and do not ignore inconvenient ideas which do not fit easily into the narrative structures. One must confront difficult ideas or problems for any generalizations by looking at exceptions and inconsistencies.

Related to the basis of justification for the thinkers and topics compared in this book is the problem of sequence. The comparisons are between roughly contemporaneous thinkers because of the chronological nature of the narrative in this book. This is not strictly necessary and there are points at which parallels or contrasts with thinkers from disparate historical periods are appropriate. Fitting all contemporary thinkers into a narrative has been difficult to sustain at points, but it was necessary to provide some form of sequential historical periodization, however forced in some cases. Not all historical periods can be said to naturally produce similar political thought, especially in the early periods where there is little or no contact between the major civilizations. The periodization is somewhat contrived and not always satisfactory. At the same time, it often appears that similar ideas and thinkers appear in historical conditions that do bear a good deal of resemblance. At least there is enough similarity to provide a useful narrative to hold the discussion together.

One task of the comparisons is to explore whether or not there is a basis to these shared characteristics. The overarching themes of the sections and implicit in the chapters, such as "first major thinkers," "first empires," "medieval," "renaissance," "reform" are originally derived from Western historical periodization and admittedly biased to a degree as a result. A better division of historical time frames or even a historical comparison of like thinkers is definitely possible. Nonetheless, the period divisions used in this book are not far removed from local historical periodization, even if these too have been influenced by Western scholarship and thought over the years, particularly Marxism, its predecessors and challengers. To be clear, I am not suggesting that there is a common human trajectory, even in the modern era. However, the purpose of the book is to provide an overall chronological narrative and viewing similar thinkers at similar times makes the most sense. The real test of the periodization is the coherence and value of the comparisons for helping us understand political thought. For that reason, loose periodization is not a problem so long as the comparison is informative and productive.

WHAT IS IT THAT IS COMPARABLE?

One "soft" version of comparative conceptualization might be the notion of equivalences, such as that used by Anthony Parel drawing on the work of Eric Voegelin.[1] Parel provides three sets of equivalences as: "the Aristotelian *politikos*, and the Confucian *junzi*, Indian *dharma* and premodern western notions of 'natural rights', the Islamic prophet-legislator and Platonic philosopher-king." One can easily question how similar each of these sets are but more important for our purposes is that this use of the concept of equivalences appears to misread Voegelin. Voegelin argued that the search for the meaning of concepts is itself dependent on the concepts it uses to decipher concepts. The process is a self-reflective one – a theory of equivalences – in which one must be conscious of the historical and cultural position of one's own enquiry. Voegelin found in the end that there were no constants in history because history is a process of discovery that itself is relative to what was found before.[2] On this reading, the quest for equivalences is ambiguous. Parel appears to be using the concept as similar or similar enough or, more worryingly, as the specific historical or cultural manifestation of the same universal idea. This is another area where the focus on differences is important. There has to be enough similarity to make it interesting but it is the differences that will be most important. One must ask: what is left after the comparison? It does not mean that two thinkers or concepts are the same once they are stripped of all historical or cultural baggage. There can be two distinct formulations with profound differences but it does not stop one from suggesting that there is a core around which both can be compared.

This is not a relativist position. In fact, the worst types of comparisons are those that try to demonstrate how different two ideas (or societies or civilizations) are. There are going to be some basic commonalities to all political realms no matter when and no matter where. It makes no sense to focus on trivial differences or differences in style and the mode by which ideas are expressed or used. The idea of a core conception implies the potential for a universal form but also the impossibility of finding it because such a form can never be defined precisely, and how the form is manifested will vary endlessly. There are, without a doubt, ideas and dilemmas with continuing significance, thus the notion of perennial issues and ideas in political thought, but it is a mistake to believe that there can be a fixed unchanging meaning and manifestation of an idea universal to all politics. At the same time, the existence of comparable ideas or sets of ideas to compare, contrast, borrow, adapt and build upon is not absurd.

---

[1] Anthony Parel (1992) "The Comparative Study of Political Philosophy," in Anthony J. Parel and Ronald C. Keith, eds, *Comparative Political Philosophy: Studies Under the Upas Tree*, Lanham, MD: Lexington Books: 12.

[2] Eric Voegelin (1990) "Equivalences of Experience and Symbolization in History," in Ellis Sandoz, ed., *The Collected Works of Eric Voegelin, Vol. 12: Published Essays, 1966–1985*, Baton Rouge, LA: Louisiana State University Press: 115–133.

A linguistic analogy of soft conceptualization is how the same word can denote similar but different meanings. For example, one can use the concepts of pinpoint, pinned down, pinwheel, and so on which are all centered on the notion of a "pin" or small sharp object with the ability to hold something in place or denotes a degree of precision or fixation, depending again on the context. This analogy is apt because the history of political thought often turns on concepts such as the use of "*ren*" (仁) as humaneness or "*li*" (禮) as ritual in Chinese political thought or "*dharma/ dhamma*" in Indian thought or "the city" in Western and Islamic political thought, which shift meaning over time and depending on context. A good example is the notion of "liberty," which has been important historically in the West but not always in the same way,[3] and has evolved as it has become a global concept despite being articulated and developed in significantly different ways.[4]

Even if one finds a concept that seems specific to a context, it is important to look for it in the other civilization with which comparison is being made. It is not a matter of unreasonably forcing similar concepts in another society into the role played in the comparator. It is simply that the role of the concept in both the comparator and the original context are put into relief when the comparison is made. Identifying differences in the conceptualization and use can only benefit the analysis. One example is concept of ritual in East Asian thought. Ritual exists everywhere, it can be conceded, but does not have the same role theoretically or practically elsewhere. As anthropologists are apt to show, ritual has surprisingly more relevance than one might think at first even in modern societies. Important ideas have some commonality across civilization and even if one could find one that did not, then that can be interesting too.

LANGUAGE

This leads us to the role of language and its analysis, which is often regarded as central to the study of political thought[5] largely as a legacy of the Cambridge

---

[3] Quentin Skinner (1998) *Liberty before Liberalism*, Cambridge: Cambridge University Press.

[4] See, for example, Alain Roussillon (2001) "'Ce qu'ils nomment 'Liberté'. . .' Rifā'a al-Ṭahṭāwī, ou l'invention (avortée) d'une modernité politique ottoman," *Arabica*, 48(2): 143–185; and Douglas Howland (2001) "Translating Liberty in 18th Century Japan," *Journal of the History of Ideas*, 62(1): 161–181.

[5] J.G.A. Pocock (1971) *Politics, Language and Time: Essays on Political Thought and History*, Chicago, IL: University of Chicago Press; and Quentin Skinner (1969) "Meaning and Understanding in the History of Ideas," *History and Theory*, 8(1): 3–53.

School and the influence of Wittgenstein on philosophy in particular. It is inevitable that understanding a text requires understanding of the linguistic context in which the original text was produced, though this does not exhaust the issues related to language. Even attacks on linguistic contextualism largely accept the validity of the practice even if the argument is that emphasis should be placed as well on other sources of possible meaning.[6]

In comparative political thought the key problem is that of translation. Few can master two or more languages to a degree that allows them to compare across civilizations effortlessly. Even then the logic of comparison based on subtle judgments of meaning has to be explained and justified. In the case of a project involving multiple ancient languages or the entire scope of the world history of political thought, reliance on translation is inevitable. This problem can be addressed to a large degree by "triangulation." Triangulation in this context is the method by which the reading of two or more translations of the same work enables one to check the robustness of meaning. Special care is needed when analysis hinges on a key word or phrase. Many key terms have complex meaning which cannot be captured in a simple direct translation so one must ensure the discussion of key concepts and terms is treated with nuance and reflects the ambiguity and multiplicity of possible meanings. In this book, I have attempted to go back to the original source in the original language where possible, though, for the convenience of readers, English language translations are usually cited (or the nearest Western language equivalent).

The main problem with lack of knowledge of the original language of a text is not an inability to translate accurately. It is more that the hermeneutic possibilities inherent in the text are often better understood in the original or at least by someone with wider experience of the language and the possibilities of the language, particularly as language was used in the society of the time in which the text was written. In any case, it helps to have some understanding of the nature of the language being used. For example, classical Chinese possesses both "lexical ambiguity" and "optional precision" which makes it difficult to interpret precisely in every case. "Lexical ambiguity" occurs for a variety of reasons but includes the situation in which some Chinese characters can be forced to be read as others because they are a homonym of a word but have a different original meaning in order to avoid repeating the same word over again. However, this leads to vagueness and works against semantic precision.[7] It is "optional precision" because Classical

---

[6] Mark Bevir (1992) "The Errors of Linguistic Contextualism," *History and Theory*, 31(3): 278.
[7] Archie Barnes, Don Starr, and Graham Ormerod (2009) *Du's Handbook of Classical Chinese Grammar*, London: Alcuin Press: iii.

Chinese often does not provide the key information on case, number, gender and other grammatical fixtures that can constrain the meaning of sentences in other languages.[8] It may not be so much that this economy of style caused few problems to contemporary readers[9] as much as it enabled the text to set fire to the imagination, increased its appeal and was only constrained by subsequent interpretation by schools of thought or "tradition."

Some works of political thought are ambiguous and that may be why they are considered great. The great works of literature tend to be open to a reading that speaks to the widest possible audience or at least a broad audience of the educated.[10] It might be too much to argue that such works are intentionally vague but certainly many works of political thought are open to interpretation and this is why they appeal to different groups. As Stanley Rosen has put it "no text worth reading wears its meaning on its sleeve."[11]

A final problem with the use of language is that some thinkers may intentionally not say what they mean. Some engage in irony so that they may mean something different and even opposite to what they appear to be saying. In a conversation we can pick up clues when a person is being sarcastic or ironic but in texts in another language or in a completely different historical context, it may not be clear. Another possibility is a hidden core meaning behind the idea or ideas. For example, the text might hide an esoteric meaning which is only obvious to those who understand its deeper structure and implications. Leo Strauss is associated with this type of approach[12] but there are also more recent proponents.[13] Strauss has been critiqued, most notably by Drury[14] as hiding his own esoteric political agenda in his revelation of esoteric meaning in ancient political thinkers. Others are not so sure that there is a clear agenda in Strauss.[15] Therefore even in this case of a scholar who explicitly recognized esoteric meaning and its interpretation, there is no consensus on what was meant and this shows the difficulties of determining if and when one should look for hidden agendas.

---

[8] Barnes et al. (2009) *Du's Handbook of Classical Chinese Grammar*: xv.
[9] Barnes et al. (2009) *Du's Handbook of Classical Chinese Grammar*: vi–v.
[10] Jonathan Bates (2008) *The Genius of Shakespeare*, London: Picador.
[11] Stanley Rosen (2003) *Hermeneutics as Politics*, 2nd edn. New Haven: Yale University Press: 142.
[12] Leo Strauss (1952) *Persecution and the Art of Writing*, New York: The Free Press.
[13] Arthur M. Melzer (2014) *Philosophy Between the Lines: The Lost History of Esoteric Writing*, Chicago, IL: University of Chicago Press.
[14] Shadia B. Drury (1985) "The Esoteric Philosophy of Leo Strauss," *Political Theory*, 13(3): 315–37.
[15] Michael Frazer (2006) "Esotericism Ancient and Modern Strauss versus Straussianism on Political-Philosophical Writing," *Political Theory*, 34(1): 33–61.

Even so, there are understandable reasons why a thinker might not set forth his or her views in a forthright manner. It might be that the thinker is trying to explain ideas to an audience which needs to be addressed in a specific way. The true intention of the author is masked by the need to communicate more effectively or cautiously. Ideas that are controversial might be masked through an argument that appears non-threatening to existing sensitivities but conceals a deeper position which challenges conventional assumptions. The notion usually takes the form that the thinker is rational but must hide their true views by reference to traditional myths and forms of piety. There is a general consensus that the medieval Muslim philosopher al-Farabi, for example, may have written his works with this concern in mind though it is also possible that he wanted to compel his readers to think for themselves and reach their own conclusions, which is another reason why an author might leave a text open to interpretation.[16]

Good translations and multiple translations with many footnotes to tease out the nuances of meaning of words and phrases can enable the reader to make a judgment about the possible meanings of a text but it is not a complete substitute for having a direct grasp of the text in the original language. Key passages can be ambiguous or have complex implications. Often translation involves simplification or adding material that at best is implicit but is added to make sense of a passage in a different language. If we rely on the translator to make decisions about what a text means in these cases, then we miss an opportunity to think for ourselves. It is such ideas and sections of text that must be the focus of our hermeneutic resources in translation or not.

METAPHYSICS

For a history of political thought, it is essential to raise those aspects of thought that are relevant to politics, broadly conceived. Politics in the narrowest sense of the term is the nature of rulers and the ruled. That is, who controls power to make major decisions with an impact on society and how those in a society relate to those with power. In doing so, it is often necessary to look at the underlying metaphysics, logic of ideas and ethics in order to enhance understanding of the political ideas of the various thinkers. Often metaphysics or logic explains or has implications for ethical or moral values which are expressed in human relationships at the basis

---

[16] Charles E. Butterworth and Thomas L. Pangle, "Foreword," in Al-Farabi; Muhsin Mahdi trans. (2001) *Alfarabi: The Philosophy of Plato and Aristotle*, revised edn. Ithaca, NY: Cornell University Press: ix–xii.

of politics. This includes the logic and ethics of being a ruler, subject or citizen. The sequence of links is as follows:

metaphysics and its logic→ethics/morals→human relations→politics

Highlighting the role of metaphysics might be contentious but comparative political thought cannot avoid discussing it. Metaphysics is simply that which cannot be explained by conventional empirical science. It is implicit in ethical and political ideas so we can best compare when we make it explicit. In doing so, one will notice differences in how societies approach the world. For example, one could make the crude generalization that Western thought is based on the notion of monism and being, whereas Eastern thought is traditionally focused on plurality and emptiness or nothingness. That is, Western thought seems to try to create logical systems that result in a single truth or being that resolves all contradiction but Eastern thought is often more dialectical, violating the notion of the "excluded middle" central to Western logic, to explore unresolvable but productive contradictions and paradoxes. This difference has been used to dismiss non-Western approaches as mysticism, which is seen as bad, but in fact there is simply a difference in approach. The real problem is that metaphysics is often hidden in modern Western thought in order to bolster its scientific credentials and to provide a contrast to the more "traditional" and "exotic" non-Western forms of thought with more explicit metaphysical underpinnings. This book will attempt to highlight metaphysics, including that in the West and in modern times, and point out the value of understanding the role of metaphysics in political thought regardless of its origins.

There are three basic metaphysical threads running through this book. One is neo-Platonism, which emerges in Antiquity, runs through the late middle ages and still has an influence today, not just in Christian and Islamic thought but also in secularized thinking in the societies in which these religions have been historically important. The second is Taoism, or more precisely, the development of Taoist philosophy by the Literati who are commonly referred to as Confucians. These ideas have been influential in East Asia and continue to linger today. The third is Indian metaphysics that starts with the *Upanisads* but also includes Buddhism as well as what is called Hindu thought. This has an influence not just in South Asia, including Southeast Asia, but also through Buddhism in East Asia (where it was sometimes combined with Taoism), and may have possibly influenced neo-Platonism as well. These traditions are important and necessary to any understanding of the history of world political thought.

The problem is that metaphysics is often mixed up with the concept of religion, which is very difficult to define in a historical sense, as we will see. I argue in this book that the modern separation of religion and political philosophy is a barrier to understanding the history of political thought, not just in the non-West but in the West as well. It is easy to point to "religion" in a modern sense when it appears in the past and in other societies, but views on what is religion are bound up with modern Western thought, explicitly and implicitly. By focusing on metaphysics I try to finesse the issue to some degree, but I often have to insist that the role of what appears to modern sensibilities to be religion in political thought is legitimate and perhaps inescapable. It is also very much related to ethics. It is possible to be ethical without being religious but the source of non-religious ethics is just as grounded in metaphysics as religious ethics, god, gods or no god.

IMPORTANCE OF DIFFERENCES WITHIN SIMILARITIES

I have tried to explore the clearest or most obvious or most noted similarities and differences between thinkers or schools of thought first. At the same time, I have tried not to allow myself to be satisfied with superficial similarities. Often the differences even in the most similar thinkers are most revealing of the nature of their thought. Initially one should make as strong a case for similarities as one can but then one must acknowledge the points on which they are different and consider why that is the case. This is the principle of *differences within similarities* which is crucial to good comparison. One should challenge similarities by pointing out the remaining differences until there are no unchallenged similarities left. Challenging apparent similarities is methodologically more significant because "negative evaluation is intrinsically more instructive than positive valuation because the justification of a negative evaluation automatically involves a contrast that the justification of the positive does not. . ."[17] It provides additional evidence of the relationship between two arguments that brings them into sharper focus. Similarity is often too flexible to ground the formation of meaningful categories and it is only a common theory or context that can provide the basis for categorization, not similarity alone.[18] Humans tend to see similarity even when it is weak or even non-existent because we use superficial similarity or analogical reasoning

---

[17] Maurice A. Finocchiaro (1981) "Fallacies and the Evaluation of Reasoning," *American Philosophical Quarterly*, 18(1): 17.
[18] Robert L. Goldstone (1994) "The Role of Similarity in Categorization," *Cognition*, 52(2): 125–157.

when processing information.[19] Given appropriate guidance, however, it is possible to identify structural similarity by focusing on underlying relations between elements of the things being compared.[20] This suggests that we must look deeper to understand the extent of any similarity and the nature of the differences is crucial to doing that.

The comparative politics literature contains hints for how similarities might be conceptualized in comparative political thought.[21] Anyone who examines political thought comparatively can sympathize with Sartori's critique of conceptual stretching, which, he notes, is also "conceptual straining."[22] The symptoms of this problem include vague and amorphous conceptualizations, that is, concepts without clear definitions and the attempt to make concepts value free, or more accurately, "universal." He particularly notes that studies of non-Western political systems have forced comparative politics specialists to use concepts drawn from the West to analyze politics outside the West which he implies may not be valid. He was concerned that by stretching concepts scholars were taking the easy path but one in which "gains in extensional coverage tend to be matched by losses in connotative precision."[23] One advantage that comparative thought has over comparative politics is the systems of thought have an internal logic which can be used to tease out meanings and provide a contrast to similar concepts in other civilizations. There is no assumption of a universal rule-bound social science that drives political processes in political thought as there has tended to be in comparative politics, at least at the time Sartori was writing.

Even so there may be some value in considering comparative politics research strategies such as those proposed by Collier and Mahon,[24] including the notion of family resemblance, radial categories, and even the Weberian "ideal type." One must proceed cautiously, however. Family resemblance makes sense only if there is a set of shared characteristics but in the case of civilizations not in contact with one another then the

---

[19] Brian H. Ross (1989) "Distinguishing Types of Superficial Similarities," *Journal of Experimental Psychology: Learning, Memory, and Cognition*, 15(3): 456–468.
[20] I. Blanchette and K. Dunbar (2000) "How Analogies are Generated: The Roles of Structural versus Superficial Similarity," *Memory and Cognition*, 28(1): 108–124.
[21] Sara Jordan and Cary J. Nederman (2004) "Between Sartori and Skinner: Methodological Problems in the Study of Comparative Political Thought," Annual Meeting of the American Political Science Association (APSA), Chicago, IL.
[22] Giovanni Sartori (1970) "Concept Misformation in Comparative Politics," *American Political Science Review*, 64(4): 1034.
[23] Sartori (1970) "Concept Misformation in Comparative Politics": 1034.
[24] David Collier and James E. Mahon, Jr. (1993) "Conceptual Stretching Revisited: Adapting Categories in Comparative Analysis," *The American Political Science Review*, 87(4): 845–855.

assumption might be misleading. Shared characteristics might be more useful in the case of diffusion and adaptation of ideas in different contexts. Radial categories assume a certain universal core upon which the category can be developed and a pure universalistic approach may not be appropriate if it assumes fixed starting points. Weberian ideal types also hold similar problems especially when the types are drawn from a theory that effectively denigrates certain types of thought, for example, viewing religion or rationality on an evolutionary scale, which will make some systems of thought seem less developed and therefore less worthy of consideration than others. Nonetheless, it makes sense to articulate and apply clearly defined concepts and extend them appropriately in order to distinguish between the meanings of a concept in any given situation.

One solution to the problem of assessing the nature and extent of similarity can be to develop a rationale for why two thinkers appear to be similar (a theory) and provide evidence that there is a similarity for the reasons posited. However, one must take care because premature theorization can also be a block to enhanced understanding.[25] At the same time, if we are going to meaningfully compare or tease out similarities then there has to be a rationale for doing so. The more robust the rationale, the more theoretically sophisticated the comparison is likely to be.

This task is aided when thinkers are compared on each topic or concept one by one rather than looking at each thinker as a whole separately. It is better to compare in fine grain point by point to tease out the similarities as well as the crucial differences. Doing a comparison of thinkers or schools of thought as a totality in discretely separate analysis tends to lack nuance and detailed engagement with the ideas being compared. It is too easy to finesse the argument when it is in broad brush strokes in two distinct blocks of discussion. In contrast, differences more clearly emerge at the level of finer conceptual and logical granularity when comparing specific ideas or approaches. For example, two thinkers may advocate "nature" as a guide to political praxis but it depends on how nature is defined and can or should be made relevant to politics. Only by comparing thinkers on the micro-level will we have deeper understanding of what each thinker meant. Every effort should be made to highlight the similarities to other thinkers and the differences within those apparent similarities at the finest grain level of analysis possible.

In this book, however, it has only been possible to provide this interwo-

---

[25] Albert O. Hirschman (1970) "The Search for Paradigms as a Hindrance to Understanding," *World Politics*, 22(3): 329–343, and though Hirschman may be misusing the concept of a paradigm, his point regarding the dangers of premature theorization, particularly in a cross-cultural context, is in general still correct.

ven, fine grain analysis in only a few places. There are practical reasons for not doing so consistently in an overview of this type. Most importantly, it would be a much longer book if the comparisons were carried out in more detail than present throughout the entire work. In addition, my aim is to be more suggestive of the potential for comparison for others than to do all the comparison work in detail. This is partly because this book is meant to help others see the scope of possible comparison and broader brush strokes are better for this task. There is also the danger that any comparisons made in detail will suggest that the comparison between two thinkers is exhaustive when in reality it is possible to compare thinkers in many different ways, even on the points raised here. I hope that the few places in which two thinkers' concepts are contrasted on finer points of difference provide some insight into how such comparison can be best conducted.

HISTORICISM AND UNIVERSALISM

This project is explicitly historicist but it is crucial to define what that means in any given situation. The simplest aspect of historical impact is context, that is, the range of historical possibilities and the nature of events and ideas that existed at the time. Obviously historical context does matter but one must explain why. All historical conditions are unique but that does not mean that they cannot be compared. One needs to make a case for or against comparability. It is not a given or impossible in any case.

One must make an effort to avoid anachronism. One must ask what did it mean then? It may require a conscious steer away from what it can mean now. At the same time current usage and meaning (significance) can be useful as a contrast and for making the ideas accessible. Certainly the relevance or possible relevance of any ideas for contemporary readers can have a great heuristic value, which will enhance understanding and engagement with the ideas.

One must take care to avoid universalism, that is, the view that there is only one meaning and purpose to similar ideas everywhere based on a shared universal basis to politics. Yet, we should also reject relativism: the view that thinkers and ideas cannot be compared at all because every context is different. The only case I can make for this middle way between universalism and relativism is the notion of an *irresolvable dialectic* where the tension between two opposing ideas are left in free play, that is, without resolution in conclusion or synthesis. It is better to allow two similar but still distinctly different concepts to stand in constructive opposition to one another rather than try to dissolve the differences by positing a universalistic core incorporating both. As noted above, dialectic methodology is underrated in Western thought if perhaps overrated in Eastern thought. It is useful, however, in circumstances where there is no easy single answer and the tension between two principles produces interesting results.

Universalistic categories such as pre-modern, early modern and modern imply progression and development in a way that is unhelpful. This is true when modernity is seen as a special case. For this reason, supposed alternatives such as "multiple modernities,"[26] "axial age,"[27] and "new axial age"[28] are more of a hindrance than an aid to the process of reading political thought comparatively.[29] In particular the notion of modernity tends to trivialize non-Western, classical or "medieval" ideas, because they are deemed traditional (so not modern) by definition. One must consciously confront the ideological and temporal limitations of such periodization. Even when the notion of ancient or medieval thought is used in this book, it is introduced explicitly and critically. As noted above, the terms ancient or medieval are used in their loosest senses because the term will not cover an exact replica of the periodization from one civilization to another.

There is a sense in which a degree of universality is necessary to comparative political thought. If there is no basis for understanding across civilizations, then the whole enterprise is pointless. Yet, there is an argument that it is not possible for someone from one tradition to comprehend another that is substantially different, an approach often associated with Richard Rorty. This is a radically historicist approach, based on the idea that philosophy itself is highly contingent and based on circumstances peculiar to the West.[30] Rorty seems to insist that any comparison is so deeply situated in its own culturally bound conceptual scheme that any attempt at comparison can be neither useful nor neutral. He seems particularly dismissive of the content of non-Western thought when he rejects Davidson's approach to understanding language that all humans hold true beliefs about those same things[31] by saying that Davidson's argument holds only for whole natural languages, not for "specialized jargons,"[32] which

---

[26] Shmuel N. Eisenstadt (2000) "Multiple Modernities," *Daedalus*, 129(1): 1–29.

[27] Karl Jaspers (1953) *The Origin and Goal of History*, New Haven, NJ: Yale University Press, and Robert Bellah and Hans Joas (2012) *The Axial Age and Its Consequences*, Cambridge, MA: Harvard University Press.

[28] Yves Lambert (1999) "Religion in Modernity as a New Axial Age: Secularization or New Religious Forms?" *Sociology of Religion*, 60(3): 303–333.

[29] Anthony Black (2008) "The 'Axial Age': What was it and what does it signify," *The Review of Politics*, 70(1): 23–39.

[30] Richard Rorty (1989) "Review of Larson and Deutsch (1988) Interpreting Across Boundaries New Essays in Comparative Philosophy," *Philosophy East and West*, 39(3): 334.

[31] Donald Davidson (2001) "On the Very Idea of a Conceptual Scheme," in *Inquiries into Truth and Interpretation*, Oxford: Oxford University Press: 183–198.

[32] Richard Rorty (1989) "Review of Larson and Deutsch": 336.

presumably prohibits access to the meaningful content of non-Western thought. James Tartaglia points out that this is not consistent with Rorty's overall orientation, which is more open-minded as accepting of dialogue and suggests that he was forced to take this position because the possibility of comparative political thought undermines his argument that philosophy is culturally specific and thus Rorty's pragmatism.[33]

Rorty's argument, however, does imply that the attempt of comparison, especially by Western thinkers in their current position of dominance, can do damage if one insists that another society compare its practices and ideas to that of another. It is true that one needs to look at who benefits (theoretically and empirically) from the approach to the interpretation taken and whether or not conceptual schema or even specific ideas can be used at the expense of others. The argument is that a single universal morality is detrimental to some. It is true that moral imperatives have their opposites: happiness is often seen to be a goal of good politics but one can argue that suffering is sometimes necessary and even helpful; altruism and selflessness are often praised but self-interest often seems a more efficient and effective motivator; equality is held by most moderns to be preferable but inequality is empirical fact and needs to be taken into account; Nietzsche has argued that pity and compassion can be used to keep others in a position of weakness; and modern Western respect for individuals can come into conflict with the needs and goals of the larger community. One might even argue that all standards of morality and political practice are against nature and distort humans (this is the Taoist argument as we will see). However, this would be true within civilizations as well as between them. All one can do is try to make sense of as many different approaches to politics and related ethical arguments to examine the range of possibilities and make one's own choices. Consideration of the broad spectrum of world political thought is the best way to do this.

THE PRINCIPLE OF CHARITY AND REFLEXIVITY

Perhaps the most important methodological consideration in comparative political thought is the principle of charity. For the most part the effort here is to attempt to reconstruct the possible meaning of the texts of each thinker. Once we have accepted that reconstruction is valid or at least plausible, we must then consider the motivations for reconstruction. This could focus on a scholarly search for truth but we must heed Gadamer's warning

---

[33] James Tartaglia (2014) "Rorty's Thesis of the Cultural Specificity of Philosophy," *Philosophy East and West*, 64(4): 1017–1038.

that we can never entirely succeed in reconstructing historical texts: "They remain fruit torn from the tree. Putting them back in their historical context does not give us a living relationship with them."[34] Instead, he urges us to be aware of what we want the text to do for us: "...the essential nature of the historical spirit consists not in restoration of the past but in thoughtful mediation with contemporary life."[35] In theory the principle of charity can be both integration (that is, how do I make sense of this thinker for myself or my audience) and reconstruction (that is, what is possible that this originally meant). This means we can define *integrative charity* as trying to making sense of the ideas of others for one's own purposes but also making the best case for these ideas in doing so. We can similarly define *reconstructive charity* as making sense of ideas using the available evidence of the intentions of the author and the influences of the times in which a text was written to formulate an interpretation. It cannot entirely escape integrative charity. For example, a logical/rational reconstruction might contradict a spiritual reconstruction. That is, if you believe that the thinker is a rational thinker and dismiss miracles as myth then one reconstruction is possible but if you think that miracles are possible, then another completely different reconstruction is possible. It depends what one is seeking to get out of the text.

It is in this situation that reflexivity is crucial. We must try to be conscious of the "baggage" or prejudgments we bring to the reading of a text. This includes one's own temporal situation (historical), cultural background (American, British, Christian, atheist, and so on) and theoretical approaches taken (virtue ethics, Marxian, Hegelian, and so on).[36] Modern readers can often misunderstand because they read texts anachronistically based on modern norms and beliefs. By acknowledging potential prejudices, we can understand possible obstacles to understanding a text.

Religion is a real problem in this study of this kind, particularly when religion is viewed anachronistically. Moderns and academics tend to be skeptical of religion. The separation of religion and secular life is a deeply ingrained notion in the West, especially in academic circles, and to a degree in all modern societies (including modern enclaves in what are called "traditional" societies). It is not just the problem of whether political thought and so-called religion should or can be separated because it is questionable in many historical periods and societies whether the two should or can for

---

[34] Hans-Georg Gadamer (1989) *Truth and Method*, 2nd edn. London: Sheed and Ward: 168.
[35] Gadamer (1989), *Truth and Method*, 2nd edn: 169.
[36] P. Bourdieu and L.J.D. Wacquant, eds (1992) *An Invitation to Reflexive Sociology*, Cambridge: Polity Press.

the purposes of analysis. Yet, modern approaches to the role of religion are based on the assumption that religion, on the one hand, and secular matters, such as political power, on the other, should be separate. In this context, non-rational and un-scientific ideas are difficult to take seriously. However, everyone has non-rational and un-scientific ideas – even the most modern of us. Again this is an area where an applied understanding of metaphysics is essential. An effort is required to understand why someone, including very intelligent individuals, would believe in ideas with which one might not agree. One should certainly not deal with the problem by means of pathology, that is, analysis based on search for causes that assumes deficiencies such as ignorance or delusion that might explain why others hold what might appear to be non-rational and un-scientific beliefs. A strong and valid case must be made for any form of thought in order to understand it. One has to believe in an argument to a degree, even just temporarily, in order to critique from inside and outside.

A similar problem occurs with the inclusion of what is usually considered "ideology" as though some approaches to political thought such as Marxism or anarchism are somehow distinctly of less worth than "standard" thinkers and texts such as Thomas Hobbes and the *Leviathan* or John Stuart Mill and *On Liberty*. The distinction between "political philosophy," which is based more on modern academic philosophical analysis, and "political thought" is ignored here as well because modern academic philosophical analysis can and must be historicized and seen as a form of political thought as well in order to be understood comparatively.

This means that another aspect of the principle of charity is to accept that there is going to be a diverse genre of works with which one must engage. Often non-Western political thought is not considered political thought at all. Buddhist sutras are a case in point. However, if you look at the range of genre, non-Western political texts are roughly similar to Western ones: advice for rulers, history, literature, theology, ethics, pamphlets, cosmology, ontology, epistemology, epics, and so on. In the West as well there are many cases where non-academic thought is considered to be part of the canon of political thought so do not dismiss the other of other civilizations because it does not seem like political thought as you know it (such as being too religious, for example, or a work of fiction, as in Homer's *Iliad*, More's *Utopia* or Rousseau's *Emile*, and so on). Many thinkers need to be taken more seriously, especially those who do not seem obviously "political" but are given the context in which they were read (here I am thinking of early Taoism, the works of Zhu Xi, and so on).

In the end, the principle of charity simply means that one must give each thinker the benefit of the doubt. Make the best case you can for their ideas, explaining or resolving any problems or contradictions rather than criticizing them for it. However, do not be fooled into thinking that charity does not permit critical analysis. In fact, it is only by comparing the charitable interpretation with existing and potential critical interpretations that the thought will be most thoroughly understood.

Any critique of the ideas of past thinkers must be based on both the evidence and reflexive sensitivity. For example, one must be particularly wary of rejecting the views of thinkers because certain views are unacceptable now but could be seen as valid in another place and another time. Even within the Western tradition, Plato and Aristotle are usually not entirely rejected because they accepted the legitimacy of slavery, nor can one completely dismiss Locke because he preached tolerance but excluded atheists. It does not mean we need to completely forgive thinkers of the past for ideas that are offensive today but it is also true that thinkers need not be held to contemporary standards to the extent we dismiss what is of potential value. In most of these cases, it is more important to consider whether the system of thought being proposed inherently leads to problematic outcomes or can be salvaged based on the overall positive contribution that potentially flows from the ideas put forward even if some ideas need to be omitted or reinterpreted.

The book also seeks to give life back to many of the ideas discussed by authors in different times and traditions. In contemporary political thought there is a tendency to create and analyze abstract concepts as ethics, democracy, authority, and so on as generic entities shorn of their original context or historical development. Even when they are discussed in historical context they are treated as quaint antique artifacts with little relevance for those living today. By bringing these thinkers and ideas back to life, and saving them from neutralization as mere conceptual background, there is hope that they can be made relevant to the world today. A "Confucian" view of the world can contribute much to understanding the role of ritual for example in modern politics. Buddhist political ethics can and has made a major contribution to environmental political thought. Differences in how law, power, deception, loyalty, belonging, and other concepts that arise again and again in the history of political thought have continuing importance today.

VALIDITY ISSUES

Validity as a methodological issue is normally defined as trying to ensure that a concept or measurement of a concept corresponds sufficiently to the phenomena that one is studying. Validity is determined by the strength or ability of the concept to cover the cases it argues can be covered by the concept.

Case selection is the first and perhaps most important aspect of validity in textual analysis. Case selection is relevant when we argue that a thinker holds a particular set of views, fits with a specific school of thought, is potentially the key figure or exemplar of a school, and most crucially when a text or passage in a text is seen as meaningful or representative of a specific view or set of views. In some cases, the categorization of the thinker into one school or another needs to be problematized and the nature of concepts being used must be distinguished from the modern English language meaning of the term. In these cases, the use of the original language is a necessity and not pretentious.

One might also make a distinction between what I call internal and external validity, though I apply it in a different way than used in other fields of inquiry. Internal validity is centered on the text. What does the thinker actually say? There is often a gap between what the secondary literature says a thinker says and what is actually written in the texts. It would be too tedious to add long quotations from original text but they are the basis for any statements and are clearly cited in this history so the reader can check the text against my reading. There is also the larger issue of viewing specific passages and ideas in the larger context of the entire work or body of work of the thinker. This requires a close and accurate reading, not just of particular passages but of the parts of the text in relation to the whole work or the entire oeuvre of the author. This often requires one to identify textual issues. One must assess accurately if the passage or text conveys the ideas of the person being studied. Often there are later accretions of interpretation that require a text to be "unpacked" and reordered.

External validity focuses on how the text and one's interpretation of the text relate to the world, both of the author and history in general. How is it relevant? Is it relevant in the ways that the author and his interpreters, then and now, appear to have intended? In the first instance it revives a role for conventional hermeneutics based on the evidence of historical circumstances. It also means that information relating to the author is important to provide context. However, this should not be entirely the focus of the study. It is discussed only if it enhances substantially understanding of the nature of the arguments made. The idea that the intention of the author is the sole arbiter of the correct meaning of the text is wrong and impossible to determine in most cases anyway. It is true that evidence drawn from the writings and history of the author and contemporaries (friendly and hostile) can enhance our understanding of the text. At the same time, it is crucial to understand what it can mean in other political contexts, including to readers today. What is the enduring appeal of the ideas that mean that they have been preserved, transmitted and seen as valuable over time, including today?

THE KEY QUESTIONS AND TOPICS

The key questions I always had in my mind when writing were: What was written of importance by these thinkers and why is it important? What are the similarities and differences between the thinkers and others who seem similar? Are they really similar and how are they different even if some similarity can be plausibly attributed? What is the basis of the similarities and differences? Finally, what contribution do they make to our understanding of political thought in general?

The general pattern of the chapters is to look at the historical context briefly, then to consider the main approaches in the period and the tendencies underlying each one. There is always a focus on metaphysics and cosmology, which is crucial, as argued above, and this is often part of a larger discussion of the role of ethical and religious systems in political thought. The chapters tend to conclude with a consideration of views of thinkers and systems of thought regarding what can be called issues of equality but are essentially how the average person and particularly women as a whole are treated. The treatment of the "masses" and women reveals much about the underlying metaphysics and ethics of a system of political thought.

The decline of teaching of the history of political thought in the past few decades is in part due to the criticism that it only focuses on "dead, old, white men." A world historic view deals with the problem of only focusing on "white" thinkers (whatever that is supposed to mean). The thinkers in this book are still mainly dead (though not all) but that is inevitable with most history. However, it became clear that a focus on the role of women in the history of political thought was essential. First of all, the role and status of women as viewed by major political thinkers reveals much about different systems of thought. There was also the problem of the fact that most thinkers were addressing a male audience. While there is no attempt in this book to anachronistically make the thinkers gender neutral, where ideas are potentially applicable to all humans, then it is fair to point this out. At the same time, views on women, both positive and negative, are clearly set out. This focus on women is not an exercise in tokenism because, as the reader will see, women play a key role in the history of political thought, not just as crucial subject matter for male thinkers but also as important contributors in their own right, which is even more obvious if one looks globally.

Overall the range of thinkers and topics covered should present the reader with a good understanding of the basic outlines of the world history of political thought. It is not perfect but it should be a good start.

PART I

Comparative studies

2. The foundational thinkers (600–400 BC)

There are three foundational thinkers in political thought: Gautama Siddhārtha (सिद्धार्थ गौतम), Confucius (*Kongzi* 孔子) and Socrates (Σωκράτης).[1] It is striking that these three thinkers were roughly contemporaneous. Gautama, who was later called the Buddha (बुद्ध), lived approximately 563–483 BC with the possibility that he died closer to 400 BC so was born around 480 BC (exact dating is not really a major issue in this context though a later date would make him a contemporary of both Confucius and Socrates). Confucius is generally agreed to have been alive 551–449 BC, and Socrates, the latest and best attested of the three, lived between 469–399 BC. All three lived to a relatively old age and experienced dramatic change in their lifetime, including profound political upheaval.

Before these three, notions of what was good, noble, correct and true were largely controlled by the ruling elite based on myths of gods and heroes with sacrificial rituals and festivals to celebrate them. These three thinkers were active at a time when there was increasing diversity in definitions of morality and legitimate government in the societies in which they lived. Each established ethical ideals that, in theory, were potentially accessible to all humans and not just the elite. In doing so, these three foundational thinkers raised questions and proposed approaches that we can truly call political thought.

WARRIOR BACKGROUNDS AND POLITICAL INVOLVEMENTS

All three were political thinkers. Confucius and Socrates are often seen as political thinkers but even the Buddha developed a system of thought with political implications and a long-term influence on the political ideas of Asian civilization and beyond. In fact, Buddha has more claim to being a

---

[1] While it is anachronistic to use Sanskrit for the Buddha because there was no writing system for the languages likely used in his time and location, it is the closest equivalent in this context.

25

political thinker than Socrates who is always accepted as such. Confucius and Socrates educated the ruling elite but Buddha also interacted with and taught key monarchs of the time. It must be noted, however, that none of them wrote texts on politics and it is only through the interpretations of their followers that the political implications emerge. Nonetheless, it is possible with careful textual analysis to discern the ethical ideas that had an influence on their followers and serve as the basis for subsequent political thought in these civilizations.

The Buddha has been identified as a member of a warrior class or caste and it is likely that he was part of a broad ruling group of citizens who had the right to confer and rule. Buddha's close relationship with monarchs demonstrates that political issues were an influence even for him and his fellow ascetic recluses. Confucius was also trained as a warrior, held minor office in his native state of Lu and trained an elite group of students who were deeply political in that they strived to serve the state or educate those who did. In this sense Confucius is the most overtly political, especially given his experience as a public official and his role in the education of others who had the potential to become public officials. Socrates was a citizen-warrior who fought in the Peloponnesian War, participated in Athenian government and spoke to a broad group of citizens in the republic.[2]

In the India of Buddha, a trend toward monarchical rule was challenging a widespread tradition of quasi-republican states. Monarch is associated with the spread of Vedic culture as it was evolving in its core homeland. The kings with the support of *Brahmin* "priestly" caste developed an ideology for centralized hierarchical monarchies that contrasted with the more diffuse political participation found in neighboring states with quasi-republican forms of government with "kings" that were ceremonial and temporary. There were two key monarchies in the time of early Buddhism: Magadha ruled by King Bimbisara and Kosala ruled by King Prasenjit. The key "republican" states were Kashi, Kuru (which switched to a republican-like form at around the time of Buddha), and Malla, where Buddha died. The sixteen states of the period called the *Mahajanapadas* (महाजनपद) were not necessarily states in the sense that one would recognize today because most were simple tribal organizations without permanent institutions and organs of government.[3] The Buddha was from one of the small republican

---

[2] As noted below in the context of India, Greek republics were not inclusive or democratic in the modern sense. They simply had systems of rule that involved arrangements beyond simple monarchy. See also the glossary of concepts at the end of the book for this and other terms.

[3] In addition to these sixteen, there were smaller republics known as *Sangh* or *Gana* (see below).

states, Sakya, with its center in the town of Kapilavastu, and was the most northerly republic nestled up against the Himalayan mountains.

It is true that these "republics" were not democratic republics in the modern sense of the word.[4] Only a limited number of families or clans had the right to participate in decision making, though this could have included most families. It is likely that all male tribe members of families who fought for the tribe were recognized as full participants in the decision making process, as one might expect of a warrior tribe. There is some evidence that women had participated in some form at times, but it is more likely that women and servants were largely excluded from decision making in a way that is comparable with ancient Greek "democracies."

One point that creates confusion in ancient accounts of these republics is that all the members of the tribe who could participate were called *rajas* or "kings" though one might be selected to act as the chief of the tribe and called the *maharaja* (महाराज). This explains the confusion caused by stories calling Buddha a prince. It is no doubt technically true as his father was a *raja* or king, but this is obviously misleading. Stories of his royal status and life of wealth and luxury were no doubt embellished to create a contrast with his later ideals. This also helps explain the classification of the Buddha as a member of the *Kshatriya* (क्षत्रिय) warrior caste from which rulers are chosen in classical Vedic culture. If he was a member of a family with traditional warrior band rights to participate in the decision making assemblies, then it is not a stretch to put him in the *Kshatriya* warrior caste but it is doubtful that the notion of caste had spread or solidified at this point, which explains why the Buddha seems to doubt or reject the notion of caste based on birth in some of his recorded sayings.[5]

These republics were also important because the concepts in Buddhist decision making such as *sangha* and *gana* appear to have been borrowed from these quasi-republican tribal polities in which the term *gana-sangha* (गणसङ्घ) was used, literally "equal assembly," meaning assembly of equals, and *gana-rajya* (गणराज्य), literally "equal government," meaning government of equals. One can obtain a sense of what the decision making processes might be like in the numerous references to assemblies, moot halls, debating chambers and similar meetings at which issues were debated as described in the earliest Buddhist canon. It is true that the tribal decision

---

[4] The discussion that follows is derived from a critical reading of J.P. Sharma (1968) *Republics in Ancient India, c. 1500–c. 500 BC*, Leiden: E.J. Brill, which is still the best treatment of the subject.

[5] *Dīgha Nikāya* 3, "Ambaṭṭha Sutta" paralleled in the *Dīrghāgama* (長阿含經) Chapter 3 (第三分) 20 (阿摩晝經) and *Majjhima Nikāya* 93, "Assalāyana Sutta" parallel in the *Madhyamāgama* (中阿含經) Chapter 12 (梵志品) 151 in "Sutta Central: Early Buddhist texts, translations, and parallels": https://suttacentral.net/ (accessed June 3, 2017).

making process was based on families, clans or federations of clans, much like the phratry (*phratria* φρατρία) and phyle (*phulē* φυλή) system that preceded Athenian democracy, so the nature of the Buddha *sangha* is different. However, it is possible that both relied on notions of seniority, in contrast to the more arbitrary if highly equalizing selection by lot in Athens. For the Buddha, seniority was based not on birth but the date of one's ordination in the Buddhist *sangha*. Thus even if one is skeptical of the Buddha basing the Buddhist *sangha* on a quasi-republican model, it is clearly plausible in terms of the decision making process which emerged.

One can sense that the Buddha prefers republics and is wary of kings but he knows he needs the protection and patronage of kings. The Buddha was most intimately involved with the rulers of the state of Magadha, specifically King Bimbisara (558 BC–491 BC) and the state of Kosala, especially King Prasenjit. Bimbisara was a great patron of the Buddha and his followers, and Prasenjit engaged Buddha in intellectual discussion and expressed an interest in his ideas. The rulers that succeeded these two kings increasingly engaged in brutal wars of conquest, destroying the small republics in the process. The Buddha is believed to have been alive at the time of the destruction of his home republic Sakya and saw the beginning of the violent interstate endgame of domination by force.

Like the Buddha, Confucius lived during a key stage in the breakdown and transformation of existing political authority. Admittedly the Zhou dynasty (周代 c. 1046 BC–256 BC) in which he lived was never a centralized government because it relied on personal bonds between the court and branches of the Zhou family and others to control localities. Princes and their branch families as well as other powerful families, including those associated with the Shang dynasty (商代 c. 1600 BC–c. 1046 BC) defeated by the Zhou, were bound to serve the court. These families were proud of their lineage and their ties to the Imperial Court, which were reinforced with rituals and offerings, including bronze vessels with inscriptions that explained the significance of the rituals. Both the Zhou court and the local nobility fostered the creation of official posts to regulate their relationships, conduct rituals, and record history and a tradition of divination carried forward from the Shang. Officials were also created to tutor princes and the sons of nobles in affairs of state. In the end, however, these feudal domains grew into independent states that vied with each other for territory and power.

The small state of Lu where Confucian grew up was the focus of his loyalties even if he wanted to return to the greater unity of the early Zhou. The state of Lu (魯) can be traced back to Bo Qin (伯禽), the eldest son of the Duke of Zhou who founded the Zhou dynasty. This connection may explain why Confucius in particular is associated with an interest in preserving ancient state rituals. Lu was relatively strong in the initial period of the breakdown of the Zhou feudal system especially under Duke Yin (722–712 BC) and Duke Huan (魯桓公 711–694 BC). Despite the fact that Lu was surrounded by the powerful neighboring states of Jin (晉), Qi (齊) and Song (楚), it was often victorious in battle and engaged in armed expeditions against other minor states. Lu was severely weakened by the division of power between three branch families descended from three sons of Duke Huan, just as other powerful families gradually undermined the leadership of many of the other states at the time. It is clear from the evidence in the collection of his sayings, the *Analects* (論語) that the issue of insubordination and the deterioration of authority concerned Confucius and his students. That is, it is important to see Confucius' concern for ritual not as the complaints of a stickler for tradition but as an expression of serious fears over the deterioration of political relations as some in the nobility attempted to usurp the prerogatives of the imperial house.[6]

Socrates also experienced dramatic political change.[7] Two Peloponnesian wars threatened Athens during his lifetime and he was intimately involved in both. In all the campaigns in which he participated, Socrates was faced with defeat but is said to have acted honorably in the circumstances. The initial stages of the Peloponnesian War were followed by a period called the Peace of Nicias, also known as the Fifty-Year Peace, based on a peace treaty between the Greek city-states of Athens and Sparta in March 421 BC but this never really stopped the conflict and it was formally abandoned in 414 BC. It was at this time (415–413 BC) that the Sicilian Expedition was undertaken by the Athenians. The expedition's primary advocate, Alcibiades (Ἀλκιβιάδης, 450–404 BC), who was associated with Socrates, was recalled from command to stand trial even before the fleet reached Sicily. Fearing that he would be treated unfairly, Alcibiades defected to Sparta. Though expedition had some early success, it ended in a catastrophic defeat for Athens. Worse, Alcibiades advised the Spartans to take actions that severely weakened Athens. As a result, the Athenians demanded more tribute from her subject allies and put stress on already tense relationships. The enemies of Athens successfully encouraged revolts in the Delian League, the alliance dominated by Athens, and thus undermined Athenian power.

In 411 BC a coup overthrew the democratic government of Athens with a short-lived oligarchy known as "The Four Hundred." The oligarchy

---

[6] See *Analects* Book 3, for example 3.2, in Confucius; Arthur Waley trans. (1938) *Analects*, New York: Vintage Books: 97.

[7] The history of ancient Greece here is a standard account of events but I have primarily used Cyril E. Robinson (1929) *A History of Greece*, London: Methuen and Co.

was supported by many powerful and wealthy families, including those who were acting in coordination with Alcibiades at the behest of the Spartans. This government of the "Four Hundred" was almost immediately undermined by conflict between moderates and extremists. The moderates wanted a broader oligarchy of "the 5,000," which included most landowners and those who could afford to arm themselves to fight. In response, the extremist leaders attempted to making a deal with Sparta to remain in control of Athens in exchange for surrendering the city. A confrontation ensued between the moderates and extremists which ended with The Four Hundred replaced by the 5,000, who ruled for several more months.

Athens was initially able to achieve a number of victories and rebuild its empire, with a major role in this success due to Alcibiades, who had changed sides to defend Athens from Sparta. However, the Sparta general Lysander (Λύσανδρος, d. 395) destroyed most of the Athenian fleet at the battle of Aegospotami in 405 BC and Athens was put under siege until they surrendered in 404 BC. For a short period of time, Athens was ruled by the "Thirty Tyrants," a regime set up by Sparta, and democracy was suspended. However, this small oligarchy was overthrown and a democracy was restored in 403 BC. It is true that this "democracy" was limited to free male citizens only so excluded foreigners, women and slaves who made up the majority of the population but Athenian democracy was based on "popular" rule by citizens, however narrowly defined, rather than a monarch or small oligarchy. This democracy was the one under which Socrates was condemned and forced to commit suicide.

SOCIAL CHANGE AND POLITICAL IDEAS

It is clear then that all three thinkers must be seen against the background of the social and political conflict of the times in which they lived. In particular, these three foundational thinkers also emerged against the backdrop of extensive social change in all three societies with greater social interchange and mobility than historically had been the case. This in turn led to the questioning of traditional values. Certainly each of the thinkers and the societies in which they lived interacted with others from different social groups and political systems. Importantly these three thinkers were not major political leaders so simply put forward political philosophies to respond to the challenges of political change as best that they could. This is reflected in what they taught.

The Buddha was originally called Siddhārtha Gautama, a man on a quest for answers to the suffering in this world. This was not unusual given that many in this period were questioning traditional belief systems.[8] Traditional thought was based on Vedic (वेदा) literature, which started from the Rg Veda and early poetic mythology of the Aryan invaders of India. The name Aryan derives from *ārya* (आर्य) meaning "noble" in Sanskrit and Vedic literature represented the culture of the ruling elite. Other Vedic poems were created with additional layers of exegis and liturgy for the *Brahmin* priests to transmit from generation to generation. At this point, it is likely that Vedic *Brahmins* did not have the authority and pervasive influence that it had later in Indian history but they would have been at the center of much intellectual discussion at the time. In fact, by the time of Buddha, a new literature, the *Upanisads* (उपनिषद्), were being written, with a nascent movement in the oldest sections of this work toward monotheism and metaphysical reflection on the nature of the self (*ātman* आत्मन्). The *Upanisads* reflect the intellectual and spiritual problems that confronted Buddha.[9] There were also a variety of cults, including those based on Vaishnavism, in which gods act in this world through avatars, namely cults of Baladeva and Vāsudeva, with which Kṛṣṇa and other legends were later integrated into what would be called "Hindu" tradition.

The challenges to the Vedic tradition included the ascetic movements of *shramana* (श्रमण) or ascetic wanders who questioned key ideas such as the natural course of morality or righteousness (*dharma* धर्म]). The Buddha seems to have been attracted to these movements initially. There were the Ājīvakas (आजीवक), founded by Makkhali Gosala (born c. 484 BC), who advocated fatalism because one's actions could not lead to salvation, now or later, so often dropped out of society. The Jains, led by Mahavira (540–468 BC), led a life of non-violence, self-denial and self-control to achieve salvation by wandering and meditation. In contrast to the ascetics, there were also the materialists, the Cārvāka (चार्वाक) school, which rejected an afterlife, reincarnation, and even spiritual salvation itself so saw gratification of natural appetites as good. All these groups engaged in a debate over the purpose of being moral and how to behave. Given all the possibilities, the Buddha's struggle to find the best answer is no doubt symbolized in this struggle with Māra (मार), the devil, who tempted him with a range of alternatives, some of which were no doubt easier for him than to put forward his own approach.

Vedic culture also had social and political tendencies related to its theology and philosophy. One was the division of society into caste or *varna* (वर्ण), literally "color." *Kshatriya*, the warriors and rulers of states, would

---

[8] Romila Thapar (1966) *A History of India, Volume 1: Early India from the Origins to A.D. 1300*, Harmondsworth: Penguin: 46–48.
[9] Patrick Olivelle, trans. (2008) *Upanisads*, Oxford: Oxford University Press.

appear to be the top of the social ladder but the *Brahmin* (ब्राह्मण) caste that transmitted Vedic culture at the time of Buddha began to place itself in a stronger position ideologically. *Brahmin* knowledge and control of ritual and dispensation of karma of the ruling *Kshatriya* caste, provided a clear source of power. The *Vaishya* (वैश्य), craft workers and traders, were next in order with the *Shudra* (शूद्र) or servant caste at the bottom. Caste may have begun to be developed from the time of the Aryan invasions, based on the subjugation of indigenous people, but caste structure appears to have been fluid still in the time of the Buddha. This may have been based on political differences as well, because those areas long held by the Aryans and deeply rooted Vedic culture tended toward monarchy but in large parts of northern India tribal confederations, which may have originally split off of the Aryan mainstream, maintained tribal practices that echo republican ideas. The Buddha often took Vedic ideas and substantially reinterpreted them in line with his philosophy.

For the Buddha, the key concept was dependent origination (*paticcasamuppada* in Pali पटिच्चसमुप्पाद /*pratītyasamutpāda* in Sanskrit प्रतीत्यसमुत्पाद), which is defined as the chains of causation that explain why we exist and perceive that we exist.[10] There are no independent things in the world because everything is the result of chains of causation. Once we understand these chains of causation in a web of cause and effect, then we can change our perception, interpretation and attachment to the things and events in the world that ensnare and entrap us. Attachment to transitory chains of cause and effect are what causes suffering because one has the illusion that the world has a permanence that we can rely on. However, everything eventually loses its luster, breaks and decays, just as everyone gets old and dies.

The Buddha proposed a way of overcoming the suffering caused by attachment to the world by knowledge, mental discipline, and right behavior in order to help others understand the nature of dependent origination and cope with its consequences. He rejected the approaches taken by others at the time, such as advocates of ascetic denial, often masochistic, or reliance on empty ritual and superstition, because they were ineffective. Once dependent origination is understood, one can try to untangle oneself from the psychological impact of attachment to it. This is not the same as indifference because dependent origination also means everyone is connected. Because everyone is connected, one must act correctly, both by avoiding the illusion of permanence and also by being compassionate and helping others. This is why the Buddha, even

---

[10] Caroline R. Rhys Davids and F.L. Woodward (1950–1965) *The Book of the Kindred Sayings* (Sanyutta Nikaya), vol. 2, Bristol: Pali Text Society: 1–94, especially 12–13.

though reaching enlightenment, chose to remain in society and teach those who wanted to follow his path (despite his initial reluctance to accept followers). He wanted to convey to others his "wisdom" (*paññā* in Pāli or *prajñā* प्राज्ञा in Sanskrit), that is, his understanding of the true nature of reality, which was the processes of dependent origination and how attachment to things that are impermanent, or *anicca* (अनिच्चा) in Pāli, *anitya* (अनित्य) in Sanskrit, leads to dissatisfaction or suffering, or *dukkha* (दुक्ख) in Pāli, *duḥkha* (दुःख) in Sanskrit. By using Buddhist wisdom, one can cope with and even overcome the nature of human existence.

One must be careful here to distinguish the Buddha's approach from the Vedic notion of *karma* (कर्म). As with many existing ideas, the Buddha critiqued and used the Vedic notion of *karma* to encourage others to think about the nature of dependent origination and the role of the individual in it. Dependent origination means that the past does matter and one contributes to the future, and that one has a responsibility to deal with the past and improve the future. This is not purely selfish focus on rebirth in a better place in the world or a better realm, however, because there is no "self" (*ātman* आत्मन्), that is, there is no pure discrete continuous and whole individual to be reincarnated. In fact, much in Buddha teaching about the consequences of following the correct path is about improving the world in general in an altruistic sense for others. It has been pointed out that the notion of reincarnation does not fit well with early Buddhist teaching, especially the idea that there is no self.[11] There is no eternal self but there is self in the sense that one can and should act. Therefore, discussions of *karma* or reincarnation in early texts must be seen as the Buddha trying to make sense of his ideas for an audience holding traditional Vedic views on *karma* and reincarnation to get them to understand his ideas. It does not mean that he himself believed in reincarnation. After his death, however, this distinction appears to have been lost and reincarnation was fully incorporated into Buddhist philosophy.

Confucius also taught at a time of dramatic change and a decline in social and political order. As we have noted, he lived during a period of increasing fragmentation of the Zhou dynasty and the loss of central authority. This is reflected in the sparse literature in the time, mainly historical records and a poetry collection, the *Book of Songs* (*Shijing* 詩經). The *Book of Songs* is an important source of early Chinese thought. Some of the "songs" are early as Shang dynasty but most are from the early Zhou period. The popular odes can also provide insight into Chinese

---

[11] 和辻哲郎 (Watsuji Tetsurō) (1927) 原始佛教の實踐哲學 (*Genshi Bukkyō no Jissen*). 東京：岩波書店 (Tokyo: Iwanami Shoten): 427–445.

political thinking, especially outside of the elite. These often suggest a degree of fatalism especially in dealing with political authority. The role of heaven (*tiān* 天) is important, taken from Shang times and central to Zhou thought. Heaven is not like a monotheistic god but it does act and is a force which appears to be beyond human control.[12] Confucius often quotes from the *Book of Songs* in the *Analects*.

Another work, likely to be contemporary to Confucius, is the *Spring and Autumn Annals* (春秋). This book is very terse, like a series of newspaper headlines or twitter feeds, and it is only through later commentaries that we can make sense of the content, such as the *Zho Commentary* (左傳), which was composed contemporary with or slightly prior to Confucius and likely to have informed his understanding. This text emphasizes heaven or *tiān* (天), divination of the will of heaven and how to obtain the favor of heaven. This is also an important text in which the concept of the Way or *Tao* (道) is also used. At this point, the Way is clearly still a generic concept, meaning the natural course of events, and its lack of development is reflected in sayings of Confucius as well. Appropriation of this concept by the Taoists and other schools of thought comes later. The Way is the flow which we can attune to, heaven is the force that drives events. They are connected but distinct. An analogy might be helpful here: A surfer riding a wave, if skillful, is following the Way (*tao*) or temporal manifestation of heaven but heaven (*tiān*) is overall force, like an ocean current that creates the waves.

Most importantly for understanding Confucius, there is a distinction in the *Annals* between ritual (*li* 禮) as behavior and ritual as ceremony (*yi* 儀) especially in the declining Zhou dynastic context, and this is also related to the role of ministers in the state. Much of what we call ritual today is ceremony in Zhou terms. However, for Confucius, ritual includes everyday ways of showing respect and therefore is intimately connected to humaneness. In fact, *li* (禮) encompasses the broader notion of respectful behavior and even etiquette, though the latter term is used too much in contemporary times to imply exaggerated emphasis on outmoded models of good behavior. The term *li* has been translated as "propriety,"[13] which perhaps made sense in the nineteenth century when it was first used but for the most part "ritual" is a better translation. Even then, for most contemporary readers, ritual retains a negative connotation of unfeeling traditional repetition and formal behavior, whereas Confucius is clear that

---

[12] See, for example, Arthur Waley, trans. (1946) *Book of Songs*, London: George Allen & Unwin: 308.

[13] For example, James Legge trans. (c. 1920) *The Four Books (*華英四書*)*, Shanghai: The Chinese Book Company: 25.

rituals, including informal ones, demonstrate a sincere effort to engage with others respectfully.

Another key concept for Confucius is *ren* (仁), which is sometimes translated as benevolence or humanness, but it is easy to agree with Waley that it often makes more sense to translate as the good or goodness.[14] Benevolence implies paternalism, which is not completely absent from the ideal, but it is a mistake to overemphasize that aspect. It is being humane but that is too narrow a definition. It is really treating others correctly, fairly, appropriately, in short, treating people well. Doing good means helping them and not hating them even if you think they are wrong or they do not reciprocate.

One final concept, though mentioned less than *ren*, is dé (德).[15] Waley translates dé as moral force, which he contrasts with physical force.[16] Confucius believed that correct behavior had a power of its own. If you act in the correct way it will encourage, teach and even compel others to do so as well. According to Confucius, if one practices *li* (禮) and *ren* (仁), they create moral force (dé 德) which can bring peace and tranquility. That is, practicing ritual respect and acting humanely will induce others to do the same and so bring order and harmony to the world. Ritual is important because it embodies humanness essential to social and political order. Those trying to do their best cultivate a sense of propriety and exercise humanness even though it is difficult, whereas the petty-minded pursue gain and avoid trouble rather than make sacrifices to uphold the good and do the right thing when necessary.[17] Confucius based his ideals on mythical rulers of the past and historical figures, such as the Duke of Zhou, who provide a standard to which others can and should aspire.

Socrates also lived in a time when traditional ideas were being challenged. Homer (Ὅμηρος) especially in his epic poem the *Iliad* (Ἰλιάς) has a clear implicit definition of heroic virtue, which can be summed by the traditional term *kalos kagathos* (καλὸς κἀγαθός), that is, the good/beautiful (καλός) and good, brave, noble (κἀγαθός), as the ideal for citizens and rulers alike. However, the definition assumes that only the noble, that is blood members of the nobility, are good and have the potential to act for the good and be seen as beautiful. However, this was challenged by the expansion of participation in Athenian politics by an increasingly wider group of citizens.

---

[14] Confucius; Waley trans. (1938) *Analects*: 27–29.
[15] For example, *Analects* Book IV 11 and 25 in Confucius; Waley trans. (1938) *Analects*: 104 and 106.
[16] Confucius; Waley trans. (1938) *Analects*: 33.
[17] Confucius; Waley trans. (1938) *Analects*: 102–105.

Socrates was also heir to the speculation of thinkers who began to question the very nature of the universe and the place of humans and gods in it. These thinkers, including those from Ionian and Italian Greek states and colonies are called pre-Socratic thinkers because they largely predate and anticipate the intellectual turmoil and freedom of the time of Socrates.[18] The earliest of these thinkers was Anaximander (Ἀναξίμανδρος 610–546 BC) who searched for a first principle and substance upon which all else is based. Heraclitus of Ephesus (Ἡράκλειτος ὁ Ἐφέσιος 535–475 BC) argued all things are in flux and only held together by a logical structure termed *logos* (λόγος) which one can only find by looking beyond changing appearances. Xenophanes of Colophon (Ξενοφάνης ὁ Κολοφώνιος 570–470 BC), suggested the idea of one God to create unity which permeates and controls the universe. Parmenides of Elea (Παρμενίδης ὁ Ἐλεάτης 510–440 BC) also posited a unity of essence and that all change was illusion. Another key pre-Socratic is Pythagoras of Samos (Πυθαγόρας ὁ Σάμιος 582–496 BC) who looked for harmony in the world and believed it could be found in numbers. Leucippus (Λεύκιππος fifth century BC) and his pupil Democritus (Δημόκριτος 460–370 BC) were atomists, that is, materialists who believed everything was made up of atoms, the small indivisible units to cause all change and substance by their interaction. As with much of the Western philosophical tradition, Socrates seems to value the principle of unity though he argues against a purely materialist approach, such as those of the atomists.

Socrates' Athens was one of many Greek city-states but also the most diverse and filled with debate. It attracted foreign merchants, craftsmen and teachers. Most in the city did not have rights to participate in political life because they were not citizens (along with slaves and women) but even non-citizens joined in debates (including women). The debates were over ideas such as reason (*logos*) and ethical norms (*ethos* ἦθος) as well as *arête* (ἀρετή) or excellence. Some of the discussion of these ideas was informed by teachers called Sophists (σοφιστής), who were teachers of oratory and rhetoric. The skills they taught were essential to enable citizens, particularly the children of the elite, to progress or survive in Athenian social and political life, particularly in the need to appeal to fellow citizens in the Assembly and when faced with litigation in the courts, which had large juries also made up of fellow citizens. The problem was that the ethics of the Sophists were questionable and were accused of teaching others how to make bad arguments seem good.

Socrates questioned all concepts in such a profound way that he stood out from the Sophists who merely preached rhetorical skill (even though

---

[18] Robin Waterfield trans. (2009) *The First Philosophers: The Presocratics and Sophists*, Oxford: Oxford University Press.

his approach was considered similar to the Sophists judging by the way he is depicted in Aristophanes in *The Clouds*).[19] Socrates relentlessly pursued the logic of ideas and practices to allow his listeners to question everything and enable them to think for themselves rather than to merely win an argument. He developed his own forms of enquiry based on keen scrutiny or *elenchus* (ἔλεγχος) and in order to reveal and confront challenging puzzles and profound doubts or *aporia* (ἀπορεία) about the nature of an ethical life, which in the Athenian context was a political life. His focus was on knowledge and how to achieve a good life defined as *eudaimonia* (εὐδαιμονία) or well-being, a concept which later Greek philosophers, particularly Aristotle, developed, but it also seemed to promise that this would make them better citizens and rulers. This set him apart from the Sophists.

Socrates argued that the exercise of virtue is a skill based on knowledge and all virtues derive from one unified ideal of virtue which should be the goal of all individuals because it is the highest good. He was not content with traditional definitions. Socrates sought to try to get to the essence of key virtues with the aim of a unified theory of virtue but demonstrated the difficulty of doing so given the snares of conventional wisdom. Key virtues he debated are piety, wisdom, temperance, courage, and justice. Socrates was dissatisfied with the answers given by others and seemed uncertain that answers can be found. Still, he seemed sure that there is a unity to virtue so that all the virtues, if correct, should constitute a single "goodness" (*agathos* ἀγαθός), which is far from Homeric or conventional notions of goodness. There is only one virtue of which other virtues are a part and it takes skill and introspection to grapple with the best possible meaning of and approach to virtue that will benefit oneself and one's community. He was looking to cultivate virtuous and just individuals to rule. Justice is a key virtue and it is absolute to the point that it is better to suffer injustice because the person acting unjustly always harms himself more than the person being badly treated. It is only through ignorance that one does evil. That is, no one does harm willingly because if they had knowledge of virtue, they would not harm others. Moreover, if one is good (with knowledgeable = virtuous) then no harm can come to you. Knowledge is key to Socratic dialogues.

---

[19] Aristophanes; Alan Sommerstein, trans. (1973) *Aristophanes: Lysistrata, The Acharnians, The Clouds*, Harmondsworth: Penguin Books.

EQUALITY AND CLASS BIAS

One crucial issue is the evidence for a class bias in the philosophy of these thinkers. Those with more status and wealth may be more likely to have the upbringing and resources to follow their advice. Indeed, all three connect personal morality to correct behavior in a way that emphasizes ability to rule well, particularly Confucius and Socrates. Moreover, in all cases, it is implied that only a rare few can do what is needed to be truly virtuous. However, there is also a sense that birth, social status and breeding are not prerequisite. All have an inherent belief in equality. One might question the extent that it is true equality, given the nature of their original audience and the apparent tacit acceptance of slavery by all three thinkers, but the fact remains that, in principle, anyone can achieve these ideals. This is how these thinkers have been interpreted and their work provides plenty of scope to do so.

As noted above, Buddha was raised in a society composed of a broad ruling group of republican citizens, even if this "republic" was limited to the warrior elite, it may have included most men and possibly women participating in consultative assemblies. An egalitarian ethos would have been natural for him. Yet, for most of his life as a teacher, he had to work with monarchs and was respectful if not wary of their power. Socrates also spoke to a broad group of citizens in Athens though in effect these citizens were still in some ways an elite of male citizens among a larger group of foreigners, women and slaves. Nonetheless, the fact that these ruling groups were limited to a minority of the population does not diminish the importance of the ideas or the potential for them to be extended to others later in history. Of all three, Confucius was the most elitist as part of a hierarchical aristocratic system of government. At the same time, Confucius represented a trend to advocate merit as a basis for office as opposed to simple hereditary aristocracy. Confucius taught the ruling class but made it clear anyone could be a superior individual because it was based on attitude and not simply status in the hierarchy.

Understanding the Buddha in relation to caste and equality is difficult because one has to remember that the concept of caste has not solidified yet in India.[20] As with the quasi-republics and the growing bureaucracy of the monarchial states, the ruling class/warrior class/official class was not necessarily a small group. *Brahmins*, or "priestly" families were not yet dependent on the state as a group, and seem to have sometimes included householders who may have been involved in commerce and agriculture.

---

[20] Debiprasad Chattopadhyaya (1968) *Lōkayata: A Study In Ancient Indian Materialism*, New Delhi: People's Publishing House.

Buddha often discusses *Brahmin* status as a spiritual goal more than a caste.[21] Those identified as "householders" appear to be property owners even if only on a modest scale. There was also a growing merchant class, especially in the major cities of the growing monarchies. There is some mention of lower orders, the poor and servants, but as in Confucius, their limited resources of time and education were a problem for fully engaging with Buddha's thought. Therefore, when Buddhist texts highlight the role of members of the ruling class, *Brahmins*, and merchants as playing a leading role in the *sangha*, it is because these groups had the capacity to educate themselves and attain enlightenment rather than an indication of an intentional class bias. In theory the *sangha* was open to all individuals, regardless of background. Of course, men in royal service did not have the right to become a monk, and, in addition, slaves, debtors and criminals were also excluded from the *sangha* but one could argue that this was more to placate the authorities and protect the movement than an ideological stance. The Buddha seemed to be reluctant to challenge all aspects of caste or political authority in order to protect his fledgling movement. Nonetheless, his ideas do challenge the caste system and imply a greater degree of equality and emphasis on the qualities of a person rather than birth or caste.

Philosophically, in fact, the Buddha was the most egalitarian of the three thinkers. The notion of dependent arising can be the basis for both equality and concern for others. If all beings are a product of a long complex string of cause and effect relationships, then all people are united by a common process that brings them into being. All individuals are also equally responsible for their own behavior as they respond as best they can to the world in which they find themselves. Buddha argues that one's status depends on behavior and not birth. This responsibility is not just to save oneself but to make the world a better place in general. The Buddha's rules (*vinaya* विनय,) for the monastic community (*sangha*) also demonstrate a desire for equality. Seniority is used as a principle but it is not based on age or status but on when one became a monk so on an implicit notion of merit based on experience. Similarly, the decision making rules in the community are based on broad consensus in which all monks have an equal say and power of veto. Again the early Buddhists were heavily influenced by republican practices especially in their internal organization. At the same time, Buddhists were not overt and articulate champions of republican ideals despite a clear affinity for associated ideas.

Confucius has more of an obvious class bias in his use of the terms *junzi*

---

[21] See footnote 4.

(君子), which is usually translated as gentleman or superior or person, and *xiăorén* (小者) as the small or mean individual. Even so, translation of *junzi* (君子) is not straightforward. It originally meant prince but became more widely a term for the sons of the high nobility and then any cultivated individual, especially in the *Analects*. The parallel with Machiavelli calling his work *Il Principe* (The Prince) is not far off but the word gentleman or gentleperson (to make it gender neutral) makes sense given that it too derives from a term for a higher social status position but has become a term for any cultivated individual. It is sometimes translated as a "noble person," which reflects its original aristocratic origin but also retains the ambiguity of signifying a form of behavior independent of status. For *xiăorén* (小者), the term small person is common but "petty individual" is closer to the meaning. However, this does not necessarily equate with class and outward status. Like Buddha, Confucius focuses more on behavior than status. Even a well-born person can act petty and that is exactly the type of person at which his criticism is aimed. Inequality does play a role in the views of Confucius because knowing the right thing to do depends on deference and knowing one's position in the status hierarchy. One could also make the case that the type of education, cultivation and lifestyle needed to be a noble person was only possible for the elite. Still, the potential to act correctly is open in theory to anyone and it contrasts with previous emphasis on strict family or status lineage as the criterion of what makes a person good.

The class bias of Socrates has been alleged.[22] It is certainly true that his views on democracy and equality were unclear. Still, he loved Athens in which there was civic involvement by a wide range of citizens, and he thrived on the free if sometimes acrimonious and litigious debate in Greek states. He was also suspicious of the Sophists, who trained the wealthy elite to manipulate the *demos*, the masses. It is true that Socrates' friends and followers, such as Plato, tended to be part of the Athenian elite but this cannot be said of Socrates who was a craftsman and would talk to anyone who would engage him, even the poor and women. Buddha was open to speaking to anyone as well.

Indeed, the views of these thinkers regarding women are also important. For example, it would be impossible to argue Buddha was a feminist because he had to be persuaded by Ananda, one of his chief followers, to allow the ordination of women as nuns.[23] Even then, women were required

---

[22] Ellen Meiksins Wood and Neal Wood (1978) *Class Ideology and Ancient Political Theory: Socrates, Plato, and Aristotle in Social Context*, Oxford: Basil Blackwell: 81–118.

[23] "The story of Mahāpajāpatī Gotamī" in Nuns (Bhikkhunī), Khandhaka (Cūḷavagga) 20, Vinayapiṭaka, *Sutta Central*, https://suttacentral.net/en/pi-tv-kd20 (accessed June 3, 2017).

to have the permission of their husband and parents before joining the order. Buddha also expressed an exaggerated fear of female sexuality, in part based on his view of sexuality as a key source of human suffering. On the other hand, one could also view his rules as a way of managing the incorporation of women in monastic organization to make it transparent and protective of the women as well as the reputation of his movement. There is even a sense in which gender discrimination itself is an obstacle to enlightenment.[24]

The attitude of Confucius toward women is less clear. It is true that all the references to filial piety attributed to Confucius concern sons but this is not surprising given the sons of the elite were his students. One must also remember that the concept of filial piety is late and not necessarily what the historical Confucius emphasized. In any case, filial piety does not exclude women. There is one passage (*Analects* 17.25) in which Confucius does seem to directly disparage women, who are compared to petty men and said to be difficult to cultivate because if one acts too familiar with them, they become unwilling to follow instruction but if one is too reserved, they become upset. Legge translates this as "girls" not women, which makes more sense but does not completely eliminate sexist implications.[25] Of course, the saying is entirely based on hearsay, and textual analysis suggests that this passage is in a late book composed long after the death of Confucius. Even if they are Confucius' own words, they are certainly atypical and not reflected in the core texts most associated with the historical Confucius. For the most part ancient Chinese is gender neutral so it is not impossible to argue the core ideas of Confucius can be interpreted as valid for women as well as men. Even if the later thought of some of the successors of Confucius in East Asia was often hostile to women, there is no evidence that this reflects the views of Confucius himself.

Socrates sometimes appears to be denigrating women as weak by comparing weak men with women. However, Socrates' student Plato was famous for considering both men and women fit as potential guardians, or philosopher-kings and philosopher-queens of his ideal state and there is also evidence that Plato was encouraged in this view by Socrates. In the dialogue *Meno*, Socrates seems to argue for gender equality and, if so, challenged the norms of Athenian and ancient Greek society in general.[26] Socrates is portrayed as telling Meno that there is no separate concept

---

[24] "Soma Sutta," *Samyutta Nikaya* 5.2, Sutta Central, https://suttacentral.net/en/sn5.2 (accessed June 3, 2017).

[25] James Legge trans. (c. 1920) *The Four Books* (華英四書), Shanghai: The Chinese Book Company: 271.

[26] Plato; Benjamin Jowett, trans. (1892) *The Dialogues of Plato*, vol. 2, 3rd edn, Oxford: Oxford University Press: 29–30.

of virtue of men versus women just as men and women can be either healthy or unhealthy. He even insists that strength can be a characteristic of women as of men. Meno tries to argue that men should employ their virtue in the state and women in the home, but Socrates insists that the same virtues are needed in both cases so the distinction is spurious. Both men and women need the same degree of virtue and, by implication, can and should exercise it everywhere.

All three thinkers focus on personal ethics and virtue in order to appeal to the elite that is, or should be, the ruling class. Nonetheless, the ethics and standards put forward can potentially be seen as good for everyone as they are not limited by class, status or even gender. Moreover, there is no distinction between the morality of the rulers and the ruled. Buddha is clear in believing that all humans can and should try to follow his path. There is clearly a benefit for all of society when the ruler adopts his ideals. The Buddha saw the ruler as a facilitator as well as a potential follower. Confucius' idea of the moral force is not only a positive influence on others, it draws others to it so it multiplies the impact. Socrates tried to convince his fellow citizens that questioning themselves and working hard to understand and practice virtuous conduct was good for the individual and society as a whole.

RELIGION AND METAPHYSICS

As noted in the introduction, the role of religion in political thought is important from the start and throughout the history of political thought. We must reject the myth that political thought, particularly Western political thought is more secular and more worthy of being considered philosophy or that the non-West is more religious and less worthy as a result. The problem is partly due to Western categorization of religion due to the division of religion and the state after the Reformation, but it is also contestable historically. Buddha seems the most religious conventionally but could be argued to be the least religious and most philosophical. Confucianism is often termed a religion but it would be incomprehensible as a category historically in East Asia, and not really a religion in any case except arguably much later (in the nineteenth century) in very limited circumstances (only a small minority in Korea and China). Certainly the historical Confucius shows no hint of acting as a religious figure even if sometimes seen or at least called in translation a holy Sage. In contrast, Socrates is explicitly religious but in modern times is not often seen as a religious figure, and certainly not to the same extent as the other two. This is as much due to his philosophy-based rational argument as it is due to the presence of others in the narrative of Western ethical thought who were much more conventionally religious. One could argue that Socrates was the most religious of all three of the foundational thinkers. Socrates relied on guiding spirit or *daimon* (δαίμων) and an inner voice (ἀποτρεπτικός), and claimed that he tried to be pious/hallowed (ὅσιος).[27] This is the basis of his views on justice and duty. Socrates was unwilling to disobey the state demands that he stop teaching philosophy because he felt to do so was sacred duty, but could not disobey the state that had ordered his own death. He viewed the state as his parents who he would harm and even do violence to it if he ran away to save his life. In this sense, he projected filial piety onto the state. Therefore, he felt he must accept the death penalty imposed on him even if unjust because injustice is not the response to injustice. Yet, Socrates was willing to disobey the state when a god or his inner divine voice told him to do so. He was certainly the most conventionally pious of all three thinkers even if he finds it difficult to define what piety is.[28] It is telling that Socrates was forced to commit suicide by his enemies and fellow citizens in democratic Athens for both corrupting youth and setting up new gods.

One area related to religion is ritual, on which all three have distinctive views. Buddha opposed animal sacrifice, but not merely because it takes the life of a living thing. In fact, he did not oppose ritual entirely but it is clear that he did not believe that ritual alone makes a difference. His focus is more on intention and psychology in one's actions. Ritual cannot change the past; only future good behavior can help. He transformed the concept to enable people to consider the consequences of their actions and reinforce good practice.

In contrast, ritual is absolutely central to Confucius because it has an important role in ordering relationships and expressing courtesy and social integration. Confucius clearly did not object to animal sacrifice, famously loving ceremony more than the sheep being sacrificed.[29] For Confucius ritual is also discussed frequently in conjunction with music, but mostly likely because music played more of a ritual role than the popular music today, that is, it was part of traditional "pomp and circumstance." There is a residual aspect of this use of music in national anthems, such as at sporting events. For Confucius ritual can also mean manners. This is also consistent with the view of personal etiquette expressed in the *Analects*. Whether the focus is on formal ritual or manners, the important aspect is that it is heartfelt.[30] Confucius goes further and suggests that the rites are

---

[27] Plato; Jowett, trans. (1892) *The Dialogues of Plato*, vol. 2: 125.
[28] Plato; Jowett, trans. (1892) *The Dialogues of Plato*, vol. 2: 65–94.
[29] 3.17 in Confucius; Arthur Waley trans. (1938) *Analects*: 98.
[30] 3.26 in Confucius; Arthur Waley trans. (1938) *Analects*: 101.

important because they are key to governing well.[31] Ritual and manners are a way of signaling and cultivating respect, building a sense of community and treating people with dignity. Ritual does not necessarily imply belief though Confucius argued it should. The implicit argument is that he felt some do not believe or believe in it for the wrong reasons, and this is something he would never do.

Socrates was also a believer in ritual though he mostly questions how it works and typically reaches no conclusion.[32] He seemed implicitly critical of the idea that it is a simple commercial transaction with the gods, or that one can make sacrifices to gain favors, and appears to agree that it is more a symbol of respect, reverence, and gratitude. However, there is a question about the meaning of his last words when he suggested that Crito (Κρίτων) should sacrifice a cock in his honor to Asclepius (Ἀσκληπιός), the god of medicine.[33] This could be taken as an ironic statement to thank him for his death as a welcome cure for life rather than a serious request. Yet there are also other examples of Socrates engaging piously in the conduct of ritual. Any ambiguity over his beliefs about its role may be imposing modern disbelief in ritual onto Socrates to make him appear more secular and acceptable.

Another striking point about all three thinkers is the tendency toward monotheism or monism. This is clear on the concept of *dharma* as the moral laws of the universe which is an important part of the Indian systems of thought and became a core concept in Buddhism, the principles of which the Buddha has claimed to understand and found solutions for human beings to cope. Similarly, the concept of the Way (*tao* 道) for Confucius has a flow and logic that makes his solutions work effectively. Even Socrates argues that there is one idea of virtue or skill that contains all the others and perhaps a single unified truth behind this logic. Of course, it is the very simplicity of the systems as developed by these thinkers that led their later followers to add a more complex cosmology in support.

TEXTUAL ISSUES

This leads to the final issue of how we can know what these thinkers really said. One must acknowledge that a good deal of care is required to identify specific ideas associated with any of these thinkers. For all three we do not

---

[31] 4.13 in Confucius; Arthur Waley trans. (1938) *Analects*: 104.
[32] Plato; Jowett, trans. (1892) *The Dialogues of Plato*, vol. 2: 90–92.
[33] Plato; Jowett, trans. (1892) *The Dialogues of Plato*, vol. 2: 266. Even though Phaedo is a late dialogue, the story is famous enough that it may reflect his actual last words.

know if any of the words attributed to them were actually uttered by them. This adds a layer of doubt about the meaning of their ideas beyond the normal problems of interpretation which will be raised for all thinkers in the history of world political thought. Detailed textual analysis would be required to explain the logic of selection of ideas assigned to each thinker in this chapter. Greater background will be provided in the next chapter so at this point the reader must be asked to accept that there is robust analysis behind the choices made here.

Buddhist texts have not been subject to as much recent scholarly analysis as Confucius or Socrates. The general rule of interpretation followed here is that texts that exist in both the Pali Canon and other traditions (particularly the Chinese Agama), ideas that are repeated, and shorter rather than longer dialogues are more likely to be earlier. In this chapter the Buddha is assumed to be a human being debating with other human beings so I have interpreted him as interacting with followers of other belief systems rather than directly in dialogue with the gods and other fantastic beings in those belief systems, as the texts sometimes suggest.[34] One example is the role of the concepts of karma or reincarnation in early texts both of which must be seen as the Buddha trying to make sense of his ideas for an audience holding traditional Vedic views on karma and reincarnation to get them to understand his ideas. As noted, it does not mean that he himself believed in reincarnation. After his death, however, this distinction appears to have been lost and reincarnation fully incorporated into Buddhist philosophy.[35]

As with the Buddha, Confucius did not write any books and we are reliant on his followers for his sayings. As his followers developed their own schools and followings, the interpretations changed and concepts evolved. It is under these later followers that views on government and other concepts emerged. *Li* (禮), *ren* (仁) and *dû* (德) are the primary early concepts of Confucius. These are well attested in the core books that are widely agreed to be closest to the historical Confucius. Analysis of the *Analects* has advanced considerably in recent years[36] and will be discussed

---

[34] See Richard Gombrich (1996) *How Buddhism Began: The Conditioned Genesis of the Early Teachings*, London: The Athlone Press, but only for the spirit of this analysis and not the detail, with which I have no doubt he would disagree.

[35] It is interesting that the emphasis in Buddhism is on reincarnation because Plato also put the concept into the mouth of Socrates in the dialogue Phaedrus (248–250), that is, reincarnation according to knowledge of the true, but it is hardly considered a key part of his philosophy. It may be that the widespread influence of what later became Hinduism was so strong that the idea became more important than it was originally in the Buddha's philosophy. See Plato; Jowett, trans. (1892) *The Dialogues of Plato*, vol. 1: 454–455.

[36] For all its limitations, the translation by B. Brooks and T. Brooks (1998) *The Original Analects: Sayings of Confucius and His Successors*, New York, NY: Columbia University Press, is an effort to make sense of the historical layers of the *Analects*.

in some detail in the next chapter, but suffice to say that Book IV and then the rest of the Books III–VIII are earliest, Books I and II reflect a tradition of one set of Confucius' followers after his death and, to paraphrase Arthur Waley, Books XIV–XVIII seem to have little original connection to Confucius or his immediate followers and are correctly regarded as late.[37] The focus in this chapter is on goodness and ritual in the texts widely agreed to be closest to the historical Confucius (Books III and IV). In contrast, filial piety is barely mentioned in the early texts including the *Analects* and not at all in the manner used by later followers of Confucius.[38] This is an important clue for understanding the role of filial piety in early Chinese thought, which will be discussed in the next chapter.

In contrast, works quoting Socrates have been the subject of detailed analysis for many years, particularly as he appears in the dialogues of Plato (Πλάτων c. 427–c. 347 BC) and Xenophon (Ξενοφῶν c. 430–354 BC). It is widely agreed that Plato's early dialogues are considered relatively reliable as a portrayal of the "real" Socrates[39] whereas Xenophon appears to lack the ability and nuance to portray Socrates' thought accurately. Certainly Xenophon's dialogues are not as sophisticated as Plato's versions, and Xenophon is said to have left Athens well before the peak of Socrates' final days so may have copied or fabricated his accounts. Nonetheless, Xenophon had known Socrates personally and may convey a sense of the core features of his personality and his work. As with any material, Xenophon's material must be used critically. This is also true of the works of Plato who often clearly uses Socrates as a mouthpiece for his own ideas. Looking at both carefully, scholars over the years have been able to produce a plausible outline of Socrates' views and this chapter has followed in that tradition.

The next chapter looks at these textual issues in more detail in order to understand the evolution of the ideas raised by these three foundational thinkers.

CONCLUSION

It is helpful to begin this history of world political thought by focusing on these three thinkers. It is easy to demonstrate that they are foundational in the sense that much of the political thought that follows in the civiliza-

---

[37] Confucius; Waley trans. (1938) *The Analects*: 21.

[38] Yuri Pines (2002) *Foundations of Confucian Thought: Intellectual Life in the Chunqiu Period (722–453 BCE)*, Honolulu: University of Hawaii Press; and Confucius; Arthur Waley trans. (1938) *Analects*: 38–39.

[39] Gregory Vlastos (1991) *Socrates, Ironist and Moral Philosopher*, Ithaca, NY: Cornell University Press.

tions that they influenced was based on issues that they raised. They are also important for similar reasons. All three arose in periods of political and intellectual turmoil. The widening of involvement of individuals outside of the elite was also a factor in this unrest but also might explain why the relatively open and one might even say egalitarian implications of the philosophies of all three thinkers are no doubt related to these historical conditions. However, there is also considerable ambiguity in the implications of their ideas, which is why there was enormous scope for interpretation and the development of different approaches as we will see in the following chapters.

3. The first "schools" of political thought (400–250 BC)

Each of the foundational thinkers of the last chapter is associated with a stream of followers and successors who often used their predecessor as a mouthpiece to express ideas that are clearly not those of the original thinker. It is a mistake to think that the Buddha was followed by a unified *sangha* which produced a pure coherent canonical oral legacy consistent with his ideas, or that the students of Confucius simply recorded his sayings and transmitted them faithfully, or that Socrates is best remembered by Plato to provide the basis of all Western thought. This chapter traces the evolution of the ideas of the foundational thinkers in ways that are revealing of the potential interpretations of their thought.

There is a tendency to simplify the legacy of thinkers and schools of thought because it makes them easier to understand but it distorts the messy reality of the emergence of ideas. One should be wary of any neat classification of coherent schools of thought in this period because it is unlikely the boundaries between different approaches were so clear. Moreover, there is a large degree of syncretism and evolutionary change in the thought associated with each of the three foundational thinkers. The tendency for simplicity often makes Western thought look more pure and logical compared to what is portrayed as pseudo-religious and confused non-Western traditions. This is not true. They are all messy in similar ways. The beginning of this chapter unpacks the early historical development of foundational ideas to expose the politics of reinterpretation.

WHOSE LEGACY?

In the previous chapter it was argued that there were three foundational thinkers so after their death the expectation is that the thinkers who follow them have derived their ideas from these thinkers. However, this is not as straightforward as one might think. All systems of thought change over time, particularly as influenced by their opponents and the need to respond to them.

All schools of Buddhist thought agree that the first Buddhist Council was in Rajagrha immediately after the death of the Buddha (After Nirvana or AN) under his trusted follower Ananda.[1] Before he died Buddha asked for the monks to abolish the minor and least important of his precepts but there was no agreement on what they were so it was decided that all his sayings would be recited so they could be preserved.[2] In many cases this resulted in multiple versions of the same teaching. Many of these sayings will be accurate reflections of the Buddha's views because oral transmission based on strict memorization and repetition can be just as reliable as the transmission of written texts. The early Buddhists also used mnemonic devices as aids to memorization, such as repeating certain phrases or grouping ideas into numerical groups. Given human fallibility some errors may have crept in but the body of sayings memorized by monks who heard him, particular those in the Kindred and Middle-Length sayings (*Samyatta Nikaya* and *Majjhima Nikaya*) that have come down to us, potentially reflect his ideas.

At the same time some of his sayings may have been altered slowly over time to accommodate what are later called "Hindu" beliefs, with which they were in competition.[3] We should also expect a degree of syncretism as Buddhism challenged and sought to propose alternatives to existing beliefs such as heaven and hell or reincarnation. The Buddha himself challenged the followers of other belief systems by questioning the basis of their beliefs through demonstrations of the logical consequences of the ideas upon which they were based. In that case, it is not a major leap to have the Buddha showing that the beliefs of others are compatible with his philosophy and even using the fiction of him directly conversing with and refuting the gods of others in person. One good example is the introduction of reincarnation into Buddhism, which has been argued to be inconsistent with other key ideas of the Buddha. The Buddha was also implicitly critical of the caste and wealth. One should note that such syncretic material most often appears in what are clearly later sections of the Canon especially the *Anguttara Nikāya* and *Dīgha Nikāya* sections.[4] In the case of reincarnation, it is even unclear whether the Buddha is focusing on

---

[1] See André Bareau (1955) *Les premiers conciles bouddhiques*, Paris: Presses Universitaires de France.

[2] See also Étienne Lamotte (1958) *Histoire du bouddhisme indien: Des origines à l'ère Saka*, Louvain: Publications universitaires, Institut orientaliste, 125–126 and Digha Nikaya 2.

[3] See Lamotte (1958) *Histoire du bouddhisme indien*, 68–69 and more recent articles by Analayo (2011) "Brahmā's Invitation the Ariyapariyesana-sutta and its Madhyama-agama Parallel," *Journal of the Oxford Centre for Buddhist Studies*, 1: 12–38 and Paisarn Likhitpreechakul (2012) "Decoding Two 'Miracles' of the Buddha," *Journal of the Oxford Centre for Buddhist Studies*, 2: 209–222.

[4] James P. McDermott (2003) *Development in the Early Buddhist Concept of Kamma/Karma*, New Delhi: Munshiram Manoharlal: 12.

intention or on actual acts, including whether one act alone can determine rebirth or if it is based on the culmination of a series of deeds.[5]

The tendency to collapse the evolution of ideas into a single canon makes Buddhist thought in this period seem one dimensional when there were likely multiple sources, layers of exposition and divergent views on key issues being resolved. It is a difficult but necessary task to try to disentangle the various threads to make the most sense of the Buddha's legacy of political thought. This also means that it will be difficult to discern a coherent early political philosophy given the diversity of influences. Even if there was a core of sayings in the "Buddhist Canon" established in the century after the death of the Buddha, it is also likely that they were slightly modified and edited many times before being committed to writing.[6] The Long Dialogues, in particular, should be seen as a later embroidering of elements of early Buddhist sayings. There are two or three Long Dialogues that are particularly relevant to the evolution of Buddhist political thought after the death of the Buddha. One is the *Aggañña Suttanta* and the other is *Cakkavatti Sihanada Suttanta*, and, to a lesser extent, the *Maha-Parinibbana Sutta* should be included here. The *Aggañña Suttanta* describes a creation myth with profound political implications but there is evidence that it is late. For example, the concept of caste (*varna*) is accepted in a way that it is not clear that the Buddha did in other sayings attributed to him.

It is likely that the first major schism in the Buddhist movement was at the Second Buddhist Council held at Vaishali, capital of the Licchavis (c. 400–350 BC). There appear to have been many Licchavi followers of Buddha and he is said to have visited them on many occasions but by this point the quasi-republican community of the Licchavis had been absorbed into the kingdom of Magadha. Some argue that there was a dispute over ten specific points of discipline at the Vaishali council but it has been convincingly demonstrated that the division was over the expansion of the *vinaya* monastic rules.[7] The Mahāsāṃghika group (महासांघिक; 大衆部) "The Great Sangha" or "the majority" wanted to leave the rules untouched but the Sthaviravāda (स्थविरवाद; 上座部) "Sect of The Elders" or "those seated higher" felt that additional rules were needed to deal with discipline problems. This seems to be borne out by differences in the *vinaya* codes of the different sects that begin to emerge at this time. However, it

---

[5] McDermott, *Development in the Early Buddhist Concept of Kamma/Karma*: 13ff.

[6] See Lance Cousins (2013) "The Early Development of Buddhist Language and Literature in India," *Journal of the Oxford Centre for Buddhist Studies*, 5: 122.

[7] Janice J. Nattier and Charles S. Prebish (1977) "Mahāsāṃghika Origins: The Beginnings of Buddhist Sectarianism," *History of Religions*, 16(3): 237–272.

The first "schools" of political thought (400–250 BC) 51

was not until around the time of King Ashoka, the most famous Buddhist *cakkavatti* or universal ruler that the divisions in the *sangha* increased and began to have long-term significance to the development of Buddhism. These will be discussed in the next chapter.

The explosion in philosophical debate that follows the death of Confucius requires considerable attention in this chapter because it constitutes the foundation of East Asian political thought as much as ancient Greek thinkers such as Plato and Aristotle are seen as the basis for Western political thought. The problem is that later observers have artificially grouped together thinkers of this period into schools that did not formally exist at the time. Affiliations and tendencies were looser in this period than the notion of schools allows. This is particularly the case of the general term for thinkers and their followers called *Ru* (儒), or "Literati," which is almost always misleadingly translated as "Confucians." Even among the direct followers of Confucius, one can identify at least two strands of thought. These strands themselves were influenced by (and influenced the development of) three other tendencies, or that of the "Taoists" (*Dao-Jiā* 道家), "Mo-ists" (followers of Mo Di or *Mò-Jiā* 墨家), and the "Legalists" (*Fǎ-jiā* 法家).

The *Analects*, as we have seen, is our main source of the ideas of Confucius, but it bears the imprint of differences among the students of Confucius and their students, and other tendencies, as it developed over time. First of all, not all of the students of Confucius played a major role in the transmission of his ideas. One early version of the *Analects*, the "Seven Chapter Analects of Qi" (齊人論語七篇) is associated with Zigong (子貢) who is mentioned the most often in our received version of the *Analects* and was among the more politically active,[8] but this book is likely a later version though it may contain some authentic material on Confucius' students from the more politically active group. Zixia (子夏) is particularly important as the most immediately influential teacher who followed Confucius.[9] For example, one of his students, Gongyang Gao (公羊高) of the State of Qi, wrote an important commentary on the *Spring and Autumn Annals* (*Chunqiu* 春秋) that was later considered a key *Ru* (Literati) interpretation of the text.

Our understanding of Confucius, however, has been more influenced by another group of followers who clearly added ideas to the *Analects* after the death of Confucius. This group, which I will term the filial piety/ mystical school, were based in Confucius' native state of Lu and had the

---

[8] Takeuchi Yoshio (武内義雄) (1939) *Rongo no Kenkyū* (「論語之研究」) Tokyo: Iwanami Shoten (東京: 岩波書店) on pages 100–101 and more specifically on page 106.
[9] Confucius; D.C. Lau trans. (1998) *The Analects*, Harmondsworth: Penguin: 213–214.

authority of access to and perhaps the support of Confucius' family. Most important amongst these is Zheng Zi (曾子). He played a major role in early *Ru* work associated with Confucius and is credited with large portions of another work, the *Great Learning* (大學), and figures as the partner in a dialogue with Confucius in the *Classic of Filial Piety* (孝經) but is mentioned relatively little in the *Analects*. His contributions to the canon of the sayings of Confucius appear to be later interpolations, but his material is attached to the "Hejian seven chapter" (河間七篇) version of the *Analects* that includes most of the core early books associated with Confucius. Therefore, the core of our *Analects* is a version that is specific to one school or tendency of thought.[10]

This is an important school because it includes Zheng, Zisi (子思 c. 481–402 BC, a grandson of Confucius), and Mencius, a key later interpreter of the ideas of Confucius. One should note that this school also includes You Zi (有子) who Lau notes held a special position in *Ru* schools associated with the Confucius school after the death of Confucius. Yet, You Zi's position as a direct student of Confucius is unclear since he only appears on one book of the *Analects* that seems to have been added much later.[11] You Zi's book is one of two books, a sort of rump version of the *Analects* associated with the filial piety/mystical school, the "Qi-Lu Two Chapters" text (齊魯二篇)[12] of which one is Book One of our *Analects* and strongly associated with You Zi (有子) and Book Ten, which is simply a collection of ritual maxims and not distinctive enough to consider a part of the earliest thought of Confucius or his followers.[13] It appears that You Zi or his followers edited the book to make the filial piety school more prominent by placing their texts earlier in a compilation of the *Analects* to constitute what are our received Books One and Two.

The most important change from Confucius was the transformation of the concept of filial piety (*xiào* 孝). Although Confucius claims to derive his views on all subjects from the practice of the ancients, and, closer to his time, the Shang and early Zhou dynasties, we have little early evidence of the type of filial piety which plays such an important role in later what the West came to call Confucianism, especially popular Confucianism. Indeed, many East Asians would cite filial piety as the central tenet of Confucianism. However, there is little early evidence of filial piety in ancient Chinese texts and even then it focuses primarily on respect for the

---

[10] According to Takeuchi (1939) *Rongo no Kenkyū*: 99 – "This is clearly the Analects of the School of Zhengzi/Zizi/Mencius."
[11] Confucius; D.C. Lau trans. (1998) *The Analects*: 214, 218–219 and Confucius; Waley trans. (1938) *Analects*: 20.
[12] Takeuchi (1939) *Rongo no Kenkyū*; 90–95.
[13] Confucius; Waley trans. (1938) *Analects*: 21.

dead.[14] In the earliest books of the *Analects*, we also find that the discussion of filial piety is isolated and ambiguous.[15] It certainly does not justify later notions of filial piety. It merely seems to suggest being polite to, and kind and supportive of one's parents. The emphasis on filial piety is in decidedly late books, which again were no doubt placed at the front of the *Analects* to reinforce their dubious authority. This includes *Analects* Book I Sections 2, 11 and Book II Sections 5, 7, 8, 20, 21 all of which place clear limits on any challenge to authority in the name of filial piety. This would have had a clear impact on the common people and on women of all status levels. This discussion gets distorted by misleading comparisons about deference to parents, elders and authority which forms the folk knowledge, East and West, about so-called Confucianism. This is reinforced by the tendency to exaggerate filial piety and its significance, especially in such works as the *24 Exemplars of Filial Piety* (二十四孝), which again features Zheng Zi (曾子), but was not written until the Yuan dynasty (1260–1368) nearly two thousand years after the death of Confucius.

Importantly, the two late books associated with You Zi and the filial piety school also have an emphasis on government. For example, in Book I, Section 12, Confucius is made to argue that the proper rituals performed by the divinely sanctioned leader can act as a force for harmony in the state and thus order. In Books II, Sections 3 and 20, and Book XIII Sections 11 and 12 the direct focus is on power of moral force – through correct behavior of the leader – contributing to order. These passages are unusual as they focus on the ruler rather than the usual focus of Confucius on the noble person and good minister. However, the strongest influence of this group is to tie filial piety and obedience to authority. It is particularly stark in the saying attributed to You Zi: "They are few who, being filial and fraternal, are fond of offending against their superiors. There have been none, who, not liking to offend against their superiors, have been fond of stirring up confusion."[16]

Mencius (孟子 372–289 BC), can be considered as the culmination of this mystical/filial school of Zheng Zi and You Zi. Like his predecessors, he clearly developed his ideas in tandem with and opposition to other schools, particularly the one led by Mozi (墨子 c. 470–391 BC) and another associated with the proto-Taoist Yang Zhu (楊朱 440–360 BC). Another proto-Taoist contemporary, Zhaung Zi (莊子 369–286 BC), may have also been in

---

[14] Confucius; Waley trans. (1938) *Analects*: 38.
[15] For example, *Analects*, Bk. IV 18–21 in Confucius; Waley trans. (1938) *Analects*: 105–106.
[16] James Legge, trans. (c. 1920) *The Four Books* (華英四書), Shanghai: The Chinese Book Company: 2–3.

the background to the development of Mencius' thought. The arguments of Mo-ists and other opponents against filial piety must have led to a reinforcement of these ideas in later versions of the *Analects*. It makes sense, then, to view the students and later followers of Confucius and his students in the context of the other thinkers emerging as the *Analects* was compiled and the other *Ru* texts were being written. Similarly, the tendency toward naturalism and even mysticism in Mencius is a response to early forms of what is later called Taoism.

Mo Di (墨翟) or Mozi (墨子) or Master Mo (c. 470–c. 390 BC) was one of the key thinkers who had a major impact on the thinking of followers of Confucius, even more so if, as is possible, Mo was also a native of the state of Lu and was in immediate conflict with immediate students of Confucius and their students. It may not have been a direct challenge at first because Mo himself and his followers appear to be from lower classes than the *Ru*. He emphasized equality and respect for everyone regardless of position or lineage.[17] This undermined the view of Confucius and his followers that ritual and order, including status and hierarchy, were central to good government. In reaction, the Zheng/You/Zisi/Mencius followers of Confucius began to emphasize the family relations and mutual affection as the strongest counter-argument they had against Mo's views of equality and universal love or impartial care (*jian'ai* 兼愛) for others.

Another counter-argument to the ideas of Confucius arose from what we now call Taoism (道教). The concept of the *tao* or "the Way" is accepted as basic to all thinkers in the Zhou dynasty. What are called the Taoists, however, have a philosophy opposed to core ideas of Confucius and his followers, particularly the value of ritual and goodness. At the very least, the so-called Taoists strongly challenged *Ru* understanding of these concepts.

The final tendency, Legalism (*Fǎ-jiā* 法家), sometimes translated as "Realism," is closely related to what we are calling Taoism that it is difficult to separate especially in the early period. For example, Laozi's *Book of the Way and Virtue* (Daodejing 道德經) is one of the most famous Taoist texts but it has many arguments that are similar to the *Fǎ-jiā*.[18] Later tradition traces *Fǎ-jiā* back to political practitioners such as Shang Yang (商鞅, 390–338 BC), who was born in the state of Wei but was made a minister of the state of Qin under Duke Xiao and strengthened that state through a combination of meritocracy and strict punishment with an emphasis

---

[17] See Mo Di, Ian Johnston trans. (2010) *The Mozi: A Complete Translation*, New York, NY: Columbia University Press.

[18] Lao tzu [Laozi]; Arthur Waley trans. (1934) *The Way and Its Power: A Study of the Tao tê Ching and its Place in Chinese Thought*, London: G. Allen & Unwin: 83–87.

on standards (*fǎ* 法). Shen Buhai (申不害) prime minister from 351 BC to his death in 337 BC and his Shenzi (申子) are often classified as a *Fǎ-jiā*, partly because of his influence on later *Fǎ-jiā* in relation to the concept of *shù* (術) defined as technique or skill in using power.[19] He also embraces Taoist ideas but much as Shang Yang focuses on *fǎ* (法) or standards, rather than law per se.[20] This Shenzi must not be confused with the work of Shen Dao (慎到, c. 350–c. 275 BC) who focuses on *shì* (勢) defined as circumstantial advantage, power or authority, which is used in ways that has affinities with *Fǎ-jiā* theory as well.[21]

Xunzi (荀子 298–235? BC) is the last well-known Warring States *Ru* scholar claiming to be a follower of Confucius. He did not travel as widely as Confucius and Mencius and there are very few dates associated with his life. He was a magistrate who continued in office for eighteen years until an assassination in 237 BC after which he lost his position for reasons that are unclear. Manuscripts discovered in an elite tomb in Guodian have revealed several texts which help put him in better perspective.[22] We can trace the Zheng/Zisi/Mencius lineage but some of these new texts suggests an alternative strand that anticipates some of Xunzi's ideas. Therefore, it is likely that there were at least two major strands of *Ru* followers of Confucius of which Mencius and Xunzi represent clear types. Xunzi's view that human nature is inherently evil is a clear contrast with Mencius who believes it is inherently good. Actually, Xunzi does not really say "evil" but he did believe that humans are originally uncultured and born with a strong desire for profit and sensuality, which can often overwhelm their potential for good. At the very least, Xunzi is skeptical of the natural goodness of basic human character (*xing* 性).[23]

Xunzi was opposed to hereditary privilege and believed that all offices should be filled based on ability.[24] However, even though he was against status distinctions based on heredity, he believed that status distinctions were important and should be given on merit. Moreover, these must also

---

[19] Creel, Herrlee G. (1974) *Shen Pu-Hai: A Chinese Political Philosopher of the Fourth Century BC*, Chicago, IL: University of Chicago Press.

[20] This concept of standards is central to section one "Authoritative Moral Force" (*wēi dé* 威德) of the fragments of Shenzi work. See http://ctext.org/shenzi/wei-de (accessed June 3, 2017).

[21] Shenzi; Eirik Lang Harris trans. (2016) *The Shenzi Fragments: A Philosophical Analysis and Translation*, New York, NY: Columbia University Press; Shenzi, M. Thompson ed. (1979) *The Shen Tzu Fragments*, Oxford: Oxford University.

[22] Paul Goldin (2005) *After Confucius: Studies in Early Chinese Philosophy*, Honolulu, HI: University of Hawaii Press: 36–37.

[23] Burton Watson trans. (1963) *Basic Writings of Mo Tzu, Hsün Tzu and Han Fei Tzu*, New York, NY: Columbia University Press: 157–171.

[24] Xunzi; Eric L. Hutton trans. (2014) *Xunzi: The Complete Text*, Princeton, NJ: Princeton University Press: 141–144.

be created and highly regulated by the ruler. Overall, however, Xunzi maintains a balance between punishments and rewards. On the positive side, he favors low taxes and freedom of individuals from arbitrary actions of the ruler, but he also favors draconian punishment to maintain order. Not surprisingly, Hughes notes that Xunzi hardly ever uses the term *dé*, moral force or virtue, which was one of the key early ideas associated with Confucius.[25]

Ironically, for all his work in rationalizing and completing the work of Confucius, Xunzi played a role in the creation of *Fǎ-jiā* (Legalism), a movement which could be seen as strongly anti-*Ru* (anti-Confucian). Two of his students, Han Fei (c. 280–233 BC) and Li Ssu (李斯, 280?–208 BC) were not only the key figures identified as *Fǎ-jiā*, but also were more successful and harmful, and had greater influence than any of the followers of Confucius. In the end, Xunzi's philosophy fostered despotic government. The authoritarian strain of Xunzi thought in later *Ru* philosophy is unmistakable.

A rough sketch of the flow of intellectual influences is shown in Figure 3.1.

Chinese thinkers in the Spring/Autumnal (771–476 BC) and Warring States (475–221 BC) periods were much more independent and decentralized than Figure 3.1 suggests. Formal schools were uncommon even if teacher–student relationships played an important role in transmission. The concept of *Ru* (儒) is a generic term which could have included all the thinkers except for the extremes of followers of Mo and Yang Chu, the mystical Taoists and authoritarian *Fǎ-jiā* (Legalists). The existence of this wider audience explains why all schools also share some key concepts, such as the Way (道), even when the divergence in their approaches to politics is dramatic.

There are similar complexities in understanding the successors to the legacy of Socrates in ancient Greece. One might argue that the Cynics (κυνισμός) are the most direct and most plausible followers of Socrates. For example, the Cynic Antisthenes (Ἀντισθένης 445–365 BC), a well-known friend of Socrates, focuses on leading a simple life in the pursuit of virtues in a way that is very similar to that of Socrates. He also argues that virtue can be taught, much like the skills of a craft, as Socrates often implied, and that only those who are virtuous should be considered noble. The Cynic Diogenes of Sinope (Διογένης ὁ Σινωπεύς) took these ideas further by living in a large storage jar with the bare minimum of possessions and viewing authority with contempt, looking for an honest man with a

---

[25] E.R. Hughes (1942) *Chinese Philosophy in the Classical Times*, New York, NY: E.P. Dutton: 248.

Mystical: Yang Chu → Zhuang Zhou (c. 369–c. 286 BC)

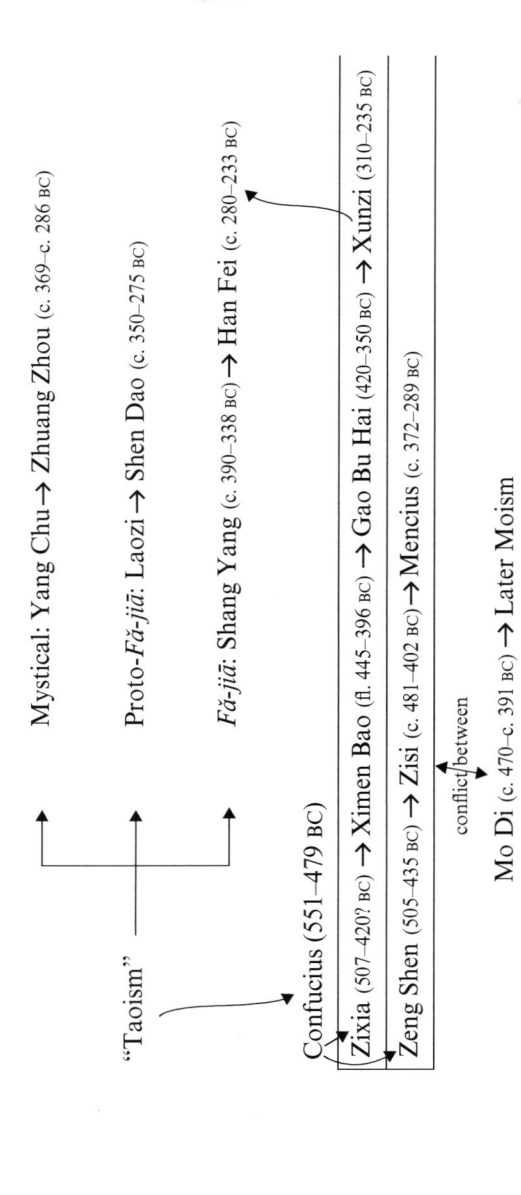

Proto-*Fǎ-jiā*: Laozi → Shen Dao (c. 350–275 BC)

Fǎ-jiā: Shang Yang (c. 390–338 BC) → Han Fei (c. 280–233 BC)

"Taoism"

Confucius (551–479 BC)
Zixia (507–420? BC) → Ximen Bao (fl. 445–396 BC) → Gao Bu Hai (420–350 BC) → Xunzi (310–235 BC)
Zeng Shen (505–435 BC) → Zisi (c. 481–402 BC) → Mencius (c. 372–289 BC)

conflict between

Mo Di (c. 470–c. 391 BC) → Later Moism

Figure 3.1 Lineages of early East Asian political thought

57

lamp in the daylight, mocking Plato and declaring himself a cosmopolitan (that is, a citizen of the world and not one state). His follower Crates of Thebes (Κράτης ὁ Θηβαῖος c. 365–c. 285 BC) is said to have been the teacher of Zeno of Citium (Ζήνων ὁ Κιτιεύς c. 334–c. 262 BC), the founder of Stoicism, which had a widespread influence on the Roman Empire and later Western political thought. The problem is that the ideas of these thinkers exist only in tantalizing fragments so tracing their lineage back to Socrates is difficult.

Plato (Πλάτων c. 427–c. 347 BC) was, on the other hand, Socrates' most well-known student and all of his works seem to have survived until present. Plato appears to have also been influenced by the ideas of Pythagoras of Samos (Πυθαγόρας ὁ Σάμιος, c. 570–c. 495 BC) from whom he developed a mystical interest in the logic of numbers that appears in some of his dialogues. From Socrates he developed a theory of forms/ideas *eidos* (εἶδος) or fixed ideas of the good against the Sophists' relativism by which they were able to twist the meaning of words to suit their purposes. Plato extends the ideas of Socrates in ways that Socrates would likely not have recognized because Socrates' approach was to question and allow those with whom he interacted make sense of the paradoxes themselves. Plato seems more sure that he knows the correct answer and simply needs to lead his student to it. Not surprisingly, Plato founded one of the first academic schools, the Academy, in 385 in a sanctuary of Athena in northern Athens.

Aristotle (Ἀριστοτέλης, 384–322 BC), a student of Plato at the Academy, was opposed to the approach of Plato in many ways. Like Socrates Aristotle attempted to understand the supreme goals or aim (telos τέλος) of human life which he saw as *eudaimonia* (εὐδαιμονία) or well-being, sometimes translated as "happiness." Yet against Plato's insistence on fixed ideas of the good, Aristotle applied practical wisdom (*phronēsis* φρόνησις) to seek out appropriate ends and goals of politics. Followers of Aristotle's approach developed into the Peripatetic school he established at the Lyceum, a temple dedicated to Apollo Lyceus, which competed for influence with the Academy and the Stoics throughout Western classical civilization.

The Cynics were slowly replaced by the Stoics. Indeed, as we have noted, the founder of the Stoic school, Zeno, was originally a Cynic. Zeno created the concept of *kathekon* (καθῆκον) meaning "appropriate behavior," "suitable actions," "action in keeping with nature," or "proper function." In this sense, he was closer to the pragmatic approach of Aristotle but retained some of the mysticism of Plato. Thus, the Cynics gave rise to the Stoics, who will be discussed in the next chapter. Sophists' approach of relativism lingered in the Skeptics so also played a minor role in the development of Stoic political thought.

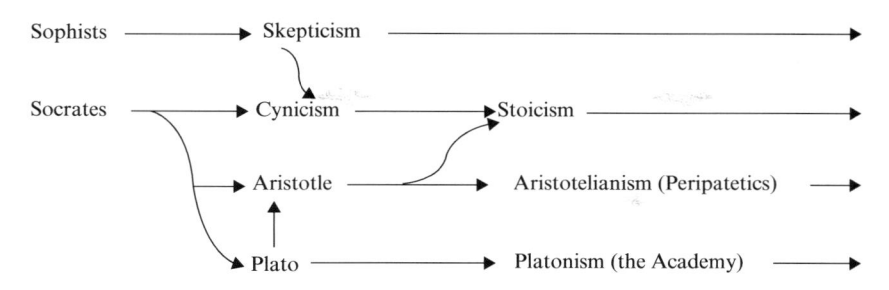

The first "schools" of political thought (400–250 BC)   59

```
Sophists    ──▶ Skepticism ─────────────────────────────▶
                     ↖
Socrates    ──▶ Cynicism ──────▶ Stoicism ───────────────▶
         ╲
          ──▶ Aristotle ──────▶ Aristotelianism (Peripatetics) ──▶
                  ↑
          ──▶ Plato ──────────▶ Platonism (the Academy) ──▶
```

Figure 3.2   The influence of Socrates on ancient Hellenic and Roman thought

Figure 3.2 suggests the flow of influence of Socrates in relation to the various schools of classical thought. Socrates is parallel to but distinct from the Sophists. The most direct influence of Socrates is on the Cynics. Plato is placed furthest from Socrates because Platonic thought is much more the work of Plato than Socrates. Aristotle is placed in between, because he is influenced by Plato, even if in reaction to his approach, and because Aristotle appears to have tapped into what he thought was the more practical focus of Socrates in contrast to the theoretical focus of Plato.

RELATIONSHIP TO POLITICAL POWER

Students of Confucius, Socrates' student Plato and Plato's student Aristotle were all involved with political rulers of their day. Only the Cynics and Taoists tended to try to avoid the politically powerful but strangely not the Buddhists who are highly dependent on royal patronage and even seem to favor monarchism. Despite the models of democratic or republican rule in both Indian and Mediterranean civilization, monarchs were seen by most if not all of these thinkers as the accepted form of government. Therefore, theories of how to best rule are prominent in each case with an ideal of the Sage rulers important for all.

In Buddhism, the default assumption that the good ruler is a monarch is clear in the *Cakkavatti Sihanada Suttanta*, which explains the evolution of kingship, based on the rise and fall of the *cakkavatti*, or universal monarch, literally a "wheel turning monarch," or *cakravartiraajan* (चक्रवर्तिराजन्), or simply a wheel mover, *cakravartin* (चक्रवर्तिन्). The story is very elaborate and suggests policies and practices that are later than those associated with the time of the Buddha. Finally, the concept of a Buddha and a ruler of the world are linked in *Maha-Parinibbana Sutta*.[26] For example, Ananada tells the Mallas of Kusinara that the remains of the Buddha must be treated like a universal monarch (*cakkavatti*) and a monument or stupa must be erected over his remains.[27] The stupa are believed to have the power to bring calmness and order to the world. They also act as a symbol of Buddhist conquest as much as the control of the state by a *cakkavatti*. Buddhism had adopted the symbols of royal power, and, at the same time, relics and objects symbolizing the Buddha were considered important to royal power. There was a mutually reinforcing relationship. Since stupas are archeologically much later than the Buddha, it again suggests that this and the other Long Dialogues are later additions to the canon.[28]

Some of the immediate students of Confucius were particularly successful and politically influential, especially in the state of Wei, and initially amongst *Ru* intellectuals as a whole. Among these were Zigong (子貢) and Zixia (子夏) who were politically active followers of Confucius. One student associated with Zixia is Ximen Bao (西門豹), a government minister and court advisor to Marquis Wen of Wei (reigned 445–396 BC). He led the State of Wei to abolish inhumane punishments, and he attacked superstition, such as his advocacy of abolition of the practice of sacrificing people to the river god He Bo. This suggests that Ximen was a rationalist following from the teachings of Zixia who again looms large as a politically active and pragmatic thinker in the early history of the transmission of Confucius' ideas. In contrast, the Zheng-Lu school, which had the most influence over the text of the *Analects*, seemed to be ignored by political leaders initially and took a much more mystical approach to power. Of the Zheng-Lu lineage, it is mainly Mencius who is portrayed as actively engaged in providing advice to kings, though often more to admonish them than actively engage them.[29]

Plato flirted with advising rulers in his ill-fated trips to the Greek colony of Syracuse to teach the rulers of the city, once where he was sold into slavery and then when he was held captive, but in neither case did his advice make a difference. Aristotle was famously tutor to Alexander the Great when he was a child but Alexander's successes and failures show

---

[26] Both the "Cakkavatti Sihanada Suttanta" and "Maha-Parinibbana Sutta" have been translated by T. W. Rhys Davids (1881) *Buddhist Suttas*, The Sacred Books of the East, vol. XI, Oxford: Oxford University Press.
[27] Rhys Davids, *Buddhist Suttas*: 155–157.
[28] Gregory Schopen (1997) *Bones, Stones, and Buddhist Monks: Collected Papers on the Archaeology, Epigraphy, and Texts of Monastic Buddhism in India*, Honolulu, HI: University of Hawaii Press: 86–113.
[29] For example, *Mencius* 1.1 in Mencius; D.C. Lau trans. (1970) *Mencius*, Harmondsworth: Penguin: 49.

little of Aristotle's influence. Even the Cynics seemed to favor the ideal of the monarch as a hero who sacrifices for the common good, for example in the emphasis of some Cynics on Hercules. Cynics might also be included with those Socratics, such as Xenophon who seemed to idealize Cyrus, the Persian Ruler, and monarchical Sparta. Of course not all Cynics favor monarchy. Although Diogenes tended to call himself a king, he did it with the implication that anyone can call themselves anything and was contemptuous of the power of real kings. Even if the stories of his interaction with Alexander the Great are a myth, it is likely that he did not revere kings. Cynics are certainly wary of the abilities of most actual monarchs.

ELITISM, CLASS AND GENDER BIAS

In the previous chapter it was noted that all three foundation thinkers had an implicit notion of equality. As the time passes, the issue of equality and class bias is raised more clearly. Most schools of political thought in this period are elitist, though potentially the philosophy of Buddhism, Mozi, the Taoists, and the Cynics could be viewed as egalitarian or at least meritocratic (even if involvement with power as a theme suggests that they were not often successful in avoiding/appealing to/using elite status).

The Buddhist "Agganna Suttanta" appears to accept the notion of caste even if it challenges traditional versions with the *Kshatriya* caste placed first in this myth (it is usually second in traditional "Hindu" accounts), with the Brahmins as ethical seekers next (usually first), and then merchants and craft workers, *Vaishya*, following them and *Shudra*, who are portrayed as hunters (and not servants as traditionally), emerge last. Within the Buddhist community itself, however, equality would have been maintained, though as noted, women were often organized separately.

The anti-Literati Mozi is sometimes seen as populist and egalitarian because he bitterly attacks the *Ru* (Literati) followers of Confucius for being a self-serving elite but it is not clear that he is against hierarchy but merely seeks a different kind. On the other hand, Mencius, who one would expect to defend traditional hierarchy and filial relations (including toward the ruler), puts a good deal of emphasis on the importance of the people (*min* 民). He considers them more important than heaven (fate) and earth (material conditions)[30] because luck will not be on your side if the people are not and even the best weapons or fortifications are useless

---

[30] Mencius; Lau trans. (1970) *Mencius*: 85.

unless one has a loyal population to use them effectively. He is even seen as a proto-democrat when he argues "the people are supreme,"[31] he recognizes the importance of popular morale for leadership ("lose the people and lose power"). There are three different elements of a nation, that is, the People, tutelary Spirits, and Sovereign, of which "The people are the most important element in a nation; the spirits of the land and grain are the next; the sovereign is the lightest."[32] In this sense the people are part of the Mandate of Heaven, the concept which Mencius develops more fully. Nonetheless, one must take care not to read democratic ideals into Mencius. He argued the ruler is responsible for keeping people in line but in doing so must not exploit them too much. Moreover, Mencius argues that women do not have the ability to engage in politics or achieve much in education but he does suggest that they may have greater ethical insight than men.[33]

The later Warring States follower of Confucius, Xunzi, with his emphasis on merit basis of hierarchy rather than hereditary succession might also seem more democratic but he was deeply suspicious of the average person and believed that good behavior is only possible through rigorous training in ritual. As part of his understanding of ritual and order, Xunzi advocates clear social roles and ritual practices for women separate from men, in part, it seems, because he believed that women played a role in creating the disorder of the age in which he lived.[34]

Plato and Aristotle were seemingly less egalitarian than Socrates. Plato was from a wealthy family and clearly opposed to democracy. In his *Republic*, it is seen as the worse form of government. Aristotle argued that some humans are "slaves by nature" (*physei doulos* φύσει δοῦλος), that is, inherently prone to follow their base instincts so are slaves to their appetites and thus need to be controlled and driven by others of a more noble character.[35] This is reflected in Aristotle's analysis of states where he suggested the need for a mixed constitution with a balance between the mob (seen in democracy), the tyranny of dictator and the avarice of an oligarchy, so not reliant on a single ruler because appetites can pervert the holders of office, even the best ones.[36] Moreover, immediately after

---

[31] Mencius; Lau trans. (1970) *Mencius*: 183.
[32] Mencius; Lau trans. (1970) *Mencius*: 121–122.
[33] Wang Robin ed. (2003) *Images of Women in Chinese Thought and Culture: Writings from the Pre-Qin Period through the Song Dynasty*, Indianapolis, IN: Hackett Publishing Company: 102.
[34] Wang Robin ed. (2003) *Images of Women in Chinese Thought and Culture*: 113.
[35] Aristotle; Earnest Barker trans. (1958) *The Politics of Aristotle*, Oxford: Oxford University Press: 11–14.
[36] Aristotle; Barker trans. (1958) *The Politics of Aristotle*: 146.

announcing that some men are slaves by nature, Aristotle declared that women are inferior to men, and though there is the notion of friendship involving women appears to be an exception this is not really developed by Aristotle further.[37] However, Plato would make women equal as guardians of his ideal Republic, and here seems to follow Socrates in a more positive view of the intellectual capacities of at least some women.

Cynics were more egalitarian in principle because they do not make the distinctions between citizen/foreigner or barbarian, and reject class- or birth-based concepts. The Stoics followed the Cynics by dividing humanity into wise and foolish with the ideal a community of the wise across humanity. Only the foolish should be considered second class citizens and even prohibited from participation in government. However, few Cynics had political power and they implied that actual rulers were often fools so that the wise must reach out to each other and do what they can to ameliorate the influence of fools. Most intriguingly, there were prominent female Cynics philosophers such as Hipparchia of Maroneia (Ἱππαρχία ἡ Μαρωνεῖτις; fl. c. 325 BC),[38] which suggests that they were much more egalitarian in a real sense than most in Greek society at the time.

COSMOLOGY AND KNOWLEDGE

In this chapter, we can avoid discussion of religion but there is a metaphysics behind the cosmology essential to understanding these schools of thought. This cosmology is also connected to knowledge, that is, one must act politically in accordance with the way the universe works and knowledge is key to understand the nature of the universe. This has implications for the skills needed by rulers and those who would pursue justice. In all cases, there is a distinction between theoretical knowledge and practical (applied) knowledge.

This is relevant to how we should interpret Buddhist texts. The Buddha, as we have seen, had a great ability to adapt his discussion of Buddhist ideas to the beliefs of those to whom he was speaking.[39] There is a concept of *upāya-kaushalya* meaning "skill in means" from *upāya* (उपाय), "expedient method," particularly to in order to teach, with *kaushalya* (कौशल्य) or "cleverness" usually associated with the later development of Mahāyāna

---

[37] Aristotle; Barker trans. (1958) *The Politics of Aristotle*: 33–38.
[38] Diogenes Laërtius; Robert Drew Hicks trans. (1925) "The Cynics: Hipparchia," *Lives of the Eminent Philosophers*, 2 volumes, London: William Heinemann: 2: 6.
[39] Gombrich, *How Buddhism Began*: 17.

Buddhism[40] though a similar approach does appear in the Pali canon.[41] It is the notion that examples and stories that provide the listener access to the concepts of Buddhism do not need to be precisely accurate. It is possible to provide a crude heuristic version of Buddhist concepts for individuals to start to grasp the ideas with the aim of refining them later. It is particularly important in Buddhism where true understanding is to be found outside the material world and beyond the conceptual framework of ordinary language.

This helps explain the logic of the advice to maintain or restore rule that is central to late canonical Buddhism in the *Cakkavatti Sihanada Suttanta*. This text tells of *cakkavatti* who orders his advisors to monitor "the Celestial Wheel" that seems to be a metaphor for the quality of the rule by a monarch which is bound to decline as complacency sets in and advanced age leads to the ruler and royal advisors to become less competent. When the Celestial Wheel declines, the King is meant to send for the prince regent and resign. Before he leaves, the old King tells the prince of his duties as Wheel-turning Monarch, which is to depend on the "Norm," honouring and respecting it, to protect the kingdom including beasts and birds. The concept of the "Norm," here used as the translation of the word *dharma* (धर्म in Sanskrit or *Dhamma* in Pali), is key in Buddhist thought. It can also be translated as "Law" but less the human law than something like the laws of physics. The words "*Droit*" in French and "*Reich*" in German more closely resemble the term *Dharma* as a source of the law, what is right, and power, or essentially Law of truth and righteousness. The sutra also contains more specific admonitions:

> Let no wrongdoing prevail; give wealth to the poor, listen to those who pursue religious life and allow them to question what is good and what is bad, what is criminal and what is not, what is to be done and what left undone, what line of action will in the long run work for weal or for woe. Deter them from evil and encourage them to do what is good. This is the duty of a sovereign of the world.[42]

Initially the kings follow this advice and the Celestial Wheel returns and rolls across the regions of the earth, followed the Wheel-turning king, and wherever this king and his army went all rival kings welcome him and ask

---

[40] Asaf Federman (2009) "Literal Means and Hidden Meanings: A New Analysis of Skillful Means," *Philosophy East and West*, 59(2): 125–141.
[41] "Sangiti Sutta" in Digha Nikaya 33, *Sutta Central*: https://suttacentral.net/en/dn33 (accessed November 15, 2017).
[42] "Simile of the Raft" in Majjhima Nikaya 22, *Sutta Central*: https://suttacentral.net/en/mn22 (accessed June 3, 2017).

them to teach them. This king, as sovereign war-lord, tells the other kings to "Slay no living thing. Do not take that which has not been given. Do not act wrongly in enjoying bodily desires. Do not lie. Drink no maddening drink. Enjoy your possessions as you have always." These enemy kings in the regions become vassals to the king, the Wheel-turner. Once the entire earth is conquered in this way, the Wheel and the king move to the royal capital and the Wheel stands as if fixed in place in the judgment hall of the king. Over time, however, the kings fail to listen to the advice of their predecessors and attempt to rule as they see fit but because the realm is ruled differently than in the past, the kingdom does not prosper. Even when the king seeks advice, it is not complete, for example, the king fails to provide for the poor and poverty became widespread. Poverty leads to theft and even though at first the king is lenient, this seems to encourage theft, but when the king punishes theft severely, it leads to widespread lying and even violence to avoid capture and punishment. As lying became widespread, this in turn led to immorality as it became common for husbands and wives, parents and children, and others to avoid telling the truth to each other. Therefore, from the king's failure to help the poor, poverty grew rife as did stealing, violence, murder, lying, evil speaking, adultery, abusive and idle talk, covetousness and ill-will, false opinions, incest, wanton greed and perverted lust, until finally there is a lack of filial and religious piety and contempt for authority, which, in turn, leads to a complete collapse of social order. Thus, even with the best of intentions, the ruler's errors can lead to moral and social decline. This order can only be restored by those individuals, Buddhists, who forego violence, lying, lust, and so on. When their influence is widespread then a new Wheel-turning monarch will emerge. In short, the text is a justification of the role of Buddhists in restoring a kingdom to its former glory and assisting the ruler in maintaining power.

It is important to remember that Confucius and the *Ru* (Literati) who followed his ideas accepted the notion of the Way (*Tao* or *Dao* 道) even if they interpreted it slightly differently from the Taoists. Even so, the *Ru* studied Taoist concepts and were influenced by them. Perhaps the most intriguing notion in Taoist political thought is *wu-wei* (無為) or, roughly, "action thru inaction." The best way to enable the Way to unfold naturally is inaction. To not do something is sometimes more likely to reach the desired goal than to try too hard. Eagerness to reach a goal can make that goal impossible to reach. The easiest example is over-eager approaches to a person of romantic interest. If you try too hard, it can have the opposite effect because trying too hard can make you look desperate; of course, it may be true that you are desperate but it is counter-productive to appear to be so. In this sense, we are all Taoists sometimes when we feel that not doing something will be likely to produce a better result than trying too hard. From a political point of view, the best ruler is one that allows events to unfold naturally so everyone says "It happened of its own accord"[43] even if selective non-intervention was key to the unfolding of events. Similarly, the ruler should be distant and not too accessible. One can see a similar tendency in the diffusion of a "presidential" form of governance, for example where a president or other political leader enters a press conference down a long distant corridor and makes a simple statement without taking questions. At the same time, *wu wei* is not always non-action. The exact exercise of *wu wei* is problematic because sometimes one must act or at least not act strategically or tactically. In theory, *wu wei* rejects action and seems to reject theoretical knowledge by aiming at something more natural but it is not always not acting. It is knowing, on a practical and natural level, when to not act and when to act.

Another paradox in the Taoist literature is that the Taoist Sage is the best person to govern but not only does this literature argue that Taoist kings should not act, there are also many stories of Taoists refusing to take political power when it is offered to them. Mencius criticized Yang Chu for being unwilling to trade even a single hair on his head for political power, or perhaps one might say, maliciously misinterpreted this as meaning that a Taoist Sage would not even sacrifice one hair off his head to save the empire if he could do so. It was the general lack of a sense of civic responsibility or duty which Mencius was criticizing. However, what the Taoists tended to argue was that political power and even all the riches of the empire are not worth anything in the long-run. A political leader hungry for power is likely to end up being a bad leader. One reluctant to take power is often more attractive as a leader and sought after for that reason.

Plato is also suspicious of the ability of humans to manage political power. He wanted strict educational regime, censored to protect the population of his ideal state. The most educated and capable of the citizens would be Guardians in charge, led by philosopher-kings who were the most knowledgeable of all. Plato seemed to cling to theoretical ideas as purer and worth pursuing even against all trials and tribulations. Plato created the expression "*sophos kagathos*" (σοφός κἀγαθός) separating external beauty from the beauty of the soul that can be found through knowledge. Plato's theory of forms/ideas (*eidos* εἶδος) clearly expresses the ideals to which he wanted the human mind to aspire and not surprisingly it plays a

---

[43] Lao tzu; Waley trans. (1934) *The Way and Its Power:* 164.

key role in the discussion of his ideal state in *The Republic* (Πολιτεία).[44] He does not underestimate the difficulty of human beings in acquiring true knowledge. For example, he uses the analogy of someone living in a cave who can only see shadows of the outside world. This is the extent of ordinary human knowledge of the real world but through understanding of the underlying ideal forms of the true world, one can begin to emerge even slightly from the cave of ignorance. He was also pragmatic to the extent that Plato's *Laws* (Νόμοι) seems to have set out the blueprint for a possible realistic state, especially when compared to the ideas of his Republic.[45]

Aristotle (Ἀριστοτέλης 384–322 BC) was a student of Plato but took a very different approach to political thought as he emphasized *phronēsis* (φρόνησις) or practical wisdom and *telos* (τέλος), or the appropriate ends and goals of politics including the ultimate goal for humans of *eudaimonia* (εὐδαιμονία) or well-being. His ethics focuses on specific virtues for which a balance between extremes is the aim. For example, courage is not recklessness out of having no fear or cowardice where fear leads a person to flee. True courage is doing one's duty without being overwhelmed with fear of the consequences. This distinction was already raised by Socrates but Aristotle applies it as a general rule to a range of virtues, including magnificence, which is not senseless liberality nor being miserly but using one's wealth sensibly to benefit others. In short, he developed principles to use *phronēsis* to achieve one's aims through intelligent moderation. Aristotle did not suggest that there is a clear fixed ideal as Plato did, only an understanding of dynamics in which one might situate oneself. Aristotle's argument is that the *telos* or goal of humans was *arête* or excellence (ἀρετή). Aristotle's *Politics* (Πολιτικά) makes the claim that humans are "political animals" (πολιτικό ζώο) so it is natural that they work together in groups, which implies the need for civic involvement and an implicit criticism of individualism and withdrawal from public life.[46]

It is possible that the distinction between theoretical knowledge as *sophia* or *ideos* conceptions, which is abstract and distant, and practical knowledge (*phronesis*), appears first possibly in the Cynics and then more explicitly in Aristotle. However, unlike Aristotle, Cynics appeared to express contempt for political power, in many ways similar to the Taoists, and just like the Taoists, this may have made them attractive to rulers. The apocryphal story of Alexander the Great standing before Diogenes the Cynic and offering him anything he wanted, and Diogenes' response was for Alexander to stop blocking his sunlight, indicates the Cynic's distaste

---

[44] Plato; Benjamin Jowett, trans. (1892) *The Dialogues of Plato*, vol. 3, Oxford: Oxford University Press: 1–338.
[45] Plato; Benjamin Jowett, trans. (1892) *The Dialogues of Plato*, vol. 5: 1–361.
[46] Aristotle; Barker trans. (1958) *The Politics of Aristotle*: 1–7.

for political power. Cynics and the Stoics who succeeded them tended to view themselves as cosmopolitans, or citizens of the cosmos rather than one state. What the ideal state was for the Cynics is unclear because though they appear to have produced a number of works, including versions of *The Republic* and books on ethics, these are now largely lost. For this reason, it is difficult to reconstruct Cynic political thought based on the small amount of material, much less than we have for the Buddhists, Taoists, *Fǎ-jiā* and even the followers of Mozi.

NATURE AND HUMAN NATURE

Perhaps the most important debate in all three civilizations in this period was over "human nature." The questions are: Is human nature basically good or bad? Would a naturally good tendency emerge if left alone or is there a need for training, punishment and great efforts in maintaining self-control? Do people need more rules or no rules?

The Buddhist view of human nature can be found in the *Aggañña Suttanta*.[47] It puts forward a vision of the state of nature usually associated with later Western political thinkers such as Hobbes, Locke or Rousseau. In this text, it is argued that originally the world consisted of only luminous beings in absolute darkness but some became greedy and desired to taste the world. This greed led to the emergence of daytime so the world would be seen, but it also led to the emergence of night-time in contrast to the day. The light of day enabled plants (creepers) to grow to satisfy hunger and when these plants were exhausted, rice was cultivated. Eating food had an impact on human bodies so that they became coarser and differentiated into male and female. The two genders became filled with lust and were soon so preoccupied with sex they felt compelled to build private dwellings to indulge in it. Many became lazy and did not gather food or rice for themselves. Others, however, set up their own plots of land greedy to have more food for themselves. When attempts were made by those without rice to seize the food or plots of others with rice, it was decided, based on the popular choice that a ruler was needed to maintain order. The key point is that society was a human invention. It emerged due to human lust, greed and the potential for violence but the choice of ruler is based on popular election. The good ruler in the Long Dialogues of the Buddha is a *cakkavatti*, a sovereign overlord who conquers, "not by the scourge, not by the sword, but by righteousness."[48]

---

[47] "Aggañña Suttanta", Dīgha Nikāya DN27, *Sutta Central*: https://suttacentral.net/en/dn27 (accessed November 15, 2017).
[48] Lakkhaṇa, Dīgha Nikāya DN30 at *Sutta Central*: https://suttacentral.net/en/dn30/.

Buddha focused on the need for self-control and power of temptation from things in the world. It might be seen as a denial of human nature but as this myth suggests, the primordial state was without desire. It was not only an error but to a lack of knowledge that led to the mistake of pursuing desires. The Buddha's system of coping with desire was simple but required considerable self-discipline and he seemed to have doubts about the ability of most individuals to master this discipline. For example, the *vinaya* rules for the community are fairly extensive and prescriptive. Nonetheless, it is a free choice whether a person wants to undertake this discipline. This concern with discipline also provides an insight into the split between the Mahāsāṃghika and Sthaviravāda wherein the latter group of senior monks felt that additions were needed to the rule of discipline (*vinaya*) but the former group did not. As time passed, senior monks probably feared for the coherence of the community in a way that most monks did not see as a threat.

The human nature debate in the Late Zhou dynasty is a key moment in the history of world political thought. In general Taoists saw virtue not as something to be cultivated, but as natural. It is not that people are naturally good, it is just that untouched by rules and moral strictures, they are better able to act as they should in accordance with the Way (the *Tao*). If the Way requires them to be evil, they should. In fact, they should not be instructed to not be evil as the lesson may have unintended consequences such as making people aware of evil (when they had not been) and may even give it a forbidden attractiveness or may make them unable to act to protect themselves.[49] Similarly it is only through simplicity that possessions and ambitions will be few so that theft and strife will be eliminated.

Naturalness is key as in Laozi, which we need to insist again, was more of a *Fǎ-jiā* (Legalist) text than a pure Taoist text. This is not surprising because *Fǎ-jiā* and Taoists shared a view that natural forces can be harnessed or finessed to build political power. Laozi and Shen Dao also exhibit the moral ambivalence of both Taoism and *Fǎ-jiā*. As such it is a clear contrast with the *Ru* trained in the classics such the *Analects* and associated texts which argue for moral force that can be fostered through ritual and cultivated behavior. For Taoism and *Fǎ-jiā*, the *Tao* (or heaven or nature) is force that is its own logic and can be used to maintain political power and order but not morality. There is an implicit ideal of craftsmanship in this view, despite the idea of "no action" because the skill is mastered by a ruler to the point of spontaneity and forgetting (which Heidegger would later appropriate). This is not the skill of Socrates,

---

[49] Lao tzu; Waley trans. (1934) *The Way and Its Power*: 166.

though he is closer in his approach, and certainly not the contrived skills of Plato's overly trained Guardians or Aristotle's "ethically" cultivated aristocrats. The better parallel are the Cynics who might appear to share some characteristics of the Taoists but the contrasts make the approach of each clearer. In fact, Zeno, who was originally a Cynic even if later identified as a Stoic, put forward the concept of *kathēkon* (καθῆκον) translated as "appropriate behavior," "befitting actions," or "convenient action fitting nature" or also "proper function," which are comparable with *ren* (仁), in terms of treating people well or correctly and the notion of the *Tao* (道) shared with the *Ru* (Literati associated with Confucius) in general but most certainly shares affinities with *wu wei* of the Taoists and *Fǎ-jiā* (Legalists).

Taoist ideas probably triggered the debates over human nature or *xing* (性). It was something that Confucius did not discuss, with one possible dubious later interpolation, but was a key debate in the period after his death. One approach appears to arise in the students of Zixia, perhaps including Gaozi (告子 c. 420–350 BCE) who appears to have been a contemporary of Mencius (c. 372–289 BCE). Aspects of his thought suggest that he was influenced by Mozi[50] because he seems to imply that there is no fixed human nature but he is more likely to be a *Ru*, possibly the missing link between the school of Zixia, who was recognized as the key transmitter of Confucius' ideas, and Xunzi, the influential follower of Confucius at the end of the Warring States period. While Gao is a suspected follower of Mo, Xunzi is seen as tied to the *Fǎ-jiā* school. However, these labels are somewhat meaningless because, once again, the lines of what was part of the *Ru* were not set at this point in time and his views are consistent with one strand of *Ru* who argue that goodness needs to be cultivated in individuals because they are not inherently good.

Mencius, in contrast, argues that feelings of sympathy, modesty, shame and right and wrong in all men are evidence of a basic tendency of individuals to be good. Each has a bud or sprout of goodness in their character and this can be cultivated. Most give in to their animal desires and destroy the potential good. In principle, however, the natural course of human development of *xing* (human nature) will, given normal nourishing conditions, be good.[51] That is, it is most natural for humans to exercise goodness

---

[50] "We must take seriously, I have argued, the possibility that Gaozi as a very young man was a disciple of Mozi. In one way, Mozi and Gaozi are obviously alike: if the Mozi is an indication, Mozi too denied that humans have any fixed moral nature." David S. Nivison and Bryan William Van Norden (1996) *The Ways of Confucianism: Investigations in Chinese Philosophy*, La Salle, IL: Open Court: 130.

[51] Paul Goldin, *After Confucius*: 38 citing A.C. Graham (1986) *Studies in Chinese Philosophy and Philosophical Literature*, Singapore: Institute of East Asian Philosophies: 7–66. See, for example, Mencius VI(A)1–7, VII(A)7&15.

and take the correct path.[52] This approach of Mencius demonstrates an affinity for the natural course advocated by Taoists, despite his tendency to criticize the thinkers with Taoist views. There is also a hint of Taoism mysticism in the connection of this natural instinct with the concept of Heaven itself. Mencius argues against the arbitrariness of Heaven and fate by pointing out that heaven or fate is not just what happens to you but how you deal with it.[53] This operates on a personal level, though there are some things, such as unjust imprisonment, which should not be accepted as the course of heaven.

In contrast, Xunxi takes the view that, as a Guodian text puts it, morality or a sense of right and wrong or righteousness (*yi* 義) is not natural but comes from outside or externally (*wai* 外) to each individual,[54] which we have seen is associated with Gaozi. In theory anyone can become a noble person or a Sage, but it is only through strict training that one can become cultured and able to this high degree. All humans need social organization to gain this culture. This is why the rites are important. In the context of the disorder of the time, rites and associated values are important to maintaining the social organization. Man has a rational and emotional side. The rites represent the values of piety, faith, refinement, respect and love. Superior men know this and this is why they uphold the rites. Rituals are important because they give gravity and meaning to key events. This is true today as well with obvious cases, such as formal court proceedings which have a clear ritual, but also weddings, graduation ceremonies and other formal events. It is true that some conservatives can insist on freezing the present forms of ritual or preserving the unnecessary detail of the past forms. The point of Xunzi is that discipline and order, not to mention harmony and beauty, can be found in following and perfecting ritual.

For Plato and Aristotle, humans must constrain their appetites to act virtuously. Particularly for Aristotle, *eudaimonia* or a sense of well-being, comes from moderation and, in a striking parallel to Xunzi, Aristotle advocates training to control one's appetites.[55] The Cynic Antisthenes believed the goal of life is *Eudaimonia*, as with Aristotle, but that this can best be achieved by living in a way that accords with nature as consistent with human reason. This involves self-sufficiency (*autárkeia* αὐτάρκεια), equanimity, *arête* (excellence). Antisthenes advocated this approach in his essay "On Kingship" in order to produce individuals who can rule well. In general, however, Cynics were known for a love of humanity, *parrhesia*

---

[52] Mencius; Lau trans. (1970) *Mencius*: 122.
[53] Mencius; Lau trans. (1970) *Mencius*: 182.
[54] Paul Goldin (2005) *After Confucius*: 38.
[55] Aristotle; Barker trans. (1958) *The Politics of Aristotle*: 323.

(παρρησία – freedom to speak one's mind or speak candidly) and indifference to the vicissitudes of life (*adiaforia* ἀδιαφορία) which can be promoted by ascetic practices (*áskesis* ἄσκησις), including *ponos* (πονος) or work, the *daimon* (δαίμων) or spirit of hard labor and toil. Some also embraced shamelessness (*anaideia* αναιδεια) and rejection of the *nomos* or the laws, customs, and social conventions and norms of society which others blindly follow. This is why Diogenes' association with "defacing currency" should perhaps be interpreted as a rejection of the state and social norms but not an articulate theoretical anarchism.[56] Cynics were called "dogs" in that they were shameless like dogs but also the watchdogs of humanity or perhaps as the haranguing loyal conscience of humanity.[57]

CONCLUSION

This chapter shows how the basic ideas of the foundational thinkers were disputed, developed and transformed into the basis of political thought in the three civilizations being examined here. Even though some of these schools of thought or tendencies were opposed to the ideas of the original thinkers, these objections were addressed by their followers. Since we are reliant on oral transmission of the ideas of all three, it is not surprising that these later debates and controversies crept into the body of sayings associated with each.

The outlines of key ideas in political thought set out here are also foundational for much of the political thought that follows. In that sense, this is a challenging chapter with the introduction of many new concepts and terms. Fortunately, the schools of thought that emerge as a result of these trends continued to use these ideas, and with repeated use and subtle (and not so subtle) modification, the nature of ideas raised by these early successors should become increasingly clear in the chapters that follow.

---

[56] Diogenes Laërtius; Robert Drew Hicks trans. (1925), *Lives of the Eminent Philosophers*, vol. 2, London: William Heinemann: 22–23, the interpretation of which depends on the interpretation of certain terms, especially παραχάραξαι (*paracharasia*) in ancient Greek.

[57] Cynic derives from the ancient Greek κυνικός (*kynikos*), meaning "dog-like," and κύων (*kyôn*), meaning "dog," which may have been the name given to them as the insult used by Plato against Diogenes, see Diogenes Laërtius; Hicks trans. (1925) *Lives of the Eminent Philosophers*, vol. 2: 40–41.

4. Political thought of the first empires (250 BC–200 AD)

This chapter examines the first major empires in the three civilizations that have been covered so far. There are outstanding similarities in each case. The relatively long-lasting empires of the Mauryan dynasty, the Han dynasty and Rome were preceded by short-lived empires. These initial attempts at empire seemed to have been essential to clearing the path for their larger successors. The change in the size of political unit from smaller states to empires also had an impact on the development of political thought. Empires required institutions and ideologies for ruling diverse people. This included the development of systems of thought based on the notions of law rooted in concepts of universality and a naturalistic cosmology rather than small group and paternalistically fostered personal morality. This situation left the political thought of previous political thinkers, which was based on personal morality as the model for rulers, in a position where it needed to be reformulated.

FIRST SHORT-LIVED EMPIRES

In all three cases (South Asia, East Asia and Europe), the first empires were preceded with short-lived attempts at large empires, namely the Nanda dynasty, the Qin dynasty and the empire of Alexander the Great. These precursors helped prepare the foundation for their more long-lasting successors by sweeping away older institutions and practices in ways that challenged established political ideas.

The Nanda dynasty 424–321 BC was founded by Mahapadma Nanda (महापद्म नंदा, 450–362 BC) who had the nickname "the destroyer of all the Kshatriyas," implying a challenge to the established ruling caste. He was said to be the son of a *Shudra* mother so by implication low-born status but this may have been a slur of his enemies. It is likely that he was not content to be a ruler over other kings based on tribute relations, because he seemed to have destroyed or deposed them to be sole ruler unlike previous practices of hegemonic rulers who were overlords in name only. The Nanda dynasty only lasted 100 years and the founder ruled for most of it, from assuming power at 25 until his death aged 88. His sons were incapable of maintaining the dynasty and it collapsed 40 year later. They were defeated by Chandragupta Maurya who founded the Mauryan Empire. The Mauryan Empire was important to the spread of Buddhism in India and brought about change in the political thought of India, which extended to South Asia and beyond.

The Qin (秦) state, which brought an end to the Warring States period in China (475–221 BC), was an even more short-lived empire. It was one of the six major states which emerged from the decline of the Zhou dynasty, but unlike the other states with claims to royal lineage, Qin was a half-"barbarian" country on the periphery of the Zhou domains. Given its position, it had the most experience in fighting aggressive nomadic tribes and this made it stronger than many of its more refined neighbors. In addition, the Qin had no qualms about experimenting with ruthless political doctrines. Indeed, the policies of Qin Prime Minister Shang Yang and subsequent thinkers called the Legalists gave Qin the wealth and military might that allowed it to challenge all the other states of the late Zhou period for control and in the end the ruler of Qin was able to declare himself emperor over all. However, the first emperor of Qin (259–210 BC) was also effectively the last. Soon after his death, intrigue among officials led to disunity. At the same time, rebel forces grew in strength – swelled by escaped convicts and bitter opponents of the regime's sweeping changes and authoritarian practices. Thus, the Qin dynasty lasted only from 221 to 206 BC. Nonetheless, it constituted the first centralized state and created the administrative basis for all subsequent dynasties, including the Han (漢) dynasty, the first major empire on the East Asian continent.

Alexander the Great, Aristotle's tutee, also founded a short-lived empire (330–323 BC) that stretched from Macedonia in the North of the Greek states to the edges of Indian civilization. Alexander is believed to have attempted to adopt the role of Persian semi-deified despot but faced resistance to this development from his Macedonian troops and died before he had consolidated power. His policy of mixing Greek and Persian civilizations was abandoned by his generals, and his heirs engaged in a struggle to assume control as the empire collapsed into a few regional states. These Greek-led states did spread Hellenistic (or Greek) culture throughout the area once controlled by Alexander, including Greek language and literature. Even Rome, which was outside of the area controlled by Alexander, was heavily influenced by the vibrancy of Greek thought as it spread through the Eastern Mediterranean. The political philosophy of the Roman Empire was largely based on Greek political thought arising out of the Hellenistic world.

REALISM AND EXPEDIENCY

The rise of these empires was also associated with the development of amoral political thought that was more successful in gaining political power than reliance on the ethical principles of the foundational thinkers and the schools of thought associated with them. In India, the emergence of *Arthashastra* demonstrates this trend and is associated with both the rise and fall of the Nanda. In East Asia, it was the development of what is often translated as "Legalism," which was the ideological basis of the Qin dynasty, but also its undoing. In the Roman Empire, there is no specific text advocating such an amoral or realist approach to politics but the possibility of such an approach informed the writing of history and political thought in the period.

The rise of Chandragupta Maurya (चन्द्रगुप्त मौर्य, 340–298 BC), who created the Mauryan Empire, is interwoven with the story of the scholar Chanakya (चाणक्य, 370–283 BC). Chanakya was purported to be a teacher in Taxila, a city that was a seat of higher learning on the edges of the area between India and the states formed by the successors of Alexander the Great. Chanakya is said to have written a major work of political thought, the *Arthashastra*, literally, "Treatise on *Artha*" under the pen name Kautilya (कौटिल्य). The notion of *Arthashastra* is based on one of the four ends or goals of human existence, which are (1) *dharma* (धर्म), as shall be frequently noted, is difficult to translate but here, put crudely, ethics; (2) *kāma* (काम) or sensual pleasure as in the famous *Kamasutra* (कामसूत्र); (3) *moksa* (मोक्ष) or "liberation"/salvation with strong religious connotation; and (4) *artha* (अर्थ), normally translated as material well-being, but includes a variety of aspects of worldly achievement, including power and wealth. It is likely that there were originally many works in the *Arthashastra* genre and the version we have today appears to be Chanakya's collation of previous attempts with added commentary, particularly the striking counter-argument "No, says Kautilya. . ." where Chanakya refutes his predecessors and provides his judgment of the correct approach.

It is possible that Chanakya is simply associated with this text because of the legend that surrounds his role in the foundation of the Mauryan Empire. The story goes that King Dhana Nanda insulted Chanakya so Chanakya decided to take revenge by destroying the Nanda Empire. Chanakya mentored Chandragupta Maurya, who based on the advice of Chanakya, used stratagems, manipulation and spies such as those in *Arthashastra* to bring down the Nanda and build the first stable empire covering most of India. Chandragupta Maurya adopted the title of *samrat* (सम्राज्) or overlord. He is credited with establishing a consistent and effective system of administration, again probably based on *Arthashastra*.

This led to prosperity and trade, and enabled him to defeat the successors to Alexander the Great's followers in India and establish a long period of peace on the subcontinent. He is said to have converted to Jainism at the end of his life and voluntarily resigned to make way for his son Bindusara to rule.

The most important ruler in the Mauryan dynasty is King Ashoka (304–232 BC). He was the son of Bindusara Maurya (c. 320–272 BC), and so grandson of Chandragupta Maurya, who founded the dynasty. It appears that he might have had early success in suppression of revolt at Taxila as Viceroy of Ujjain in a way that made him stand out from the other princes and provided the basis for his claim to the throne. Much of the legend surrounding Ashoka seems to be embroidered to provide a stark contrast with his later conversion to Buddhism. In his rise to power after the death of this father he was not the eldest or heir apparent and is said to have killed 99 half-brothers in order to win the throne. His early rule was alleged to be one without ethics where he put to death 500 ministers and regularly used a torture chamber. One story is backed by evidence from his own proclamations, primarily his violent destruction of the state of Kalinga (260 BC) about which he expresses remorse over his excesses and led to his conversion to Buddhism. However, it is possible that Ashoka still relied on aspects of *Arthashastra* advice, including the use of "spies" to monitor his officials and the populace of the empire, even after his possible adoption of the Buddhist faith.

The *Arthashastra* argues that *artha* is the basis of all else so must be given priority. It is the sort of amoral pragmatism found in Machiavelli (with which it is often compared) but over one thousand years earlier.[1] It is extremely prescriptive and provides detailed advice on all aspects of political rule. It is unusual in that it has a dualistic tendency as sometimes it seems to be advising the ruler and at other times it seems to be addressing the advisors of the ruler. This is clear in passages such as those that argue the ruler must constrain an appetite for food, sex, wealth, power, and so on because it can lead to infirmity and conflict with others. This is not only advice for the ruler to follow but also a suggestion for advisors to create "healthy" outlets for the ruler's appetites.

The general assumption of the *Arthashastra* is that all rivals must be destroyed or neutralized. There is no notion of healthy contestation. In order to defeat rivals, it recommends extensive use of spies and deception. This is the area in which a lack of ethics is most stark. It also seems to value short-term success without much thought of long-term consequences. In

---

[1] The best translation remains R.P. Kangle trans. and ed. (1960, 1963, 1965) *The Kautiliya Arthasastra*, Three Parts, Bombay: University of Bombay Press.

particular, use of spies and deception could lead to mistrust and suspicion in a way that would be damaging overall and lose effectiveness.

The symbolic role of the *danda* or rod of punishment is emphasized, though this is a key feature of much ancient, non-Buddhist Indian political thought.[2] The *danda* has deep religious and symbolic meanings beyond the scepter of rulers. It was based on the ancient notion of the power of the king to punish the wicked in order to maintain order by acting against those who threaten it. It is simultaneously the rod of peace, the rod of death and the rod of punishment. The king is in battle is the *danda* meant to defeat and punish enemies. The *danda* of the king is also the source of legal authority, though in the *Arthashastra* this authority is mostly delegated to judges and others by the monarch.

While various Chinese dynasties claimed to be based on the Literati learning starting with Confucius, there is more Legalism (*Fǎ-jiā* 法家) in the actual workings of the Literati state than many would like to admit, and it was Legalists not the Literati who enabled China to be unified under one emperor. Moreover, there is a strong undercurrent of Taoism in *Fǎ-jiā* thought as noted in the previous chapter. The Taoist influence is also clear in *Han Feizi* (韓非子), the most well-known and authenticated Legalist text. Han Fei (韓非, 280–233 BC) was a member of the ruling family of the state of Han, so he was part of the nobility rather than the lower gentry as in the case of most Literati. Though very much interested in Taoism, he was a student of the Xunzi, a follower of one strand of Literati thought associated with Confucius. Han Fei studied the policies of Shang Yang and hoped to implement them to strengthen his native state of Han. He was eventually sent to Qin as an envoy and was well-liked by the ruler of Qin who may have considered offering him a post in his government. However, he was put in prison and effectively poisoned by a former fellow student of Xunzi, Li Ssu (李斯, 280?–208 BC), another Legalist.

The focus of the Legalists was not so much law per se as developing a consistent set of punishments and rewards, which is why the definition of *fa* (法) as "standards" rather than "law" also makes sense. The Legalists appealed to both immediate and long-term self-interest. They held out the possibility of rewards for those who enhanced the power of the state through their activities. Those who spied on their neighbors, produced wealth and goods, or fought bravely for the state were rewarded. Legalists hoped that the incentive structures of the state would encourage valorous productive behavior that would make the state strong and prosperous.

One of the key aspects of the Qin state was far-reaching standardization.

---

[2] Ariel Glucklich (1988) "The Royal Scepter ('Daṇḍa') as Legal Punishment and Sacred Symbol," *History of Religions*, 28(2): 97–122.

The realm was divided into administrative units, prefectures and counties, directly administered by state officials. Old feudal titles, rights and land holdings were abolished and land was freely bought and sold. All in the state were subject to the same law regardless of status and tax rates were made uniform. A new standardized system of weights, measures and currency was created to promote commerce and exchange – following from the experience of the Qin state. Finally, the writing system was also with the style and form of Chinese characters proscribed at this time. All these innovations – the administrative units, measures, characters – were standard throughout East Asia until very recently (until after the end of World War II in 1945).

This standardization also extended to attempting to establish a uniform system of thought. Except for practical books on agriculture, medicine and a few Legalist administrative guides, other books were burnt. One reason we have such unreliable copies of earlier works is that many were destroyed in this campaign. Of course, the numerous Literati (Confucian) were opposed but the consequences were brutal and swift. In 212 BC, 460 such scholars were buried alive as a lesson to all others. Given the strict laws and heavy penalties for opposing the new regime, the prisons were soon full of convicts. These were employed in massive construction projects, including the first sections of what has come to be called the Great Wall of China.

It might be a surprise, then, to learn that the ultimate goal of the Legalist ruler was non-activity just as it was with the Taoist Sage-king. In fact, it was the essentially Taoist ideas which created a metaphysical basis for sweeping change. The difference with Taoists is that it was not the natural flow of the "Way" that was the source of action through non-action, but a consistent and immediate system of punishments to ensure people would obey without question and even act to aid the state before the ruler needed to ask. The idea was that if the rule of law is enforced unforgivingly and consistently, order will be established, as Han Fei noted:

> The best penalties are those which are severe and inescapable, so that the people will fear them. The best laws are those which are uniform and inflexible, so that the people can understand them. Therefore, the ruler should never delay in handing out rewards, nor be merciful in administering punishments . . . He establishes the standard, abides by it, and lets all things settle themselves.[3]

Inculcation of habit and fear were to be the basis for behavior so that there would be no need for the state to constantly act. If the ruler deliberates or

---

[3] Watson; Burton trans. (1963) *Basic Writings of Mo Tzu, Hsün Tzu and Han Fei Tzu*, New York, NY: Columbia University Press: 96–117.

acts, it must be in stealth without revealing his preferences so that there is no opportunity for ministers to become "yes men" because as Han Fei argued: "Tao exists in invisibility; its function lies in unintelligibility. Be empty and reposed and have nothing to do. Then from the dark see defects in the light. See, but never be seen. Hear, but never be heard. Know, but never be known."[4] Like the Taoists, there is a sense in which a laissez-faire attitude prevails in the belief that if outlets were made available for the people to gain reward in the service of the state, then people will take advantage of them. People will work for wealth and military glory out of self-interest. Rulers need simply put in place the optimal combination of rules and selective intervention to maintain order. There is also mysticism behind this realism, which enables it to transcend and overcome traditional ethical barriers.

Even when the Literati gained influence in the Han dynasty, there was still a strong dose of Taoist thought, for example, in the work of the seminal thinker Dong Zhongshu (董仲舒, 179–104 BC), who was credited with making the Han dynasty "Confucian." The main text that he is associated with is the *Luxuriant Dew of the Spring and Autumn Annals* (春秋繁露), an elaboration on a commentary on the Warring States period text, the *Spring and Autumn Annals* (春秋 Chūn Qiū), a historical record of the state of Lu.[5] This text was a record of events, allegedly edited by Confucius, with each meant to have profound meaning. However, by itself the *Annals* appears nothing more than a collection of events so is usually accompanied by a commentary. Dong favored the political *Commentary of Gongyang* (Gongyang Zhuan 公羊傳), which as we have seen can be traced back to Confucius' most scholarly and political student, Zixia. This Commentary was considered more suitable in support of Dong's advocacy of centralization of power and meritocratic government than the *Commentary of Zuo* (Zuo Zhuan 左傳), which is more exciting as a narrative but closer to a Taoist or laissez-faire interpretation.

In Dong's exegesis, there is still a strong element of contingency, with aspects of Yin-Yang and divination as necessary to know when to act in ways consistent with Taoist and *Fǎ-jiā* thought, even if coupled with Literati values of humaneness (*ren* 仁) and righteousness or justice (*yi* 義). Dong argued that there are times and circumstances when each form of thought is appropriate. In doing so, he seemed to be attempting to

---

[4] E.R. Hughes (1942) *Chinese Philosophy in the Classical Times*, New York, NY: E.P. Dutton: 260–262.

[5] Dong Zhongshu; Sarah A. Queen and John S. Major ed. and trans. (2015) *Luxuriant Gems of the Spring and Autumn*, New York: Columbia University Press. Note that the texts I am attributing to Dong are only Chapters 1–13, 30, 32, and 74–75.

reconcile the views of Confucius and his followers such as Mencius, who disdained violence, with the necessity of using force to maintain order without going to the extremes of the *Fă-jiā*. Punishment in particular was seen as contrary to Confucius' views.[6] Dong's texts often mention "punishment" (fá 罰) but this should be read as a metaphor for all use of violence by the state. It is telling that Dong's *Pearls of the Spring/Autumnal Annals* starts with a justification of the killing of Xia Zhengshu (夏徵舒) of the state Chen (陳) by King Zhuang (莊) of Chu (楚) because he could not let his crime go unpunished, and goes on to chronicle other examples of correct punishment. There is also a Taoist aspect of waiting until the need for force is obvious as the only alternative and then using it without hesitation. Dong is trying to justify the value of Literati thought for the rulers of the Han as distinct from Taoist and *Fă-jiā* thought by showing it supplements and enhances other forms of thought.

Initially it might seem that the political thought of the Roman Empire offers nothing comparable to the *Arthashastra* and *Fă-jiā* (Legalism). Machiavelli is the natural Western comparator to these approaches but obviously Machiavelli comes much later in history. Indeed, it is interesting the Indian and East Asian thought dealt with this *realpolitik* approach earlier in history. Yet, *realpolitik* did exist in the rise and fall of the Roman Republic and this meant that Romans were aware of these issues. Machiavelli relies heavily on Roman history in his work, most notably in his *Discourses on the First Ten Books of Livy*, drawing heavily on the Roman historian Livy. It is also likely that Machiavelli was influenced by Cicero's *De Officiis* and its discussion of expediency.[7] Cicero denies that there is a conflict between expediency (*utile*) and morality. This is not because he is arguing that it is not expedient if it conflicts with morality due to the possibility of bad consequences in the long-run so amorality is inexpedient in that sense or that expediency can achieve goals for the common good so is moral. Cicero's approach is fundamentally different from the *Arthashastra* and Machiavelli, at least, because expediency for the latter two is what is advantageous in promoting a particular policy at a given time. In contrast, Cicero argued that one must act in a way that is good for order, justice and morality even if the immediate and personal consequences are inconvenient. Thus, expediency is irrelevant. Cicero may have been thinking of several cases where he had to take a principled stand. One is the controversy over his order for immediate strangulation in

---

[6] See Confucius, *Analects* 2(3) as portrayed by the Zheng/Zisi school though other followers such as Zi Lu (子路), were more willing to sanction punishment (*Analects* 13(3)).

[7] Marcia L. Colish (1978) "Cicero's De Officiis and Machiavelli's Prince," *The Sixteenth Century Journal*, 9(4): 80–93.

prison of the Catiline conspirators who tried to overthrow his Consulship rather than waiting for appeals process to be completed and a formal judicial execution to be carried out. Cicero believed that the danger of the conspiracy was so great that delay would be disastrous. This incident led to attacks on Cicero for illegality later in his career but he always stood by his decision. In fact, Cicero was forced into exile twice and unsuccessfully tried to defend the Republic as it was being destroyed by civil war by working with various dubious allies. In all these cases, he was firm in his political convictions and remained steadfast in what he was trying to achieve despite the consequences for himself. In his mind, expediency and doing the right thing were not opposed. He was aware that others advocated expediency as a strategy absent of morality but rejected this approach.

PUBLIC/PRIVATE ETHICS AND THE LAW

The intrigues of *Arthashastra*, the draconian nature of *Fǎ-jiā* philosophy and brutal *realpolitik* of the Roman Empire all created a dilemma for those politically involved and political thinkers who wrote for the political class in these societies. There was now a divergence between private ethics and demands of public power, and this had an impact not only on the elite of officials and politicians but also the general population as well. In some ways, these "realistic" policies were failures. This is least clear in India due to a lack of historical record but one can surmise that the logic of the *Arthashastra* led to the bloodbath of the Kalinga War, remorse over which is given source of Ashoka's decision to convert to Buddhism. One can imagine that the use of monks and women for spies as advocated by the *Arthashastra* and practiced in the Mauryan Empire, would have also created suspicion and mutual distrust. *Fǎ-jiā* policy successfully brought order to China but the excesses of the Qin regime led to its swift demise. The civil war in Rome as a result of the unfettered scramble for power between powerful men such as Julius Caesar, Pompey the Great, and Marcus Licinius Crassus, must have made the foundation of the Imperium under Octavian as *princeps* ("first citizen") as *Augustus* ("the venerated") welcome but with unclear implications of the position of older republican-based ethical politics. The result in all these cases was both the further development of existing ethical systems into forms of law-like philosophies and institutional checks and balances, though largely depending on the training and personal restraint of those in power.

Ashoka was a Buddhist, or at least, strongly favored Buddhism, and has been viewed across Asia since as a model Buddhist ruler. There is ample evidence for Ashoka's support for the Buddhist monastic community (the *sangha*) with generous donations, humanitarian construction projects, and evangelical missions. He even made public declarations against schisms within the Buddhist community, though his own reported involvement in the Third Buddhist council (c. 250 BCE) at Pataliputra is seen as the origin of major divisions in the *sangha*. Ashoka was likely the role model for the *chakravartin*, a great enlightened world ruler, in the theory of Buddhist kingship elaborated in the Long Dialogues of the Pali canon and stories of righteous rule in the Buddhist *Jātaka Tales* (जातक), both of which were written around this time. Ashoka's mature approach to the ethics of kingship should be seen in opposition to the ideas of statecraft of *Arthashastra* though the influence of the logic of such work is likely to have lingered in how his empire was organized and administered.

What we know about Ashoka is based on the edicts he published in various locations across the empire. One underlying principle advocated by Ashoka was "*dhamma*" (the Pali term for *dharma*). As noted above, *dharma* is difficult to define and it is also true in the case of Ashoka's conception of "*dhamma*." It seems to be correct behavior though there are hints that it is not a problem to interpret it according to one's own beliefs. Ashoka seems to have sincerely respected all beliefs, including what later came to be called Hinduism as well as Jainism and Buddhism. The definition *dhamma* provided in one of Ashoka's edicts provides a clue: "good behavior to slaves and servants, obedience to mother and father, generosity toward friends, acquaintances, and relatives, and toward *shramanas* and *Brahmans*, and abstention from killing living things."[8] The idea is that everyone should know what is good and should follow it as if this was unproblematic. Ashoka's use of the concept of *dhamma* is more prescriptive, even if he recognizes that different systems of belief may define *dhamma* differently, because there is an implicit universalistic core that he insisted all must follow. In order to implement this policy, Ashoka appointed *dhamma-mahāmattas*, officials in charge of overseeing implementation of the *dhamma* policy. It is unclear what these officials did but it is likely that Ashoka relied on the established Mauryan bureaucracy based on principles from the *Arthashastra* with the implication that these officials were monitoring if not spying on the population in order to actively impose his *dhamma* policy.

Even though the specific policy did not long survive Ashoka himself, it had an influence on Indian thought in general. One example might be the *Manusmṛti* (मनुस्मृति) or "Laws of Manu" and *Dharmasastra* (धर्मशास्त्र). There is no doubt the much of the material in the *Dharmasastra* texts is

---

[8] N.A. Nikam and Richard McKeon ed. and trans. (1959) *The Edicts of Asoka*, Chicago, IL: University of Chicago Press: 45.

ancient and predates Ashoka. It is clearly an extension of Vedic literature but it was not written down until the third century AD. However, given the emphasis of Ashoka on *dhamma*, and evidence from within the texts, it is not absurd to suggest that the impetus for the emergence of this literature in its current form was a reaction to Ashoka's policy of *dhamma*. The "Laws of Manu" emphasize traditional Vedic gods as the basis for kingship as including "lasting elements of Indra, the Wind, Yama, the Sun, Fire, Varuna, the Moon and Kubera."[9] Indra (इन्द्र) is the leader of the gods, god of rain and thunderstorms, who is much like Zeus in Greek mythology, which is not strange as they share an Indo-European cultural root, and both serve as a model of rule. Yama (यम), the god of death, ruler of the departed, is also paralleled in the Greek god of the underworld, Hades, though significantly in the India version he is the one who exercises the *danda* (दण्ड) as the "rod of Yama," the lord of death, particularly over mortals. The god Varuna (वरुण), the god of water and oceans, plays a much bigger role than the Greek god Poseidon, because he is omniscient, catching liars, and has a thousand eyes spying on and watching all. Varuna is also the lord of punishment (*isa dandasya* ईश दण्डस्य) who wields the scepter (*danda*) even over kings.[10] The god Vishnu (विष्णु), a key deity in later Hindu thought, later inherits these same qualities from Varuna. Purity is guaranteed for a king and all who serve him, even when they must engage in impure practices such as killing, and the fact that a king gains one-sixth of the religious merit of the people he helps, both reflect what later are known as Hindu ideals.[11]

Although these texts use the term law more loosely in the sense of a guide for behavior, they do emphasize the legal authority of the king even more than in *Arthashastra*. The *Manusmṛti* and *Dharmasastra* also outline the responsibilities of the monarch, such as the King's responsibility for theft in that if a thief is not caught the king must pay for any loss incurred by those who experience a theft. Also the king is subject to the law and pays the highest fines for misconduct. One must be careful to note that this is not universal law. Manu provides options with considerable relativity in application. The main feature of the "Laws of Manu" is caste differentiation and argue for the protection of and advice from Brahmins. It is an example of an early attempt to build ideological support for the importance of the caste system and the pivotal role of the Brahmin caste within it.

For Dong, in the Han dynasty, there is a natural order and policies

---

[9] Wendy Doniger O'Flaherty trans. (1991) *Laws of Manu*, Harmondsworth: Penguin.
[10] Ariel Glucklich (1988) "The Royal Scepter (Danda) as Legal Punishment and Sacred Symbol," *History of Religions*, 28(2): 108.
[11] O'Flaherty trans. (1991) *Laws of Manu*: 109–110.

must be implemented as appropriate according to circumstances. There is no strong ideological insistence on either draconian punishment or universal benevolence. The Han Legal code became the basis for legal systems throughout East Asia but it was also infused with a synthesis of *Fă-jiā* ideas and Literati terminology. Dong does place some ethical ideas above the law to a degree, for example, filial piety may lead an individual to break the law to help someone in their family and exercising leniency in these cases is an opportunity to demonstrate the emperor's benevolence.[12] Tradition was maintained by the use of the ancient text of the *Spring and Autumn Annals* as the basis for legal precedents.[13] In the end, however, Dong and the Literati state in the Han dynasty aimed at maximum flexibility in interpretation to foster a natural harmony. The power of the ruler is limited by both the fact that he is locked into a system of officials and advisors upon which he must depend and the mandate of heaven suggests direct responsibility for any failures, both as a result of failed policies but also misfortune.[14] Respecting good ministers is particularly emphasized as the basis for maintaining power, with failure to heed expert advice as potentially threating the very existence of the state.[15] Dong's approach was open to hermeneutic flexibility because it was more focused on unity and integration than enforcing social control due to his concern with finding the right balance to accommodate human nature (*xing*). Even so, human nature must be cultivated to serve the state. Dong clearly stated: "Moral education is the foundation of government, deciding cases is indeed the fullest, most palpable expression of government."[16]

The philosophy of the Stoics was very influential amongst the Roman elite and served to allow them to advocate public service and maintain a separate private ethical sphere. There is a Stoic contempt for existing institutions, which might be expected given that the founder of Stoicism, Zeno of Citium (Ζήνων ὁ Κιτιεύς, 334–262 BC), was originally a Cynic. However, Zeno also saw himself as continuing the Socratic movement and taught an increasingly sophisticated philosophical system in the Athenian

---

[12] Sanft, Charles (2010–2011) "*Chunqiu jueyu* Reconsidered On the Legal Interest in Subjective States and the Privilege of Hiding Family Members' Crimes as Developments from Earlier Practice," *Early China*, 33/34: 141–169.

[13] Norman P. Ho (2010) "'Stare Decisis' in Han China? Dong Zhongshu, the Chunqiu, and the Systematization of Law," *Tufts Historical Review*, 3(1): 153–169.

[14] R.R. Vuylsteke (1982) "The Political Philosophy of Tung Chung-shu (179–104 BC): A Critical Exposition," PhD dissertation, Hawaii, HI: University of Hawaii: 191.

[15] Dong Zhongshu; Queen and Major trans. (2015) *Luxuriant Gems of the Spring and Autumn*, Chapters 7 and 8 (Book 5A/B).

[16] Ho (2010) "Stare Decisis in Han China?": 156.

marketplace under the colonnades (*stoa*).[17] His Cynic background might explain why he is accused of advocating abolition of temples, courts, schools and currency, and insisting on loose unisex clothing that would not leave the body completely covered. These ideas may have formed part of his ideal Republic, which he set out in a text by that name of which only fragmentary reports survive. He appears to have been the first to advocate Νόμος φύσις (natural law) and he certainly seems to believe that human *telos* is to live naturally in a community. The ideal political community appeared to be restricted to only Stoic Sages, and since Stoic Sages are rational and follow providence, there would be no need for law or institutions, which also explains his advocacy of the abolition of temples, courts, schools, and currency. In reality, however, Stoics seem to have taken the view that they are a potential cosmopolitan community of Stoic Sages. This community transcended ordinary states but since a Stoic must live in such states, then they are required to be politically involved in existing states in order to improve them where possible.

Therefore, the Stoics seem to have accepted the views of Polybius, who pointed to the institutional strengths of the Romans that enabled their empire to grow so quickly and successfully.[18] Polybius emphasized the need for an institutional balance between the *demos*, aristocrats or oligarchs and a strong monarchy or leader, with more power for the latter in times of war and crisis. The institutions of the Roman Republic (509–27 BC) provided this balance: the popular forces were the Plebeians who selected the Consul, the aristocratic Patricians controlled legislative power in the Senate and the institution of the temporary Dictator was required for periods of crisis and war. These political institutions of the old Republic, before the emergence of great power brokers like Julius Caesar, Pompey, and Crassus, were the ideal set of institutions based on a balance between popular, aristocratic and executive power though more as a composite state with pure forms of each, than a balanced state with checks and balances against each other. Cicero has a more favorable image of kingship than most Roman republicans and Stoics but his ideal political leader follows the pattern of the philosopher-king in Plato's *Republic* aimed at raising the moral standard of the state.

---

[17] Paul A. Vander Waerdt (1994) "Zeno's Republic and the Origins of Natural Law" in Paul A. Vender Waerdt ed., *The Socratic Movement*, Ithaca, NY: Cornell University Press, Chapter 11. Given the fragmented nature of the evidence for Zeno's work, this discussion is also informed by H.C. Baldry (1959) "Zeno's Ideal State," *The Journal of Hellenic Studies*, 79: 3–15 and Anton-Hermann Chroust (1965) "The Ideal Polity of the Early Stoics: Zeno's 'Republic'," *The Review of Politics*, 27(2): 173–183.

[18] A.A. Long and D.N. Sedley (1987) *The Hellenistic Philosophers*, vol. 1, Cambridge: Cambridge University Press: 433.

Law was also important because, as Cicero argued, "Law is the highest reason, rooted in nature, it is the mind and reason of the prudent man, and it distinguishes justice and injustice"[19] but he also emphasizes that in Roman law it is both equity and choice that the law enables. Cicero also accepts the logic of the Stoic conception of natural law, and that "just" laws applied to all, are a restraint on tyranny. This law is also universal in keeping with the Roman concept of *ius gentium* or "law of the peoples" or "law of nations," which transcended the legal practices of individual communities and tribes to form a core of law that could apply to everyone everywhere. It was not a formal legal code but a practical outgrowth of Stoic natural law thinking that the Romans found useful in dealing with other nations. Cicero insisted that wealth and ability will always be unevenly distributed but law should be the same for all because it is law that determines justice and freedom. We must be slaves to the law so we are free and can enjoy a harmonious life with others.

As important as formal and informal institutions was the ability of human beings to control emotions. This was especially essential for rulers and officials. For early Stoics such as Chrysippus of Soli (Χρύσιππος ὁ Σολεύς 280–207 BC), the goals that most individuals pursued in life should be considered indifferent (*adiaphora*) because they were not relevant to higher moral aims. Among the indifferent goals are health, riches, and honor. These Stoics argued that it is possible to be sick and poor but still be a good person. Conversely, a wise person can enjoy wealth and honor but does not need them. The Stoics were aware that most individuals would prefer to be rich and healthy rather than poor and ill, but they argued that this was simply a matter of emotions (*pathe*) to prefer one over the other. Stoics believed that one had to control one's passions because emotions cloud our judgment and prevent us from doing the right thing. In this sense, emotions were viewed by these early Stoics as contrary to nature.

The thinkers of Middle Stoa, such as Panaetius of Rhodes (Παναίτιος ὁ Ρόδιος, 185–c. 109 BC) and Posidonius of Rhodes (Ποσειδώνιος ὁ Ρόδιος, c. 135–51 BC), in contrast, seemed to accept a role for emotions and even argue that passions are a natural part of human life. Ethics involves placing reason over passions but not eliminating them. Posidonius had an influence on Cicero who attended his lectures. Even though it would be difficult to argue that Cicero was a Stoic, like the Stoics, Cicero believed that political life is the high expression of human achievement and political activity is the highest calling.

As Rome grew successful and wealthy, there was a tendency to excess

---

[19] Marcus Tullius Cicero; James E.G. Zetzel trans. (1999) *On the Commonwealth and On the Laws*, Cambridge: Cambridge University Press: 111.

and luxury so the Romans looked to the Greeks who had a more sophisticated set of philosophical ideas as teachers to enable them to learn how to act and rule more wisely. The Scipionic Circle that formed around the politician Scipio Aemilianus found Stoicism to be a sophisticated system of thought to preserve and promote the best of Roman ideals, such as courage, fortitude, self-denial, discipline, and so on. Therefore, later Roman thinkers were often Stoics, though this also indicated the limits of philosophy in the context of the Roman Imperial state. For example, Seneca (c. 4 BC–65 AD) developed a humanistic version of Stoic philosophy without the demand of perfection or lack of human feelings advocated by more extreme Stoics but he found it difficult to put these ideals into practice in his personal life and the political realm in which he operated. Seneca was born into a powerful Roman family in what is now Spain, he came to Rome at a young age and rose to high office along with the other members of his family. He was caught in the midst of dangerous conflicts with the emperors Caligula and Claudius, which ended in banishment to Corsica. He was recalled to Rome by Claudius' fourth wife Agrippina to tutor her son Nero, then 12 years old. Agrippina was able to ensure Nero rather than the heir apparent Britannicus became emperor. Seneca became one of two trusted advisors of Nero, the other being the praetorian prefect Sextus Afranius Burrus (1–62 AD). However, both he and Burrus were unable to stop Nero from murdering his mother, and, worse, they appeared to defend him afterward. In the end, Nero became suspicious of Seneca, and despite retiring to one of his rural properties, Seneca was accused of plotting against Nero and was forced to commit suicide. Both his early involvement with the emperor and inability to have a positive impact on the regime raises questions about Stoic philosophy and ethics.

Later Stoa also experienced the same limitations. Epictetus (55–135 AD) was a former slave who had been banished from Rome and forced to exile in Greece. His *Discourses* were written down by his follower Arrian (c. 86–c. 146 AD). Epictetus seems to argue that reason alone is good and the irrational is evil. Evil is caused by error and we have a compassionate duty to point out and correct error whenever possible. We were given rationality and a soul by divine providence and one must try to fit with the universal order of the world as providence unfolds. However, we also have a duty to serve our country and our friends. The polis is the universe in which one has a responsibility to all fellow human beings. Our role is to compassionately correct and improve the order of the world with reason. The philosophy of Epictetus was particularly influential with the Stoic Roman Emperor Marcus Aurelius (lived 121–180 AD/ruled 161–180 AD), who quotes from Epictetus' *Discourses* extensively. Yet Marcus Aurelius' book, often translated as "Meditations" but in fact meaning "notes to myself", revealed his struggle to control his emotions and act with a sense of duty to public service. Clearly for Roman Stoics, the ideal of political involvement was often overwhelmed by their personal struggles with their emotions. This included both a former slave Epictetus and a Roman emperor.

THE ELITE, THE PEOPLE AND WOMEN

All the philosophies discussed in this chapter – Ashoka's *dhamma*, Dong's Literati synthesis and Roman Stoicism – were intended to guide all in society but were often most accessible only to the elite. The content of the philosophies also tended to reinforce hierarchy and the position of those already with high status and power. There is a high degree of paternalism in the thought of the main thinkers in all three civilizations.

Ashoka himself states that "All are my children. Just as I seek the welfare and happiness of my own children in this world, I seek the same things for all people."[20] For the most part this is directed at charitable work that is aimed at the whole of the community without discrimination. For example, he commissioned his officials to:

> work among soldiers and their chiefs, the ascetics and householders, the poor and aged, to secure the welfare and happiness, and release from imprisonment those devoted to [*dhamma*]. They are also commissioned to work among prisoners to distribute money to those who have many children, to secure the release of those who were instigate to crime by others, and pardon those who are very aged.[21]

Rulers also have a duty to the people and Ashoka reminds people of his public works for the welfare of the people, though mainly he says to promote his *dhamma* policy.[22] This policy had its compassionate side but it was also in support of the existing social order and not a challenge to it so when in Rock edict XI talks of the gift of *dhamma*, the establishment of human relations on *dhamma*, the distribution of wealth through *dhamma* or kinship in *dhamma*, he means that one needs to treat slaves and servants well, be obedient to one's mother and father, and give liberally to friends, acquaintances, priests, and ascetics.[23]

In East Asian Literati thought, the people are more a force of nature,

---

[20] Nikam and McKeon eds. and trans. (1959) *The Edicts of Asoka*, Chicago, IL: University of Chicago Press: 53 and 61–62 (Kalinga Edicts I and II).
[21] Nikam and McKeon eds and trans. (1959) *The Edicts of Asoka*: 59.
[22] Nikam and McKeon (1959) *Edicts of Asoka*: 64.
[23] Nikam and McKeon (1959) *Edicts of Asoka*: 44–45.

controllable and malleable unless one does not deal with public affairs correctly. In the case of the Literati, this meant managing ritual and relationships successfully but in the case of Taoism, the goal of good governance was *wu wei* and simplicity. In the *Huai Nanzi*, the ruler and Sage are most important to the state but the interests of all people and lower classes should not be ignored because both rulers and Sages can arise from the lower orders as well.[24] Dong is perhaps the most meritocratic in the role of the Literati in his advocacy of the selection of officials by ability. At the same time, he suggests "the people" must be kept under control through moral force based on ritual and hierarchy with each knowing the proper role and place. Dong reinforces the hierarchical tendency of Literati thought by using Yin-Yang thought to classify the emperor (*jun* 君), father and husband as yang while ministers (*chen* 臣), son and wife are classified as yin. These social roles constitute an absolute social hierarchy called the "three bonds" (san gang 三綱). Dong's metaphysics reinforces the overriding influence of filial piety in the structuring of relationships.

The Stoics in principle seemed to have believed in an egalitarianism which appealed across the community. Much like the mandate of heaven and the work of Dong, Panaetius argued that there may be variation in states but ones which do not promote the Stoic form of goodness are likely to lose the support of the people in them. This view is echoed to a degree by Cicero in his admonition to "let the welfare of the people be the ultimate law."[25] In *The Republic*, Cicero hints of meritocracy: "A just and wise king, or a select group of leading citizens, or the populace itself (though that is the least desirable type) can still, it seems, ensure a reasonably stable government, provided no forms of wickedness or greed find their way into it."[26] But he also argues that "nature has decreed not only that men of superior character and ability should be in charge of the less endowed, but also that the latter should willingly obey their superiors."[27] With a few exceptions, Stoicism and Ciceronian philosophy were the preserve of the elite.

There is greater variation in the three civilizations over the position of women. For example, Ashoka is associated with a prominent role for women, including his third wife and second queen, Karuvaki (or Charuvaki) who is mentioned for her charitable work in his inscriptions.

---

[24] Evan Morgan (1933) *Tao – The Great Luminant: Essays from Huai Nan Tzu. With Introductory Articles, Notes, Analyses*, Shanghai: Kelly and Walsh: 223–224.

[25] Cicero; M. Griffin and E. Atkins trans. (1991) *On Duties*, Cambridge: Cambridge University Press: 61.

[26] Cicero; Niall Rudd trans. (1998) *The Republic and the Laws*, Oxford: Oxford University Press: 20.

[27] Cicero; Rudd trans. (1998) *The Republic and the Laws*: 23.

Ashoka's eldest daughter Saṅghamittā (Saṅghamitrā संघमित्रा in Sanskrit) by his first wife, Devi, together with her brother Mahinda became monks and traveled on a mission to Sri Lanka to disseminate the teachings of Buddha in the reign of King Devanampiya Tissa (250–210 BC). There with other nuns she established the lineage of *bhikkhunis* (a fully ordained female Buddhist nuns), including ordination of several of the women in Tissa's court at Anuradhapura. This became the basis for female monastic orders throughout South Asia. Romila Thapar notes that the Mauyan royal bodyguards included women and that women were used as spies, though the latter would only be further evidence of the influence of the *Arthashastra* which suggested that unlikely figures, such as monks and holy men, were most effective as spies.[28] In short, the evidence for an enhanced position for women under Ashoka is intriguing but inconclusive.

It has been argued that Dong's use of Yin-Yang was aimed at justifying the subordination of women.[29] In theory, the Yin-Yang approach can be interpreted as the pairing of mutually complementary if opposite forces and there is some element of this view in Dong's *Luxuriant Dew*. However, it is true that Dong's emphasis is primarily on the negative portrayal of yin and the positive connotations of yang. Yin, and hence women, are clearly and firmly placed in a subordinate position to yang, represented by men.

For Zeno the community of the wise includes Stoic women Sages, not as in Plato's *Republic*, where women trained to be part of the guardian-philosopher ruling class despite their weaknesses, but because women are by nature equal to men. There is evidence that some Stoics did advocate and practice equality between the sexes even if this aspect of Stoic thought was softened by later Stoic thinkers.[30] In fact, the reputation of the Stoics as possible champions of women may have been overstated by some scholars, except possibly in the area of education where there is some sense of equality, following from Plato's view that men and women can be trained as guardians of his ideal state. It is unlikely that most Stoics went this far.[31] Though not strictly a Stoic, Cicero shared many of their ideals and yet still had particularly negative views of the involvement of women in public life. There are some examples of politically active women in Rome but the general trend among the educated elite was to engage in the rhetorical

---

[28] Romila Thapar (1990) *A History of India, Volume 1: Early India from the Origins to AD 1300*, Harmondsworth: Penguin: 84.

[29] Robin R. Wang (2005) "Dong Zhongshu's Transformation of 'Yin-Yang' Theory and Contesting of Gender Identity," *Philosophy East and West*, 55(2): 209–231.

[30] C.E. Manning (1973) "Seneca and the Stoics on the Equality of the Sexes," *Mnemosyne*, 26(2): 170–177.

[31] David M. Engel (2003) "Women's Role in the Home and the State: Stoic Theory Reconsidered," *Harvard Studies in Classical Philology*, 101: 267–288.

strategies to discredit them reflecting the standard Roman view of politics as a male domain.[32] Cicero does mention some positive female role models including prominent educated Roman women but the roles they played, as mothers and wives, are very conventional and in keeping with traditional Roman conceptions.[33]

COSMOLOGY AND METAPHYSICS

Cosmology was central to political thought in all three empires. To a large degree this cosmology is syncretic. In each civilization there were debates over the correct understanding of metaphysics. In the case of Indian Buddhism, these differences had long-term implications.

The Buddhist cosmology underlying Ashoka's *dhamma* policy is most likely found in the texts discussed in the last chapter as they were probably developing around the time he was in power. This period was also when many of the divisions in early Buddhism had begun to emerge. In fact, in one of his edicts he speaks directly to the Buddhist *sangha*, primarily against schism though the way it is written it appears to be directed at aberrant individuals rather than groups.[34]

As noted in the previous chapter, the *Mahāsāṃghika* (Majority) split with *Sthaviravāda* (Elders) over the issue of *vinaya* monastic rules. Within the *Mahāsāṃghika* there were differences over whether *Mahāyāna* (महायान, 大乘) teachings should be incorporated formally into their official literature. *Mahāyāna* thought focuses on Bodhisattvas or beings who had obtained *bodhicitta[a]* (बोधिचित्त), that is, awakening that led them to compassion to seek enlightenment for all sentient beings. These beings were in effect super-human and could achieve things that the training of normal human monks could not. The *Mahāsāṃghika* split during the reign of Ashoka based upon the degree to which they accepted the authority of these *Mahāyāna* texts. The *Ekavyāvahārikas* (एकव्यावहारिक, 一説部), accepted the *Mahāyāna* sūtras as the words of the Buddha (*buddhavacana*). In contrast, the *Kukkuṭika* or *Kukkulika* or *Golulaka* (鶏胤部) sect did not accept the *Mahāyāna* sūtras as *buddhavacana*.[35] *Mahāyāna* is important

---

[32] S. Ige (2003) "Rhetoric and the Feminine Character: Cicero's Portrayal of Sassia, Clodia and Fulvia," *Akroterion*, 48: 45–57.
[33] Edward E. Best, Jr. (1970) "Cicero, Livy and Educated Roman Women," *The Classical Journal*, 65(5): 199–204.
[34] Nikam and McKeon (1959) *Edicts of Asoka*: 66–68.
[35] Joseph Walser (2005) *Nāgārjuna in Context: Mahāyāna Buddhism and Early Indian Culture*, New York: Columbia University Press: 51.

to East Asian political thought and will be covered in more detail in the chapters that follow.

The *Sthaviravāda* (Elders) also experienced splits around this time. One of the most important was the emergence of the *Pudgalavāda* or "Personalist" school of Buddhism around 280 BC. This school argued that each individual must constitute a *pudgala* (पुद्गल) or "person," which was essential for karma, rebirth, and nirvana to be possible. This approach, which seemed to contradict Buddha's argument that there was no self (*ātman*), was opposed by other schools of Buddhism that believed that any "person" only exists as nominal label for the *skandhas* (स्कन्ध), that is, the combination of outward physical form, sense perception, feelings and consciousness that most mistakenly associate with coherent permanent individual but in reality are a bundle of transient phenomena. *Pudgalavāda* agree that there is no *ātman* but they argued that their notion of *pudgala* is neither the same as nor different from the *skandhas* (स्कन्ध). The *Vatsīputrīya* group of *Pudgalavāda* emerged as an important force during the time of Ashoka and its successor, the *Sammitīya*, became the largest school of Buddhism in India.

The *Sarvāstivāda* school also split from *Sthaviravāda* around the time of Ashoka. They argued that all dharmas – past, present and future – exist simultaneously, which denies any reality to an individual "self" fixed in a particular place and time. However, it is unclear if it formed from a schismatic group in the *sangha* that had been expelled and migrated to northwestern India evolving into the *Sarvāstivādin* school, or it was actually one of Ashoka's missions to Gandhara in northwestern India and evolved out of interaction with non-Buddhist schools in the area.[36] Eventually the *Sarvāstivāda* became powerful based on the patronage of the Kushan emperor Kanishka the Great (कनिष्क 127–163 AD) during which time they were greatly strengthened when he held a 4th Buddhist Council where *Mahāyāna* formally split from *Theravāda*.

Finally, *Theravāda* (also School of the Elders) emerged from the *Vibhajjavāda* group, which itself had emerged from *Sthaviravāda* during the reign of Ashoka, in opposition to the *Sarvāstivādin*. The *Vibhajjavāda* and its successor the *Theravāda* believed that humans could find enlightenment as *arhats* ("one who is worthy" or "perfected person" who has achieved nirvana) but that Buddhahood was difficult if not impossible. The *Vibhajjavāda* and *Theravāda* therefore focused on monastic training as the basis for enlightenment as the goal for normal human beings. In contrast, *Sarvāstivādins* shared the view of *Mahāsāmghika* that *arhats* are

---

[36] Joseph Walser (2005) *Nāgārjuna in Context: Mahāyāna Buddhism and Early Indian Culture*, New York: Columbia University Press: 51.

imperfect and fallible. The *Vibhajjavāda* may have been favored by Ashoka who expelled its opponents after the Third Council Buddhist council held in his reign. This is supported by the fact that the Theravāda school spread to Sri Lanka as a result of a well-attested mission sent by Ashoka. As a result, Theravāda became the dominant form of Buddhism in South Asia, later spreading into Southeast Asia. These divisions in the Buddhist *sangha* influenced the direction of political thought in the broad regions of the India subcontinent, South and Southeast Asia, and Central and East Asia in the centuries that followed.

Even after the fall of the Qin and into the early Han dynasty, a mixture of *Fǎ-jiā* ("Legalism") and Taoism was still predominant. This is apparent in texts such as the *Huangdi Sijing* (黃帝四經) or "The Yellow Emperor's Four Classics," which could be found in the Chinese texts at Mawangdui in 1974. Particularly the *Jing Fa* (經法) "The Constancy of Laws," suggests this approach. These appear to be representative of the Huang–Lao (黃老) "school" of political thought, based on the purported thought of the mythical Yellow Emperor Huang-di (黃帝) and Laozi (老子) the supposed author of the *Classic of the Way and Virtue*, the *Fǎ-jiā* Taoist text. This was reinforced by the fact that Literati thought of the time reflected the views of Xunzi rather than that of Mencius.[37] Even if we cannot say there was a formal Huang–Lao school of thought, this type of thinking predominated in the early Han. Taoism was important in the period of rule of emperors Wen and Jing (*Wén Jǐng Zhī Zhì* 文景之治, 180–141 BC), primarily due to the influence of Empress Dou, who was Emperor Wen's wife and Emperor Jing's mother. Taoist influence on government was strong until her death in 135 BC, during the reign of her grandson Emperor Wu of Han. Her policies are best known for reductions in taxation and other burdens, and policies that led to peace and stability.

The most significant development in this period was the emergence of a Taoist cosmology that had a depth of argumentation and explanation that it was lacking in Literati theory. This cosmology to the fore in the *Huan Nanzi* (淮南子), a text attributed to a Han royal prince Liu An (劉安 ?–122 BC) but more likely by the group of scholars around him.[38] Liu An was interested in all systems of thought including that of the Literati but this works' greatest contribution is to explain how Yin-Yang principles could integrate earlier creation myths as well as the Taoist, Literati and other

---

[37] Janice J. Nattier and Charles S. Prebish (1977) "Mahāsāṃghika Origins: The Beginnings of Buddhist Sectarianism," *History of Religions*, 16(3): 237–272.

[38] Yu Mingguang (2002) "Xunzi's Philosophy and the School of Huang Lao: On the Renewal and Development of Early Confucianism," *Contemporary Chinese Thought*, 34(1): 37–60.

forms of thought. The result is both rationalistic but also largely Taoist. The Literati doctrines are reduced to fixed categories within the system.

If we look at the *Huai Nanzi* it might at first seem that Taoism is predominant and as we have seen Taoism is also consistent with *Fǎ-jiā* thought as well. In fact, some scholars argue that it is primarily a *Fǎ-jiā* document on political rule. Others suggest that it is based on the Literati thinker Xunzi rather than pure *Fǎ-jiā* Legalism,[39] which makes sense because there is a strong Literati flavor to sections of the texts,[40] including those that echo the *Great Learning*, a major Literati text. Utilizing the people is a *Fǎ-jiā* concept found in *Han Feizi* but at the same time the tone of this passage is more Literati in its sympathy with the people. There are also sections that are even more reflective of Literati thinking with an emphasis on family, and use of the term "mind" is not unlike Mencius. Overall the text is clearly Taoist in intention though once again the *Tao* is part of the thought of Confucius and the Literati as well. Liu An, who organized the scholars behind the *Huai Nanzi*, was forced to commit suicide in 122 BC over his alleged involvement in a plot against the throne. His demise coincided with the rise of Literati influence in the Han state.

There is no question that Dong Zhongshu was representative of Literati circles but the work attributed to him also combines aspects of *Fǎ-jiā* Legalism, Taoism and Literati thought. Taoism in particular is used to provide a more substantial metaphysics and cosmology for this political philosophy.[41] For example, one often quoted text of Dong's *Luxuriant Gems* is Book 19 "Establishing the Primal Numen" (立元神第十九) which was probably not written by Dong.[42] Superficially it seems to provide a very Taoist set of ideas to guide the ruler. It starts by pointing out that the ruler is the basis for the state and the pivot of all things. Anything he does, even erring by one millimeter, will have drastic consequences. Therefore, he must be attentive to the small and the subtle. But there is also a sense in which he must stop his own passions and preconceptions from interfering with his policymaking, though this is stated in a poetic and mystical way, indicating that "He must calm his essence and nourish his spirit" (安精養神), with spirit often translated as "numen." The ruler must be tranquil

---

[39] John S. Major, Sarah Queen, Andrew Meyer and Harold Roth (2010) *The Huainanzi: A Guide to the Theory and Practice of Government in Early Han China, by Liu An, King of Huainan*, New York, NY: Columbia University Press.

[40] Roger T. Ames (1983) *The Art of Rulership: A Study in Ancient Chinese Political Thought*, Honolulu, HI: University of Hawaii Press.

[41] William Theodore De Bary, Irene Bloom and Joseph Adler (1999) *Sources of Chinese Tradition, vol.1 from Earliest Times to 1600*, 2nd edn, New York, NY: Columbia University Press: 269.

[42] Wang (2005) "Dong Zhongshu's Transformation of 'Yin-Yang' Theory and Contesting of Gender Identity": 213.

and non-active (寂寞無為) to the extent that he stills his body and does not cast a shadow (*xiuxing wujianying* 休形無見影). He then silences his voice and does not emit a sound (捨聲無出響) and with an empty (open?) mind he contemplates with his subordinates (officials) what has occurred and what may be to come. He considers the opinions of the wise and seeks out the views of his people until he obtains an understanding of their hearts and what they are feeling (得其心遍見其情). In short, the ruler should shut up and listen to what his advisors are saying especially when keeping in mind the context of what the people are thinking, which is completely understandable Literati advice but is given with a heavy dose of Taoist mysticism.

Often Five Elements thought is also attributed to Dong but this too is a later addition. Even so, one can see why some might have thought it is consistent with Dong's approach and it still associated with the Han Synthesis. The Five Elements or Five Phases (五行 or *wǔxíng*) school began in the Warring States period. The elements are wood, fire, earth, metal, and water (*mù, huǒ, tǔ, jīn, shuǐ* 木, 火, 土, 金, 水) and were used for describing interactions and relationships between phenomena. The doctrine of Five Phases has both generating (*shēng* 生) and overcoming (*kè* 克) cycles of interactions. In the generating cycle, wood generates fire (by combustion); fire generates earth (ash); earth generates metal (mining of metal ore); metal generates water (by condensation); water generates wood (growing trees). In the overcoming cycle, wood rots to become soil (earth); earth absorbs water; water extinguishes fire; fire melts metal; metal (axes and saws) cuts wood. The role of these elements was later grafted onto Dong's text to reinforce the naturalist cosmology behind this synthesis of political ideas.

One should note that the cosmological emphasis of Dong and his successors did not go unquestioned. Wang Ch'ung (王充 27–100 AD) in the Later Han published his influential book *Lun Heng* (論衡) or "Balanced Debates," which looked coldly and rationally at the *Analects* and other Literati works. He did not believe that Confucius and his followers were particularly more intelligent than people in his time and he was willing to criticize sections of the *Analects* and related works for being nonsense. At the same time, he criticizes the *Fǎ-jiā* Han Feizi for being unwilling to consider morals and rituals. However, he also opposed the questionable quasi-Taoist logic that pervaded the work of Literati such as Dong, particularly superficial analogies between heaven and earth, on one hand, and men and women, on the other, or the notion of the Five Elements or seasonal variation in relation to government policies. Wang's book survives because it was a provocative critique of Han Literati cosmology from a purely rational perspective and the Literati valued it as such. It also demonstrates that the Literati were not a uniform group as the mistranslation "Confucian" implies.

Stoic political thought was also directly related to their cosmology. One key concept was the notion of "providence," literally, "forethought" or *pronoia* (πρόνοια) in Greek or, in Latin, *providentia* from "foresight," from pro- "ahead" and videre "to see" but meaning that there is a purpose to the universe that is known or foreseen by divine forces. Chrysippus of Soli argued that nothing happens by accident but that there is still personal choice and action within the confines of fate. Providence is based on divine reason and associated with *logos*, which Stoics saw as divine reason. This *logos* is active and organizes matter (*hyle* ὕλη), which is passive and inert. Chrysippus argued that *pneuma* (πνεῦμα) was how matter was structured, both living and inanimate. Pure *pneuma* was itself *logos*, which emerges when the cycles of generation and destruction occasionally end in conflagration (*ekpyrôsis* ἐκπύρωσις). The unity of the cosmos is held together by God who is a single active principle that governs the whole cosmos and provides the causation that allows *pneuma* to function. In fact, the universe is God and follows law-like or logical processes even if they are unintelligible to us. This divine *pneuma* is the soul of the cosmos but it differentiates into *pneuma* of different grades to produce everything in the world. The *pneuma* of the human soul (*pneuma psychikon* πνεῦμα ψυχικόν) is high grade *pneuma*. This provided an opportunity for humans to understand the universe and find their place in it. For the Stoics, the goal of human life was to live harmoniously with nature (*physis* φύσις). One natural aspect of the universe is for humans to form communities to maintain order and cooperation for the common good. Thus, the Stoic is bound to follow this natural law, this order of the cosmos which transcends particular states or regimes.

Some modern writers suggest that Cicero did not really believe in the gods[43] but it is more likely that he viewed the official gods and rituals as the divine aspect of institutional arrangements for ensuring harmony, regardless of his personal views, much like the view of Dong and the Literati in general on the role of ritual. Cicero explains the nature of the gods but sees them as serving the state. Cicero's detailed regulation of religion required belief in timeless gods, a religious hierarchy and strict laws though he advocates concessions to differences in urban and rural practice, with rural practice based on existing local and ancestral practices. For Cicero, religion was a duty related to politics. In fact, one has a moral duty to use divine reason within and to put it to use in the service of the

---

[43] W. Hooper (1917) "Cicero's Religious Beliefs," *The Classical Journal*, 13(2): 88–95.

commonwealth.[44] Cicero argued that humans and gods have the ability to reason in common so humans can perceive justice and must act on that basis. The "Dream of Scipo," which serves as the culmination of Cicero's Republic, describes how the divine is the spiritual peak of all human endeavor, especially politics. This is the metaphysics behind his morality and his politics.

CONCLUSION

We can see that the development of these empires were the natural culmination of the political thought of earlier schools of thought. The problem was that the forms of thought that created the empires were not related to the moral thought of the foundational thinkers and, instead, reflected the amoral *realpolitik* that they rejected. Even so, these empires provided the context in which the political thought of the foundational thinkers and the schools that derived from them could flourish.

In the end, however, these systems of thought were still limited to the elite and failed to satisfy the thirst for answers of the mass publics created by the empires. It was in this context that more sophisticated and complex systems of metaphysics were developed and the beginnings of what we can call religions, both of which had a transformative impact on political thought.

---

[44] Cicero; Rudd trans. (1998) *The Republic and the Laws*: 118, 119.

5. Metaphysics, "religion" and the decline of empires (200–500)

The demise of all three empires – Mauryan, Han and Rome – saw the rise of "religious" movements. These movements involved both sophisticated elite metaphysical debates as well as explicit mass belief systems, the latter of which is why they appear religious to us. Even with the failure of Ashoka's religious policy and fall of the Mauryan Empire after his death, the spread of Buddhism continued in India with increasing theoretical sophistication. Ashoka's policies also sparked a rethinking and revival of what later became called Hinduism. In East Asia, Taoism joined with local beliefs and rituals to become a more systematic system of thought with both popular or "religious" elements as well as further developments in elite philosophy. In the Roman Empire, neo-Platonism was a philosophy for the educated elite, but Christianity infused with neo-Platonism became a religion for the masses. Related to the spread of ideas was syncretism: Hinduism borrowed from Buddhism and Buddhism assimilated ideas from Hinduism, Taoism from the Literati and Buddhism, and Buddhism from Taoism and Literati; and Stoicism and neo-Platonism (not to mention paganism) entered into Christianity, while religious cults influenced neo-Platonism. As we have seen syncretism is common in all civilizations as powerful forms of thought compete and accommodate each other.

This chapter also demonstrates the problems of the relationship between religion and political power. One important change was that new forms of thought begin to appeal to the masses in a time of uncertainty so foster unrest and challenge elite practices and beliefs. There was also often a contrast between the mundane politics of the corrupt and flawed material world, and the ideals promised by religions and advanced philosophies. All three civilizations (Indian, East Asian and Roman) struggled with the tendency to reject the real world in favor of private and quietist notions of contemplation, including Christian monasticism in the later Roman Empire and post-Han dynasty "Pure Conversation." While some sought withdrawal, others argued one must remain engaged in politics. There was a struggle for religious movements to find support from the state while they seemed to undermine it. There was the problem of finding a role for the enlightened elite (including rulers) in these new forms of thinking.

Political thought reflects the attempt of many to deal with connection of the soul, mind, spirit, and so on to the *tao*, divine, godhead as the basis for morality, improvement, and political and social order. As a result, in all three civilizations there was a more complex metaphysics which gave birth to what are later seen as the scholastic tendencies in Indian Buddhism, Literati neo-Taoism and late Roman neo-Platonism.

THE CONTEXT OF IMPERIAL DECLINE

When the Mauryan Empire collapsed, it had many imitators but these never held control to the same extent, and it was not until the Gupta dynasty that an empire on the same scale was re-established. The key works of Buddhism were compiled and written down in this period leading to greater scholarly development, whereas Jainism, in contrast, retained a simpler liturgy and remained in the community to a larger extent than the Buddhists. What became Hinduism, appears to have done both, developed its literature and philosophy but also deepened its links with local communities. Indeed, by the Gupta Empire, there was a "Hindu" revival, as part of what Ghoshal identifies as a period rich in political thought.[1]

The Gupta (गुप्त) did not create a true empire, because its control of the Indian subcontinent was limited to a system of alliances based on often nominal subordination. This dynastic state, founded around 320 CE by Chandra Gupta, lasted until 550 CE and at one point or another claimed at least nominal control over most of India. Due to political stability, the economy, science and the arts flourished and the near final versions of the key Indian epics are thought to have been written around this period. Two key works in the Hindu canon are the *Mahabharata* (महाभारतम्) and the *Ramayana* (रामायणम्). The *Mahabharata* reached its final form by the early Gupta period (c. fourth century). *Ramayana*, a version of which is included in the *Mahabharata*, contains even older Vedic material, but is adapted at this time as a key piece of Hindu literature on kingship. In fact, both the *Mahabharata* and the *Ramayana* constitute major works of Hindu political thought. This was also an important period in the development of Buddhist and Hindu theory that later had important political implications. One such development, particularly relevant to South Asian political thought, was the establishment of Vaishnavism. The Hindu god Vishnu became the supreme god and others with great powers, such as Krishna, are seen as avatars of Vishnu. It was in the Gupta period that this

---

[1] U.N. Ghoshal (1959) *A History of Indian Political Ideas: The Ancient Period and the Period of Transition to the Middle Ages*, Madras: Oxford University Press: 307–396.

form of thought was fully developed and began to be spread throughout South Asia. In fact, both Buddhism and Hinduism spread throughout South Asia and formed the basis for political rule in a number of states.

Buddhism spread slowly in East Asia but eventually grew to become a powerful institutional force that had major implications for the state. The initial political implication of Buddhism in East Asia was a negative one: the alienation of the Buddhist community from the state. This is because this community was cut off from productive activity, given its dependence on donations. As we have seen, a role of the Buddhist ruler was developed in the earliest Buddhist literature as a patron of the Buddhist community and promotes its basic values. Buddhists want rulers that tolerate its existence at least. However, that does not mean that they want to be subordinate to rulers and the state. At first the Buddhist monks were keen to preserve their autonomy and integrity. For example, when a former official to the Eastern Jin emperor set up his own dynasty and demanded that the monks of the Donglin Temple (東林寺) pledge their obedience to him, the abbot Huiyüan (慧遠 334–416) wrote his *A Monk Does Not Bow Down Before A King* (*Shamen bu jingwangzhe lun* 沙門不敬王者論) in 404[2] in which he insists that monks do need to observe the law but need not bow before the emperor because that would make them seem as if they are seeking favor in this world, a world which is none of their concern. Interestingly enough, Huiyüan does suggest that those in the lay community should obey the customs and traditional teachings of their family as well as the authorities. However, outside the family and the requirements of the authorities, the teachings of the Buddha should be followed. In particular, monasteries where monks and nuns are seeking enlightenment should not be forcibly subject to the ruler. He concludes his argument by claiming that Buddhism has the same goals as the Literati even if they seek to attain those goals differently. In the end, the local ruler was not able to make Huiyüan submit to his demands and the reputation of his argument spread.

Others wrote similar defiant texts but not all monks resisted political authority and some sought to work with it. The "Humane King Sūtra" (*Renwang Huguo Jing* 仁王護國經), for example, argues for a mutually reinforcing relationship between rulers and Buddhism. It points out that wisdom, also valued by the Literati, is one of the virtues of a good ruler, and one which Buddhism will enhance.[3] There were other texts

---

[2] William Theodore De Bary, Irene Bloom and Joseph Adler (1999) *Sources of Chinese Tradition, Volume 1: From Earliest Times to 1600*, 2nd edn, New York: Columbia University Press: 426–429.

[3] See Charles D. Orzech (1989) "Puns on the Humane King," *Journal of the American Oriental Society*, 109(1): 17–24.

that became more important to the relationship between Buddhism and the state such as the "Golden Light Sūtra" (*Suvarṇaprabhāsottama Sūtra* सुवर्णप्रभासोत्तमसूत्रे or *Jinguangming Jing* 金光明經) and "Flower Garland Sutra" (*Avatamsaka Sutra* महावैपुल्यबुद्धावतंसकसूत्र or *Huáyán Jīng* 華嚴經). Even if Buddhism never completely supplanted the Literati at most East Asian dynastic courts, both Buddhism and Literati thought became part of the foundations of political thought in East Asia and were often adopted as a set package of advanced political thought in this period.

It is common but misleading to call this system of thought "Chinese" Buddhism because it was first adopted and fostered by kingdoms on the periphery of the old Literati world order which followed the collapse of the Han dynasty. In fact, the short-lived Northern Zhou (北周 557–581) state, which aimed at recreating the ancient Zhou dynasty in the model of the Literati ideal, was also the most hostile to Buddhism. Buddhism had a more profound influence in the tribal states which emerged on the periphery of the old imperial world order, though in combination with Literati institutions and practices. For example, three new kingdoms emerged on the Korean peninsula and each incorporated elements of Literati systems of rule and Buddhism, even earlier than states in the area we now call China. The Korean states are usually referred to as the "Three Kingdoms": Goguryeo (高句麗 37 BC–668 AD), Baekje (百濟 18 BC–660 AD) and Silla (新羅 57 BC–935 AD). Goguryeo, the closest to China overcame Han military-command control in 313, and Baekje had already formed as a centralized kingdom by about 250 absorbing the Mahan tribal confederacy. Similarly, Silla expanded by subordinating neighboring chiefdoms to form a strong independent federation. In addition to the Three Kingdoms, there was a smaller tribal confederacy, the Gaya, which survived at the tip of the Korean peninsula. The Three Kingdoms period ran from 57 BC until Silla's triumph over Goguryeo in 668. During this period, all of the three adopted both Literati forms of rule complemented with Buddhism, though with varying degrees of success.

Goguryeo adopted Literati rule under King Sosurim (小獸林王 ?–384, r. 371–384). A Literati training university (*taehak* 太學) was set up in 372 and a Code of Laws (律令) was adopted along the lines of the Han dynasty in 373. Parallel to these developments, King Sosurim welcomed the Buddhist monk Shundao (順道) from former Qin (前秦), which itself was one of the Sixteen Kingdoms based on a "barbarian" ethnic group which emerged in the breakup of the Han dynasty, and adopted Buddhism as the official faith in 372. Literati institutions that accompanied the introduction of Buddhism allowed for the centralization of authority with the monarch and Buddhism was used as the ideology to pacify opposition and assimilate native beliefs. Nonetheless, it must be remembered that the Literati system included a significant dose of Legalism as is seen in Goguryeo at the height of its power under Gwanggaeto the Great (廣開土太王 r. 391–412), who was notable for his military campaigns of territorial expansion. In this and other tribal states, Buddhism supplemented Literati/Legalist systems of rule to produce a degree of centralization of authority and a more stable political order.

In contrast, the decline of the Roman Empire, which was occurring at this time, led to the development of a new system of thought, neo-Platonism. Plotinus, the creator of neo-Platonism, was deeply engaged with the political elite with his lectures and seminars attended by many in the Roman elite, including Senators. He also maintained friendly relations with the Emperor Gallienus (Publius Licinius Egnatius Gallienus Augustus c. 218–268) who ruled Rome with his father Valerian from 253 to 260 and alone from 260 to 268. Plotinus used his relationship with Gallienus and the emperor's wife Salonina to propose the creation of an ideal city to be called Platonopolis. The problem was that Rome itself was in turmoil. Emperor Gallienus was the successor to a string of short-lived imperial reigns, and he himself lost large parts of his empire to revolts and barbarian invasions, and was eventually assassinated in a conspiracy involving his own commanders. Political conditions were not conducive to the realization of political ideas. It may be one reason why the metaphysical and spiritual side of neo-Platonism was subsequently transmitted and emphasized over the political.

The obscuring of the political and the rise of the metaphysical is apparent in later neo-Platonist thinkers. For example, the neo-Platonist philosopher Hypatia (Ὑπατία c.350/370–415), head of the neo-Platonic school in Alexandra, was subsequently believed to be more of a mathematician but can also be considered a prototype philosopher-queen.[4] She tried to help settle a dispute between Orestes, the Roman governor of Alexandria, and Cyril, the Bishop of Alexandria, but given the fact she had the ear of the governor, she was viewed as an enemy of Cyril by Cyril's more extreme supporters so was kidnapped by a Christian mob that took her to a church and murdered her. Her death symbolized the end of intellectual tolerance in the Roman Empire and the precarious position of neo-Platonist philosophy. This is not surprising because the empire itself was under attack. For example, Synesius (Συνέσιος) of Cyrene c. 373–c. 414, a student of Hypatia, was compelled to act as an envoy to Emperor Arcadius (Ἀρκάδιος 377–408) in Constantinople to appeal for assistance in defending his community in North Africa as the empire withdrew military support from

---

[4] Dominic O'Meara (2003) *Platonopolis: Platonic Political Philosophy in Late Antiquity*, Oxford: Clarendon Press: 83.

its frontiers. While he was there he wrote *De regno* (On Kingship), which attempted to appeal to Arcadius to fight corruption and to urge Arcadius to stem the increasing power of barbarians in the Byzantine (East Roman Empire) army. Synesius obtained assistance from the powerful praetorian prefect Aurelianus and his advice to Aurelianus can be found in *Aegyptus sive de Providentia*, an allegoric work depicting Aurelianus as the good Osiris and the Goth military advisor to Arcadius, Gainas, as the evil Typhon. The story is that Osiris and Typhon both started with the same soul but Typhon became evil and self-interested so took power from Osiris, despite the latter being more worthy of it. Even when all seemed bleak, however, the crimes and excesses of Typhon led divine providence to take power from Typhon and return it to Osiris.[5]

The position of later writers is also intimately related to the tribulations of the late Roman Empire. For example, St. Augustine of Hippo (354–430) wrote his *City of God* in response to the charge that the rise of Christianity had weakened the empire after the sack of Rome by the Visigoths in 410. Augustine spent his last days in Hippo under siege from the Vandals, a Germanic tribe that engaged in marauding attacks on different provinces of the Roman Empire. Similarly, the last important neo-Platonist and Christian thinker in the period, Boethius (c. 480–524), acted as a Consul in the Ostrogoth kingdom, which had taken over northern Italy from Rome, but he was imprisoned as a spy for the Eastern Roman Empire and eventually executed by King Theodoric the Great.

It was in this context that metaphysical systems of thought were developed. These promoted and reinforced the development of "religion" on the popular level but also had implications for political thought because, as we have seen, it is difficult to separate religion, metaphysics and political rule anywhere in this period and others.

THE RISE OF THE METAPHYSICS IN INDIA

India after the Mauryan Empire saw a revival of Vedic philosophy at the same time that Buddhist philosophical speculation reached its peak in India. The two key "Vedic" or "Hindu" works one must consider in this context are the *Mahabharata* and the *Ramayana*. The *Ramayana* is more focused on *kshatravidya* (क्षत्रविद्य), or the (acquisition of) science or wisdom necessary to be a ruler, than the *Mahabharata*, which focuses on duty, and for that reason the latter was closer to the Buddhist conceptions

---

[5] W.S. Crawford (1901) *Synesius: The Hellene*, London: Rivingtons: 439–452 for a translation of "Aegyptus sive de Providentia."

of rule. This includes the *rajavritta* (राजावृत्तित्व) or true/correct behavior of kings, such as truth and compassion. In the *Ramayana*, kings are gods in mortal form and become a model for divine kingship. The *Mahabharata* follows the *Arthashastra* tradition of combining straightforwardness with deception. The *Mahabharata* contains material from various dates, including some that predate Buddhism, but the received version clearly reflects the experience of Ashoka and the Mauryan dynasty if only to reject the Buddhist non-violence of Ashoka in order to demonstrate the need for violence to maintain order and secure justice. The *Mahabharata* is also a consciously Brahmin appropriation of popular warrior caste myth.

The central narrative in the *Mahabharata* is of the Kurukshetra War and the fates of the Kaurava and the Pandava princes. Mahabharata means "the great tale of the Bhārata dynasty" and one Brahmin clan appears to get the most attention: Bhrgus or Bhargavas.[6] There are several odd aspects of the epic but central is the relationship of the Bhrgus to *kshatriyas* and the gods ranging from "intimate friendship to murderous hostility."[7] The Bhrgus, a Brahmin clan, seem to violate caste rules because they marry into the *Kshatriya* warrior caste and behave as if they are *kshatriya*.[8] There are other inversions with *kshatriyas* becoming Brahmin, though they tend to remain as Brahmin, whereas eventually the Bhrgus give up *kshatriyas* status and return to the Brahmin caste.[9]

The main political text can be found in the Shanti Parva (शान्ति पर्व) or "Book of Peace" section of the *Mahabharata*.[10] The key figure is Yudhishthira (युधिष्ठिर), leader of the Pandava princes in the Kurukshetra War. He loses his kingdom in a game of dice and is forced into exile. His efforts to regain the kingdom are the basis of the War and the entire story of the *Mahabharata*. It is widely acknowledged that Yudhishthira is modeled on moral doubt about violence as personified by Ashoka.[11] Indeed,

---

[6] Robert Goldman (1977) *Priests and Warriors: The Bhrgus of the Mahabharata*, New York, NY: Columbia University Press: 1–2.
[7] Goldman (1977) *Priests and Warriors*: 94.
[8] Goldman (1977) *Priests and Warriors*: 99.
[9] Goldman (1977) *Priests and Warriors*: 111–112.
[10] The *Mahabharata* is traditionally attributed to Vyasa (व्यास), literally the "compiler," who is also a character in work. A full English translation is Vyasa; Kisari Mohan Ganguli trans. (1883–1896) *The Mahabharata*, Calcutta: Bharata Press, but there is a more recent effort at translating this work including the key sections of political thought in Vyasa; James L. Fitzgerald trans. (2004) *The Mahabharata*, vol. 7, Chicago, IL: University of Chicago Press, though this volume contains only Book 11 (The Book of the Women) and part of Book 12 (The Book of Peace).
[11] Nick Sutton (1997) "Aśoka and Yudhisthira: A Historical Setting for the Ideological Tensions of the Mahābhārata?," *Religion*, 27(4): 333–341 and Alf Hiltebeitel (2001) *Rethinking the Mahābhārata: A Reader's Guide to the Education of the Dharma King*, Chicago, IL: The University of Chicago Press.

after Yudhishthira has won the war, he is filled with heavy grief over the dreadful carnage. He declares that he detests the life of the *Kshatriyas*, with the greed for valor, and lust for wrath that is required to be successful in war. The desire for sovereignty, he argues, is not worth the cost. Worse, he and his companions have been reduced to acting like a pack of dogs fighting one another for a piece of meat. However, he has lost interest that was to be gained as a result of this sacrifice. He goes on to praise forgiveness, self-restraint, humility, non-violence and other practices of those who have renounced life and dwell in the forests. His companions try to persuade him that the role of a ruler can also include forgiveness, compassion, and even non-violence, but they insist that those who seek to disrupt the legitimate order for their own selfish purposes must be slain so the righteous can govern the earth.

The centerpiece of the Book of Peace is the long speech by the elder Bhishma to Yudhishthira on the subject of *rajadharma* (royal duties, or more accurately, correct royal duties). *Rajadharma* becomes the ethical justification for the amorality in the logic of the *Arthashastra* so that the skills and tactics set out in the *Arthashastra* are subordinated in the *rajadharma*.[12] *Rajadharma* depends on *dandaniti* (sciences or art of government with roots in punishment). The rod of chastisement (*danda*) is righteousness itself. Without the *dandaniti*, chaos will result and the dharma of the world will be lost. Everything is dependent on the rod of chastisement. There are some who can only be restrained by *danda* to stop them committing unspeakable evil. If the rod of chastisement did not protect people, the world would sink into the darkness of hell. A king who fails to uphold righteousness himself trespasses against morality. The true king must slay those that deserve death, and also make gifts to persons deserving of charity and protect his subjects according to the law.

There is also a cosmology of the origins of kingship in the *Mahabharata* very much like the Buddhist one but with more emphasis on the decline of original dharma and the need for the ruler to keep order. In the *Mahabharata*, the original set of kings failed to uphold the *dandaniti* and after several failures, illustrative of what not to do, one upheld the *dandaniti* so was called "king" (*raja*) and *Kshatriya* because he protected Brahmin. There are also parallels with the Buddhist genesis myth with the significant difference that kingship in the Buddhist text is based on mutual agreement (a sort of social contract) but in *Mahabharata* it is a divinely led creation. For the *Mahabharata* the king is the source of divinely inspired dharma

---

[12] S.J. Tampiah (1977) *World Conqueror and World Renouncer: A Study of Buddhism and Polity in Thailand against a Historical Background*, Cambridge: Cambridge University Press: 30.

and benefits the whole world by maintaining it. Without him chaos will ensue. People have an obligation to support him and the king must act to preserve the social order. Thus the *Mahabharata* reflects both the Buddhist literature on the subject and the *Arthashastra* and *Dharmasastra* literature in a way that is original yet also more synthetic and comprehensive of the tradition.

There are two places in the *Mahabharata* in which higher level metaphysics are used to justify the role that the ruler is meant to play, no matter how unpleasant exercising that role might be. One is in the "Bhagavad Gita," the section of the *Mahabharata* where Yudhishthira is about to go into battle but has lost the will to fight. The god Kṛishṇa becomes Yudhishthira's chariot driver and relates a vision of symbolic stages leading to a higher mystical union with the divine godhead with each level more beautiful and terrifying, to inspire Yudhishthira to realize that the troubles of this world are not important. While it is often seen as allegorical of ethical and spiritual struggles, central to this discussion is the concept of fulfilling one's duty as a warrior and potential ruler, that is, to fight and kill those who are acting unjustly and deserve punishment.

The remainder of the *Mahabharata* focuses on Yudhishthira overcoming his doubts and acting as a good ruler, but his real reward comes as he ascends to heaven. The overall point is that his own feelings do not matter. He must perform his duty. It is even foolish for him to worry about his own soul. It is true that ignorance, desire, and evil acts arise from the state of union between soul and body, but the body is destructible and the soul is not. However, this does not mean the soul remains as it is forever. The soul is more like small rivers falling into larger ones, and the larger ones rolling into the ocean, in the same way the soul reaches its emancipation when it is received into the Universal Soul. Those who perform their duty can move toward liberation but those who do not, will remain to suffer in the physical world.

Buddhist metaphysics in India also progressed significantly in this period. For example, the Buddhist thinker Nāgārjuna (नागार्जुन 龍樹 c. 150–250 AD) built on the ideas of the Buddha but provided a more philosophical basis that is important later in East Asia. One key concept is of emptiness (*śūnyatā* शून्यता) in the sense that any one thing or individual at any given moment is dependent on an incalculably large number of factors in order to come into existence so that the reality of any single point of time, in terms of both physical things and the character of individuals, is so insignificant in the context of that chain of events that it is effectively "empty" of any real content. Nāgārjuna stops us from being overwhelmed with this realization with his "Treatise on the Middle Path" (*Mādhyamika-śāstra* मध्यमकशास्त्र *Zhong Lun* 中論), that is, a path between the notion that everything exists as a concrete reality and nothing exists as reality, or, between nihilism (nothing exists) and realism (all that is experienced is permanent and "real"). The path between these two extremes is the "middle way." This builds on the Buddha's idea that it is wrong to believe the self exists forever, which is "eternalism," and also that there is no self at all, which he termed "annihilationism." There must be enough of a self to act and have an impact, as was demonstrated in Chapters 2 and 3. In fact, it can be argued that this notion of the "emptiness" of existence creates the space in which moral action becomes possible. If all the causes that have existed before determined all that will happen in the future, then that is determinism. By arguing that existence is empty and reflecting on that fact, it means that we will then have the ability to attempt to begin to detach ourselves from the chain of causation and from sources of suffering. At the same time, Nāgārjuna permits us to believe in reality, that is, reality for us, but opens the way to understand its true nature as infinite chains of cause and effect in order to cope with it. Nāgārjuna's three treatises, including that of the middle path, are very important in later East Asian Buddhist political thought.

Another important Gupta school of Buddhism is the *Yogācāra*, which has roots in the *Saṃdhinirmocana Sūtra*, but was given its essential form by two Brahmin-born half-brothers Asaṅga and Vasubandhu, of which the work of Vasubandhu has potentially more political implications. *Yogācāra* is also sometimes called the Consciousness-only school because one key concept is *Vijñapti-mātra(tā)* (विज्ञानवाद) or "mere representation of consciousness" but this does not mean that *Yogācāra* is similar to Western idealist philosophy. It simply means that the unenlightened see the world through the mere representation of things in their consciousness rather than seeing its true nature. The work of Vasubandhu (वसुबन्द fl. fourth century) reflects debates within *Sarvāstivādin* school in general and the *Yogācāra* school in particular. He confirms the logic of the emptiness of existence by noting that there is no creator god because there can be no one uncaused cause that can account for complexity of dependent origination so the meaning of individual existence cannot arise from a divine source. He goes on to argue that Yogācāra views emptiness in a positive sense of lack of duality between what one perceives and what is real, and not only in a negative sense of the relative unimportance of any given link in the chain of causation of dependent origination. For this reason, Vasubandhu puts forward a "doctrine of universal momentariness" which means that all experience of the world is momentary but also infinite.

Vasubandhu also argued strongly against the *Pudgalavāda* or "Personalist" sect of Buddhism that was still very popular at the time. He insists that there is no "self" (*ātman*) only the five aggregates (*skandhas*).

However, Vasubandhu goes further by explaining eight forms of consciousness, including the five senses (each as one form of consciousness), mind (in the sense of perception), *manas* (मनस् or self-consciousness), and storehouse consciousness. The last is a central concept because our own consciousness cannot explain the world as we experience it, especially the nature of things and people we perceive as external to ourselves, so store consciousness (*ālayavijñāna* आलयविज्ञान) is necessary to explain how karma unfolds in ways that are not immediately explainable by individual action. Vasubandhu posited that karma is stored as seeds (*bīja* बीज). Our experience of the world results from the development of these seeds that are "perfuming" (*vāsanā* वासना) the world. It is the sum total of these seeds and their state of perfuming that constitutes the "receptacle world" (*bhajanaloka* भजनलोक), that is, the totality of good and evil actions that determines the apparently "outside" world as we experience it. Store consciousness also determines the potential of each person to achieve enlightenment, though he suggests that some beings, *icchantika* (इच्छन्तिक), are incapable of achieving enlightenment, except perhaps with the assistance of a Buddha or bodhisattva.[13] Tampiah has suggested that Vasubandhu inherently contains the possibility of a *Yogācāra* political thought with king (that is, *cakkavatti*, a virtuous wheel-rolling world ruler) as a corrective factor but it is not clear how much of Tampiah's interpretation is purely his own.[14] In fact, Vasubandhu in his *Abhidharmakosa* argues that *cakkavatti* are extremely rare[15] but Tampiah's interpretation is plausible if one considers the later political influence of the school in certain times and places as we will see in the next chapter.

The *Yogācāra* school also created a "three-body" doctrine for the nature of Buddha's power by arguing that Buddhahood has three aspects: (1) *nirmāṇakāya* (निर्माणकाय) or "transformation body" (manifestation in our physical world); (2) the *sambhogakāya* (सम्भोगकाय) or "enjoyment-body" or "bliss body" (manifestation in different realms, such as the Pure Land associated with a specific Buddha); and (3) the *dharmakāya* (धर्मकाय) or "dharma-body." *Yogācāra* emerged from the *Sarvāstivādins* who saw

---

[13] Note for later: This notion of *icchantika* is rejected by the Tiantai school in East Asia, which argues that potential Buddhahood is inherent in all sentient beings. This disagreement led Tz'u-en (慈恩, 632–682) the first patriarch of Yogārcāra in China, to propose two types of nature: the latent Buddhahood found in all beings (*lǐ fó xìng* 理佛性) and the Buddhahood in action (*háng fó xìng* 行佛性).

[14] Tampiah (1977) *World Conqueror and World Renouncer*: 38; This also applies to Tampiah's reference to Paul Mus (1964) "Thousand-Armed Kannon A Mystery or a Problem," *Journal of Indian and Buddhist Studies* (印度學佛教學研究), 12(1): 447–453, though there seems more potential for political thought in Mus' interpretation.

[15] Vasubandhu; Leo M. Pruden translation from French translation of Louis de La Vallée Poussin (1988) *Abhidhramakośabhāsyam*, vol. 2. Berkeley, CA: Asian Humanities Press: 484.

the historical Buddha's physical body (*rūpakāya* रूपकय) as impure and improper for taking refuge in, so sought refuge in the *dharmakāya* or "truth body" of the Buddha, which is beyond normal human conception and part of the higher law of the universe that the Buddha taught. This was also the view of the *Mahāsāṃghika* school and became a tenet of *Mahāyāna* Buddhism. It becomes important politically because rulers often invoke the power of the Buddha or other Buddhas in either *sambhogakāya* or *dharmakāya* form. One early example was the Vairocana (वैरोचन), a Buddha seen as the embodiment of the concept of Emptiness. The Vairocana is often interpreted, in texts such as the Flower Garland Sutra, as a *dharmakāya* that constitutes the transcendental source of Buddha power from which Buddhas arise and to which they can return. As such, Vairocana is considered a Primordial Buddha. In East Asian Buddhism, Vairocana was gradually superseded by the Amitabha Buddha, who could also appear as a *sambhogakāya*. This notion of different bodies was used later to suggest that rulers were avatars of Buddhist beings and might possess their extensive powers.

TAOIST AND "DARK LEARNING" METAPHYSICS IN EAST ASIA

At the end of the Han dynasty, religion also played a more important role in East Asia. For example, Taoist thought, which as we have seen, was created by the elite as political thought in the Warring States period and developed by subsequent scholars, begins to take on a more popular and thus religious dimension at the end of the Han dynasty. A good example of this transition is the political text entitled "The Great Peace" or *Taiping Jing* (太平經). There are two versions of the early *Taiping Jing*, both of which underscore its origins as a political text. One is by Gan Zhongke (甘忠可 fl. late first century BC) who submitted his *Tiānguān lì Bāoyuán Tàipíng jīng* (天官歷包元太平經) as a memorial to the Han dynasty Emperor Cheng (32–7 BC). The other is a text by an unknown author, the *Tàipíng Qīnglǐng Shū* (太平清領書) presented to Han Emperor Shun (漢順帝 126–145 AD). The version that still exists today was preserved by later religious Taoists and does not include all the original material of these two original texts due to being edited and transmitted selectively over centuries, but even a cursory reading makes the political origin of content apparent.[16]

Popular movements were behind the shift in Taoism toward what

---

[16] Barbara Hendrischke (2015) *The Scripture on Great Peace: The Taiping jing and the Beginnings of Daoism*, Berkeley, CA: University of California Press.

appears as more of a religion. For example, Zhang Jue (張角 d. 184), the leader of the Yellow Turban Rebellion (*Huáng jīn zhī Luàn* 黃巾之亂), advocated "Taiping Daoism" (太平道) at the end of the Han dynasty, influenced by the same logic as the *Taiping Jing*, mobilizing common people in revolts that severely weakened the government. This period also saw the rise of the Five Bushel Sect (*Wudou mi dao* 五斗米道) founded by Zhang Ling (張陵 34–156) (no relation to the Yellow Turban Zhang Jue), which was a Taoist movement that formed the basis for what became the Taoist religion with the leader of the movement, Zhang Tao Lin, known as the Heavenly or Celestial Teacher or Master (*tiānshī* 天師). Zhang Ling created holy talismans to cure and protect his followers, wrote commentaries and other works (now lost) to create a Taoist scripture and reformed local ritual practices by abolishing blood sacrificing and consolidating the pantheon of local spirits or deities (*shen* 神) who had long been the basis of local beliefs and veneration. The Five Bushel Sect was centrally funded and had an administrative hierarchy. It became a mass movement among farmers who were asked to donate five ancient Chinese measures of rice (a bushel is used to translate the approximate measure) and for this reason they were also known as the rice pirates but more commonly as the Five Bushel Sect. The sect created a network of inns where followers could stay and eat free of charge but if there was any infraction of strict rules, the perpetrators were punished by being made to do road work or work on the *tao*, which can mean literally path, way, or road. The movement was continued by Zhang Ling's son, Zhang Heng (張衡 78–139) and his grandson, Zhang Lu (張魯 d. 216). Zhang Lu established an independent state as part of a rebellion against the Han dynasty in 184 AD but gave loyalty to the leader of the founder of the Wei dynasty in exchange for honors, a fiefdom and recognition by the government (Zhang Lu even lived at Court). The movement spread over the next two centuries to all of East Asia, growing to be a major religious force which still exists today (the present Heavenly Master is a theoretical descendant of Zhang Ling, the founder, and lives in Taiwan). It seriously challenged Literati by claiming that their Heavenly Master and not an impersonal heaven, is the source of political legitimacy.

The religious tendency in Taoism led to more elaborate myths, such as the myth of the Mountain Hermits (*xian ren* 仙人) or Spiritual Hermits (*shen xian* 神仙), often translated as the Immortals who live above the clouds on or near mountain tops. Originally there were five Immortals who lived 7,000 *li* (里) apart. These are individuals who, through Taoist practices, have transcended mortal life. A Taoist paradise was also created, though it resembles a series of city halls rather than a paradise in the Western sense. The Jade Emperor (*Yù Huáng* 玉皇 or *Yù Dì* 玉帝) is the ruler of Heaven and all realms below heaven including that of us mortals. He can also be referred to as a Heavenly Master (*Tiān Gōng* 天公). One important and popular Immortal is the Queen Mother of the West (*Xiwangmu* 西王母), Queen of the Immortals, who was modeled on an ancient goddess predating organized Taoism and first mentioned in the *Zhaungzi*. Belief in this goddess probably arose in the West of China and was transmitted along the silk road about the time of the early Roman Empire. She may reflect pre-historical matriarchal power structures reflected in practices of ethnic minority groups in China (including some until relatively recently) and the myths and legends of Vietnam, Korea and Japan. In fact, initial contact between Japan and the continent was linked to the legitimacy of the sacred Japanese female ruler Himiko (卑弥呼) and associated with the Imperial ancestral goddess Amaterasu (天照), so that the Queen Mother of the West, as represented on mirrors, appears to have played an important ritual role in pre-historic Japanese polities.[17]

At the same time, Literati thought was evolving with the most prominent philosophy of the period called *Xuánxué* (玄學), or, crudely, "Neo-Taoism." This approach spread further in the Northern and Southern Dynasties period (420–589) which began when the Jin ruling house fled south to a capital in Jiankang (modern Nanjing). After the Jin collapsed in 420, there were two different short-lived dynasties in the north and in the south, both of which claimed the mandate of heaven and thus control of all under heaven. The term *Xuánxué* is variously translated as the Dark, Mysterious or Illusory Learning and is really a relatively loose label for all the diversity of thinkers of the period.[18] It flourished particularly in the Southern dynasty of Emperor Wen of Liu Song who officially recognized *Xuánxué* as a part of the curriculum of the imperial academy as integral but distinct from "Confucian" or Literati thought (*ru* 儒). That is, *Xuánxué* was a form of Literati thought supplemented with Taoism and other ideas. As a philosophy, it was more rationalist than the religious Taoism discussed above, but still heavily influenced by earlier political Taoism. This was partly due to the "old text, new text" controversy and the rationalists such as Wang Lu in the Han dynasty. *Xuánxué* thought was developed primarily through commentaries on texts such as the *Yijing*, Laozi's *Classic of the Way and Virtue* (Tao Te Jing), and the *Zhuangzi*. The aim is to reveal the deeper meaning in these texts that appear to be dark and mysterious. In doing so, key *Xuánxué* scholars, such as He Yan, Wang Bi and others in

---

[17] Gina L. Barnes (2014) "A Hypothesis for Early Kofun Rulership," *Japan Review*, 27: 3–29.
[18] In modern Chinese, *Xuánxué* is associated with astrology, geomancy and similar popular Taoist practices so care must be taken in how the term might be misunderstood even by modern East Asians.

the Wei-Jin dynasties developed a sophisticated reinterpretation of Literati thought based on Taoist metaphysics.

He Yan (何晏 c. 195–249) is considered one of the founders of *Xuánxué* along with Wang Bi. He Yan's "Commentary on the Analects" (*Lunyu He-shi Jijie* 論語何氏集解) is the most complete text of his to survive but it may be the work of several scholars and not his alone. He is also known through quotations from essays "On the Nameless" (無名 *wuming lun*) and "On the Tao" (道論 *dao lun*) found in the works of others. He argued that since the *Tao* is nameless and has no form, it is complete and the source of all things, including energy and matter (*qi* 氣), that make for both form and spirit, light and shadow, and make it possible to measure everything. This follows Laozi but provides more concrete theory to explain how the *Tao* is manifest. The concept of *qi* (氣) is important and plays a central role in later East Asian thought. *Qi* is both matter and energy, because it is a basic element of everything in the universe, physical and non-physical. It is both quantitative and qualitative because it gives everything unique properties. Han Ye argued that it is the properties of the *qi* that constitutes a thing and determines if it is refined or crude, heavy or light, thick or thin, and so on. It provides the "nature" (*xing* 性) of things and all phenomena in the world, including the nature of the political community and political actors within it. As we have seen, the debate over human nature (*xing*) goes back to the Warring States period and the generation of scholars a century after Confucius. He Yan explains the process in terms of *qi* (氣) that determines an individual's "capabilities" (*cai* 才), which includes all talents, intellectual capacity, physical abilities, emotional stability and sense of morality (論語何氏集解 15.29). This link between *xing* and *cai* was central to the debates among the *Xuánxué* Literati. The pinnacle of *cai* was the Sage (*shèngrén* 聖人), who has exceptional *qi* to the extent the Sage can commune with the virtues of heaven and earth (論語何氏集解 14.35 and 16.8). He Yan appears to be influenced here by the *Yijing* (*Book of Changes*) in that the presence of the virtue of heaven and earth is necessary for a stable and prosperous political community. Since the Sage has the nature to see and reach this standard, they are necessary to create the best political forms.

Wang Bi (王弼 226–249) is perhaps the most well-known of the *Xuánxué* school and a crucial link between classical and later East Asian thought. His commentaries on the Laozi's *Tao Te Jing* and the *Book of Changes* include concepts that were essential for a new metaphysics of Literati thought.[19] Wang argues that nothingness (*wu* 無) is a position

---

[19] Wang Bi; Richard John Lynn trans. (1994) *The Classic of Changes: A New Translation of the I Ching as Interpreted by Wang Bi*, New York, NY: Columbia University Press, and Wang Bi; Richard John Lynn trans. (1999) *The Classic of the Way and Virtue: A New*

from which the *Tao* can be best understood. The *Tao* is both nothingness and unity of "one." The *Tao* is an unseen source that gives sustenance and vitality to the world just as the roots of a tree anchor and nourish the branches. However, it does not have an identifiable source so seems to arise from nothing. Wang Bi posits the concept of principle (*li* 理) as the logic behind the operation of the *Tao*. Things happen for a reason. When we see something happen it is manifest through *qi* (氣) but it is due to the workings of *li* (理). The unfolding of the *li* (理) of the *Tao* has a varying impact on different individuals because a person's *qi* endowment varies (Wang Bi commentary on *Lunyu* 17.2). Nonetheless, all *qi* comes from the *Tao* and the *Tao* is internal to all things. Since the order and harmony inherent in *li* tends toward stillness and stability, by overcoming the desires that distort human relationships and psychology (such as power and greed), one can arrive at a tranquil core through the *li* (理). By overcoming excessive or unnatural desires, humans can cultivate their original condition, their basic nature, or using a term from Zhuangzi, our nature as "self-so" (*zìrán* 自然), or as it is, in and of itself, so needing no more than that.

This does not mean Wang Bi rejects normal emotions, however. The Sage has the same five emotions (happiness, anger, sadness, pleasure and desire) as ordinary people. However, because his intelligence (*shenming* 神明), or, literally, spiritual enlightenment, is superior, he also possesses gentleness and amiability, and, therefore, can identify with nothingness (*wu*). A Sage also responds appropriately to situations with sadness or pleasure but does not become overwhelmed by them. It does not mean that he is not responsive at all.[20] He Yan suggests that it is very difficult, if not impossible, to become a Sage but Wang Bi suggests that a Sage is not too different from ordinary people. The Sage is best placed to run a state because the state as a sacred instrument (*shenqi* 神器) but Wang interprets *shen* as something without form or restriction, not as spirit or god (as the term *shen* is usually translated), so perhaps more the state as unfettered action as in sovereign, and *qi* (器) as a concrete way (or, literally, instrument) to order and integrate.[21]

Another *Xuánxué* thinker was Guo Xiang (郭象 d. 312) who wrote the most influential commentary on the text of the *Zhuangzi*. Guo Xiang's heavily edited version of the text was so well-received that it is the only

---

Translation of the Tao-te Ching of Laozi as Interpreted by Wang Bi, New York, NY: Columbia University Press.

[20] De Bary, Bloom and Adler (1999) *Sources of East Asian Tradition*, vol. 1: 214.

[21] Wing-tsit Chan (1979) "Introduction" in Ariane Rump trans. *Commentary on the Lao Tzu by Wang Pi*, Honolulu: University of Hawaii Press: ix.

complete version we have today. Guo's focus is on Zhuangzi's views on naturalness (zìrán 自然). Guo distinguishes between underlying principles, such as humaneness (ren 仁) and rightness (yi 義), and the actual manifestation of these principles at any one time. Humaneness and rightness are principles of human nature but human societies and the life of those in them changes, and can be different compared with the past when the classics were written. If one insists on a fixed interpretation of things, then one will develop prejudices and hypocrisy, but if one exercises a principle appropriate for the time, then one will truly understand the nature of the underlying principle. Thus, the rituals of the ancient kings met the needs of their time but as time has passed, they simply become the source of false affectations and poor imitation. This suggests that the practices of a Sage in government must naturally evolve with the times.[22]

At the same time as the *Xuánxué* school was developing, the Literati ideal of a duty to serve the government was undermined by political intrigue, which often had potentially deadly consequences. Both loyalty to Cao Wei and attempts to win favor in the Jin dynasty were fraught with danger. Some scholar-officials decided to pursue an alternative lifestyle of personal freedom through spontaneity, enjoyment of nature and refusal to become embroiled in politics. Their self-imposed exile to the countryside inspired artists and others seeking escape from political turmoil. "Pure conversation" (qīng tán 清談), known as "empty chat" where Literati would meet and talk about philosophical issues free from the constraints of authorized interpretations or conventional societal opinion in a sort of free association. It was practiced widely among intellectuals until it was overtaken by interest in or opposition to Buddhism. The tendency to emphasize aesthetic pleasure, nature and spontaneity led to it being considered a hedonistic trend. Some of the individual members of the group are based on real persons but stories surrounding the group as a coherent movement are based on myths created by later writers, such as in the *New Tales of the World* (*Shishuo Xinyu* 世說新語).

Those who have been associated with the group put forward a political theory of escapism with a critique of Literati culture. Over time the legend of the Seven Sages of the Bamboo Grove (*zhulin qixian* 竹林七賢) had spread throughout East Asia: Xi Kang Liu Ling, Ruan Ji, Ruan Xian, Shan Tao, Wang Rong and Xiang Xiu. Each was influential. For example, Xiang Xiu's (向秀 c.223–c.275) commentary on the *Zhuangzi* was the starting point of the version produced by Guo Xiang. Perhaps the most notable was Xi Kang (嵇康; 223–262), a musician who wrote on

---

[22] De Bary, Bloom and Adler (1999) *Sources of East Asian Tradition*, vol. 1: 215–216.

music, politics and ethics as well as neo-Taoist topics such as longevity, in such works as *Yangsheng Lun* (養生論) or "Essay on Nourishing Life"), *Shengwu Aile Lun* (聲無哀樂論) or "On the Absence of Sentiments in Music," *Qin Fu* (琴賦) or "A Composition on the Qin [a musical instrument]," and *Shisi Lun* (釋私論) or "Discourse on Dispelling the Self." Ji Kang acquired a reputation for challenging Literati orthodoxy and the social norms of his time. He took a government post in the Cao Wei dynasty but demonstrated nothing but contempt for the work and his colleagues, and rudely refused to work for the subsequent Jin dynasty. When he attempted to defend a friend from false charges, he was himself put to death. This suggested that Xi Kang's disdain for official life eventually led to his execution.

The final thinker in this period to consider is Ge Hong (葛洪, 283–343) and his book the *Baopuzi* (抱朴子) or "The Master who Embraces Simplicity."[23] Ge Hong was a minor official during the Jin dynasty (263–420). The *Baopuzi* reflects the Literati struggle to reconcile their personal interests and their role as public servants. The "Inner Chapters" focus on health, longevity and personal salvation through esoteric knowledge, whereas the "Outer Chapters" are an eclectic mix of subjects including politics, and so on, though more often than not a reflection of the more concrete concerns of former Han dynasty Literati elite living and working under the Jin dynasty. Ge Hong is important as a source for Bao Jingyan (鮑敬言) who could be seen as an early anarchist philosopher, but it is entirely possible that Ge Hong made him up because he puts forward very standard Taoist arguments against authority and it may have been safer for Ge Hong to put his words into the mouth of a fictional person rather than be associated with them personally.[24] What is interesting about Bao is that he questions how the Literati know what Heaven is meant to have mandated, particularly the supremacy of rulers over the people, which he viewed as simply the use of force and wiles to control simple people. Heaven had nothing to do with it. In fact, he argues that originally there were "no rulers and officials" (*wu jün wu chen* 無君無臣) and people were free and at peace. All beings participated in a mysterious equality/sameness

---

[23] The only full English translation of this work is by Jay Sailey (1978) *The Master who Embraces Simplicity: A Study of the Philosopher Ko Hung, AD 283–343*, San Francisco, CA: Chinese Materials Center, but it is not widely available and I had to use a Japanese translation by 葛洪 (Ge Hong) 本田済訳 (Honda Wataru trans.) (1990) 『抱朴子 内篇・外篇』 (Baopuzi naihen/gaihen) 全3巻 (3 volumes), 東京：平凡社 (Tokyo: Heibon Sha).

[24] Joseph Needham (1956) *Science and Civilization in China, Volume 2: History of Scientific Thought*, Cambridge: Cambridge University Press: 435 translates a large portion of the text on Bao. See also Kung-chuan Hsiao; Frederick W. Mote trans. (1979) *History of Chinese Political Thought, Volume 1: From the Beginnings to the Sixth Century AD*, Princeton, NJ: Princeton University Press: 623.

(*xuantong* 玄同) and forgot themselves in the *Tao*. Power and profit was not pursued so war, contagious disease and deceit did not arise. People led long happy lives.

NEO-PLATONIST METAPHYSICS IN THE ROMAN EMPIRE

In the declining Roman Empire, neo-Platonism emerged to provide a complex metaphysical system with a strong political orientation. The creator of neo-Platonism, Plotinus (Πλωτῖνος 204–270), was born in Roman Egypt and his ideas are a synthesis of Greek philosophy with Egyptian and other Eastern ideas including possible Indian influences. What follows is related by his student Porphyry who edited Plotinus' major work the *Enneads* and the biography by Porphyry comes at the beginning of the text. Born in Egypt Plotinus traveled to Alexandria to study philosophy at the age of 27 where he studied under the Platonist Ammonius but also engaged with other schools including the Stoics. He became interested in Persian and Indian philosophy, this led him to join the army of Gordian III that aimed at attempting to conquer Persia but with the failure of this expedition Plotinus was temporarily stranded in the East. Plotinus eventually found his way back to Rome. We cannot be sure of the extent he was able to study Persian and Indian thought during his time in the East, because although knowledge of Persia and India must have been available in the eastern areas of the Roman Empire in such cities as Alexandria, there are no direct references to Persian or Indian sources or concepts in the work of Plotinus left to us. Nonetheless, there is a basis for comparison and hints of some influence.

The starting principle in neo-Platonism is the One (τὸ ἕν) which is the source and end of existence but is not being itself. It is "beyond being" (*epekeina tes ousias επέκεινα της ουσίας*, see Plato's *Republic* 509b). It is the logical extension of Aristotle's view that all things have a teleology and that must include the totality of things in the universe. The One itself cannot be directly understood because to think is to use concepts and the One is beyond all conceptualization. At the same time, the individuality of all things comes from the One. The One is the source of all things and by returning to the One all things can achieve completion and perfection. The One is the ultimate unity which has no distinctions as the highest form, incorporating all that is good. The One and individual things are not separate, however, because things arise in the One, participate in the One even as individuals, and return to the One. In order to achieve the ends of human existence, the soul of each individual must undertake a divine quest to realize union with the One through the Intellect (*Nous* νοῦς or Mind). However, the One is so simple, it cannot be grasped easily by the Intellect. In striving to grasp the One, Intellect produces the Soul (*Psyche* ψυχή). The Soul is also a mind, but unlike the Intellect does not understand its connection to the whole. The Soul is focused on its own world and relationship to it causes Time to come into existence. Just as when Intellect tries to grasp the One, it produces the Soul, when the Soul attempts to join with the Intellect, it produces the body in the material world.

There is no explicit political text by Plotinus. O'Meara points out a reference to politics in the *Enneads* must be broadly construed because it seems to include rule of the individual over their body (passions), their household and the polis.[25] This parallels Aristotle in the *Politics*, and the division between the legislative as in Plato's *Laws* (which focuses on the law of an ideal state) and the judicial as in Plato's *Republic* (which focuses on the ideal of justice and the elite who are trained to seek it). It would also not be strange if neo-Platonism was political because Plato was and is considered at the source of Western political thought. In fact, it is the absence of politics in neo-Platonism that needs explanation. In the work of Plotinus the definition of politics (Πολιτική) is subordinated to the ordering of appetites in the soul, seemingly drawing on a similar analogy in Plato's *Republic* but the conceptualization of Plotinus on this point is ambiguous in that it hovers at the level of the personal rather than as the basis for the political.[26] There is one intriguing exception in the use of the concept of *kairos* (καιρός), or appropriate action for the circumstances by Plotinus,[27] which parallels aspects of *wu wei* (無爲) in Taoist political thought, because it suggests that the neo-Platonist must act in the real world sometimes and not only focus on the divine alone.

The successors of Plotinus provide further clues to the politics of neo-Platonism.[28] For example, Iamblichus (Ἰάμβλιχος 245–c. 325), a Syrian whose name literally means "He is king," probably pointing to royal lineage, elaborated stages of development of the Intellect needed to bring it progressively closer to the One. The divine hierarchy descended from the One through to living beings and the material world, which is how the soul became material in the form of human beings. Souls can return to divine One by *theurgy* (θεουργία), literally, "divine-working" to achieve oneness or *henosis* (ἕνωσις). Neo-platonic theurgy seems to have originally

---

[25] O'Meara (2003) *Platonopolis*: 40–44.
[26] Plotinus; A.H. Armstrong trans. (1966) *Plotinus*, vol. I, 2nd edn, Cambridge: Harvard University Press: 144–145.
[27] Plotinus; A.H. Armstrong trans. (1966) *Plotinus*: 206–207.
[28] Jeremy M. Schott (2003) "Founding Platonopolis: The Platonic Politeia in Eusebius, Porphyry, and Iamblichus," *Journal of Early Christian Studies*, 11(4): 501–531.

been inspired by Julian the theurgist, alive in the reign of Emperor Marcus Aurelius, but in his *De Mysteriis*, Iamblichus developed theurgy based on Platonic principles. Many are similar to magic ritual practices of the time, such as sympathetic harmony with the cosmos, and invocations of gods, *daemons* (spirits), the souls of heroes, and angels, and so on which Platonic philosophers normally rejected (following from Republic II and Laws X). However, Iamblichus believed that these practices contained the power to move gods and were worthy of emulation. He then developed a curriculum to aid the Soul in the process of grasping the Intellect and the One, starting from practical knowledge and rising through to mathematics and cosmology. Some elements of the training included ritual practices and meditation on specific ideas, words or objects. Yet, according to O'Meara, political life was seen as a preparatory stage in the development of the Soul, and even after attaining higher levels of divine knowledge, there was an obligation for the enlightened to "descend back into the cave," using Plato's terminology, to legislate and guide based on divine experience.[29] The parallel with the role of bodhisattva is uncanny though a bodhisattva is almost purely spiritual whereas the divinely focused neo-Platonist training was clearly political, at least in one stage. It would be a mistake to think that neo-Platonism was primarily if not exclusively spiritual.

Neo-Platonism also became an influence on the rise of Christianity in the late Roman Empire. The process of accommodation of Christian thought with classical learning, particularly Greek philosophy, was begun by the Jewish thinker Philo of Alexandria (Φίλων ὁ Ἀλεξανδρεύς, c. 25 BC–c. 50), and considerably advanced by early Church Fathers such as Titus Flavius Clemens (c. 150–c. 215), known as Clement of Alexandria (Κλήμης ὁ Ἀλεξανδρεύς) and Origen (Ὠριγένης), or Origen Adamantius (Ὠριγένης Ἀδαμάντιος, 184/185–253/254). Origen was important for his position as an early ascetic Christian theologian but also for his views, which the Church later rejected, such as the pre-existence of souls and the final reconciliation of all creatures, including perhaps even the devil, through the apokatastasis (ἀποκατάστασις), that is, the reconstitution, restitution, or restoration to the original or primordial condition, including of Souls to the One in later neo-Platonism, such as in the work of Proclus (Πρόκλος 412–485).[30]

The Christian who firmly tied neo-Platonism to Christianity was St. Augustine (354–430), who wrote one of the most important works of

---

[29] O'Meara (2003) *Platonopolis*.
[30] Not everyone would agree on this point, see: Ilaria Ramelli (2009) "Origen, Patristic Philosophy, and Christian Platonism. Re-Thinking the Christianization of Hellenism," *Vigiliae Christianae*, 63: 217–263.

political thought in the West. St. Augustine was brought up as a Christian but, like most men of the elite at the time, he was trained in classical tradition. Christianity theology at the time was fairly loose and contained many popular beliefs so less attractive than more sophisticated classical philosophy. Augustine looked at various philosophies but he found them wanting. It was only when he adopted the Christian faith that he felt complete and had a set of beliefs that was profound and true, though influences from Manicheanism, for example, lingered in his strong distaste for sexuality and other sensual, worldly pursuits as well as his sharp separation of true believers and sinners. This dualistic distinction between good and evil gave him greater rhetorical power and skill in motivating and organizing others. Based on his background in philosophy, Augustine was also able to engage the elite, and others followed his example. From this point forward, neo-Platonism and Christianity developed in parallel and Christianity became increasingly intertwined with philosophy.

The *City of God* is Augustine's main "political" work which was written to answer the charge that the sack of Rome by barbarians was caused by Christianity weakening the Roman Empire.[31] He rejected the idea that permanent order can be maintained by any human regime and that we are always condemned to suffer in this life. Humans want peace and happiness but their bodily lusts and desires tear apart bonds of friendship and loyalty. All must submit to a political authority for their own safety but those who live in the "city of man" can never be truly happy or at peace. Even rulers and their subordinates have to engage in actions of questionable morality to maintain order. They often have to resort to violence (and worse) to catch and punish the wicked. The peace they maintain harms their souls and only keeps the wicked in check because the nature of the world does not allow for the problem, which is essentially lusts and desires, to be addressed. Augustine argued that the adoption of Christianity by Rome does not remove this problem of human frailty. Only salvation in the next world, the city of God, will bring true peace.

St. Augustine goes further and insists that it is a matter of indifference to Christians whether they live under one type of political regime or another. They should cooperate with any regime in order to limit violence and disorder. Any stable regime that is formed is based on God's Providence and must be obeyed. Christians are like travelers who must obey the laws of the countries they visit without comment because it is none of their business. Of course, Christians must help their fellow humans through such activities as charity as befits their beliefs. Ultimately, however, even the best

---

[31] St. Augustine; John Healey trans. and Ernest Rhys ed. (1945) *City of God*, London: J.M. Dent.

regime and the efforts of Christians in this world pales in comparison to the peace and happiness found in the city of God. There are areas where St. Augustine seems to favor political authorities. He does not believe that regimes can legislate mercy, though he does advocate its exercise when possible. He also explains the conditions under which it is just for Christians to go to war, despite the pacifist message of early Christianity. Finally, he argues that Christian authorities should compel heretics to stop spreading ideas contrary to the Church because it will confuse the faithful. St. Augustine may not be attractive to modern secular readers but his positive arguments for faith and the virtues of the city of God, especially as found in his extensive writings, can be persuasive. He demonstrated that free will produced sin in the world and that God sent Jesus as the incarnation of himself to free men from sin if they would only listen and follow his divine guidance.

St. Augustine was not the end of Hellenic philosophy, and, in fact, he uses many of the concepts and logic of classical philosophy even if reaching Christian conclusions. There is clear evidence of neo-Platonism in his book *Confessions* and his approval of aspects of neo-Platonism in his *City of God*. Christian neo-Platonism continued to have a respected role. There are also important differences, however. Augustine accepts the neo-Platonist quest to seek the One, though he sees it as God and he vehemently argues against the use of spiritual guides, *daemon*, to do so. He takes the view that these *daemon* are "demons" and he literally seeks to demonize them as entirely evil. This put him at odds with most others in the period, including Jews and neo-Platonists, who believed in *daemons* as both helpful and evil spirits that were integral to the workings of the universe.[32] St. Augustine's attack on *daemons* was an attack on these other systems of belief. St. Augustine was also skeptical about angels. He does not reject the idea of angels but refuses to believe that such beings can help one to move closer to God. Thus, St. Augustine completely rejects the neo-Platonist view that human will and pursuit of knowledge can move one closer to the One, which he saw as a faint image of God.

Following St. Augustine, neo-Platonism become more absorbed into Christian theology and lost its political focus in the West. It was an Islamic philosopher who eventually exploited the full potential of neo-Platonism as the source of a political philosophy, al-Farabi, who will be discussed in the following chapter.

---

[32] Norman Bentwich (1910) *Philo-Judaeus of Alexandria*, Philadelphia, PA: The Jewish Publication Society of America: 151.

CONCLUSION

In each of the three major civilizations – Indian, East Asian and Classical Greco-Roman – metaphysics developed toward the end or in the aftermath of an empire. It may just be a coincidence but it is also possible that the end of political stability led to an interest in finding philosophical foundations to provide more certainty in troubled times. The metaphysical systems developed also had a long-lasting influence, not only for the hundreds of years of the medieval period in which they were clearly dominant, but also linger in the underlying metaphysical assumptions of more recent thinkers, whether they deny it or not. These relatively abstract systems are key to what comes next.

6. The integration of "religion" and political thought (500–1000)

It is tempting to refer to this period in all three major civilizations as the early medieval period. In all three it followed an "ancient" period and the disintegration of major empires. They also all manifest what we moderns would call religious beliefs in the form of organized and institutionalized ethics. Debates about how to reconcile politics and religious beliefs dominated all three and at roughly the same period in world history. Differences arise in how the relationship unfolded and the solutions to the balance between religious authority and political authority played out, including how the spiritual community and its relationship to political authority was universalized, devolved or compartmentalized.

The focus in this chapter is on East Asia and early Islam. It fills a lacuna in existing histories of political thought arising from an excessive focus on Western political thought. There is little innovation in the West at this period. The Church used its enormous power to narrow the intellectual debate. For example, Pope Gregory the Great or Gregory the First (c. 540–604), who was Pope from 590 to 604, was well educated but wrote only in Latin and did not read or write Greek, and though he appears to have been familiar with Latin authors, natural science, history, mathematics and music and may have trained in law, his writings typify the end of philosophy and learning in the West at the beginning of the so-called "Dark Ages" where superstition and dogma overtook classical learning. One might object to the term "Dark Ages" because there was beautiful craftwork and epic literature produced in the period but it is dark in the sense that philosophy was effectively dead and the classical legacy of ancient Greece and Roman largely and maliciously destroyed in the West. For this reason, it was common for histories of political thought to jump from St. Augustine (354–430) to John of Salisbury (1120–1180) as if not much of importance happened in between. Yet, this period is outstanding in East Asia for the peak of Buddhist political thought and foundational for Islamic political philosophy so it would be negligent to ignore.

BUDDHISM AND THE STATE IN CONTINENTAL EAST ASIA

At this point it is instructive to review the rise of Buddhism in East Asia to demonstrate that its position in Literati controlled dynasties on the continent was still tenuous at the time it was developing in the Korean peninsula and Japan. As powerful patrons of continental East Asia began to endow Buddhist monasteries with extensive tracts of land from the fourth century onward, Literati officials began to become alarmed at the growth of tax exempt lands. The Buddhists argued that they owed nothing to the state or families, which also outraged Literati officials, but few rulers in the Northern and Southern Dynasties (*Nán-Běi Cháo* 南北朝) period (420–589) were able to curb the growing power of the Buddhist establishment.[1] The first serious conflicts were in the Northern Wei (北魏 446–452) and Northern Zhou (北周 574–578) in which the suppression of Buddhism was attempted in earnest. In both cases, the popular reaction was so strong that subsequent rulers rescinded anti-Buddhist laws and future rulers were wary of opposing the Buddhists. Northern rulers were generally pious, but were trying to subordinate Buddhism to the state,[2] and though there is some evidence that a few favored other systems of thought, they rarely sought an exclusively Literati state without Buddhist influence.

One leader who understood the ideological potential of Buddhism was Yang Jian (楊堅 541–604). He was an official in the Northern Zhou who married into the royal family and seized the throne on the pretext of a regency of his grandson, the legitimate heir to the throne. He proclaimed a new dynasty, the Sui (随 581–618), and himself as its first emperor, Emperor Wen (文帝 581–604). He went on to overthrow the Southern dynasty and reunited most of continental East Asia under a centralized administration controlled directly by the emperor. Importantly, Yang Jian was born in a Buddhist monastery and raised by a nun. He had witnessed the reaction caused by the attempted suppression of Buddhism in 574–578 in Northern Zhou and on assuming the throne, he immediately began building temple complexes, required contributions to the casting of images and copying of sutras and dropped restrictions on the ordination of priests. These policies encouraged the spread of Buddhism. Yang Jian's son, the Emperor Yang (煬帝 604–617), however, was overly ambitious and even tyrannical, so was assassinated and the Duke of Tang seized control and

---

[1] Stanley Weinstein (1987) *Buddhism Under the Tang*, Cambridge: Cambridge University Press: 3.
[2] Weinstein (1987) *Buddhism Under the Tang*: 4.

established the Tang dynasty (618–907), one of the most important and long-running dynasties in East Asia. The first Tang emperors were initially not supporters of Buddhism but were wary of the potential reaction to attempts to curb the *sangha*. Often expedient patronage was balanced with modest attempts to reduce the wealth, size and privileges of the clergy and their establishments. Over time, however, the influence of Buddhism over the Tang state increased to the point that it is the dynasty most identified with Buddhism.

In the early years of the dynasty it appeared that there was a strong Literati influence as can be seen in The Great Tang Code (唐律), first published in 624, with a commentary (*Tang-lu-shu-yi* 唐律疏議) added in 653. This code created a legal system which became the model of law not just for later dynasties but also for the other major states of East Asia. It is primarily a Legalist document that is modified by a realistic Literati ("Confucian") approach. The preface sets out its main principles, which are a combination of Taoist and Legalist ideas, but other concepts, such as mention of consciousness could suggest Buddhist influence. The emphasis on a need for the agreement of the masses and moral teachings are Literati. As one might expect, there are also many aspects that are Legalist given its role in the Han Literati synthesis, and with its emphasis on social hierarchy and capital punishment it is clearly not a very Buddhist text.[3]

Soon after the publication of The Great Tang Code, Emperor Taizong (太宗 r. 626–649) allowed Buddhism to once again come to the fore. As a young prince, he killed two of his brothers, including the crown prince and forced his father to abdicate. This was a clear violation of Literati principles of filial piety and may explain why he decided to patronize the Buddhist establishment. At the same time, he could be considered a rationalist because a text associated with his name opposes superstition and belief in signs from heaven. Taizong's reign is seen as one of the most peaceful and prosperous in East Asian history, the so-called "Reign of Zhenguan" (*Zhēnguān Zhī Zhì* 貞觀之治). It is recorded in the *Zhenguan Zhengyao* (貞觀政要), an important text for political and administrative guidance in East Asia even if largely unknown in the West. There are few deep philosophical principles put forward but it is a key exemplar of advice to rulers of the practical sort that one finds in other civilizations, including Islamic and Western civilizations. It is attributed to the editorship of the court historian Wu Jing (吳兢 670–749) based on the sayings of Emperor Taizong. More plausibly it is the record of advice by the emperor's top advisors (*zhong chen* 重臣) such as Wei Zheng (魏徵 580–643), Fang Qiao

---

[3] Wallace Johnson, trans. (1979) *The Tang Code: Volume One: General Principles*, Princeton, NJ: Princeton University Press.

(房諱 579–648), Du Ru-hui (杜如晦 585–630), Wang Gui (王珪 571–639), and others in response to questions from Taizong.

A parallel, if not earlier, integration of Buddhism and Literati rule was occurring around the same time in the kingdom of Silla on the Korean peninsula. Silla had adopted Literati institutions early but, and perhaps because of this fact, Buddhism came to Silla the latest of the three states on the Korean peninsula. Yet by the time of King Beopheung (法興王 514–540), Buddhism had become well-known in Silla, at least among the elite, after it had been introduced earlier by Goguryeo monks during the reign of Maripgan Nulji (訥祇麻立干) in the fifth century. At this time Buddhism was still struggling for recognition in other states in the area formerly controlled by the Han dynasty and there was naturally resistance from the Silla aristocracy. One of King Beopheung's ministers, Ichadon (異次頓), who was a Buddhist convert, contrived to have himself executed as a martyr to promote Buddhism as the official creed of the state. Ichadon prophesized that when he was killed milky white blood would flow from his body, and when he was executed, the prophecy came true. King Beopheung was able to use this miracle to suppress opposition to Buddhism and make it an official state ideology though its position would not be solidified until the reign of King Jinheung (眞興王 526–576, r. 540–576). At the same time, both Beopheung and Jinheung were also seen as good Literati ("Confucian") rulers.[4] This is because Buddhism came to these states as part of a package of Chinese civilization including the Literati/Legalist aspects of state organization. King Beopheung instituted Literati-style reforms including the *golpum* or bone rank system (骨品制度) in 520 based on the Tang cap rank system similar to the one introduced later in Japan but whereas the Japanese version regularized the aristocracy in relation to the Imperial House, the Silla version was more strictly hereditary within ranks and thus acted almost as an aristocratic caste system. It is obviously an adaptation of Tang administrative law but was used to reinforce existing bloodline and lineage arrangements. Only the first two ranks were termed "bone" (*gol* 骨) ranks – "sacred bone," or *seonggol* (聖骨) being a segment of royal Kim family pure royal blood, and "true bone," or *jingol* (眞骨), which included the rest of the royal family, and the Park and Seok families – but it is used to describe the whole system. Below these were numbered Head Ranks (*dupum* 頭品) 6, 5, 4 and then, presumably, commoners, but it seems slaves were not included. Similarly, King Jinheung further encouraged the growth of Buddhism but once again it was not the only system of belief. Buddhism is usually associated with a band of young warriors he

---

[4] William Theodore De Bary ed. (2008) *Sources of East Asian Tradition, Volume 1: Premodern Asia*, New York, NY: Columbia University Press: 493.

created, Hwarang (花郎), due to their belief in the Maitreya Buddha but, as throughout Silla at the time, the system of thought was syncretic. This is reflected in the Five Commandments for Secular Life (*Sae Sok O-Gye* 世俗五戒) created by Wŏn Gwang (圓光 541–630?) which constituted the code of practice for the Hwarang:

1. Loyalty to one's sovereign (*sagun ichung* 事君以忠)
2. Respect for parents (*sachin ihyo* 事親以孝)
3. Trust among friends (*gyo-u isin* 交友以信)
4. Never retreat in battle (*imjeon mutwae* 臨戰無退)
5. Never take a life without reason (*salsaeng yutaek* 殺生有擇).

Loyalty and filial piety in the first two slogans are Literati ("Confucian"), admonitions to courage are a Legalist-Literati hybrid and the qualified reverence for life is Buddhist. The historical chronical *Samguk Yusa* (三國遺事) also records that Hwarang members learned the Five Cardinal Literati Virtues, the Six Arts, the Three Scholarly Occupations, and the Six Ways of Government Service (五常六藝 三師六正), reflecting a Literati curriculum.

Buddhism, at the same time, was clearly a central part of state ideology. Temples were built, often financed and sponsored by high ranking nobility, such as Buddha State Temple Bulguksa (佛國寺) including its Stone Grotto Seokguram (石窟). Hwangyongsa (Imperial Dragon) temple (皇龍寺) played a central role in supporting the power of the monarchy and Buddhism's role in state protection. The nine stories of its wooden pagoda were meant to symbolize submission of nine nations to Silla.[5] The foundations of Buddhism in Silla were further strengthened by the monk Jajang (慈藏 590–658) who played a major role in solidifying the Korean *sangha*. He was born into the aristocracy but he rejected joining government service and instead traveled to the Tang dynasty in 636 to study Buddhism as part of an official delegation. When he returned in 643 he was appointed as Great State Overseer (*taeguksa* 大國統) to bring order to the *sangha*. He built Tongdosa Temple (通度寺) and introduced the Tang monk robes. He is also credited with building of the Imperial Dragon Temple pagoda (*Hwangnyongsaji* 皇竜寺址) as a symbol of Silla overcoming its enemies, with dragons particularly important to connecting Buddhism in support of royal power.[6]

---

[5] Bae-yong Lee (2008) *Women in Korean History*, Ewha Womans University Press: 140.
[6] Hung-gyu Kim (2012) "The Rhetoric of Royal Power in Korean. Inscriptions from the Fifth to Seventh Centuries," *Cross Currents: East Asian History and Culture Review*, 2, e-journal at https://cross-currents.berkeley.edu/sites/default/files/e-journal/articles/final_kim.pdf (accessed November 16, 2017).

Like its rival Silla, the Baekje Kingdom, also adopted Literati institutions but Buddhism had more of an influence than in neighboring Silla or Goguryeo. Buddhism was brought to Baekje by the Indian monk Marananta (摩羅難陀) from Eastern Jin in 384. The first Buddhist temple was built and 10 monks trained one year later. The dangers of Buddhism were made apparent when King Gaero (蓋鹵王 ?–475, r. 455–475) fell under the control of the monk Dōrim (道琳), who turned out to be a spy from Goguryeo. Dorim used King Gaero's passion for the game of *baduk* to befriend the king and persuaded him to divert resources from defense to Buddhist construction projects. Baekje was weakened and forced to retreat when attacked and the Seoul region fell to the neighboring state Goguryeo with the capital hurriedly moved to Ungjin. The weak monarchy led to open aristocratic clashes including those between members of the aristocracy descended from Buyeo ethnic group and local Mahan-based clans. There was a brief revival of Baekje in the Sabi (泗沘) Period (538–660) under King Seong (聖王 ?–554, r. 523–554) when central control was strengthened through administrative reorganization to limit the political power of the clans of the nobility. At the same time, in 528, Seong announced that Baekje officially adopted Buddhism as its state belief system while attempting to reform the Buddhist establishment by asking the monk Gyeomik (謙益) to go to India in search of original texts of monastic (*vinaya*) rules. The disciplinary school is important politically because clear rules of discipline governing monastic life were believed to serve the state as well because it would establish clear standards for belief and behavior of the increasingly influential monastic orders.[7]

King Seong of Baekje's successors also promoted Buddhism but began to promote newer forms imported from the Tang. For example, King Wideok (威德王 525–598, r. 554–598) favored the monk Hyŏn'gwang (玄光) who had studied under Huisi (慧思 515–577), the third *Tiāntai* patriarch, and though Hyŏn'gwang focused on the "Lotus Sutra" and the "Three Treatises", *Tiāntai* interpretation and practice was still an innovation compared to the more established text-based schools of Buddhism. Hyŏn'gwang teachings helped to smooth the harmonization of Buddhism with indigenous and Literati ritual and political practice. The following monarch, King Beop (法王 ?–600, r. 599–600), was so devout a Buddhist that he was named the "dharma king." Beop prohibited all killing, including hunting and butchering of animals for food and went so far as to order the release of hunting falcons and the burning of fishing implements and hunting weapons. Like King Gaero he is criticized for pursuing

---

[7] Ki-Baik Lee; Edward W. Wagner trans. (1988) *A New History of Korea*, Cambridge, MA: Harvard University Press: 60.

construction projects at the expense of national defense, with the implicit argument that he gave priority to Buddhism and personal aggrandizement over good rule. Not long after his death the country was invaded in 660 and conquered by Silla. One suspects that these lessons regarding too much interest in Buddhism and its consequences are the emphasis of later Literati historians.[8]

Baekje had particularly strong intellectual and trade links with both the Tang dynasty and Japan. King Seong had sent the mission which led to the official introduction of Buddhism to Japan (538), and King Mu (武王 580–641, r. 600–641) sent the Buddhist monk Gwalleuk (觀勒) to Japan in 602 with texts on Buddhism, astronomy, history, and geography. Internal unrest often led to migration of major Baekje families to Japan and in fact the Baekje royal family fled to Japan when the country was destroyed. The mother of Emperor Kammu (see below) was Takano no Niigasa (高野新笠 c. 720–790), a descendant of King Muryeong (武寧王 462–523, r. 501–523) of Baekje. Baekje noble families appear to have developed family connections with the major family groups in Japan such as the Ōuchi clan (大内氏), the Sue clan (陶氏), Soga clan (蘇我氏) and others, all of whom played a central role in the adoption of Buddhism and the Literati state in Japan. Their support was crucial because the introduction of Buddhism and the Literati system of rule became a source of aristocratic conflict in Japan. Buddhist and Literati ideas and institutions were a direct threat to established native great families or clans (*uji* 氏) and the native Shintō (神道) belief system that supported Imperial rule. In this context, it is striking how one relatively obscure family, the Soga, who actively promoted the new ideas, was able to gain high office in the Imperial household. Thereafter, they fought vigorously to oust their rivals and established control over the Imperial House.

A lot of credit for the adoption of Buddhism and the Literati system of rule in Japan is given to one individual, Prince Shōtoku (聖徳太子 572–622). One must take care not to accept the obvious hagiography in accounts of Prince Shōtoku, which no doubt exaggerates his importance, but there is a clear logic to the ideas with which he is associated, and even if he represents a collection of like-minded individuals, the impact of the movement is clear. Shōtoku was the second son of Emperor Yomei (用明天皇, r. 585–587). Empress Suiko (推古天皇 554–628, r. 593–628), appointed Prince Shōtoku, her nephew, as regent, delegating

---

[8] Though both the more mythological *Samguk Yusa* (三國遺事) and the more factual *Samguk Sagi* (三國史記) were compiled before the complete dominance of Literati thought, the latter in particular reflects the views of the Literati and the former may have been edited later to do so as well.

all powers to him. He used his position to implement radical reforms based on the Literati model with the aim of strengthening imperial authority. At the same time, Shōtoku proclaimed that the imperial court would promote Buddhism in 594 and provided imperial support to the building of Buddhist temples, including Hōryūji (法隆寺), which still exists today and is the oldest temple in Japan. In 604, Shōtoku replaced *kabane* (姓) ranks based on *uji* (氏) clan lineage groups (*uji-kabane* system) with a system of 12 cap ranks for courtiers so essentially turning the great *uji* families into court officers. Shōtoku also dispatched diplomatic missions to the Sui dynasty and led to the exchange of scholars and monks, who had an influence on the government, including the Taika (大化) Reforms of 645, which led to a full Literati legal system. In 620, Shōtoku also played a role in the compilation of two historical chronologies, *Tennoki* (天皇記) and *Kokki* (国記), explaining the Imperial lineage and bolstering its right to rule. These books are now lost but became the basis for the *Kojiki* (古事記) and *Nihonshoki* (日本書紀) which established the legitimacy of the historical lineage of Imperial family in Japan.

Shōtoku's most important contribution to political thought was his "Seventeen Article Constitution" (*Jūshichi Jō Kenpō* 十七条憲法).[9] At first glance, this is a progressive document in many senses, for example, suggesting that wide-consultation is the best method of deliberation for important decisions (Article XVII). Most of it, however, is a mixture of Legalism, Literati thought, Taoism and Buddhism. Legalism is the easiest to find with the focus on rewards and punishments as well as meritocracy and the need for surveillance (Articles VI and XI). Even the Literati ("Confucian") aspects focus on need for loyalty and benevolence rather than flattery and deception (Article VI). There is also an emphasis on harmony at the outset of the document which is taken directly from the *Analects*[10] but this is a late passage and reflects Taoist influences. Indeed, the Taoism, Yin-Yang thought and hierarchy implicit in the Han synthesis are present throughout the document (Article III). This emphasis on harmony is not distinctive to Japan and is clearly derivative of the Taoist literature of the Han dynasty and after. Moreover, given the context in which Shōtoku was operating with religious, powerful *uji* families and political intrigue, including assassination, the emphasis on harmony is an aspiration rather than a fact.

The Buddhist element is stated clearly in Article II: "Sincerely reverence the Three Treasures. The Buddha, the Law, and the religious orders

---

[9] De Bary, William Theodore, Donald Keene, George Tanabe and Paul Varley (2001) *Sources of Japanese Tradition, Volume 1: From Earliest Times to 1600*, 2nd edn, New York, NY: Columbia University Press: 50–54.

[10] Confucius; Waley trans. (1938) *Analects*: 86.

(*sangha*) are the final refuge of all being and the supreme objects of reverence in all countries." Shotoku is portrayed as primarily a Buddhist inspired ruler with some of the rationalizing influences of Literati thought (in its post-Han/early Tang form). Some Japanese authorities on Shōtoku see him as attempting to emulate the great Buddhist ruler Ashoka. His *Commentaries on Three Sūtras* (San Gyō Kisho 三經義疏), which are often listed as attributed to him rather than definitely his work, do indicate the nature of the Buddhism accepted into Japan at the time.[11] The first sutra, the "Lotus Blossom of the Fine Dharma Sūtra" (Myōhō Renge Kyō (妙法蓮華經)) is extremely important in subsequent Japanese thought based on a simple message of salvation. The second, "Vimalakīrti Sūtra" (jp. *Yuima Kyō* 維摩經) is less famous but important because Vimalakirti was a lay follower of Buddha who lived an ordinary life yet still achieved wisdom beyond most monks. Lay belief takes a lead role in this sutra and stresses that the truth of Buddhism can be found in secular life.[12] This was an important lesson for members of the Japanese aristocracy by stressing that Buddhism did not reject the world completely because this life also presented an opportunity to demonstrate the good deeds that make for a better world for the ruler and others, both now and in the future.

By the Nara period (709–795 AD) the influence of Buddhism in Japan was considered central even if it was not yet well-known outside the capital and the Imperial Court. It was closely associated with the Tang dynasty and was dominated by continental monks and priests. Therefore, Buddhism was an elite religion dependent on a professional priesthood and a close connection to the Imperial house. The mass of people would have been relatively unaffected, at first at least. In fact, teaching it to the common people was specifically prohibited by law. Instead, Buddhism was expected to serve the state. One important text, particularly in Japan was the "Golden Light Sutra" or "The Sovereign King of Sutras, the Sublime Golden Light" (*Suvarṇaprabhāsottamasūtrendrarājaḥ* सुवर्णप्रभासोत्तमसूत्रेन्द्ररराज). It also offers protection to the ruler who governs well because the Four Heavenly Kings (四大天王) assist rulers who promote and practice Buddhism. Historically, Buddhism in Japan as in the rest of East Asia emphasized its role in protecting the ruler and the state.[13]

The rise of Islam would seem to move us toward the involvement of another religion in politics but Islam initially had little explicit political

---

[11] Excerpts from these works can be found in De Bary et al. (1999) *Sources of Japanese Tradition*, vol. 1, 2nd edn: 55–62.
[12] Hajime Nakamura (1969) *A History of the Development of Japanese Thought: From AD 592 to 1868*, Tokyo: Kokusai Bunka Shinkokai: 264–265.
[13] De Bary et al. (1999) *Sources of Japanese Tradition*, vol. 1, 2nd edn: 107.

The integration of "religion" and political thought (500–1000)

theory. The prophet Muhammad (محمد c. 570–632) set out a moral order in the *Quran* (القرآن). He also established defined *shari'a* (شريعة) as divine law which applied to all members of the community of *ummah* (أمة). This law was revealed in both the *Quran* and *hadith* (حديث) or "Reports" of what Muhammad or his key followers had said in certain circumstances. There are six hadith collections, the *Al-Kitāb as-Sittah* (الكتب الستة), literally "the six books," the order of authenticity which varies between different schools of interpretation or doctrine. This law was comprehensive in the sense that it involved detailed personal action on a daily basis and simple in that the rules were relatively clear. It should be noted that all the hadith collections are relatively from a late date after Muhammad and based on oral tradition with some ambiguities and even contradictions. Nonetheless, hadith are important to different Islamic schools of thought, especially in Islamic jurisprudence, and these can have political implications or interpretations.

After Muhammad's death, there needed to be a successor, requiring both a Leader (*Imām* إمام) and his Deputy (*Caliph* or *khalīfah* خَلِيفة). The first four Caliphs, from 634–661, oversaw the spread of Islam to Persia, Egypt, Syria and North Africa. These are termed the "Rightly Guided" or *Rashidun* caliphs (ٱلْخُلَفَاءُ ٱلرَّاشِدُونَ): Abū Bakr, Umar, Uthman, Ali, Hasan ibn Ali (624–670). Ali was married to Mohammad's daughter, and considered heir apparent to Muhammad by some but the influential 'Umar ibn al-Khattāb (عمر بن الخطاب b. 583–d. 644) put Abu Bakr (بكر أبو c. 573–634) in control as first Caliph and effectively created the institution of Caliph in doing so. Umar himself became Caliph after Abu Bakr and oversaw the early expansion of Islam. He was well respected because he lived a simple life, avoiding the luxuries that his position could have provided, and advocated a system of welfare for all (including non-Muslims). Umar's successor, 'Uthmān ibn Affan (عثمان بن عفان b. 576–d. 656), was considered by some a bad ruler and when he was assassinated by his enemies there was a dispute over succession that led to civil war in Islam, the *Fitnat Maqtal 'Uthmān* (فتنة مقتل عثمان), literally "Fitna of the Killing of Uthman." Eventually Ali ibn Abī Ṭālib (علي ابن أبي طالب b. 601–d. 661), often simply known as Ali, who as noted above was married to Mohammad's daughter, was chosen as Caliph. Ali seems to have been very educated and wrote many important works, but he in turn was assassinated by a member of 'Uthman's family. Ali's son, Hasan ibn Ali (حسن ابن أبي b. 624–d. 670), succeeded Ali as Caliph but abdicated a little more than half a year later when he was forced to cede power to the Umayyads (الأموية). The Umayyad dynasty emphasized their legitimacy as successors to the Caliphate through kinship with 'Uthman. They were opposed by those subsequently called the Shi'a who believed that the ruler should be an Imam, a particularly pious and wise spiritual leader, someone like Ali who also had a blood connection to the prophet Muhammad, and not just the hereditary successor of a monarch or someone who came to power by assassination and force. Under the Umayyad's, who controlled the Caliphate from 661 to 750, the Shi'a were excluded from power.

Since the *Quran* and *hadith* do not contain explicit political thought, the Umayyad Caliphate tended to rely on the political ideas of advisors from the Sassanid Persian Empire, which had fallen to Islamic rule. Persian political theory was based on a patrimonial state centered around an absolute monarch. A good example of this influence of Persian thought in Islam is the role of ibn Muqaffa' (بن المقفع), a Persian and Zoroastrian (died c. 756), who in his translations and short prose works on politics and administration advocated a Persian approach to political thought so that he places the monarch's powers over Islamic Law.[14] At the same time, classical political thought of ancient Greece and Rome, primarily in the form of late Roman neo-Platonism, constituted an alternative to Persian political thought. Neo-Platonism and the whole of the classical tradition back to Aristotle and Plato still thrived in these areas and Islam helped to keep the classical philosophical tradition alive to the extent that neo-Platonist pagan philosophers forced to flee persecution by Christians after the fall of Rome were welcomed in Islamic territories. Neo-Platonist ideas also influenced philosophers and Sufi thinkers in Islam. The earliest Islamic philosophy argued that the process of *ijtihad* (اجتهاد) or "finding the truth" was found in all spheres including the political. Political power and Islam were thus intimately related from the beginning. Indeed, the founders of the Abbasid Caliphate (الخلافة العباسية) strategically supported intellectual debates as part of their strategy to undermine the Umayyad Caliphate, particularly to mobilize non-Muslim population to support the Abbasids. When the Abbasids came to power in 750, they continued to encourage philosophical and metaphysical speculation, including classical Greek and Roman philosophy.

The most prominent example of Abbasid patronage of classical learning is Harun al-Rashid (هَارُون الرَّشيد, 763/766–809 r. 786–809), the fifth Abbasid Caliph. He created the "House of Wisdom" (بيت الحكمة; *Bayt al-Hikma*) that included Jewish and Christian as well as Muslim scholars. One of the philosophers working in the House of Wisdom was al-Kindī (الكندي c. 801–873). Under the direction of the Abbasid Caliphs, he translated ancient Greek scientific and philosophical works into Arabic, and is credited with creating the Arabic philosophical vocabulary. Al-Kindī saw

---

[14] Said Amir Arjomand (1994) "'Abd Allah ibn al-Muqaffa' and the 'Abbasid Revolution'," *Iranian Studies*, 27(1/4): 9–36.

no conflict between Islam and philosophy[15] in his efforts to use the best knowledge of the day in the service of Islam. Islamic philosophers such as Al-Kindī must be distinguished, however, from the so-called "rationalist" Mutazilite (المعتزلة) scholastic theologians who were not philosophers but did have some regard to Islamic philosophy, ancient Greek philosophy and Indian philosophy but within a framework of Islamic belief. They were particularly important when the majority of the population ruled by the Caliphate were non-Muslims and served as a bridge between Islamic theology and philosophy. Like the philosophers, Mutazilite theologians were favored by the early Abbasid Caliphate.

It is important to note, therefore, that philosophy in Islam developed in parallel with so-called traditional approaches to Islamic jurisprudence (*fiqh* فقه) shaped by *ulama* (علماء) who are, roughly, "legal scholars" or sometimes called "jurists," though not always in official judicial roles. One might make the parallel with Plato's ideals of the law and philosopher-magistrates though *ulama* were more decentralized and based on popular choice than Plato would have allowed. This decentralized approach to law allowed Islam to distance itself from discussion of rulers and led to ambivalence about political power and political thought. There are five Islamic schools of jurisprudence (*fiqh* فقه) named after their founders: Hanafi (677–767), Maliki (711–795), Shafi'i (767–820), Hanbali (780–855) and Zahiri (815–883/4). The earlier schools are mostly flexible/liberal, whereas the later schools are mostly conservative or traditionalist. For example, the Hanafi is the oldest school, focused on reason, and most "liberal." The Shafi'i also allows for flexibility in interpretation but *jus ad bellum* for *jihad* (جهاد) is disbelief (*kufr* كفر) and not injustice, unlike the other schools. All the schools hold most opinions in common, but there are some hadiths accepted by one or more schools and rejected by the others. They also vary considerably over the role that analogy or reason (*qiyas* قياس) can play in deciding difficult cases. There are also separate schools of jurisprudence for Shi'a Islam.

As a result of popular movements led by the leaders of later conservative schools of *fiqh*, Abbasid Caliphate increasingly distanced itself from non-traditional philosophical approaches, especially by the tenth century when the Caliphate was also under pressure from the Shi'a inspired Fatimids who led a successful revolt against the Caliph and conquered Tunis (909), and Sicily, North Africa and Egypt (969), and even went on to control Medina and Mecca. Only Iraq and Arabia held out against them. The Fatimid state practiced religious toleration and the pursuit of learning. In fact, the early

---

[15] Al-Kindī; Alfred L. Ivry trans. (1974) *al-Kindī's Metaphysics*, Albany, NY: State University of New York Press.

years of the Fatimid Caliphate (909–1171) opened space for a wider discussion of political ideas. It is in this context that we can best understand the work of the key Islamic political philosopher al-Farabi (الفارابي b. 872–d. 951). Thus, it is a mistake to see Islam as the end of classical learning and philosophy when initially it engaged and even promoted philosophy far more than Christianity, particularly in this period.

METAPHYSICS AND POLITICAL THOUGHT

Both Buddhism and Islam pursued metaphysics in order to accommodate their beliefs with politics. This is clear in forms of political thought that were developed during the earliest dynasties in which Buddhism and Islam were influential. For example, as the Tang dynasty was being formed and consolidated, Buddhist ideology was becoming more sophisticated, particularly if viewed in the wider East Asian context. The Flower Garland (*Huayen* 華嚴) school is a case in point. The school was founded by Dushun (杜順 fl. c. 600), who was a native of Qingzhou which had relatively recently been incorporated into the Tang dynasty so was on the edge of the empire. Based on the text of the *Mahāvaipulya Buddhāvataṃsaka Sūtra* (महावैपुल्यबुद्धावतंसकसूत्र) or "Great Vaipulya Sutra" of the Buddha's Flower Garland, this school argues that all beings are interrelated in the form of a large wreath of flowers, so they emphasize community, connectedness but also individuality. The Buddhist state (ch. *fuguo* jp. *bukkoku* kr. *bulguk* 佛國) would be one that realized this spiritual communion. It would break down aristocratic and local rivalries without resulting in the loss of identity of each person and place. The approach was notably developed further by Wŏnhyo (元曉 617–686) of Silla. Wŏnhyo's focus was to demonstrate the underlying unity in various approaches to Buddhism by an attempt at the "harmonization of conflict" (*hwajaeng* 和諍) to unify the competing schools of Buddhist thought debated amongst monks. One must remember that monks, usually members of the aristocracy, tended to form factions and tried to argue their approach was superior to the others in an attempt to gain influence at Court. This was true not just in Silla but in Japan and other states of East Asia as well. Of course, the attempt to resolve these conflicts was itself a political strategy but also one more likely to be seen favorably by the political authorities, who were concerned with the factionalism at Court. This included factions based on traditional clan loyalties but increasingly also involved conflict between Buddhist monks and supporters of older forms of rule, including the Literati.

It is worth pausing here to consider the various Buddhist sects in East Asia at the time. Most sects or schools of thought focused on a text. We have already seen that *Vinaya* (戒律) focuses on texts relating to monastic discipline, which again was appealing to rulers attempting to control monks. The other text-based schools were the "Three Treatises" (三論) of Nagarjuna, "Storehouse Treatise" (俱舍論) of Vasubandhu, "Nirvana Sutra" (涅槃經), Consciousness Only/ *Yogācāra* (唯識瑜伽行), and "Flower Garland Sutra" (華嚴). All of these were originally based on Indian texts. The *Tiāntai* (天台) sect was developed in East Asia and focused on the text of "Lotus Sutra" (法華經) but significantly also developed a liturgy or set of practices which was very popular amongst the lay aristocracy, so was considered a sect (ch. *zong*, jp. *shu*, kr. *jong* 宗) and not a doctrinal school of text study (ch. *xue*, jp. *gaku*, kr. *hak* 學). Other later important sects were the Chen Yen/Shingon (眞言) or Esoteric (密教) Buddhism, Pure Land (浄土) of both the Maitreya (मैत्रेय or 彌勒菩薩) and the Amitābha (अमिताभ or 阿彌陀佛), and Chan (jp. Zen, kr. Seon, vt. Thiền 禪). Historically, these three (Chen Yen, Pure Land and Chan) developed in East Asia during the early Tang dynasty but are more appropriately discussed later. However, something might be said about Chan at this point.

Chan is closely related to Flower Garland thought but Chan was also influenced by Literati thought including the re-evaluation of Literati texts by neo-Taoists. For example, Daōsheng (道生 c. 360–434), one of the sources of Chan, seems to imply a short-cut based on the text of the *Analects* Book XI, 18: "As for [Confucius' follower Yen] Hui, he was near (perfection), and frequently 'empty'."[16] He argued that it is a mistake to be too obsessed with the meaning of a text rather than the meaning of the teaching which is beyond words. Words must be forgotten once the goal is obtained. "The purpose of words is to explain the Truth (*li* 理) but once truth is entered, words may be suspended."[17] Chan also argues that all *icchantikas* (non-believers) possess the possibility of achieving Buddhahood so are endowed with Buddha nature.[18]

The word Chan simply means "meditation" from the Sanskrit *dhyāna* (ध्यान) so was originally a meditation school. The early patriarchs of Chan are relatively obscure until we get to the sixth Huineng (惠能 638–713) who is the founder of the schools of Chan which survive. One key text, the "Platform Sutra of the Sixth Patriarch" (六祖壇經), includes the story of how Huineng was forced to flee his temple when he was unexpectedly chosen as the successor of the true Chan lineage and was attacked by jealous rivals

---

[16] Confucius; Waley trans. (1938) *Analects*: 157.
[17] Yu-Lan Fung; Derk Bodde trans./ed. (1983) *History of Chinese Philosophy, Volume 2: The Period of Classical Learning from the Second Century BC to the Twentieth Century AD*, Princeton, NJ: Princeton University Press: 270.
[18] Fung; Bodde trans. (1983) *History of Chinese Philosophy, Volume 2*: 271.

who refused him the position.[19] By the middle of the eighth century, monks claiming to be among the successors to Huineng, formed the Southern school, and were opposed by Shenxiu (神秀?–706), who headed the Northern school after Huineng fled. The story in the "Platform Sutra" appears to have been created by a successor to Huineng to legitimize the Southern school and win influence at the Imperial Court. In 796 an imperial commission decreed that the Southern school of Chan represented the orthodox line of transmission. The "Platform Sutra" suggests that though less educated than other monks, Huineng understood the true essence of Chan. Huineng is said to have argued that one must find the purity of "Original Mind" (ben-xin 本心) through "Stability" (ding 定) and "Insight" (hui 惠), that is, the stability that quiet sitting allows as the basis for meditation and then enlightenment must be found through sudden insights. It is a mistake, he argued, to become attached to the *dharma* as manifest in written texts and intellectual concepts. In fact, one key aspect of Chan is that it believes that enlightenment can be found even while doing everyday activities. The practical implications of this belief was that Chan monks were not averse to engaging in secular activities, including working to maintain themselves, rather than only relying on alms or the endowments to support them. The practical knowledge and discipline of Chan monks made them trusted officials and advisors to rulers and local elites in much of East Asia.

Chan Buddhism was transmitted to Silla in the Korean peninsula where it was called "Seon" Buddhism through the efforts of Beomnang (法朗 fl. 632–646), student of Daoxin (道信 580–651) where it was popularized by the monks Sinhaeng (神行 704–779) and Dōui (道義 d. 825). The greatest contribution, however, is made by the monk Gyunyeo (均如 923–973) of Flower Garland school (*Hwaeom* 華嚴宗) in creating the theoretical basis for the reconciliation of Flower Garland and Seon (Chan/Zen), which would have been important to avoid conflict among the Buddhist schools and maintain support from the Silla monarchy, and in fact, would have strengthened the position of the central authorities.

There is a similarly clear link between metaphysics and political thought in Islam. This is particularly outstanding in the work of al-Farabi, called the second teacher (after Aristotle who is considered the "First Teacher" or *al-mu'allim al-awwal*, المعلم الأول) because al-Farabi's work was considered equal to that of the ancients by subsequent Islamic scholars such as ibn Sīnā, ibn Rushd and the Jewish medieval philosopher Maimonides. Al-Farabi led the effort to reconcile ancient thought and revealed religion.

---

[19] John R. McRae trans. (2000) *The Platform Sutra of the Sixth Patriarch*, Berkeley, CA: Numata Center for Buddhist Translation and Research and Philip B. Yampolsky trans. (1967) *The Platform Sutra of the Sixth Patriarch*, New York, NY: Columbia University Press.

His approach constituted a unique philosophical approach even if deeply rooted in the neo-Platonism of late Roman antiquity with additional influences from the Peripatetic school of Aristotle. For example, the concept of happiness (*saada* سعادة) is central to al-Farabi's political philosophy and is closely related to Aristotle's *eudaimonia* or well-being, also often translated as happiness. In a virtuous society *(al-ijtima al-fadil* الاجتماع الفاضل) and a virtuous city (*al-madinah al-fadila* المدينة الفاضلة) everyone cooperates to achieve happiness by doing what is good. When all nations collaborate to create the conditions for universal happiness, it is a virtuous world (*al-ma'mura al-fadila*). A virtuous society protects not only the person but also the souls of all its inhabitants. In contrast, "vicious" societies are of four types: ignorant, wicked, errant, and misguided. In the ignorant city (*al-madınah al-jahilah* المدينة الجاهلية), inhabitants only cooperate to fulfill their basic desires, regard gaining wealth as the primary aim of life, pursue fame and distinction, and seek to be free by doing what one likes without regard for others (the latter of which he identifies with democracy). The erring city (*al-madınah al-dallah* المدينة الضلالة) aims at the high ideals of the virtuous city but holds false beliefs that mislead the population. Such cities are usually founded by rulers who have falsely received revelation or acquired understanding of correct beliefs but are mistaken in their application. In the wicked city (*al-madınah al-fasiqah* المدينة الفاسقة), everyone claims to be pursuing the high ideals of the virtuous city but its inhabitants still behave the same as those in the ignorant city. Finally, is the misguided city (*al-madınah al-mubaddilah* المدينة المبدلة), which, though originally virtuous, changes in time into its opposite.

Al-Farabi appears to have been advocating rule by philosophically trained guardians on the Platonic model who can lead the virtuous state because they are morally perfect. The perfect human being (*al insan al kamil* الإنسان الكامل), according to al-Farabi, has refined his intellect and cultivated perfect moral virtues. In Islamic thought, the term "al-Insān al-Kāmil" is often used as an honorific title to describe Muhammad. It literally means "the person who has reached perfection" so it can be used to indicate an ideal human being, pure in thought and faithful to the truth, in contrast with those who are trapped by sensory stimulus and the material world. Al-Farabi divides *aql* (عقل) or mind (from the Greek *nous*, which as we have seen is also a key concept in neo-Platonism) into six categories. First, there is prudence; this is the ability to act for the good when necessary. Second is common sense; "obviousness" and "immediate recognition" of what to do in a situation. Third is natural perception, which allows us to be certain about basic principles of motion and so on. The fourth is "conscience," in which good can be distinguished from evil based on life experiences. The fifth is intellect of which there are different types. The highest and most important is the *aql al-faal* (عقل فعال), active intellect or the creative mind, which was responsible both for "actualizing the potentiality for thought in man's intellect and emanating form to man and the sublunary world."[20] This is similar to the Universal Soul of Plotinus. Al-Farabi argues that the perfect ruler will have a soul that is united to the active intellect. He extends this requirement in various degrees to all the classes that make up the virtuous city or state.

RISE OF EARLY POPULAR RELIGIOUS FORCES FOR AND AGAINST THE STATE

Literati and Buddhist metaphysics were seen as necessary for the state. In Islam, too, the metaphysical basis for rule was being created. Nonetheless, religious ideas could be wielded both for and against the state. In Islam, philosophers, and the "rationalist" Mutazilite theologians (*al-kalam* الكلام) who were not philosophers but did have some affinity with Islamic philosophy, ancient Greek philosophy and Indian philosophy were favored by the early Abbasid Caliphate, but this closeness to the Caliphate was their undoing. Caliph al-Mamun (d. 833) who instigated an inquisition or *Mihna* (محنة) in support of *Mu'tazila* ideas, reinforced traditionalist animosity of the Mutazilites, particularly influenced by the jurist Ahmad ibn Hanbal who was imprisoned and tortured at the time.[21] As these traditionalists were influential with the general population of Muslims, the result was a popular reaction against the Mutazilites. The Mutazilites are often contrasted with the "traditionalist" Asharite (الأشعرية) movement but in fact, the Asharites were created by a student of the Mutazilites who used philosophical arguments to defend the traditionalist view. The Asharites focused on the *Sunnah* (سُنَّة), originally meaning "way of life" but usually interpreted as the practice or tradition of Islam according to the prophet Muhammad. This is the basis of an emergent Sunni consensus which would become the mainstream of Islam. Even though it was not as enamored with philosophy and relatively conservative, it was not fundamentalist. It merely incorporated the general popular consensus of Islam at the time it was created and modified it in line with common practice through the centuries.[22]

---

[20] Ian Richard Netton (1998) "Al-Farabi, Abu Nasr" in Edward Craig and Oliver Leaman eds, *Routledge Encyclopedia of Philosophy*, vol. 3. London: Routledge: 554–558.
[21] John Abdallah Nawas (2015) *Al-Ma'mūn, the Inquisition, and the Quest for Caliphal Authority*, Atlanta, GA: Lockwood Press; also see Christopher Melchert (2006) *Ahmad ibn Hanbal*, Oxford: One World: 8–18.
[22] See Richard C. Martin and Mark R. Woodward (1997) *Defenders of Reason in Islam: Mu'tazilism from Medieval School to Modern Symbol*, Oxford: Oneworld Publishers; Sophia

In Japan, initially, Buddhism was an elite religion and it was prohibited for commoners to learn about it or Buddhist monks to work among the masses. However, these rules were openly flouted by unofficial Buddhist monks or lay practitioners who brought Buddhism to the common people through simple preaching and good works demonstrating the spirit of Buddhism. The most outstanding of these was Gyoki (行基 668–749). He is credited with founding charity hospitals, orphanages, and old people's homes; constructing canals, irrigation ponds, bridges and harbors. He built a network of free clinics and lodgings which were run by his followers. His social work was suppressed in 717 but controls were relaxed in 731, and by 741 he was able to meet with Emperor Shōmu and by 742 he was involved in construction of the state-sponsored temple Todaiji. Due to his success in this project and widespread popularity he was appointed as the first *Daisōjō* (僧正) or Great Priest in 745. In fact, Emperor Shōmu (聖武天皇 701–756) was particularly supportive of Buddhism and built state-sponsored monasteries (*kokubunji* 国分寺) and nunneries (*kokubun niji* 国分尼寺) in each province. The official name of the monasteries was *Temples for Protection of the State by the Four Heavenly Kings Golden Light Sutra* (金光明經四天王護国之寺) where the monks recited the "Sovereign Kings Golden Light Sutra" regularly to protect the country. These temples were symbols and instruments of central authority throughout Japan during the Nara period (710–794). Shōmu also sponsored the creation of the sixteen-meter high statue of the Vairocana Buddha in the Tōdaiji Temple of Nara, and, at the opening ceremony in 752, he declared himself a servant of the three treasures – the Buddha, Buddhist teachings and the Buddhist community – effectively declaring Japan a Buddhist nation.

In contrast, the golden age of Tang was under Emperor Xuanzong (唐玄宗 712–756) who when he came to power attempted to control Buddhist abuses associated with his predecessors, especially those with economic implications. Under Xuanzong, members of the aristocracy were refused the right to petition for permission to establish Buddhist or Taoist temples on their estate, which had been used as a thinly veiled subterfuge to remove land from the tax rolls. Restrictions were placed on the construction and even repair of monasteries. A strict distinction was attempted between villages and monasteries with religious instruction restricted to monasteries and village temples closed. At the same time, Xuanzong also realized the need to support religious establishments, both Buddhist and Taoist. His tendency was to be interested primarily in the esoteric tradition in Buddhism which is closer to Indian and Tibetan traditions, and also has

---

Vasalou (2008) *Moral Agents and their Deserts the Character of Mu'tazilite Ethics*, Princeton, NJ: Princeton University Press.

more of an affinity with Taoism. Initially his economic and administrative reforms produced great prosperity. His capital, Ch'ang-an, was the world's greatest city at the time with a population of 1,000,000 which was unprecedented at that period in history. However, as Xuanzong aged, he became infatuated with a young imperial consort, Yang Yuhuan (楊玉環) 719–756, whose family began to gain power as a result. When a local revolt began, a Turk named An Lu-shan (安祿山, 703–757) – who had risen to the command of the main imperial armies – was sent to put them down, he took the opportunity as a favorite of consort Yang to rise in rebellion himself and the emperor was forced to flee. Ultimately Lady Yang was denounced and strangled while the emperor resigned in favor of one of his sons but stability was not soon restored.

Toward the end of the Tang dynasty, loyalist and rebel forces fought for years and led to the decline of the old aristocracy and the rise of military adventurers and regional warlords. As the government and local commanders sought new sources of funding, they engaged in the indiscriminate sale of ordination certificates in an attempt to raise funds. This increased the size of the Buddhist establishment but also had the effect of weakening the integrity of Buddhism as a whole. In fact, at the end of the Tang dynasty considerable wealth found its way to Buddhist monasteries, despite attempts to reduce the number of clergy and prohibit existing clergy from passing on their personal wealth. Eunuchs and officials in charge of regulation of church assets often kept property destined for the treasury or accepted bribes to ignore the law. In addition, local military commanders continued to profit from the sale of ordination certificates so that paper monks with exemptions from taxation continued to be a problem. As the dynasty collapsed, constant fighting led to widespread destruction of monasteries and literature. This meant that Buddhist sects, such as Pure Land and Chan, which did not require extensive literature and ritual objects as central to their activities, were better able to survive and even flourish, as we shall see.

In Japan, in contrast, it was the rise of Tendai and Shingon Buddhist sects that weakened the grip of the aristocracy on the Buddhist establishment, though, in the process, helped to reinforce central Imperial authority. For example, Emperor Kammu (桓武天皇, 737–806, r. 781–806), similar to Xuanzong, sought to fight excessive Buddhist influence but he also was careful to promote new forms of Buddhism to strengthen the power of the state. At first glance, Kammu initially appears to be a Literati reformer. He is associated with changing the syllabus of the university to provide a stronger rationale for the Imperial government by basing the curriculum on two newly imported commentaries on *Spring and Autumn Annals* (春秋), the *Gongyang zhuàn* (公羊傳) and *Guliang zhuàn* (穀梁傳). Based on these commentaries, the emperor reorganized the government on Literati/ Legalist lines including sending expeditions to fight barbarian tribes (*Ezo* 蝦夷) in the north of Japan. He also tried to escape the influence of the Buddhist monasteries that had become increasing powerful and were not above intimidating officials to get their way. As a result, Kammu relocated his capital twice in order to escape influence of the powerful Nara Buddhist establishment – because while the capital moved, the major Buddhist temples and their officials stayed put in Nara. Moreover, Kammu declared limits on the number of Buddhist priests to be ordained and the building of temples by members of the aristocracy. One should not think of Kammu as anti-Buddhist, however. At the same time as curbing the power of the Nara sects, he encouraged other Buddhist monks knowledgeable regarding current trends in Buddhist thought to undermine Nara Buddhism by propagating alternatives more conducive to centralized imperial rule. This led to two new Buddhist sects, Tendai (天台) and Shingon (真言), competing for Imperial patronage.

In 806 the monk Saichō (最澄 767–822) established a branch of the Chinese *Tiāntai* (天台宗) sect, called Tendai in Japan. Together with the Shingon sect, it became the dominant sect of the Heian period (794–1185). Saichō succeeded in winning institutional autonomy for the sect and altered the character of Buddhist monasticism by replacing the traditional precepts for monks with the simpler *Mahāyāna* bodhisattva ones. Emperor Kammu supported Saichō's activities as a counterweight to the influence of the Nara temples. Kammu's official recognition of the Tendai temple Enryakuji (延暦寺) on Mt. Hiei however, stipulated that the new sect was limited in that the state-regulated system of ordination still required that all novice monks go to Nara to be tested and to receive final ordination. Between 818 and 819 Saichō petitioned the court in three works, known collectively as the *Sange gakusho shiki* (山家學生式 or Regulations for Student-Monks of Mt. Hiei) for permission to set up an independent ordination hall on Mt. Hiei.[23] This proposal aroused strong opposition from the Nara monks, and the court withheld its reply.

Saichō and his followers have left us with an important body of literature on what appears to be an obscure debate on aspects of Buddhism between Saichō and Tendai monks against the Hossō (Yogācāra) school of Buddhism and one of its monks, Tokuichi (徳一 760–783). In fact, it reveals the politics of the development of Buddhism and its role in the early Heian period. Tokuichi was from a prominent aristocratic family, like many Nara monks, and defended established monastic practices of

---

[23] Dengyō Daishi Saichō; Shōshin Ichishima ed. (2013) *The First Mahāyāna Precepts Platoform at Mt. Hiei*, Tokyo: Tendai Buddhist Sect Overseas Charitable Foundation.

Nara Buddhism and its claim to a monopoly on legitimization of the state. Saichō, in contrast, made Buddhism more accessible in a way that would attract more individuals including those who were less wealthy and well-connected than the aristocrats that had hitherto joined Buddhist monasteries by providing an ideological basis for transforming monks into higher beings, worthy of reverence, and, at the same time, into officials who could serve the state. Tokuitsu appears to have argued that Buddhahood for humans exists as an ideal but in reality no human can become a Buddha.[24] Hossō doctrine identified five types of practitioners and the religious goals they might ultimately aspire to reach, with an important distinction made between Buddha-nature in principle (ch. *lĭ Fó xìng*, jp. *ri-Busshō* 理佛性) and Buddha-nature in practice (ch. *háng Fó xìng*, jp. *gyō-Busshō* 行佛性). Like other conservative and aristocratic approaches, this implied that some, particularly the uneducated and poor, were *icchantikas* who lacked Buddha nature or, at least, the right type of Buddha nature. Saichō, in contrast, argued that through Tendai and Esoteric practices Buddhahood was possible for everyone even in their present lifetime. This was in stark contrast to the Hossō view that Buddhahood required eons of practice through rebirth and that some would never attain it. Saichō interpreted of the "Lotus Sūtra", based his commentary on the story of the Naga girl in his arguments for *sokushin jōbutsu* (即身成佛) or realization of Buddhahood with this very body, which suggested that anyone can attain Buddhahood.

It was Saichō's proposals for changes in monastic discipline that were no doubt the underlying basis of his debate with Tokuitsu. First of all, Saichō also criticized the *Dharmaguptaka Vinaya* (*Sifen lü* 四分律), which were the rules of ordination of the established state sponsored Kokubunji (国分寺) temple system by saying that they were a Hīnayānist formula that hindered progress toward enlightenment. He wanted them replaced with the *Mahāyāna* "Brahmā Net Sutra" (*Brahmajala Sūtra* or in Chinese, the *Fanwang-jing* 梵網經) which outlines ten major precepts (*shi zhong jie* 十重戒) for bodhisattvas and the 48 minor precepts, essentially a set of moral rules to follow to advance along the bodhisattva path. These constitute the "Bodhisattva Precepts" (菩薩戒) which Saichō argued were a higher ethical path for monks compared with the traditional monastic rules. Second, he wanted the power to ordain Tendai monks at their own temple complex on Mt. Hiei. Third, Saichō argued that the ordained Tendai monks would be required to remain for twelve years within the

---

[24] See Takahashi Tomio (高橋富雄) (1990)「徳一と最澄」- もう一つの正統仏教 (Tokuichi and Saichō – Another Legitimate Buddhism) 東京：中央公論社 (Tokyo: Chuō Kōron Sha).

monastery's boundaries to ensure they were disciplined and well trained. Fourth, after the twelve years on Mt. Hiei, Saichō wanted his monks to be given government posts as teachers or administrators in the provinces. Finally, his Tendai temples would be closely allied to the Court through the appointment of lay administrators (*zoku bettō* 俗別当) from court officials. This would give the Tendai sect great influence throughout the country, which was no doubt the reason for vehement opposition to Saichō's proposals by the Hossō and other Nara schools because his plans would reduce their power and influence. Initially the Imperial Court hesitated to make the changes but soon after Saichō died, the changes were approved as a tribute. Eventually Saichō's rules replaced the traditional rules for most monks in Japan.

The real competitor to Saichō's Tendai sect was not the Nara schools but Kūkai (空海 774–835), the founder in Japan of the Shingon sect (真言宗), who had acquired a mastery of esoteric Buddhism in Tang monasteries. Kūkai was born into a declining aristocratic family in a provincial town. At age 18 he entered the university in Heian with the aim of becoming a court official but soon quit. He justified his action by writing a book in which he compared the three main systems of East Asian thought – Literati, Taoist and Buddhist – entitled *Sangō shiiki* (三教指帰) or "Principles of the Three Teachings" in 798.[25] It was based on his personal experience of studying all three. In this work, Kūkai comes across as an egalitarian and humanist with scholarly erudition, but the book also has a subtlety and sense of humor which made his discussion of the philosophies come to life. In 804, he sailed as part of an official mission to the Tang dynasty as a student monk and studied Shingon, which synthesized Indo-Chinese esoteric (*mikkyō* 密教) Buddhism based on other forms of thought including Madhyamika, *Yogācāra* (Hossō), and Flower Garland. When Kūkai returned to Japan, he was presented with the temple of Toji (東寺) by the Emperor Saga (r. 809–823), which became the headquarters for Shingon Buddhism. In return, Kūkai created a ritual to protect the state (*chingo kokka* 鎮護國家). Every year he convened the *Geango* (夏安居) during which monks and nuns gathered to recite the "Sutra for Safeguarding the Nation, the Realm and the Chief of State" (*Shugo-kokkaishu-darani-kyō* 守護国界主陀羅尼經) over a three month period. Previously, the temples around Japan read the "Golden Light Sutra" and prayed for the protection of the state but while he was studying in the Tang dynasty Kūkai translated the "Perfection of (Transcendent) Wisdom Sutra" (*Prajñāpāramitā* from the Sanskrit प्रज्ञापारमित or 般若波羅蜜多 as Kūkai was fluent in both

---

[25] Yoshito S. Hakeda (1972) *Kūkai and His Major Works*, New York, NY: Columbia University Press.

Sanskrit and classical Chinese) and created new rituals to supersede previous ones. Kūkai made a special effort to educate the population outside of the aristocracy and his philosophy of egalitarianism and humanism also expanded the appeal of Buddhism to the masses.

WOMEN AND POLITICAL POWER IN BUDDHISM AND EARLY ISLAM

Although East Asian Buddhism retains some texts that view women negatively, such as "The Forty Two Chapter Sutra" (*Shisierzhang jing* 四十二章經) and "The Blood Tray Sutra" ("Xuepen jing" 血盆經), key *Mahāyāna* Buddhist texts have also been used to empower women, such as the "Lotus Sutra" (*Miaofalianhua Jing* 妙法蓮華經) and "Vimalakirti Sutra" (*Weimojie Jing* 維摩詰經).[26] In fact, a clear tendency for Buddhism to be closely related to the political power of female rulers in East Asian history can easily be missed because most research on the interrelationship between women, Buddhism and political power tends to focus on individual cases and is buried in national histories.

In 634 Queen Seondeok (善德女王 ?–647, r. 632–647) became the first female ruler of Silla in a time of war and unrest. As with her predecessors, she strengthened ties to the Tang court and sent officials there to learn the latest governing techniques but she also promoted Buddhism and completed the building of Buddhist temples. However, in 647, Lord Bidam (毗曇 ?–647) led a revolt against her rule arguing that "female rulers are incapable of being good rulers" (女主不能善理) and used the sighting of a shooting star as heaven's sign that the queen's reign must end. The revolt was put down within two weeks, and Bidam and thirty of his men were executed but Queen Seondeok had also died soon afterward for reasons that are unclear. Another woman, Seondeok's cousin, next ascended the throne as Queen Jindeok (眞德女王) and reigned from 647 to 654. The circumstances that permitted female rulers to come to power in Silla appears to be the absence of male heirs to the throne from the sacred or hallowed bone (*seonggol*) rank so that when the last ruler in that rank, Queen Jindeok, passed away, the system was ended. However, it is also clear that both of these female rulers were keen supporters of Buddhism and found it more amenable to the reigns rather than Literati thought.

---

[26] Masatoshi and Makiko Ueki trans. Robin R. Wang ed. (2003) *Images of Women in Chinese Thought and Culture: Writings from the Pre-Qin Period through the Song Dynasty*, Indianapolis, IN: Hackett Publishing Company: 266–293.

The most important female monarch in East Asia, and the only Chinese empress, Wu Zetian (武則天 684–705), was also strongly associated with Buddhism. She started her career as a thirteen-year-old concubine to one of the early Tang emperors. Her father had been a successful merchant who supported the Tang rebellion against the Sui but her mother was from an influential pro-Buddhist branch of the deposed Sui imperial family. Normally, she would have been forced to become a nun upon the death of the emperor who had originally recruited her but she was employed by the new emperor's wife to lure the emperor away from another concubine to whom he had become excessively attached. She used her new high-ranking position to rise to power, allegedly by poisoning her rivals. When the emperor was incapacitated after 660, she seized effective power and, after the emperor's death, she enthroned and removed his two sons successively to finally establish herself as the first and only ruling empress of China. Given that she was raised primarily by her devoutly Buddhist mother, it is not surprising that Wu Zetian systematically moved to raise the status of Buddhism at the Imperial Court. Given the early Tang ruling family ties to Taoism, however, it was perhaps natural that she would have turned to Buddhism to bolster her own claims to the throne. Buddhist monks even produced sutras which supported the right of a woman to rule and interpreted auspicious omens as indicating that the mandate of heaven had passed to her. At first, Buddhism was declared equal to Taoism but eventually Buddhism was placed above Taoism, and the Hua-yen (Flower Garland) sect in particular was favored with imperial patronage.

Initially Buddhist monks provided legitimacy to her reign by citing the text of the "Great Cloud Sutra" in which a queen is praised by Buddha as the incarnation of the Maitreya bodhisattva (मैत्रेय or 彌勒菩薩).[27] This Buddha has millennial connotations and suggests a new era, which is consistent with the new dynasty name she founded as well as the rise of a woman as ruler. Moreover, at Longmen Stone Statue Grotto (龍門石窟) she had an impressive statue created with herself as the Vairocana Buddha.[28] As noted in the previous chapter, the Vairocana is a celestial Buddha who is often interpreted, in texts like the "Flower Garland Sutra", as a *dharmakāya* (धर्मकाय, lit. "truth body" or "reality body") as one of the three bodies (*trikaya*) of the Buddha in *Mahāyāna* Buddhism. One of Empress Wu's key advisors was Fazang (法藏 643–712). His rapid rise to power from a novice to a key figure at court was due to his willingness to

---

[27] Keith McHahon (2013) "Women Rulers in Imperial China," *Nan Nü*, 15(2): 200–201.
[28] Amy McNair (2007) *Donors of Longmen: Faith Politics and Patronage in Medieval Chinese Buddhism*, Honolulu, HI: University of Hawaii Press: 111–122.

promote Flower Garland thought under imperial patronage.[29] His essay "On the Golden Lion" (*Huayan jinshizi zhang* 華嚴金師子章), produced for her Court, could easily be interpreted as accepting the equality of all beings and noting that subordination even to a female ruler, would not be a threat to the identity of men.[30]

Buddhism was also associated with the power of women rulers in Japan. Though all the credit for the introduction of Buddhism and the establishment of Literati systems of rule usually goes to Prince Shōtoku, he had been appointed by Empress Suiko and may have been given prominence in the reform process to avoid harming her position if he failed. The importance of the translation of the "Srīmālā Sūtra" (*Shōman kyō* 勝鬘經), one of the commentaries attributed to Shōtoku, is also revealing as Srīmālā was an Indian queen as well as a lay believer.[31] Clearly more significant was when Emperor Shōmu, the great patron of early Japanese Buddhism, abdicated in favor of his daughter, Empress Kōken. She first ruled as Empress Kōken from 749 to 758 and abdicated in favor of her second cousin, Emperor Junnin, but six years later she returned to power for a second reign (764–770) as Empress Shōtoku (not be confused with Prince Shōtoku) during which time she delegated power to a Buddhist monk named Dōkyō. Dōkyō was originally the member of a provincial aristocratic family and he appears to have gained the confidence of the retired Empress Kōken in 761 so when she reassumed power as Empress Shōtoku, Dōkyō was able to gain increasing political power and by 769 he was the most powerful man in the court bureaucracy, even exercising imperial prerogatives. At this point, Empress Shōtoku tried to abdicate her throne in favor of Dōkyō.[32] Dōkyō was only able to hold on to power so long as the Empress was alive so when she passed away in 770, he was forced to leave the capital and died three years later while serving in a lowly post at a temple in the provinces.

In short, in mainland East Asia, the Korean peninsula and Japan, there were women who rose to the highest positions of power and both supported and were supported by the Buddhist establishment at the same

---

[29] Jinhua Chen (2003) "More than a Philosopher: Fazang (643–712) as a Politician and Miracle Worker," *History of Religions*, 42(4): 320–358.
[30] Wing-Tsit Chan (1963) *A Sourcebook in Chinese Philosophy*, Princeton, NJ: Princeton University Press, 409–411.
[31] Diana Y. Paul and John R. McRae trans. (2004) *The Sutra of Queen Srimala of the Lion's Roar: The Vimalakirti Sutra*, Honolulu, HI: University of Hawaii Press. Also, Alex Wayman and Hideko Wayman, trans. (1974) *The Lion's Roar of Queen Srīmālā*, New York, NY: Columbia University Press.
[32] Ross Bender (1979) "The Hachiman Cult and the Dokyo Incident," *Monumenta Nipponica*, 34(2): 125–153.

time in East Asian history. This was not a coincidence given the exchange of ideas and the role of Buddhism in all the relevant states.

In early Islam, in contrast, the position of women was less prominent and there is considerable controversy over how to view women in Islam in this period.[33] Muhammad himself seemed to be favorably disposed as his first converts were often women. His teachings raised the status of women when compared to the common practices of the time, for example, by protecting female orphans, allowing widows to remarry, and so on. There is much in the *Quran* that supports this view, including an emphasis on love between couples and how marriage brings stability to make religious piety possible. The attention given to women by Muhammad is clear in "Sūrat an-Nisā" (سورة النساء), the fourth chapter of the *Quran*, the name of which derives from the numerous references to women in the chapter. Indeed, it was not until the reign of the conservative Caliph Umar that the separation of men and women in prayer was ordered, likely following Christian and Jewish practice, and Umar also refused Muhammad's surviving wives the right to make pilgrimage out of fear that they were a source of potential unrest, perhaps because they were critical of his regime. One might also note that the mother of Harun al-Rashid, al-Khayzuran bint Atta (الخيزران بنت عطاء d. 789), was able to exercise considerable influence over the governments of her husband and two sons who became Caliph. However, the strongest support for a political role for women comes in the work of al-Farabi, who, in his *Mabādi' ārā' ahl al-madīna al-fāḍila* (كتاب آراء أهل المدينة الفاضلة), clearly states that women have equal intellectual capacities as men, which following from the rest of the text also implied that they can reach perfection and serve as rulers as well.[34] This fits very well with the predisposition of neo-Platonism to accept and encourage female philosophers as much as it is al-Farabi's acceptance of Plato's idea that women should be among the philosopher-guardians who rule the ideal state. Therefore, there is plenty of evidence that the early Islamic view of women is not entirely negative and includes potential to empower women in theory if not in practice.

---

[33] See the early work by Gertrude H. Stern (1940) "Muhammad's Bond with the Women," *Bulletin of the School of Oriental and African Studies*, 10(1): 185–197 and Nabia Abbott (1942) "Women and the State in Early Islam," *Journal of Near Eastern Studies*, 1(1): 106–126, both of which are still valuable sources.

[34] Al-Farabi; Richard Walzer, trans. (1985) *Al-Farabi on the Perfect State: Abū Naṣr Al-Fārābī's Mabādi' Ārā' Ahl Al Madīna Al-fāḍila*, Oxford: Clarendon: 197.

CONCLUSION

Buddhism eclipsed Literati thought in East Asia. The stress on harmony is one that is given added emphasis in Literati thought as a result of the Buddhist challenge. Islamic philosophy under al-Farabi was the continuation and peak of neo-Platonist thought of antiquity. One can see why Islamic philosophers saw (and still see) themselves as the natural continuation of ancient Greek and Roman civilization when, in contrast, Christian Europe had descended into religious anti-intellectualism. In both Literati thought in East Asia and Christian political thought in Western Europe, the influence of Buddhism and Islamic classical learning respectively are the basis for new forms of political thought. This is true even if they were simply a reaction to these forms of thought but it is also true that Literati and Western thought were changed into something different as a result of their interactions, respectively, with Buddhism and Islam.

7. Late "medieval" political thought (1000–1300)

Neither the previous chapter nor this one should suggest that the concept of medieval thought is appropriate for all the areas covered and it would be misleading to argue that South Asia, East Asia and Europe and the Middle East were the same in this period. Nonetheless, it is not uncommon to use the term medieval for the history of most areas of the world at this time. Again, in this chapter as in the previous one, it is medieval in the sense that it is still part of that middle period between the ancient and the modern.

This is also the period in which specific forms of thought become dominant, including what will be called Hinduism in South Asia, Zhu Xi's "neo-Confucian" orthodoxy in East Asia, the rise of the opponents of philosophy (*falsafa*) in Islam and "Thomist" Catholicism after St. Thomas Aquinas. Buddhism, which had effectively dominated East Asia for centuries, was being challenged by the revival of a reformulation of classical Literati thought during the Song (宋) dynasty which spread throughout East Asia. At the same time, popular forms of Buddhism became prominent though they lacked much political significance everywhere except in Japan. The dominance of Hindu political philosophy is reinforced by local social practice, and even fleeting success of Jainist political philosophy seemed to have reinforced this point. In Islam, a conflict between popular and elite approaches played a role in shaping the trajectory of Islamic political thought, just as the split between popular Buddhism and elite Literati thought did in East Asia, and with just as profound consequences. In contrast, Europe is still dominated by elite debates that do not really have much widespread influence until the Reformation.

As with the previous chapter, one must be careful not to dismiss the thought in this period as worthlessly obscure or so esoteric as to be meaningless. As we will see later, the denigration of medieval thought started with the Reformation and the Enlightenment. Readers today are still influenced by Reformation and Enlightenment prejudice against metaphysics. The different approaches to metaphysics in each civilization reveal much about how the world was viewed and the political ethics believed to be required. We can still learn from such metaphysics, especially if we take seriously the insights provided and consider the long-term impact of these approaches that linger today.

DOMINANT FORMS OF POLITICAL THOUGHT

It might seem strange to start a discussion of dominant forms of political thought with Jainism, because the Jains have always been a relatively small minority in India. Nonetheless, Jainist political thought is the most notable in this period in India and it demonstrates the degree to which there was a standard tradition in Indian political thought. The key authors are Somadeva (fl. 959–966), author of the *Nikivakyamritam*, and Hemachandra (1089–1172), the author of works on grammar (both Sanskrit and Prakrit), science, logic, mathematics, philosophy, epic poetry, devotional works on eminent monks, and a book of political thought, *Laghvarhanniti*. Both of these Jain thinkers draw heavily on the *Arthashastra/Dharmasastra* tradition but they also had to reconcile the need to rule with ascetic and non-violent Jain philosophy. The most important of these works is the *Nitivakyamrtam* (नीतिवाक्यामृत) translated as "Nectar of the Science of Polity" of Somadeva (सोमदेव fl. 959–966).[1] Somadeva was also the author of the *Upasakadyayana* (उपासकाध्ययन) on lay followers or *upasaka* (उपासक), a central work of the *shravakacara* literature, that is, instructions and prescriptions for *shravakas* (श्रावक) of Jain ascetics of the Digambara (दिगम्बर or "sky clad") sect of Jainist ascetics who wear no clothes. For Somadeva, political philosophy is only of use in the material world but does follow certain principles. A king should not be weak because he would be useless and will go to hell for the sin of not doing the right thing. There is a general sense that the power and violence of a good king is an evil that is justified for the greater good. Violence is inevitable in human affairs so the skill of the king is to constrain it. He opposes war, especially aggressive war, as unacceptable, however. The second key Jainist political thinker in this period is Acharya Hemachandra (अथवा हेमचन्द्रसूरि 1089–1172) who was a member of the Śvētāmbara (श्वेतांबर or śvētapaṭa श्वेतपट) meaning "white-clad" Jainist ascetic or monks who wear white robes. He rose to prominence under the reign of Jayasiṃha (जयसिंह, r.c. 1092–1142), who assumed the title *Siddharāja* (*siddhis* सिद्धि is a Jainism term used to refer to the liberated souls) and greatly expanded the sphere of the Chaulukya (चालुक्य) dynasty in the Indian region of Gujarat, through a combination of military power and diplomacy. Hemachandra was also an advisor to

---

[1] Somadeva; Oscar Botto trans. (1962) *Il Nitivakyamrta di Somadeva Suri*, Torino: Universita di Torino, Faculta di Lettere e Filosofia, Fodanzione Parini-Chirio.

Jayasimha's successor Kumarpal (कुमारपाल 1143–1173). Kumarapala was born in a Shaivite family, but had become a patron of Jainism at some point in life. Kumarapala spent his early life in exile disguised as an ascetic to avoid persecution by Jayasimha Siddharaja. It may be that this was the context in which he met Hemachandra. Kumarapala succeeded Jayasimha upon his death, with the help Hemachandra, and ruled for almost three decades. Like his predecessor Kumarapala subdued a number of neighboring kingdoms. Hemachandra's influence appears to have led Kumarapala to accept Jainism as an official religion of Gujarat but not as the only religion. Kumarapala also patronized Shaivism according to inscriptions. Even so, it is likely that Kumarapala showed an interest Jainism to gain the support of the Jain community in his territory and fostered its growth in this period.

Hemachandra's main work of political thought is the *Laghvarhanniti*.[2] Strangely it is not included in the official collection of Jain works and has not yet been translated into a Western or East Asian language (it is only available currently in Hindi translation). It is still possible to glean some sense of Hemachandra's view on kingship from his *Lives of the Jain Elders*.[3] In this work he follows a very orthodox approach to power. The notion of a good ruler is related to the ideal of a good lay Jain follower, though sometimes the powers of a king seem to go beyond the average abilities of a lay follower, for example, in the tale of the thoroughbred horse where the moral of the story is that the single-minded pursuit of correct behavior is more beneficial and more effective than any fortification or guards, and that even a king can gain from it.[4] Hemachandra skillfully combined Jainist ethics and traditional Indian political thought.

ISLAMIC POLITICAL THOUGHT IN THE LATE MEDIEVAL PERIOD

One early Islamic philosopher was ibn Sina (ابن سينا b. 980–d. 1032), known in the West as Avicenna. He was a medical doctor and his main work of political thought is found in his "Book of Healing" (Kitāb al-Shifa' كتاب الشفاء) in Book X of his *Metaphysics*. In many respects, ibn Sina simply takes ideas from Aristotle and adapts them to revealed religion but there

---

[2] U.N. Ghoshal (1959) *A History of Indian Political Ideas: The Ancient Period and the Period of Transition to the Middle Ages,* Madras: Oxford University Press: 475–493.
[3] Hemachandra; R.C.C. Fynes trans. (1998) *The Lives of the Jain Elders,* Oxford: Oxford University Press.
[4] Hemachandra; Fynes trans. (1998) *Lives of the Jain Elders*: 93–97.

is a hint of neo-Platonism (perhaps just asceticism) when he suggests that happiness is obtained when the soul turns itself away from the body and returns to its true substance. Unlike late Roman neo-Platonists, however, he is clear that the role of the ruler is crucial in enabling this process.[5] In turn, the Caliph as ruler can demand the obedience of those he rules.

Perhaps the most influential political thought, in terms of actual political practice, was that associated with Nizam al-Mulk (نظام‌الملک b. 1018– d. 1092), a Persian scholar who became a vizier in the Seljuq Empire. The Seljuq dynasty (1016–1153) was formed by a Turkish tribe, which had only converted to Islam around 985, but had taken control of Persia and established an empire in 1050–1051. Nizam rose to hold almost absolute power under two Seljuq sultans. He became the key architect of Seljuq rule and his administrative arrangements remained in Persia until the nineteenth century. Nizam's influence was reinforced by his educational policy. He founded schools (*madrasa* مدرسه) in major cities of the Seljuk Empire. These were named "nezamiyehs" or "nizamiyah" after him and emphasized religion and Islamic law, based on Sunni and the conservative Shafi'i school of interpretation. The "nizamiyah" focused on arguing against what were considered unorthodox approaches, whether it was Shi'ite or *falsafa*. Successful students were often hired for government posts, particularly in policing (*hisbah* حسبة, literally "accountability") and "legal opinions" (*istifta'* استفتاء). The philosophy of Nizam appears to be set out in his *The Rules for Kings* (*Siyar al-Muluk* سیرالملوک in Arabic; *Siyasat-nama* سیاست‌نامه in Persian, literally, "The Rules of Nizam al-Mulk"), which is attributed to Nizam even though it is unlikely that he wrote any of it.[6] The first section of the book was probably written by al-Ghazali, who is discussed below, and the second half by a Persian author who appears to have been a government secretary writing after Nizam's death,[7] who reinforced Persian, rather than the Greek or Roman thought, as the basis of conservative Islamic political thought, particularly the traditional Persian political idea that religion and government are twins.

Al-Ghazali (الغزالي, b.1058–d.1111) was a prominent Islamic scholar and

---

[5] Avicenna; Michael E. Marmura trans. (1963) "Healing: Metaphysics X, Chapter 4" in Ralph Lerner and Muhsin Mahdi eds, *Medieval Political Philosophy: A Sourcebook*, Ithaca, NY: Cornell University Press: 103.

[6] Despite the assumptions of the introductory essay in the English translation, Hubert Darke trans. (2002) *The Book of Government, or, Rules for Kings: The Siyar al-Muluk, or, Siyasat-nama of Nizam al-Mulk*, 3rd edn, Surrey: Curzon Press, as was pointed out at the time it was published: Moshe Perlmann (1964) "Review of The Book of Government or Rules for Kings: The Siyāsat-nāma or Siyar al-Mulūk of Niẓām Al-Mulk by Hubert Darke," *Journal of the American Oriental Society*, 84(4): 422.

[7] See also Patricia Crone (1987) "Did al-Ghazali Write Mirror for Princes? The authorship of the Nasihat al Mulūk," *Jerusalem Studies in Arabic and Islam*, 9: 167–191.

administrator who was hired by Nizam al-Mulk to bolster the Caliphate by successfully defending Sunni orthodoxy against the Shi'a inspired Fatamids. Al-Ghazali's work requires deeper consideration. He excelled in his studies under the top theologians and jurists of his time but appears to have had a crisis of confidence over the role of reason in religious belief, and as a result he became an ascetic and studied Sufism or *Taṣawwuf* (تصوف). That is, he did not start as a sufi but it seemed to have filled a need for him during his period of doubt over the role of rationality in Islam. Sufism is a form of mysticism and asceticism that stresses a more direct spiritual relationship with God than can be obtained by mundane means. It was only in the time just before al-Ghazali that the doctrines of Sufism were written down, including the *Kashf al-Mahjûb* (كشف المحجوب) of Al-Hujwiri (الهجويرى c. 1000–d. 1076), and the *Risâla* (رسالة "Journal," "Pamphlet," or "Book") of Al-Qushayri (القشيري b. 986). Al-Ghazali played a major role in promoting mainstream acceptance of Sufism in his "Revival of Religious Sciences" (*Iḥyā ulūm al-dīn* إحياء علوم الدين) and in his "Alchemy of Happiness" (*Kimiya-yi Sa'ādat* كيمياى سعادت) written in Persian.

It would be wrong to think that only Islam produced anti-rational and mystical thinkers such as al-Ghazali. We have seen them in East Asia and in South Asia. They also existed in the Christian world. St. Augustine, particularly his *De Trinitate* and his *Confessions*, were an important source for much medieval mysticism based on a conservative interpretation of both neo-Platonism and Christianity. The influence of Plotinus and later neo-Platonists was evident in works such as that of Pseudo-Dionysius the Areopagite (c. 500), which was the basis for mystical Christian theology. Much of the anti-intellectualism of the early medieval period in the West was strongly influenced by this type of thought. What is different about al-Ghazali is that he argues directly against the *falsafa*, such as al-Farabi and even ibn Sina, in his *The Incoherence of the Philosophers* ("Tahāfut al-Falāsifa" تهافت الفلاسفة). He argues that rational argument can play a role once the foundations of one's position are known but these foundations can only be obtained by a leap of faith derived from mystical experience. Despite his attack on philosophers, however, he was clearly influenced by neo-Platonism. Al-Ghazali was influential because he reinforced popular and official distrust of *falsafa* by promoting mysticism, and insisting on reliance on the decisions of *ulama* educated in the *Quran* and *hadith* but not in wider philosophical traditions. As we have seen, the *ulama* were often the most educated members of many Muslim communities and had direct contact with the masses but were also suspicious of *falsafa*. They were popular, in the sense they were close to the populous, but not democratic in a political sense, and were often an important if informal part of the state where they were paid out of public funds. In this way, the policies of Nizam al-Mulk and his successors as well as the nizamiyah schools he founded, all worked against *falsafa*. Al-Ghazali merely gave the arguments against *falsafa* more of an intellectual foundation even if his Sufi beliefs retain lingering influences from the very neo-Platonism that he had rejected in *falsafa*.

Al-Ghazali did not mark the end of Islamic philosophy but it was marginalized. For example, ibn Rushd (ابن رشد), known in the West among Latin scholars as Averroes (1126–1198) taught and worked as an official in Muslim Iberia, and held political ideas that were Platonic with logic and other philosophical arguments rooted in Aristotelian principles. He wrote a commentary on the *Ethics* of Aristotle, used later in the West, but could not get a copy of Aristotle's *Politics* so used Plato's *Republic* to provide an Aristotelian critique of Plato to examine the ideal state. Although the critique is in the form of a commentary, ibn Rushd used the text to make sense of politics in Islam. For this reason, it is striking that he accepts so much of Plato's political philosophy including the advocacy of a regime of strict education, equality of the sexes (at least in terms of guardians), and censorship, especially of poetry and the other arts that might have a bad influence.[8] Ibn Rushd had a great influence in the Christian West, which at the time did not have access to these works of ancient Greek political theory and initially only knew key Platonic and neo-Platonist arguments as developed by ibn Rushd through translation from Arabic to Latin. Ibn Rushd also attacked al-Ghazali in his book *The Incoherence of Incoherence* (Tahāfut al-Tahāfut تهافت التهافت) by demonstrating the weak logic used by al-Ghazali to denigrate philosophical thought. Ibn Rushd believed that there is one truth even if philosophy and religion express it in different ways. Philosophy can be useful even in understanding religious texts where metaphor is used and teasing out the true meaning is difficult. In this sense, he did seem to place philosophy in a superior position and implies that philosophers have a better understanding of the true meaning of even religious texts compared to those uneducated in philosophy.

Ibn Rushd's metaphysics was widely debated in later Western thought and was called Averroism. He seemed to advocate the idea that all humans share the same mind or soul. This arises through the neo-Platonist idea of the Intellect but ibn Rushd takes it further to imply a shared consciousness and even that the seemingly individual soul is part of one universal soul. The influence of Islamic philosophy led to an Aristotelian revival in Christian scholarly circles culminating in the figure of St. Thomas Aquinas who accepted that the logical arguments of philosophy can be

---

[8] Ibn Rushd; Ralph Lerner trans. (2005) *Averroes on Plato's Republic*, Ithaca, NY: Cornell University Press.

reconciled with Christian revelation but rejected Averroism. In contrast, Islamic political thought subsides at the point where Islam rejects philosophy at the same time as it begins to re-emerge in Western Europe. Still, it must be remembered that Islam had kept the classical tradition alive. That is, even if the classic texts were better preserved in the Byzantine Empire, from which they were made available around the time of the Renaissance, initial medieval Western interest in classical authors, especially Aristotle, can be attributed to scholarship fired by Islamic commentary on classical texts and ideas. In fact, it is only after John of Salisbury (1120–1180) that we have the first "Western" political thinkers since St. Augustine, a gap of hundreds of years. John of Salisbury is important because his *Policraticus* suggests a right to tyrannicide, that is, the right to kill tyrannical rulers, which would put Christian morality above the divine authority of kings. From the time of John of Salisbury, however, responses to Islamic thought come to the fore and influence the direction of European political thought.

THE RISE OF "NEO-CONFUCIANISM"

The Song dynasty (宋朝 960–1279) or, more precisely, the Northern Song (北宋 960–1127) was established after a coup d'état against a boy emperor but as usual, Literati trained officials ran the government and maintained an influence at the Imperial Court. The Literati advice of this time can be seen in works, such as the "Comprehensive mirror to aid in government" (*Zizhi tongjian* 資治通鑒), written in the Northern Song period by the Literati scholar and official Sima Guang (司馬光 1019–1086) and was an important contribution to the genre of "mirrors for princes." This book has long been seen as an important work of political thought in East Asia but its interpretation of history and practical advice is based on the standard Literati view of politics. More importantly, it failed to challenge the rise of Chan Buddhism, in particular, as a competitor for the hearts and minds of the Literati. By the time of the Southern Song (南宋 1127–1279), which was created when two barbarian dynasties in the north forced the Song dynasty to retreat to the south, several thinkers began to develop a new system of political thought to woo the Literati away from Chan Buddhism. This new system of thought, often translated as "neo-Confucianism" was so powerful, it not only outlived the Song dynasty, it also spread to the rest of East Asia to become the predominant system of political thought for centuries.

Neo-Confucianism is a Western term that refers to the system of thought that in East Asia is usually called "Song Learning" (宋學) or the "Song-Ming Principle School" (宋明理學) based on its development in the subsequent Ming dynasty (明代). It is also called the "Teaching of the Way" (daōxue 道學) though this term is potentially confusing to the uninitiated who might mistake it for Taoism. It does have roots in the "Dark Learning" (*Xuanxue*) of neo-Taoism and in later Literati thinkers, such as Han Yu of the Tang dynasty, but significantly these earlier ideas were revived by Ouyang Xiu (欧陽修 1007–1072) of the Northern Song. Ouyang was involved in the composition of two histories, "Historical Records of the Five Dynasties" (*Wudai Shiji* 五代史記) and "New Book of Tang" (*Xīn Tángshū* 新唐書) which were modeled on classical texts such as the *Spring and Autumn Annals*. He also contributed to an epigraphical movement that sought to decipher ancient bronze and stone inscriptions, as part of his advocacy of a return to the study of ancient texts. Crucially he interpreted these texts in aid of his strongly anti-Buddhist stance. The Southern Song thinkers went further than Ouyang to create a much more elaborate cosmology and philosophy linked to a system of training for Literati as the ethical standard for official post holders.

The cosmology of neo-Taoism was adapted by Zhou Dunyi (周敦頤 1017–1073) to provide Literati thought with the metaphysical foundations which it lacked compared to that of Buddhism. His key contribution was the "Explanation of the Diagram of Highest Motion" (*Taiji tushuo* 太極圖說). This diagram explains how phenomena including the Five Elements and *yin* (陰) and *yang* (陽) arise out of the extreme polarity of nothingness, silence and motionlessness, or *wuji* (無極). Yet, at the same time, all phenomena can also achieve supreme polarity (*Taiji* 太極), which is the highest potential of all things. Zhou's approach had clear Buddhist influences. For example, stillness is connected to the Taoist notion of "non-action" but it also links to the Buddhist notion of "no desire." No knowledge is like the Chan or Zen meditation of emptying of the mind that paradoxically leads to enlightenment. If the mind lacks selfish desires, it becomes straightforward and reaches higher levels of comprehension. Just as Buddhism sought to help individuals reach higher levels of Buddhahood, the new school of Literati sought to allow people to reach Sagehood. Zhou's method of achieving Sagehood is like the Chan (Zen) monks based on living naturally and acting naturally.[9] The key role played by Zhou was to emphasize the order of the universe as revealed in the *Book of Changes* (*Yijing* 易經), a book of divination. He explains the process by which Heaven influences all things, including human beings, and how the Sage rulers can tap into heavenly endowed humanity and righteousness, through the rites (*li* 禮) to bring order (*li* 理) to people. In addition to the

---

[9] Yu-Lan Fung; Derk Bodde trans./ed. (1948) *A Short History of Chinese Philosophy*, New York, NY: Free Press: 272.

Yijing, one of the other key texts on which Zhou focused upon was the "Doctrine of the Mean" *Zhongyong* (中庸), a relatively obscure section of the *Book of Rites* associated with Zizi, the grandson of Confucius and teacher of Mencius.

The second major figure in the rise of neo-Confucianism is Zhang Zai (張載 1020–1077) who was a student of Literati thought but was attracted to Buddhism and Taoism. Eventually he decided that the approach of the Literati was the correct path, and he also felt compelled to draw on the *Yijing* to develop a more sophisticated metaphysics to challenge the Buddhists. He was particularly important for his emphasis on the nature of *qi* (氣), which here we have to translate as "psycho-physical substance," that is, the real material and electromagnetic phenomena that make up the universe, which includes the bio-chemistry that makes up our psychology, our minds, and, by extension, ideas and relationships. Literati critics of Buddhism tend to want to assert that there is no distinction between matter and mind. Whereas Buddhism implied that mind was constant but matter decays (such as one's body), Zhang's argument was that reality is made of both in a state of flux. When one dies or something is destroyed, it returns to the *Taixu* (太虛) or "great vacuity" or "great void." That is, everything emerges from this "nothing" then collapses back into it only to re-emerge again at the appropriate time. There is both decay and regeneration.

Finally, the stage for neo-Confucianism was set by the Cheng brothers. They were important because they reformulated key concepts in Literati thought into a more systematic philosophy. Cheng Yi (程頤 1033–1108) was the more stubborn and difficult of the two brothers so that he made powerful enemies to the extent that he was banned from teaching and banished from the capital. Cheng Yi identified the eternal forms of idealized concepts as *li* (理), which is usually translated as "principle," in the sense of the rational principles that govern the universe. It is the principles or logic of reality that give it order and meaning. This was mentioned by earlier writers, as we have seen, but Cheng Yi makes it central to Literati thinking. Cheng Hao (程顥 1032–1085) was more relaxed than his brother. He did not like to study so took to reading Taoist and Buddhist popular works but these always drove him back to the Literati classics. As with his brother, he was a student of Zhou Dunyi. Nonetheless, he too had trouble with the authorities and so was transferred to a series of minor provincial posts as punishment. The Cheng brothers are also the first to call for the investigation of things (*géwù* 格物) in order to find the principles (*li* 理) behind them. The Cheng brothers were severe critics of Buddhism by arguing that the Buddhists talk of principle but reject human relationships and act selfishly by abandoning the world because they are driven by a fear of death. Neo-Confucians embrace normal life in the real world and seek the underlying principles of life in order to understand how to live it well (humanely or virtuously).

THE DEVELOPMENT OF CHAN (OR ZEN/SEON/THIEN) BUDDHISM IN EAST ASIA

As in the rest of East Asia, the Song dynasty made use of the Chan Buddhist establishment despite growing Literati distaste for Buddhism. The early Song dynasty strengthened its control over the country, particularly in remote areas, by employing Chan (禪) Buddhist monks to carry out administrative tasks. The *Wu-shan Shicha* (五山十刹) System or "Five Mountain Ten Monastery" system was developed during the Southern Song based on a form of bureaucracy that was adopted by temples throughout the country, including a system of temple ranks and administrative procedures.[10] Originally there were five "houses" (五家) of Southern school Chan starting in the Tang dynasty: Guiyang (潙仰宗), named after Guishan Lingyou (771–854) and Yangshan Huiji (813–890); Linji (臨濟宗), named after Linji Yixuan (d. 866); Caodong (曹洞宗), named after Dongshan Liangjie (807–869) and Caoshan Benji (840–901); Yunmen (雲門宗), named after Yunmen Wenyan (d. 949); Fayan (法眼宗), named after Fayan Wenyi (885–958). Initially the Linji school was the dominant school within Chan, due to support from Literati and the Imperial Court in the late Tang period. During the twelfth century, however, Caodong began to distinguish itself from the Linji school as both competed for dwindling support from the Literati in the context of the Song court attempts to limit Buddhist influence on society.

In the Silla dynasty, on the Korean peninsula, provincial revolts gave rise to a militarized aristocracy that aimed at putting down growing civil unrest. Military aristocratic factions reduced kings to figureheads until the dynasty collapsed and power was only reconsolidated when a few provincial warlords competing for power nominally resurrected the ancient Three Kingdoms of Korea. The kingdom that won out in the power struggle between these new three kingdoms was called Goryeo (918–1392). Seon in the Goryeo period was based on the "Nine Mountains" (*Gusan* 九山) system. The pattern of Chan/Zen/Seon schools in East Asia was for them to be established in times of unrest in isolated mountain locations, usually with the support of a local militarized aristocracy and in Goryeo it was no different. This isolation was reinforced by the fact that, initially, Seon and

---

[10] Philip Yampolski (2003) "Zen. A Historical Sketch" in Takeuchi Yoshinori ed. *Buddhist Spirituality. Later China, Korea, Japan and the Modern World*, Delhi: Motilal Banarsidass: 3–23.

other meditation schools were viewed by the *Gyo* (教) or doctrinal schools with suspicion and alarm due to the potential threat of the new sect to the long-standing influence of the doctrinal schools in government.

There is no question that Buddhism was the dominant belief system of the Goryeo period. That is, even most Literati official-aristocrats believed in Buddhism and saw it as a supplement and complement to Literati principles of rule, especially as a source of ritual. With only a few exceptions, Goryeo was strongly Buddhist and Buddhist ritual was court ritual, such as the *Yeondeunghoe* or Lantern Ritual (燃燈会) and the *P'algwanhoe* or "Eight (Rules of Discipline) Receiving Ritual" (八関会). Buddhism was supported by the royal family, who in turn were supported by the Buddhists. Buddhist monks were exempt from corvée labor, and at one point received a stipend, but were required to pass examinations to obtain ordination and posts within the monastery. The monasteries were tax exempt and accumulated considerable land and slaves, becoming massive enterprises, much like medieval European monasteries. A royal or national head monk, called the State Preceptor (*Guksa* 國師) was also selected by the Court. When the dynasty came under attack from the Khitans and Mongols, monks engaged in copying all the known Buddhist Texts to protect the kingdom, Eighty Thousand Tripitaka Koreana (*Palman daejanggyeong* 八萬大蔵經), which are still preserved in Haeinsa Temple (海印寺).

Seon achieved an opening to gain dominance in Goryeo just as the Flower Garland school (*Hwaeom*) gained its greatest success in harmonizing the differences between the doctrinal schools in a way that weakened the existing schools and made the Flower Garland school more influential. There was an affinity between the Flower Garland school teachings and that of Seon, reinforced by the Flower Garland school's tendency to try to create unity by rising above and resolving doctrinal disputes. The work of the monk Gyunyeo (均如 923–973), in particular, furthered the reconciliation of Hwaeom and Seon, continuing the legacy of Uisang and Wŏnhyo. As we have seen, the Flower Garland thought was a political ideology as much as a Buddhist text school. Gyunyeo also seems to have used Flower Garland thought to justify the centralization of power in the monarch through the unification of administrative practice between the capital and the other local areas. Yet, it would be a mistake to assume that Flower Garland thought was used instrumentally. Gyunyeo emphasized mutual dependency of all the beings and established the theory of the absoluteness of the teaching of One Vehicle, emphasizing the perfection of the "Flower Garland Sutra" against the other Buddhist doctrines which, he argued, are imperfect and provisional.

The Doctrinal schools were also weakened by the arrival of the Cheontae or Tiāntai (天台宗) sect, which we have seen provided an attractive liturgy to segments of the ruling elites in the Tang dynasty and in Heian Japan. The sect was brought by Uicheon (義天 1055–1101) and he was appointed "Great Enlightened State Preceptor" (*Daegak Guksa* 大覺國師) from 1055 to 1101. Uicheon was also the fourth son of King Munjong of Goryeo and like most other monks in this period had initially studied Flower Garland thought. After studies in the Song dynasty and returning to Goryeo in 1086, Uicheon viewed Cheontae as a way to reconcile Doctrinal or Text schools and Seon schools by pointing out that Cheontae sees all experiences in the sensory world as expressions of Buddhist *dharma*, and therefore can be part of a path to enlightenment. Tensions between Seon monks and Uicheon continued during Uicheon's lifetime but eventually Cheontae was recognized as another meditation school, giving rise to the term "Five Doctrinal Schools/Two Sects" (*Ogyo Yangjong* 五教兩宗), the sects being Seon and Cheontae.

It was Jinul (知訥 1158–1210) who is considered to be the most influential figure for Seon Buddhism in Goryeo. He saw the *sangha* was in crisis due to divisions over doctrinal disputes and the influence of external forces weakening the disciple of the monks and nuns. Jinul argued that Goryeo Buddhism as a whole had been invaded by superstition, fortune-telling and payments for prayers to attain worldly gain, with many monks and nuns motivated by greed. Jinul created the "Samadhi and Prajna society" (*Jeonghyesa* 定慧社) to establish a community of practitioners who were more lofty-minded and disciplined, which led to the founding of the Songgwangsa monastery (松広寺) at Mt. Jogye. What distinguished Jinul's movement was that it was aimed at commoners whereas Cheontae was much more aristocratic. Like the Cheontae sect, Jinul believed that Buddha nature was present in all beings but went further in arguing that since Buddha nature is innate then one need only search for it in oneself so only meditation and not complex Cheontae ritual was the best path to awakening.

Chan or Zen came latest to Japan and only became a major branch of Japanese Buddhism through the work of Eisai (栄西 1141–1215) and Dogen (道元 1200–1253), both of whom faced strong resistance from the powerful establishment sects of Tendai and Shingon Buddhism. It is best to look at the two Zen schools established by Eisai and Dogen respectively, Rinzai and Soto, separately. The Rinzai (臨済) sect of Zen was conspicuous in both the imperial capital, Kyoto, and the shogunal capital at the time, Kamakura. These cities saw the rise of the Five Great Temples (*Gozan* 五山), which were active intellectual centers as well as monasteries. The *Gozan* system started based on three monasteries in Kyoto and two in Kamakura but eventually increased in number so that there were five monasteries in each city. Eisai founded Japan's first Rinzai temple and was abbot of two of the key temples in Kyoto. Eisai was originally a Tendai monk but when he traveled to the original sect temple on Mt. Tiāntai, he become aware of Chan (known in Japan as Zen) ideas. When he returned to Japan Eisai attempted to gain the support of the Imperial Court by writing a treatise in 1198 entitled "On Promoting Zen and Protecting the Nation" (*Kozen gokoku ron* 興禪護国論), which extolled the benefits for Zen for the nation and the rulers of a nation who promoted Zen. In it he argues that the Zen lineage in India and China was known for its tightly linked succession of proper *dharma* heirs. Thus the true *dharma* propagated by the Buddhas of old was handed down along with the correct ritual forms of Buddhist ascetic training made manifest in the Zen sect. The substance of the *dharma* is kept whole through master-disciple relationships, and confusion over correct and incorrect monastic decorum was thereby eliminated. This once again emphasizes the discipline of monks. He cites the "Benevolent Kings Sūtra" to argue that the wisdom that Buddhas provide to rulers as a secret jewel for protecting the realm is none other than Zen. At the more practical level he emphasizes upholding morality and selecting a morally pure person to be monastic leader but also that the chanting of the "White Parasol" or *Handara* (白傘) magical spell was their ritual for protecting our kingdom's rulers. The White Parasol refers to the Sitātapatrā (सितातपत्रोष्णीष or 白傘蓋仏頂), a powerful figure who was said to have formed from the topknot on the head of Gautama Buddha and is associated with non-violent *cakravartin* (universal monarch) rule.[11] As Eisai's influence grew, he faced increasing opposition of traditional schools of Buddhism such as Tendai and Shingon, which maintained close connections with the Imperial Court. Even though the Imperial Court was politically powerless with the rise of the Kamakura Shogunate, they still had influence in the key monastic communities, especially around the old capital in Kyoto. As a result, Eisai left Kyoto for Kamakura in 1199, where the powerful Shogun and his warrior caste (samurai) were very receptive of Zen teachings. Hōjō Masako (北条政子 1156–1225), the politically influential widow of the first Kamakura Shogun Minamoto no Yoritomo (源頼朝 1147–1199), sponsored Eisai's building of Jufukuji (寿福寺), the first Zen temple in Kamakura.

In this way, Zen stressed its purity in contrast to the established sects such as Shingon and Tendai, which had incorporated a lot of disparate elements, even non-Buddhist elements, into their rituals and practices. Zen monastic rules and practices also required more discipline on the part of their monks. Finally, Zen cultivated useful abilities in its monks, for example, they were expected to farm and cook their own food, and not rely on unearned income like other sects, which put them into more sustained

---

[11] Eisai (2004) "Promote Zen to Protect this Kingdom's Rulers" in Donald Lopez trans. *Buddhist Scriptures*, Harmondsworth: Penguin Books: 321–322.

contact with commoners. It made Zen monks useful as disciplined and educated local agents of political authority at a time when discipline and education were rare, and as we have seen there was a precedent in the relationship between Zen and the state in the Song dynasty. The monks of the *Gozan* temples also studied and preserved so-called *Gozan* literature, which acted as a repository for broader East Asian culture for the ruling class in times of instability. This included non-Buddhist scholarship such as the Literati classics and the neo-Confucian philosophy of Zhu Xi (1130–1200). In fact, Japanese Zen monks kept neo-Confucianism alive in Japan despite deteriorating political conditions over the next few centuries.

A second Zen sect also emerged, the Sōtō (曹洞) school founded by Dōgen. He also traveled to China and he attained enlightenment under master Rujing (如淨 1163–1228). After his travels in China, Dōgen initially worked near to Kyoto but faced hostility and political intrigues in the old capital so he traveled to Echizen (now Fukui Prefecture) and founded Eiheiji (永平寺) or "Temple of Eternal Peace." Like Eisai, he wrote a "Defense of Zen" as good for the nation though this text is now lost. What makes Dōgen interesting is that he wrote in Japanese at a time when classical Chinese was still the language of Buddhism, indicating his attempt at broader appeal. By the end of the Kamakura period, a Zen monk Muso Soseki (夢窓疎石 1275–1351) was declared State Preceptor (*Kokushi* 國師), the highest accolade for a Buddhist priest given by the Imperial house since the Nara period. Eventually, all the abbots of the main Zen temples were granted the title State Preceptor by the Imperial Court.

In Dai Viet, the emperors of the Lý (李) dynasty (1009–1225), were devout Buddhists but also were strongly influenced by Literati from the Song dynasty. The first national university, the "Imperial Academy" (Quốc Tử Giám 國子監), was built in 1070 during the reign of Emperor Lý Thánh (李聖宗 1023–1072) under Song dynasty influence. It emphasized the Literati classics and students were selected by examination, with most students being the children or close relatives of existing officials. The same year led to the opening of the first university in Vietnam, the "Temple of Literature" (*Văn Miếu* 文廟), which became the basis for training and selection of civil servants rather than based on aristocratic or royal connections. Yet, Lý emperors were also Buddhist rulers who actively supported the *sangha* and participated in Buddhist ritual. Monks were exempt from taxes and military duty. Buddhism also developed popular forms associated with indigenous magic, spirits, and medicine though there was some opposition in the *sangha* to what was viewed as this "corruption."[12]

---

[12] George Dutton, Jayne Werner and John K. Whitmore eds (2012) *Sources of Vietnamese Tradition*, New York, NY: Columbia University Press: 77.

The subsequent Tran (陳) dynasty (1225–1440) was more directly influenced by the Song dynasty because it was formed by one of a number of immigrant families from modern Fujian in what was part of Song territory. The Tran not only had become very wealthy as merchants, they also secured prominent positions of power in the Lý dynasty court, and took advantage of the mental illness of the last Lý emperor and the weakness of the crown prince set to succeed him. After massacring the extended Lý royal family and putting down various revolts, the dynasty almost immediately had to confront an attempted invasion by the Mongol Emperor Kublai Khan. It was in this context that the Tran dynasty produced one of its most prominent figures, the Thien (Chan/Zen) teacher Tuệ Trung Thượng Sĩ (慧中上士 1230–1291). Tue Trung was born Trần Tung (陳嵩), the eldest son in a branch of the royal Trần family and was the elder brother of Queen Nguyên Thánh Thiên Cảm (元聖天感 d. 1287) who was wife of King Trần Thanh Tong (陳聖宗 1240–1290) and mother of King Trần Nhân Tông (陳仁宗 1258–1308), and of Trần Hung Daō (陳興道 1228–1300), the latter of whom was the commander of Tran dynasty troops that successfully resisted the attempted invasion of the Mongolian Emperor Kublai Khan. Trần Tung had himself been a general in this war, fighting the campaigns of 1285 and 1288. After the war, he became a monk. He was trained by a teacher of Wu Yantong (無言通 759?–826, known in Vietnamese as Vô Ngôn Thông) lineage of Thien Buddhism. Wu Yantong, like most Zen lineages permitted monks to farm, which helped them to survive the Great Anti-Buddhist Persecution at the end of the Tang dynasty so they relied less on donations than other sects. Tue Trung had been well educated before becoming a monk and his ability to explain the Buddhist teachings made him a notable figure in the spread of Thien Buddhism to individuals from a range of backgrounds. Most notably Tue Trung influenced Trần Nhân Tông, the king who after abdication founded the first indigenous Vietnamese school of Buddhism, Trúc Lâm (竹林, literally, Bamboo Grove) though interestingly his posthumous reign name is the Humane Trần King (陳仁宗) indicating that Literati culture was still very influential. Drawing on Chan teaching Tue Trung emphasized non-duality and the limits of formal meditation and ritual in reaching enlightenment. Tue Trung authored an *Analects of Tue Trung Thuong Si* (Tuệ Trung Thượng Sĩ Ngữ Lục 慧忠上士語錄) in the form of a dialogue.[13]

---

[13] Dutton, Werner, and Whitmore (2012) *Sources of Vietnamese Tradition*: 54–56.

DOMINANT FORMS OF METAPHYSICS

The metaphysics developed in the period is essential for understanding much of what follows in East Asian and Western thought for the next several hundred years. For this reason the focus must be on Zhu Xi (朱熹 1130–1200) and St. Thomas Aquinas (1225–1274) who are the two towering figures in their respective civilizations and whose influence is difficult to overestimate.

Song philosophy reaches its peak in the work of Zhu Xi. He was extremely prolific and his commentaries dominated official views on Literati thought until 1911 and still inform understanding of classic texts in East Asia up to the present. Zhu Xi was promoted and demoted several times as a public official because he was so outspoken about incompetent officials in the higher civil service. Moreover, his teachings were initially viewed as controversial and attacked by the establishment. He was popular with scholars, however, and after his death his philosophy was adopted as the official interpretation of the Literati tradition by the Song dynasty and subsequent dynasties. Zhu used Dark Learning (*Xuanxue* 玄學) concepts from Wang Bi as well as Song thinkers such as Zhou Dunyi and the Cheng brothers to argue that the world is a combination of ideal principles (*li* 理) and things made of material-force (*qi* 氣). The two are interdependent but principle is higher because it is not corporeal and thus not prone to corruption and impurities. Since *qi* (氣) is corruptible and *li* (理) is not, then *qi* (氣) is the source of evil, lust and other problems, but all men can potentially strive to uncover *li* (理) as a standard to avoid corruption. It is very tempting to put a Platonic gloss on Zhu's theory because there are similarities with Platonic theory of ideas. The *T'aiji* (太極) or Supreme Ultimate is the summation of all the *li* (理) in the world – nature, man, heaven. Human nature comes from heaven but nature is nothing but principle (*li* 理). Zhu likens it to a post held in the government in that it has a statutory purpose but it is up to the individual to fulfill the ideal of that role as best they can. However, he also defined human nature more concretely in terms of filial piety, specifying the key bonds of human society and the state, that is, between ruler and minister, father and son, and husband and wife, and the Five Constant Virtues (*wǔ cháng* 五常) or humaneness or benevolence (*rén* 仁), rightness or righteousness (*yì* 義), propriety or ritual (*lǐ* 禮), wisdom (*zhì* 智) and fidelity or trust (*xìn* 信). Since Buddhists reject the human relationships of this world, Zhu Xi argued, the neo-Confucian approach is better because it shows honest and real affection rather than see human interaction as a barrier to enlightenment.[14]

---

[14] William Theodore De Bary, Irene Bloom and Joseph Adler (1999) *Sources of Chinese Tradition, Volume 1: From Earliest Times to 1600*, 2nd edn, New York, NY: Columbia University Press: 713.

Zhu Xi was challenged by an opposing school which was created by his friend, Lu Jiuyuan (陸九淵 1139–1193) who argued that mind is not corrupt *qi* because it is an active partner with principle (*li*). Mind is not a stuff but shares the supreme ultimate with *li*. Jiuyuan insisted that the mind is not as impure as Zhu Xi suggested and that Zhu Xi's dualism between the mind and principle is mistaken. Since Lu's notion of the mind has similarities with Chan Buddhism, the more orthodox Zhu Xi was forced to defend his friend from the false charge that he was a Chan Buddhist. By placing emphasis on the mind, however, Lu did establish a basis for accommodation with the more psychological approach of Buddhism. In contrast to Buddhists, however, Lu wanted the mind to act to make the world a better place and not reject it. Lu wants people to "honor their moral nature" by acting in accordance with what the mind can reveal to them. This is where there is contrast as well with the more bookish and conservative Zhu Xi who reportedly admitted that Lu's students were mostly concerned with putting their beliefs into practice whereas his emphasized contemplation of principle over action.[15]

The greatest figure in Western medieval political thought is St. Thomas Aquinas (1225–1274), who was heavily influenced by Islamic thought. This is true even if his work was a reaction against Averroist philosophy because it clearly had an impact on his arguments in response. Aquinas rejects ibn Rushd's metaphysics by pointing out that Aristotle was arguing that the individual intellect cannot be independent of the physical body. However, Aquinas still believed that humans must use rationality and logic to understand God's creation and our place in it because God reveals himself through nature. This is "general revelation." Where rationality conflicts with revealed religion, such as in scripture or miracles, then these supernatural means of God's revelation must be given special priority. This is "special revelation." Some individuals may also experience direct revelation of God's will to them.

Aquinas did not accept tyrannicide, against John of Salisbury, because he considered it a danger to order. People had to put up with a tyrant unless higher authorities, ultimately God, changed the tyrant's heart or removed him from power. It may be that Aquinas did not worry too much about rulers because out of four sources of law, human law was only one. That is, he saw eternal law (God as reason/rationality), natural law (the logic of the created world – the way things work empirically, very similar to some meanings of *dharma*), and divine law (the gift of God's grace-revelation-revealed truth) as more important than human law. It may be

---

[15] De Bary, Bloom and Adler (1999) *Sources of Chinese Tradition, Volume 1*: 719.

true that human law should be derived from eternal, natural and divine law but human law is created by the ruler, as law maker and judge. The ruler seems to mean absolute monarch but Aquinas also stated that forms of mixed rule (perhaps influenced by Cicero and/or Aristotle) are best. Moreover, Aquinas argued the Pope should retain the power to educate and guide the moral development of all people even if he must hand the sword of justice to secular rulers.

As with Zhu Xi, who followed Mencius in his belief that all humans are inherently good, Aquinas also believed that natural law gives all humans a natural inclination to the good.[16] Also, as in Zhu Xi, the natural tendency toward the good can be distorted or even "blotted out" by evil persuasion, vicious customs and corrupt habits.[17] Both viewed the nature of the physical world as an obstacle to finding the best way of behaving, including ruling others. Zhu Xi favored principle over the material nature of *qi*. Aquinas saw the divine as perfect and the sinful nature of humans make them unable to reach a divine level of perfection, though the notion of the Sage (and of the Imam) are closer to perfection than Aquinas would have admitted, though perhaps the wise (rational) and divinely anointed ruler might come close. The difference is that the focus of Aquinas was on heaven whereas Zhu Xi and the neo-Confucians in general were reacting against the Buddhists so stress the value of what can be achieved in this world rather than in the afterlife.

Aquinas follows Aristotle in viewing individuals in terms of the quality of their ability and tacitly accepts the idea that some are slaves by nature.[18] He views human souls has holding the lowest rank amongst intellectual substances (presumably angels and others are higher) because even though humans receive knowledge of divine providence, it is imperfect and an effort must be made to improve on it. This is hindered by the corporeal nature of human existence and the weakness of the human intellect. Only higher spirits can assist in attaining high forms of intellect. Aquinas also makes a distinction between humans in terms of how "those who excel in

---

[16] Aquinas; Fathers of the English Dominican Province trans. (1920) "Question 94: The Natural Law, Article 2: Whether the Natural Law Contains Several Precepts, or Only One?" *Summa Theologiæ* of St. Thomas Aquinas, at New Advent: http://www.newadvent.org/summa/2094.htm (accessed June 5, 2017).

[17] Aquinas; Fathers of the English Dominican Province trans. (1920) "Question 94: The Natural Law, Article 6: Whether the Law of Nature can be Abolished from the Heart of Man?" *Summa Theologiae* at: http://www.newadvent.org/summa/2094.htm (accessed June 5, 2017).

[18] Thomas Aquinas; Vernon J. Bourke trans. (1955) "Book Three: Providence, Chapter 81: On the Ordering of Men Among Themselves and to Other Things," *Summa Contra Gentiles*, New York, NY: Hanover House. Online edn. Joseph Kenny: http://www.dhspriory.org/thomas/english/ContraGentiles.htm (accessed November 17, 2017).

understanding naturally gain control, whereas those who have defective understanding, but a strong body, seem to be naturally fitted for service" quoting Aristotle and scripture. For Aquinas, those who gain power by strength or sensual affection and not intellect can only bring disorder. Zhu Xi focuses more on the positive effort to cultivate oneself to attain Sage learning (*sheng xue* 聖學), the ultimate aim of which was individual attainment of Sagehood. In many respects this is a political goal as the exemplars are Sage-kings or Sage-rulers as explained through the transmission of this learning from the early wise emperors Yao and Shun through to Duke of Zhou and then through Confucius and Mencius to Zhu Xi. Moreover, Zhu Xi focused on education of the civil servants as is the case with most Literati thought. It is an aid to one's ability to rule or help others rule well.

POPULAR FORCES AND VIEWS ON WOMEN

In contrast with the elite tendency of Chan/Zen/Seon/Thien, the Pure Land sect, which grew to prominence in this period in East Asia, appealed to the masses. This popular form of Buddhism fit with the millennialist concept of the Final Dharma Age (ch. *Mò Fă*, jp. *Mappō* 末法), which is considered the "degenerate" Latter Day of the Law of Dharma. *Mappō* was believed to begin 2,000 years after Sakyamuni (the historical Buddha) died and was to last for "10,000 years." The Japanese calculated the start of this age as 1054 AD. Since the power of the dharma will be weaker in this period, the world will be in chaos and the teachings of the Buddha will be inadequate to attain enlightenment. It has apocalyptic implications, creating a sense of urgency, and not just a sense of despair. Radical things must be done in response.

Although often traced back to Hui-yuan (334–416) the spread of the Pure Land Buddhism to the general population came much later. It was not until Shantaō (善導 613–681) that there was a systematic approach to reciting passages of relevant sutras, meditating on Amitābha and his Pure Land (净土), and chanting his name. This became known as *nien-fo* in Chinese (念佛) or *nembutsu* in Japanese, *yeombul* in Korean and *niệm phật* in Vietnamese but originally came from the Sanskrit concept of *buddhānusmṛti* (बुद्धानुस्मृति), which means "mindfulness of the Buddha" usually achieved by repeating the simple incantation "Namo Amitābhāya" (नमोऽमिताभाय or 南無阿彌陀佛), literally, "Homage or Devotion to the Buddha of the Infinite Light." *Nien-fo* or *nembutsu* is usually associated with a vow made by Amitābha Buddha (the Buddha of Everlasting Light), who was a previous incarnation of Siddhartha Gautama, the historical Buddha, that sentient beings who sincerely and joyfully entrust themselves to him and want to be born into his Pure Land need only call his name several times, though his vow does contain an exclusionary clause that those who commit the five gravest offences and abuse the right *dharma* are excluded.[19] This invocation of Amitābha Buddha was considered a natural corollary of one's keeping the Buddha in mind (念佛). This was appealing because it did not require the rigorous training usually demanded of monks. With the decline of elite patronage at the end of the Tang dynasty and the massive increase in the numbers of clergy due to sales of tax exemption ordination papers, this accessible form of Buddhism grew popular on the East Asian continent.

There are different Buddhas ruling different Pure Lands on which one can call but Amitābha's Pure Land (浄土) of Sukhāvatī is said to be the most beautiful of realms according to the "Longer Sukhāvatīvyūha Sūtra" (sk. सुखावतीव्यूह; 無量寿經 ch. Wúliángshòu Jīng, jp. Muryōju Kyō, kr. Muryangsu kyŏng, vt. Vôluợngthọ kinh). To arrive in this Pure Land is not only to guarantee that one will reach enlightenment, but also that one can return as a bodhisattva to assist others. Other Pure Lands, such as Akṣobhya's pure land of Abhirati associated with Shingon, or the Pure Land of Maitreya, often associated with the aristocracy and royalty, have also been important in East Asia, but Amitābha's has been by far the most popular. For example, Korea saw the introduction of Pure Land (called *Jeongto* in Korean) of both Maitreya and Amitayus. Unified Silla and Tang were close and many monks traveled freely and studied new developments in Buddhism such as Seon and Pure Land Buddhism. In Japan, Pure Land grew out of the Tendai (Tiāntai/Cheontae) sect after the ninth century which culminated in the Kamakura period (1185–1333) with the establishment of independent Pure Land sects. This was possible in large part because the influence of the Tendai sect was in decline along with the fortunes of the court aristocracy as political power decentralized.

One of the first and most prominent Japanese monks to spread this idea was Hōnen (法然 1133–1212). He established the Japanese *Jōdo* (Pure Land) sect in Japan. It was based on teaching common people and emphasizing the need for Amida Buddha to help people reach enlightenment because they cannot do it on their own. Hōnen became a novice at the Tendai complex on Mt. Hiei at the age of twelve, sent there after the murder of his father. He acquired a reputation for great knowledge but the more he studied, the more he was dissatisfied with the Tendai approach. This led him to Commentary on the "Meditation Sutra" (ch. *Kuan wu-*

---

[19] Hisao Inagaki trans. (2017) *Larger Sutra on Amida Buddha (Daimuryojukyo, or Larger Sukhavativyuha Sutra)*, http://web.mit.edu/stclair/www/larger.html (accessed June 28, 2017).

liang-shou ching shu, jp. *Kammuryōju-kyō sho* 観無量寿經疏) by Shandao (613–681) in which there is a passage that argued simply and wholeheartedly keeping in mind the name of Amida whether walking, standing, sitting or lying down never abandoning this name for one moment, even for a short time, will fulfill the Amida Buddha's vow. He became convinced that the Pure Land was the only approach possible for people in the age of *mappo*. During the rest of Hōnen's life he gained many followers and his teachings increasingly drew criticism from the Buddhist establishment in Nara and the Tendai monks of Mt. Hiei. He was also forced into internal exile temporarily, between 1207 and 1211, due to his disciples converting two Imperial ladies in waiting to Pure Land Buddhism. He defended his approach in the *Senchaku Hongan Nembutsu Shu* (選択本願念佛集) or "Passages on the Selection of the Nembutsu in the Original Vow," which can be viewed as the official declaration of the establishment of the *Jōdo* (Pure Land) sect.

One of Hōnen's most important followers was Shinran (親鸞 1173–1263). Shinran was the son of a noble who was orphaned at the age of nine. After twenty years as a monk at Mt. Hiei, Shinran abandoned monastic life because he felt that one so full of evil passion and ignorance as himself could not achieve anything. Indeed, he came to believe that the life of a monk was ill suited to enable anyone to attain enlightenment. At the age of 29, when he quit as a monk, he met Hōnen and learned much from him but Shinran decided that Hōnen's interpretation of Amida Buddha's Primal Vow was incorrect and established the *Jōdo Shinshu* sect or the *True* Pure Land Buddhist sect. Shinran argued that attempts to achieve enlightenment through meditation or monastic discipline and study were a mistake because no one can overcome the obstacles to enlightenment by oneself, regardless of the amount of training one has or efforts one expends. He saw it as yet another form of "self-power" (*jiriki* 自力) along the lines practiced by the older schools which advocated rigorous meditation, difficult austerities and strict adherence to the monastic precepts. Even Hōnen's approach – to repeat *nembutsu* innumerable times in order to attain birth into the Pure Land – makes the mistake of putting an emphasis on one's own abilities, which only reinforces the self as an obstacle. This is delusional because one's own pathetic efforts are nothing compared to the absolute perfection of Amida's Pure Land. Shinran believed that the average people need more realistic role models and methods to reach enlightenment than the established Buddhist sects provided them. A simpler doctrinal formula was necessary, he argued, to bring Buddhism to the masses in which one relied on a power greater than oneself, the "other power" (*tariki* 他力) of the Amida Buddha. In fact, he argued even one sincere repetition of *nembutsu* could lead to salvation. Shinran's approach was, of course, attacked by the Buddhist establishment, which in turn meant that the government was against him as well – as we have seen the two were intimately related. Moreover, there was little basis for accommodation because he argued that people should follow only one school (his, of course) because the others would only mislead them. As a result, he was exiled from Kyoto and traveled widely. Eventually, he settled near present day Tokyo and followed his own view that monks should marry and lead normal lives, by doing so himself and fathering six children. Shinran said that Prince Shōtoku, who is credited with bringing Buddhism to Japan, came to him in a dream and declared Japan a Buddhist nation. This advocacy of reliance on "other power", then, was intended to be empowering politically as well, as an aid in Shinran's fight with the Buddhist establishment and the state. This was developed further by his successors.

Another independent outgrowth of Tendai was the Nichiren sect, founded by a monk, Nichiren (日連 1222–1282), who had studied at Mt. Hiei and based his religious beliefs on the "Lotus Sutra". Nichiren was the most nationalistic of the Japanese Buddhist monks and directly confronted political authority even more directly than the other sects. Nichiren was a fisherman's son but chose to study Buddhism, eventually traveling to the political center of Kamakura, and then on to Kyoto and Nara, to master the full range of Buddhist literature. In 1253, he adopted the name Nichiren (literally "Sun-Lotus") when he advocated chanting "*Nam-myoho-renge-kyo*" (南無妙法連華經), or "Homage to the Mystical Dharma of the Lotus Sutra," as a *nembutsu*. This sect of Buddhism was not only new but it was a Japanese sect that had no direct links to Buddhist developments in China – in fact his name Sun Lotus is from Land of the Rising Sun (Japan) and Lotus for the "Lotus Sutra". Not only was his approach a Japanese form of Buddhism with him at the head but his thought had political and nationalist implications. One of his earliest and most famous works, *Rissho Ankoku Ron* (立正安國論), which is translated various ways but generally as "On Establishing the Correct Teaching for the Peace of the Nation," consists of a dialogue between a host and his visitor. It is assumed that Nichiren is the host and the visitor represents a high government official. It sets out the problems that beset a nation that follows false teachings and how adoption of Nichiren's views will save the nation.

Nichiren was known for his intolerance of other sects, even more so than the *Jōdo* sects, who were similarly exclusivist. His attacks were directed at Hōnen and the Pure Land Sect as well as Shinran and the True Pure Land Sect despite the fact they advocated similar *nembutsu* approaches. He also attacked Shingon, which was still influential in the aristocracy. Shingon used rituals with secret or complex layers of meaning based on mantras and mudras, and included purification rites and exorcism. These practices were normally reserved for the elite and taught to only a select few to preserve the mystery of the ritual. Nichiren had particular confrontations with mixed Shinto-Shingon temples and others who he termed New Shingon "sorcerers," who he encountered at the Hōjō family (Kamakura Shogunate) sponsored temples. He also objected to a Shingon temple that taught *nembutsu* to the common people because he argued its priests also practiced sorcery. For their part, the Shingon and Shintō priests despised Nichiren because he revealed exoteric mudras, mantras, and mandalas and made them accessible to ordinary people. Given his fierce and uncompromising attacks on the establishment and other sects, it is not surprising that he was persecuted and so were his followers. Nonetheless, his and other forms of *nembutsu* Buddhism spread among the masses and empowered them to accept it and fight existing authority that was backed by older forms of Buddhism. As a result, these forms of Buddhism contributed to the further decline of political power in medieval Japan as we will see in the next chapter.

Neo-Confucian views of authority were general hierarchical with the "people" as a force to be dealt with carefully but mainly to be strictly controlled. The same can be said of Islam with the possible exception of ibn Rushd. His notion of a universal Soul and Intellect has implications for the underlying unity of humans and has potential egalitarian implications but these seem to be offset with the notion that some individuals have better access to the One through Intellect than others. What evidence we have of his actual exercise of political power, ibn Rushd was generally liberal. He was trained in the Maliki school of jurisprudence, which gives more weight to the consensus of the people, originally defined as the people of the city of Medina in Muhammad's time. Most importantly, he clearly accepted Plato's view that women should be among the ruling guardian elite in the ideal state, thus following al-Farabi in a high evaluation of women's capacity for intellect.

Negative views of women in Islam and Christianity seem to be derived mostly from Aristotle. For example, ibn Sina's discussion of women follows the sequence of discussion of the household at the start of Aristotle's *Politics* but he goes even further in denigrating women directly. Women should be veiled and secluded because they are easily deceived and less inclined to obey reason but also female promiscuity causes well-known harms (perhaps referring to uncertainty over the paternity of children) whereas jealousy is the only problem when men are promiscuous. The woman should not be the bread-winner and it should be legislated that women are to be dependent on men.[20] The *Siyar al-Muluk*, attributed to Nizam al-Mulk but most likely a Persian secretary with rather un-Islamic views,[21] very crudely rejects women's involvement in political affairs and goes so far to argue that whatever a woman says, the opposite should be done. It is a hysterical and incoherent attack on women with a deep-rooted anger, which says more about the author than Islam.[22] For al-Ghazali's views of women, it is best to examine "The Revival of the Religious Sciences."[23] The discussion is from the male point of view only and is relatively patronizing but it has none of the exaggerated fear of women in the passages of the second half of the *Siyar al-Muluk*. Al-Ghazali argues that it is best if a woman is timid because it will keep her separate from her friends and fearful of going anywhere without her husband[24] but that a husband should treat his wife with kindness and playfulness[25] and avoid excessive anger when dealing with one's wife or prying into their secrets.[26] There is also a sense that the sexual pleasure of the woman also matters.[27] It is true that he states that when a husband wants sex, she cannot refuse, with the main reason put forward to prevent the husband's infidelity.[28] Women are also admonished to avoid extravagance and ask the husband's permission before giving food to charity, but engage in good works in the husband's absence. Interestingly, al-Ghazali argues that a wife should not grieve excessively when her husband dies and no longer than four months and ten days![29] The key problem for al-Ghazali is controlling sexual passion, which he noted is more a problem for the man. In fact, he has a long section in "The Revival of the Religious Sciences" (*Ihya Ulum al-Din* احياء علوم الدين) on the controlling appetite, meaning excessive eating and controlling sexual passion of the man, but eating was seen as much if not more of a problem. Thus, even the arch conservative al-Ghazali had much more nuanced views on men and women than one might think.

In contrast, St. Thomas Aquinas, in his essay on whether or not it was a mistake for God to have created women, argued against Aristotle's view

---

[20] Avicenna; Michael E. Marmura trans. "*Healing* from Metaphysics X, Chapter 4" in Lerner and Mahdi eds (1963) *Medieval Political Philosophy*: 106.
[21] Patricia Crone (1987) "Did al-Ghazali Write Mirror for Princes? The Authorship of the Nasihat al Mulūk," *Jerusalem Studies in Arabic and Islam*, 9: 167–191.
[22] Hubert Darke trans. (2002) *The Book of Government, or, Rules for Kings: The Siyar al-Muluk, or, Siyasat-nama of Nizam al-Mulk*, 3rd edn, Surrey: Curzon Press: 179–186.
[23] Al-Ghazzali; Fazal ul Karim trans. (1993) *Revival of Religious Learnings: Imam Al-Ghazzali's Ihya Ulum-id-Din*, 3 volumes, Karachi: Daral Ishaat.
[24] Al-Ghazzali; Fazal ul Karim trans. (1993) *Revival of Religious Learnings*, vol. 2: 31.
[25] Al-Ghazzali; Fazal ul Karim trans. (1993) *Revival of Religious Learnings*, vol. 2: 33.
[26] Al-Ghazzali; Fazal ul Karim trans. (1993) *Revival of Religious Learnings*, vol. 2: 35.
[27] Al-Ghazzali; Fazal ul Karim trans. (1993) *Revival of Religious Learnings*, vol. 2: 38.
[28] Al-Ghazzali; Fazal ul Karim trans. (1993) *Revival of Religious Learnings*, vol. 2: 43.
[29] Al-Ghazzali; Fazal ul Karim trans. (1993) *Revival of Religious Learnings*, vol. 2: 44.

that woman was a misbegotten man but still insisted that women are merely there to help men and accepts Aristotle's view that women must be subordinate to men. Aquinas even sounds slightly Taoist in his argument that "the active power of generation belongs to the male sex, and the passive power to the female".[30] Aquinas relies heavily on Aristotle, as did ibn Sina, and this can explain the relatively negative view of women for both. Al-Ghazali, who is somewhat influenced by neo-Platonism, has a less negative view of women but was clearly not as egalitarian as al-Farabi with regard to women's intellectual capacity.

Pure Land Buddhism could be considered to hold very egalitarian views regarding women, especially for the time. Hōnen was exiled to Shikoku due to his disciples converting two of Imperial ladies in waiting. The cause of his exile is characteristic of his thought because Hōnen demonstrated an extraordinary interest in the spiritual salvation of women, regardless of social status. This is reflected in the greater participation of women in the Japanese Pure Land sects compared to other sects. There is some controversy over Shinran's views of women, however because in some texts he appears to accept the Amida Buddha's Thirty-Fifth Vow, which states that women will have to be reborn as men in order to achieve enlightenment. It is not possible to simply explain away this text so all one can say is that it is not representative of the general True Pure Land view of women.

CONCLUSION

This period is very important in terms of developing the basic political orientations of Hindu, Christian, Literati and Islamic political thought for many centuries to come. The impact of this period still lingers today in identifiable ways. The involvement of Chan/Zen/Seon Buddhism with the establishment can be contrasted with the popular empowerment of Pure Land Buddhism. Zen viewed itself as able to protect the state with the practical aspect of their skills in support of local and national political establishments a natural corollary. Buddhist sects believed that they were tapping into extraordinary sources of power such as the Pure Land for Pure Land followers, the "Lotus Sutra" for Nichiren or "Parasol Sutra" for Zen. God and Allah perform the same role for Christianity and Islam. In contrast, there is no notion of divine in neo-Confucianism though the role of the "Supreme Ultimate" as origin of all and source of heavenly good is not too different. Buddhas, Christian God and Allah in Islam are

---

[30] St. Thomas Aquinas (1920) *The Summa Theologiæ*, 2nd revised ed. Online edition 2016 by Kevin Knight at http://www.newadvent.org/summa/ (accessed November 17, 2017).

simply more anthropomorphic and paternalistic than the neo-Confucian cosmology. All systems of thought agree that human law is inferior to divine forces but they disagree over the extent to which one must tolerate evil rulers and what can and should be done to reform the world.

Neo-Platonism in ibn Rushd (Averroes) is more egalitarian with the notion of a shared divine soul of all beings and this extends to viewing women as equal in intellect. In contrast, the influence of Aristotle's views on what he sees as inferior individuals and particularly women, had a profound impact on both Islam and Christianity. Zhu Xi is also hierarchical with his reinforcement of ideas of filial piety and obedience to imperial power but more open about the potential for all individuals to work toward Sagehood. For this reason, Zhu Xi is somewhat less discriminatory with regard to women than Aquinas despite the image of Confucianism, particular neo-Confucianism, as patriarchal.

Therefore, we can see that metaphysics matters in how one views the world and how it is constituted. Buddhism retains its power to empower the masses, neo-Confucianism to maintain hierarchical power. Aristotle's metaphysics as manifest in his politics is used in support of conservative Catholicism and Sunni Islam. In the next few chapters, the dominant approaches are challenged but they continue to linger in the background.

8. Renaissance and revival (1300–1540)

This chapter discusses the political thought of the Renaissance and other forms of political renewal around the world. In all these cases there was a decline of the old order and the need for rebirth, specifically, the collapse of the Mongol Yuan dynasty in East Asia, attacks from Bedouins, Turks, and other non-Arab peoples on established Islamic settlements, and the decline of the Holy Roman Empire, the territorial ambitions of the Papacy and the rise of city-states in Italy and nation-states in Western Europe. The conflict between political power and religious belief also became more intense in this period. East Asian Buddhism was confronted by militant neo-Confucianism, Islam by non-Arab forms of political organization and social ethos, and Europe saw increasing conflict between the Church and the state.

It is in this context that there was a revival of classical thought but largely reinterpreted to find practical solutions to current problems. The thinkers who arose were often trying to advise rulers, though generally unsuccessfully, including Barani, Griots of Mali, Kitabatake, ibn Khaldūn and Machiavelli. These last two are indisputably key figures in world political thought, and had a great impact: Machiavelli was influential more immediately and since, but ibn Khaldūn grew in significance later (eighteenth and nineteenth centuries forward). In many ways, all of these thinkers were merely producing typical "mirror for prince" advice for rulers. Yet, it is also significant that history plays more of a role in the work of the key thinkers in this period. Once again, the question of the role of the people, the masses, was raised with hints of "modern" views of the purity and strength of simple people versus the corruption of the civilized. There was also an increased emphasis on the role of women who are both reviled and praised to a greater degree than in the past. The term Renaissance might seem Western but it aptly covers many of the developments around the world in this period.

THE REBIRTH OF POLITICAL THOUGHT IN AN ERA OF DRAMATIC CONFLICT

In East Asia, regime change and the impetus for innovation in political thought arose due to the rise and fall of the Mongol Yuan dynasty. In Japan, the Kamakura Shogunate (1185–1333) fell indirectly due to the attempted invasion of the Mongols because the regime had to maintain its vigilance and defensive fortifications against possible future Mongol attacks, which put a severe strain on its resources. Growing unrest led to an attempt to restore to power the Imperial Court that had been sidelined under the military-based Kamakura government. In 1324 Emperor Go-Daigo (後醍醐天皇 1288–1339) led an uprising, and though he was soon defeated and sent into exile on an island off the coast of Japan, he escaped and was assisted by attacks from other warlords on Kamakura. Ultimately, the emperor was betrayed by one of the powerful military family allies who initially supported him, the Ashikaga. This family went on to create their own Shogunate, often called the Muromachi (室町) or Ashikaga (足利) Shogunate (1338–1573). Go-Daigo and his children tried to re-establish the Imperial Court with his remaining followers but the Ashikaga set up a rival Court based on a different line (branch family) of the Imperial family so that, for about 60 years, there was a Southern Court, of Go-Daigo and his successors (son and grandson) and a Northern Court backed by the Ashikaga. The Southern Court only succumbed when Go-Daigo's grandson naively accepted a deal to alternate power with the Northern Court, but when the Northern Court surrendered as part of the agreement, the Ashikaga did not honor it. The Southern Court/Northern Court conflict (*Nanboku no sōran* 南北朝の争乱) was mainly notable for the effort of one of Emperor Go-Daigo's advisors, Kitabatake Chikafusa, to legitimize the regime using a combination of neo-Confucian logic and native Japanese ideas.

The decline of the Yuan dynasty helped bring about the demise of the Goryeo kingdom in Korea, especially given the association of the regime with the Mongols and the role of Buddhism in supporting the state while the Mongols dominated. The idea that Buddhism was particularly corrupt is probably an exaggeration of later Literati historians but the complicity of Buddhists in Mongol domination led to Buddhism going on the defensive in both China and Korea. In this context, the Literati began to become interested in neo-Confucian, including its vigorous attacks on Buddhism. Neo-Confucianism or Song learning had already been introduced into Goryeo as early as the thirteenth century by the scholar An Hyang (安珦 1243–1306). An Hyang visited China under the Mongol Yuan dynasty and used the opportunity to transcribe the collected writings of Zhu Xi, which he brought back to Korea. However, the key figure in the neo-Confucian revival was Yi Saek (李穡 1328–1396) who played a crucial role in the local adaptation of Zhu Xi philosophy to Korea. He studied neo-Confucianism in the Yuan dynasty and opened an academy after his return to Goryeo. Many of his students, such as Gwon Geun (權近 1352–1409), transformed neo-Confucian into an ideology for overthrowing the Buddhist kingdom of Goryeo and establishing neo-Confucian Joseon. Of these, the most important of these students was Jeong Dojeon (鄭道傳 1324–1398). This has been called the Korean Renaissance, with some justification.[1]

Conflict and regime change is also the context in which Islamic political theorists wrote. It is important to point out that this thought focused on the defense of Islamic states and not aggression. In fact, after the initial conquests of Muhammad and his immediate successors, generally Islam spread through relatively peaceful means, mainly by trade and educational activities, in Africa from the eighth to the seventeenth century and Southeast Asia from the thirteenth to the sixteenth century. Within Ghana, for example, Muslims were employed as administrators even though kings continued to rely on traditional religious ritual in support of the state. Islam was also involved in the creation of the Mali Empire in the thirteenth century, when a Mande (Mandingo) leader, Sundiata, of the Keita clan absorbed the remains of the Ghana Empire and established the empire, a story considered in some detail below. The Mali Empire became very prosperous due to control of the regional salt and gold trade. It expanded to the point it drove the Tuareg, a Berber people, out of Timbuktu and established the city as a center of learning and commerce. The peak of Mali's power was the fourteenth century, when Mansa Musa (c. 1280–1337, r. 1312–1337) made his hajj (حج) pilgrimage to Mecca with 500 slaves, each holding a bar of gold. Mansa Musa also brought back Islamic scholars who tied Mali more deeply into the Islamic civilization. After the reign of Mansa Suleyman (r. 1341–1360), however, Mali started to decline. Mossi cavalry raided from the south and the Tuareg attacked from the north. At the same time, the empire of Great Fulo (1490–1776) arose in the west. In 1546 the Songhai Empire (c. 1464–1591) conquered the ancient Mali capital of Niani, and though it was recovered temporarily, it was lost again to attacks by the Bambara, which led to the final collapse of the Mali Empire in 1670.

The Mamluk empires were important to the story of the expansion of Islam in the Near East and India. The *mamluks* (مملوك) were slaves who were taken from their parents when very young and trained under strict religious and military education to become Muslim soldiers. Since they had no family ties or social status and, given their discipline and education, they often became trusted officials. After training ended, they were attached to the patron who had purchased them and funded their

---

[1] Soyoung Lee (2010) "Art of the Korean Renaissance, 1400–1600," The Metropolitan Museum of Art: http://www.metmuseum.org/toah/hd/kore/hd_kore.htm (accessed November 17, 2017).

education. Patrons hired them out or used their services to gain influence and wealth. The *mamluk* was bound by ties of loyalty to the patron and to his fellow *mamluks* under the same patron. Eventually some of these *mamluks* rose to high office and a few formed their own dynasties, including the Khwarazmian dynasty in Persia (1077–1231), the Mamluk Sultanate in Cairo (1250–1517) and the Mamluk Sultanate in Delhi (1206–1290).

The Islamic political thinkers in this chapter all operated in this context, including Ziauddin Barani and ibn Khaldūn. Ziauddin Barani (ضياء الدين بَرَني b. 1285–d. 1357) was from an aristocratic Muslim family, which had held high government posts for generations under the Tughlaq dynasty (سلسل تغلق c. 1320–1414) of the Delhi Sultanate, particularly toward the end of the dynasty when it was in decline and soon to be overwhelmed by the Timurid dynasty (تيموريان 1370–1507), founded by Timur (known as Tamerlane in the West). Barani never held an official post, but was a *nadim* (companion) of Muhammad bin Tughlaq for seventeen years and was close to his Amir, Khusro. After Tughlaq was deposed, Barani wrote books to gain the attention of the new sultan, Firuz Shah Tughluq, but Barani failed to obtain a post and died in poverty in 1357.

The work of ibn Khaldūn (بن خلدون b. 1332–d. 1406) was also heavily influenced by the political changes of his time. From the tenth to thirteenth centuries, there was a large-scale migration of Bedouins who began to attack Islamic settlements in North Africa. This was also the time during which the Ottoman Empire (1299–1453) began its rise. The Ottomans began in the late eleventh century as a group of small Muslim emirates of Turkic origins that arose in different areas of Anatolia and were employed to defend Seljuq Sultanate of Rûm on its border with the Byzantine Empire, leading to the migration of many Turks to Asia Minor. However, in 1073 and following the victory of the Seljuqs over the Byzantines at the Battle of Manzikert, the Ottomans threw off Seljuq authority and created their own state. Established Muslim states in the Middle East were also under attack by Timur who eventually ruled an extensive area including Mesopotamia, Anatolia, the Caucasus, Persia and large parts of Central Asia as well as northern India. Ibn Khaldun had direct experience of all these new forces and it is reflected in his political analysis.

The context of the Renaissance in Europe was the decline of the Holy Roman Empire, the increasing territorial power of the Papacy, and the rise of city-states in Italy. Conflict between the city-states (and the Papal state) in the Italian peninsula led to often brutal wars, usually made worse by the use of mercenaries. There was also the period in which Europe saw the emergence of nation-states and centralizing monarchs, such as Henry the VIII in England. Most important for Italy and Machiavelli, was the rise of France as a major European power and French intervention in Italy.

HISTORY AND ITS ROLE IN POLITICAL THOUGHT

History plays a major role in the development of political thought in this period. Of course, works of history existed prior to these times such as the work of Ssu Ma in the Han dynasty, the *Kojiki* and *Nihongi* in ancient Japan, and the ancient Greek historians, such as Thucydides and Polybius, and the Roman historians, such as Livy. Indeed, the works of history in this period sought to emulate these classics but there was much more emphasis on using history to find regular patterns of historical dynamics than in previous works.

East Asian history in this period, including that written by the Literati, appears to have been influenced by Chan (Zen) Buddhism. There is a strong emphasis on the historical succession of Chan lineage as a key aspect of the legitimacy of the sect with the argument that Chan had a pure traceable lineage that went back to its founder, Bohdidharma (बोधिधर्म 菩提達磨 fl. c. 5–6 centuries), and then back to the Buddha. Although this focus on lineage may have been influenced by (and been an influence on) family temple ancestor worship of the family of Confucius and other great Literati families, the idea that each monk is ordained by a monk that ultimately can trace lineage back to Buddha existed before contact with Literati culture. The legitimacy of direct lineage and the documentation of succession has an influence on the role of history in later political thought and was important to development of similar efforts at historical reconstruction, fabricated or not, in much of East Asia, and not just amongst Buddhists. Kitabatake Chikafusa's work *Jinnō Shōtōki* or *Chronicle of the Direct Succession of Gods and Sovereigns*, which will be considered below in some detail, follows this logic of legitimacy through unbroken succession. In Dai Viet, too, the Thien (Chan/Zen) inspired historical work, *Outstanding Figures in the Zen Community* [of Vietnam] (*Thiền Uyển Tập Anh* 禪苑集英, c. 1337) follows this pattern. More important from a political point of view is the *Collection of Stories on Spirits of the Departed in the Viet Realm* (*Việt Điện U Linh Tập* 粵甸幽靈集), compiled by Lý Tế Xuyên (李濟川 fl. 1400), which not only explains the role played by key historical figures but also their spiritual significance. Again, the influence of Chan or Zen on the development of East Asian historical tradition and in turn on political thought is notable.

In Africa, written history did not appear until much later. Initially, we are dependent on Islamic historians, such as ibn Khaldūn, for information on Africa. However, there is a rich African oral tradition, and as in the case of the oral transmission of early Buddhism, its validity should not be dismissed. The epic of Sundiata, for example, tells the story of Sundiata Keita (c. 1217–c. 1255) and the founding of the Mali Empire. As an epic, it is only semi-historical, but it appears to be a well-attested oral tradition, transmitted by generations of *griots* (story-tellers and official advisors), with some versions written down in the 1890s but most recently collated from different versions starting in the 1960s.[2] The same issue arises for the constitution set forth by Sundiata, the *Kouroukan Fougan*, which has been reconstructed from oral tradition in a regional workshop held in Kankan, Guinea in 1998 under United Nation auspices.[3] These texts are discussed further below but have historical and political significance.

Islamic political history, in contrast, was well developed in the period covered by this chapter. For example, Ziauddin Barani wrote history of the Delhi Sultanate up to the time of his contemporary Sultan Firuz Shah Tughlaq (1309–1388) called *Tarikh-i-Firuz Shahi* (تاريخ فيروز شاهي) or Firuz Shah's "History" in 1357,[4] which was the complementary work to his political theory in his *Fatwa-i-Jahandari* (فتاوى جهانداري)[5] discussed below. Ibn Khaldūn wrote many works but viewed his history of the world, *al-Kitābu l-'ibar* (الـعبر كتاب) literally "Book of Lessons") as his greatest achievement. However, it is *The Muqaddimah* (مقدّمة) or "Prolegomena" to this history where he sets out the basic principles of historical dynamics as he understands them, which we examine below.[6]

History was also essential to the development of Renaissance political thought in Italy. Leonardo Bruni's (1370–1444) *Historiae Florentini populi* (History of the Florentine People) is the first to use the division of history into Ancient, Medieval and Modern though it follows Petrarch, who saw the end of the classical period of Greek and Roman learning as a plunging into darkness (*tenebrae*). This History not only removed the heavy hand of Christian interpretation from history, making it the first secular history since ancient Rome, it also constitutes a work of political thought including themes that are later developed by Machiavelli.[7] Bruni's biography of Cicero, as well as his studies of Dante and Petrarch, demonstrated the meaning of humanism because they put humans at the center of historical

---

[2] D.T. Niane (2006) *Sundiata – an Epic of Old Mali*, 2nd edn, Harlow: Longman-Pearson.
[3] S. Kouyaté ed. (1998) "La charte de Kurukan Fuga," http://www.frabenin.org/IMG/pdf/kurukan_fuga.pdf (accessed May 20, 2017).
[4] Ziauddin Barani; H.M. Elliot trans. and John Dowson ed. (1871) "Tarikh-i Firoz Shahi" in *The History of India, by its Own Historians: The Muhammadan Period*, vol. III, London: Teubner and Co.: 93–269.
[5] Ziauddin Barani; Mohammed Habib and Afsar U.S. Khan trans. (1961) *The Political Theory of the Delhi Sultanate including a translation of Ziauddin Barani's Fatawa-i Jahandari, circa, 1358–9 AD*, Allahabad: Kitab Mahal: 1–116.
[6] Ibn Khaldûn; Rosenthal Franz trans. (1958) *The Muqaddimah: An Introduction to History* (Bollingen Series, XLIII), 3 volumes, New York, NY: Pantheon Books.
[7] James Hankins (2009) "A Mirror for Statesmen: Leonardo Bruni's History of the Florentine People," Unpublished paper, Harvard University. https://dash.harvard.edu/bitstream/handle/1/2958221/BruniHistoryHJ.pdf?sequence=4 (accessed May 20, 2017).

attention rather than metaphysics or divine providence. Of course, history is essential to understanding the work of Machiavelli, as we will see below, including his own Florentine Histories (*Istorie fiorentine*) as well as his works "The Prince" (*Il Principe*) and "Discourses on the First Ten Books of Titus Livy" (*Discorsi sopra la prima deca di Tito Livio*), based on the work of the Roman historian Livy. Renaissance Florence also produced Francesco Guicciardini (1483–1540), best known as a historian who focused on official documents and systematic analysis of people and events. Guicciardini was a friend of Niccolò Machiavelli and they seemed to have influenced each other, though Guicciardini was mainly critical of Machiavelli because Guicciardini thought Machiavelli erred in drawing clear conclusions from complex events and that Machiavelli was wrong to consider ancient Rome an ideal state. Guicciardini also wrote a "History of Florence" (*Storia Florentina*) as well as works of political analysis, such as the *Ricordi politici e civili*, *Dialogo del reggimento di Firenze*, and *Discorsi politici*.

For these thinkers, history becomes the substitute for metaphysics. That is, what has existed in history begins to constitute evidence for what is possible as empirical fact or regularity, rather than metaphysical speculation regarding the ideal of what is possible. This is why ibn Khaldūn and Machiavelli may seem modern and are associated with modernity. However, in all these civilizations, there was still conflict between religion and political power with religion playing an important role, even in these apparently secular writers.

BELIEFS AND AUTHORITY IN THE RENAISSANCE

It would be anachronistic to suggest that these thinkers set out to substitute historical or philosophical truths for religious or metaphysical dogma because religion still played a role. It is true, for example, that neo-Confucianism was associated with the suppression of Buddhism but even though Emperor Go-Daigo staffed his Court with scholar-political nobles who were familiar with Song neo-Confucianism, such as Kitabatake Chikafusa, at the same time, he had two of his sons appointed in posts at the top of the Tendai religious hierarchy. Indeed, one of his portraits shows him in monk robes and holding the instruments of Buddhist worship used by monks. Zen had not assumed the dominant position in Japan that it had in the Song and late Gyoreo dynasties nor had popular religions such as True Pure Land Buddhism begun to undermine political power. For this reason, Kitabatake's neo-Confucianism is less pronounced and obscured by his attempt to legitimate imperial rule by referring to traditional beliefs.

Kitabatake Chikafusa (北畠親房 1293–1354) wrote the *Jinnō Shōtōki*

(神皇正統) or "Chronicle of the Direct Succession of Gods and Sovereigns" in 1339, to attack the Ashikaga Shogunate. This was because the Ashikaga had become the enemy of his patron Emperor Go-Daigo and, perhaps more importantly, Kitabatake aimed at portraying the conflict between the Ashikaga and the emperor as a struggle between the warrior class and the more refined nobility of the Court.[8] In it he analyzes the reigns of Japanese emperors in order to support Go-Daigo's claim to power. Even though much of the logic in Kitabatake's writing is Literati thought, mainly the Han/Tang Literati synthesis as well as clear elements of Song dynasty Literati thought,[9] as with many Japanese writers, such as Nichiren, there is an appeal to national pride. This nationalist aspect was later highlighted by Japanese extremists but it is not key to Kitabatake's argument. The core of Kitabatake's claim is the unbroken lineage of the Imperial house. In fact, the logic of the work is largely neo-Confucian in inspiration even if it includes passages which in retrospect appear nationalistic. In fact, excessive emphasis on nationalism can lead one to ignore other important aspects.

The *Jinnō Shōtōki* focuses on the centrality of political rule based on the emperor and not on Buddhist power. Of course, there are Buddhist aspects, such as when Kitabatake claims that the "Diamond Mountain" in the "Flower Garland" (*Kegon*) Sutra refers to the Kogōn mountain in Japan, but this is merely a passing reference to the "Flower Garland Sutra", which, as we have seen, has been used often in East Asia as a way of bolstering central authority by providing for the integration of disparate elements in the political system into a sense of political community subordinated to the monarchy. Kitabatake's discussion of the Imperial regalia (mirror, jewel and sword), however, is more reminiscent of Literati theories of rule when he states that:

> The [Great Sun] Goddess's commands on the Three Regalia must indicate the proper methods of governing the country. The mirror does not possess anything of its own but, without selfish desires, reflects all things, showing their true qualities. Its virtue lies in its response to these qualities and, as such, represents the source of all honesty. The virtue of the jewel lies in its gentleness and submissiveness; it is the source of compassion. The virtue of the sword lies in its strength and resolution; it is the source of wisdom. Unless these three are joined in a ruler, it will be difficult indeed to govern the country.[10]

---

[8] Kitabatake Chikafusa; H. Paul Varley trans. (1980) *A Chronicle of Gods and Sovereigns: Jinnō Shōtōki of Kitabatake Chikafusa*, New York, NY: Columbia University Press.

[9] 下川玲子 (Shimokawa Ryōko) (2001) 「北畠親房の儒学」 (Kitabatake no Jugaku), 東京: ぺりかん社 (Tokyo: Perikan Sha).

[10] W.T. De Bary, Donald Keene, George Tanabe and Paul Varley eds (2010) *Sources of Japanese Tradition, Volume 1: From Earliest Times to 1600*, 2nd edn, New York, NY: Columbia University Press: 362.

These three virtues are similar to that of the *Book of History*, an early Literati classic, though they do not map onto the following three principles in a way that does not require some modification: (1) correctness and straightforwardness; (2) strong rule; and (3) mild rule. It is true that Kitabatake's focus is on the legitimacy of the claims of Imperial lineage by tracing them back to the Sun Goddess Amaterasu, which is emphasized over the ideologies of Buddhism and Literati ideas, but this notion of lineage is consistent with both Buddhist and Literati ideas of legitimacy. In fact, one could argue that Kitabatake is trying to unify the different system of thought in Japan to bolster the claims of the Imperial house. In the short-run, however, neo-Confucianism did not really take hold in Japan, which makes sense given that the victor in the struggle for power against Go-Daigo and his advisors, the Ashikaga Shogunate was better served with existing Buddhist and Literati ideas and practices.

The tension between religious establishment and the political elite, that is, between Buddhism versus neo-Confucianism is starker in Korea. The key figure in the introduction of neo-Confucianism in the Joseon state in Korea was Jeong Dojeon. His father was a high government official but his mother was a concubine, and not a wife, which made it very difficult for Jeong to secure office himself at first. His situation improved when he became a student of Yi Saek. Like Yi, Jeong Dojeon opposed Buddhism as corrupt, nihilistic and antinomian based on arguments from Han Yu, the Cheng brothers, and Zhu Xi. In his *Bulssi Japbyeon* (佛氏雜辨) or "Array of Critiques Against Buddhism," Jeong argued that the government, including the king himself, exists for the sake of the people. Its legitimacy could only come from benevolent public service.[11] If the king and his ministers failed to rule well by following the correct path, then they can be overthrown. This was used to justify the destruction of the Goryeo along the lines of the mandate of Heaven in classical Literati thought. Jeong divided society into three classes: a large lower class of agricultural laborers and craftsmen, a middle class of Literati, and a small upper class of bureaucrats. Anyone outside this system, including Buddhist monks, shamans, and entertainers, he considered a threat to the social fabric. Even though Buddhists may use similar terms to the Literati, Jeong insisted that Buddhists deny the existence of reality and are not interested in making the world in which we live a better place.

It is in response to this text that the monk Gihwa (己和 1376–1433) wrote his defense of Buddhism. Gihwa was the student of the last Korean

---

[11] Jeong Dojeon; Charles Muller trans. (2005) "Array of Critiques against Buddhism" (Bulssi Japbyeon) http://www.hm.tyg.jp/~acmuller/jeong-gihwa/hyeonjeongnon.html (no longer accessible).

State Preceptor Muhak (無學 1327–1405) and he followed on from Jinul's attempts to unify Seon (Zen) and *Hak* (學 or text-based) Buddhism. In his *Hyeonjeong non* (顯正論) or "Exposition of the Correct," Gihwa countered the rise of neo-Confucianism with a defense of Buddhism and criticized neo-Confucians for a lack of clarity in regard to the relative merits of reflection on the ideal and the realization of these ideals.[12] Gihwa argues that the fundamental values of the three teachings (Literati, Taoism and Buddhism or 三教 ch. *sanjiao*, kr. *samjiào*) are not different, and Buddhism can correct the mind and lead to cultivation as much as Literati thought so can also regulate the family, govern the state, and bring peace to the world. He goes on to point out that Literati claim to reject rewards and punishments as incapable of reforming humans yet still rely on them but Buddhism goes further by reforming the inner mind to steer people away from evil behavior. Buddhism is also superior in that it prohibits harming other beings.

Gihwa was fighting a losing battle. The rise of neo-Confucianism and its attack on Buddhism is credited with undermining the legitimacy of the Goryeo dynasty and served to create the foundation of the next dynasty, the Joseon. When Yi Seonggye (李 成桂 1335–1408) established himself as founder of the Joseon dynasty he did so with the support of the neo-Confucian movement, including most prominently Jeong Dojeon, and was quick to suppress Buddhism (崇儒廃佛). Increasing restrictions were placed on Buddhists with the number of temples reduced from hundreds to 36, Buddhist monks and nuns were forced out of cities and begging for alms was outlawed, age restrictions were placed on entry into the *sangha* so that only those older and less economically productive could become monks, and Buddhist funerals were banned, particularly for the elite, in order to cut off a key source of income for monks. The original doctrinal or text-based schools (*gyo* 教) were forced to merge with either the Seon (Chan/Zen) and Cheontae (Tiāntai/Tendai) sects and eventually Cheontae was forced to merge with Seon. There were subsequent limited revivals of Buddhist influence in the Joseon dynasty, most notably under King Myeongjon (明宗 1534–1567, r. 1545–1567) and his mother, Queen Munjeong (文定王后 1502–1565), who was the patron of the Monk Bou (普雨 1515–1565), a promoter of a form of *yeombul* Seon (念佛禪), a Seon/Pure Land hybrid, which was popular with the masses but disdained by the elite, especially Literati. Monks were also able to gain some respect when they formed an effective fighting force of "Righteous Monks" (*uisa* 義士) during the Japanese invasion of Joseon in the sixteenth century. Still,

---

[12] Gihwa; Charles Muller trans. (2005) "Exposition of the Correct" (Hyeonjeong Non), http://www.hm.tyg.jp/~acmuller/jeong-gihwa/hyeonjeongnon.html (no longer accessible).

for most of the Joseon dynasty, Buddhism was completely subordinated to the state and merely tolerated in a limited form.

Buddhism was still dominant when neo-Confucianism arrived in Dai Viet and initially the two co-existed. During the Trần dynasty (1225–1400), in which Buddhism was predominant, Literati education and systems of rule were still important and played a role in the training of government officials. The National Educational Academy (Quốc Học Viện 國學院) was established in June 1253 to teach more of a neo-Confucian curriculum based on the Four Books (四書) and Five Classics (五經) to potential future Court officials (thái học sinh 太學生). However, the attempt of neo-Confucian Literati to gain more influence in Dai Viet came at the end of the reign of the devout Buddhist Emperor Trần Minh (陳明宗 1300–1357). Even though Trần Minh's period of rule combined both Buddhism and Literati thought with influences from neo-Confucianism, and he was one of the most successful emperors of Đại Việt, both in his own right, when he ruled from 1314 to 1329, and when he acted as regent and co-ruler with his sons, the Trần Hiến Emperor (陳憲宗 1319–1341, r. 1329–1341) and Trần Dụ Emperor (陳裕宗 1336–1369, r. 1341–1369), he was also blamed for the subsequent decline of the Tran dynasty by the Literati due to what they argued was his excessive support for Buddhism. This is not completely surprising because this attack on the legacy of Trần Minh by the Literati was part of a systematic attack on Buddhism as part of a campaign to remove Buddhist influence from government inspired by Song neo-Confucianism.[13] For example, the Literati official Truong Han Sieu (張漢超 ?–1354) expressed open opposition to the influence of Buddhism at Court and the need for neo-Confucian reform.[14] When the Le (黎) dynasty formed in 1428, Literati influence became dominant with King Le Thanh (黎聖宗 1442–1497) adopting a clear neo-Confucian ideology, earning his reign the Literati epitaph "Flood of Virtue" (*Hong Duc* 鴻德), which became the basis for the "Good Book of Government of the Hong Duc Era" (*Hong Duc thien chinh thu* 鴻德善政書) compiled in 1540 but based on Le Thanh's reign a half century earlier. At the end, however, even though Buddhism was removed from the highest levels of influence of the late Tran dynasty, the Le dynasty still retained ties to the Buddhist establishment and Buddhism was not suppressed to the degree it was in Joseon Korea.

In Islam, we also see the beginnings of the tension between fundamentalism and political authority. For example, the preacher ibn Taymiyyah (ابن تيمية), who was born in 1263 in the Seljuk Sultanate of

---

[13] Dutton et al., eds (2012) *Sources of Vietnamese Tradition*: 68–70.
[14] Dutton et al., eds (2012) *Sources of Vietnamese Tradition*: 57–58.

Rum but died in 1328 in the Mamluk Sultanate of Cairo, was often in conflict with the authorities for his fundamentalist beliefs. His surname is based on a female ancestor, Taimiyatu, famed for her scholarship and piety. Ibn Taymiyyah was a student of the conservative Hanbali school of Islamic jurisprudence, and his *Political Shariyah on Reforming the Ruler and the Ruled*[15] (al-Siyāsah al-sharʻīyah fī iṣlāḥ al-rāʻī wa-al-raʻīyah السياسة الشرعية في إصلاح الراعي والرعية) is about consistency in applying the shari'a law as a prerequisite to political order. It is notable for insisting that the law must be applied without regard to social or political status and that the fines that allowed rich Muslim to escape the full punishment of shari'a law were effectively bribes in that they undermine the law by creating effective exemptions. Ibn Taymiyyah therefore insisted on strict punishments including stoning for adultery and cutting off hands and legs for theft as well as criminalizing drinking wine, flirting, and so on. He was also strongly opposed to lucky charms, relics and veneration of saints, including pilgrimage to saint's tombs. In order to enforce this strict code, he advocated a strong state to protect both religion (*din* دين) and manage mundane life in this world (*dunya* دنيا) as opposed to heaven. However, ibn Taymiyyah also insisted that rulers need guidance and are prone to error so need correcting as much as the ruled. His views on the fragility of political authority and duty to engage in *jihad* can partly be explained by the pressing external threat of the Mongols. His opposed rationalism in religion put a heavy emphasis on conservative views on the law, sin and bribery. Even in his own time, his views were considered extreme and he was often imprisoned for "literalism" by Mamluk Sultanate, and, in fact, he died in prison as a result.

Ziauddin Barani (ضياء الدين بَرَني b. 1285–d. 1357) in the Tughlaq dynasty (سلسله تغلق), from 1320 to 1414, of the Delhi Sultanate (سلطنة دهلي), from 1206 to 1526, was also very pious but not as extreme in his views as ibn Taymiyyah. His political theory is found in his book *Fatwa-i-Jahandari* (فتاوى جهان داري).[16] In it he argues that the final end of political society is the worship of God. It is God who raises up rulers to rule so a ruler must depend on God. He adopts the Persian notion of religion and temporal rulers as twins, which is natural given the Persian origins of the Delhi Sultanate. Yet, he goes further to argue that the world cannot be made right by rulers alone because prophets and learned religious scholars are also necessary to aid kings. The problem is that kingship is incompatible with some religious ideas and must often violate them. Thus, he seems

---

[15] Ibn Taymiyyah, Umar Farrukh trans. (2006) *The Political Shariyah on Reforming the Ruler and the Ruled*, Dijon: Dar ul Fiqh.
[16] Barani; Habib and Khan trans. (1961) *Fatawa-i Jahandari*: 1–116.

to agree with the criticism that the Sultanate is a Persian invention and un-Islamic, but in the absence of an effective Caliphate, the Sultanate must assume this role because, he argues, a king is necessary. It is only by the grace of God that the Sultan will be protected and redeemed by God in the future so must believe in God and do God's work. The king must demonstrate ability by appointing harsh officials to oversee the operations of government but also the king must appoint wise advisors to guide him. Good and evil are always locked in battle and evil cannot be eliminated. Only the king can keep evil in check. Rulers who are themselves evil will be punished by God.

Ibn Khaldūn was more focused on historical and social dynamics though the non-Muslim reader might feel that the constant references to God are a sign of piety and not mere ritual invocation. Khaldūn does note that the existence of these social dynamics are part of the world created by God and the fact of existence "attests to the necessity of group feeling for the caliphate" and that "The religious law would hardly ever make a requirement in contradiction to the requirements of existence. And God, He is exalted, knows better."[17] In short, his social science is compatible with the will of God, a position not unlike that taken by Christian scientists in the modern era.

In Europe at the time of the Renaissance, the role of religion was more directly and concretely institutionalized in the form of the Roman Catholic Church. Moreover, the Church had by this period acquired territory and, through mercenaries, military power to defend and expand its interests, particularly on the Italian peninsula. The political thought of Dante, Marsiglio of Padua, William of Ockham and Nicholas of Cusa were all centered on attempts to redefine the role of the Church in a way that aimed at reducing its secular involvements. Although usually considered medieval thinkers, the attack on papal authority and the case for the predominance of secular authority is the basis for both the Renaissance and the Reformation. Dante's (1265–1321) *De Monarchia* is a straightforward case for secular authority over the Papacy based on the idea of a universal empire of peace led by the Holy Roman Emperor.[18] This authority must be derived directly from God given to secular leaders and not through the Pope, as the Papacy argued. Similarly, the *Defensor Pacis* or "The Defender of the Peace" of Marsiglio or Marsilius of Padua (1275–1342) is based on naturalism and rationalism drawn from Averroism and Aristotelianism to argue for the

---

[17] Ibn Khaldûn; Rosenthal trans. (1958) *The Muqaddimah*: 402.

[18] Dante Alighieri; Aurelia Henry trans. (1904) *The De Monarchia of Dante Alighieri*, Boston, MA: Houghton, Mifflin and Co.; and Dante Alighieri; Prue Shaw trans. (1996) *Dante: Monarchy*, Cambridge: Cambridge University Press.

complete subordination of the Church to the secular state.[19] One should also note that William of Ockham (1287–1347) argued for the freedom of Christians from the pretentions of a worldly Papacy.[20] He defended Franciscans, so-called Spirituals, who advocated clerical poverty and had been excommunicated by Pope John XXII. William of Ockham looked to secular authority to defend minority views against papal inquisitions because Ockham viewed papal political power as an heretical innovation. Finally, Nicholas of Cusa (1401–1464) was involved in the movement for conciliar reform (including the Councils of Constance 1414–1418 and Basel 1431–1449) by trying to heal the rifts in the Church, including those arising from popular revolts led by Wycliffe and Hus, discussed in the next chapter. Nicholas argues that it is the whole body of the Church and not the Pope which should decide the direction of the Church through an agreement that maintains a harmonious concordance amongst all its parts – papacy, clergy, lay followers, and so on.[21] The Pope represents the unity and authority of the church but this must be brought into harmony by conciliation with the body of the church. In all these thinkers, there are elements of the case for ancient liberties and traditions mobilized against the arbitrary acts of the powerful but real reform of the Catholic Church did not occur until the Reformation tore it apart, as we shall see.

Despite his reputation, even Machiavelli recognizes the importance of religion, though one might suspect that he gives more role to *fortuna*, or luck, than divine providence.[22] Machiavelli does believe that there is a large degree of ability to choose and choose wisely despite the vagaries of fortune, because luck only rules half our lives. One can anticipate misfortune and prepare for it, though most individuals tend to stick to the practices that made them successful and fail to see the need to change until it is too late. Machiavelli's rejection of traditional moral norms is more problematic because, he argues that:

> [A] prince, especially a new one, cannot observe all those things for which men are esteemed, being often forced, in order to maintain the state, to act contrary

---

[19] Marsilius of Padua; Annabel Brett trans. (2005) *Marsilius of Padua: The Defender of the Peace*, Cambridge: Cambridge University Press.

[20] William of Ockham; John Kilcullen trans. and Arthur S. McGrade eds (1992) *William of Ockham: A Short Discourse on Tyrannical Government*, Cambridge: Cambridge University Press; and William of Ockham; John Kilcullen trans. and Arthur S. McGrade ed. (1995) *William of Ockham: "A Letter to the Friars Minor" and Other Writings*, Cambridge: Cambridge University Press.

[21] Nicholas of Cusa; Paul E. Sigmund (1996) *Nicholas of Cusa: The Catholic Concordance*, Cambridge: Cambridge University Press.

[22] Niccolò Machiavelli; Robert Adams trans. (1977) *The Prince*, New York, NY: Norton: 70–72.

to faith, friendship, humanity, and religion. Therefore it is necessary for him to have a mind ready to turn itself accordingly as the winds and variations of fortune force it, yet, as I have said above, not to diverge from the good if he can avoid doing so, but, if compelled, then to know how to set about it.[23]

This does not mean that Machiavelli sees no role for religion because he praises the Romans for relying on religion to reorganize their city, carry out enterprises and stop internal dissension. Moreover, a kingdom that relies only on the skill of its ruler is more fragile than one based on a fear of God. A ruler must organize the kingdom to maintain itself and in this process religion has a role.[24] Machiavelli seems morally neutral here and only interested in what works but so does ibn Khaldūn even if he is more conventionally pious. Ibn Khaldūn also saw a positive role for religion but primarily in the way it can promote social cohesion.

ETHICS, RIGHT AND WRONG WAYS TO RULE

The actual mechanics of rule for the main thinkers in this chapter, however, are distant from religion or metaphysics. They are still conscious of ethics, in terms of the right and wrong ways to rule, but these are based on their reading of history and sociopolitical dynamics. For example, Kitabatake believed the problem with Japan at the time he was writing was conflict created by an unlimited number of people claiming a limited amount of land. He viewed the land constables (*shugo* 守護), de facto owners of land, and their stewards (*jitō* 地頭), who both were in theory agents of the Imperial Court, as land-hungry, and writes that the practices that developed at the beginning of the Kamakura period were against rational principles of government. Kitabatake wanted to return to the Tang Literati inspired governmental structures of the Taihō Era and the Ritsuryo state. Ancient Japan and other states organized on Imperial centralism had the land owned in theory by the state in the name of the emperor even if it was distributed (and often redistributed) to the nobility in accordance with their office at Court. From Kitabatake's point of view, the self-serving behavior of those who nominally owned and managed the land was not proper behavior because they should not be land owners, they are merely there to serve the emperor. Kitabatake did not seek to abolish the distinction between great warrior families (*bushi* 武士) and court nobility (*kuge*

---

[23] Niccolò Machiavelli; William K. Marriot trans. (1908) *The Prince*, London: J.M. Dent: 143–144.

[24] Niccolò Machiavelli; Ninian Hill Thomson trans. (1883) *Discourses on the First Decade of Titus Livius*, London: Kegan Paul, Trench and Co.: 50–51.

公家) but he saw the existing system of land tenure and tax collection as the basis for undue power of the *bushi*, and he viewed the power of the *bushi* and the Shogunate as a threat to the power of Imperial House. The emphasis on land holding is Mencian in origin, thus Literati (Confucian) but of course based on later Chinese Imperial practice, which also advocated the subordination of officials, such as the *bushi*, to the Court as part of a centralized state.

The rise of neo-Confucian Learning did not necessarily lead to a more ethical approach to rule in the Joseon dynasty. For example, Jeong Dojeon, the key figure in the adoption of neo-Confucianism was killed in the First "Strife" of Princes, the very unfilial bloody battles among princes of the Court to gain power, when he tried to advocate the supremacy of ministerial rule over direct rule by the king. There were some strong Literati inspired rulers, such as King Sejong (世宗 1397–1450, r. 1418–1450), the fourth and perhaps greatest monarch of the dynasty, who used the neo-Confucian approach to reform the legal code, encouraged science and technology, established economic stability and is credited with the creation of the Korean alphabet, Hangul. He also engaged in typical Legalist inspired activities such as the dispatch of military campaigns to the north where he put in place the *Samin* Policy (徙民政策) to attract new settlers to the region by colonizing disputed lands in the north of the Korean peninsula and attacked Japanese pirates in the seas around Korea. In contrast, King Sejo (世祖 1417–1468, r. 1455–1468) seized power from his brother in a coup d'état and assassinated the Literati scholar-officials who protested his actions. He generally weakened the role of Literati ministerial advice and strengthened the powers of the Court by promoting and enriching a small oligarchy that became known as the Hungu faction (勳舊派). Attacks on the Literati intensified in the reign of Prince Yeonsan (燕山君 1476–1506, r. 1494–1506), who carried out purges (*sahwa* 士禍) against leading Literati, torturing and executing many. Lower ranking officials were finally able to remove him and this gave rise to the Sarim Faction (士林派) of Literati-officials, who were in favor of a strict interpretation of neo-Confucianism. The Sarim Faction rose to dominance in the reign of King Jungjong (中宗 1488–1544, r. 1506–1544) under the Sarim Official Jo Gwangjo (趙光祖 1482–1519). The subsequent period is known for a flourishing of neo-Confucian scholarship, particular the work of two key scholars, Yi Hwang (李滉 1501–1570) and Yi I (李珥 1536–1584).

In West Africa, the "Epic of Sundiata" is revealing of the logic of rule.[25] It is a story about Naré Maghann Konaté, a Mandinka king who one day

---

[25] D.T. Niane (2006) *Sundiata – an Epic of Old Mali*, 2nd edn, Harlow: Longman-Pearson.

received a hunter at his court who prophesized that if Konaté married an ugly woman, she would give birth to a son who would be a powerful ruler. Konaté already had a son, Dankaran Toumani Keïta but when he met an ugly, hunchbacked woman named Sogolon, he married her and she gave birth to another son, Sundiata Keita, who seemed to be set to fulfill the prophecy. Keita was unable to walk as a child but was given the honor of his own *griot* advisor/storyteller so that the two would grow up together and trust and nurture one another. When Naré Maghann Konaté (c. 1224) died, his first son, Dankaran Toumani, assumed the throne despite Konaté's wishes that Sundiata be king. Faced with this usurpation of his rightful place, Sundiata learned to walk and grew stronger. The new king Dankaran Toumani began to view Sundiata as a threat, and forced Sundiata and his mother into exile. Yet, Dankaran Toumani was himself forced from the throne by an attack by a Sosso sorcerer king who ruled over and oppressed the Mandinka people. The Mandinka appealed to Sundiata to help them and Sundiata and his allies fought and defeated the Sosso. Sundiata was crowned with the title *Mansa*, or "king of kings" and his reign constituted the beginning of the Mali Empire. Sundiata is also believed to have brought together a *Gbara* (assembly) of nobles and notables and presented them with an oral constitution known as the *Kouroukan Fougan*.[26]

The *Kouroukan Fougan* recognized the ruling clans (lineages) as representatives of the *Gbara*. There were sixteen clans in the *Djon-Tan-Nor-Woro* (quiver carriers) or warriors who protected the kingdom. There were also four clans in the *Mori-Kanda-Lolou* (guardians of the faith) who were advisors in Islamic jurisprudence. There were four *nyamakala* clans who were effectively guilds, including metalworking and tanners. There were four clans of *djeli* (masters of speech), the *griots*, who remembered and recited history, with history important to the legitimacy of the empire. There were also five clans of *marabouts* who as teachers of Islam were to be respected. Finally, there were representatives of different age groups who were to be involved when the king was to make important decisions. All these clans and groups were represented in the *Gbara*.

In the *Kouroukan Fougan*, the people are exhorted to be satisfied with the work of their lawful representatives. The constitution also guarantees the right to life and physical integrity so murder is punished with death. There is a system of supervision to fight against laziness and idleness. Emphasis is also placed on the need for *sanankunya* (joking relationships) and the *tanamannyonya* (blood pacts) which are the basis for mutual

---

[26] Kouyaté ed. (1998) "La charte de Kurukan Fuga."

respect in society. *Sanankuya* is a long-standing West African social tradition where playful banter should be exchanged and was seen here as a civic duty. The main aim appears to be promotion of tolerance and solidarity. All members of society, not just parents, were responsible for the education of children by transmitting societal values and basic education, and particular emphasis was put on not offending the talented (*nyaras*). There was also an emphasis on ethics. One article of the constitution insisted that vanity indicates weakness and humility is associated with greatness. Citizens were told that they can kill the enemy in war, but must not humiliate him. Members of society must never betray one another and keep their word of honor, though "Lies that have lived for 40 years should be considered like truths." Finally, there was a basic equality in the constitution in that anyone who breaks the rules will be punished and all members of society are required to ensure the effective implementation of the law.

Despite the constitutional position of Islamic scholars, conversion of the population to Islam was gradual. Since the power of the ruler was rooted in traditional spiritual concepts, Sundiata did not openly convert to Islam but Muslims with literacy skills were employed in the Court as secretaries and accountants. Islam was openly practiced by Sundiata's son Uli I (1225–1270), who made a pilgrimage to Mecca, but *Mansas* continued to allow a role to be played by traditional gods, rituals and festivals.

In the more established Islamic kingdoms of Mediterranean North Africa, individuals such as ibn Khaldūn were trained in philosophy including al-Farabi and ibn Rushd as a result of which ibn Khaldūn became interested in Plato and Aristotle. He had one of the best Islamic educations of his day including logic and mathematics under the top scholars of his time, and far in advance of the West at the time. In the *Muqaddimah* (مقدّمة) or "Prolegomena" to his world history, ibn Khaldūn puts forward the theory that all civilizations, no matter how great, eventually decay. Civilizations are replaced by groups, usually viewed as barbarians, who have a cohesive form of social solidarity that is the basis of their strength. This is the basis for ibn Khaldūn's central concept of *asabiyya* (عصبيّة) often translated as "social cohesion." This solidarity is common in tribes and similar small kinship groups; but other groups with a sense of shared endeavor can also manifest this solidarity. Shared religious beliefs can enhance this cohesion. Ibn Khaldūn classifies human societies or *al-umran* (العمران) into two types, civilized life or urbanism (*hadara* حضارة) and nomadic life (*badawa* بداوة). Urban life is easier and more attractive but it leads a society to become accustomed to luxury and unwilling to make sacrifices to fight. Nomadic society is attracted to the wealth of urban areas and attempts to conquer them. The group solidarity of small nomadic bands makes them strong and successful in battle. However, once nomads conquer an urban area, they became accustomed to luxury and become as weak over time as those they conquered. They, too, are in turn conquered by new nomadic groups. In this way, there is a historical system of success, domination, decay and demise. The period of domination can be prolonged promoting religious ideology or the urban civilization can delay its decay by attempts to incorporate of dynamic cultures, such as nomads, into their civilization.

In Europe, the Renaissance starts with Petrarch (1304–1374), who is considered the "Father of Humanism" due to a strong interest in collecting ancient Greek texts. It should also be remembered that many humanists were associated with the Catholic Church in this period, including Petrarch. By the mid-fifteenth century humanist education was widespread. The advent of mass printing in the early sixteenth century further promoted humanism and created the basis for the Reformation as well. The renaissance of classical learning gave impetus to the rediscovery of neo-Platonism, which was already deeply rooted in Christianity, so that it was re-established in its own right as part of the European intellectual environment. This process was greatly aided by attempts to reconcile the Orthodox and Catholic Churches which led to meetings in the late fifteenth century between Greek scholars from Constantinople and Cosimo de' Medici and the scholars that he patronized. One member of the Medici entourage, Marsilio Ficino (1433–1499), was the key figure in resurrecting Plato for the Renaissance by translating all of Plato's dialogues into Latin from Greek, making them widely available to a wider audience. He also translated the works of Plotinus which were also made newly available in Western Europe. The neo-Platonist Giovanni Pico della Mirandola (1463–1494), a student of Ficino, was also able to translate out of ancient Greek and had an understanding of Hebrew and Arabic, which might explain why Pico came into conflict with the Church but Ficino did not because Pico suggested that Arabic understanding of neo-Platonism had great value in opposition to the stance of the Church. Ignoring Arabic thought placing an emphasis on classical Greek and Roman thought became the basis of a "civic humanism" based on active and patriotic citizenship combined with ethics and an emphasis on classical education.[27]

The work of Niccolò Machiavelli (1469–1527) also needs to be seen in this context. His most famous work is *The Prince*, which is, in a sense, simply an example of the "mirror for princes" genre but goes far beyond the conventions of this type of work. Machiavelli was advising not an existing

---

[27] Hans Baron (1955) *The Crisis of the Early Italian Renaissance: Civic Humanism and Republican Liberty in an Age of Classicism and Tyranny*, Princeton, NJ: Princeton University Press.

ruler or a prince but someone who wanted to create a new state or transform an existing state into one that they can control. In fact, Machiavelli is the first to use the term "state" in the contemporary sense (though he also uses the term as status as was the practice of his time). He argues that to gain power one must have skill, or *virtû*. This is not ethical skill, despite the similarity to the word "virtue," because it can include criminal skill, as in the skill of being a good or successful criminal.[28] The would-be prince must also develop military skills and possess a loyal army not relying on mercenaries, who are fickle. The prince must also choose good advisors, avoiding sycophants who will only say what the prince wants to hear. In some ways, the tactics of Taoism in using silence to tease out the best advice is suggested by Machiavelli. Most famously, Machiavelli appears to reject ethics, because a reputation for compassion and generosity can sometimes be less effective than a reputation for cruelty and parsimony. In the end, a balance is needed to avoid both contempt, which would come from being too soft, and hatred, which would be the result of cruelty and miserliness. There is an ethics in terms of the need to keep one's promises (most of the time) and to the restraint to keep away from that most valued by subjects, mostly their property and their wives, though this is for practical and not moral reasons.[29] In his *Discourses*, Machiavelli favors a more republican form of government though he does not seem sure that the Florentine people are ready to rule themselves and he argues a strong leader is needed to create the conditions for a republic, including fostering a sense of civic duty in a people that have grown corrupt and disengaged from power after years of domination by the nobility.[30] Still, the people are important to Machiavelli and to all the other writers.

POPULAR FORCES, THE MASSES AND WOMEN

Neo-Confucians were somewhat more sympathetic to the people than one might expect. Kitabatake's concern about land holdings is also related to the plight of the tenant farmers on the land. Kitabatake's patron, the Emperor Go-Daigo, also mobilized popular forces to fight the entrenched power of the warrior clans that controlled Japan. The most notorious of the popular forces mobilized were the so-called *akutō* (悪黨) or organized

---

[28] Neal Wood (1967) "Machiavelli's Concept of Virtù Reconsidered," *Political Studies*, 15(2): 159–172.
[29] Machiavelli; Marriot trans. (1908) *The Prince*: 149.
[30] Machiavelli; Thomson trans. (1883) *Discourses on the First Decade of Titus Livius*: 65–77.

groups of commoners who were viewed as having nefarious power over the economic or political activity in local areas. It would have included organized criminals but also local guilds and monopolies, as well as groups of disgruntled warriors and local elites who rallied to the Imperial cause. It also included some peasants. Even Jeong Dojeon in early Joseon Korea carried out land reform and freed slaves, though slavery and land inequality persisted as *yangbang* Literati dominance increasingly formed a sort of caste system as the Joseon period progressed. In terms of women, however, the advent of the Joseon dynasty was a set back because it significantly reduced the freedom of women.[31]

Sundiata Keita's *Kouroukan Fougan* constitution was clearly more progressive. It may even have reserved the 30th seat in the Gbara assembly for a female representative since, although its specific allocation is unknown, the constitution states women are to be represented at all levels of government. The *Kouroukan Fougan* also has a special emphasis on special protection of women, children, the poor and slaves.[32] For example, one article indicates that when your wife or your child runs away, stop running after them if they enter a neighbor's house. The constitution insists that women should not be treated in an offensive matter and should be involved in the management of society. Divorce is permitted for the impotence of the husband, the madness of one of the spouses, or the husband's incapability of assuming the obligations due to the marriage. Slaves are not to be ill-treated. It is stipulated that "We should help those who are in need" and even declares that it is not robbery if someone takes food when they are hungry so long as they do not attempt to take more away than can fit in their hands (not in a bag or pocket). Nonetheless, the constitution still places men and property in a superior position. The law of primogeniture is followed and succession is patrilineal so that a son should not take priority when one of his father's brothers is still alive. Protection of property is emphasized based on five ways to acquire property: purchase, donation, exchange, as wages and inheritance, though any object found without a known owner becomes common property after four years.

In contrast to the progressive nature in the Islamic-influenced Mali Empire, ibn Khaldūn's views on the mass of humanity and the position of women is more matter of fact. In small groups, individuals may be involved in hierarchical relationships but these are based on a form of social solidarity that can only work with relatively small groups.[33] When a

---

[31] Martina Deuchler (1995) *The Confucian Transformation of Korea*, Cambridge, MA: Harvard University Press: 231–281.
[32] Kouyaté ed. (1998) "La charte de Kurukan Fuga."
[33] Ibn Khaldûn; Rosenthal trans. (1958) *The Muqaddimah*, vol. 1: 201–203.

group becomes larger or more powerful, royal authority is the natural goal of group feeling. Royal authority makes possible living in cities and mass society by suppressing natural mutual aggression and injustice (though he notes, "save such injustice as comes from the ruler himself").[34] The Caliphate goes further and forces the masses to act as required by religion in their interest both in the next world as well as in this world.[35] The Caliphate fosters the group feeling which is necessary to the preservation of a Muslim political community and enables (the community) "to fulfill what God expects of it."[36] However, when the Caliphate developed into royal authority, the first thing the dynasty did was to bar the masses from access (to the ruler). The rulers feared that their lives were in danger from attacks by rebels or simply feared that the masses would overwhelm them with numerous demands.[37] The creation of the office of Wazir provided the administrative system necessary for a mass society. The masses are then used to construct monuments and large buildings because human beings desire them and they bolster royal authority. Ibn Khaldûn implies that these are not essential but are created to impress the masses (no point in creating such things for the few), and is merely observing that large-scale labor and cooperation is needed to build them. These tasks reinforce and justify the creation of dynasties and royal authority.[38]

At the same time, ibn Khaldûn has a higher evaluation of the average person than he does of scholars. He argues that politicians must pay attention to the political realities of the outside world where facts can be unclear and will not conform to universal ideals. Scholars, on the other hand, often commit errors and the same is true of the educated, intelligent and politically alert. The average person is more sound in judgment when he or she is not interested in speculation and judges a situation according to its particular circumstances limited to what is perceivable by the senses. Such individuals are more trustworthy when considering politics and have the right outlook in dealing with fellow human beings.[39] Indeed, he argues that scholars are, of all people, those least familiar with the ways of politics. Ibn Khaldûn's references to women are even more matter of fact and often in situations where their behavior could be interpreted as exemplary. His discussion is also gender neutral in the sense that he argues that most religious laws apply to women as they do to men. He insists that even if women are not directly addressed by a text, they are included by

---

[34] Ibn Khaldûn; Rosenthal trans. (1958) *The Muqaddimah*, vol. 1: 202.
[35] Ibn Khaldûn; Rosenthal trans. (1958) *The Muqaddimah*, vol. 1: 385–388.
[36] Ibn Khaldûn; Rosenthal trans. (1958) *The Muqaddimah*, vol. 1: 414.
[37] Ibn Khaldûn; Rosenthal trans. (1958) *The Muqaddimah*, vol. 2: 6–8.
[38] Ibn Khaldûn; Rosenthal trans. (1958) *The Muqaddimah*, vol. 2: 233–240.
[39] Ibn Khaldûn; Rosenthal trans. (1958) *The Muqaddimah*, vol. 3: 308–310.

way of analogical reasoning. Even if men control them in other aspects of their life, as far as the duties of worship, everyone must control his or her own actions, male or female.

The Renaissance is important to the development of the Western European republican and popular government tradition. For example, Bruni, speaking on the constitution of Florence, advocates that everyone has and should have an equal hope of gaining honor, as long as they prove themselves industrious, mentally able and serious-minded. With civic equality, there is no need to fear of force or injustice, to have equality before the law for all citizens. This "cannot happen in the rule of either one or a few." Not only do kings lack the virtues often attributed to them, the hope of honor spurs free citizens to action and denied that hope, the people decline into inertia.[40]

Even in *The Prince*, Machiavelli seems to recommend gaining power by popular support rather than through the support of the aristocracy.[41] A leader supported by the people does not have to share power with those who consider themselves his equal or better. Siding with the aristocracy is likely to involve one with promoting their interests, whereas popularity can be gained by defending the people against the predations of the aristocracy. Besides, the people are great in number so constitute many possible enemies but the nobility is relatively few and are easier to cope with. One can be abandoned by the people but the aristocracy can not only abandon but also attack and destroy. One always needs popular support to some extent because one is always compelled to live among people but the nobility can be put at a distance or their power removed. One needs to keep the people friendly but mainly by leaving them alone. The problem is that one comes to power based on popular support; the people will demand things but if a leader seeks popular support when they were expecting that the leader was serving the interests of the nobility, then they will be grateful rather than expectant. By granting the people favors, or even better, making them dependent on him in some way, the people will remain supportive and provide some security in adversity.

Machiavelli is even more supportive of popular government in his *Discourses on the First Ten Books of Livy* where he seems to advocate a mixed form of government, noting that in the Roman Constitution tensions between the populace and Roman Senate made the Republic free and powerful.[42] The authority of Tribunes was a bastion of liberty because

---

[40] L. Bruni (1996) "Oration on the Death of Nanni Strozzi (1428)" in P. Viti ed. *Opere Letterarie e Politiche*, Torino: Utet: 716–718.
[41] *Prince* (Chapter 9).
[42] Machiavelli; Thomson trans. (1883) *Discourses on the First Decade of Titus Livius*: 16.

they had the right of public accusation to call powerful citizens to account. He stresses the importance of the army of a state being manned by the people, not professionals or mercenaries, because they are more reliable due to what is at stake for them. In this way, a republic should be heavily armed, have excellent laws, but also build an empire and allow foreigners access to her privileges. Much of Machiavelli's political thought hinges on the character of a people. People accustomed to being ruled by one man, if by some chance become free, have difficulty holding on to their liberty. A corrupt people who become free can only hold on to freedom with great difficulty. Only laws and institutions can protect a people – for those not constrained by law must be kept in check by authority regardless if it is more or less arbitrary. In fact, dictatorships can be beneficial especially if people give up their freedom willingly and are led by outstanding individuals. In the end, strong republics and fine men sustain the same outlook, no matter what happens, and never lose their dignity.

Machiavelli's misogynistic views are well documented and have been extensively discussed in academic literature.[43] Pitkin is no doubt correct that there are both contextual and deep-seated psychological reasons for Machiavelli's negative views of women.[44] It is notable, however, that the writings of thinkers such as Machiavelli have not been used to imply that the entire Western tradition is misogynistic but the less extreme views of Islamic writers are used to condemn the entire Islamic tradition. There is one individual who is a useful contrast to Machiavelli and that is Christine de Pizan (1364–1431) who is said to be the first feminist because her *The Book of the City of Ladies* (Le Livre de la Cité des Dames, c. 1405) discussed the contribution women can make to society if they were listened to.[45] It is true that most of her views on power and women are largely conventional, especially given that she tends to write in the traditional "mirror for princes" genre. Nonetheless, she has the claim to be the first female political philosopher to whom we can directly attribute a major text and stands in important contrast to the misogynist Machiavelli.

---

[43] See for example, Arlene W Saxonhouse (1985) *Women in the History of Political Thought: Ancient Greece to Machiavelli*, New York: Praeger and Michelle Tolman Clarke (2005) "On the Woman Question in Machiavelli," *The Review of Politics*, 67(2): 229–255.

[44] Hanna Fenichel Pitkin (1999) *Fortune is a Woman: Gender and Politics in the Thought of Niccolo Machiavelli*, 2nd edn. Chicago, IL: University of Chicago Press.

[45] Christine de Pizan; Kate Langdon Forhan ed./trans. (1994) *The Book of the Body Politic*, Cambridge: Cambridge University Press.

CONCLUSION

Even though the term "Renaissance" is European in origin, there are still intriguing similarities with developments in other parts of the globe that have led a number of scholars to use the term for other areas of the world as well, particularly in East Asia. The turmoil that is the backdrop for the thinkers in this chapter is not unique but how the various thinkers reacted to change is. The role of historical study is especially outstanding in that history is transformed from justifying the claims of monarchs or religious dogma into a general history based on factual analysis and hypotheses about the nature of human beings, though less so in East Asia than in Italy and Islam. It is also easy to see this historical writing as a tendency toward objective analysis separated from ethical injunctions but there are still ethical and religious principles driving these thinkers, even Machiavelli. These developments set the stage, however, for more dramatic conflict involving religion. However, instead of the intellectual elite, popular forces play a larger role and transform the nature of political thought further.

PART II

The interdependence of modernities

9. Popular religious revolt and state building (1450–1670)

Religious revolt in Japan and the Reformation in Europe in the fifteenth and sixteenth centuries on the surface appear to be comparable.[1] In both cases the older institutionalized religions and the political ideas with which they supported the political establishment were challenged by forms of thought linked to an appeal to the masses. Where political order was fragmented, diversity in forms of thought grew, including radical political thought, though not where it was repressed by a strong state. To this we add the case of Wang Yangming thought, which is not religious so might seem odd to discuss in this context, but there are elements of this thought that can benefit with comparison to Japanese and European religious conflict in this period, particularly its popular appeal and related tendencies to reinterpret traditional thought and encourage forms of individualism in ways that challenged traditional political authority.

WARRING STATES AND SACRED SPACES IN JAPAN

As authority broke down in Japan in the Warring States (*sengoku* 戰國) period (1467–1600), Buddhists increasingly insisted on the interdependence between the royal and Buddhist realms (*ōhō butsuhō izon* 王法佛法依存) by arguing that the laws or dharma of the king or monarch are mutually dependent on the laws or dharma of Buddhism just like two wings of a bird are necessary to fly.[2] Rather than an appeal by the Buddhist monasteries for complete autonomy, it was a plea for the links between both to be strong and to maintain a good working relationship.

As we have seen, the Imperial Court had long been associated with Buddhism, first with the Nara schools of Buddhism and then with Tendai and Shingon. During the Kamakura and Ashikaga Shogunates, Zen was

---

[1] See, for example, Galen Amstutz (1998) "Shin Buddhism and Protestant Analogies with Christianity in the West," *Comparative Studies in Society and History*, 40(4): 724–747.

[2] 佐藤弘夫 (Satō Hirō) (2010) 日本中世の国家と仏教 (*Nihon Chūsei no Kokka to Bukkyō*), 東京：吉川弘文館 (Tokyo: Yoshikawa Kō Bunkan).

incorporated after some initial resistance. We have also seen that there was opposition from the existing Buddhist establishment to the emergence of each new sect, with both Shinran of the True Pure Land and Nichiren of Nichiren Buddhism, and their respective followers persecuted. However, as True Pure Land and Nichiren spread, they also converted local powerful figures to their sects and this encouraged others in the local area to join as well, most voluntarily, but also based on community and family pressure. There were even local areas which declared themselves Buddha realms (*bukkoku* 佛國), partly a symbolic act, like a local city declaring itself a "fair trade" city or "nuclear free zone" but also had a powerful effect of declaring the area of be a Buddha land. In this way, the mutual dependence of the secular and the Buddhist was deepened in the eyes of many.

With the onset of the Ōnin Rebellion (応仁の乱 1467–1477), Japan's political fragmentation spread. Yet it is important not to exaggerate the anarchy and lawlessness of the period. This period in Japanese history is probably more comparable to political complexity of the Middle Ages in European history with overlapping feudatory ties even if it was far from the ideal of the centralized bureaucratic empire of the Literati. In fact, Japan was possibly relatively more peaceful than Europe at the time with the death and destruction greater in the Hundred Years' War in Europe (1337–1453) or England during the War of the Roses (1455–1487). Nonetheless, Japan in the sixteenth century saw the locally powerful lords increasingly competing for territory and influence. War was always threatening but some large religious communities, such as the Tendai complex on Hieizan (near Kyoto), or commercial towns such as Sakai (now part of Osaka) were able to achieve a degree of independence. The Papal States and commercial city-states such as Genoa in Italy in the same period, or the various German states before German unification in the nineteenth century might be comparable. The County Palatine of Durham and even some charter cities such as London at early periods in English history experienced varying degrees of political autonomy. While it may be an exaggeration to suggest that Sakai and other enclaves were exactly the same, some areas of Europe, particularly in Germany and Italy under the Holy Roman Empire had comparable degrees of political autonomy.

One key figure in this period in Japan is Rennyo (連如 1415–1499). In 1457, Rennyo succeeded his father as head of Kyoto's rundown True Pure Land (*Jōdo Shinshū*) main temple of Honganji (本願寺). Directly related by blood to Shinran, the founder of the sect, Rennyo followed Shinran's teachings on the saving grace of Amida Buddha and taught that there was no need for religious practice beyond saying the *nembutsu* in gratitude. This meant that his teachings particularly appealed to peasants and the lower classes in general. In 1457, Rennyo began to engage in active missionary work in Omi Province leading to a dramatic revival in the temple's fortunes. However, his success in promotion of the unorthodox Jōdo Shinshū form of Buddhism offended the older Tendai temples, and Rennyo was forced to flee to Omi when Honganji was attacked by Tendai Enryakuji monks in 1465. It is notable that Rennyo started his proselytizing during and his success came after the Ōnin Rebellion had begun in 1467, when the old Imperial capital of Kyoto was laid waste and the country descended into political turmoil. In 1471, Rennyo decided to escape the violence by moving to Yoshizaki in Echizen Province where he built a popular temple that attracted many converts and helped the sect to grow widely in the northwestern part of the main Japanese island of Honshu. Five years later, he returned to the region around Kyoto and set up new Honganji branch temples.

Rennyo did not directly advocate disobedience to civil authority and, in fact, he sought accommodation with various political authorities and other sects, but he continued Shinran's attempt to bring Buddhism to the people. He was considered a great organizer, who wrote many pastoral letters to explain True Pure Land doctrine in clear and easy to understand Japanese. He stressed that his followers should view the True Pure Land faith as the only true teaching and not engage in syncretic practices with other Buddhist sect practices or Shintō kami worship, though he is careful not to attack other sects directly. In fact, he spends considerable effort to implore his followers not to attack others openly.[3] There is evidence that the political impact of his work concerned him, but it was a natural consequence of what he taught. He was successful in empowering people to resist authority because they could create a sense of quasi-religious community, which bound them together for mutual aid and defense, and enabled them to create new links with the local authorities as political order declined. The initially aristocratic revolts led to an empowerment of the lower orders of society and also enabled women to play a role in transforming the community, though religious based popular groups were still dependent to a large degree on local powerbrokers, often *bushi* themselves, called *kokujin* (國人), who were often True Pure Land believers and collaborated in shedding off central authority from the Shogunate and their agents.

By the time of Rennyo, he believed that Buddhism had deteriorated so much that people only sought simple superstitious devices to gain salvation, and unscrupulous monks were no better than gangsters who

---

[3] De Bary et al. (2010) *Sources of Japanese Tradition*, vol.1: 229; Rennyo; Ann T. Rogers and Minor L. Rogers trans. (1996) *Rennyo Shōnin Ofumi: The Letters of Rennyo*, Berkeley, CA: Numata Center for Buddhist Translation and Research: 68.

sold dubious amulets and other charms as part of a spiritual protection racket. Rennyo appealed not only to the peasantry, as is often assumed based on the standard translation of *ikki* (一揆) as "peasant revolt" but also to organized groups of commoners (*akutō* 悪黨), such as transport workers or others who had sliced out a territory and controlled it to maximize revenue in the area under their control.[4] Given the increasingly ambiguous status of political order, these groups created local order and made economic activity possible. The notion of radical spiritual autonomy which Rennyo implicitly promised was welcome to these people.[5]

Sporadic revolts were termed *ikkō ikki* (一向一揆) or "single-minded revolts" because of the religious fervor of the True Pure Land believers leading them to attack with unrestrained vehemence. In 1488, a True Pure Land community carried out an *ikkō ikki* that effectively took control of an entire province. They then went on to defeat the warriors who had been sent by the Ashikaga Shogunate to stop them. As a result of these successes, the revolts spread. Revolts were carried out separately by True Pure Land followers and by Nichiren followers with both contributing to the decline of political authority. In fact, one of the last of the revolts, the Temmon Hokke Rebellion (天文法華の亂) occurred in 1536 when True Pure Land believers threatened the city of Kyoto and provoked the formation of Nichiren believer militias who ruled the city for the next four years. This short period of Nichiren rule was called the Lotus Uprising (*hokke ikki* 法華一揆) in contrast to the True Pure Land Buddhist *ikkō ikki*. The revolt only ended when a counter-attack by warrior-monks of the Tendai complex of Enryakuji on Mt. Hiei attacked and defeated the Nichiren militias, destroying most of the city in the process, which is called the Tenmon Persecution (*Tenmon hōnan* 天文法難) by Nichiren followers.

In the context of this unrest, a realist approach, similar to that of the *Fǎ-jiā* (Legalists) or Machiavelli, was used by Oda Nobunaga (織田信長 1534–1582), the first of three powerful Japanese Warring States lords or *daimyō* (大名), to re-establish central authority in Japan. By seizing the key strategic points at the center of the main island of Honshū, Oda was able to create an unchallenged combination of territorial claims and alliances that helped secure his victory in the Battle of Nagashino in 1575.

Oda focused on destroying independent power bases of those areas not controlled by *daimyō* with whom he was allied. He seized control of the Imperial family through his occupation of Kyoto in 1568, and though this was more a symbolic than a real strategic advantage, it is notable that

---

[4] 五木寛之 (Itsuki Hiroyuki) (1994) 蓮如—聖俗具有の人間像 (Rennyo: Seizoku Guyū no Ningenzō) 東京: 岩波書店 (Tokyo: Iwanami Shoten): 57–61.
[5] The example in Itsuki's *Rennyo* above is from the area around Lake Biwa near Kyoto.

he felt the need to legitimate his political ambitions with reference to the Imperial House and not other sources such as Buddhism. He attacked and destroyed the powerful Tendai monastic complex on Hieizan in 1571 signaling the end of Tendai's political influence and prominence, and the end of monasteries as independent political power bases. Oda legitimated his attack on the monastery by claiming that Buddhist monks were not living up to their ideals and he was preserving the "Way of Heaven" (*tendō* 天道), a concept with Literati overtones. His suppression was brutal and spared no one, including monks, lay persons, and children. Even when countless beautiful women and young boys who denounced the monks were led before Nobunaga, they were not reprieved and had their heads chopped off one by one. Oda went on to suppress the *ikkō ikki* communities during the period 1573–1580. Finally Oda undertook the notorious Azuchi Disputation (*Azuchi Shuron* 安土宗論) in 1579 where he ordered a debate between the Nichiren and True Pure Land representatives to settle the frequent disputes between the two sects. Nobunaga judged that Nichiren was the source of most of the disturbances and had Nichiren Buddhist leaders executed. He also forced Nichiren Buddhists to pay reparations to the True Pure Land sect and prohibited Nichiren followers from arguing with other sects.

In 1582, however, Oda died in mysterious circumstances and was replaced by Toyotomi Hideyoshi (豊臣秀吉 1536–1598), a common foot soldier who had risen to prominence under Oda. In 1588, Toyotomi conducted a nationwide sword-hunt (*katanagari* 刀狩) and effectively disarmed the peasantry leaving only a small elite of samurai retainers of *daimyō* in possession of swords. In 1595, he conducted a nationwide cadastral survey (*kenchi* 検地) which assessed the productive capacity of the land as the basis of a system of fixed taxation and regularized the income of *daimyō* and the samurai officials who served them. Hideyoshi's power was so complete that he embarked on a campaign to invade Korea as the first step to conquering continental East Asia. He was victorious until the Koreans and their Ming dynasty reinforcements began to appear with their own firearms, and fought back the Japanese. When Hideyoshi died in 1598 the Korea expedition was abandoned as Japanese forces returned to scramble for control of Japan.

It was Tokugawa Ieyasu (徳川家康 1542–1616) who emerged victorious as the final unifier of Japan. His decisive victory at the Battle of Sekigahara (1600) is the starting date for the Tokugawa period (1600–1868) and by 1603, Tokugawa Ieyasu took the title of Shogun. In 1615, the last pocket of resistance was removed with the fall of Osaka Castle and the death of Hideyoshi's son who had been a potential rallying point for resistance. However, the unification of Japan in the late sixteenth and early seventeenth century was not unification in the sense of centralization. It was a stalemate where the Tokugawa regime ruled key areas of Japan, but powerful *daimyō* still controlled independent domains in which they were nearly sovereign. The result was a sort of stillborn decentralized absolutism. The fact that these many key areas of the country were independent and outside of direct Tokugawa control led to the development of spies which both the Tokugawa and their enemies used to keep track of each other. Neo-Confucianism quickly became the favored ideology of the Tokugawa regime in order to maintain order and justify Tokugawa rule. Yet, Japanese neo-Confucianism was tame in comparison with the Song version because it had a less intimate relationship with the state in terms of the selection of public officials through examination based on a Song neo-Confucian curriculum.

RADICAL NEO-CONFUCIANISM IN THE MING DYNASTY

The Ming dynasty, in contrast to Japan, had achieved a degree of stability earlier in the fifteenth century. Zhu Yuanzhang (朱元璋 1328–1398), the founder of the Ming dynasty, was the son of tenant farmers and orphaned in his youth so became a novice in a small Buddhist monastery. He was forced by circumstances to leave the monastery to become a wandering healing monk who eventually became caught up in semi-religious uprising of which he became the successful leader. First, he became a local warlord, then proclaimed a new dynasty at Nanking and drove the remaining Mongols from the north of China back into Mongolia. The Ming dynasty suppressed the forms of esoteric Buddhism patronized by the Mongol Yuan dynasty, and Chan became predominant and at the popular level monks, such as Hanshan Deqing (憨山德清 1546–1623) promoted a combination of Chan and Pure Land methods, including the use of the *nianfo*. The Ming officials were wary of religious influence to the extent that they limited the ordination of Buddhist and Daoist clerics to twenty per locality in the early part of the dynasty.

The Ming emperors ruled in an autocratic style which they inherited from the Mongols. That is, they exercised power arbitrarily when they chose to do so, but for the most part they were content to allow the Literati-trained bureaucracy to administer the empire on their behalf. These officials were not completely trusted, however. They were constantly in fear of purges and summary execution so were docile agents of the rulers and always fearful of failing to act in their best interests. This distrust of Literati officialdom and early Ming social policy was a natural extension of the social and religious roots of the founder of the dynasty. Slavery was abolished and huge land-holdings were confiscated to be distributed to tenant farmers. Local communities were charged with collecting taxes and managing local affairs rather than giving too much power to Literati officials. The political and social peace created by the Ming led to an increase in commerce and general prosperity. It also led to a cultural blossoming of painting and literature to meet the tastes of the new middle-class created in these circumstances.

It was in this context that a new movement arose from the "School of the Mind" form of neo-Confucianism created by Lu Jiuyuan (陸象山 1139–1193), the friend and opponent to Zhu Xi, the founder of orthodox neo-Confucianism. It has been noted earlier that Lu argued that the mind or heart (*xin* 心) is not a crude approximation of an ideal principle but an active partner with principle. Mind is not stuff (*qi* 氣) and instead shares the ultimate with principle (or *li*, 理). Mind is not a source of impurity that a focus on principle must overcome, as Zhu Xi suggested. Also in contrast to Zhu Xi's students, Lu Jiuyuan's were better at putting ideals based on principle into practice, as Zhu Xi himself admitted. Lu's approach was adopted and expanded by the Ming thinker Wang Yangming (王陽明 1472–1528) who said he was attempting to liberate Zhu Xi's orthodoxy from its bookish nature and use it as a force in the world. It is certainly different from the conservatism of the Zhu Xi approach, despite Wang's claim that he merely intended to continue and improve Zhu Xi's teachings.

Wang's approach was sometimes referred to as the "Mad Chan" school of neo-Confucianism,[6] which is not surprising because it shares some ideas with Chan Buddhism, for example, from the "Platform Sutra". Wang Yangming school of neo-Confucianism is also referred to as "intuitionism."[7] We can see why this might be the case if we think back to the origins of some of these ideas in the School of the Mind. However, it is misleading to use the term "mind" in this context. The actual Chinese character (*xin* 心) can also mean heart in the sense of feeling soul of humans rather than the cold rational mind. However, in Wang Yangming's neo-Confucianism, the "mind" is not an abstract mind nor is the "heart" merely an emotional heart, it is a mind and heart that acts together as one. Wang Yangming's distinctive contribution to neo-Confucianism is taking

---

[6] Youru Wang (2017) *Historical Dictionary of Chan Buddhism*, Lanham, MD: Rowman and Littlefield Publishers: 36.

[7] Wang has been attacked by Qing dynasty thinkers as "intuitionist," see W.T. De Bary ed. (2008) *Sources of East Asian Tradition, Volume 2: The Modern Period*, New York, NY: Columbia University Press: 24; In a more positive and comparative context, see John Zijiang Ding (2011) "Self-Transformation and Moral Universalism: A Comparison of Wang Yangming and Schleiermacher," *Journal of East-West Thought*, 1(1): 101.

principles, mind, heart and intuitions and putting them into effective action.

Wang Yangming came from a family with a long line of officials among his ancestors and extended family. Initially when he was being trained as a Literati scholar, he was very interested in Taoism and Buddhism. In 1499, at the age of 28, he passed the examination for the "presented scholar" (進士), ranking second in his class. He was immediately appointed to the Department of Public Works. At the time, China was being invaded by semi-nomadic tribes from the Northwest, so he wrote a memorial to the emperor with ideas on national defense. While the memorial was rejected, his ideas on strategy, finance and morale became widely known and he was soon made a Divisional Chief for the Department of Justice. At the Department of Justice, he worked with prisoners who had been influenced to oppose the regime based on Taoist and Buddhist ideas and he was effective in rehabilitating them because he understood how these philosophies could lead to mistaken political views that he could counter and correct. In 1504, he was appointed to conduct provincial examinations in Shantung, and his questioning of candidates on the range of Literati canon and current problems was so profound that his reputation with other civil servants soared. He was soon made Division Chief Assistant of Military Personnel in the Department of Military Affairs. His problems began, however, when he defended several officials who opposed a palace eunuch who seemed to be attempting to usurp the powers of the emperor. As a result, he was banished to the extreme south of China in Lung-ch'ang (modern Kuei-chou) which was then inhabited by barbarian Miao tribes. He ran an insignificant dispatch station. He had no books and was forced to do his own chores in primitive conditions, Wang searched his own mind to find a clearer interpretation of neo-Confucian concepts such as the investigation of things and knowledge.

For Wang, Zhu Xi separated *li* (理), or principles or rationality, from *qi* (氣) or the empirical "stuff" in the world. Zhu Xi insisted that the aspects of ourselves related to *qi* (feelings and desires) must be controlled by a focus on principle. The inherent knowledge of principles within us can be supplemented through the investigation of things outside of us, but we must be aware of the distinction between perfect principles inherent in things in theory and imperfect real things in the outside world, and, thus, Zhu Xi maintains a distinction between principle/thingness (*li/qi*) and inside/outside. Wang, in contrast, argues that we ourselves, including feelings, desire, substance, things and ideas, are the source of our principles, so things in the world (*qi*) and the principles (*li*) behind them are the same (*qi-ji-li* 氣即理). This means that heart-mind and principle are also the same (*xin-ji-li* 心即理), in fact, "the heart-mind *is* principle."[8] That is, our principles (rationality) must come from our human mind. From Wang's point of view, there need be no conflict between the School of Principle of Zhu Xi and the School of the Mind of Lu Jiuyuan. It also means that we do not need to seek the highest good outside of ourselves. There are no things/events outside the mind (*xin-wai-wuwu/shi* 心外無物 / 事) and no principles outside the mind (*xin-wai-wu-li* 心外無理) because we are part of the world and the world is part of us. We are all connected together if we would just realize it. Our mind is connected to all things, great and small, and we have a responsibility that derives from that. If one intuitively understands this connection, one will act as part of the world from the beginning. At the same time, Wang has a problem, similar to Mencius, in explaining people who act badly. To do so he makes a distinction between those who have the natural insight into that which connects us all and those whose understanding is blocked. If so, one must strive to work to attain knowledge of what is good (*liángzhī* 致良知) by removing obstacles to restore the original substance of the mind.

By 1510, Wang's term at the dispatch station had ended and he was made a magistrate in Lu-ling (modern Kiangsi) where he gained a remarkable reputation again. He had an audience with the emperor and was promoted to Division Chief Assistant in the Inspections Division of the Civil Personnel Department (1511) and a few years later (1514) he was Senior Lord of the Bureau of State Ceremonies. When repeated campaigns failed to suppress bandits and rebels in the southern areas of Kiangsi and Fukien, Wang was promoted to Senior Censor in the Censorate and Governor in the region. He not only pacified the area, but rehabilitated the rebels and bandits as well as reforming the tax and education systems. He even put down a rebellion by a nephew of the emperor, Prince Ning. The last success, however, caused jealously in the Imperial Court because the emperor had wanted to lead the expedition against Ning himself but Wang had acted so quickly and successfully he effectively pre-empted involvement by the emperor. Wang was charged with treason, and even though he was cleared, he was demoted, constantly attacked and forced into virtual retirement. He was later recalled to service in order to put down another rebellion in the South, but died due to long-term ill-health after this, his final success. In any case, we can understand why the principles of the mind as tested in the real world are important to him. To sum up, one could view Wang Yangming's views in the slogan: thought and action as one (*zhi xing heyi* 知行合一). Wang wanted people to go back to the

---

[8] Philip J. Ivanhoe trans. (2009) *Readings from the Lu-Wang School of Neo-Confucianism*, Indianapolis, IN: Hackett Publishing: 137.

natural realization of the bonds that lay behind concepts such as filial piety. Such concepts should not be conventional formulas, which one must study as in the case of exaggerated paragons of filial piety, because one can lose the natural sense of an affectionate bond upon which it is based. One has to rely on one's natural, even intuitive, understanding of the right thing to do and then do it. Indeed, one cannot know the true meaning of principles unless one acts upon them.[9] Knowing there is a principle to act upon is important, but all principles must be practiced and understood in action.

THE CHRISTIAN REFORMATION IN EUROPE

The first major movement toward the Reformation in Europe began with two university lecturer clerics; one in Oxford, John Wycliffe (c. 1320–1384), and one in Prague, Jan Hus (c. 1369–1415). They not only openly advocated radical change in the Catholic Church, they also inspired popular revolts, specifically the Lollards in the Peasant Revolt of 1381 in England and the Hussite Wars 1420–1431 in Czech lands. Both uprisings were brutally suppressed, particularly where the Roman Catholic Church sent troops to suppress uprisings in Eastern Europe. As a result, reformist sentiment went underground (for example, most Czechs held onto Hussite beliefs but practiced them secretly). Even though these revolts were unsuccessful, the essential arguments of these movements re-emerged with the Reformation, which formally starts with Martin Luther (1483–1546).

Even though he wanted to reform the Church, Luther was politically conservative and supported the rights of local political authorities. He argued that the "secular sword of authority" has always existed and is necessary to keep non-Christians in order.[10] Even though Luther believed that True Christians do not need the sword of authority to behave correctly, they need it to be protected from others. True Christians must naturally obey the authority of a True Christian ruler. Even if the authorities are not True Christians, one must not give up one's true beliefs but must suffer the injustice of persecution passively. These views were reinforced by his abhorrence of the popular revolts that began based on demands for Church reform, such as the German Peasant's War (1524–1525) and the emergence of the Anabaptist movement (1525–1540). The German

---

[9] For a deeper exploration of the implications of Wang's approach see A.S. Cua (1982) *The Unity of Knowledge and Action: A Study of Wang Yang Ming's Moral Psychology*, Honolulu, HI: University of Hawaii Press.

[10] Harro M. Hopfl trans./ed. (1991) *Luther and Calvin on Secular Authority*, Cambridge: Cambridge University Press.

Peasants' War began on December 27, 1521 when preachers influenced by Thomas Müntzer (1489–1525) appeared in Wittenberg from Zwickau to put forward an apocalyptic and radical vision of Christian community, based on equality and common ownership, and when combined with existing social unrest, led to the Peasants' War in southern Germany.[11] This new movement believed in divine inspiration beyond the Bible so that a literal interpretation was too limiting. It is true that the political thought of these preachers was limited to living as a good Christian in harmony with others so hardly a radical threat to the authorities but, nonetheless, the revolts they inspired were brutally suppressed, and the leaders tracked down and executed. Next, the Anabaptist movement rose in religious revolt. Anabaptists are named after those who believed only in adult baptism but often include a variety of other opponents of the established church. They were opposed to forced membership in any church, even a Lutheran or Protestant church, as well as the Roman Catholic Church. They were the first movement to insist on the separation of faith and the state. They were more literalist in their interpretation of the Bible, though this is a criticism that was also leveled at Luther. Anabaptism was punishable by death but it survived as an underground movement and avoided confrontation with the authorities. Many fled, especially Germans to the American colonies, Pennsylvania in particular, where the Quaker William Penn had established a tolerant colony for Quakers and others. These became known as the Pennsylvania "Dutch" (a corruption of "deutch" or German), more widely known as the Amish.

John Calvin (1509–1564) is the next major Reformation political thinker. He first published his *Institutes of Christian Religion* in 1536 but revised it many times with some subtle changes to his position on the relationship between believers and political authority.[12] He consistently pointed out that the liberty promised in heaven means that liberty in this life is not important because one's place in the hierarchy and status in this world means nothing in the next. Nonetheless, politics is still relevant to Christians because rulers, law and the people determine if there is to be a basic order under which all might live. The most frequently changed passage was Book IV, Chapter 20, Section 8 where he suggested that "private men" have no right to debate the best type of government but then goes on to say that amongst the types – monarch, aristocracy and popular rule – aristocracy is the best because one person with power can easily

---

[11] Michael G. Baylor, trans./ed. (1991) *The Radical Reformation*, Cambridge: Cambridge University Press.
[12] Harro M. Hopfl trans./ed. (1991) *Luther and Calvin on Secular Authority*, Cambridge: Cambridge University Press.

lose self-control but several persons can assist, instruct and admonish each other to curb individual license. This might seem anti-democratic but he tended to use the "republican" word magistrate for the ruler, with the monarch as the superior magistrate but lower officials as inferior magistrates or just magistrates in general so he implied a broad aristocracy of officialdom.

French Protestants, called Huguenots, were inspired by the writings of John Calvin but faced both government and popular persecution. The French Wars of Religion began with a massacre at Vassy on March 1, 1562, when a large number of Huguenots were killed and wounded. This was followed by the St. Bartholomew's Day Massacre of August 24 to October 3, 1572 when Catholics killed thousands of Huguenots in Paris. Similar massacres took place in other towns across France in the weeks following. The exact number of fatalities will never be known but the killing occurred on a very large scale. To add insult to injury for the Huguenots, an amnesty was granted in 1573 that pardoned those involved in the killings. It is in this context that the Huguenot tract *Vindiciae contra tyrannos* was published in 1579, which argued that individuals can violently resist a bad ruler (that is, one who does not have the correct religious beliefs or persecutes believers of the correct form of religion such as the Huguenots) because such a ruler will destroy the commonwealth if not stopped.[13] However, this resistance must be led, as noted by Calvin, by an inferior magistrate (as opposed to the superior magistrate who is the monarch). It was one of the first Protestant tracts to openly call for rebellion against a Catholic monarch.

POLITICAL THEORY AND POLITICAL ORDER

The establishment of the Tokugawa Shogunate in Japan solidified secular power but the ideological basis of the regime was initially unclear. Eventually neo-Confucianism was chosen but the process of adoption was not as straightforward as in the Song and Ming dynasties or in Joseon Korea. The Literati in Japan were never as powerful as on the East Asian mainland. In fact, neo-Confucian thought during the Warring States period in Japan was preserved, transmitted and studied primarily by Zen Buddhist monks, and therefore, when the specialists in this thought were mobilized by the new Tokugawa regime for ideological support, they initially recruited

---

[13] Stephanus Junius Brutus; George Garnett trans. (2003) *Vindiciae, contra tyrannos: Or, Concerning the Legitimate Power of a Prince over the People, and of the People over a Prince*, Cambridge: Cambridge University Press.

Zen monks. In fact, the early Tokugawa Literati were only permitted to hold office as monks and were regarded with suspicion if they took Literati thought to be a distinct system of thought in contrast to Buddhism. The authorities initially feared that Literati thought, particularly neo-Confucianism was similar to Christian ideas, which had been considered subversive to political order and a potential tool of foreign powers, and so was viewed with suspicion if not outright persecution. Even the requirement of registration at Buddhist temples was used not just against Christians but also initially against dedicated Literati enthusiasts.[14]

It was Fujiwara Seika (藤原惺窩 1561–1619) who liberated neo-Confucianism from the confines of the Zen temple, though he himself had been a Zen monk and had learned Confucian doctrines in a Zen temple in Kyoto. Fujiwara had become dissatisfied with Zen Buddhism, and was more attracted by neo-Confucian literature so he left the temple and began to study and teach neo-Confucianism as an independent philosophy. He tried to travel to Ming China to study neo-Confucianism but the attempt ended in failure. He then engaged in an exchange with the Korean Literati Gang Hang (姜沆 1567–1618),[15] and based on this activity he established an independent school of systematic neo-Confucianism which up to that point had been simply a part of the general education of Gozan Zen monks. Fujiwara's approach is primarily Zhu Xi neo-Confucianism but it incorporated some elements of the Wang Yangming school. Fujiwara Seika fostered the adoption of neo-Confucianism by using *waka* poetry and Japanese classical texts to persuade both Hideyoshi Toyotomi and Tokugawa Ieyasu of the need for neo-Confucianism. He was asked by Ieyasu to serve him as an official but he refused and instead recommended his student Hayashi Razan (1583–1657) who entered Ieyasu's service as an advisor on legal and historical precedents. Razan was also permitted in 1630 to establish a private neo-Confucian school with the financial support of the Tokugawa Shogunate, and later in 1690 this became the official Tokugawa college, the Shōheikō (昌平黌). Initially only samurai officials affiliated with the Shogunate were permitted to study, but later samurai from the different domains (*han* 藩) and commoners were also admitted. Local lords in their domains founded their own *han* schools in the years that followed. After his death, the Hayashi family received a hereditary appointment to the Shogunate as neo-Confucian advisors. It was they who maintained the orthodox line of Tokugawa neo-Confucianism.

---

[14] Beatrice Bodart-Bailey (1993) "The Persecution of Confucianism in Early Tokugawa Japan," *Monumenta Nipponica*, 48(3): 293–314.

[15] See Ja-hyun Kim Haboush and Kenneth R. Robinson (2013) *A Korean War Captive in Japan, 1597–1600: The Writings of Kang Hang*, New York, NY: Columbia University Press.

Razan political ideas – as seen in such works as *Honchō hennen-roku* (本朝皇胤紹運録) or "Chronological History of Japan" and *Honchō tsugan* (本朝通鑑) or "Survey History of Japan," completed by his son Gahō (鵞峰 1618–1688) – served to provide a Literati interpretation for the legitimacy of the Tokugawa Shogunate, based upon the concept of *Tendō* ("way of heaven") of the late Warring States period. *Tendō* became the Japanese equivalent of the "mandate of heaven" (天命 ch. *tian-ming*, jp. *tenmei*). Razan emphasized the neo-Confucian and earlier Literati view that the order of heaven and earth needs to be replicated in the relationship between rulers and subjects. This is expressed in the conventional formula of the Five Relationships – those between "ruler and minister [lord and retainer], parent and child, husband and wife, older and younger brother, and friends" and the view that:

> Rulers should love their people; ministers should serve their rulers; fathers should be compassionate toward their sons; husbands should manage external matters, while wives should handles the family's internal affairs; elder brothers should teach their younger brothers, and younger brothers should follow their older brother's instructions; friends should associate with one another on the basis of rites and justice.[16]

The two central moral ideals of Confucianism were "loyalty" (忠 jp. *chū*, ch. *zhōng*) and "filial piety" (孝 jp. *kō*, ch. *xiao*) but in contrast to continental neo-Confucianism, Tokugawa thinkers like Razan placed as much emphasis on loyalty (*chū*) in support of feudal lord-vassal relations as they did for *kō*, which was a family ethic.

Neo-Confucianism in Japan also had an impact on Buddhism, though not to the extent that it did in the Song and Ming dynasties and was certainly less repressive than in Joseon Korea. Instead, Buddhist temples in Japan were compelled to act as part of the state. All Japanese were required to register with their local temple, known as *terauke seido* (寺請制度), which effectively recorded all deaths and births. The monitoring of religion by domains was made mandatory in 1664, with the requirement of each major domain to appoint a magistrate of temples and shrines (*jisha bugyō* 寺社奉行). This was done to control Buddhism but also to enforce the prohibition of Christianity, which had some success in the late sixteenth and early seventeenth centuries in making converts but was soon considered a subversive religion promoted by Western powers to undermine Japan.

In the later Ming dynasty, in contrast, it was Wang Yangming thought

---

[16] De Bary (2010) *Sources of Japanese Tradition*, vol. 2, 2nd edn: 58.

that produced unrest. In order to understand the impact of Wang Yangming thought in this period, it is helpful to start with distinguishing between three main subsets of successors.[17] The most radical group, considered to be the "left-wing" of the Wang Yangming movement, was the Realization or Actualization (*Xiànchéng* 現成) School, the "right-wing" was the Quietist or Tranquility (*Gui-ji* 歸寂) School, and between the two was the Cultivation or Enlightenment (*Xiūzhèng* 修証) School aimed at making Wang's thought acceptable to the authorities.

The most important member of the Cultivation school was Youyang Nanye (欧陽南野 1496–1554) who held highest official position of all of Wang Yangming's students and helped to secure initial official toleration for Wang's unorthodox views. He focused on how one can exercise inherent knowledge of the good (*liángzhī* 良知). He argued that knowledge is different from will (*yi* 意) and innate knowledge is different than simple perception so suggested that access to inherent knowledge of the good is only possible through investigation of things but as part of the process of rectification of the heart (*zheng xin* 正心) and not as something external as in the Zhu Xi school approach. However, one must follow this process without expectation of either action or quietude. Therefore, he adopted middle course between the activist Realization School and quiescent Tranquility School.

One of the key members of the Tranquility School was Nie Shuangjiang (聶雙江 1487–1563) who emphasized the need for moral effort (*kung-fu* 功夫) to realize *liángzhī* (良知), which defined as original substance (*běntǐ* 本體). For Nie, such effort is essentially quietude because he viewed the heart/mind (*xin* 心) to be quiet and the ultimate substance in the world, and therefore the practice of quiet sitting (*jingzuo* 靜坐) and the quest of inner quietude as the basis for *liángzhī* (良知).[18] Another figure associated with this school is Wan Si-mo (萬思默 fl. early seventeenth century), who was part of the second generation of Wang Yangming's followers. He used the *Classic of Changes* (Zhouyi 易經) to structure Wang Yangming thought with the aspects of the philosophy associated with concepts in the book,

---

[17] Much of what follows draws on 岡田武彦 (Okada Takehiko) (2004) 王陽明と明末の儒学 (Ōyōmei to Meisue no Jugaku) 東京: 明德出版社 (Tokyo: Meitoku Shuppan Sha); For an English summary see Takehiko Okada (1973) "The Chu Hsi and Wang Yang-ming Schools at the End of the Ming and Tokugawa Periods," *Philosophy East and West*, 23(1/2):139–162.

[18] Rodney Leon Taylor and Howard Yuen Fung Choy (2005) *The Illustrated Encyclopedia of Confucianism: N–Z*, New York, NY: Rosen Publishing: 452. See also Fukuda Shigeru (1995) "On the Position of Nie Shuangjiang (聶雙江) and Luo Nian'an (羅念庵) in the Wang-yangming School (陽明學派)," *Journal of the Bulletin of the Sinological Society of Japan*, 47: 133–148.

with the aim of reaching tranquility, thus placing him in that School.[19] Nie also wrote "A Brief Outline on Statecraft" (*Jing Shi Yaolüe* 經世要略) of 1610 applying his approach to practical affairs including governing.

Wang Yangming became very popular but it was not without its critics. There was increasingly fierce criticism of Wang Yangming thought by figures such as Chen Qinglan (陳清瀾 1497–1567)[20] and Luo Qinshun (羅欽順 1465–1547).[21] Perhaps the most important criticism came from the Dong Lin School (*Dong lin xue* 東林學) which upheld the Zhu Xi School of Principle orthodoxy and became increasingly influential in opposition to Wang Yangming toward the end of the Ming dynasty. In fact, by the rise of the next dynasty, the Qing, Wang Yangming thought was heavily suppressed.

Wang Yangming thought also failed to gain much influence in Joseon Korea. It was studied by a few scholars such as Nam Yeongkyung (南彦經 1528–1594) and Lee Yo (李瑤 1536–1584) who used it to critique the excessively ritualistic side of Zhu Xi thought by contrasting it to the more active Wang Yangming approach. Chong Chedu (鄭齊斗 1649–1736) was the leading exponent of the Wang Yangming school in Joseon Korea and went so far as to reject the Zhu Xi school that was dominant in the country at the time. As with Wang, he argued that principle (*li* 理) and matter/force (*qi* 氣) are inseparable and that the unity of thought and action as a form of pragmatism should be given emphasis, which he applied by studying astronomy, literature and social relations. He was permitted to do this, due to living in relative isolation on Kanghwa Island (江華島) and possibly with the support of local authorities.[22] It also seems that Chong taught some members of the Li (李), the ruling family of Joseon, which might also suggest he was protected by the authorities despite his unorthodoxy, but Wang Yangming remained a minority interest in Joseon. The only information on Wang Yangming most Joseon scholars would have had access to were critical evaluations by orthodox neo-Confucians who used Wang Yangming thought as a "foil" to reinforce the orthodox (Zhu Xi) interpretation, with Yi Hwang in particular a key figure in doing so.

---

[19] See Zhang Zhao-wei (2009) "Wan Ting-yan's Yi-ology Based on Mind/Heartology," *Studies of Zhouyi and Ancient Chinese Philosophy* 3. http://211.86.56.178:8080/english0/periodical/200903.asp#8 (accessed April 10, 2017).

[20] See T'ang, Chun-i (1973) "The Criticisms of Wang Yang-ming's Teachings as Raised by his Contemporaries," *Philosophy East and West*, 23: 163–186; Chen Qing-lan; Chen Jian (陳建), Zhang Bo-xing (張伯行) and Zuo, Zong-tang (左宗棠) eds (1968) *Chen Qing-lan Xiansheng Xuebu Tongbian* (陳清瀾先生學蔀通辯) 12 volumes (卷). Taipei: Yi wen yin shu guan (藝文印書館).

[21] See Kim, Youngmin (2003) "Luo Qinshun (1465–1547) and His Intellectual Context," *T'oung Pao*, 89(4/5): 367–441. Also De Bary ed. (2008) *Sources of East Asian Tradition*: 451.

[22] Ki-baik Lee; Edward W. Wagner trans. (1988) *A New History of Korea*, Cambridge, MA: Harvard University Press: 243.

The relationship between political thought and political order in Europe at this time, in contrast, is intimately related to religion, including Jean Bodin, King James I of England and, most importantly, Thomas Hobbes. Jean Bodin (1530–1596) wrote his *La Six Livres de la Republique* ("Six Books of the Republic") in 1576, clearly influenced by the religious conflict in France. He follows the tradition, derived from Aristotle, of rooting politics in the household. It is the family who owns property and families are the foundation of the state. The father was an authoritarian figure who ruled the family in a private realm that was based on natural law. Similarly, a state or commonwealth (*republique*) only exists where all private subjects are under the rule of a common sovereign. This constitutes a political community with a unity beyond differences in religion, ethnicity, and so on. There can be only one sovereign. If a king is sovereign, then a parliament is only advisory, if the parliament is sovereign then the king is its instrument. Bodin takes this sovereignty to be the unlimited, perpetual, unconditional right to make, interpret and execute law. He considers it essential to the well-ordered state. Bodin also assumes that this power will only be exercised in accordance with natural and divine law. He does not discuss what happens if they conflict. His goal is to create a transcendent authority which all can obey without question for the common good. It is an appeal for religious toleration based on an overarching sovereign as a source of unity. In fact, the warfare between French Catholics and Protestants did not end until 1598, when Henry of Navarre assumed power as Henry IV and issued the Edict of Nantes. The Edict declared Catholicism as the state religion of France, but promised to treat Protestants with equality as royal subjects, and provided a large degree of religious freedom within majority Protestant regions. To some degree this compromise is consistent with Bodin's thought.

In England, conflict over religion was central to the late Tudor dynasty (1485–1603). At the end of the dynasty, however, the political thought was relatively undeveloped so that Richard Hooker's (1554–1600) *Of the Lawes of Ecclesiastical Politie*, written in 1594, seems a step backward when compared to Bodin because Hooker insists that there can be no separation of church and state, which is a very medieval approach. He argued that there is one community in which church and state are one so to be a member of one is to be a member of the other. So long as it is a Christian state, there is no reason for a Christian to object to the type of Christianity which is up to the sovereign to decide. This book is a justification for the Tudor compromise of a state church under the national sovereign. It is not religious toleration by the state but asking for toleration by different dissenting sects of the mode of state church. The political works of James I of England, simultaneously James VI of Scotland (1566–1625), were an even greater retrograde step to insist on the unfettered divine right of kings. He argued that kings are breathing images of God on earth, they are God's lieutenants, and even called gods by God. The king is the head without which a body is useless. God appoints the king as law giver so they are above the law and responsible only to God. The power of the king is supernatural and not subject to debate. The king's right descends to rightful heirs. This cannot be altered for any reasons, even utility.

In contrast, Thomas Hobbes' (1588–1679) *Leviathan or The Matter, Forme and Power of a Common Wealth Ecclesiasticall and Civil* (usually, *Leviathan* for short), a radical rethinking of political order, was published in 1651, after the execution of James I's son Charles I in 1649 and the end of the English Civil War (1642–1651) in which those supporting the Parliament defeated the Royalists. Rather than rely on traditional modes of political thought Hobbes argues for a focus on first principles from natural civil philosophy and rejects the "vain philosophy" of the ancients and scholastics, primarily Aristotlean and neo-Platonist metaphysics.[23] Hobbes argues that everything starts with motion and that motion leads to passions, passions to speech, speech to discourse. Discourse is used as justification for motions and passions but also fosters beliefs and faith in solutions. Discourse, in turn, leads to intellectual virtues (and defects), to "Forms of Knowledge" and ultimately "Religion." From this logic, Hobbes posits that the natural condition is equality but without law and power to enforce the law, equality leads to a war of all against all so that life is "solitary, poor, nasty, brutish and short."[24] This situation leads to two laws of nature. The first law is to seek peace and the second law is to surrender liberty to secure peace, and this in turn requires the mutual transfer of rights which is the definition of a "Contract." From this follow other laws of nature, such as justice. Yet, despite these natural laws, Hobbes argues that there needs to be an authority to provide security and order. This cannot be done by one group or a multitude. There must be one sovereign to which all are subject (following Bodin). The sovereign is absolute and perpetual. The sovereign alone can make law, interpret law and decide succession. Finally, he argues that all authority is still based on consent, because even in the event one is oppressed by a tyrant, there remains the choice to flee or kill oneself as an alternative to consent.

---

[23] Thomas Hobbes (1651) *Leviathan, or the Matter, Forme, & Power of a Common-wealth Ecclesiasticall and Civill*, London: Andrew Crooke, at the Green Dragon in St. Pauls Churchyard: 78.

[24] Hobbes (1651) *Leviathan*: 415–437.

THE EMERGENCE OF ARGUMENTS FOR POPULAR POWER AND GOVERNMENT

As noted above, Actualization or Realization (*Xiànchéng* 現成) School can be considered the left-wing of the Wang Yangming movement. The term *xiànchéng* (現成) jp. genjō) probably was derived from Chan/Zen, for example in the *genjō kōan* (現成公按) translated as "Actualizing the Fundamental Point," in an essay by the Japanese Zen teacher Dōgen in which he argues that *genjō* represents all phenomena that comprise the universe, including our subjective understanding of the world and the objective world itself. The *Xiànchéng* (現成) School of Wang Yangming, therefore, seeks to realize the ideals of neo-Confucianism by using our subjective understanding to reach out and have an impact on the world as it is now. The two important direct students of Wang Yangming in this school were Wang Longxi (王龍溪 1498–1583) and Wang Xinzhai (王心斎 1483–1541) both of whom demonstrate this radical and partially Chan Buddhist tendency.

Wang Longxi could certainly be accused of tilting the philosophy toward Buddhism. He argued that people have inherent knowledge of the good, but his arguments are suspiciously like those Buddhists who argue there is a Buddhahood in all people. In doing so, he slightly distorts Wang Yangming. For example, Wang argues that: "The absence of good and evil characterizes the original substance of mind. The presence of good and evil characterizes [the mind's] exercise of thought. Knowledge of good and evil characterizes [the mind's] intuitive knowledge. The doing of good and ridding of evil characterizes [the mind's] correction of things,"[25] that is, acting on knowledge of good returns to the original substance. Wang Longxi rewords this as:

> Once it is realized that the mind is devoid of either good or evil, then its thinking, its knowledge, and the things (it corrects) all likewise become devoid of either goodness or evil ... the nature conferred by Heaven is so purely and utterly good that the motivation for mental activities and responses is spontaneous and cannot be helped; hence "goodness" cannot be ascribed to it. For it, evil is certainly absent, but goodness too cannot be held to exist.[26]

This is more Buddhist in its denial of good than Wang Yangming's original. Wang Longxi even makes this affinity between Wang Yangming and Buddhist salvation explicit in other passages. It is also radically egalitarian:

---

[25] Fung, Yu-Lan; Derk Bodde trans./ed. (1983) *History of Chinese Philosophy, Volume 2: The Period of Classical Learning from the Second Century BC to the Twentieth Century AD.* Princeton, NJ: Princeton University Press: 624.

[26] Fung; Bodde trans. (1983) *History of Chinese Philosophy*, vol. 2: 624.

The innate knowing of the mind-and-heart partakes of the holy, the sagely. It is the spirituality of nature, supremely empty and divine, utmost nothingness and transforming power. Requiring neither study nor deliberation, as the Heavenly it is what comes naturally. At the lowest level it can be readily understood by even ignorant men and women: in its highest reaches it goes beyond the comprehension of even sages and worthies so that they liken it to the sun or moon shining in the heavens.[27]

This is almost Taoist in origin but that should not be a surprise given the affinity of Chan Buddhism and Taoism.

Wang Xinzhai goes further in extending this philosophy to the masses. He argued that the streets were full of Sages who needed neither books nor examinations to know how to do the right thing. Wang Xinzhai shares a belief in the essential goodness of all people similar to Wang Longxi, but Xinzhai and his followers are more faithful to the original Wang Yangming in avoiding an extreme Buddhist interpretation and merely suggesting that it was not enough to know principles, it was also important to act upon them. However, some of the arguments promoted a radical egalitarianism that might even be seen to be similar to Mozi:

> To make the self secure, one must love and respect the self, and one who does this cannot but love and respect others. If I can love and respect others, other will love and respect me. If a family can practice love and respect, then the family will be regulated. If a state can practice love and respect, then the state will be regulated, and if all-under-Heaven can practice love and self-respect, then all under Heaven will be at peace.[28]

Wang Xinzhai and his followers were particularly keen to spread this message to merchants and even peasants. He founded the Taizhou School (泰州學派) which cut across all social and intellectual barriers in China from commoners to the highest officials. Wang Xinzhai's school produced thinkers such as He Xinyin (何心隱 1517–1579),[29] Luo Rufang (羅汝芳 1515–1588) and, most notorious of all, Li Zhi (李贄 1527–1602).

Li Zhi had a particularly strong Chan influence and denied the distinctiveness of neo-Confucianism by arguing that the three teachings (*sānjiao* 三教), that is, Literati, Taoism and Buddhism, all have a single message. Li Zhi's works included *A Book to Burn* (焚書), and, in 1602, after he was put in prison and committed suicide, the book was banned and, as

---

[27] De Bary et al. (1999) *Sources of Chinese Tradition*, vol. 1, 2nd edn: 857–858.
[28] De Bary et al. (1999) *Sources of Chinese Tradition*, vol. 1, 2nd edn: 861.
[29] 森紀子 (Mori Noriko) (1977)「可心隱論--名教逸脱の構図」(He Xinyin Ron – Meikyō Itsudatsu no Kōzu)『史林』(Shirin), 60(5): 650–689; Ronald G. Dimberg (1974) *The Sage and Society: The Life and Thought of Ho Hsin-yin*, Honolulu, HI: University of Hawaii Press.

he predicted, all confiscated copies burned, though some remained in private hands and were copied secretly.[30] He criticized the orthodox neo-Confucian encouragement of the bureaucracy, which he insisted was only used to oppress. He preached equality and liberty, and was emulated by others who attracted large crowds of followers – so much so that governments felt they had to suppress the Wang Yangming school as a whole. He challenged the Literati to embrace real life and not a rarified notion of what life should be based on some unrealistic ideal. As he argued in an essay on "The Legitimacy of Being Self-Interested," the true gentleman should be familiar with:

> the desire for goods, sexual satisfaction, for study, for personal advancement, for the accumulation of wealth; the seeking out of the proper geomantic factors (*fengshui* 風水) that will bring blessings to their children—all the things that are productive and sustain life in the world, everything that is loved and practiced in common by the people, and that they know and say in common.[31]

By the time of Li Zhi, however, the Ming dynasty was in decline and these ideas – or any similar ideas – were easily a threat to its stability. This helps explain the suppression of Wang Yangming thought in continental East Asia.

Wang Yangming also had an impact in Tokugawa Japan where it lingered much longer. Nakae Tōju (中江藤樹 1608–1648) can be considered the first major teacher of Wang Yangming (王陽明 jp. Ōyōmei) in Japan. Originally the son of a farmer in Omi province, Nakae was adopted at the age of nine by an uncle who was the samurai retainer for a minor lord. In 1617 he moved with his grandparents to another domain. However, when he was 27, he returned to Omi with the excuse that his mother was ill and he had to be filial. He then set up his own school in the Tōju mansion from which he derived his working name. Initially he followed the teachings of Zhu Xi but slowly began to be persuaded by Wang Yangming's version of neo-Confucianism, particularly his theory of obtaining knowledge of things from the things themselves (and not just speculation). He is also known for teaching the most prominent Wang Yangming follower in the early Tokugawa period, Kumazawa Banzan.

Kumazawa Banzan (熊沢蕃山 1619–1691) was born the son of a *rōnin* in Kyoto, and when he was eight he was adopted by a maternal uncle. After being taught by Nakae Tōju, he returned to his home domain, led by a local

---

[30] 李贄 (Li Zhi); 増井経夫訳 (Masui Tsuneo trans.) (1969)『焚書：明代異端の書』(Funsho – Meidai Itan no Sho) 東京：平凡社 (Tokyo: Heibon Sha).
[31] De Bary et al. (1999) *Sources of Chinese Tradition*, vol. 1, 2nd edn: 871.

lord who favored Wang Yangming thought, and set up a domain school, one of the first such schools in the country. In 1649, he accompanied his lord to Edo (Tokyo). He created an association for educating commoners in 1651 which led to the establishment of the first school in Japan for commoners in 1670. During a flood and famine in 1654, he worked on relief efforts. He then became involved in efforts to help poor farmers and agricultural policy in general. However, his reforms were criticized by older advisors of his lord and his advocacy of Wang Yangming thought was attacked by Tokugawa officials, including Hayashi Razan. As a result, he went into hiding. However, pressure from his opponents within the domain and in the Tokugawa regime led to him being ejected from the domain. Kumazawa went to Kyoto in 1658 and set up his own school but once his fame as a teacher spread again he was forced out of Kyoto in 1661 and for the rest of his life was hounded from place to place. However, he continued to write, including criticism of Tokugawa policy. He died at the age of 74 still under attack from the Tokugawa authorities. Kumazawa Banzan was important because he transformed Wang Yangming studies from a means for individual spiritual enlightenment under Nakae Tōju into a method for political reform. Following from Wang Yangming ideas, Kumazawa saw the human mind (jp. *shin* 心) as embodying the principle (jp. *ri* 理) and insisted that one must act on that basis. Kumazawa believed to do so meant to apply Wang Yangming ideas to political theory with the goal of reforming government. For example, he believed that merit and not heredity should be the basis for the selection of officials for government posts. He also opposed *sankin kotai* (参勤交代) or "alternative attendance" where the lords of all domains were forced to spend part of the year in residence in the capital, because Kumazawa viewed it as a waste of resources. He also believed that the laws that prohibited samurai from engaging in farming or commerce based on strict class rules were harmful to the samurai's ability to understand problems of the Japanese economy and particularly communities that were primarily agricultural. The Tokugawa regime, however, saw Kumazawa's ideas as destabilizing. Indeed, any teaching of Wang Yangming in general was supposed to be suppressed but the Shogunate only had full control of its own domains and not of all of Japan due to the decentralized nature of the Tokugawa regime so as a result Wang Yangming thought continued to be taught, particularly in domains outside of direct Tokugawa control.

Similar to the Wang Yangming philosophy, the English Civil War created an opportunity for republican and even radical egalitarian ideas to flourish. The earliest of these movements, the Quakers, predates the Civil War, but helped to create the basis for later developments. Quakers practiced radical equality to the extent of they refused to use respectful language (rejecting the use of "thee" and "thou") and treated everyone equal, such as charging everyone the same price for items that they sold, which was not the common practice at the time. Quaker Meeting Houses also operated without priests so that anyone could stand and speak. The more radical group called the Levellers, however, grew out of the New Model Army which had defeated the forces of King Charles I, and was drawn from the rank and file soldiers who demanded a wide extension of the franchise, the abolition of the monarch and House of Lords, equality before the law and religious toleration. The Diggers, also called the True Levellers, went so far as to occupy unused land held by aristocrats and other wealthy landowners. Use of violence and legal action to evict them was not immediately successful due to popular support but eventually the landowners got their way. One thinker who shared the True Leveller perspective, though he was not necessarily one, was Gerrard Winstanley (1609–1676). He favored a sort of primitive libertarian communism.[32] He was not against the state but attacked the state in so far as it protected the wealth and privileges of a few. In the Civil War, the removal of the king led to the transfer of crown lands to the state so for Winstanley it was a natural next step that the land of the aristocracy should be confiscated as well. This land must be owned in common for the benefit of all the people, including those who had fought in the Civil War.

Most political thinkers in this period were less radical but there is a pronounced tendency in favor of republican or at least constitutional monarchy. For example, James Harrington (1611–1677) in his *Oceana* (1656), also argues that landownership is important because it determines regime type. A few landowners make others dependent on them (as Machiavelli argued), but many landowners provide for a free and stable state (as Aristotle claimed). He favored the division of large estates through restrictions on inheritance. This reform must be based in law to create a large gentry to counter-balance and replace the aristocracy. Nonetheless, this does not mean he was necessarily opposed to monarchy.[33] Similarly, John Milton (1608–1674) in his *The Ready and Easy Way to Establish a Free Commonwealth* (1660) argued that a ruler must only act on behalf of the people and when one does not, that ruler can be removed. This was compatible with constitutional monarchy but might have seemed dangerously democratic republican at the time. Milton also opposed state funding of the church because he saw it as a source of religious corruption. Religion

---

[32] Gerrard Winstanley; Christopher Hill ed. (1973) *Law of Freedom and Other Writings*, Harmondsworth: Penguin Books.
[33] Rachel Hammersley (2013) "Rethinking the Political Thought of James Harrington: Royalism, Republicanism and Democracy," *History of European Ideas*, 39(3): 354–370.

should be based on individual conscience. The church should be concerned with spiritual matters and the state with secular matters so that the two are distinct and separate. Finally, Algernon Sidney (1623–1683) in his *Discourses Concerning Government* (1698) shared Milton's view that power should be based on the consent of the people and that the best leadership was by those of natural ability and not necessarily heredity. Again nothing Sidney wrote was incompatible with constitutional monarchy but he was executed for opposing the monarchy, in part due to this work, even though it was only published after his death.

WOMEN IN THE ERA OF RELIGIOUS REVOLT

In East Asia, this period of revolt seems to have empowered women and allowed them more freedom, though with some qualification. As we have seen in previous chapters in the case of Hōnen and Shinran, Pure Land Buddhism and True Pure Land respectively, particularly in Japan, took an interest in the salvation of women. There was some ambiguity over the reasons why women are particularly in need of salvation and that problem continues in the case of Rennyo. Rennyo generally expresses a keen consciousness of the need to provide salvation for women but in some of his letters he seems to be accepting the view that women are in particular need of help by rebirth in Pure Land because they are more defiled than men when he uses the term *nyonin shōki* (女人正機), often interpreted as women have a special need for compassion. This is reinforced by comparison with Shinran's theory of *akunin shōki* (悪人正機), that those who are evil are especially in need of Buddha's compassion, but the general tone of Rennyo's letters is to make a special effort to involve women and make them welcome as an important part of the True Pure Land Buddhist community in a way that empowered rather than excluded.[34] The radical Wang Yangming thinker Li Zhi rejected the idea that women were inferior to men in innate intelligence, and argued that many historical women such as Empress Wu were actually superior. He also criticized orthodox neo-Confucian discrimination against women but he did not believe women should be emancipated and praised widows who chose suicide over remarriage.

The rise of the Tokugawa Shogunate in Japan and Qing dynasty on mainland continental East Asia led to many more restrictions on women

---

[34] Matsumura Naoko; Maya Hara trans. (2006) "Rennyo and the Salvation of Women," in Mark L. Blum and Shin'ya Yasutomi eds, *Rennyo and the Roots of Modern Japanese Buddhism*, Oxford: Oxford University Press: 60.

in contrast to the previous period. Tokugawa rules inspired by neo-Confucianism, put more restrictions on women compared to the previous era but these were probably worse for the samurai and *daimyō* families than the bulk of the population who often continued traditional practices. The Tokugawa era retained a nostalgia for the freer and more decadent times for both men and women in the previous Momoyama-Aizuchi period.[35] Even though the rigid division of the sexes loosened at the end of the Tokugawa period, it appears a strict version was advocated if not enforced in early Tokugawa.[36] A similar transformation occurred in the early Qing dynasty with a return to more orthodox neo-Confucianism. Gender roles were more restrictive and works of popular culture in the early Qing implied that the fall of the Ming dynasty was due to its feminine qualities and the failure of women to uphold traditional roles.[37]

Luther in many ways was like Shinran in that he married to demonstrate the problems with Christian thinking of his time, just as Shinran did not believe that living life as a monk was necessarily good for achieving salvation and was probably a hindrance. It is in relation to marriage that Luther considered himself to be helping women escape from the ideal of virginity of the Catholic Church, but marriage could be as oppressive as the virgin ideal, and Luther himself believed that women were to be "quiet, pious and submissive."[38] The other great protestant reformer Calvin saw women as inferior in many ways, arguing that they are more prone to such sins of vanity and sexual seduction, and were made as inferior by God.[39] At the same time, Calvin seems to view women as equal to men before God in terms of the need for redemption, much like Rennyo, but with a less positive overall view of women as Rennyo. Yet, Calvin is radical in rejecting St. Paul's advice that women must be silent in church and cover their heads as not central to the Christian thinking.[40] At the same time, Calvin excludes woman from positions of authority within the church.[41] Here is difficult to compare because the Buddhist church is much less insti-

---

[35] Neil Francis McMullin (1977) "Oda Nobunaga and the Buddhist institutions," PhD dissertation, Vancouver, BC: University of British Columbia: 291.

[36] Sumiko Sekiguchi (2010) "Confucian Morals and the Making of a 'Good Wife and Wise Mother': From 'Between Husband and Wife there is Distinction' to 'As Husbands and Wives be Harmonious,'" *Social Science Japan Journal*, 13(1): 95–113.

[37] Wai-Yee Li (1999) "Heroic Transformations: Women and National Trauma in Early Qing Literature," *Harvard Journal of Asiatic Studies*, 59(2): 363–443.

[38] Susan C. Karant-Nunn and Merry E. Wiesner-Hanks (2003) *Luther on Women: A Sourcebook*, Cambridge: Cambridge University Press: 13.

[39] Mary Potter (1986) "Gender Equality and Gender Hierarchy in Calvin's Theology," *Signs: Journal of Women in Culture and Society*, 11(4): 725–739.

[40] E. Jane Dempsey Douglass (1984) "Christian Freedom: What Calvin Learned at the School of Women," *Church History*, 53(2): 155–173.

[41] Potter (1986) "Gender Equality and Gender Hierarchy in Calvin's Theology": 729.

tutionalized but women would have been active in some form, especially in the period Rennyo was alive, more than would have been possible in Calvin's time or afterward. Certainly, later Calvinists, such as John Knox (c. 1514–1572), the Scottish Calvinist leader, were clear in their negative view of women. Knox was brutally critical of female rulers in the context of working against both Mary Queen of Scots (Mary Stuart 1542–1587) and Elizabeth I of England (Elizabeth Tudor 1533–1603).[42] However, the work of the Calvinist Thomas Hobbes has aspects that can be given a feminist reading because even though he does justify the subjection of women by men, his justification is that it is convention and not nature or even custom that requires this arrangement.[43] Hobbes' views appear to have inspired Margaret Cavendish to make the argument that women can be educated to be just as capable as men to participate in civil society.[44] In contrast, the Republican Milton held conventional Puritan, or at best contemporary "humanist" views on women, which were not so advanced as one might think.[45]

The exception to the subordination of women in the West was the more radical dissenting sects. Winstanley and the Diggers began to rethink the position of women in society though it is never given the focus or thought necessary to constitute a fully radical departure from conventions of the time so are not as progressive as they might first appear.[46] It was the Quakers who adopted a position of radical equality with all members, including women, free to speak in the Quaker Meeting Houses, and leading to the development of the radical female theology of Quaker women such as Dorothy Waugh, Sarah Tims, Mary Fisher and Elizabeth Wilson in the late seventeenth century.[47] Indeed, the Quakers were a major force behind the eventual emergence of the women's rights movement in the US and beyond.[48]

---

[42] John Knox (1790) "The First Blast of the Trumpet against the Monstrous Regiment of Women" (1571) in *The History of the Reformation in Scotland and Other Works*, Edinburgh: H. Inglis: 437–451.

[43] Gabriella Slomp (1994) "Hobbes and the Equality of Women," *Political Studies*, 42(3): 441–452.

[44] Karen Detlefsen (2012) "Margaret Cavendish and Thomas Hobbes on Freedom, Education, and Women," in Nancy J. Hirschmann and Joanne H. Wright eds, *Feminist Interpretations of Thomas Hobbes*, University Park, PA: Pennsylvania State University Press: 149–168.

[45] Paul N. Siegel (1950) "Milton and the Humanist Attitude Toward Women," *Journal of the History of Ideas*, 11(1): 42–53.

[46] Elaine Hobby (1999) "Winstanley, Women and the Family," *Prose Studies*, 22(2): 65.

[47] Hobby (1999) "Winstanley, Women and the Family": 66.

[48] Nancy A. Hewitt (1986) "Feminist Friends: Agrarian Quakers and the Emergence of Woman's Rights in America," *Feminist Studies*, 12(1): 27–49.

CONCLUSION

The parallels between the Reformation in Europe and religious revolt in Japan are intriguing but the differences are greater than the similarities. In Europe, states were torn between continuing a strong relationship with the Catholic Church or recreating a national church based on Protestantism. Much of the political thought of this period in Europe reflects theorizing in support of centralized political authority or a more decentralized commonwealth depending on the orientation of the thinker toward the religious nature of the state they favored or opposed. This intellectual ferment produced some fundamental rethinking of political theory but needs to be seen as somewhat parochial in its context. In Japan, the diversity of the Buddhist sects meant that there was no established sect and the success of the True Pure Land and Nichiren sects was limited to specific localities and successful only because of the breakdown of central authority. The adoption of neo-Confucianism by the Tokugawa Shogunate, and its regulation of the Buddhist sects, meant that religion was removed as a possible source of political dissent. Neo-Confucianism came late to Japan and was never embraced to the degree it was in Joseon Korea, for example, but it was an off-the-shelf solution that required minimal adaptation to the Japanese context.

More interesting from the point of view of political thought in East Asia was Wang Yangming thought. It constituted a serious challenge to political authority in the Ming dynasty and in the Tokugawa Shogunate. Its philosophy of radical egalitarianism did not constitute a full political philosophy because it relied too much on seeking autonomy without addressing the nature of political authority. In this sense, Wang Yangming thought, particularly in the late Ming dynasty, has affinities with the radical thought of the Levellers, Quakers and Winstanley, with similar limitations. Republican political theory was articulated more explicitly in Europe but it took the Enlightenment, particularly the thought of John Locke, to give popular government a theoretical (or metaphysical) basis to explain how popular freedom can be compatible with political authority.

10. Enlightenment and historicism (1670–1790)

The age of the "Enlightenment" in the West is important because it is also the period in which the different civilizations of the world began to come into more intimate and sustained contact. It is also when the West is meant to have developed a much more secular and philosophical approach to the world with the beginnings of modern notions of science and empirical epistemology. This is contrasted with religion, superstition, scholasticism and metaphysics, which is meant to be prevalent in the non-West. However, even in the West, religion was still an important influence behind opposition to scholasticism and metaphysics.[1] The icon of Western science, Isaac Newton, believed in a metaphysics that, for him, complemented rather than contradicted his physics.[2] Moreover, what is supposed to be modern may not be. Take for example, Descartes and his rational analysis of existence, starting with the premise "I think, therefore I am." Reason and rationality were debated long before the seventeenth century everywhere as we have seen. Neo-Confucianism is premised on the concept of rational understanding of the universe through principles (*li* 理) to the extent that a key Enlightenment figure such as Voltaire could hold up the Qing state as a form of successful secular rational rule. Even Descartes' skepticism is not new as Buddha dealt with this challenge in ancient India. In fact, Buddhists would be the first to point out that Descartes could not be sure that there is even a self or an "I" that thinks. Descartes' logic is predicated on a coherent continuous entity, such as the Christian concept of a soul, as its foundation. It is no wonder then that he is able to use this basic point to reconstruct and justify a Christian god from this seemingly skeptical or rational premise.

We must start with the rise of new modes of textual interpretation in East Asia, Islam and the West, including approaches that appear to be historicist, but in all cases challenge orthodoxy and provide the basis for

---

[1] Alister McGrath (1987) *The Intellectual Origins of the European Reformation*, Oxford: Basil Blackwell.
[2] Edwin A. Burtt (1925) *The Metaphysical Foundations of Modern Physical Science: A Historical and Critical Essay*, London: Kegan Paul, Trench, Trubner.

later thought. This chapter is premised on anti-scholasticism and empiricism, not only in John Locke, one of the leading figures of the Western Enlightenment from whom one might expect it, but also East Asian and Islamic thinkers. One helpful comparison is between Locke and Shāh Walīullāh who both start their analysis of politics from the evolution of society and reach similar conclusions about tolerance and authority. The final aspect of the Enlightenment that requires attention is the hidden metaphysics in the Western Enlightenment, which can be seen more clearly by comparison with Eastern ideas and thinkers who may have influenced the emergence of some of the key ideas of the Western Enlightenment in the first place. Once again, the role of women, which is increasingly prominent around the world, is also a useful corrective to the assumption that the West is superior.

TEXTUAL CRITICISM, INTERPRETATION AND HISTORICISM

One feature that is striking in political thought of this period (roughly, the seventeenth and eighteenth centuries) is the role of philology and textual analysis as the basis for new interpretations of texts in order to challenge orthodoxy. The role of hermeneutics in the Reformation and Renaissance has already been discussed but the Enlightenment was also a product of reinterpretation and, more importantly, greater awareness of the historical context in which texts are created. Awareness of history hints at early forms of historicism, though strictly speaking historicism as a concept emerges much later. Nonetheless, textual issues and radical reinterpretation were a key part of this period including in the European Enlightenment.

Textual issues were central in East Asia. This was clear even when Emperor Kangxi (康熙帝 1654–1722) of the newly formed Qing dynasty ordered the compilation of the Kangxi Dictionary (*Kāngxī Zìdiǎn* 康熙字典) in an attempt to win over the Chinese elite, of which Literati were a large part. Many scholars and former officials still refused to serve the new dynasty out of loyalty to the defunct Ming dynasty but Kangxi asked scholars to work on the Dictionary without taking up an official position in the new dynasty. As a result, many found themselves gradually taking on more and more responsibilities until some were incorporated into the civil service. Those who refused were initially left alone, which included a number of Literati scholars taught by the Wang Yangming follower Lou Rufang, namely, Huang Zong-xi (黃宗羲 1610–1695), Gu Yanwu (顧炎武 1613–1682), and Wang Fuzhi (王夫之 1619–1692). This group also tended to be critical of the failures of neo-Confucianism in the late Ming dynasty and focused on an evidential approach (*kǎozhèng* 考證). This led them to also approach the texts of ancient classics using critical philology to attempt to read the texts as they were originally written and not based on neo-Confucian (Song dynasty) interpretations. This approach was called "Han Learning" (漢學) due to their belief that the Han dynasty period interpretation of the texts was better than later versions.

Wang Fuzhi, for example, wrote commentaries on the early Literati classics (including five on the "Yi Jing" or *Book of Changes*) in an attempt to reconsider the orthodox interpretation but he was unable to completely escape the influence of neo-Confucians such as Zhang Zai and Zhu Xi. Nonetheless, Wang's approach put more emphasis on *qi* (氣 or real stuff, energy or material force), which can be perceived and for which there is evidence, and argued that *li* (理), or principle, form, or idea, is only manifest in real things, that is, *li* is derived from *qi*, as others critical of Zhu Xi and the Song Learning in general have argued. However, Wang takes this further by insisting that moral values only arise from concrete human practice. In contrast to Zhu Xi, Wang claims it is not necessary to reject emotions that arise from the joys and vicissitudes of human life, as the Buddhists do, but one must respond to them appropriately. Wang thinks that we must use our senses rationally to understand the world in which we live but he does so by implicitly rejecting the intuitionism of Wang Yangming as well as the quietist speculation on principle of Zhu Xi. This led Wang Fuzhi to advocate reform because he believed that political authority should be based on rational understanding of how human beings can best live together and opposed fatalist interpretations of the operation of the Tao (道). Similarly, Gu Yan-wu supported this approach by using philology to reconstruct the phonological system of ancient Chinese and recover the sense of old rhymes and texts based on his belief that Song (neo-Confucian) thinkers had misread and distorted the meaning of ancient texts. As with Wang Fuzhi, he focused on practical activities and advocated personal responsibility for making the country better as a goal for everyone, not just officials or the Literati, by working to improve things on a practical level.

The Han Learning approach reflected the persistence of tensions between the Literati and the new dynasty. The new dynasty adopted orthodox Zhu Xi thought and made it even more bureaucratic and authoritarian in order to serve the requirements of state. This is apparent in the "Sacred Edict" (*Sheng Yu* 聖諭) set out by the Qing. It starts with filial piety and put great emphasis on harmony and moderation but it also opposes non-orthodox teaching and insists on deference to hierarchy. Neo-Confucianism was useful for the Qing. The system of training, examination and recruitment was in place and it could be used to manage and legitimate any regime. However, Qing rule still had its dangers for the Literati. For example, Lü Liuliang (呂留良 1629–1683), who had been a fierce opponent of the Manchu invasion and the Qing efforts to establish a new dynasty, appeared to have relented a few years after the official establishment and stabilization of the new state, but he still refused to take office in the new regime. The fifth Qing Emperor Yongzheng (雍正帝 1678–1735), initially ignored Lü Liuliang's stance because, although it was known that he took a principled stand against serving the Qing, Lü still supported orthodox neo-Confucian values of loyalty and service to the state. Lü eventually felt compelled to become a Buddhist monk to avoid trouble with the authorities but continued to teach and write until his death. However, when a rebellion occurred said to be inspired by Lü's works, Emperor Yongzheng had his grave destroyed and his works attacked officially. His poems were considered to contain coded messages against the Qing so the next emperor, Qianlong (乾隆帝 1711–1799), ordered the banning and burning of all his works as part of a general literary inquisition. This attack on Lü and others needs to be put in context. Banning and burning literature was not new in China, and it is not surprising that Qing rulers were sensitive regarding widespread anti-Manchu feelings among the Chinese. However, early occasional repression became more systematic under Emperor Qianlong's reign and extended to suppression of challenges to Song learning neo-Confucian orthodoxy.

Due to this repression of unorthodoxy, scholars emerged who subtly challenged the foundations of neo-Confucian orthodoxy by undermining its foundations rather than confronting it head on. One was the Yan-Li school (顏李學派) of "learning by practice" (*xi xing* 習行). Yan refers to Yan Yuan (顏元 c. 1635–c. 1704). Yan's father had gone away to fight when he was young and not returned, and when a close relation of his died, he felt compelled, based on his studies, to follow the strict mourning ritual of "Family Rites of Zhu Xi" (*Zhuzi Jiali* 朱子家禮) to the extent that he refused food and drink. However, he fell ill and nearly died. This led him to think that neo-Confucian ideals were unrealistic and turned instead to "actual writings, actual activities, actual forms, and actual use" (*shiwen, shixing, shiti, shiyong* 實文、實行、實體、實用). He argued that it was the lived moral principles of Confucius and his followers rather than abstract ideas in books that mattered. Yan Yuan advocated the "six arts" (*liuyi* 六藝), that is, the classical education of the Zhou dynasty (1122–256 BC), which included Rites (*li* 禮), Music (*yue* 樂), Archery *(she* 射*)*, Charioteering (*yu* 禦), Calligraphy (*shu* 書), and Mathematics (*shu* 數). To this, he added a practical education in applied disciplines such as warfare, agriculture, industrial crafts, finance, and hydrology.

Ideas of Yan Yuan were developed by his follower Li Gong (李塨

1659–1733), who had been trained in music, archery, mathematics, calligraphy and military sciences. In 1690 he passed the civil service exam (*jǔrén* 举人) but did not take up office and became a wandering scholar instead in order to disseminate Yan's and his own ideas. Li Gong argued that all things have both conditional principle and chronological principle *(tiao-li ri-li* 條理日理), so principle itself depended on the situation. That is, there is potential principle which is inherent in a thing and the contemporary manifestation of principle in a thing. A concrete entity, with potential and in time, must exist for principle to be manifest so in this sense *qi* (氣) precedes *li* (理). This is why he believed that classical texts must be supplemented with an understanding of actual practice (*xi xing* 習行). From his point of view, this is why neo-Confucianism failed to help previous dynasties. "True knowledge" (*zhen zhi* 真知) consists of learning what can work and must precede action (*xue sheng xing, xue xian xing* 學勝行，學先行).

Another important thinker is Dai Zhen (戴震 1724–1777), who is best known for his commentary on Mencius published in 1776, the *Mengzi Ziyi Shuzheng* (孟子字義疏証). He used "evidential learning" (*kaozhen* 考証學) methods to interpret the text of Mencius and key concepts, such as principle (*li* 理), humanness (*ren* 仁) and righteousness (*yi* 義). Dai Zhen believed that Mencius argued goodness in human nature is innate but this is not the same as being derived from Heaven and principle. The Song neo-Confucians, such as Zhu Xi, and their successors adopted the Buddhist view that desires were obstacles even though neo-Confucians claimed to be opposing Buddhism. By attempting to deny desires and emotions, the neo-Confucians made a mistake because the path to Sagehood is to understand a range of feelings and experience the failures and successes of one's desires. It is this experience that allows one to reform the world and rule it well.

Finally, there is Zhang Xue-cheng (章學诚 1738–1801), who takes a thoroughly historical approach. Zhang argued that the classics need to be read keeping in mind the origins of the text, that is, the circumstances that gave rise to the texts and how they were transmitted and interpreted in response to changing circumstances over time. In contrast to the neo-Confucians who viewed principles in Literati texts as embodying fixed principles, Zhang suggested that the ideas reflect an attempt to cope with the needs of the time in which they were written. He pointed out that the (six) major classics of ancient literature are nothing more than historical texts (*liù jīng jiē shǐ* 六經皆史) from which lessons can be derived but only by adapting the lessons for the world as it is now and not as it was in the past. He was also not widely known in his own time with his most important works, *On Literature and History* (*Wenshi tongyi* 文史通義) and *The General Meaning of Bibliography* (*Jiaochou tongyi* 校讐通義), not published until 1832, and became important only then because they represented a pragmatic alternative to neo-Confucian orthodoxy. Even if there is a tendency of recent scholarship to see Zhang as more modern than he really was,[3] he did contribute to a critical trend in Literati studies that made possible the reinterpretation of the classics outside of neo-Confucian orthodoxy.

A similar, parallel and possibly connected development in the interpretation of Literati classics also occurred in Japan at this time. Of course, Literati thought was more eclectic and less orthodox neo-Confucian in Japan than in the Qing and certainly compared to that in Joseon Korea. However, as in the Qing, there was a return to ancient texts in Japan that formed the basis of a critique of neo-Confucianism. Yamaga Sokō (山鹿素行 1622–1685) is considered the founder of the ancient learning (*kogaku* 古學) approach in Japan. He was born the son of a *ronin* (浪人) or masterless samurai in Aizu in the Mutsu domain. He went to Edo aged six and was taught by official and orthodox Literati scholar Hayashi Razan but also undertook military studies, Shinto, among other disciplines. For reasons that are unclear, he was sent into internal exile to Harima domain where he was allowed to teach but was limited to propagating his better known works on military education and Buddhism. In his surviving texts, he maintains the orthodox neo-Confucian emphasis on personal moral discipline and political practice with an emphasis on investigation of things (*gewu*) and finding the principle (*li*) to guide political goals and actions. At the same time, Yamaga did not believe that personal morality was the only basis of rule. Most importantly he began to question the methods of Zhu Xi and other neo-Confucians by moving away from a purely introspective approach as the source of principle toward more focus on external standards as found in ancient texts though did not reject the Zhu Xi approach entirely. Others, such as Itō Jinzai (伊藤仁斎 1627–1705), however, went even further. For example, Itō Jinzai emphasized Confucius and rejected later texts, such as the *Great Learning* central to Zhu Xi's approach. He believed that such texts contradicted or distorted the ideas of Confucius. In fact, he rejected the neo-Confucian philosophy of Zhu Xi in its entirety.

The most important figure in Japan in this context, however, is Ogyū Sorai (荻生徂徠 1666–1728). Half a century after Ito, Ogyū Sorai began to advocate the "study of ancient words and phrases" (*kobunjigaku* 古文辞學) and produced his radical antithesis to the Zhu Xi school. These critical arguments gradually undermined the metaphysical basis of the Tokugawa orthodoxy and led to its theoretical weakening. Ogyū originally criticized Ito Jinzai but toward the end of his career, Ogyū was the most

---

[3] Wong, Young-tsu (2003) "Discovery or Invention: Modern Interpretations of Zhang Xuecheng," *Historiography East and West*, 1(2): 178–203.

forceful advocate of the ancient learning approach. There were significant differences, however. Whereas Ito Jinzai still respected the *Analects* and *Mencius* as the basic texts, Ogyū Sorai felt the Five (or Six) Classics, which predated Confucius, were more important as the depository of China's classical heritage as they contained essential facts. The *Four Books*, including *The Great Learning* and the *Doctrine of the Mean* as well as the *Analects*, were for him no more than interpretations of these primary sources. Interpretations must be supported by facts, however, before they can be accepted as definitive explanations of the Way so if the facts are disregarded and interpretations alone are the focus, over-generalization and poor judgment are likely to result.[4]

An important aspect of Ogyū Sorai was that he was an active political advisor. He had been born in Edo (Tokyo) into the family of a physician to the Shogun Tokugawa Tsunayoshi (徳川綱吉 1646–1709) and Sorai's brother was physician to the Shogun Tokugawa Yoshimune (徳川吉宗 1684–1751). Initially in 1696, he was recruited by the Shogun Tsunayoshi under the patronage of Yanagizawa Yoshiyasu (柳沢吉保 1659–1714) but upon Yanagizawa's death, Sorai left government service and set up a private school, the *Kenenjuku* (蘐園塾). After 1722, he returned to government to become a close advisor to the Shogun Tokugawa Yoshimune. It was for Yoshimune that he wrote his "Political Discourses" (*Seidan* 政談) which appears to be the practical application of his political thought. Sorai is a conservative, which is not surprising given his background and position.[5] He justifies social hierarchy and the subordination of servants, though there are some hints of meritocracy[6] and he is also concerned about the damage to society caused by poverty[7] with the admonition that wealth should be used for the public goods and that rulers are responsible for dealing with unemployment and homelessness[8] as well as controlling the wealth of merchants.[9] His works "Distinguishing the Way" (*Bendō* 弁道) and "Distinguishing Terms" (*Benmei* 弁明), however, constitute a rigorous

---

[4] Both the translations by Tucker (Ogyū Sorai; John A. Tucker trans. (2006) *Ogyū Sorai's Philosophical Masterworks: The Bendô and Benmei*, Honolulu, HI: University of Hawaii Press: 139) and Najita (Tetsuo Najita trans./ed. (1998) *Tokugawa Political Writings*, Cambridge: Cambridge University Press: 3) are limited here. Tucker weakens the force of Sorai's views by using the word "meanings" instead of "interpretation," whereas Najita slightly overstates by using the term "spiritual meaning."

[5] Ogyū Sorai; Olof G. Lidin trans. (1999) *Discourse on Government (Seidan)*, Wiesbaden: Harrassowitz Verlag.

[6] Ogyū Sorai; Lidin, Olof G. (1970) *Ogyū Sorai: Distinguishing the Way (Bendō)*, Tokyo: Sophia University Press: 78–82.

[7] Ogyū; Lidin (1970) *Distinguishing the Way*: 13.

[8] Ogyū; Lidin (1970) *Distinguishing the Way*: 55–56.

[9] Ogyū; Lidin (1970) *Distinguishing the Way*: 46.

and systematic effort to analyze the basic philosophical concepts of Literati thought with an emphasis on what words meant in ancient times compared to what they had come to mean in his day. This gave Sorai the hermeneutic flexibility to reinterpret texts, including making sense of them in a way that benefits rather than constrains.[10] Indeed, Sorai's most notable and influential student, Dazai Shundai (太宰春台 1680–1747), was more radical in that he advocated Japan open to world trade to increase national wealth because otherwise the only alternative was the redistribution of wealth.[11]

The tendency in this period to approach what seemed to be timeless principles but to analyze them in historical perspective is very similar to the work of Giambattista Vico (1668–1744). Indeed, Najita in his preface to Ogyū's political writings likens him to Vico as a historicist.[12] That is, Ogyū believed that ideas were created and not universal, given and timeless. However, he found that the Ways of the Ancient Kings, reflected in the earliest classics (that is, *Analects* and before) are the best guide to follow for human conduct. One might rightfully be reluctant to accept this characterization, and, of course, it is anachronistic to say that Sorai was a historicist but one could argue that it is true of Vico as well. However, if one does not insist on the strict definition of historicism as the name of the German historical movement in the nineteenth century and adopts a looser definition, then historicism was perhaps more common in East Asia than Europe at this time and only a few thinkers such as Vico stand out as similar in the West.

Vico's arguments are striking, particularly because they challenged the prevalent Enlightenment tendency to elevate science over the humanistic study of human societies.[13] He posited the *verum factum* principle, that is that truth is verified by creation not empirical observation. Only those who create a thing can fully understand it, so this is why God understands all because he created everything. This explains why we can comprehend mathematics, law and history as creations made by other humans like us. Understanding of human history requires recognition that it is a process of cultural development; once we understand how things have arisen, then we can fully appreciate them. Vico advocates "reconstructive imagination" to empathize with others and enter their minds by using our ability to *fantasia* (imagine). Even ideas that are foreign to us in place and time can be

---

[10] Ogyū; Lidin (1970) *Distinguishing the Way*: 11 and Najita trans./ed. (1998) *Tokugawa Political Writings*: 112–113.
[11] Najita trans./ed. (1998) *Tokugawa Political Writings*: 141–153.
[12] Najita trans./ed. (1998) *Tokugawa Political Writings*: xiii–liv.
[13] Vico, Giambattista; Thomas G. Bergin and Max H. Fisch trans. (1968) *The New Science of Giambattista Vico: Revised Translation of the Third Edition (1744)*, Ithaca, NY: Cornell University Press.

grasped because all humans were created by God so what humans in turn create can be understood by other humans. He particularly emphasizes *phronêsis* (practical wisdom) rather than abstract theory to make sense of human creations, including politics. He used this to make sense of classical literature to demonstrate what it might have meant then and not what it meant to readers in his own time.

DEVELOPMENT OF HUMAN SOCIETY, TOLERANCE AND JUSTICE

It is this tendency to reconstruct the historical development of human society that helps us understand the work of John Locke (1632–1704) and Shāh Walīullāh (شاه ولي الله b. 1703–d. 1762). This pair of thinkers may appear to be a surprising choice for comparison and could even be viewed as unfair. Locke is usually assumed to be the champion of science and rationality at the foundation of liberal democracy, whereas Shāh Walīullāh supports *jihad* or war against infidels, which has been associated with Islamic fundamentalism. To some degree this characterization is true but it points to the problem of hindsight reinterpretation of the work of individuals that ignores the original historical context in which they lived. That is, there are elements of toleration, science and innovation in the work of Shāh Walīullāh and of tradition and faith in Locke, so it is more how the societies adapted their ideas and the context in which they did so that is important to fully understanding the significance of these figures. At this point we must point out the differences and similarities while holding back on making judgments based on how we know the ideas were used subsequently. It is only in the context of later historical developments that current interpretations make sense.

In his seminal "Second Treatise on Government," Locke begins with the distinction between the state of nature, in which individuals must reason with each other as equals, and the state of war, which he sees as a situation where reason is not possible and one is under immediate threat so must kill or be killed. The state of nature is the condition where there is no authority but the state of war can occur whether there is a central authority or not. Using evidence from non-Western cultures, particularly native Americans, he argues that natural condition is the state of nature with reasoned interaction between equals. However, the state of nature changes with the development of property. Once someone adds labor to a piece of land to cultivate it or build a dwelling, then property comes into existence. He also considers the theory that family relationships are the basis for political society, particularly the authority of the father over the family, and demonstrates that the father's role in a family is not the same as political authority. He describes political society as "Those who are united into one body, and have a common established law and judicature to appeal to, with authority to decide controversies between them and punish offenders, are in civil society one with another."[14] Once there is such a body united and able to legislate to make laws for the public good, it is no longer the state of nature. Locke goes on to declare that, therefore, absolute monarchy is inconsistent with civil society and civil government because it would not make sense to leave the state of nature just to give arbitrary power to one individual. In fact, his evidence points to all societies originally being formed as a social pact to unite as one and not the surrender of power to an individual. The reason that they are willing to join in society with others is "to unite for the mutual preservation of their lives, liberties and estates, which I call by the general name – property. This is the purpose of government."[15] This is based on the will of the majority even if they give power to a few select individuals (an oligarchy) or to an individual (a monarchy). However, no matter to whom the community has given power, it is "limited to the public good of the society" and "can never have a right to destroy, enslave, or designedly to impoverish."[16]

Locke also insists that a conqueror is not a legitimate ruler because one cannot give consent when it is extorted by unlawful force. He seems to suggest that if those conquered are incorporated into one people under the same laws and freedom, then there is less of a problem, though this is implied and not explicit. On the other hand, use of simple force to rule is pure despotism. No one will be able to dispute their rights to be governed by consent in such a situation, but there is no legitimacy in a situation where authority is based on whatever brute force gives to the stronger over the weaker. Those who were forced to submit and their descendants always have the right of freeing themselves from tyranny and creating a government to which they consent. He gives the example of Grecian Christians (under the Ottoman Empire) and asks rhetorically if they, therefore, should have the right to throw off "the Turkish yoke."[17] One wonders, however, if he would have extended this right to the people colonized by Britain, including the Irish in his day, not to mention the vast areas of the British Empire in the nineteenth century. The main purpose of his

---

[14] John Locke (1759) *The Works of John Locke esq.* vol. 2, London: D. Browne, C. Hitch and L. Hawes, J. Shuckburgh, A. Millar, J. Beecroft, John Rivington, James Rivington and J. Fletcher, J. Ward, R. Baldwin, J. Richardson, S. Crowder, P. Davey and B. Law, T. Longman, E. Dilly, R. Withy, T. Payne, and M. Cooper: 191.
[15] Locke (1759) *Works*, vol. 2: 202.
[16] Locke (1759) *Works*, vol. 2: 205.
[17] Locke (1759) *Works*, vol. 2: 222.

argument is domestic so he can use this example of oppressed people elsewhere to argue that any usurpation and tyranny, international or domestic, where sovereign authority is used not to protect the people, but instead for personal "ambition, revenge, covetousness, or any other irregular passion" then the people are at "full liberty to resist the force of those who, without authority, would impose anything upon them."[18]

There is a vigorous debate in the literature over the influence of religion on John Locke's political thought, with much of it centered on supporting or refuting the work of Jeremy Waldron.[19] Some even suggest that his religious views are completely irrelevant. For example, it can be pointed out that even though Locke asserts frequently in the "Second Treatise" that God's will is the source of natural law, in his *Essay Concerning Human Understanding* he describes the psychological processes whereby we develop our concept of God but the implication is that it is devoid of real meaning so that any emphasis on God is merely to support public belief in the myth of divine natural law as essential to political stability.[20] In fact, some go so far as to say the *Two Treatises on Government* are a clear and strong case against revelation as the source of authority.[21] Yet, at the same time, Locke requires all members of a political community to belong to a religion, for example, by opposing atheism because there is no basis on which an atheist could make a sacred bond or oath in the absence of belief in a superior power that would guarantee their word, though even this could still fit with the purely pragmatic use of religion in Locke.[22] It may be that the religious aspect of Locke is even more fundamental to his logic. It can be argued that even his tendency to secularization is based on the Protestant distinction between the spiritual kingdom of God and the worldly kingdom of secular society.[23] Traditionally Catholics and most

---

[18] Locke (1759) *Works*, vol. 2: 228.
[19] Jeremy Waldron (2002) *God, Locke, and Equality: Christian Foundations of John Locke's Political Thought*, Cambridge: Cambridge University Press, and Paul. E. Sigmund (2005) "Jeremy Waldron and the Religious Turn in Locke Scholarship," *Review of Politics*, 67(3): 407–418 and J.W. Tate (2013) "Dividing Locke from God: The Limits of Theology in Locke's Political Philosophy," *Philosophy and Social Criticism*, 39(2): 133–164. See also Joshua Mitchell (1990) "John Locke and the Theological Foundation of Liberal Toleration: A Christian Dialectic of History," *The Review of Politics*, 52(1), 64–83, Kim Ian Parker (1996) "John Locke and the Enlightenment Metanarrative: A Biblical Corrective to a Reasoned World," *Scottish Journal of Theology*, 49: 57–73.
[20] William T. Bluhm, Neil Wintfeld and Stuart H. Teger (1980) "Locke's Idea of God: Rational Truth or Political Myth?" *The Journal of Politics*, 42(2): 414–438.
[21] Stanley C. Brubaker (2012) "Coming into One's Own: John Locke's Theory of Property, God, and Politics," *The Review of Politics*, 74: 207–232.
[22] Elissa B. Alzate (2014) "From Individual to Citizen: Enhancing the Bonds of Citizenship Through Religion in Locke's Political Theory," *Polity*, 46(2): 211–232.
[23] Jakob De Roover and S.N. Balagangadhara (2008) "John Locke, Christian Liberty, and the Predicament of Liberal Toleration," *Political Theory*, 36(4): 523–549.

Muslims would find this distinction incomprehensible or dangerous. It is based on the idea of a personal relationship with god and not the need for a comprehensive spiritual community with authority to create the conditions for a better life now and in the hereafter.

Shāh Walīullāh also sets forth a theory of the development of political society that shares many features with that of Locke but draws on the Islamic intellectual tradition. The key work for understanding Shāh Walīullāh's political theory is "The Book of the Conclusive Argument from God" (*Kitāb Ḥujjat Allāh al-Bālighah* كتاب حجة الله البالهة).[24] This is based on his universal history of human development in which there are certain basic forms of sociopolitical organization and levels of moral development. It is a more detailed, sophisticated and nuanced theory than Locke. Shāh Walīullāh identifies four stages in human development or *irtifāqāt* (ارتفاقات). First is when nomads and forest dwellers form small social groups with a common language, practice monogamy, bury their dead and live in dwellings. This also includes the initial stages of agriculture (digging wells, planting trees, domestication of animals) and simple exchange (barter). Second is urbanization and the creation of cities run by wise rulers. These societies have the resources to refine their conduct in such areas as aesthetics and different forms of wisdom (*hikmah* حكمة). Science or thought is put into eating, dressing, business, agriculture, virtues/morals to guide behavior. Efforts are made to protect the community from external aggression (organization of defense). However, as the division of labor increases[25] and more complex forms of exchange requires authority to maintain justice,[26] it leads to the next stage of *irtifāqāt*. The third stage is where humans develop the science of ruling or political science of a city/state (*siyāsat al-madina* سياست المدينه). With larger and more complex societies, including the need to organize society to cooperate for collective goals, obedience to a ruler is required. This is because at this stage, the state requires all members of society to be as a single person in terms of binding themselves into a whole but since unanimity is impossible with a large group of individuals, obedience to a single authority is required upon which everyone should agree. The more disputatious and violent the society, the more need for a single authority.[27] This authority is required to carry out tasks for common

---

[24] Full translation is: Shāh Walīullāh; Marcia K. Hermansen trans. (2005) *The Conclusive Argument from God: Shāh Walī Allāh of Delhi's Ḥujjat Allāh Al-Bālighah*, New Dehli: Kitab Bhavan. Key passages on political thought have also been translated in Muhammad Al-Ghazzali (2008) *The Socio-Political Thought of Shah Wali Allah*, New Delhi: Adam Publishers & Distributors.

[25] Al-Ghazzali (2008) *The Socio-Political Thought of Shah Wali Allah*: 158.

[26] Al-Ghazzali (2008) *The Socio-Political Thought of Shah Wali Allah*: 159–160.

[27] Al-Ghazzali (2008) *The Socio-Political Thought of Shah Wali Allah*: 161.

benefit, such as public works (defensive walls, inns, forts, ports, bazars, bridges, wells, fountains, boats on river banks, and so on), giving incentives to traders and merchants to continue to supply necessary goods to society through cordial persuasion, ensuring that outsiders are treated fairly, ensuring farmers do not leave their land, encouraging craftsmen to excel in their products and improve them, and fostering the education of society in learning various arts and sciences, such as calligraphy, mathematics, history, medicine, and other useful branches of knowledge. However, excessive amounts should not be spent on supporting soldiers, scholars, poets and ascetics who do not benefit society. Heavy taxes that are ruinous to farmers, merchants and artisans must be avoided. Taxes should be fair and convenient. Although less explicit about consent, his view was similar to Locke in the view that the ruler must act for the people.

The fourth level is the highest level of civilization. It emerges because the conflict between smaller states leads to competition that eventually ends in the creation of empires, such as that of Alexander the Great or Rome. For Shāh Walīullāh, however, the ideal is the creation of a Caliphate, which will act most wisely for the benefit of all humans in this situation. The Caliphate should avoid action that is not intended to achieve a specific purpose. For example, the Caliphate cannot be expected to depose all tyrants and oppressive rulers so must engage them with truces, treaties, and tribute relations. Waging war must be reserved for dealing with those tyrants that are particularly unjust or brutish.[28] The ideal ruler for Shāh Walīullāh seems to be an Imām as someone who can and would understand the collective interests of civilization and the affairs of the city-state but such individuals are rare. Such an Imām realizes that since human development is universal, the origin and essence of all religion is one even if the prescribed laws may vary[29] so the leader (*Imām*) requires the substance of his *shari'a* to be:

> like a natural course of life for the people of virtuous realms, whether they be Arab or non-Arab. . . the substance of this *sharī'ah* should also conform to his own community's existing heritage of the knowledge of *irtifāqāt*. In ascertaining this conformity, the conditions of the majority of the people in the community is to be kept in view.[30]

The Imām must build on existing conditions to inspire others to follow *shari'a*.[31] Shāh Walīullāh was incredibly tolerant of differences within Islam (Sunni, Shia, Sufi, and so on) and potentially this extends to other

---

[28] Al-Ghazzali (2008) *The Socio-Political Thought of Shah Wali Allah*: 173
[29] Al-Ghazzali (2008) *The Socio-Political Thought of Shah Wali Allah*: 193.
[30] Al-Ghazzali (2008) *The Socio-Political Thought of Shah Wali Allah*: 226.
[31] Al-Ghazzali (2008) *The Socio-Political Thought of Shah Wali Allah*: 227.

faiths as well, particularly Abrahamic faiths (Judaism and Christianity). In this sense, he is as tolerant as John Locke. Locke is only interested that those of other faiths are free to worship, which Islamic rulers would normally permit in any case.

The *Kitāb Ḥujjat Allāh al-Bālighah* does have an entire chapter on *jihad* but it has a mainly defensive rationale at first, though there is also some sense of a civilizing mission at points in the text. As noted above, the ideal ruler focuses on *jihad* against tyrants and he also indicates that it is important that those being conquered accept it as the preferred alternative, which is not unlike Locke's view of conquest. However, most of his discussion of *jihad* involves spiritual disposition of those fighting and how to manage the gains of war. There is a discussion on the ethics of fighting such as not breaking truce agreements, and that women and infants should not be killed, and killing the elderly should be avoided if at all possible, as well as the need to avoid cutting down trees or setting fires, and no killing of animals without a clear military rationale.[32] Without trying to deny a potential aggressive interpretation of this discussion of *jihad*, it also needs to be seen in the context of a declining Sultanate against an aggressive and ruthless enemy, the rise of the anti-Islamic Maratha Confederacy that fatally weakened the Sultanate and led to the formation of the Maratha Empire (1674–1818). It is in this context that Shāh Walīullāh's work led to an Islamic intellectual revival in South Asia though it did not save the Sultanate itself.

One should pause here to consider a more conservative interpretation of Islam, one that was the minority then, as now, that of Muhammad ibn ʿAbd-al-Wahhab (محمد بن عبد الوهاب b. 1703–d. 1792). Muhammad ibn ʿAbd al-Wahhab focused on the idea that God was a single unique indivisible entity and, therefore, to rely on any other form of divine or spiritual power other than God violates the notion of *tawḥīd* (توحيد) or the "unity" of God. This led him to a strict interpretation of Islam that did not permit reverence of the graves or shrines of Islamic saints or great figures in Islamic history as well as natural monuments and phenomena. Even to ask and expect God (Allah) to help is seeking the divine in a way that is other than through pure faith and submission. This led him and his successors to declare other Muslims who did not share his views as *takfir* (تكفير), a form of verbal excommunication by insisting that another Muslim is an unbeliever.[33] Despite resistance to his ideas, Muhammad ibn ʿAbd

---

[32] Al-Ghazzali (2008) *The Socio-Political Thought of Shah Wali Allah*: 273.
[33] Even if it is true, as Tarikk Firro (2013) "The Political Context of Early Wahhabi Discourse of Takfīr," *Middle Eastern Studies*, 49(5): 770–789, has demonstrated that *takfiri* discourse was significantly shifted to an even more intolerant interpretation of *takfir* by ibn

al-Wahhab was able to develop a relationship with Muhammad ibn Saud (محمد بن سعود d. 1765) in which ibn ʿAbd al-Wahhab gave religious sanction to the efforts of ibn Saud to conquer the Saudi Arabian peninsula and ibn ʿAbd al-Wahhab was given authority in religious matters. Muhammad ibn Saud successfully dominated the Saudi Arabian peninsula (hence the name) and the Saudi family have continued to rule the area with the support of the descendants of ibn ʿAbd al-Wahhab, who control religious institutions. The contrast between ʿAbd al-Wahhab and Shāh Walīullāh is striking even if they appeared to have been training as jurists at the same time in Medina. Shāh Walīullāh argues that Islam must be reinterpreted to suit the current age, which is consistent too with his training in Hanafi jurisprudence with its emphasis on the role of reason. This contrasts with the more fundamentalist approach of ʿAbd al-Wahhab, who was trained in the conservative and literalist Hanbali School of jurisprudence. One must not make the mistake of conflating different forms of Islam into one or ignoring the relative quality of some thinkers in comparison to the West.

DID THE ENLIGHTENMENT HAVE NON-WESTERN FOUNDATIONS?

There is evidence that the Western Enlightenment was influenced by non-Western sources. Even if the direct influence is weak, similarities in the types of arguments should force us to look at the metaphysical foundations of the Enlightenment in the West. That is, even though Enlightenment thinkers tended to reject traditional neo-Platonist and Aristotelean metaphysics in favor of more rational foundations based on logic, these logical foundations were grounded in assumptions that are metaphysical in character. This is a common tendency in modern Western political thought.

We have already noted use of the example of Native Americans on Locke's political theory, and there is a strong suggestion that Locke's *Essay on Human Understanding*, a work of epistemology that had some bearing on this political thought, was influenced by the work of ibn Tufayl (بن طفيل d. 1185) also known as ibn Tufail (Aben Tofail or Ebn Tophail), whose neo-Platonist inspired novel *Ḥayy ibn Yaqchān* (حي بن يقظان), had just been translated in Oxford when Locke was working there and contains

---

ʿAbd al-Wahhab successors, who emphasized violence as an acceptable way of dealing with religious and political opponents, the potential for abuse was present in ibn ʿAbd al-Wahhab's thought from the beginning.

speculation on how observation and experience can lead to knowledge of the world.[34]

French thinkers such as Montesquieu (1689–1755) also used non-Western examples, though in Montesquieu's case, they are used to highlight his view of French politics, and rely on the stereotype of oriental despotism so are hardly comparative political thought. In his *Persian Letters* (1721) for example, he attempts to examine and find the basic bonds that hold society together and puts an emphasis on fear and love, and in doing so, suggests a similar role in French as in Persian political society.[35] Similarly, the comparative history and sociology in his *De L'esprit des Lois* (The Spirit of the Laws, 1748) relies on non-Western cases.[36] There is some subtlety in Montesquieu's work that may be overlooked if one adopts the stereotype of oriental despotism as based on fear and an unconstrained despot. Montesquieu uses the notion of despotism based on fear to the European context but he also seems to realize that there is more complexity and nuance to how regimes work so that despotism can use intermediating political institutions, cultural practices, countervailing elites and separate social spheres to its advantage.[37] The focus on factors such as climate, where hot areas tend to despotism and cold areas to liberty seem to doom non-European areas of the world to despotism. However, Montesquieu could be said to be avoiding the universalism of most liberals by pointing out that political institutions must be adapted to political cultures rather than insisting that all societies should adopt the same political institutions and ideals.[38]

It is East Asian Literati thought, however, that played a significant role in the European Enlightenment, particularly in France and among the most radical elements. Baruch De Spinoza (1632–1677, in Latin

---

[34] Ibn Tufayl, Muhammad ibn 'Abd al-Malik (1686) *The History of Hai Eb'n Yockdan, an Indian Prince: or, the Self-Taught Philosopher*, London: for Richard Chiswell, and William Thorp, Bookseller in Banbury, which is also the likely source of Defoe's *Robinson Crusoe* (1719); "One could call this work, with perfect justification, a case study for the main thesis of Locke's Essay" according to Gül A. Russell (1993) "The Impact Of The Philosophus Autodidactus: Pocockes, John Locke, And The Society Of Friends" in Gül A. Russell ed., *The "Arabick" Interest of the Natural Philosophers in Seventeenth-Century*, Leiden: Brill: 224.

[35] Orest Ranum (1969) "Personality and Politics in the *Persian Letters*," *Political Science Quarterly*, 84(4): 606–627.

[36] Montesquieu; Melvin Richter (1977) *The Political Theory of Montesquieu*, Cambridge: Cambridge University Press.

[37] Roger Boesche (1990) "Fearing Monarchs and Merchants: Montesquieu's Two Theories of Despotism," *The Western Political Quarterly*, 43(4): 741–761 and Corey Robin (2000) "Reflections on Fear: Montesquieu in Retrieval," T*he American Political Science Review*, 94(2): 347–360.

[38] Keegan Callanan (2014) "Liberal Constitutionalism and Political Particularism in Montesquieu's 'The Spirit of the Laws'," *Political Research Quarterly*, 67(3): 589–602.

Benedictus De Spinoza) was the first to praise aspects of Chinese thought as a form of rationalist monist deism but it took Pierre Bayle (1647–1706) and Nicolas Malebranche (1638–1715) to pursue the idea based on access to the *Confucius Sinarum philosophus* (1687),[39] which was the first translation of the Literati classics in the West and gave an insight, if not always entirely accurate, to the nature of Literati thought.[40] This work certainly had an influence on important European thinkers such as Gottfried Wilhelm Leibniz (1646–1716),[41] and greatly influenced radical enlightenment.[42] This included Voltaire (1694–1778) who held up the Qing Literati as paragons of rational secular government and put Chinese history at the start of this world history in *Essai sur les moeurs et l'esprit des nations*.[43] It is in this context that we must consider the thought of two key Enlightenment thinkers.

A central figure in the Scottish Enlightenment who is sometimes overlooked in conventional histories of political thought is David Hume (1711–1776). Hume had great influence based on his thorough-going skepticism. He challenged the assumptions of the thinkers that we have discussed to this point, and, as a result, is considered a very modern thinker. At the same time, he tacitly accepts the inequality of society and takes an aristocratic view that the passions of the poor and uneducated must be contained.[44] Indeed, he argued that passions are what drive human beings and not reason as supposed by most thinkers we have examined. Therefore, the study of morals and politics must be based on understanding human psychology and sociology. Reason is only used once passions have been aroused and given a direction. He also warned against conflating what one thinks ought to happen with what actually exists, the so-called "is–ought" problem, that is, empirical statements about what exists, cannot be used

---

[39] Thierry Meynard S.J. ed. (2011) *Confucius Sinarum Philosophus (1687): The First Translation of the Confucian Classics*, Roma: Institutum Historicum Societatis Iesu.

[40] Yuen Ting Lai (1985) "The Linking of Spinoza to Chinese Thought by Bayle and Malebranche," *Journal of the History of Philosophy*, 23(2):151–178. See also David E. Mungello (1980) "Malebranche and Chinese Philosophy," *Journal of the History of Ideas*, 41(4): 551–578 and Gregory M. Reihman (2013) "Malebranche and Chinese Philosophy: A Reconsideration," *British Journal for the History of Philosophy*, 21(2): 262–280.

[41] See Casey Rentmeester (2014) "Leibniz and Huayan Buddhism: Monads as Modified Li?" *Lyceum*, 13(1): 36–57 and Daniel J. Cook (2015) "Leibniz, China, and the Problem of Pagan Wisdom," *Philosophy East and West*, 65(3): 936–947.

[42] Jonathan Israel (2007) "Admiration of China and Classical Chinese Thought in the Radical Enlightenment (1685–1740)," *Taiwan Journal of East Asian Studies*, 4(1): 1–25 and Jeffrey D. Burson (2015) "Unlikely Tales of Fo and Ignatius Rethinking the Radical Enlightenment," *French Historical Studies*, 38(3): 391–420.

[43] Voltaire; Jacqueline Marchand ed. (1962) *Essai sur les moeurs et l'esprit des nations*, Paris: Editions Sociales.

[44] Hume's political thought is concisely laid out in Hume's own words in David Hume; Fredrick Watkins ed. (1951) *Hume: Theory of Politics*, Edinburgh: Nelson.

to justify normative statements about what should be. Hume's *Natural History of Religion*, published posthumously, rejects the idea of teleology and divine design that underpinned natural law theory used by many political thinkers and also much of the science of the period.

There is a robust if indirect case that Hume's skepticism might have been influenced by Buddhism, with Hume's questioning of a coherent "self" as the basis for his reconsideration of the nature of human morals one of many striking similarities with Buddhism in his work.[45] There is the possibility that Hume was influenced by Buddhism while he was writing the *Treatise* in the French town, La Flèche, where there was a Jesuit Royal College which was associated with Ippolito Desideri, who had a deep understanding of Buddhist philosophy he had gained as a Jesuit missionary in Tibet for many years.[46] The links with French Enlightenment thinkers and East Asian thought through the work of Jesuits is well-known so it is not impossible that Hume was similarly influenced.

Similar issues have been raised with the work of Adam Smith (1723–1790). Adam Smith's *An Inquiry into the Nature and Causes of the Wealth of Nations* (1776) in which he adopts the logic of "laissez-faire" derived from the physiocrats Francois Quesnay (1694–1774) and the Marquis de Mirabeau (1715–1789) by arguing that the forces of supply and demand will lead to a balance in prices, wages and employment automatically through an "invisible hand."[47] This justifies his view that governments should not interfere with markets except to collect the bare minimum of taxes and protect property. It has been suggested that there is a Taoist inspiration for this concept given the similarity to *wu wei* or action by inaction because the physiocrats, from whom Smith drew much inspiration, were interested in China, including François Quesnay who wrote *Le Despotisme de la Chine*, first published in *Ephémérides du Citoyen* in 1767.[48] Nonetheless, it is unlikely that there is a direct connection between laissez-faire and Taoism because neither Quesnay nor others mention it

---

[45] David Hume; L.A. Selby-Bigge ed. (1896) *A Treatise of Human Nature*, Oxford: Clarendon Press: II. ii. 5 (363). See also N.P. Jacobson (1969) "The Possibility of Oriental Influence in Hume's Philosophy," *Philosophy East and West*, 19(1): 17–37; and James Giles (1993) "The No-Self Theory: Hume, Buddhism, and Personal Identity," *Philosophy East and West*, 43(2): 175–200.

[46] Alison Gopnik (2015) "How an 18th-Century Philosopher Helped Solve My Midlife Crisis: David Hume, the Buddha, and a search for the Eastern roots of the Western Enlightenment," *The Atlantic*, https://www.theatlantic.com/magazine/archive/2015/10/how-david-hume-helped-me-solve-my-midlife-crisis/403195/ (accessed May 22, 2012).

[47] Adam Smith (1945) *An Inquiry Into the Nature and Causes of the Wealth of Nations*, Woodstock Ontario: Devoted Publishing: 206.

[48] François Quesnay (1888) *Œuvres économiques et philosophiques de F. Quesnay, fondateur du système physiocratique*, Paris: Peelman and Co.: 563–660. English translation in Lewis A. Maverick trans. (1946) *China: A Model for Europe*, San Antonio, TX: Paul Anderson.

in their published writings. It is more likely that the notion came from Smith's *The Theory of Moral Sentiments* (1759) in which he suggests that ordinary human judgment is sound and, thus, will make correct decisions and adjust as appropriate in the absence of outside interference. He also argues that law cannot create virtue, that is, one cannot legislate morality. These ideas that underlie the assumptions of his political economy, sound very similar to Confucius, Mencius and other Literati who argued for the basic goodness of human beings and the inability of law to make individuals moral. In Smith, the argument for non-interference is based on a recognition of the limits of human action, though again, this is very close to the Taoist notion that interference often has unintended if not contrary consequences. This appears to be a case of similarity rather than causation though one should also note that there is a literature on the origins of the notion of the concept of the division of labor in Adam Smith that makes a strong case that the idea originated in Persian thought,[49] and one might also note that similar ideas were raised by ibn Khaldūn and Shah Walī Allah well before they were raised by Smith. Therefore, it is not the ideas of Smith that were unique. It was only how they began to be applied to political economy in Europe at the time that is notable.

This is not to say that all notions of rationalism and liberty in the Enlightenment have exact parallels in Islam and East Asia. For example, Jeremy Bentham's (1748–1832) utilitarianism is based on a purely rational argument and a rejection of tradition that would have been abhorrent outside the West as it was inside. Bentham's *A Fragment on Government* (1776) is part of an attack on the legal theory of Sir William Blackstone who emphasized the importance of tradition and precedent in common law. Bentham argued that the legal system needed to be reformed to make it more rational and consistent, in order to maximize public welfare and individual liberty. Such overarching principles and not the dead weight of tradition should guide the law and legal reform. Bentham is also famous for his "greatest happiness" principle that viewed the purpose of life is to maximize pleasure and minimize pain so that the best government would seek to make possible the greatest happiness for the greatest number.

This brings us to perhaps the most important and influential Enlightenment thinker, Immanuel Kant (1724–1804). In many ways Kant is a reaction to the skepticism of Hume and the rationalism of Bentham because such approaches tend to undermine the moral foundations of society. Though he follows Hume in his skepticism, Kant is unwilling to accept the pessimistic conclusion that the limitations of human knowledge

---

[49] Hamid Hosseini (1998) "Seeking the Roots of Adam Smith's Division of Labor in Medieval Persia," *History of Political Economy*, 30(4): 653–681.

require us to accept that arbitrary passions are what lead our moral decision making. Kant puts forward a metaphysics of morals to allow us to posit a transcendent logic that allows beings to comprehend the world. Since it is only possible to perceive phenomena (things as they appear to us) and not possible to get at *noumena* (things in themselves, as independent of any perception by others), then there have to be some a priori rules that allow us to grasp the nature or order of things in a logical system. This is the transcendental analytic. Therefore, Kant argues that morality and standards of what is "good" cannot come from nature or even God. It comes from an act of will that chooses freely to take up the duty to follow universal moral law. In order to do this, we must consider universal reasons (ones that apply to all individuals) that are the basis for our moral actions.

One key text in Kant's political thought can be found in the *Metaphysics of Morals* (Die Metaphysik der Sitten) of 1797. Kant suggests that the key universal law is to treat others as ends and not means, that is, not to view others for what they can do for you (or you can get out of them) but work with them to help them achieve their goals. Of course, these cannot be goals at one's own expense (or they would be treating you as an end) so the aim is to find a way of assisting one another to achieve each other's ends (goals, ambitions, and so on) in what has been translated as a *Kingdom of Ends* (Reich der Zwecke) by which he means "union of different rational beings unified in a system by common laws."[50] This constrains individuals but also provides the context in which they can perfect their moral duty.

Kant bases his *Reich der Zweche* on "recht," normally translated as "law" or "jurisprudence" but also meaning justice and right (as in the right thing to do), in many ways similar to "dharma" or the Law in this general interrelated and almost organic sense, as the way things are and can be. Thus, Kant's political theory is a theory of law or, at least, *rechtslehre* or doctrine of jurisprudence.[51] Kant divides the law into private and public law. Private law includes those rights that humans possess from nature (*naturrecht*) both in terms of the possession of property and in relation to living with others. Public law focuses on the establishment of the state, where there must be a sovereign who guarantees the liberty and equality of the members of the state. For this reason, Kant opposed pure democracy due to the possibility that majority rule would undermine individual liberty. Yet, though his notion of sovereign implied a monarchy, following

---

[50] Immanuel Kant; Thomas K. Abbott trans. (1879) *A Theory of Ethics*, London: Longman, Green: 74.

[51] Immanuel Kant; Mary Gregor trans. (1996) *The Metaphysics of Morals*, Cambridge: Cambridge University Press.

from classical authors such as Aristotle, Kant favored mixed government with elements of aristocracy and monarchy as the ideal. There remains a possible conflict between one's moral duty and loyalty to the state as a union of men under law. In such cases, one must follow one's duty but also be obedient to authority as much as possible. This compromise between duty and authority is not much different from Literati ethics in which one must obey the commands of the ruler but also try to advise the ruler if a mistake is being made, that is, obey but reprimand, even to the point that one's protest over a policy could result in one's death. This is no doubt a typical intellectual moral response to working with absolutist rulers.

There are also aspects of Kant's thought that have parallels with Buddhism even if there is little evidence of direct Buddhist influence on his thinking. One should point out that the early Western Buddhist scholar Edward Conze was dismissive of any comparison of Buddhism with Kant. Conze admitted the type of skepticism raised by Kant and earlier Buddhists has parallels[52] but rejects comparison because the context, that is, the historical conditions that produced each system of thought, and the purpose of the ideas in each case was different but, of course, neither of these points eliminates the possibility that the ideas are comparable.[53] In fact, there are many affinities of Kant's philosophy with Literati thought, particularly neo-Confucianism and, more specifically, Wang Yangming thought. More important for the argument here is precisely that these ideas are historically situated so that they can be compared and, at the same time, it demonstrates that it was not the rejection of metaphysics that made the Western Enlightenment possible but a different kind of metaphysics in each case that gave rise to similar approaches to common problems of human existence, ethics and politics. In fact, one recent study has found that some of the problems faced by Kant can be dealt with more effectively by using Buddhist inspired philosophical reasoning.[54] In the end, we can only say that in Kant, as in the rest of the thinkers of the Enlightenment, there are intriguing connections and certainly the basis for dialogue between the West and philosophical traditions outside the West.

---

[52] Edward Conze (1963) "Buddhist Philosophy and Its European Parallels," *Philosophy East and West*, 13(1): 9–23.

[53] Edward Conze (1963) "Spurious Parallels to Buddhist Philosophy," *Philosophy East and West*, 13(2): 105–115.

[54] Laura E. Weed (2002) "Kant's Noumenon and Sunyata," *Asian Philosophy*, 12(2): 77–95. However, as we will see the political thought that emerged from the Kyoto School, which is at the basis of this comparison, is not without its problems.

THE POSITION OF WOMEN IN ENLIGHTENED SOCIETIES

The Enlightenment is the first period in the West where we have female political thinkers, such as Mary Astell (1666–1731), who though a conservative member of the status quo elite, is a notable participant in the debates of her time.[55] However, even though other areas of the world did not have women writers such as Astell, who were also the exception in the West at the time, it did have women exercising power and with spaces and prerogatives not available to women in the West. In fact, political policies and ideologies to reinforce the subordination of women are often a testament to the potential power of women in these areas as seen in the fears articulated by prominent male political thinkers. It is a mistake, however, to assume that women were treated worse outside the West. It is a mistake to see non-Western women as exotic, erotic and passive, but it is also the modern Western myth that women outside the West are oppressed and the West is more enlightened about the role and potential of women, particularly in this period, and that non-Western women are universally and objectively worse off in any period. For example, in Tokugawa Japan, there is a recognition of the value of earlier female poets and writers with some prominent women involved in the literary and critical scene. Even if Ogyū Sorai's political advice to rulers, *Seidan* (政談), insists on trying to cut the ties of the ruling class to entertainers and what he saw as inappropriate women, the practice was so widespread that it was difficult for the Tokugawa regime to control.[56] This is why he feels compelled to attack the pretentions of elite women while discussing the virtue of mistresses and how to control women generally.[57] It has long been accepted that the restrictions on women in Tokugawa were most strictly applied to the elite samurai class and that peasant women were not necessarily treated so harshly.[58] Even if the extent of peasant freedom is disputed, it was clearly as great if not greater than enjoyed by the majority of women in the West. Certainly the demands of strict Christian morality and fear of accusations of witchcraft were not as much an issue in Japan as in the West.

---

[55] Mary Astell; Patricia Springborg ed. (1996) *Political Writings*, Cambridge: Cambridge University Press.
[56] Ogyū Sorai; Olof G. Lidin trans. (1999) *Discourse on Government (Seidan)*, Wiesbaden: Harrassowitz Verlag: 105–107.
[57] Ogyūi; Lidin trans. (1999) *Seidan*: 277–285.
[58] For example, see Laurel L. Cornell (1990) "Peasant Women and Divorce in Preindustrial Japan," *Signs*, 15(4): 710–732 and Anne Walthall (1991) "The Life Cycle of Farm Women in Tokugawa Japan" in Gail Lee Bernstein ed. *Recreating Japanese Women, 1600–1945*, Berkeley, CA: University of California Press: 42–70.

India in this period saw several female rulers. For example, Maharani Ahilya Bai Holkar (महाराणी अहिल्या बाई होळकर 1725–1795) was a Maratha Queen of the Malwa kingdom after her husband and only son died. She already had been taught to read and write by her father, which was unusual, but her father-in-law also taught her how to administer government and wage war, with her personally leading her armies into battle. There is also the case of Mamola Bai (1715–1795), a member of the Rajput community of ruling families who acted as regent and ruled Bhopal for nearly 50 years on behalf of two stepsons after the death of her husband. One should also note Joanna Nobilis Sombre (c. 1753–1836), popularly known as Begum Samru (बेगम समरू), but born with the name Farzana Zeb un-Nissa, who took control of the mercenary army of Europeans and Indians of her husband when he died, and fought the British until she was given rule of Sardhana in Uttar Pradesh. Even in the Mughal Empire, women such as Zeenat-un-Nissa (زینة النساء b. 1643–d. 1721), the second daughter of Emperor Aurangzeb (أورنكزيب b. 1618–d. 1707), was given the title of Padshah Begum (پادشاه بیگم), a special honorific designation of the most revered female of the empire, and was entrusted to give advice to the emperor and administer this household. In fact, the Begum title was given to many women, including female relatives and consorts of the emperor, which enabled them to exercise varying degrees of authority. In fact, it can easily be argued that women played an important but unacknowledged role as administrators, patrons and brokers throughout Mughal history.[59] However, Dalal points out, this arose in the eighteenth century due to changes in the conception of female space, for example, relaxation of the prohibition of courtesan and female performers from the *harem* and entertainment quarters in large cities such as Delhi, which allowed skilled women access to the rulers in ways that were not possible in previous centuries.[60] Moreover, the property rights and commercial activities of women in Mughal India appear to be more extensive than that in the West of the time, that is, up until the coming of the British systematically removed these rights and weakened the position of women.[61] The British also discriminated against female rulers though many successfully gained or regained power after the failure of the men put in place by the British.[62]

---

[59] Urvashi Dalal (2015) "Femininity, State and Cultural Space in Eighteenth Century India," *The Medieval History Journal*, 18(1): 126.
[60] Dalal (2015) "Femininity, State and Cultural Space in Eighteenth Century India": 133–134.
[61] Indrani Chatterjee (2016) "Women Monastic Commerce and Coverture in Eastern India Circa 1600–1800," *Modern Asian Studies*, 50(1): 175–216.
[62] Abida Sultaan of Bhopal (1980) "The Begums of Bhopal," *History Today*, 30: 30–35.

Shāh Walīullāh's views of women are traditional but indicate the need for mutual respect between men and women. In his discussion of the second level of *irtifāqāt*, Shāh Walīullāh discusses women in the context of marriage, children, possession and companionship. The instinctive need for sex requires contact and fellowship between man and woman, and mutual cooperation is necessary to take care of children.[63] His division of labor between the sexes is certainly very traditional. He considers the woman better able to nurse children, more skillful in ordinary matters and possessing a greater capacity for sacrifice but the woman is also said to be of lighter intellect, eager to evade hardship, and more complete in modesty and attachment to the house. The man, on the other hand, has more accuracy in intelligence, a stronger ability to protect his reputation, and greater courage when challenged but, on the negative side, also tends to wander more, debate excessively and jealously pursue aims. In his view men and women are considered essential to each other and should develop a spirit of camaraderie in which they share equally. However, he regards the custodianship of men over women as natural with "no difference between Arabs and non-Arabs." Although divorce is acceptable to Shāh Walīullāh, he believed it was necessary to impose restrictions so that the institution of marriage is not taken lightly, and to prescribe an intervening period (*iddah* العدة) between divorce and remarriage to protect lineage from confusion and doubt.[64] For the most part, the focus of Shāh Walīullāh tends to be on the misbehavior of men, obligations of the husband to live amiably with their spouses and protect their private life from indecency and disgrace but he also notes the obligations of the wife to be chaste, loyal to the husband and focus on the general welfare of the house.[65] Overall the emphasis is on the inappropriate behavior in men.[66] Sexual offenses, including sodomy and tribady are also mentioned, which lead people from healthy outlets and amount to the reversal of human nature like turning a male into a female and vice versa. Finally, Shāh Walīullāh argues that young women should not be allowed to fight in wars but that they can contribute to military efforts if their lives are not put into immediate danger. Older women are, however, allowed to fight in war if necessary.[67]

The journals of Lady Mary Wortley Montagu (1689–1762), who traveled to the Ottoman Empire in this period, seem to imply that in some ways

---

[63] Al-Ghazzali (2008) *The Socio-Political Thought of Shah Wali Allah*: 154.
[64] Al-Ghazzali (2008) *The Socio-Political Thought of Shah Wali Allah*: 156.
[65] Al-Ghazzali (2008) *The Socio-Political Thought of Shah Wali Allah*: 162.
[66] Al-Ghazzali (2008) *The Socio-Political Thought of Shah Wali Allah*: 171.
[67] Al-Ghazzali (2008) *The Socio-Political Thought of Shah Wali Allah*: 272.

women were freer under Islam than in the West at the time.[68] It is possible that this included the freedom to have affairs,[69] which may have been possible, but it seems more likely to have meant freedom from harassment and constant supervision by husbands and male family members. Women in Ottoman society appeared to have had a degree of anonymity in public and, at the elite level she saw, lived in gender-segregated spheres where women had control of their daily lives to a larger degree than in the West.

In Europe, the male figures of the Enlightenment were generally ambivalent about women though there is some sense of questioning the position of women in society. For example, Montesquieu's *Persian Letters* question the subordinate position of women, especially as based on religious values, which was as true in the West as in Islam at the time. Indeed, Montesquieu's analysis of the position of women is useful in how it demonstrated that the behavior of women is constrained by custom and tradition and shows that many of the features of femininity used as evidence of their inferiority are created by the disadvantaged position in which they have been put rather than inherent in women.[70]

Locke has a fairly egalitarian view of women in that he views marriage as a voluntary agreement, mainly for sex to create children but more importantly to provide support and assistance for the upbringing of children and other shared interests. He credits the strength of this relationship as based on the wisdom of God. However, Locke advocated giving power to the man because someone must be in charge and it "naturally falls to the man's share as the abler and the stronger."[71] He also acknowledges that sometimes the views of husband and wife may diverge and in those cases the wife should retain her share of common interests and property, and this demonstrates that the husband's power is not absolute and there are circumstances in which a wife is at liberty to separate from her husband. Civil authority then can intervene, which again shows the limits of the husband's authority, though the law still strongly favored the man in this period. Kant's views on women emphasize the inferiority, submissiveness and moral weakness of women in contrast to his general egalitarian

---

[68] Lady Mary Wortley Montague (1764) *Letters: Written During Her Travels in Europe, Asia and Africa to Persons of Distinction, Men of Letters, etc in Different Parts of Europe*, London: T. Becket and P.A. De Hondt.

[69] Afsaneh Najmabadi (2006) "Gender and Secularism of Modernity: How Can a Muslim Woman Be French?" *Feminist Studies*, 32(2): 251.

[70] Susan Tenenbaum (1973) "Montesquieu and Mme. de Stael: The Woman as a Factor in Political Analysis," *Political Theory*, 1(1): 92–103 and Susan Tenenbaum (1982) "Woman through the Prism of Political Thought," *Polity*, 15(1): 90–102.

[71] Locke (1759) *Works*, vol. 2: 190.

theories.[72] In fact, it demonstrates that the Enlightenment in Europe was in many respects theoretical rather than real for most women.

None of the discussion above should imply that the status of women was good in areas outside the West. The point is simply that women may have been treated better in some places than in the West at the time and conditions also varied within each society. Male dominance was a fact in all civilizations at the time. There are hints in Enlightenment thinkers of the basis for viewing women as equal, but as we have seen such thinking was not necessarily more advanced in the West at the time even if these ideas were subsequently expanded to include women. Certainly there is a lot of material to suggest that Westernization and modernization starting with the Enlightenment did not always mean improvements in the social or political status of women in much of the world, and may have made the situation worse especially as a result of imperialism.

CONCLUSION

An examination of political thought around the world at the time of the European Enlightenment suggests that there were many challenges to orthodoxy and reconsiderations of the basis of political theory. Of course, in all cases, the new theories were a continuation of older work. Just as Shāh Walīullāh drew on the work of ibn Khaldūn, Locke's work is unthinkable without Hooker and Hobbes. The parallels between the textual reinterpretation and historicism in East Asia and that of European thinkers, such as Vico, is clearly recognizable. The case for Islamic, Indian or East Asian influences on Enlightenment writers is relatively weak in terms of direct impact but some inspiration for rationality and secularism was drawn from outside the West, and there is an uncanny similarity with many key ideas that the West was highlighting and those that had been raised elsewhere before. Indeed, key Islamic and East Asian thinkers were revisited as the challenge from Western imperialism grew more serious because they suddenly seemed more relevant. At the same time, Western imperialism undermined the ability of non-Western societies to draw on their intellectual heritage by denigrating non-Western systems of thought as we will see.

---

[72] Susan Groag Bell and Karen M. Offen eds (1983) *Women, the Family, and Freedom: The Debate in Documents*, Stanford, CA: Stanford University Press: 110–115.

11. Revolution, romanticism and reform (1760–1860)

The "Age of Revolution" follows the "Age of Enlightenment." This makes sense not only from the point of view of Western thought because by this period the world was increasingly interrelated philosophically. The conflicts between beliefs and state power, the new hermeneutics of interpretation and rationalism of the new sciences all led to questioning of existing political arrangements and demands for change. Some of these issues were rehearsed in the English Civil War and the Commonwealth, but in England republicanism was not successful. However, the revolutions in the Americas, not just in North America but also in Latin America, were successful anti-colonial and republican experiments. The French Revolution was perhaps the most profound in its attack on existing political forms from the point of view of ancient states and its repercussions were felt across Europe and also beyond.

Revolution led to new ways of thinking and the creation of new political forms but these changes also led to the rise of counter-revolutionary conservatism and romanticism. This new conservatism was particularly strong in Europe and demonstrates that it was not the world outside the West which was slow to accept the promise of the Enlightenment and revolution. Romanticism was initially revolutionary in how it reimagined the nature of power and the need for freedom or autonomy under new forms of community and sovereign power. In fact, it was often not the revolutionaries but the Romantics who advocated enhanced rights for women. However, romanticism often ended as a new form of conservatism as it often ended the subordination of the individual to the nation.

Both revolution and reaction led to a series of movements toward reform everywhere around the world even if there were significant differences in the pace, extent and nature of change. For example, early proposals for reform in the Ottoman Empire tended toward enforcing stricter religious observance and centralization of authority. East Asian states felt that they should isolate themselves from the West to protect their societies until they realized that this was not the answer. The fate of reform was ultimately tied with imperialism, but in this stage, initiatives for change were often internal.

THE GLOBAL AGE OF REVOLUTION

There were two great revolutions in the late eighteenth century, the American and the French. The American is not as dramatic and far-reaching as the French. In fact, it is largely an effort to reject the claims of Britain through demands based on traditional notions of English rights and liberties, though these are often justified based on ideas drawn from the English and French Enlightenment. Nonetheless, there are aspects of the American experience that are worth mentioning in this context. In particular, it is useful to consider the thought of Thomas Paine, Thomas Jefferson and the Federalist/Anti-Federalist debate in the late eighteenth century.

Thomas Paine (1737–1809) was perhaps the most radical or well-known radical approach to politics in pre-revolutionary America. His *Common Sense* (1776) was fervently anti-monarchical and made a strong case for independence in a popular tone suited to mass democracy and the not academic theorizing of most of the founding fathers. Indeed, the elite were appalled at Paine's work. For example, John Adams replied to *Common Sense* in *Thoughts on Government, or in full Thoughts on Government, Applicable to the Present State of the American Colonies* (1776) by opposing Paine's idea of a single legislative body as conducive to tyranny and rejected Paine's view that men who did not own property should be allowed to vote and run for public office.

Thomas Jefferson (1743–1826) too was fairly radical for his time.[1] He idealized the independent yeoman farmer as the model of republican virtues of common sense, hard work and honesty. He viewed the corrupt and elitist political establishments based around monarchy to be the root of problems in Europe. He feared that the inhabitants of cities, especially financiers and industrialists, would place commerce and profit above the interests of their fellow citizens so he favored a decentralized political system, with democracy at the state or local level where possible. The church was also a potential source of elitism and corruption so he advocated separation of church and state at the federal level and incorporated it in the *Virginia Statute for Religious Freedom* he authored. He also believed that all males in the Commonwealth should be educated in order to promote cultural unity and enable citizens to fully enjoy a free press and debate essential to democratic society. Jefferson did limit the right to vote to those who owned property but he wanted to make it easier for the poor to obtain land so that everyone who worked and paid taxes would

---

[1] Thomas Jefferson; Terence Ball ed. (1999) *Jefferson: Political Writings*, Cambridge: Cambridge University Press.

effectively be entitled to participate in government. At his most radical, he believed that rebellion and violence was often necessary by asking "what country can preserve its liberties, if the rulers are not warned from time to time, that this people preserve the spirit of resistance? Let them take arms" because the "tree of liberty must from time to time be refreshed with the blood of patriots and tyrants. It is its natural manure."[2]

It was against this ideal of decentralized democracy and resistance to power, that *The Federalist Papers* were written by Alexander Hamilton (1757–1804), James Madison (1751–1836), and John Jay (1745–1829) supporting ratification of the United States Constitution to provide for a stronger central government after the failure of the decentralized Articles of Confederation to create effective government.[3] The greatest controversy was caused when the Federalists opposed listing the specific rights of citizens in the Constitution because, as Alexander Hamilton argued (Federalist No. 84), specifying certain rights might be interpreted as limiting rights to only those mentioned. In the end, James Madison proposed amendments to the Constitution, which became the basis for the Bill of Rights, to deal with objections raised by critics of the Constitution, particularly the so-called Anti-federalists, who wrote their own papers against the dangers of strong central government powers without protection of the rights of individuals.[4] The Bill of Rights set out individual rights of citizens and explicitly notes that these rights are not the only ones and others are delegated to individual states of the United States or to the individual. While many of the rights were based on earlier documents, such as the Magna Carta, or the immediate experience of what the American colonists had felt were the abuses of power of the British King, the creation of individual rights for all citizens to protect them from interference by the state was an important development in political thought.

The debate in the American colonies was heavily influenced by European thinkers, mainly British, but also French thinkers such as Montesquieu, Voltaire and others. One key source of thinking was also the controversial Jean Jacques Rousseau (1712–1778). Rousseau's background demonstrates both the complexities of the man and his ideas, and why he might appeal to Americans attempting to create a new democratic society. He was originally a citizen of Geneva, one of the Swiss cantons run effectively as

---

[2] Thomas Jefferson letter to William S. Smith dated November 13, 1787 from Thomas Jefferson collection, Library of Congress, http://www.loc.gov/exhibits/jefferson/105.html (accessed May 25, 2017).
[3] Alexander Hamilton, James Madison and John Jay (1961) *The Federalist; or, The New Constitution*, London: Dent.
[4] David Wootton ed. (2003) *The Essential Federalist and Anti-Federalist Papers*, Indianapolis, IN: Hackett Publishing Company.

a democratic republic based on the vote of male "citizens" but as in the case of the ancient India and Greek republics, the bulk of the population were women or foreigners who had no say in government. Even worse, the city was controlled by a few wealthy families. Due to family circumstances Rousseau left Geneva and converted to Roman Catholicism which caused him to lose his citizenship of Geneva. He achieved notoriety in France in 1750 when his essay "Discourse on the Arts and Sciences," won first prize in a competition. This led Rousseau to become involved with Denis Diderot (1713–1784) and the Encyclopedistes, but he soon came to view them as atheists and materialists, and opposed to Rousseau's own views on the soul and divine nature of universe. Rousseau returned to Geneva in 1754, reconverted to Calvinism and regained his official Genevan citizenship. In 1755, Rousseau completed another essay, the "Discourse on the Origin and Basis of Inequality Among Men," which elaborated on the arguments of the "Discourse on the Arts and Sciences." However, Rousseau's initial literary success came with his novel *Julie, ou la nouvelle Héloïse*, published in 1761. In 1762, Rousseau published his key political tract, *The Social Contract* (Du Contrat Social: Principes du Droit Politique). In May, the same year, he also published *Emile: or, On Education*, which advocated religious belief but rejected original sin and divine revelation. In fact, Rousseau suggested that all religions are good if they encourage virtue though it was better to stay with the religion of one's own family and community if possible. These views were attacked by both Protestants and Catholics so he was forced to flee Geneva again, traveling to Luxembourg, then Britain and finally to France, where he was permitted to stay so long as he did not publish.

Rousseau argued that people are naturally free but have been made unfree. Even the sciences, letters, and arts merely "spread garlands of flowers over the iron chains with which men are burdened, stifle in them the sense of that original liberty for which they seem to have been born, make them love their slavery, and turn them into what is called civilized peoples."[5] God provides order and harmony in nature so that young people in particular should embrace their natural feelings to overcome the alienation, competitiveness and prejudices of modern society. Rousseau suggests that humans have innate goodness that can be found by seeking the seed of divinity. It will enable all to experience the freedom that will cultivate consciousness for a better society. However, this freedom can ultimately only be found within a community. This might seem a contradiction but the community would be based on what Rousseau calls the *volonté*

---

[5] Donald A. Cress trans./ed. (2011) *Jean-Jacques Rousseau: The Basic Political Writings*, 2nd edn, Indianapolis, IN: Hackett Publishing: 6.

générale ("general will") in that it would transcend individual and private but also enable the individual to be free.

Despite the potential totalitarian possibilities for the vague notion of submission to the general will, the term had been used as a term to identify the common or public interest in the French legal tradition so was not a complete invention or necessarily sinister. It is even more difficult to make a direct link between Rousseau and the events of the French Revolution and its immediate aftermath but one can see how it might appear that certain excesses of the revolution, particularly the actions of Robespierre and the Terror, could be traced to Rousseau. Yet, it is probably the work of others, such as Abbé Emmanuel Joseph Sieyès (1748–1836), particularly his *What is the Third Estate?* (1789), that was a much more immediate and definable influence on the French Revolution.[6] In this tract, Sieyès argues that the nobility (aristocracy) is a fraudulent institution. They dominate the Royal Court, own the land and have access to the tax revenue of ordinary people but are effectively parasites. It is the "Third Estate" or the commoner class, who produces goods and provides services, and should really be the sovereign power.

Most narratives of political thought put the focus on the European and North American experience with revolution but there is considerable value in looking globally. This includes cases where democratic government was less successful despite promising leaders and ideals. This is especially true of the Latin American political thought. For example, a revolution in Haiti in 1791 was led by the black slave Toussaint L'Ouverture (1743–1803) who had been educated in Enlightenment thought and used the opportunity of the French Revolution to liberate the slaves on Haiti and declare independence from France.[7] Another important example is the political thought of Simón Bolívar (1783–1830). For Bolívar, the problem was that his fellow citizens feared strong executive power, but from his point of view the danger was that weak federal governments would degenerate into power bases for local powerbrokers or strongmen, *caudillos*, which is what eventually occurred. At the same time, Bolívar was conscious of the need to avoid putting authority in the hands of one ruler. As the military leader who liberated many areas of South America from Spanish colonial rule, he had great influence and could have used it to assume power but he wanted to use his influence to foster democracy in Latin America instead.

---

[6] Abbé Emmanuel Joseph Sieyès (1987) "What is the Third Estate?" in Keith M. Baker ed., *Readings in Western Civilization, Volume 7: The Old Regime and the French Revolution*, Chicago, IL: University of Chicago Press: 154–179.

[7] C.L.R. James (1980) *The Black Jacobins: Toussaint L'Ouverture and the San Domingo Revolution*, London: Allison & Busby.

He refused to take power and offered it to the representatives of the people who he had liberated. His logic for refusing to take power himself is clear:

> The continuance of authority in the same individual has frequently meant the end of democratic governments. Repeated elections are essential in popular systems of government, for nothing is more perilous than to permit one citizen to retain power for an extended period . . . herein lie the origins of usurpation and tyranny. Our citizens must with good reason learn to fear lest the magistrate who has governed them long will govern them forever.[8]

Bolívar points out the peculiar position of the subjects of Spain in the Spanish colonies in Latin America who simply by being born in a colony were not permitted to rule themselves so were ruled by the Spanish and kept as colonial subjects in ignorance. Unable to learn to rule themselves, they could gain no knowledge of government and civic virtues. For such people, if liberty is gained, it is soon lost. He argued that only democracy was able to foster and preserve liberty. However, he rejected the constitution of the United States because the people of the US had already become accustomed to liberty. Of all the choices of political regimes, he felt that the British system was most appropriate for Latin America. That is, he advocated an elective legislative Congress for the representatives of the people, along the lines of the British House of Commons, together with an unelected Senate chosen by the Congress but with Senators holding office as a hereditary position, as in the British House of Lords. The Senate was not intended to be an aristocracy of wealth but a chance for a group of individuals who had distinguished themselves in the wars of independence to develop the knowledge and skill to protect liberty without being swayed by the popular demands of public opinion through constant re-election and the corruption inherent in elective public office. The Senate would also serve as a check on the power of the President because the Senate would be the sole legislative power, though as in the British House of Lords for most of its history, it also appeared to include powers of judicial oversight. It would also permit a strong executive without fear that it would degenerate into tyranny. Bolívar, the revolutionary, realized that the new constitution needed to be based on practices and institutions that would enable Latin Americans to learn how to exercise and protect liberty. In a sense, he aimed at creating a new tradition suited to the people he had liberated.

---

[8] Simón Bolívar; Gerald E. Fitzgerald trans. (1971) *The Political Thought of Bolívar: Selected Writings*, The Hague: Martinus Nijhoff: 47.

REACTION TO REVOLUTION: CONSERVATISM AND ROMANTICISM

Revolution led almost inevitably to reaction and the rise of conservative thinkers. At the same time, it would be a mistake to think of these thinkers as merely conservative reactionaries clinging to tradition. For example, Edmund Burke (1729–1797), often considered a key founder of conservatism, was generally sympathetic to the demands of the American colonists prior to the America War of Independence and relatively enlightened in his views on Ireland. His focus was always on maintaining ancient English liberties, which he defined as freedom from the arbitrary demands of tyranny, rooted in the English constitutional and legal precedent. Such liberty was bound up with the traditional practices that worked well for the English people, and though they may need to be reviewed and reformed, this must be done slowly and carefully. Only gradual and moderate reform has any chance of success. For this reason, Burke was appalled at the unfolding developments in the early years of the French Revolution and argued vehemently against those in Britain who sought a similar revolution. With the progress of the Revolution in France to the period of the terror and the guillotine, his worst fears seemed to be borne out. The French sought to gain their liberty but Burke believed that liberty can only be rooted in tradition because without tradition, liberty will result in disorder and the use of force.

Other European conservatives went even further. Joseph-Marie de Maistre (1753–1821), claimed that monarchy is divinely sanctioned so can be the only legitimate form of government and to reject Christianity is to invite anarchy and bloodshed, such as in the French Revolution.[9] His innovation was to tie monarchy and Catholicism to nationalism. In his *Considérations sur la France* (Considerations on France) of 1797, he insists that France has a divine mission from the time of Charlemagne as the principal instrument of good fighting evil on Earth. The failures of the revolution underscored the failure of France to fulfill this mission. In 1809, he published his "Essai sur le Principe Générateur des Constitutions Politiques et des Autres Institutions Humaines" (Essay on the Generative Principle of Political Constitutions and other Human Institutions) in which he argued that constitutions are not the product of human reason but come from God through the actions of his agents on earth. Rational logic cannot produce arrangements that result in effective government. As in Burke, there is an organic unity to traditional systems of rule and these

---

[9] Bela Menczer trans. (1962) *Catholic Political Thought 1789–1848*, Notre Dame, IN: University of Notre Dame Press: 59–76.

are based on a necessary element of irrational belief in sacred authority that enables government to be stable and endure. The basis of such a system must not be widely questioned or it will collapse.

Revolution and reform also gave way to religious-based conservative reaction in Spain and Latin America. However one must not assume that it was because these societies were less able to foster change. Indeed, it was because the movement for reform was strong in places that the counter-reaction was so strong. For example, Juan Donoso Cortés (1809–1853) was initially a liberal influenced by Jean-Jacques Rousseau but after the beginning of the First Carlist War, a civil war in Spain from 1833 to 1839, he became alarmed at the rising at La Granja of low paid sergeants in August 1837 who threatened a much more radical turn toward a Spanish revolution.[10] By 1851, when he wrote *Ensayo sobre el catolicismo, el liberalismo, y el socialismo considerados en sus principios fundamentales* (Essays on Catholicism, liberalism and socialism considered in their fundamental principles) in reaction to the uprisings across Europe in 1848, Donoso Cortés was a full-fledged conservative. This had affinities with Ultramontanism which argues that all systems of philosophy are made by humans and cannot really address the ultimate questions of meaning and destiny to solve the problem of human destiny so that humanity must accept absolute dependence on the Catholic Church for social and political salvation. Donoso Cortés' work was not only important in Spain, it also had an influence in Latin America, for example in the conservative government of the Ecuadorian President Gabriel García Moreno (1860–1875) when together with ideas of the French thinkers Joseph de Maistre and Louise G.A. de Bonald (1754–1840), Dosono Cortés helped to create the ideological foundations of theocratically inspired traditional states. The Moreno government was religious in nature, centered in the Catholic Church and even encouraged the Jesuits to return after their initial expulsion. From this we can say that it would be a mistake then to see the Islamic world or India or China as particularly weighed down by religion in this period. Religious feelings were part of the reaction to revolution and reform in the West.

EUROPEAN ROMANTIC POLITICAL THOUGHT

The German Romantics are the most important of the European Romantic thinkers, due to the wide influence that they exercised, not just in Europe

---

[10] Menczer trans. (1962) *Catholic Political Thought 1789–1848*: 157–182.

but around the world, and for the power of their arguments. Most of the German Romantics were initially fairly sympathetic to the French Revolution but the excesses of the Jacobins and the threat of French dominance under Napoleon led them to a more conservative position. There was also a strong rejection of the cold rationality of the Enlightenment. Romantics rejected abstract conceptualization and dispassionate analysis and preferred instead engaging with the real world, discovering its mysteries and accepting reality as it is. In terms of politics, they believed that the State must be the founded "character" of the people and not the will of a simple majority. They spoke of the autonomy of the unique individual but insisted that individuals can only find true freedom in organic harmony with the whole of society.

In order to make sense of German Romantic political thought, one must first examine the thought of Johann Gottlieb Fichte (1762–1814). Fichte was not formally a part of the German Romantic movement and, in many ways, the Romantics were reacting against him, but it still makes sense to examine him as a preface to a discussion of German Romanticism because some of the political logic is similar. Fichte initially seems to be following Kant but takes Kant's arguments to extremes. While Kant posited the autonomous individual, Fichte argued that the only and ultimate reality is that of the self-active ego. Whereas Kant argued for a "kingdom of ends" where all individuals worked to enable others to achieve their mutually compatible ends, Fichte argued that self-awareness requires one to acknowledge the existence of others and limit one's freedom out of respect for others. In many ways Fichte follows Kant but the subordination of the individual to the whole is even more pronounced. In his *Theory of the State*, he argues that this collectivity must be self-sufficient, even autarchic, and demand the recognition of other states as an equal. These theories are tempting to link to Fichte's nationalism. He gave a series of "Addresses to the German Nation," speeches in Berlin under French occupation, in which he warns Germans against accepting the idea of a universal empire and implores them to fulfill the destiny of the Germans to unite and achieve greatness as a nation.[11]

Novalis (1772–1801) was perhaps the most important early German Romantic. He died young but published mainly works related to political thought before his death. His theory of the state is driven by "Faith and Love," the title of one of his essays,[12] and this includes exalting the king as

---

[11] H.S. Reiss trans. (1955) *The Political Thought of the German Romantics: 1793–1815*, Oxford: Basil Blackwell: 44–125.

[12] Frederick C. Beiser trans./ed. (1996) *The Early Political Writings of the German Romantics*, Cambridge: Cambridge University Press: 35–48.

the "pure life principle of the state," the beauty of which will be reflected on all citizens who should consider themselves officers of the state. He goes on to insist that "the true king is a republic and the true republic is a king" so that the rejection of monarchy is a mistake. The king should be many-sided, well-instructed, well informed and as impartial as possible, in short to be a perfect human being who interacts with the young and seeks out the educated. Everyone should be an artist and a true prince is an artist of artists who directs and supports them. Novalis represents the earliest form of German Romanticism in its emphasis on the organic nature of the state driven by aesthetic ideals where the best politics are beautiful politics. Novalis also hints at the shift from aesthetics to religion in his "Christianity of Europe" but this is not the religion of any organized church, it is more a spiritualism of the joy that can be found in all religions and the hope that good things are possible on earth.[13] This thought was developed, if in more conservative directions, by Friedrich Schlegel (1772–1829).[14]

The clearest representative of English Romantic political thought is Samuel Coleridge (1772–1834), who was very much influenced by the German Romantics, particularly Schlegel. As with other Romantics, he was initially somewhat radical, but soon turned toward Romantic conservatism. He did not oppose some social and political reforms, which he believed were essential to maintain a stable and cohesive society, but change should not come at the expense of traditional institutions, which have a natural origin and suitability as a result. He opposed rampant industrialization and unregulated free markets that threatened the quality of life and the atomization of society. In this context, a superior ideal is needed to unite the nation so that it did not lose its way. He believed that a revived national Church could serve as the leading spiritual, moral and cultural force of the nation and raise the level of society both morally and compassionately.

To this discussion of English romanticism, one might add the case of Thomas Carlyle (1795–1881) who was not strictly speaking a Romantic but his views on leadership and democracy are very much part of the conservative and Romantic nexus of the early nineteenth century. His *On Heroes, Hero-Worship, and The Heroic in History* extolls the roll of the "Great Man" as the basis for history, which in his pantheon includes Muhammad who impressed him with the ability to take nomadic tribes of Arabia and weld them into a powerful nation in such a short time. This emphasis on the role of the great men also is reflected in his contempt for democracy by pointing out that the policy or party which gains the most voters is

---

[13] Beiser trans. (1996) *The Early Political Writings of the German Romantics*: 61–79.
[14] Beiser trans. (1996) *The Early Political Writings of the German Romantics*: 95–168.

not necessarily right and that governments should instead be led by those who are the most capable and knowledgeable, though there is some sense in which he views democracy as a possible tool to select this elite. After a crisis of faith, Carlyle rejected Christianity but was more of a deist than atheist because he also appears to have a metaphysical belief in the power of supernatural forces to produce great leaders out of chaos.

It might seem odd here to place the thinkers of American Romantic political thought alongside of conservative British thinkers or relatively reactionary German Romantics. Figures like Ralph Waldo Emerson (1803–1882) and Henry David Thoreau (1817–1862) are fairly liberal and even radical in many respects. However, the legacy of American Romanticism promotes individualism and anti-intellectualism at the basis of much subsequent populism, which often benefits conservatism. Ralph Waldo Emerson was interested in a range of systems of thought, including neo-Platonism, Hinduism and, to a lesser degree, "Confucianism." He sought, together with fellow "transcendentalists" (a term taken from the German Romantics) to explore these ideas with the goal of reaching a higher form of understanding that rejected the cold rationality of Hume and even Kant in favor of attaining an inner spiritual sense of what it is to be human. As with Rousseau, he believed that society makes people corrupt so it is best to be self-reliant and not worry too much about conformity with societal expectations. Emerson had an influence of Henry David Thoreau. It is true that Thoreau was in many ways a radical who advocated civil disobedience in opposition to the US war with Mexico. His book *Walden, or Life in the Woods*, is seen as progressive from the point of view of environmentalism and individual freedom. Yet Thoreau also fits with American populist conservatism in many ways in his view that only the solitary individual is sincere and that complexity should be distrusted to the extent that simplicity is the solution of every problem.

JAPANESE ROMANTICISM? THE KOKUGAKU MOVEMENT

The Japanese *Kokugaku* (國學) or "nativist" movement was not influenced by events in Europe or the Americas but there is an indirect Western influence and many uncanny parallels with Western Romanticism. In addition to the ancient learning school and other movements toward the reinterpretation of texts mentioned in the previous chapter, the Tokugawa Shogunate also allowed Western learning to enter Japan in the form of Dutch books. Access to Dutch learning or *Rangaku* (蘭學) was initially only permitted for a few, mostly physicians, in order to take advantage of Western medical knowledge. Eventually a number of Japanese became proficient enough in Dutch to monitor scientific and political developments. *Rangaku* was more a curiosity than a threat to the regime, though it was tightly controlled. The contrast between *Rangaku* and Literati thought was likely another reason for the development of *Kokugaku* or "nativist" thought.

Another possible source of *Kokugaku* was *Fukko Shintō* (復古神道). While earlier Tokugawa Shinto schools relied on Taoist, neo-Confucian and even Buddhist methods in the ritual and liturgy, *Fukko Shintō* scholars studied the philology of the ancient Japanese, that is the Japanese language before the arrival of Chinese writing, through poetry and other works that had been phonetically transliterated from Japanese into Chinese characters in ancient Japan. The aim was to recover the earliest form of Shinto in what they believed was its original, pure and natural form, untainted by Chinese, Indian and other influences. Kada Azumamaro (荷田春満 1669–1736), the first to use the term "*Kokugaku*," was involved in *Fukko Shintō* and he extended the idea of finding the purity of the original Japanese to the study of Japanese ancient classical literature, written in Japanese, as opposed to most Literati works, which were written in classical Chinese. His research focused on the ancient theology, teachings and beliefs, from which he believed he found the Japanese Shinto spirit of antiquity, free from Buddhist and Confucian influences. Similarly, Kamo Mabuchi (賀茂真淵 1697–1769), a student of Kada Azumamaro, studied Japanese language classics, also focusing on ancient philology, though he had originally been a critic of Literati thought from a Taoist perspective. As both an advocate of *Fukko Shintō* and *Kokugaku*, his research focused on the hermeneutics of classical language, particularly poetry such as waka (和歌) and the *Man'ōyshū* (万葉集), a collection of ancient Court poetry written in Japanese, to discover clues to ancient Japanese thinking.

Motoori Norinaga (本居宣長 1730–1801) was the most well-known and influential of the early *Fukko Shintō/Kokugaku* group. Son of a merchant of Matsusaka in Ise province, Norinaga was a medical student in Kyoto from 1752, but also became interested in literature and poetry. Even when he set up a doctor's practice, he also lectured informally on Japanese literature with popular success. Motoori believed that language is closely connected with one's experience of the world. Therefore, spoken colloquial Japanese should be preferred to Chinese writing which he believed to be too abstract and so distanced humans from lived experience. Since human intellect was weak, it cannot truly grasp the great principles of life or the universe, which can only be understood by celestial deities.[15] He believed

---

[15] John S. Brownlee (1988) "The Jeweled Comb-Box: Motoori Norinaga's Tamakushige," *Monumenta Nipponica*, 43(1): 37.

that language should be the living language of ordinary people and not the archaic stilted language of the Literati. In fact, the tendency of intellectuals and the establishment to force people to follow Literati models of behavior meant that people who "had been straight and pure, became dirtied and crooked."[16] He goes on to insist that:

> All living things in this world, even lowly birds and insects, instinctively know well and perform those acts which they must each perform, this all comes through an august spirit . . . human beings are born into this world as especially gifted beings, and in correspondence with these gifts, know what they are supposed to know, and do what they are supposed to do. Why compel people to obey further than this?[17]

This approach will be familiar as the naturalism of Taoism and perhaps even Wang Yangming but Motoori explains it in terms of national spirit.

Through his study of ancient Japanese writing and poetry, Motoori found a sensitivity to things in the world which was evidence that Japanese experience things more directly. He felt this made Japan superior to other nations. For him, Japanese culture was the intellect of the world while the remaining cultures were the lowly brute bodies. However, of Noringa's 90 works and 260 volumes, there are only a very few passages of this type of nationalist rhetoric. In fact, it was later thinkers who took his ideas further in this direction, such as Hirata Atsutane (平田篤胤 1776–1843). Hirata was 26 when he first read Motoori's works and determined at that point to become Motoori's successor. Hirata never met Motoori but he did try to legitimate his connection to Motoori through interaction with Motoori's genuine successors. Whereas Motoori focused on literary criticism, Hirata was more interested in theology. The Japanese classics were conceived as developing a worldview based on the Way of the Gods (*Shintō*). In doing so, he constructed a *Shintō* cosmology which revealed the truth of existence that was relevant to the whole world and not just to Japan. In fact, it was superior to that of any other nation. Hirata argued that Japan should be the true Mecca of the world because *Shintō* was the original religion. Hirata and his school politicized the study of *Shintō*, and the doctrine of "national character" through their study of ancient Japanese history and morality, and a belief in *reikon* (霊魂) or holy spirits of the ancient dead who they believed could give Japan untold power. It was a short step from this type of thought to viewing the Japanese emperor as a god, particularly as the Imperial lineage is based on a myth that it stretches back to the Sun

---

[16] Motoori Norinaga; Ann Wehmeyer trans. (1997) *Kojiki-den: Book 1*, Ithaca, NY: Cornell University Press: 222.
[17] Motoori; Wehmeyer trans. (1997) *Kojiki-den*: 224.

Goddess Amaterasu who gave birth to the first emperor of Japan, Jinmu Tennō (神武天皇).

The *Kokugaku* movement spread widely in the late Tokugawa period. There are three main schools associated with *Kokugaku*. First was the Mito School (水戸學), which technically precedes *Kokugaku* as it started with the national history commissioned by the *daimyo* of Mito, Tokugawa Mitsukuni (徳川光圀 1628–1701) who attracted scholars to the domain to write his history, but under his successors, such as Tokugawa Nariaki (徳川斉昭 1800–1860), the Mito School was closely aligned with *Kokugaku*. The Mito domain was controlled by one of the key branch houses of the ruling Tokugawa family with strong links to the government. The second *Kokugaku* school was the Edo School (江戸學), including Katō Chikage (加藤千蔭 1735–1808), a student of Kamo Mabuchi who worked closely with Motoori Norinaga, and Murata Harumi (村田春海 1746–1811), who was also a student of Kamo and became the successor as leader of his school. This school was particularly influential with the elite in the social and cultural circles of Edo's *shitamachi* (下町) or downtown, the most developed commercial area in what is now Tokyo. This community was characterized by an artistic, petite bourgeois flavor. The Edo School put more stress on applying scientific methods to the study of modern culture, instead of an interpretative approach to classical studies. Finally there is the Hirata School (平田學) of Hirata Atsutane, who did much to spread *Kokugaku* on the popular level. The Hirata School was based in the Yamanote (山の手) or uptown section of Edo, which was the residential area of the samurai class. They also emphasized the superiority of Japan and this consciousness of a sense of Japanese-ness in contrast to foreign culture was a factor in the emergence of *Kokugaku* in later political debates. The spread of *Kokugaku* ideas was aided by the fact that Tokugawa Japan was a highly literate society with literacy at the time surpassing all European nations. Despite severe censorship, the publication of public debate on moral philosophy was common. *Kokugaku* was potentially dangerous for the Tokugawa regime because it could be viewed as a veiled critique of the regime itself. It was certainly a new discourse that challenged the official discourse of Tokugawa regime's Literati ideology.[18]

---

[18] Harry D. Harootunian (1988) *Things Seen and Unseen: Discourse and Ideology in Tokugawa Nativism*, Chicago, IL: University of Chicago Press.

REFORM IN INDIA AND THE ISLAMIC WORLD

Where revolution was not possible, the trend was to look to reform to bring about change. In India, British hegemony meant that reformers such as Raja Ram Mohan Roy (রাজা রামমোহন রায় 1772–1833) had to engage the British government and public opinion as much as if not more than local political elites to fulfill liberal ideas. This involved trying to repeal British efforts to impose press censorship so that freedom of the press could be enjoyed in India as it was in Britain and ideas could be freely discussed and debated. At the same time, he wanted to use British influence to improve India. Rammohun Roy was also a liberal in the economic sense of free trade and saw the rational reforms of Jeremy Bentham as a potential positive influence. He listed the advantages and disadvantages of British rule to point out the good aspects of British involvement in India with the main disadvantage being the lack of British interest in and engagement with Indians themselves.[19]

The early nineteenth-century champion of Muslim India, Syed Ahmad Khan (سید احمد خان 1817–1898), held similar views. Sir Syed, as he was commonly known, pioneered modern education for the Muslim community in India which helped to foster a generation of Muslim leaders. He had joined the British East India Company's civil service but courted controversy when he wrote a piece on causes of the infamous Indian Mutiny of 1858 which rejected the idea that it had been a conspiracy of disgruntled Muslim élites and instead argued that the British East India Company had expanded too aggressively into India. He believed that the British administrators and politicians who made policy for India lacked an adequate understanding of Indian culture. In his other writings, however, he stressed that the future success of Muslims in India required that they overcome their fears of modern science and technology. His educational plans included both traditional educational values and modern science.[20]

This interplay between learning and reform is also clear in the initial reaction to the technological rise of the West throughout the Islamic world. It was not uncommon for Muslim travelers to visit the West even before the nineteenth century. We have also seen the impact of advanced Islamic science, mathematics and philosophy on the West in previous centuries. By the nineteenth century, however, Islamic rulers began to feel that they were falling behind and some regimes, particularly the Caliphate,

---

[19] Raja Rammohun Roy; Jogendra Chunder, ed. (1901) *The English Works of Raja Rammohun Roy*, 3 Volumes, Calcutta: S. Roy.

[20] Stephen Hay, ed. (1988) *Sources of Indian Tradition*, vol. 2, 2nd edn. New York, NY: Columbia University Press: 180–195.

felt a need to respond. Students were sent to Europe to learn languages, science and technology. The desire to learn and reform was clearly present. The most prominent example was that of the Ottoman Sultan and Caliph Mahmud II (محمود ثانى b. 1785–d. 1839) and his Decree of *Tanzimat* (تنظيمات) or literally, "Reorganization," an ambitious program of reform.

The Ottoman Empire which controlled the Caliphate was in fact a loose confederation with key semi-autonomous centers of power in what today is Tunisia and Egypt. The ruler of Egypt was Mohammed Ali Pasha (محمد علي باشا b. 1769–d. 1849), an Albanian commander in the Ottoman army, who became governor (*wāli* والي), and declared himself *Khedive* (خديو) or Viceroy of Egypt and Sudan, and sent one of the first major missions of students to France to gain a firmer knowledge of the West. The Imam attached to this group was Rafi' Rifa'a al-Tahtawi (رفاعة رافع الطهطاوي b. 1801–d. 1873) who wrote an account of his travels that served as an important early engagement of Islamic thought with Western ideas and practice.

Al-Tahtawi's account became a starting point of the interpretation of Western political ideas in Arabic. He explains his journey in a matter of fact way. He suggests several areas where he thinks the French deficient but he was ingenious in explaining political concepts through traditional Arabic terms which make Western political institutions and practices understandable and even acceptable to an Islamic audience. Of course, he had a rich tradition of political thought to draw upon. Nonetheless, he also reinterpreted terms, such as hurriyya (حُرِّيّة) which effectively created the notion of personal political liberty that later Arabic writers and thinkers found useful.[21] Al-Tahtawi was not a reformer but his work inspired others. By the mid-nineteenth century, theories of constitutional change were being created throughout the Middle East.

The first attempt was that of Ahmad ibn Abi Diyaf (أحمد بن أبي الضياف b. 1804–d. 1874) who started with the argument that reason and rationality must guide political thought in Islam. He then goes on to discuss three types of rule – Absolute, Republican and Authority Limited by Law. Relying heavily on ibn Khaldūn, Absolute rule is defined as tyrannical rule though the picture he paints is close to traditional forms of rule in the Ottoman Empire and other Islamic states. The short section on Republican rule argues that it is too much based on the will of the people though that might suit certain peoples. It is Authority Limited by Law that is the best according to ibn Diyaf because it is in accordance with the legal thought of Islam but it also has the potential for constitutional and therefore limited government through constitutional monarchy rather than republicanism.

---

[21] Rafi' Rifa'a al-Tahtawi; Daniel L. Newman, trans. (2002) *An Imam in Paris: Al-Tahtawi's Visit to France (1826–31)*, London: Saqi Books: 199.

One might argue that there are problems with this interpretation because it seems to twist traditional religious concepts into constitutional ones but he argued that his views are consistent with the spirit of Islam and there are no explicit Islamic principles violated in such an interpretation.

The second, and more famous attempt at Islamic constitutional theory is that of Khayr al-Din al-Tunisi (خير الدين التونسي b. 1820–d. 1890). He was born in Caucasus in the early 1820s raised as a *mamluk* slave for the Ottoman Empire. In Constantinople he picked up Turkish and was sold to Ahmad Bey (باي أحمد c. 1784–1850), the ruler of Tunisia and Algiers in 1839. The Bey had him trained in administrative and military sciences at which time he mastered French under the French foreign military advisors sent to Tunisia. He was subsequently sent to Paris for four years by the Bey. This was a time when the West was putting pressure on the Bey to establish a modern legal system. An attempt was then made to write a constitution but the *ulama* sensed that their political influence would be weakened in the process and withdrew from the constitutional commissions. It was in this context that Khayr al-Din was propelled into a central position in the process. He had gained a reputation for dealing effectively with the French, had been an envoy to the Ottoman court and demonstrated considerable skill as a local administrator. As a result, he was named to the presidency of the Grand Council and participated in the commission that drafted the 1861 constitution. Even though it was not a particularly liberal constitution, it restricted the power of the Bey, though his power outside the capital of Tunis was limited by traditional arrangements in any case. Khayr al-Din resigned in 1862, however, when he was unable to defend his view that the new Constitution required ministers to be responsible to the Grand Council and not directly to the Bey. It was in this period out of power that he wrote his book *The Surest Path to Knowledge of Condition of Countries* (Aqwam al-masalik li ma'rifat ahwal al-mamalik أقوم المسالك فى معر الممالك), a comparative study of government which also provides a summary of his political thought including how to approach reform in the Islamic tradition. It focused on how both Islam and Western thought and practice agreed that the political power of rulers must be constrained to prevent tyranny and assure the best forms of rule benefit all people.

In Persia (Iran) in the 1850s the role of the *ulama* (jurists) was reduced and constitutionalism began to be introduced. This constitutionalism was justified in terms of traditional Islamic law and philosophy by such individuals as Malkom Khan (ملکم خان b. 1833–d. 1908) and Mirza Yusef Khan (میرزا یوسف خان d. 1895). Mirza Yusef Khan's key work, *Yek Kalameh* (یك کلمه), literally "One Word," viewed the best political system to be one based on law and a constitution could be interpreted as an extension of

Islamic practice of *shari'a* law.[22] This was a common interpretation in favor of constitutionalism.

INITIAL ATTEMPTS AT REFORM IN EAST ASIA

In East Asia the threat from the West was a growing but by no means the only source of pressure for reform. Law and education played less of a role here because both were already highly valued in neo-Confucian state ideology. The problem was the nature of knowledge and institutional change needed to move forward. Moreover, East Asian initiatives toward reform even in this period demonstrate that the Enlightenment and liberalism are not the only sources of reform, though pressures from liberal powers were an impetus for change.

Initial Chinese reform efforts were weakened by the lack of analysis of logic of reform beyond traditional ideas. For example Gong Zizhen (龔自珍 1792–1841) was famed as a reformer for his attacks on the existing civil service examination system, the rituals and organization of the Imperial Court, opium traffic and other issues but his analysis relied on the revival of the notion of the moral leadership from the earliest Literati thought and the appearance of wise rulers guided by wise ministers.[23] More important was the rise of so-called "Statecraft" (*jing-shi* 經世), including such figures as Wei Yuan (魏源 1794–1857) and Feng Guifen (馮桂芬 1809–1874) who advocated a focus on practical, concrete matters in the present rather than a focus on ideals and examples from the past.[24] That is, moral leadership was important but laws, rules and practical policies are also needed in order for leadership to be effective. It could be argued that this was another infusion of Legalism into Literati ideology though with a more pragmatic bent.

It was only when Zeng Guofan (曾國藩 1811–1871), a largely orthodox neo-Confucian combined these new ideas in a way acceptable to conservatives that progress on reform began.[25] Since Zeng came from within the establishment and espoused its basic principles, it was possible for him to

---

[22] Mirza Yusef Khan; A.A. Seyed-Gohrab and S. McGlinn trans. (2010) *One Word – Yak Kaleme: 19th Century Persian Treatise Introducing Western Codified Law*, Amsterdam: University of Amsterdam Press.

[23] William Theodore De Bary and Richard Lufrano (2000) *Sources of Chinese Tradition, Volume 2: From 1600 Through the Twentieth Century*, 2nd edn. New York, NY: Columbia University Press: 179–183; see also Judith Whitbeck (1976) "Three Images of the Culture Hero in the Thought of Kung Tzu-chen" in P. Cohen and J.E. Schrecker eds, *Reform in Nineteenth Century China*, Cambridge, MA: Harvard University Press: 26–30.

[24] De Bary and Lufrano (2000) *Sources of Chinese Tradition*, vol. 2, 2nd edn: 184–212 and 235–239.

[25] De Bary and Lufrano (2000) *Sources of Chinese Tradition*, vol. 2, 2nd edn: 240–241.

borrow ideas from movements critical of orthodoxy such as the "Back to Han" movement of the late eighteenth century. Even his emphasis on the moral correctness of officials as the basis for his reform was also combined with elements of the Statecraft school in its recommendations for reform. Zeng became one of the leaders of the Self-Strengthening (*Ziqiang* 自強) or Western Works (*Yangwu* 洋務) Movement from 1861 onward which developed Western military technology and practices to strengthen the Qing state. This suggested that the West was superior to the Qing in some respects, which was an anathema to many conservatives, but the value of this initiative was demonstrated when Zeng was able to use the modern military he developed with others to suppress the Taiping Rebellion which plunged southern China into civil war from 1850 to 1864. This restored stability and demonstrated the value of Western technology.

In late Tokugawa Japan, Aizawa Seishisai (会沢正志斎 1781–1863) and others advocated reform even though he was from the Mito domain, a core part of the Tokugawa house but, as noted above, Mito was also a bastion of *Kokugaku* (nativist) thinking. Aizawa's *Shinron* (新論) or "New Theses" (1825) were aimed at strengthening the state, especially national defense, by fostering latent popular spirit, which is the basis of his slogan "Revere the Emperor, Expel the Barbarian" (*sonnō jōi* 尊皇攘夷) that became the rallying cry of the so-called Loyalist movement and led to calls for the emperor to replace the Tokugawa shogun as the leader of Japan as the basis of national renewal to fight the threat of Western encroachment. Aizawa also developed the idea of "*kokutai*" (國体) or national essence that became an important concept in modern Japan, defining the basis of the nation. The loyalist movement verged on terrorism and fanaticism but was very useful for the forces that sought change. However, it was more moderate thinkers such as Sakuma Shōzan (佐久間象山 1811–1864) who represented the compromise that was eventually reached where it was recognized that Japan needed Western science even if Japan needed to adopt technology as it attempted to retain Eastern or native Japanese ideals. Others like Yokoi Shōnan (横井小楠 1809–1869) put the argument for reform in terms of national interest to overcome conservative opposition.[26]

East Asia had to deal with the Western threat without the intellectual background of either India or Islam in Western political ideas. Liberalism reached this region relatively late and did not contribute to the early reform debates. The argument that neo-Confucianism limited the response to the West has some validity but it is clear that there were a variety of forms of thought which had potential to create alternatives to orthodoxy. East

---

[26] De Bary et al. eds (2005) *Sources of Japanese Tradition, Volume 2: 1600–2000*, 2nd edn. New York, NY: Columbia University Press: 616–651.

Asian thought alone was not an obstacle to modernization. One might even speculate that the absence of Western political ideas was initially more helpful to the reform process, especially in Japan, than if the full force of Western ideas had guided the debate.

EARLY LIBERAL REFORM IN EUROPE AND LATIN AMERICA

The impression of slow and fitful efforts at reform in India, Islamic areas and East Asia should not lead to the conclusion that these areas were behind the West. One must not forget that reform is still unfolding slowly and fitfully even in Europe at this time. For example, Britain was still struggling with political reform throughout the nineteenth century. In the chapter on the Enlightenment we discussed the utilitarianism of Jeremy Bentham but in the nineteenth century he becomes much more specific about the changes needed in the British political system through a series of tracts and essays. In this period, it is Bentham's friend James Mill who develops further the logic of the utilitarian political program. In his "Essay on Government" Mill put his faith in the middle classes who he believed would dominate if electoral participation was expanded. Like Bentham, he was less interested in traditional or institutional forms of restraint on political power because he believed that a legislature that was elected by the majority of the people would naturally act in the best interests of all the people.[27] The liberal reform movement culminated in the British Reform Act of 1832 which was the first step in the fairer political system, even if this was only a partial victory for liberalism and Britain was still not what one could term a liberal democracy.

The more important role for Britain was its status as a great power and its political leadership in Europe and the world. James Mill's reform program did not just focus on domestic reform. It was international in scope. He joined the agitation against the activities of the reactionary powers in Europe and supported the struggles for independence in Latin America. He even employed Andrés Bello (1781–1865), a Venezuelan exile in London who was one of the first prominent reform leaders in Latin America. Bello worked with Mill on Bentham's papers and met Bentham numerous times. Although Bello did not share Bentham's atheism or Mill's utilitarianism, and so might be viewed by some as not a liberal but a conservative, the same rationalization project found in Bello's philology,

---

[27] James Mill (1825) *Essays on Government, Jurisprudence, Liberty of the Press and the Law of Nations*, London: J. Innes.

grammar and legal work point to the influence of his utilitarian patrons while in England.

Despite the revolution, political reform was also only fitfully making progress in France. The kinds of issues being raised can be seen in the thought of Benjamin Constant (1767–1830). Constant was the first thinker to refer to himself as a liberal but his political thought centers around how to increase political liberty without the excesses of the French Revolution such as the political Terror and Napoleonic expansionism. He feared that unbridled freedom and democracy would lead to mob rule. He did not expect that modern states could emulate the liberty and democracy of the ancient Greeks because it was too time consuming and required generous resources devoted to only a small part of the population. A modern political notion of liberty needed to be consistent with what was possible in large states with a degree of political equality and liberty for all citizens. His alternative was a form of constitutional monarchy with an elective legislature and cabinet government appointed by the monarch but drawn from and responsible to the legislature. Unlike the British radicals, he viewed human feelings as more complex than simple self-interest and argued that feelings of self-sacrifice and compassion also needed to be inculcated into citizens of a liberal society so that self-interest and mob mentality would not gain the upper hand. His views were incorporated into the constitutional arrangements of 1832 which Rafi' Rifa'a al-Tahtawi saw as radical new reform. It was as new for France and for Europe as for anywhere in the world.

In the rest of Europe, however, movements for reform were much weaker than in Britain and France. In Germany, for example, the Enlightenment was associated with absolutism, and then during the resistance to Napoleon, with centralizing bureaucracy so that liberalism in Germany initially depended more on centralizing monarchy than liberalism elsewhere to counteract the influence of traditional elites.[28] Yet, once Napoleon was defeated, liberals faced heavy censorship and liberal reform stalled. The aspirations of the middle class drove the liberal agenda forward but there was also a sense amongst the middle class that political order was essential to social cohesion and unity must be given priority over reform.[29]

Initially as the Spanish fought to gain independence from France there was reaction against liberal ideas which many associated with the French revolutionary tradition that had been imposed upon them by Napoleon. After independence, the *Liberales*, the first political group to use the label

---

[28] James Sheehan (1978) *German Liberalism in the Nineteenth Century*, Chicago, IL: University of Chicago Press: 35–36.
[29] Sheehan (1978) *German Liberalism in the Nineteenth Century*: 19–34.

"liberal" fought against the monarchies of Ferdinand VII (1784–1833) and his daughter Isabella II (1830–1904) which followed the departure of the French. This led to civil war between Queen Isabella's reactionary uncle Infante Carlos and *Liberales* in the so-called Carlist Wars. The frequent intervention of the military led to frequent political instability even if the soldiers and officers involved were often on the side of the liberals.

Military officers also played a role in Russia where they had been encouraged by the reforms of Alexander I (1777–1825) and their experiences in the West during and after the Napoleonic Wars but when Alexander died, the throne passed not to his eldest son, the more liberal Constantine who would defend the new Constitution, but to the less liberal Nicholas I (1796–1855) who would destroy it, about 3,000 soldiers led by liberal army officers such as Colonel Pavel Pestel protested. The so-called Decembrists rallied in Senate Square in St. Petersburg but were forced to flee from artillery fire from troops loyal to Nicholas. The leaders, including Pestel, were arrested and executed. The rule of Nicholas I was as illiberal as the Decembrists had feared. Freedom of speech was heavily suppressed. The only exception was when another officer, Peter Chaadayev (Пётр Чаадаев 1794–1856), wrote a series of his letters which circulated privately but were eventually published without his knowledge, and though he was forced to resign his commission, he had become too famous to be arrested. He was closely watched by the authorities, prohibited from publishing and even declared insane but his very presence was a sign that alternative views were possible. Chaadayev's views were more philosophical than political and he was hardly a champion of liberalism. His advocacy of Roman Catholicism and attacks on the backward character of the Russian people upset the nationalists and authorities who relied on nationalism to maintain political control.[30] Of course, as Chaadayev argued, Russia was out of the mainstream of European developments but even in Europe we can see that reform was slow and uneven. There is no sense in which Europe as a whole was more politically advanced than most of the rest of the world.

Europe was a major influence on Latin America and it is not unusual to link European romanticism with liberalism in Latin American during this period but this is misleading because reform in this part of the world focused on legal and constitutional change along liberal lines just as much as in Europe, and was in fact more advanced than much of Europe. The notion of Latin American political romanticism no doubt arises from stereotypes but also the passionate hatred for tyrants,

---

[30] Peter Yakovlevich Chaadayev; Mary-Barbara Zeldin trans. (1969) *Peter Yakovlevich Chaadayev: Philosophical Letters & Apology of a Madman*, Knoxville, TN: University of Tennessee Press.

such as that of the Argentine dictator Juan Manuel de Rosas. Esteban Echeverria's (1805–1851) writings, for example, focused on terror and blood, suggesting that the violence of Rosas' dictatorship was akin to a slaughterhouse. Similarly, another Argentinian, Domingo Faustino Sarmiento (1811–1888), who was forced into exile in Europe and then Chile by the Rosas regime, expressed his opposition in similarly colorful prose. However, there were also more staid figures, such as Andrés Bello, the Venezuelan with whom Sarmiento worked for reform, who as we have noted had worked for Bentham and James Mill.

Another key figure in Argentina and Chile was Juan Bautista Alberdi (1810–1884) who was part of the same group of liberal intellectuals. Like them Alberdi fled Argentina and traveled first to Paraguay then to Europe; and, finally, to Chile. In Montevideo he worked as a lawyer and journalist supporting French intervention against the Government of Rosas and writing articles in several newspapers in which he supported military actions against his country. Soon he was forced to flee to Paris. On return from Europe, he settled in Chile where he worked as a lawyer and studied the Constitution of the United States. When Rosas and his supporters were removed from power, Alberdi contributed a paper entitled "Bases y puntos de partida para la organización política de la República Argentina" to the delegates to the Constitutional Assembly in Argentina which had a profound impact on the debate because he argued that simply writing a constitution or making laws could not change a people unaccustomed to ruling themselves so that education, property rights and economic development were more important than citizenship rights.[31] In this way, we can see a Romantic transformed into a conservative who was also an economic liberal reformer.

In Mexico, in contrast to the secular and literary figures of the southern cone, it was a Catholic priest, José Maria Luis Mora (1794–1850) who initially promoted constitutional and legal reform. He soon turned to education as a key means to further liberal goals by advocating teaching of the Bible in Spanish and attempts to translate it into other indigenous native American languages as means to raise the educational level of the population in the first steps of liberal reform.[32] He opposed the scholasticism and elitism of the existing educational system, and the privileges of existing Catholic institutions because he wanted to use the resources of the Church

---

[31] Jeremy Adelman (2007) "Between Order and Liberty: Juan Bautista Alberdi and the Intellectual Origins of Argentine Constitutionalism," *Latin American Research Review*, 42(2): 86–110.

[32] Susan Schroeder (1994) "Father José María Luis Mora, Liberalism, and the British and Foreign Bible Society in Nineteenth-Century Mexico," *The Americas*, 50(3): 377–397.

to open education to all the people of Mexico. Some viewed his activities as bordering on the promotion of Protestantism but he still saw a key role for the Catholic Church and a form of anti-clericalism was not uncommon even among Catholic priests because the goal was to strengthen and renew the Church through radical reform.

The same combination of liberalism and Catholicism can be found in Father Félix Varela y Morales (1788–1853) of Cuba who advocated education and self-expression as well as the abolition of slavery and resistance to tyrannical government.[33] His scholarship embraced all fields of knowledge even if it reserved a special role for Catholic theology. He promoted the use of Spanish vernacular, encouraged experimental method and critiqued scholasticism. His work discussed contemporary intellectual issues without resorting to irreligion. He was protected by the Bishop of Havana who was himself dedicated to public health, welfare and education. In 1820, he also benefited the restoration of the Spanish Constitution of 1812 to become an expert in constitutional law and was selected as one of three representatives of Cuba in the new legislative body, the Cortes. When the new liberal regime in Spain collapsed, however, he was forced to flee to New York where he provided intellectual support to resistance to tyranny. Varela argued that oppressed subjects have the right to free themselves from an unjust ruler and his emphasis on education and openness to science and debate were firmly in line with liberal thought. He fought to maintain this Catholic liberalism even as Latin America shifted to secularism and many Catholics sought refuge in conservative authoritarianism.

WOMEN IN REVOLUTION, ROMANTICISM AND REFORM

The revolutionary period began with Mary Wollstonecraft's (1759–1797) *A Vindication of the Rights of Woman: With Strictures on Political and Moral Subjects* (1792), which was the most articulate and clearest statement yet of the rights of women. But she was also writing at the same time that Marquis de Condorcet (1743–1794) published his "On the Admission of Women to the Rights of Citizenship" in 1790 and Marie Gouze (1748–1793), under the pen name Marie-Olympe de Gouges, used the logic of the Declaration of the Rights of Man to write her "Declaration of the Rights of Woman and of the Female Citizen"

---

[33] This and much of what follows is drawn from Joseph J. McCadden (1964) "The New York-to-Cuba Axis of Father Varela," *The Americas*, 20(4): 376–392.

(1791).[34] Germaine de Staël (1766–1817) was very influential in political circles in France both prior to and after the revolution. What is most interesting about Mme. de Staël's political thought is that she insisted that women were an important but often ignored category in politics.[35] That is, she tries to make women visible as a part of the political world even if often it meant a focus on how they are excluded and oppressed. It is easy to understand this view when one considers the thought of someone like Thomas Jefferson. Jefferson did not think women should even discuss politics, because they would have to mix with men in public meetings and this would lead to moral depravity,[36] and because they could not fully participate in politics, there was no reason that they should be able to vote or hold office.[37] Jefferson's views on the education of women were also relatively conservative though he did support it in a limited form.[38] There is a stark contrast here with the role played by Manuela Sáenz (1795–1856), who was involved in the revolutionary movement with Simón Bolívar, and though historically she was often dismissed as simply being Simón Bolívar's lover and somehow inappropriately involved politically, she did play an important role as is now recognized.[39] Even if one argues that Bolívar's analysis of different political tendencies reinforced gender hierarchies,[40] he did assign women to the realm of human rights, philanthropy and philosophy in a position that was superior to masculine forms of authority.[41]

As one might expect, political reformers also addressed the condition of women including those in India and Latin America. Raja Rammohan Roy made great strides in promoting the rights of women. He supported

---

[34] Texts by the two can be found in Susan Groag Bell and Karen M. Offen eds (1983) *Women, the Family, and Freedom: The Debate in Documents*, Stanford, CA: Stanford University Press: 97–109.

[35] Susan Tenenbaum (1973) "Montesquieu and Mme. de Stael: The Woman as a Factor in Political Analysis," *Political Theory*, 1(1): 92–103.

[36] Thomas Jefferson to Samuel Kercheval, September 5, 1816 in which he dismisses the political rights of slaves in the same breath. https://founders.archives.gov/documents/Jefferson/03-10-02-0255 (accessed May 20, 2017).

[37] "The appointment of a woman to office is an innovation for which the public is not prepared, nor I." Thomas Jefferson to Albert Gallatin, January 13, 1807 http://founders.archives.gov/documents/Jefferson/99-01-02-4862 (accessed May 20, 2017).

[38] Homer H. Young (1956) "The Founding Fathers on the Education of Women," *Rice Institute Pamphlet, Rice University Studies*, 43(1): 48–63.

[39] Pamela S. Murray (2001) "'Loca' or 'Libertadora'? Manuela Sáenz in the Eyes of History and Historians, 1900–c. 1990," *Journal of Latin American Studies*, 33(2): 291–310 and Karen Racine (2012) "For Glory and Bolívar: The Remarkable Life of Manuela Sáenz," *Journal of Latin American Studies*, 44(1): 184–186.

[40] Catherine Davies (2005) "Colonial Dependence and Sexual Difference: Reading for Gender in the Writing of Simón Bolívar (1783–1830)," *Feminist Review*, 79: 5–19.

[41] Davies (2005) "Colonial Dependence and Sexual Difference": 7.

women's education, inheritance rights for women, opposed polygamy and most notably worked with the British to ban *sati* and permit widows to remarry. Father Felix Varela y Morales established self-help programs for women. Yet, there is a relative conservatism in both cases. This dilemma of reformist conservatism in regard to women is even more pronounced in the case of James Mill. James Mill's "Essay on Government" was radical for the time in how it advocated full suffrage rights for all male heads of household. Yet, he dismissed the rights of women by arguing that either their fathers or husbands would secure women's interests on their behalf.[42] William Thompson (1775–1833) in the *Appeal of One Half the Human Race* (1825) points out that Mill's arguments – that each person is the best judge of one's own interests so must make decisions for themselves and that power over others without consent is generally abused – apply to women as well as men, and not as Mill implies, is inapplicable to "one half the human race," that is, women.[43]

In contrast, what we have called the Romantic tendency in various societies supported the participation of women. It should be remembered that it was a female writer, Murasaki Shikibu (c. 973–1014), who was the center of Motoori Norinaga's textual analysis at the formation of the *Kokugaku* movement. In fact, the literary scene in late Tokugawa Japan included many women and *Kokugaku* not only welcomed women, it enabled many to become actively involved.[44] German Romantics "championed many modern social values, such as the emancipation of *women*, sexual freedom and the right of divorce."[45] Ralph Waldo Emerson signed the "Declaration of Principles" put forth by the first National Women's Rights Convention held at Worcester Massachusetts in 1850 and he delivered a speech to the Women's Right Convention in 1855 that made clear his view that the women's movement was "no whim, but an organic impulse . . . a right and proper inquiry . . . honoring to the age." He noted the many examples of exceptional women from all civilizations and all times in history drawing on a wide reading of texts from around the world.[46] Among the Latin

---

[42] James Mill (1825) *Essays on Government, Jurisprudence, Liberty of the Press and the Law of Nations*, London: J. Innes: 21.

[43] William Thompson, Anna Wheeler, Richard Taylor and John Stuart Mill (1825) *Appeal of One Half of the Human Race, Women, Against the Pretensions of the Other Half, Men*, London: Longman, Hurst, Rees, Orme, Brown and Green, and Wheatley and Adlard.

[44] P.F. Kornicki, Mara Patessio and G. Rowley (2010) "The Female as Subject: Reading and Writing in Early Modern Japan," Ann Arbor, MI: Michigan Monograph Series in Japanese Studies No. 70, Center for Japanese Studies, University of Michigan: 19.

[45] Frederick C. Beiser trans./ed. (1996) *The Early Political Writings of the German Romantics*, Cambridge: Cambridge University Press: xiii.

[46] Ralph Waldo Emerson; Joel Myerson and Ronald Bosco eds (2010) *The Later Lectures of Ralph Waldo Emerson, 1843–1871*, vol. 2. Cambridge, MA: Harvard University Press: 15–29.

American reformist Romantics, Domingo Faustino Sarmiento saw female education as essential for national progress and his writings appear to challenge conventional gender boundaries.[47]

The attitudes of English and French Romantics toward women were less positive. Carlyle portrayed politically active women in the French Revolution as typically hysterical and crazed in order to demonize them,[48] not to mention that his focus was always on "great men," never great women. Coleridge's views on women might have been typical of the period in which he lived but he also consciously opposed well-known alternative perspectives on women that were widely available at the time.[49] Perhaps most notable in his views on women is Rousseau who was revolutionary, Romantic and conservative, and often regarded as the key political thinker of this period. Rousseau rejects citizenship rights for women, largely because he wants them to fulfill a function in the private sphere and does not want them to be mixed up with the public sphere.[50] It may be true that he does not claim that men and women are different, merely playing different roles,[51] but it still remains that women are put in an inferior position. Despite the relative public freedom of women in the West, the way that they were viewed in Western political thought varied widely at this time so was not uniformly "advanced" compared to the rest of the world.

CONCLUSION

The American and French Revolutions can be seen as the natural consequence of the Enlightenment but must also be seen as producing a reaction, and not just in Europe. Political romanticism at first embraced the ideals of revolution in Europe but turned against the apparent emptiness of lofty slogans of liberty and fraternity when repression and imperialism were the result. The Romantics began to feel failure to realize the ideal of the revolution was due to the cold rationality of its logic. In this criticism, they were joined by conservatives who wanted to slow the pace of change

---

[47] Christopher Conway (2015) "Gender Iconoclasm in Echeverria's La cautiva and the Captivity Paintings of Juan Manuel Blanes," *Decimononica*, 12(1): 116–133.

[48] Henriette M. Morelli (2005) "An Incarnated Word: A Revisionary Reading of 'The Insurrection of Women' in Thomas Carlyle's The French Revolution," *Women's Studies*, 34(7): 533–550.

[49] H.J. Jackson (1993) "Coleridge's Women, or Girls, Girls, Girls Are Made To Love," *Studies in Romanticism*, 32(4): 577–600.

[50] Catherine Larrère (2011) "Jean-Jacques Rousseau on women and citizenship," *History of European Ideas*, 37(2): 218–222.

[51] Penny A. Weiss (1987) "Rousseau, Antifeminism, and Woman's Nature," *Political Theory*, 15(1): 81–98.

and preserve customs and practices that gave coherence and order to society that the revolutions undermined. Romanticism also gave way to nationalism where language and culture was mobilized in support of the state. This was true in Latin America and Japan as well as in Europe.

Only the staunchest conservatives could ignore the need for reform in the face of political and industrial revolution. This reform might require strengthening of the authority of the state or taming Romantic nationalism but for most it meant liberal reform. In East Asia, India and the Islamic world, reform was needed to make the technological and economic progress necessary to deal with the pressing threat of Western imperialism. It was unclear how much this progress had to be linked to political change. That is, did the success of the West depend on its political freedoms or could development occur in civilizations with alternative political arrangements? The question was never adequately answered because the onslaught of Western imperialism overwhelmed nascent efforts at reform and the dominance of the West was cemented with systems of political thought that explained why the West was superior, as we will see in the next chapter. This included a new argument that the West was superior in part because it treated women better.

12. Imperialism and liberalism (1820–1920)

The nineteenth century was clearly the time that the West rose to prominence in many ways. It had what might be called its positive side in the advance of science, the industrial revolution and doctrine of liberalism. On the negative side, however, was rampant imperialism based on notions of racial and cultural superiority. The West used political thought to redefine the world to suit its interests by dividing it into superior and inferior races based on the misuse of science and pseudo-science. Liberalism was also complicit in or even the impetus for Western imperialism that swept the globe in the nineteenth century. Even worse, it is likely that imperialism also undermined potential liberal reform in many parts of the world. The relationship between liberalism and imperialism is one of the major issues in nineteenth-century political thought.

It is not difficult to demonstrate the connection between liberalism and imperialism. It is not simply that key liberals such as James Mill and his son John Stuart Mill worked directly for the British East Indian Company and their ideas served to guide and foster British imperialism in the nineteenth century. It has been argued that liberals, including John Stuart Mill, embraced imperialism because their political doctrine was universalizing so undermined respect for differences between civilizations.[1] John Stuart Mill in his *On Liberty* goes so far as to exclude from the benefits of liberty "backward" races and argues that "despotism is a legitimate mode of government in dealing with barbarians" which is consistent with his own involvement with British imperialism in India.[2]

It was also not just Britain in which the link between liberalism and imperialism was strong. German imperialism as it developed in the late nineteenth century also appears to have had liberal origins.[3] In addition to the obvious British, French and even German forms, Dutch imperialism

---

[1] See, for example, Lynn Zastoupil (1994) *John Stuart Mill and India*, Stanford, CA: Stanford University Press, and Jeanne Morefield (2004) *Covenants without Swords: Idealist Liberalism and the Spirit of Empire*, Princeton, NJ: Princeton University Press.
[2] John Stuart Mill (1859/2001) *On Liberty*, Kitchener, Ontario: Batoche Books Limited.
[3] Matthew P. Fitzpatrick (2008) *Liberal Imperialism in Germany: Expansionism and Nationalism, 1848–1884*, Oxford: Berghahn Books.

provides the earliest and clearest case of a liberal imperialism. The Dutch state was easily the most liberal in Europe in the nineteenth century but liberal economic policy in the Dutch East Indies seemed to harm rather than help the mass of colonial subjects. Just as the Dutch used market forces led by Western entrepreneurs, they also exploited local rivalries to expand their influence and control in the East Indies in a civilizing mission similar to the tactics the British used in India, Burma, Ceylon and Malaysia, and the French in Africa and Indochina. Liberalism was a philosophy of imperialism.

Initially liberalism embraced the development of all people. It even led to great strides in viewing women as more equal than at any other time up to that point in history. This early feminism was not the exclusive preserve of the West though an exaggerated view of the relative equality of women in the West did have an impact. In many ways, the West was just as behind as anywhere. On the other hand, the rise of liberalism had the perverse effect of encouraging racism. It was easy to twist the argument that some races and areas of the world were too undeveloped to be suited for liberal politics into forms of racism. Many liberals believed that these races and peoples could develop over time to take up liberal political institutions but doubts about the potential for development due to the physical characteristics or religious beliefs led to racism and chauvinism. Worse, it was argued that there was a scientific and philosophical basis to Western superiority.

SCIENCE AND CLASSIFICATION

What was meant by science itself had begun changing in the nineteenth century. The perception grew that science was becoming Western primarily driven by the requirements of states and bureaucracies to adopt new military technologies in which Europe had a temporary edge at the time.[4] Yet, the notion of science was also applied to the study of societies and the classification of civilizations. That is, if education was required for human beings to develop and utilize new technologies, then the same could be true of whole societies and races. A "scientific" approach was applied to the questions of difference in political and social arrangements. Why is one type of society more successful than another? If there is to be progress, how should it unfold? Since religion has been important to the evolution

---

[4] Marwa Elshakry (2010) "When Science Became Western: Historiographical Reflections," *Isis*, 101(1): 98–109. A similar argument is made by S. Irfan Habib and Dhruv Raina (1989) "Copernicus, Colombus, Colonialism and the Role of Science in Nineteenth Century India," *Social Scientist*, 17(3/4): 51–66. Both make the link between Western "science" and colonialism.

of civilizations, then it was natural to analyze religion as a source of and hindrance to political progress. As the previous chapter has shown, religion was still important everywhere in the nineteenth century so it is a mistake to contrast a secular West with religious-based political thought outside the West. Moreover, as we have seen in previous chapters, religion has been central to the political thought of all civilizations.[5] It would be strange if it suddenly disappeared as an influence. However, now the nature of these religions was analyzed and classified. If it did not meet Western standards or the needs of modern technology and industry, then a set of beliefs was considered inferior if not worthless.

Of course, separating religion from political and social progress does not even make sense in the nineteenth century. For example, it would be impossible to make sense of the work of individuals such as Rammohun Roy or Rafi' Rifa'a al-Tahtawi without a discussion of Hinduism or Islam respectively. Roy's philosophy was based on a reinterpretation of Hindu tradition for modern times, strongly influenced by his interaction with Unitarianism. Indeed, throughout the nineteenth century and later religion was important to Indian political thought as a source of renewal. The relationship between political thought and religion is more complex in the case of Islam but another Indian thinker, Syed Ahmed Khan, demonstrated how it might be done as we have seen in the previous chapter. In East Asia, the Western notion of religion itself, let alone its separation from politics, is completely problematic. There continue to be debates today on whether "Confucianism" is a religion or not, but it is clear that Literati thought, now called "Confucianism," was traditionally more philosophy and ideology than theology. It is true it has a complex metaphysics and set of moral beliefs but it is clear that most Literati scholars and officials tended to find spiritual solace in Taoism or Buddhism. Yet even these were not religions in the Western sense. Taoism was also an ideology though it did incorporate folk religious elements in China and Korea. Buddhism has always been more of a philosophy than a religion though, as noted above, it is happy to incorporate other forms of thought, including those which might be deemed religious, to spread its message. One must ask if religion in the Western sense is an appropriate category for any of the East Asian forms of thought.

---

[5] When I first explained the basic outline of this *World History of Political Thought* with a major publisher, the thought systems of the world ("Confucianism," Buddhism, Islam, etc.) were frequently mentioned so I was asked if I was writing a history of religion rather than a history of political thought. In fact, the two are inseparable. It is indicative of the depth of separation in the modern Western secular mind that the two are not seen as intricately linked. As we have seen the basic premise of the book is that a range of beliefs – moral, metaphysical, etc. – informs political thought and always has.

Yet there was one East Asian reformer who recognized the need to deal with the Christian conception of religion. The political thought of the statesman and reformer Kang Youwei (康有為 1858–1927) can be seen as an attempt to create a "Confucian" religion to counteract the Christian-based ideologies of the West.[6] His work is part of the "New Text, Old Text" controversy in the late Qing built on the "back to the Han" movement of the early Qing to revive older interpretations of Literati thought grounded in a simpler Taoist metaphysics that made Confucius more of a spiritual icon than a great Sage. Yet, Kang was also a radical reformer. Kang's *Da Tong Shu* (Book of the Great Unity 大同書) of 1884 proposed a utopian future world in which rectangular administrative districts would be governed based on direct democracy with the ultimate principle of loyalty to a central world government. Some of his views on the role of the state suggest early forms of communism but he also invokes traditional Literati ideas of humanness (*ren* 仁). Kang was also an enthusiast for technology which he saw as the means of progress toward a humane and equal society. As a whole Kang reveals a faith in technological progress that we have seen in other thinkers of the century. By drawing on a rich tradition of Literati and Buddhist ideas, however, he also tried to elevate East Asia thought above other forms. His hierarchy of religions places Christianity and Islam at the bottom and Literati thought, Taoism and Buddhism in order toward the top. He even predicted that in the future what he termed "lower" religions, such as Christianity and Islam, will disappear because he viewed them as too primitive compared to Buddhist metaphysics.

World thought became the subject of classification in the West and thought outside the West was always portrayed as worse than that of the West. Western thinkers tried to put other civilizations in their place according to their religious underpinnings, but they themselves never escaped from dependence of religious thought. For key Western thinkers, religion was still central to their political philosophy. For example, it is easy to see Kang Youwei's hierarchy of religions as fanciful but similar attempts by European thinkers such as Hegel were and are taken seriously even if the conclusions flow from their own religious beliefs in each and every case. These views have implications for how liberals and their opponents view the world.

Auguste Comte's (1798–1857) entire theory of politics is based on a classification of religions which he used to make sense of the world and prescribe reforms. He views the evolution of human thought as comprised of three

---

[6] Fung Yu-lan (1948) *A Short History of Chinese Philosophy*, New York: The Free Press: 322–325.

stages.[7] The first is the "Theological" which includes forms of animism and polytheism and/or simple forms of monotheism. The second stage is the "Metaphysical" where more sophisticated philosophical underpinnings are given to religious beliefs. The final stage is the "Positive" in which science and logic overcome theology and metaphysics. Curiously Comte still felt compelled to suggest his own "Religion of Humanity" with a form of priesthood to keep an eye on the moral progress of a society and the state. He also seemed to suggest that this "religion" can draw on "Theological" stage beliefs because they are more natural to the human mind.[8]

Georg Wilhelm Friedrich Hegel (1770–1831) also had a grand scheme of history, and a sense of evolution and progress found in liberalism and the Enlightenment but he clearly rejected liberalism, particularly in his mature works. At the same time, his work was also an attempt to come to terms with the Enlightenment and in a context that is hostile in some aspects to reform. It is also highly abstract. He started with the premise that nothing is completely real except the whole (like a complex organism) called "The Absolute" and he focuses on the development of the "Spirit" as the essential historical force which develops in the Absolute.[9] He viewed history as an unfolding of freedom in the Absolute. At the same time, there is no freedom without law because freedom is only possible through submission to law. The "Spirit" and thus the law is formed differently as different stages of historical development. In "Oriental" despotism only one, the despotic ruler, is free. The implication is that all oriental forms of rule take this form, ignoring much of the nuance in political forms outlined in Islam, India and East Asia demonstrated in this book. The implication was that all non-Western societies were despotic based on arbitrary rule by one. This type of state only allows for the development of the rule or ruling group and all others are not free in the sense that they are not free to develop as individuals. The historical "Spirit" of ancient Greece and Rome is aristocracy where some, a select group, are free. In such forms of rule, the assumption is that only a select group can be free. In Hegel's own Germany, however, it is a monarch through which all are free. This is not democracy or even constitutional monarchy, but freedom for all comes through the monarch who embodies the will of all. For Hegel, this "German Spirit" is the spirit of the new world. Only the Germans incorporated the true spirit of man fighting the effete aristocratic Roman Empire.

---

[7] Auguste Comte; Gertrud Lenzer ed. (1975) *Auguste Comte and Positivism: The Essential Writings*, New York: Harper: 198ff.

[8] Comte; Lenzer ed. (1975) *Auguste Comte and Positivism*: 381–389.

[9] G.W.F. Hegel; Arnold V. Miller and J.N. Findlay trans. (1977) *Phenomenology of Spirit*, Oxford: Clarendon Press.

The Germans produced Protestantism to overcome the corrupt Catholic Church. Germans are an exemplary example of the principle of nations as central to historical development.

Many of Hegel's ideas also have resonance with ideas from the great classical civilizations including the Indian.[10] Certainly some of Hegel's ideas show the influence of Eastern thought even if he is firmly in the Western philosophical tradition. Freedom is the starting point which indicates that there is some influence of the Western Enlightenment and even liberalism in Hegel's thought. The difference is that whereas Western liberals and the Enlightenment thinkers contrast the individual with society or the state, Hegel views the freedom of the individual as only possible through society and the state.[11] This might sound oppressive and limiting to the individual but even a free individual is most likely to be free due to upbringing, education, skills, employment or wealth, friends and colleagues, citizenship and political associations, and other aspects of society and the state which make it possible for an individual to be free. The individual must cooperate in the family, educational establishments, and society institutions and relationships, and this cooperation sometimes means adapting one's behavior and views to make them work best for everyone. No one is as completely free and isolated as some Enlightenment and even some Romantic thinkers argue. Hegel argues that in fact we cannot be free without our involvement and interaction with others in a mutually supportive way.[12] Nonetheless, he recognizes the dialectical relationship between our private wants and needs and the demands of society and the state.

If religion is so central to Western political thought in the nineteenth century and beyond then why is Western thought so strongly associated with secularism? The answer to this question is best revealed in the thought of John Stuart Mill. J.S. Mill was brought up by his father using an extreme utilitarian philosophy that lacked an emotionally nurturing aspect. This upbringing caused Mill to experience a psychological breakdown which he only overcame by embracing aspects of romanticism. Overall, however, Mill tended to favor science. Even his views on Comte demonstrate

---

[10] For the influence of Indian thought in Germany at the time see B.L. Herling (2006) *The German Gītā: Hermeneutics and Discipline in the German Reception of Indian Thought, 1778–1831*, New York: Routledge. On the influence on Hegel specifically see Lucia Staiano-Daniels (2006) "Illuminated Darkness: Hegel's Brief and Unexpected Elevation of Indian Thought in 'On the Episode of the Mahabharata known by the name Bhagavad-Gita by Wilhelm von Humboldt'," *The Owl of Minerva*, 43(1/2): 75–99.

[11] Hegel, Georg Wilhelm Friedrich; Thomas Malcolm Knox trans. (1967) *Hegel's Philosophy of Right*, London: Oxford University Press.

[12] The argument, as we have seen, is not new. A similar version was discussed in the Flower Garland school of Buddhism in medieval East Asia.

acceptance of science and rejection of the "Religion of Humanity." Only toward the end of his life did Mill return to some acceptance of religion.

It is in Mill's most famous work, *On Liberty* that the roots of the tension between religion and freedom are most clearly expressed.[13] Even more significant is that Mill feared that democracy was as much a threat to liberty as despotism. The tension between freedom and democratic government is most clearly represented in the United States, as Alexis de Tocqueville (1805–1859) noted by suggesting that there is a danger of the "tyranny of the majority" when the overwhelming majority in democratic society tries to impose its views on others. It is this fear of the tyranny of the majority which most strongly motivates J.S. Mill. His concern is more with the suppression, socially or through the government, of unpopular views. He makes strong and systematic arguments in support of allowing individuals to believe and express even the most objectionable views. Even blasphemy is not exempt though the examples given are more on atheism and only indirectly on blasphemy. He does recognize that the beliefs of other cultures are just as valid as widely held beliefs in Victorian England and for that reason those who express them, no matter where, must be respected. The natural solution to this problem is to insist that religious views should be separated from government. At the same time, it is unlikely that Mill's toleration of challenges to deeply held religious beliefs could be tolerated in much of the world then and even now. The counter-argument to Mill is that certain religious views are foundational of the society that believes in them. If one's religious belief includes principles or symbols that are inviolable and sacred, then it is understanding that attacks on these principles and symbols could be viewed as dangerous and harmful. *On Liberty* remains one of the strongest arguments for individual rights ever written but the difficulty of persuading those with deeply held religious beliefs to tolerate criticisms or perceived insults to those beliefs is still a major problem in political thought.

In many ways, Herbert Spencer (1820–1903) is a culmination of these trends in liberalism and theories of development of civilization. He was the son of a non-conformist teacher but received very little formal education. After a series of jobs including railway engineer and journalist, he published his first book *Social Statics* in 1851, which argued that as societies become urbanized and industrialized, the need for the state will disappear.[14] He was very much inspired by Comte's system of thought,

---

[13] John Stuart Mill (1859) *On Liberty*, London: J.W. Parker and Son.

[14] Herbert Spencer (1868) *Social Statics, or, The Conditions Essential to Human Happiness Specified, and the First of Them Developed*, London: Williams and Norgate.

particularly his notion of sociology, which Spencer adopted as his own. Yet Spencer also sought to unify all forms of science into one, including biology which was reinforced by his reading of Charles Darwin's theory of evolution that fit with his ideas of progress. Spencer is the one who coined the term "survival of the fittest" in his *Principles of Biology* and it was subsequently adopted by Darwin himself.[15] However, Darwin's theory is about reproductive success and not necessarily producing the strongest so the concept of survival of the fittest tended to reinforce beliefs in "Social Darwinism" in which certain people, including races or civilizations, are more suited to survive than others. Spencer himself was not a simple Social Darwinist. Even as he aged and grew much more conservative politically, he opposed imperialism, in part because of his influence in places such as India and Japan where he sought to advise those in power in the face of imperialism, but suggested that the people in areas outside the West were not ready for freedom and democracy. He was also a classical liberal in his opposition to attempts to legislate to deal with social problems due to his belief that such attempts would have unintended consequences that would distort natural processes and his conviction that only a free market system has been proven to produce the best outcomes for society.[16] This seems to be founded on a Puritan ethic that distinguished between those who were deserving and undeserving or civilized and uncivilized in ways that fit with his views of conventional morality. That is, if there were negative consequences arising from the free market or interaction of nations, it was due to the deficiencies of those who were unsuccessful rather than the system itself.

TWO OTHER "PROBLEMS" OF CLASSIFICATION: GENDER AND RACE

Just as religious traditions were beginning to be classified and analyzed in the nineteenth century so were types of groups and individuals. Explicit in liberalism is the notion that some groups or individuals are capable of development and enjoying liberty but others are not. In most cases it is simply that education is needed to cultivate the tolerance and communal values needed for a free society but the major Western thinkers do seem to dismiss large segments of humanity. The criteria used for exclusion is

---

[15] Herbert Spencer (1894) *The Principles of Biology*, vol. 1, London: Williams and Norgate: 444–445.

[16] Herbert Spencer (1969) *The Man versus the State with Four Essays on Politics and Society*, Harmondsworth: Penguin Books: 112–150.

vague and this causes problems. This is manifest in the discussion of two categories in nineteenth-century liberal thought: gender and race.

Liberalism seems to have encouraged feminism. In the history of this issue in the West, John Stuart Mill looms large, but sexual equality is something that even John Stuart Mill still struggled to persuade the British public to accept and other contemporary thinkers, such as Comte, were strongly opposed to it. There are reasons to believe that Mill was inspired and assisted in these arguments by his long-time friend and eventual wife, Harriet Taylor Mill (1807–1858), who may deserve more credit for his keys works than she is often given.[17] Her work advocating giving women the vote preceded other examples by at least a decade.[18] Nonetheless, the rise of liberalism provided a backdrop for women to begin to articulate a clear political position in favor of full equality of political rights. The first strong arguments in favor of women's rights began to be articulated in Egypt by Qasim Amin (قاسم أمين b. 1863–1908) in the late nineteenth century and the 1905 Iranian Revolution gave rise to calls for women's equality. In China the Hundred Days' Reform movement, led by Kang Youwei and others led to demands for women's rights and the New Culture movement, the peak of liberalism in early nineteenth-century Republican China, saw demands for women's liberation. The utopia of Kang Youwei set out in his *Book of Great Unity* favored sexual equality and advocated the family be abolished in favor of state-run nurseries and schools, and that marriage be replaced by one-year contracts of equal partnership between women and men, so that women could gain independence. In Japan, a "New Woman Association" (*Shin Fujin Kyōkai* 新婦人協会) was formed by Ichikawa Fusae (市川房枝 1893–1981) and Hiratsuka Raicho (平塚らいてう 1886–1971) after World War I in 1919 at the beginnings of the liberal era of the so-called Taisho Democracy. By 1923 there was a federation of hundreds of women's organizations and calls for universal suffrage.

It was not until the 1920s even in the US and Britain that universal suffrage was achieved. It is true that some experiments occurred earlier at the height of the Enlightenment toward the end of the eighteenth century but these were limited in scope. Western countries such as New Zealand, Finland and Norway or states or regions in Australia or the United States had given women the vote at the end of the nineteenth or earlier in the twentieth century but by that time agitation for universal suffrage was

---

[17] Alice S. Rossi ed. (1970) *Essays on Sex Equality by John Stuart Mill and Harriet Hardy Taylor Mill*, Chicago, IL: University of Chicago Press.

[18] Barbara Leigh Smith Bodichon (1866) *Reasons for the Enfranchisement of Women*, London: Chambers of the Social Science Association.

widespread around the globe. It is interesting that Turkey gave women the right to vote in 1926 before full women's suffrage was achieved in Britain (1928) and well before France (1944). Yet it became part of the Western myth that other races, civilizations and religions were behind in their treatment of women despite the fact improvements in gender equality were accomplished only relatively recently in the West and against strong opposition. It is clear there is a relationship between liberalism and women's rights and that is why the mid-nineteenth century stands out as a period in which the political rights of women were stated with increasing clarity and depth.[19]

The women's rights movement also had links to issues of race. Many of the women's rights activists, particularly in the United States, were initially politicized through their involvement with the Abolitionist movement. For example, the Grimké sisters, Sarah (1792–1873) and Angelina (1805–1879), were leading figures in both the abolitionist and early feminist movements in the USA. It has also been argued that there is an implicit political thought in the work of Harriet Beecher Stowe (1811–1896), particularly her famous *Uncle Tom's Cabin*, which was credited for changing American thinking about slavery.[20] The paradox is that given that liberalism enhanced discussion of women's rights, including advancing the political consciousness of women who were fighting against slavery, it seems strange that liberal ideology appears to have been a step backward for racial equality.

The Abolitionist movement was one founded on the notion of equality of all humans, though the source of the view that all are equal was as much drawn from Protestant Christian beliefs as from liberalism. The most effective points made in the political philosophy of the ex-slave Frederick Douglass (1818–1895) are his emphasis on the dignity due to all humans and how slavery robs this dignity from the slave.[21] He argued that an individual requires at the very least some basic autonomy to allow one to develop one's full potential. This is the minimum that any form of liberalism must recognize. At the same time, the abolition of slavery did not mean the end of racism. The end of slavery came earlier in Latin America than in Europe and the United States but in Latin America distinctions regarding race and indigenous peoples were still problematic. Even liberals such as José Maria Luis Mora, who had a deep concern for

---

[19] This is not to denigrate the work of Mary Astell and Mary Wollstonecraft which have already been fully discussed, contextualized and appraised in the previous chapter.

[20] William B. Allen (2009) *Rethinking Uncle Tom: The Political Thought of Harriet Beecher Stowe*, New York: Rowman & Littlefield.

[21] Frederick Douglass (1855) *My Bondage and My Freedom*, New York: Miller, Orton & Mulligan.

the education of indigenous Indians in Mexico, often expressed views that appear discriminatory.[22] This racialism was not limited to Europe and Latin America. For example, Kang Youwei's utopian vision includes a strong hint of racism because he wants racial differences to be dissolved by a eugenics program to eliminate "brown and black" racial groups and produce a fair-skinned homogeneous human race with similar appearance and intelligence.

As we have already seen, there is implicit in liberalism, and backed by pseudo-science and the classification of civilizations and races, the notion that some races were more suited to development or at least the less capable races need to be mentored or controlled by more capable races. A powerful combination of seemingly scientific ideas and liberalism developed into Social Darwinism where the less fit were to make way for the more fit. Important liberals including J.S. Mill argued that race determined the possible pace and extent of political progress, though Mill himself used race in a very loose sense. However, there is no mistaking the racialism of the even more influential Herbert Spencer, who, in response to a Japanese government request for his views on interracial marriage, argued that racial mixing will only have bad results from a "biological" point of view and should be absolutely prohibited.

There is little doubt that the nineteenth century is the period in which theories and ideologies of racism became most developed. It is worth mentioning the social and political thought of Joseph Arthur Comte de Gobineau (1816–1882) in this context.[23] He put forward a theory of the Aryan master race in which he argued that the original Aryan invaders of India were a pure master race that had been degraded during the time that Buddhism dominated India, which led to notions of equality and racial intermarriage with what Gobineau termed inferior races. He believed that French aristocrats were a pure bred race that had avoided intermarriage so were superior to the masses of the French who were a mixed breed of Mediterranean and other races. He argued that mixing of what he assumes are the three main races – yellow, black and white – leads to chaos and degradation. The Aryan race, based on his interpretation of the original meaning of Aryan as "light," means that the "white" race is the best: most intelligent, beautiful, and capable of creating beauty (as in art, music, and so on).

Liberalism is associated with science in this period and we can see that pseudo-sciences supported the view that there were inherent racial differ-

---

[22] Charles A. Hale (1965) "Jose Maria Luis Mora and the Structure of Mexican Liberalism," *The Hispanic American Historical Review*, 45(2): 196–227.

[23] Arthur de Gobineau; Michael Denis Biddiss trans. (1970) *Gobineau: Selected Political Writings*, London: Cape.

ences. Liberals also argued that individuals and races might not be suited to the freedom unless they were educated or otherwise their capacities for using freedom constructively were developed. Phrenology, another pseudo-scientific approach, provides a suggestive parallel for the impact of liberalism on the concept of race. Phrenology is the study of the mind through the shape of the head. Bumps in the skull were used to "read" a person's mental abilities and orientations with an enlarged bump meaning that the mental activity associated with that area was being used extensively. It was very popular throughout the world, particularly in Germany, Britain and the United States but also in India in the early part of the nineteenth century. It was similar to liberalism in that it allowed for self-improvement and upward mobility. It suggested that education exercises and enhances beneficial "organs" of the brain while repressing base mental ideas. The problem was that phrenology was also used as justification for European superiority over other races because non-white races had shapes that indicated they were ruled by the lesser organs of the mind. Another pseudo-scientific approach to race was ethnology. One reason why Dadabhai Naoroji (दादाभाई नौरोजी 1825–1917) felt compelled to establish the East India Association in 1867 was to counter racialist propaganda by the Ethnological Society of London which, in its session in 1866, had tried to prove "scientifically" the inferiority of the Asians to the Europeans.

Race had the biggest impact in African political thought and this is associated with the settlement of former black slaves in Africa in the nineteenth century.[24] Those who had adopted British and American political ideals and institutions, often came into conflict with "tribal" Africans who had no experience of slavery, partly over land rights, but also because they were Christian or "whiter" so felt far superior to the indigenous population. One returnee who sided with the Africans against the "mulatto" ruling caste was Edward Wilmot Blyden (1832–1912). Blyden had been born into a family of free, educated blacks on the Danish Caribbean island of St. Thomas in 1832. He went to study in the United States but was denied entry to university due to his race so went instead to Liberia in 1850. Believing that racial equality was impossible in the United States, Blyden twice joined missions of American immigrants to Liberia but he also championed the cause of native Africans in Liberia who were denied citizenship rights unless "acculturated" and who had been discriminated against in various ways.[25] Perhaps the most important thinker who argued against racism in

---

[24] Peter Boele Van Hensbroek (1999) *Political Discourses in African Thought: 1860 to the Present*, Westport, CN: Greenwood Press.
[25] Edward Wilmot Blyden (1970) "African Life and Customs" in Langley, J. Ayo ed. *Ideologies of Liberation in Black Africa 1856–1970: Documents on Modern African Political*

the nineteenth century was James Africanus Beale Horton (1835–1883). Africanus Horton was a polymath who had been a British Army officer, mining entrepreneur, banker and was a trained medical physician. He contributed heavily to proposals for African self-government in the 1865 report of a Select Committee of the British House of Commons. He was also a supporter of the so-called Fanti Federation of 1870 and took the side of the Ashanti in the second Ashanti War in 1873–1874. The failure of the Fanti Federation and the narrow defeat of the Ashanti marked the beginning of massive colonial expansion into Africa. His most important work is *West African Countries and Peoples* written in 1868 to counter the emergence of white racism and the errors in the political ideas underpinning African colonialism but was ignored at the time.[26]

We can see from the experience of thinkers from around the world that the problem of imperialism is crucial to understanding in nineteenth-century political thought. Furthermore, imperialism flows naturally from the liberalism espoused in the nineteenth century. Once imperialism and ideas of the classification of civilizations overwhelmed all areas of the world, attempts at reform became even more distorted and tenuous. Liberalism promotes reform but liberal imperialism often made reform impossible.

IMPERIALISM AND THE FAILURE OF LATE NINETEENTH-CENTURY INDIAN AND ISLAMIC POLITICAL REFORM

Parallel to and reinforced by the liberal view on race was the expansion of Western imperialism in the nineteenth century. This also has an impact on how we view the political thought of the colonized areas of the world. For example, the most important contributors to political thought on freedom in nineteenth-century India have been viewed as too collaborationist despite their appeals for Indian dignity and autonomy. Mahadeo Govind Ranade (महादेवगोविन्द रानडे 1842–1901) founded the Poona Sarvajanik Sabha (National Association) and later was one of the originators of the Indian National Congress that eventually led the movement to Indian independence but Florence Nightingale could write: "the Poona Sarvajanik Sabha . . . pretends to represent the people [but] merely represents the money lenders, officials, and a few effete Mahratta

---

Thought from Colonial Times to the Present, London: Rex Collings: 78–87.
[26] J.A.B. Horton (1868) *West African Countries and Peoples*, London: W.J. Johnson.

landlords."[27] Similarly Dadabhai Naoroji (दादाभाई नौरोजी 1825–1917), the first Asian MP in British parliament, who spoke in favor of Irish Home Rule, wrote about "Poverty and Un-British Rule in India" in which he criticized the impact of British imperial rule in India. He was ultimately elected president of the Indian National Congress but was considered too moderate by many in the movement.

The differences between Indian moderates and the radicals are usually personalized by examining two individuals, Gopal Krishna Gokhale (गोपाल कृष्ण गोखले 1866–1915) and Bal Gangadhar Tilak (लोकमान्य टिळक 1856–1920). Gokhale had been educated in English and read a range of Western political thought. He was a great admirer of John Stuart Mill and Edmund Burke in particular.[28] Like most Indian moderates of the period he was highly critical of British rule but he argued in terms respectful of English political theory and institutions in the same way as his mentor Naoroji. In contrast, Tilak opposed the moderates in the Indian National Congress especially on the question of the need for immediate self-government. When two Bengali youths tried to assassinate a top British colonial official, Tilak defended the act and called for immediate *Swaraj* or self-rule. This led to him being arrested for sedition and sentenced to six years' transportation to a penal colony in Burma and a 1,000 rupee fine. Even while in the prison he continued to agitate for self-rule and wrote the *Gita Rahasya*, a key work of Hindu political radicalism in the period. Neither the moderates nor radicals were able to secure self-government despite years of agitation in the late nineteenth and early twentieth century.

The failure of reform in the Ottoman Empire can also be largely traced to Western imperialism as can be seen most clearly in Tunisia with the fate of the authors of the two major works of political thought associated with reform. As we saw in the last chapter, the work of Khayr al Din and Bin Diyaf indicated an impetus toward reform in the Middle East but it is telling that both works were written after the demise of the constitutional experiment in Tunisia. This political thought appears to have been written in the hope that further opportunities for reform would come in the future and aimed at building a theoretical basis for constitutionalism. It is true that these reforms were opposed by conservative *ulama* and local political leaders but the main problem was that Tunisia, Egypt and most of the rest

---

[27] "Florence Nightingale to Henry Fawcett esq. 1880," University of Illinois, Chicago, http://www.uic.edu/depts/lib/specialcoll/exhibits/nightingale/transcripts/T_FN_to_HF_1880_1.shtml (no longer accessible).

[28] Stanley Wolpert (1962) *Tilak and Gokhale: Revolution and Reform in the Making of Modem India,* Berkeley, CA: University of California Press: 22.

of the Middle East increasingly came under the control of Western imperial powers, particularly the British, and this effectively killed indigenous reform. For example, Khayr al-Din al-Tunisi was ultimately foiled in all reform attempts in Tunisia and the Ottoman Empire largely due to the actions of France and Britain, which led to Western colonial control of Egypt, the Sudan and Syria. Therefore, reform was put on hold as they felt compelled to deal with the problem of imperialism in preference to reform.

The legacy of imperialism for Islamic political thought is even clearer in the case of Sayyid Jamal-al-Din al-Afghani (سيد جمال الدين افغاني b. 1839– d. 1897). Al-Afghani could be portrayed as an opportunist but he was never part of the political elite, even if he tried to ingratiate himself with various officials, including those of imperialist powers such as Britain or Russia. It would be a mistake to say that he was unable to implement reform and had to rely on others to initiate the reform process because it was his reformist zeal which alienated him from the various rulers with whom he tried to work. Because imperial powers and established Islamic rulers would not listen to him, he increasingly felt compelled to emphasize strong pan-Islamic views in order to mobilize support. His pro-Islamic writing has more bulk than his moderate reformist work but it is clear that al-Afghani was speaking to different audiences.[29] Like many great thinkers, his work can and has been read two ways, both as an advocate of reforming or modernizing Islam and of anti-imperialist, reactionary Islam.

This mixed legacy is manifest in al-Afghani's student Muhammmad' Abduh (محمد عبده b. 1849–d. 1905) and indirectly through Abduh's followers. Abduh's early teaching work demonstrates the wide range of influences on his thought such as ibn Miskawayh's (مسكويه 932–1030) *Tahdib al-aklāq wa-taṭhir al-aʿrāq* (Refinement of Morals and Cleansing of Ethics تهذيب الأخلاق و تطهير الأعراق), which is an Islamic version of ancient Greek ethical philosophy, Guizot's *History of Civilization in Europe* and ibn Khaldūn's *Muqaddima*, as well as Rousseau, Spencer and Tolstoy. He angered conservatives because he accepted change and even admired aspects of European civilization but he also believed that it had to be linked to the principles of Islam. The moral foundation of individuals needed to be strengthened to cope with modernity. It was not a question of Islam or the West. It was how one could be a good Muslim in a modern society. Hourani speculates that Abduh built his argument on the positivist philosophy of Comte which was popular at the time, but there is no direct

---

[29] Sayyid Jamāl ad-Dīn al-Afghānī; Nikki R. Keddie trans. (1983) *An Islamic Response to Imperialism: Political and Religious Writings of Sayyid Jamāl ad-Dīn "al-Afghānī"*, Berkeley, CA: University of California Press.

evidence of this.[30] Nonetheless, Abduh's thought is another attempt at renewing Islam for the modern age.

Of Abduh's followers, one of the most important is Ahmed Lutfi al-Sayyid (أحمد لطفي السيد b. 1872–1963). Like other Arab intellectuals of the time, he was influenced by Comte, but more importantly by Mill and also Aristotle (with a hint of Tolstoy). Drawing on traditional Islamic thought he condemned despotism and autocracy because it prevented human moral nature from developing. He believed that religion is essential to the development of this moral nature but it can only unfold in a state with political freedom in which it is possible to fulfill one's role in society. Political freedom includes a free press and political expression but also limited government and a judiciary independent of executive authority. For him Islam cannot be the basis of political authority so the Caliphate cannot be restored. Like al-Tahtawi he valued both the ancient Egyptian and Arab Islamic influences in Egypt, so is more nationalist than Islamic, and doubted that pan-Arabic or pan-Islamic principles could form the basis for a strong political system. He tended more toward nationalism than previous Egyptian thinkers. In fact, it is important not to forget that there were many Arab Christian thinkers in the reform movements but that as the Middle East increasingly fell under Western imperial control, anti-imperialism, nationalism and the Islamist reaction choked off the potential of Arabic liberalism by the 1920s.

ONE SUCCESS, MANY FAILURES IN ASIAN AND AFRICAN REFORM

Imperialism came later to East Asia and Africa when compared to the Near East and the so-called "Eastern Problem." East Asia's successes also indicate that political space and dealing effectively with the pressures from Western powers was key to successful reform. In particular, it is worth dwelling on the Japanese case because it was widely seen as an example for other nations across the globe of a political philosophy which permitted modernization but still allowed Japan to maintain cultural integrity and autonomy. At the same time, as in India and the Middle East, the modernization of Japan occurred in the midst of strong Western political and military pressures.

Reform in Japan received its main impetus from both *Kokugaku* and Ōyōmei (Wang Yangming) thought. Among the Ōyōmei thinkers is

---

[30] Albert Hourani (1962) *Arabic Thought in a Liberal Age, 1798–1939*, Oxford: Oxford University Press: 137ff.

Yoshida Shōin (吉田松陰 1830–1859) whose belief that there was value in all persons, including those samurai who did not hold office, and even farmers and merchants, is in keeping with Wang Yangming political thought but also consistent with liberalism. Yoshida also believed that it was important for Japan to gain technology from the West. Japan had to master the technology and absorb it as its own. His radical pro-emperor stance influenced young samurai in the anti-Tokugawa domain of Chōshū to make an alliance with the Imperial Court to overthrow the Tokugawa Shogunate. The urgency for action and recognition of the pragmatic need to seize both institutional and technological opportunities is characteristic of the Japanese Ōyōmei political philosophy.

Western political ideas were also seeping into Japan. For example, Sakamoto Ryoma (坂本竜馬 1835–1867), who was initially part of the "Loyalist" movement which wanted to "expel the barbarians," soon realized the importance of Western technology and worked with Katsu Kaishu (勝海舟 1823–1899) to establish a modern Japanese navy. He also helped to negotiate a secret alliance between two key domains, Choshu and Satsuma, which were independent of the Tokugawa regime, with the aim of unifying the nation based on a restoration of power of the Japanese emperor, who was merely a figurehead under the Tokugawa system. Ryoma was important because he saw beyond the loyalties to individual lords and their domains to a centralized state with equal citizens. He realized that technological advances required that individuals be able to contribute to society based on their ability not hereditary position. He is credited with an "Eight-Point Plan" (*Senchū Hassaku* 船中八策) which formed the blueprint for the modern Japanese government. These eight points were the core of the Meiji Restoration, though the democratic implications of a parliament and a written constitution were delayed by conservatives who opposed reform.

Many in the new Meiji leadership had been students of Yoshida Shoin and reflect his Ōyōmei pragmatism. One of their first acts was to send the Iwakura Mission (*Iwakura Shisetsudan* 岩倉使節団) during 1872–1873 when a delegation of Japanese leaders toured the West to learn what they could about how to take advantage of Western knowledge. This mission included many of the key figures in the Meiji Restoration who went to study Western technology, law and political systems, among other subjects in an attempt to seek out models for reform. The Iwakura report admitted that Japan was backward in many respects and that it needed to learn from the West. It also pointed out that the rise of the West was relatively recent, that is, only the 50–100 years prior. They also noted many Japanese strong points, such as the lack of religious bigotry. The Meiji leadership was nationalistic but highly pragmatic.

The views of Fukuzawa Yukichi (福澤諭吉 1835–1901) are representative of many in the Japanese elite at the time. In principle, his views were egalitarian with a strong commitment to education as the best way to enable Japan to escape Western control, though he is skeptical of giving too much education to women or peasants because it might have the opposite effect of weakening the state. In order to do this, however, Fukuzawa unashamedly favored Western learning over classical Chinese learning but interpreted the West in ways that were easy for the Japanese to accept. In his *Outline of Civilization* (Bunmeiron no Gairyaku 文明論之概略) of 1875, he acknowledged that the West was not perfect but that since the West had evolved to an advanced stage of civilization, Japan needed to consider what it could learn from the West and how to improve upon it. He even advocated that Japan should leave Asia (*datsua* 脱亜) behind intellectually. Fukuzawa was a conservative and shared the views of the Meiji leadership in that new ideas should be adopted but primarily to strengthen the state and maintain order.

When the leaders of the new Meiji government looked to the West, therefore, they only adopted the ideas they thought were most appropriate to give stability and structure to the state. Itō Hirobumi, a member of the Iwakura Mission, found German political institutions most attractive for emulation and established a close relationship with Lorenz von Stein (1815–1890) and his student Albert Mosse (1846–1925) of the *Staatswissenschaft* school of German constitutional thought.[31] Not surprisingly Germans played a major role in the formation of the Meiji state and writing of the Meiji Constitution.[32] At the same time, Anglo-Saxon thinkers such as Herbert Spencer were important sources of liberal influence with Spencer directly corresponding with Japanese leaders such as Itō Hirobumi (伊藤博文 1841–1909) and Kaneko Kentarō (金子堅太郎 1853–1942). Spencer's advice was typical of Western liberals of the time in that he argued that the Japanese are not sufficiently developed to be capable of practicing liberal democratic government. This implicit Social Darwinism had a profound impact on Japanese thought. For example, Katō Hiroyuki, a key translator and official in the Meiji government, and thereafter the head of the prestigious Law School at Tokyo Imperial University and Privy Councilor, wrote the *Jinken Shinsetsu* (人権新説) or "New Doctrines of Human Rights" in 1882, which demonstrated a shift from his initial support of a theory of natural rights to social evolution and even Social Darwinism which fit with the statist ideology of the Meiji leadership.[33]

---

[31] Takii Kazuhiro (2010) "Itō Hirobumi wa Nihon no Bisumaruku ka?" *Yūroppa Kenkyū*, 9: 203–210.
[32] Johannes Siemes (1969) *Hermann Roesler-The Making of Meiji State*, Tokyo: Charles E. Tuttle Co.
[33] Joseph Pittau (1969) *Political Thought in Early Meiji Japan, 1868–1889*, Cambridge, MA: Harvard University Press: 118–119.

The opposition to the Meiji elite was expressed through pressure for popular involvement in the political process, in both populist East Asian Ōyōmei and Western liberal strands. Some of the key opposition leaders arose from within the elite itself. For example, when one of the top Meiji leaders, Saigō Takamori (西郷隆盛 1828–1877), advocated a vigorous Japanese expansionism, it was rejected as too dangerous by the Meiji elite and Saigō's populism, as manifest in his *Last Instructions* (大西郷遺訓), based on Ōyōmei thought was also considered a threat to political stability. An armed revolt led by Saigō was easily put down by a professional army. On the other hand, when Inoue Kowashi (井上毅 1843–1895), cabinet minister in the Meiji government, quit the government after his draft for a new constitution was considered too radical by the rest of the Meiji leadership, the peaceful propagation of his ideas under his leadership fueled pressures for liberal reform.

Outside the elite, there were other thinkers who were even more at the mercy of censors and the police. Nakae Chomin (中江兆民 1847–1901) is probably the most important in this context. He had studied in France and upon his return wrote his most famous work *A Discourse by Three Drunkards on Government* (Sansuijin Keirin Mondō 三酔人經綸問答) which is a conversation between a Gentleman of Western Learning and a Champion of the East moderated by Master Nankai, who asks probing questions and makes interesting observations about the absurdities of both positions. The Gentleman of Western Learning advocates progress, democracy and pacificism, whereas the Champion of the East argues for the samurai ethos, Literati values and military adventure. Nakae, in the guise of Master Nankai, concludes that while liberal values and democracy are the future, Japan must carefully introduce them to avoid being swamped by new ideas – creating nihilism and making Japan vulnerable by undermining native values. The book reflects a sharp understanding of both Western and Literati thought as well as acknowledging the challenges of the new world Japan faced. It is strongly egalitarian and evinces a strong belief in evolution, similar to Fukuzawa but more political and more radical. However, it was only by having the participants as drunkards saying outrageous things that the book could get by the censors. Readers of the book understood Nakae's message and he was propelled to a prominent position in the radical wing of the Freedom and People's Rights Movement (*Jiyūminken Undō* 自由民権運動).

The movement for Freedom and People's Rights involved groups of varying political sentiment and only constituted a weak liberal movement. In fact, the most vigorous elements were right-wing groups inspired by Saigō Takamori and Ōyōmei thought, and political opportunists such as Itagaki Taisuke, another former member of the Meiji government. Nakae opposed these tendencies but the attractions of power were too strong for most of the politicians involved. Thus, when democracy became stronger in the 1920s, Japan's liberalism was still fragile, as shown in the failure of the notion of *Minponshugi* (民本主義), a form of constitutional monarchial democracy advocated by Yoshino Sakuzō (吉野作造 1878–1933), which came under intense criticism as Japan drifted toward military-dominated government in the 1930s. If anything, the populist Ōyōmei strand represented a different approach which aided Japanese imperialism and even potentially fascism as we will see. Social Darwinism, one outgrowth of nineteenth-century liberalism, also justified imperialism by Japan.

Despite the ultimate failures of the Japanese model, it was attractive as a successful indigenous response to the West with what seemed to be judicious borrowing, reform and reaffirmation of national and racial values. However, the contrast of Japan with the other nations of East Asia is stark. China too attempted a "Tongzhi Restoration" (同治中興 c. 1860–1874) prior to the Japanese. Some of the individuals who sought to change China, such as Liang Qichao (梁啟超 1873–1929) attempted to build upon traditional East Asian thought by considering how to incorporate the best of Western political practice and technology but were also strongly influenced by the Japanese. Liang drew heavily on the work of Kato Hiroyuki in particular, and subsequently influenced Korean nationalists in the 1900s. This was manifest in his focus on the evolution of peoples and the need for group unity. In his *Theory of New People* (Xin Min Shuo 新民說) he goes so far as to argue that freedom only has meaning for a group and not for the individual. It is only through submission to the group or nation that a people can avoid becoming slaves of other peoples, which suggests a hint of Hegel and also earlier Romanticism.

The final effort of reform in the Qing dynasty was in 1898 with Kang Youwei as one of the key architects. Kang, along with his student, Liang Qichao attempted to implement the so-called Hundred Days' Reform. The reforms were radical but were firmly opposed by the conservatives in the Chinese state and soon failed. Kang faced execution and fled to Japan where along with Liang, he organized a "Protect the Emperor Society" (*Baohuanghui* 保皇會), promoting constitutional monarchy and competed with the revolutionary leader Sun Yat-sen's (孫逸仙 1866–1925) "Revive China Society" (*Xingzhonghui* 興中會) and "United China League" (Tongmenghui 同盟會) for funds and support, particularly in the overseas Chinese communities. After the Qing dynasty fell and the Republic of China was established in 1912 under Sun Yat-sen, Kang seemed an anachronistic figure and permanently damaged his reputation by cooperating in a failed military coup in 1917. Kang had gone from being considered a radical reformer to a reactionary in less than 20 years. The debate had moved beyond Kang and Liang's ideas rooted in Literati thought. As with most areas of the world the 1920s in China saw the last flourish of nineteenth-century liberalism. The debates over democracy in China were based on a new set of Chinese thinkers with a much more organic synthesis of Chinese and Western ideas. The problem was that soon China disintegrated into a period of interference from foreign powers, especially Japan, and the rise of warlordism and civil war.

The Japanese case demonstrates that imperialism was crucial to success or failure of reform efforts. Only a few nations maintained their independence in Africa and Asia during the nineteenth century: Persia, Ethiopia, Siam, and Japan. China and Korea were arguably independent but were compromised by persistent foreign intervention. Moreover, countries like Japan were successful due to selective modernization and not the adoption of liberalism. Crucially geographical position helped. The success of most states which remained independent was due both to early or concerted attempts at modernization and a strategic position which left them in a buffer zone between European empires so they were untouched by direct control by European powers. For example, in the Middle East only Persia was successful temporarily in retaining a degree of independence as a buffer between Russia and Britain in south Asia even if it too came under Western domination by the early twentieth century. Competition between European states led to complete control of India and eventually Burma so that Siam was left as a buffer between the British Empire and French influence in Indo-China. This political space gave Siam an opportunity for relatively independent development. For example, King Mongkut (1804–1868), famous as the modernizing monarch portrayed in the play "The King and I," and his son King Chulalongkorn (1853–1910), used their diplomatic skills to manage the pressures from Western powers and buy time to undertake reform so that Siam was the only country in Southeast Asia to avoid European colonization. The same dynamics applied to Africa, the last area to be colonized by the West. Of the indigenous regimes of Africa, only Ethiopia was successful by carving out an empire by playing off the conflicts of competing Western powers, mostly due to the fact that the country was useful in helping the British to control the Sudan and fight the Italians in Somalia. Only a few countries had the political space and resources to cope with Western imperial pressures. This, and not the quality of their political thought, was the main factor in determining whether an area was colonized or not.

Where imperial powers did take control, the damage was significant. Even the relatively benign forms of British rule in Africa were problematic. This was argued most forcefully by Joseph Casely Hayford (1866–1930) who insisted that whatever the intentions of the British, the view of indigenous people was that British imperialism

> may overwhelm them, and play havoc with all that is dear to them of law, custom and practice; it may reduce them to the condition of bondsmen and captives in their own fair domains and make them a people of no reputation, a by-word and a reproach among men; but for all these things, they would rather have the ills that they know of than fly to others that they know not of. What is more, they know what evils there are, are such that they can cope with, and that, truth being on their side, they will triumph [over] in the end.[34]

Hayford's *Gold Coast Native Institutions* described sophisticated Ashanti and Fanti political arrangements, including "checks and balances" and methods of political deliberation, which were being undermined by the British. He recognized that the Gold Coast had to modernize and deal with the flaws in existing practices and institutions but that its indigenous tradition was key to success in modernization. Any healthy development, however, was blocked by colonial administration. The British came on a liberal "civilizing mission" but since this required the suppression of the indigenous civilization, it was doomed to failure.[35]

By the end of the nineteenth century it was clear that liberalism and imperialism were not a healthy combination. Liberalism is grounded in the right to be left alone and to develop autonomously both as an individual and as a people, whether as a nation or race. Liberalism imperialism meant that the more powerful or advanced society controlled and "reformed" the less advanced but a colonialized people could not develop a liberal society because the process of colonial rule distorted and stunted relations in society and with the state. Still, it was difficult for Western countries to wean themselves from empire. The longer they waited the worse the problem became. More radical action to fight for autonomy and independence seemed to be necessary.

LATE NINETEENTH-CENTURY REFORM IN EUROPE AND LATIN AMERICA

The final problem of liberalism in the nineteenth century is clear even in those areas not under colonial control. As the industrial revolution

---

[34] Joseph Casely Hayford (1970) *Gold Coast Native Institutions. With Thoughts upon a Healthy Imperial Policy for the Gold Coast and Ashanti*, London: Frank Cass: 6.
[35] Peter Boele Van Hensbroek (1999) *Political Discourses in African Thought: 1860 to the Present*, Westport, CN: Greenwood Press.

progressed in Britain and France, the problem of economic inequality, acerbated by liberalism, overwhelmed the impetus for reform. In 1848 revolution spread throughout Europe. Liberals demanded progressive constitutions, more representative assemblies, and freedom of the press but workers demanded protection from exploitation as their interest diverged from the middle-class and industrialists who promoted liberalism. Liberals were firmly in charge in Britain with the Liberal Party formed in 1859, and under the leadership of William Ewart Gladstone (1809–1898), the Liberals carried out educational reform and introduced the secret ballot in elections. Even the Conservative Party appealed to a wider constituency as a result by developing a new populist conservatism under Benjamin Disraeli (1804–1881). Disraeli was a conservative but he also modernized the conservatism of Burke for the nineteenth century. As with Burke he is suspicious of grand schemes of reform based on abstract ideals but he also recognized that change had occurred and the nation needed to adapt to it but the only sound basis for reform were the long-serving principles behind existing institutions, which had served the nation well for years. In this way, working-men were given more representation in the House of Commons, not as part of a drive toward equality as much as the recognition of an expanded notion of "the Commons."

Conservative reform was also the pattern of reform in Germany where social and political stability were sought through the efforts of Otto Van Bismarck (1815–1898) and others to create a legal basis for the unity of the German state. This led political thought of the period to focus on three issues: national identity, rivalries between the different German states, and the "claims of popular self-government."[36] Bismarck sought to solve both these problems through the struggle to unify Germany. This was clearest in his famous speech to the Prussian Chamber of Deputies Budget Committee on September 30, 1862, where he argued Prussia must "concentrate and maintain its power for the favorable moment" and that "the great questions of the time will not be resolved by speeches and majority decision . . . but by iron and blood."[37] Bismarck succeeded in his plans through the Franco-Prussian War of 1870–1871. He did play off the various political parties to suppress the power of the Catholic Church and the growing socialist movement, but this weakened the liberal parliamentary system and merely served to strengthen the state.

Italy, in contrast, also unified in the late nineteenth century, and though the birth of modern Italy was not without violence or the interference of

---

[36] Peter Pulzer (1997) *Germany 1870–1945: Politics, State Formation, and War*, Oxford: Oxford University Press: 3.
[37] F.B.M. Hollyday (1970) *Bismarck*, New York: Prentice Hall: 16–18.

imperial powers, the political system that emerged was much more liberal than in Germany at least until the 1920s. It may be because the unification movement was inspired by Giuseppe Mazzini (1805–1872) who advocated liberal republicanism. Crucially, Mazzini's liberalism was cosmopolitan and religious.[38] However, by the end of the nineteenth century, he appeared to be an anachronism. The nationalism which he fostered was now more inward looking and liberalism was the ideology of the middle-class which favored the approach of the politician Cavour (1810–1861) rather than radical liberal idealism of Mazzini. Even so, many in Europe and beyond continued to be inspired by him, for example the Indian independence movement leader, Vinayak Damodar Savarkar (विनायक दामोदर सावरकर 1883–1966).

Even though Europe might seem the more likely refuge of liberalism, the fact is it was arguably strongest in the former European colonies of Latin America. Yet even here there were two problems. One was the strong man or *caudillo* tradition from pre-independence political rule and the other was the divisions in society along socio-economic and ethnic lines. Liberalism was victorious in Latin America and arguably more completely than in Europe, but it was not as effectively institutionalized as in most European liberal regimes. The ideological basis for this liberalism was also more theoretical. For example, in Ecuador, it is a combination of liberalism and romanticism which is strongest. When the conservative and theocratic President Gabriel García Moreno (1860–1875) was overthrown by the Liberals, he was replaced by Eloy Alfaro (1842–1912), a populist strongman who carried out extensive sociopolitical reform, based on the philosophy of one of his key ministers, José Peralta (1855–1937), an important follower of the German Romantic thinker Karl Christian Friedrich Krause (1781–1832).[39]

It is the Positivism of Auguste Comte which has the strongest influence on liberalism in Latin America. Interestingly enough, Positivism was less important in Chile and Argentina, both of which developed strong liberal democratic constitutional systems earlier in the nineteenth century, despite the presence of important Comteans such as José Victorino Lastarria (1817–88), a student of Bello in Chile, and Agustin Alvarez (1857–1914) in Argentina. Several other smaller countries also had exponents of Positivism, such as Enrique José Varona (1849–1933) in Cuba. The two countries with the strongest Positivist influence were Mexico and Brazil.

---

[38] See, for example, Joseph Mazzini (1907) *The Duties of Man and Other Essays*, London: J.M. Dent and Sons.
[39] O. Carlos Stoetzer (1998) *Karl Christian Friedrich Krause and his Influence in the Hispanic World*, Köln: Böhlau.

In Mexico, the Positivist movement is associated with the doctrine of "scientific politics" in the newspaper *La Libertad*, the so-called La Libertad group of 1878, drawing inspiration from Auguste Comte. They wanted to go beyond the formal structures of the Constitution of 1857, and go further in fully implementing liberal constitutionalism in Mexico. The most important "Positivist" thinkers were Ignacio Ramirez (1818–1879), Gabino Barreda (1820–1881), Justo Sierra (1848–1912), and José Yves Limantour (1854–1935). Comte's Positivism also played a key role in the Brazil republican revolution.[40] Positivism had been introduced to Brazil by Luis Pereira Barreto (1840–1923) and Comte's "Religion of Humanity" was promoted in particular by Raimundo Texeira Mendes (1855–1927).

It was the role of supporters of positivism in the military, however, which is outstanding in Brazil. Prior to 1889 Brazil was a monarchy, ruled by the liberal king, Pedro II (1825–1891), but republicanism was strong amongst the Brazilian elite and most republicans were awaiting the death of Pedro II to make a move to prevent his daughter Isabel from ascending the throne. This republicanism was an elite form of liberalism that focused on political rights for the wealthy even if it was also supported by intellectuals and the military. It was largely irrelevant to most of the population who were poor and lived in isolated rural communities controlled by local elites. For his part, Pedro II allowed republicans to operate freely and become public officials. He even went so far as to hire the republican military officer Benjamin Constant (of Brazil, 1836–1891) as a tutor for his grandsons. Constant was one of a number of military instructors who propagated the political ideas of Auguste Comte among Brazil's military cadets. When Pedro II refused to give up power, Constant and others in the military decided to carry out the successful republican military coup d'état of November 15, 1889. Constant is considered the founder of the Brazilian Republic and responsible for the Constitution of 1891. The new republic also adopted Comte's positivist slogan of "Ordem e Progresso" (Order and Progress), which is still emblazoned on the Brazilian flag. In Brazil, as in Europe, however, as liberalism gained the upper hand problems of economic inequality and ethnic divisions persisted and deepened. In Latin America, this made the *caudillo* strongman or the military the most attractive political forces for unity, rather than wealthy liberal politicians but even when the strongman or military espoused liberal ideals, it undermined liberalism because the tendency toward authoritarian imposition of liberalism is contrary to the spirit of liberalism.

---

[40] Miguel Jorrin and John D. Martz (1971) *Latin American Political Thought and Ideology*, Chapel Hill, NC: University of North Carolina Press: 138–144.

CONCLUSION

We can see then that liberalism began with the best intentions of reform and application of Enlightenment principles to society and politics. These attempts at reform met with resistance but some of the problems of liberalism were of its own making. Racism and Social Darwinism promoted imperialism and slowed reform everywhere. Economic inequality and nationalism fostered by liberalism, also undermined the appeal of a pure universalistic liberal movement. Liberalism was meant to succeed by leaving people free of interference by the state but imperialism and socio-economic inequality made it difficult for all to develop their potential and it often seemed to have made things worse. Religious liberalism and liberal social reform initially inspired but ultimately failed to help. This led many thinkers to more extreme solutions. The next few chapters look at the emergence of extremism on the left and the right, often running parallel to, and, in the end, overwhelming, nineteenth-century liberalism.

13. Social unrest and the rise of the left (1810–1930)

This chapter outlines the spread of radical ideas, particularly Western forms of socialism and anarchism. However, one must resist the notion that radical attempts at reform were largely a Western phenomenon until the twentieth century. Revolutionary action to help the disadvantaged has been advocated all over the world. One example is the revolt in early nineteenth-century Japan by Ōshio Heihachirō based on Wang Yangming thought. Ōshio Heihachirō (大塩平八 1793–1837) was an assistant police inspector for a magistrate (奉行所与力) in Osaka. He was dismayed that tax collectors and other officials openly accepted bribes which led to an increased levy of excessive taxes on those who could not bribe. The wealthy became richer, while poverty in lower classes continued to be a problem. Merchants in Osaka benefited from highly profitable loans to *daimyo* (regional lords) and were appointed to high level positions even though they were not of samurai status. Worse, from the point of view of Ōshio, merchants and officials did not help the poor: "Knowing no want themselves, they have lost all fear of Heaven's punishment and make no attempt to save those who are begging and starving to death on the streets."[1] Ultimately Ōshio quit his position as a police official in order to espouse his teachings and set up a private academy called the *Senshindō* (洗心洞). His Wang Yangming beliefs required him to not simply have moral ideals but also put them into action, especially when he began to see people starving during Tempo famine. He sold his book collection to feed the poor but it was not enough so he decided to lead a rebellion even though he knew the consequences would be death for him and his family. In 1837 Ōshio decided to kill officials he viewed as tormenting and harassing peasants, and execute the rich merchants in Osaka, who despite their elevated social status and wealth, did nothing to help the plight of peasants. He planned to confiscate the wealth of the merchants and redistribute it to the landless peasants in neighboring domains. First he attacked the Shogun's office in

---

[1] William Theodore De Bary, Carol Gluck and Arthur Tiedemann eds (2005) *Sources of Japanese Tradition, Volume 2: 1600–2000*, 2nd edn, New York, NY: Columbia University Press: 471.

Osaka, and set fire to it. Then he mobilized a force of about 300 from the town and surrounding countryside to attack the houses and businesses of rich merchants to confiscate their wealth. As a result of his actions and the ensuing unrest, a quarter to a fifth of Osaka was burnt to the ground. Ōshio was finally discovered a few months later after he and one of his followers had committed suicide rather than surrender.

Ōshio became a national hero and inspired similar revolts throughout Japan (despite heavy Tokugawa regime censorship). His written work, *Senshindō Sakki* (洗心洞箚記), based on his lecture notes, was already circulated widely by the time of his revolt, which both made it difficult to control its distribution and increased readership of the work dramatically.[2] He argued that people think that heaven is in the sky but this is not the only place heaven exists. It is also in the spaces between stones or the space between living bamboo. This universe is not just plants and organic matter, it goes through humans, into their mouths, ears, everywhere. There is no difference between the small *taikyo* (taixu 太虛) that ordinary people have and that of the Sages. He taught that if one can shake off one's desires and return to the *taikyo*, heaven is already living in your heart. Everyone can attain the status of a Sage. *Taikyo* or *taixu* (太虛), as we have seen, is a sort of ether or medium of nothingness out of which all is generated. Given its status as the source of all, it connects all things and can also be a source of purity for an impetus toward reform and action. There is also a notion of equality as all humans share the same source. This is not so different from Mencius' view that everyone is a potential Sage, though the focus on eliminating desire is distinctly Buddhist rather than the traditional Confucian emphasis on ritual, proper relationships, study, and so on. For Ōshio, however, eliminating desire is the main thing because once it has been accomplished the eternal immovable can be known:

> When one's heart has returned to the *taikyo*, one goes beyond good and evil to attain true knowledge because one's heart is one with heaven's righteousness: If one's heart returns to the *taikyo*, one continues to exist even if the body dies. One need not fear the death of one's heart/soul. One fears nothing. Then one knows *tenmei* (the will of heaven).[3]

Based on this philosophy it should be clear why Ōshio would ignore his official status and do what he thought was right to help the poor and

---

[2] Ōshiō Heihachirō (大塩平八郎); Yoshida Kōhei trans. (吉田公平訳) (1998) *Senshindō* (洗心洞箚記) 2 volumes (上下). Tokyo: Tachibana Publishing (東京: たちばな出版).

[3] Although the characters are the same (i.e., 天命), this is not the mandate of heaven in continental Literati thought.

suffering of Osaka regardless of the consequences for himself. Social revolution was not limited to the West.

UTOPIAN SOCIALISM

About the time of Ōshio's revolt, Europe saw the emergence of modern socialism, which is usually traced back to what later socialists and communists, such as Karl Marx and Fredrick Engels, termed "utopian socialism." This type of socialism is associated with three major figures: Henri de Saint-Simon (1760–1825), Charles Fourier (1772–1837), and Robert Owen (1771–1858).

Henri de Saint-Simon wanted to develop a state-technocracy supported by industrialists in order to wipe out poverty. Industrialization had created potential for the spread of material comfort but only if technological progress and increased productivity was made to benefit all in society. He advocated a new politics in order to foster cooperation through the decentralization of political power and administration based on an objective "science of production." Science (including both technological and administrative science), industrialization and a new religion would all be used to support these developments leading to a utopian socialist society.

In his "Eighth Letter" in *L'Industrie* (1817), Saint-Simon argued that the production of useful things is the only reasonable objective of industry.[4] However, government tends to undermine industry when it interferes in production. For example, wars and conflict decrease production of useful things even if they produce more armaments, and similarly imperialism reduces production of useful things because resources are put into the subordination of others. Therefore, only so long as productive industry is pursued, the moral state of society is improved. Humanity is a society of workers but in industrial society there are two types of people, working people and non-working people. Working people should occupy the top rank in society.[5] Since those that produce, create useful things and pay taxes are the only useful members of society they should be the only ones who should vote. The ideal society has full employment and no domination of any individual by others, with three classes: owners, workers, and the wise and artists (the latter of whom would rule society).

During his lifetime the views of Saint-Simon had very little influence and only a few devoted disciples at the time of his death. The most

---

[4] Claude-Henri de Saint-Simon (1817) *L'industrie ou Discussions politiques, morales et philosophique*, Tome 2, Paris: Bureau d'Administration: 78–89.
[5] Claude-Henri de Saint-Simon (1823) *Catechisme des industriels*, Paris: de Sétier: 2.

important of his followers were Benjamin Olinde Rodrigues (1795–1851) and Barthélemy Prosper Enfantin (1796–1864) who together had received Saint-Simon's last instructions. Based on their efforts, the sect began to grow, and before the end of 1828 held regular meetings not only in Paris but in many provincial towns in France. It attempted to expand into England and attracted the attention of the British intellectual elite. John Stuart Mill was initially attracted to but ultimately felt the need to distance himself from the movement.[6] Eventually its suppression in France led to the withdrawal of the movement from England. Nonetheless it continued to have an influence abroad, notably in the Middle East (particularly in Tunisia, Egypt and Morocco).

One industrialist, Charles Fourier (1772–1837), adopted his own approach to these issues at the time of Saint Simon. He argued that cooperation among workers will lead to higher productivity. The greatest incentive to work will arise from distributing wealth according to the fruits of one's work, but in jobs based on one's interests and desires. He believed that poverty was the root of all social problems but that religion and philosophy has tended to glorify poverty rather than address its causes and recognize the damage it does.[7] He could be accused of anti-Semitism because he believed Jews were parasitic merchants even if one could argue he was bitterly opposed to merchants in general, and he engaged in inaccurate anti-Islamic tirades as well.[8] He can be considered a feminist because he argued all jobs should be open to women as well as men, and women should have complete sexual freedom. He never married because he believed traditional marriage damaged women. For those who could not find a partner, he advocated a system of meeting for casual sex and defended homosexuality as a personal preference.

Robert Owen (1771–1858) believed that mechanization gave rise to the danger that human labor would be replaced and most reduced to poverty and powerlessness. His alternative was the formation of communities of workers to take control of machine-based production for the benefit of the community as a whole. His approach is very much utilitarian (and not surprisingly one of his investors was Jeremy Bentham) in the way he views human beings as important input into the industrial process. Human labor has been given less attention by industrialists, he argues, than inanimate machines. Working conditions in factories, particularly

---

[6] Richard Pankhurst (1957) *The Saint Simonians, Mill and Carlyle: A Preface to Modern Thought*, London: Sidgwick & Jackson.

[7] Charles Fourier; Ian Patterson trans. (1996) *Fourier: "The Theory of the Four Movements"*, Cambridge: Cambridge University Press: 182–224.

[8] Fourier; Patterson trans. *Fourier: "The Theory of the Four Movements"*: 200–201.

for child workers, was so poor that illness and disability was the result, which undermined productivity. He proposed radical plans to improve the conditions of workers in factories by connecting the factories to communities organized by parishes, by counties, or by the state. Families were to have their own private apartments but only to take care of children up to the age of three, after which they became the responsibility of the community. Everyone was to be paid the same wage but would also receive extra support according to need. The benefits of the wealth of the community would be shared in common. His factory town of New Lanark in Scotland was his showpiece attempt at creating such a community and others were attempted in the United States. His utilitarian views extended to religious beliefs, which undermined his support from the British political establishment that viewed poverty as a test by God of the character of the poor. In the end, he had only limited success in creating these utopian communities himself but his ideas inspired cooperative movements and worker-friendly community experiments by other industrial philanthropists.

SCIENTIFIC SOCIALISM OR MARXISM

Such utopian plans, however, were rejected by Karl Marx (1818–1883) and Friedrich Engels (1820–1895) who believed that they had discovered a more scientific approach to socialism.[9] Marx also distinguished between socialism, where industry is controlled by and for the people, and communism, in which the benefits of industry are shared across society. Following Hegel, Marx argued the development of socio-economic relationships had developed in stages, but unlike Hegel, who Marx viewed as an idealist, Marx believed that the dialectical tensions in society were not in the unfolding of "Absolute" but were rooted in the historical material conditions of each stage.[10] He noted that the slave-based economy of ancient times created tensions between slaves and slave owners and the resultant economic contradictions caused the slave economy to collapse. He suggested that that same process led to the collapse of feudalism and the peasant economy. With the rise of the industrial economy, a process in which the conflict between workers and capitalists would once again create contradictions and will cause the collapse of capitalism and usher in socialism and communism. In order to prepare workers to take full advantage of

---

[9] Friedrich Engels (1908) *Socialism, Utopian and Scientific*, Chicago, IL: Charles H. Kerr.
[10] Karl Marx; N.I. Stone trans. (1904) *A Contribution to the Critique of Political Economy*, Chicago, IL: Charles H. Kerr: 11–13.

this process, Marx and Engels wrote the *Communist Manifesto*, which was a call to revolt and appeal to workers to organize.

Marx's political thought is relatively undeveloped as the focus of most of his work was to critique capitalism, particularly in the later part of his life. The term "dictatorship of the proletariat" was used by Marx and Engels but it meant nothing other than that workers, as the majority and the class best suited to the task, would have to reform political institutions for the benefit of society rather than meaning a dictatorship to repress non-working-class elements.[11] The notion that once the socialist revolution was complete, that there would be a "withering away of the state" was based on Hegelian notions of the end of history where social revolution under the working-class would lead to equality and thus the need for the state to repress and control would be eliminated.[12] However, when Marx engaged in analysis of actual political events, such as in his *The Eighteenth Brumaire of Louis Napoleon* (Der 18te Brumaire des Louis Napoleon), he recognizes that the unfolding of political events is not entirely in human control with the weight of the past a powerful constraint on remaking society.[13]

Friedrich Engels' *The Origin of the Family, Private Property and the State*, was important in how it connected capitalism to the social ills and problems of the family, the subordination of women and private property in modern society.[14] He begins by identifying key stages in human society that closely follows Lewis H. Morgan's book *Ancient Society* (1877). Engels summarizes the stages as "savagery" (where products are gathered in their natural state), "barbarism" (when animals are domesticated and agriculture developed) and "civilization" (in which work is applied to the products of nature in increasingly sophisticated ways). Engels connects these stages to changes in the family over time. As bourgeois law requires strict rules governing relationships and inheritance, monogamy is increasingly enforced and women are compelled to enter into disadvantageous contractual relationships. Since the emphasis in these relationships is property rights, the narrow constraints of monogamy, immorality and prostitution are the natural result. The proletariat, however, can be freed from these constraints by engaging in voluntary relationships based on

---

[11] Karl Marx (1970) "Critique of the Gotha Program" in *Marx/Engels Selected Works*, vol. 3, Moscow: Progress Publishers: 13–30.

[12] Friedrich Engels; Emile Burns trans. (1947) *Herr Eugen Dühring's Revolution in Science (anti-Dühring)*, Moscow: Progress Publishers: 315.

[13] Karl Marx; Daniel De Leon trans. (1907) *The Eighteenth Brumaire of Louis Napoleon*, Chicago, IL: Charles H. Kerr.

[14] Friedrich Engels; Earnest Untermann trans. (1902) *The Origin of the Family, Private Property and the State*, Chicago, IL: Charles H. Kerr & company.

sex-love because they have little property to preserve within bourgeois legal structures. Monogamy would still be the norm because the elimination of class differences in communism would eliminate the demand for prostitution and end the legal control of women by men so partners would be free to choose a suitable partner for life based on love, reinforced with sexual bonds, through mutual consent.

ANARCHISM AND SYNDICALISM

Parallel to the development of Marxian socialism was the emergence of anarchism and syndicalism. The first self-declared "anarchist" was Pierre-Joseph Proudhon (1809–1865). He famously argued that all "property is theft," that is, the only legitimate source of property is work and not speculation or rentier accumulation.[15] He argued for a form of mutualism with workers' associations or cooperatives rather than nationalization by the state (or private ownership). He viewed revolution as a process of transformation and not as a sharp break with the past requiring violence, in contrast to Marx who saw violence as inevitable. Proudhon was compelled to adopt a form of federalism as a late addition to his thought in order to have a larger system to coordinate worker cooperatives, which by nature were limited to the local level.[16]

The two most prominent anarchists, however, were both Russians: Mikhail Bakunin (Михаил Бакунин 1814–1876) and Peter Kropotkin (Пётр Алексéевич Кропо́ткин 1842–1921). Bakunin was adamant that any revolution must aim at dissolution of the state, especially the police and army. Unlike Marx who believed that revolution would transfer state power to the working class, Bakunin was suspicious of any state power and those who controlled state powers involving force and violent compulsion.[17] In his mind, Marx's "dictatorship of proletariat" would be just as bad as any other authority. In fact, socialism and absolute authority would be the worst possible outcome. Instead he advocated small local associations of free equal individuals linked to one another by mutual alliances of cooperation. He insisted that such a future was not a dream because he believed that the ideals could be realized through action based on a clear vision of the future rooted in real possibilities, such as building

---

[15] Pierre-Joseph Proudhon (1876) *Works of P.J. Proudhon, Vol. 1: "What is Property?"*, Princeton, NJ: Benjamin R. Tucker: 11.

[16] Pierre-Joseph Proudhon (1863) *Du principe fédératif et de la nécessité de reconstituer le parti de la révolution*, Paris: E. Dentu.

[17] Mikhail Bakunin; Marshall Shatz trans. (1990) *Statism and Anarchy*, Cambridge: Cambridge University Press.

on existing workers' unions and cooperatives that were flourishing in the late nineteenth century. Peter Kropotkin (Пётр Кропо́ткин 1842–1921) argued that evolution of species, including humans, has been based on cooperation and not competition as those influenced by liberalism tend to insist.[18] He does not deny competitive aspects of humans but argues they are not dominant or natural. Effort should not be expended on competition and should instead be directed at dismantling the state, and institutions like the church that repress. He also believed that the economy must be based on exchange based on cooperation with self-sufficiency the goal for localities, regions and countries as far as possible.

Though originally Russian, both Bakunin and Kropotkin were active mainly in Western Europe. Their greatest influence was in Western European countries such as Spain, France, Italy and Germany. Germany might be said to have an early anarchist, Johann Kaspar Schmidt (1806–1856), better known by his pen name, Max Stirner, though his philosophy of egoism predates anarchism as a concept and not only does it fit uncomfortably with anarchism as political thought, it contains racist assumptions about human development that we have seen are typical in nineteenth-century thought.[19] Most anarchism, in contrast, is egalitarian, particularly the European thinkers who had a major influence on the rest of the world. For example, Johann Joseph "Hans" Most (1846–1906), a German émigré spread his notion of the "propaganda of the deed" in Europe, United States and beyond. Alexander Berkman (1870–1936) was a Russian émigré and together with fellow Russian Emma Goldman (1869–1940), wrote widely on anarchism for an American audience and influenced others in Europe, Latin America and Asia. Another important US anarchist was Voltairine de Cleyre (1866–1912) who was known for her idea of "anarchism without adjectives," that is, not linked to communism, socialism or syndicalism, and her advocacy of "direct action," that is, action to challenge and break down authority must be used to achieve goals and not just theory and education. As with many anarchists, her critique of society extended to a feminist attack on oppressive and unequal laws restricting women and even societal expectations for gender roles and notions of beauty that she believed repressed women. Anarchism also played a role in the Mexican Revolution. Ricardo Flores Magón (1873–1922) called for "Land and Liberty" (*Tierra y Libertad*), which was

---

[18] Peter Kropotkin (1907) *The Conquest of Bread*, New York, NY: G.P. Putnam: 35–36 and Peter Kropotkin (1972) *Mutual Aid: A Factor of Evolution*, New York, NY: New York University Press.

[19] Max Stirner; Steven Tracy Byington trans., David Leopold ed. (1995) *Stirner: The Ego and its Own*, Cambridge: Cambridge University Press.

taken up by the famous rebel Emiliano Zapata (1879–1919), who played a leading role in the Mexican Revolution and inspired the agrarian movement *Zapatismo*. Flores Magón's syndicalism mirrored the direction of the Mexican labor movement and fit with philosophy of the International Workers of the World (IWW), which was influential in the United States in the period.[20] In fact, it was while organizing for the IWW in the US that he was arrested during World War I for obstructing the war effort and died in a Kansas prison during the suppression of the left by the US government in the aftermath of war.

Anarchism as a philosophy flourished in Europe, the United States and Mexico; it also had an impact in East Asia, where it was closely tied to feminism.[21] The focus in Japan tends to be on the men, such as Kōtoku Shūsui (幸徳秋水 1871–1911) who worked against a strong current of public opinion in Japan that supported Japanese efforts to expand its influence in Asia, including war with the Qing dynasty (Sino-Japanese War) and with Russia (Russo-Japanese War) as well as Japanese colonization of Taiwan and Korea. Kōtoku was fiercely anti-war and anti-imperialist.[22] Moreover, he opposed the ideological center-piece of the Japanese state, the emperor. He viewed the emperor as the lynch-pin of capitalist repression. His strategy was to engage in direct action to agitate for goals including universal suffrage. Yet, the work of his partner, Kanno Sugako (管野須賀子 1881–1911), tends to be mentioned only in relation to him, though she too was arrested in a round-up of anarchists after an attempted assassination of the emperor, the High Treason Incident (*Daigaku Jiken* 大逆事件) and was later executed the same as him as a result.

Kōtoku had influenced others, such as Ōsugi Sakae (大杉栄 1885–1923) who Kōtoku had encouraged to study Bakunin and Kropotkin, the latter of which he particularly favored to the extent he translated Kropotkin's autobiography into Japanese. Ōsugi was careful not to advocate changes that were illegal but continued to critique capitalism and individualism.[23]

---

[20] Ricardo Flores Magón; David Poole trans. (1977) *Land and Liberty: Anarchist Influences in the Mexican Revolution*, Sanday: Cienfuegos Press.

[21] Hélène Bowen Raddeker (2005) "Anarchism, Feminism and Subjectivity in Imperial Japan: The Gendered Circumstances, Identities and 'Destinies' of Three Infamous Women," *Lilith: A Feminist History Journal*, 14: 27–40.

[22] Kōtoku Shūsui; Robert Thomas Tierney trans. (2015) *Monster of the Twentieth Century: Kōtoku Shūsui and Japan's First Anti-Imperialist Movement*, Berkeley, CA: University of California Press. Also important, but as of yet untranslated, is his *Heiminshugi*, 幸徳秋水 (Kōtoku Shūsui) 神崎清訳 (Kamisaki Kiyoshi trans.) (2014) 平民主義 (Heiminshugi), 東京: 中央公論社 (Tokyo: Chuō Kōron Sha).

[23] Ōsugi's autobiographical works have been translated in Ōsugi Sakae; Byron K. Marshall trans. (1992) *The Autobiography of Osugi Sakae*, Berkeley, CA: University of California Press and Osugi Sakae; Michael Schauerte trans. (2014) *My Escapes from Japan*,

Again, Ōsugi tends to overshadow the work with whom he associated, most likely because of his scandalous extramarital relationships with Kamichika Ichiko (神近市子 1888–1981), a leading radical feminist, and the feminist anarchist Itō Noe (伊藤野枝 1895–1923), which he justified based on his philosophical and political beliefs, including free love. In fact, Itō is an important writer apart from Ōsugi, and even though her initial writing was more focused on feminism, she was an active anarchist activist in the years before her death.[24] Ōsugi and Itō were murdered by the police in the chaotic aftermath of the 1923 Great Kanto Earthquake. One should also note the work of Hatta Shūzō (八太舟三 1886–1934) who advocated "Pure Anarchism" (*junsei museifushugi* 純正無政府主義), that is, not anarchism as a form of syndicalism in an extension of the labor movement or as part of building a socialist society but anarchism for its own sake. It is anarchism for the complete freedom and autonomy of the individual from the demands of the state in opposition to the statist tendency of socialists and communists.

One final outstanding Japanese woman anarchist was Kaneko Fumiko (金子文子 1903–1926). She and her partner Park Yeol (朴烈 1902–1974) were also imprisoned in the wave of arrests and killings after the Great Kanto Earthquake. Park survived to be released a few years later but Kaneko committed suicide in prison after rejecting an Imperial pardon. Kaneko's anarchism was based on her view that any group with power will use it to oppress others so the best one can do is challenge the powerful and try to help those who are oppressed.[25] Even when imprisoned she insisted that she alone would decide her fate even if it meant her own destruction. Kaneko had lived in both Japan and Korea and reacted against the oppression of the poor in general and Koreans in particular. This led her to a relationship with Park who was a Korean anarchist but chose to engage in resistance against authority in small ways rather than dramatic acts.

The most important Korean anarchist in the colonial period was Kim Jwa-jin (金佐鎭 1889–1930), who established the Army of Northern Military Administration (北路軍政署軍) and successfully created an area in Manchuria run by anarchist cooperative councils until attacked by Japan from the south and his former allies, the Chinese Soviet Republic, from the north.[26] Korean anarchism is usually discussed in the context

---

Tokyo: Doyosha. His writings, however, are only available in Japanese: 大杉栄 (Ōsugi Sakae) (1996) 大杉栄評論集 (Ōsugi Sakae Hyōron Shū), 東京：岩波書店 (Tokyo: Iwanami Shoten).

[24] 伊藤野枝 (Itō Noe) (1996) 伊藤野枝全集第 2 巻 (Itō Noe Zenshū, 2 volumes), 東京：學藝書林 (Tokyo: Gakugei Shorin).

[25] Kaneko Fumiko; Jean Inglis trans. (1991) *The Prison Memoirs of a Japanese Woman*, Armonk, NY: M.E. Sharpe.

[26] Ha Ki-Rak (1986) *A History of Korean Anarchist Movement*, Taegu: Anarchist Publishing Company.

of Korean nationalism but it was part of a network of anarchist activism in East Asia, particularly Japan and China.[27] Chinese anarchists were active primarily overseas as exiles initially, with some in Paris, such as Zhang Renjie (張人傑 1877–1950), Li Shizeng (李石曾 1881–1973), Wu Zhihui (吳稚暉 1865–1953), all of whom later become nationalists and anticommunists, and others in Tokyo, such as Liu Shifu (劉師復 1884–1915), Liu Shipei (劉師培 1884–1919) and He Zhen (何震 1884–c. 1920), the last an important feminist writer.[28] The Tokyo group put more emphasis on links with traditional Chinese thought such as Taoism. In general, anarchism grew to be very popular within China itself until the 1920s among students and intellectuals.[29] However, it was soon eclipsed by the rise of the Chinese Communist Party due to the success of the Bolshevik revolution in Russia.[30]

REVISIONIST AND CHRISTIAN SOCIALISM

European, East Asian and North American socialism, communism and anarchism was largely met with repression but there were also attempts to address the problems raised by radical socialism and anarchism through reform. For example, after an attempt at repression of socialism by the German state failed, the development of the Bismarckian welfare state was more successful at dampening the radical ardor of German workers. This was part of the background to the work of Eduard Bernstein (1850–1932), who in his *Evolutionary Socialism: A Criticism and Affirmation* (Die Voraussetz un gen des Sozialismus und die Aufgaben der Sozialdemokratie), challenged Marx's predictions that capitalism would soon collapse.[31] Marx had opposed reform movements because he believed that they only delayed the inevitable demise of capitalism even if they appeared to improve working conditions in the short-run. Bernstein pointed out that Marx predicted that monopolies would form in industry

---

[27] Dongyoun Hwang (2016) *Anarchism in Korea: Independence, Transnationalism, and the Question of National Development, 1919–1984*, Albany, NY: State University of New York Press.
[28] William Theodore De Bary and Richard Lufrano (2000) *Sources of Chinese Tradition, Volume 2: From 1600 Through the Twentieth Century*, 2nd edn, New York: Columbia University Press: 389–394.
[29] Arif Dirlik (1985) "The New Culture Movement Revisited: Anarchism and the Idea of Social Revolution in New Culture Thinking," *Modern China*, 11(3): 251–300.
[30] Robert A. Scalapino and George T. Yu (1961) *The Chinese Anarchist Movement*, Berkeley, CA: University of California, Berkeley, Center for Chinese Studies.
[31] Edward Bernstein; Edith C. Harvey trans. (1911) *Evolutionary Socialism: A Criticism and Affirmation*, New York, NY: B.W. Huebsch.

but many smaller and medium-sized enterprises not only survived, some even thrived. New firms were constantly emerging often displacing others. Moreover, Bernstein pointed out that the middle class was not disappearing as Marx argued it would, and that entrepreneurs were emerging from the proletariat to join the middle class. Important reforms, such as limitations on hours of labor and old-age pensions, were improving the condition of the working class and making life for workers better now was a more sensible aim than revolution that was unlikely to occur. For this reason, Bernstein advocated working class involvement in parliamentary politics to achieve socialism through both the development of capitalism and its regulation by increasing workers' rights and control of industry and the state by peaceful means. A similar development occurred in the United Kingdom; the Fabian Society, led by Beatrice Webb (1858–1943) and Sidney Webb (1859–1947), advocated slow progress toward social change, including an emphasis on voluntary cooperatives. Its members, such as George Bernard Shaw (1856–1950), advocated liberal social imperialism where Britain would lead its colonies on the path to socialism much as the liberals advocated imperialism to promote liberal reform.[32] One also might note the activities of William Morris (1834–1896), who was a self-declared Marxist but his involvement with the Arts and Crafts movement and his commercial activities are hard to reconcile with Marxism even if his political writings against the impact of industrialization and the need to improve the conditions and status of workers, particularly skilled craft workers, can be read as compatible with both.

Another alternative to Marxism was Christian Socialism. This included such figures as Frederick Denison Maurice (1805–1872), leader of the movement who wrote *The Kingdom of Christ* (1838), Charles Kingsley (1819–1875), author of *The Water-Babies* (1863), Thomas Hughes (1822–1896), author of *Tom Brown's Schooldays* (1857), and Frederick James Furnivall (1825–1910), co-creator of the *Oxford English Dictionary*. One should also include Francis Bellamy (1855–1931), a Baptist minister and the author of the original version of the United States' Pledge of Allegiance, and his brother Edward Bellamy (1850–1898), the author of an early science fiction critique of contemporary society, *Looking Backwards, 2000–1887* (1888). The most explicit work from this movement was *Practical Christian Socialism* (1854) by Adin Ballou (1803–1890).[33] One of the most influential British Christian socialists was John Ruskin (1819–1900), who was an extremely popular writer if an eclectic socialist.

---

[32] George Bernard Shaw (1900) *Fabianism and the Empire*, London: Grant Richards.
[33] Adin Ballou (1854) *Practical Christian Socialism: A Conversational Exposition of the True System of Human Society*, Hopewell, MA: The author.

In Russia, Count Leo Tolstoy (ЛеоТолстой 1828–1910) was not only influential in his own country but perhaps even more so in the rest of the world as both a Christian socialist but also a pacifist. Arab Christians, such as Salāmah Mūsā (سلامه موسى b. 1887–d. 1958) and Farah Antoun (فرح انطون b. 1874–d. 1922), also promoted socialism in the Middle East and were successful in spreading the philosophy even if their political efforts were not immediately successful.[34]

Japan was one of the first countries outside the West in which socialism began to play a significant role, even if among a minority of the elite, and was also strongly linked to Christianity. Christianity in Japan in the late nineteenth and early twentieth centuries had a much greater influence than the number of converts in the population would indicate, which has never risen to more than one percent of the population. The reasons for the great respect earned by early Christians in Japan since the end of the nineteenth century were several. They established high-quality schools with a high standard of discipline, and provided access to the poor and outcasts via scholarships or no fees policies. The moral character of Christians, especially their tendency to be teetotalers and avoid sexual excess was much admired. They also engaged in great personal self-sacrifice on behalf of others, especially the poor. However, a widespread view was that it was unreasonable to ask a normal person to do that so they were special people and not a realistic personal option for most. Christians promoted labor unions and tenant farmer unions but were respectful of employers and landlords, and tried to work within existing legal and political frameworks to accomplish change. They did not let personal pride come in the way of small changes to improve people's lives. They were willing to compromise while still insisting on faith to basic principles of dignity, truth and justice. Of course, Japanese Christians were not universally respected, and were even considered suspect because a few refused to bow to portraits of the emperor, viewed as a living god to many Japanese, because Christians believed in only one God in Heaven.

One of the most important Christian socialists was Abe Isoo (安部磯雄 1865–1949). Abe graduated at Doshisha, and went to serve in a church in Okayama in 1887. He was astonished at seeing Japanese from a traditional caste similar to India's "untouchables," the *burakumin*, taking an active part in the life of the church alongside former members of the elite *samurai* class. Abe had known Christianity stood for the equality of all people but seeing this reality of the oneness of people in the congregation of

---

[34] See Kamel S. Abu Jaber (1966) "Salāmah Mūsā: Precursor of Arab Socialism," *Middle East Journal*, 20(2): 196–206 and Donald M. Reid (1974) "The Syrian Christians and Early Socialism in the Arab World," *International Journal of Middle East Studies*, 5(2): 177–193.

Okayama Christians, he was awed by the power of Christian religion. He was sent to study at Hartford Theological Seminary along with a number of other Japanese. He introduced baseball into Japan to give university students something moral to do with their free time rather than drinking alcohol or visiting prostitutes. He continued to foster moderate Christian socialism and work to alleviate poverty in Japan by promoting self-help groups, including labor and tenant unions. Abe was an important influence on Katayama Tetsu (片山哲 1887–1978), the lawyer and union rights advocate in pre-war Japan who became an early post-war Japanese prime minister as the leader of the Japanese Socialist Party. Kagawa Toyohiko (賀川豊彦 1888–1960) who advocated unionism and cooperatives as an alternative to capitalism, might also be mentioned in this context.

Many early Japanese Christian socialists were radicalized and moved away from Christianity. An important example is Katayama Sen (片山潜 1860–1933). Katayama had graduated from Yale Divinity School and returned to Japan to organize the first modern trade union and in 1897 helped to organize the "Preparatory Association for the Establishment of Labor Unions" (*Rōdō Kumiai Kiseikai* 勞働組合期成會). In 1901, Katayama joined the Social Democratic Party (*Shakai Minshu Tō* 社會民主黨) formed by Abe Isoo, Kōtoku Shusui and others, but it was suppressed by the government on the very same day it was formed. Katayama left Japan in 1903 and though he attended the Amsterdam Congress of the 2nd Socialist International in 1904, he subsequently drifted away from moderate socialism and began to oppose parliamentarianism. He was imprisoned and forced into exile after the outbreak of World War I and took refuge in the United States. Katayama's journey from Christian socialist to radical Marxist was typical of many Japanese intellectuals in this period.

WORLD REVOLUTIONARY MARXISM

Revolutionary Marxism was crucially transformed as a result of the work of Vladimir Lenin (Владимир Ленин 1870–1924). Lenin opposed the trend toward the revisionist socialism in the rest of Europe. He argued in his *What Is To Be Done?* (Chto delat'? Что делать?), that it was unlikely that the working class could be organized simply for economic goals through unionism or social democratic parties so the working class required a "vanguard" party, tightly organized and disciplined in order to foster the revolutionary potential of the proletariat. By World War I it was clear that the major countries of the world were locked in a battle with each other and, in contrast with Marx's theories, Lenin did not believe that revolution would occur first in the most advanced capitalist nations such as Britain or Germany because the profits from imperialism, including investments in less developed nations, were being sent back to advanced capitalist countries to effectively buy the quiescence of the working class. Lenin believed that the spark for revolution needed to be lit in countries like Russia in order to foster the collapse of the entire world capitalist system, as argued in his book *Imperialism, The Highest Stage of Capitalism: A Popular Outline* (Imperializm, Kak Vysshaya Stadiya Kapitalizma Империализм, как высшая стадия капитализма).[35] By the time the Third Communist International was held in Moscow in 1919 with revolutionaries from all over the globe in attendance, the Bolshevik model of revolutionary change was validated with the success of the Soviet Revolution in Russia and it was subsequently widely emulated around the world.

The Russian revolution provided the background from which different approaches to revolution emerged. For example, Leon Trotsky (Лев Троцкий 1879–1940) had played a key role in the Bolshevik movement and made important theoretical contributions such as the concept of building a "united front" because the communist vanguard party as conceived by Lenin would require alliances with other radical and reformist groups to secure revolutionary aims, and the notion of "permanent revolution," in a sense different from that used by Marx, in that he believed that revolution was still possible in countries where capitalism had not developed because bourgeoisie is weak and cannot perform its role in eliminating feudalism, so it would have to be led by the proletariat instead.[36] Trotsky argued that undeveloped countries could be led to revolution, in contrast to the approach of Joseph Stalin (Иосиф Сталин 1878–1953) and the Soviet leadership, that capitalism had to develop in a country before it was possible to have a revolution. This was because Stalin wanted to avoid supporting international revolutionary activity on a global scale and concentrate instead on defending the Soviet state against a hostile world full of powerful capitalist states. Under Stalin, the aim was to focus on building "socialism in one country" (*sotsializm v odnoy otdelno vzyatoy strane* Социализм в отдельно взятой стране).

There were important alternatives to Stalinist communism in Europe however, both direct and indirect. It is also worth mentioning the work of Rosa Luxemburg (1871–1919) in this context. Luxemburg was a

---

[35] Vladimir I. Lenin (1970) *Imperialism, The Highest Stage of Capitalism: A Popular Outline*, Peking: Foreign Languages Press.

[36] Leon Trotsky; R.T.C. trans.? (1964) *The Essential Trotsky*, London: Unwin Books, and Leon Trotsky; George Breitman (1969–1975) *Writings of Leon Trotsky*, 14 volumes, New York, NY: Pathfinder Press.

revolutionary Marxist opposed to revisionist socialism much like Lenin but she was also against Lenin's approach to revolution. She was concerned that the one-party state run by Bolsheviks was violently suppressing even legitimate revolutionary groups in order to monopolize power and had undermined any chance of Russian democracy.[37] In contrast, she participated in the "Free Socialist Republic" (*Freie Sozialistische Republik*) in Berlin, and advocated an amnesty for all political prisoners and the abolition of capital punishment. In Italy, Antonio Gramsci (1891–1937) cooperated with the Soviet Union as leader of the Italian Communist Party but his thinking was very different from the crude historical materialism put forward by Stalin. He focused on how cultural hegemony is key to the legitimization and maintenance of the capitalist state. For Gramsci our knowledge of the world is not based primarily on our relations with objective things, but from the social relations of those using things in that world.[38] Therefore, philosophy and science cannot give us access to a single unchanging reality. A theory is only "true" in the sense that it "works" in a given historical situation.

It is essential at this point, where many accounts of communist political thought might stop, to consider the impact of communism outside Europe. For example, Katayama Sen sought refuge in the United States after his release from prison in Japan, and received help and inspiration from a group of Russian revolutionaries whom he met in New York City. In 1916 Katayama met Trotsky and Bukharin in New York and this led Katayama to reject Christianity completely. Katayama's apartment became a place of social gathering and a classroom for Marxist-Leninists, and many Japanese students who studied with him in New York later became prominent Marxist activists in Japan. In 1919, he joined the Independent Communist Party of America and helped to found the Communist Party of Mexico. He also organized Japanese communists in the US and encouraged the formation of the party in Japan, and as such is considered the father of Japanese communism, which was a force in Japanese politics for most of the twentieth century. Katayama himself was never able to return to Japan. In 1921 he emigrated to Moscow, where he lived until 1933. When he died in Moscow in 1933, he received a Soviet state funeral.

The communist movement in India was less successful. For example, one of the key founders of the Communist Party of India, M.N. (Manabendra

---

[37] Rosa Luxemburg (1971) *Selected Political Writings of Rosa Luxemburg*, New York, NY: Monthly Review Press.

[38] Antonio Gramsci (2000) *The Modern Prince and Other Writings*, New York, NY: International Publishers and Antonio Gramsci; Joseph A. Buttigieg and Antonio Callari trans. (2011) *Prison Notebooks*, 3 volumes, New York, NY: Columbia University Press.

Nath) Roy (মানবেন্দ্রনাথ রায় 1887–1954) became increasingly alienated from the Soviets and left the Communist Party to pursue his own version of radical socialism. Toward the end of his life he wrote *Reason, Romance and Revolution* in which he put forward a vision of a "New Humanism" though strangely the two volumes of this work are entirely focused on the history of Western thought.[39] Another early Indian Communist Party leader, M.P.T. (Mandayam Parthasarathi Tirumal) Acharya (1887–1951) also left the Party of India to promote anarchism. The other party founders were forced into exile in the Soviet Union and died as a result of Stalin's purges in the 1930s.

In the Middle East, three important communist parties formed. The Egyptian Socialist Party (الحزب الاشتراكي المصري) was the earliest in 1921 and joined Comintern in 1922. The Communist Party of Palestine (الحزب الشيوعي الفلسطيني) was organized by both Jews and Arabs in 1923, and the Syrian–Lebanese Communist Party (الحزب الشيوعي السوري اللبناني) formed in 1924. These tended to be small parties and had relatively little political influence but were part of the trend in the spread of socialist thought among intellectuals and political leaders in the Arab world.

One of the most important countries to be influenced by Marxist-Leninist communism was China. Socialism had been introduced to a degree in China through the work of Sun Yat-sen (孫逸仙 1866–1925), particularly his "Three Principles of the People" (*Sān Mín Zhǔyì* 三民主義), which were *mínzú* (民族), *mínquán* (民權), and *mínshēng* (民生).[40] *Mínzú* is often translated as "nationalism" but is not straightforward given the division of China into a large number of ethnic groups with a predominant ethnic "Han" majority (though the notion of "Han" as an ethnic group itself is problematic). Sun seemed to view this nationalism in the sense of unity as a nation that transcended ethnic divisions. *Mínquán* is often translated as "democracy" but it is literally only people's rights. These are protected through a complex institutional structure. Political power (*zhèngquán* 政權) of the people is expressed through elections (*xuǎnjǔ* 選舉), recall of public officials (*bàmiǎn* 罷免), initiatives (*chuàngzhì* 創制), and referenda (*fùjué* 複決). However, these are contrasted with government (*zhìquán* 治權) as the actual administration of power. Following Western constitutional theory, including that of Montesquieu, together with Literati institutions, Sun identified five powers of government (or yuan 院). The Law Making (*lìfǎ* 立法) or Legislative Yuan (a law-making body but not necessarily a legislature

---

[39] M.N. Roy (1987–1988) *Selected Works of M.N. Roy*, 2 volumes. Oxford: Oxford University Press.

[40] Sun Yat-sen; Frank W. Price trans. (1927) *San min chu i, The Three Principles of the People*, Shanghai: China Committee, Institute of Pacific Relations.

in a parliamentary sense), the Administrative or Executive Yuan (*xingzhèng* 行政), the Legal or Judicial Yuan (*sīfǎ* 司法), the Examination Yuan (*kǎoshì* 考試), for selecting public servants and the Control (*jiānchá* 監察) Yuan for overseeing public officials. Sun was not opposed to democracy but like developmental liberals he believed that the Chinese masses were not ready to cope with democracy. He believed that three stages of development were required: military rule (*jūnzhèng* 軍政), preparatory rule (*xùnzhèng* 訓政), and only then constitutional rule (*xiànzhèng* 憲政). In 1894 when the Revive China Society was formed, Sun only had two principles: nationalism and democracy. He did not pick up the third idea, *mínshēng* (民生), literally "people's life" often translated as "welfare," until his three-year trip to Europe (1896–1898) and can be seen as a form of socialism. That is, it includes social welfare but also the interests of workings in industry and greater equality of land holdings for the Chinese peasant farmers through redistribution and restrictions on large landlords and monopoly capitalists. In these views, he was influenced by the American political economist Henry George (1839–1897) as well as Karl Marx. Sun Yat-Sen played a key role in the 1911 Chinese Revolution that saw the end of the Qing dynasty and the formation of the Republic of China.

It was after World War I, however, that communism gained a predominant influence in China. The roots of the party can be found in the New Culture Movement and May 4 protests. In 1915, in response to Japanese attempts to gain concessions to control China, young intellectuals, inspired by "*New Youth*" (*Xinqingnian* 新青年), a monthly magazine edited by the iconoclastic intellectual revolutionary Chen Duxiu (陳獨秀 1879–1942), began agitating for the reform and strengthening of Chinese society. As part of this New Culture Movement (*Xīn Wénhuà Yùndòng* 新文化運動), they attacked traditional Literati ideals and instead advocated Western approaches. This included not only embracing Western science and democracy but also the full range of Western ideas including liberalism, pragmatism, nationalism, anarchism, and socialism. Chen and Hu Shi proposed a new vernacular writing style (*baihuawen* 白話文) to replace classical Literati writing (*wenyanwen* 文言文). On May 4, 1919, more than 3,000 students from 13 colleges in Beijing held a mass demonstration against the decision of the Versailles Peace Conference to transfer the former German concessions in Shandong province to Japan, and against the Chinese government's acquiescence in the decision. This was followed by demonstrations which occurred throughout the country and boycotts of Japanese goods. The campaign soon gained mass support and spread New Culture Movement ideals, which challenged traditional Literati norms, leading to calls for the emancipation of women and the emergence of a vernacular literature.

The key figure in New Culture Movement was Lu Xun (魯迅 1881–1936), a novelist and essayist, who had studied medicine in Japan but was appalled at the apathy of fellow Chinese to the plight of Chinese suffering so decided to become a writer. He read Nietzsche in 1906 and some of his early essays are clearly influenced by him but it was his anti-traditionalist "Diary of a Madman" (*Kuángrén rìj* 狂人日記) that placed him in a leading role in the New Culture Movement.[41] He taught at various universities in China but was often forced to move due to the turmoil of the Chinese civil war. By 1929 he was a Marxist and broadly supportive of the Chinese Communist Party (CCP). In fact, other figures in May 4 and New Culture Movements became the founders of the Chinese Communist Party. This included Chen Duxiu, who was originally a Trotskyite, though after arrest and imprisonment he became a libertarian socialist and began to drift away from the CCP. Li Dazhao (李大釗 1888–1927), the other co-founder of the CCP, was originally a Kropotkin-influenced communist anarchist, but after the failure of the May 4 movement and anarchist experiments of the period, he became a Marxist, as with many Chinese anarchists, due to the success of the Bolshevik revolution in Russia. He died after he was captured in a raid on the Soviet embassy in Peking (Beijing) and was executed on the orders of the warlord Zhang Zuolin in 1927.

CONCLUSION

Throughout this book there have been thinkers around the world who suggest approaches comparable to anarchism or socialism or communism but it is only in the nineteenth century that these forms of political thought emerge unambiguously. Beginning the chapter with the case of Ōshio Heihachirō was intended to make the point that the concepts are not wholly a Western phenomenon. At the same time, these philosophies were more formally articulated in the West first. The most likely reason for emergence in the West first was industrialization, which makes sense when considering the background and ideas of Saint-Simon, Owen and Fourier. It also explains Marx and Engels. One might argue that it makes sense of the early emergence of these ideas in Japan here because Japan was one of the first countries to industrialize outside of the West. This explanation cannot explain the spread of these ideas in the twentieth century in general, however. By the early twentieth century, socialism was taken up by most thinkers in the world, especially in opposition to

---

[41] Lu Xun; William A. Lyell trans. (1990) *Diary of a Madman and Other Stories*, Honolulu, HI: University of Hawaii Press.

Western imperialism, as we will see. The appeal of communism was in its strong organizational focus, which was often necessary as well given that communist parties tended to be isolated or repressed in most areas of the world. In this context, the success of the Chinese Communist Party is most outstanding and the contrast with the initial failures of the Indian Communist Party is instructive. In a future chapter, this comparison will be pursued. For the next chapter, however, the focus is on the role of political philosophy in the development of ultra-nationalism and fascism, which were most prominent in Germany and Japan, where, as we have seen, the left had been a major force.

14. Ultra-nationalism, fascism and philosophy (1880–1950)

This chapter examines a group of important controversial thinkers including Nietzsche, the Kyoto School and Heidegger together with less sophisticated right-wing and Fascist thinkers. By framing these thinkers together, it is easy to think that this chapter is uncritically accepting the flawed argument that they are clearly related to one another. There are connections but these are not straightforward. The main question raised by this chapter is why similar thinkers, particularly in Germany and Japan, have given rise to a similar controversy over their complicity and cooperation with fascism and ultra-nationalism that taints their philosophical legacy.

There are certainly close connections between the ideas of the German and Japanese thinkers. Nietzsche was a source of inspiration for both Heidegger and the Japanese scholars in the Kyoto School. This is due to the fact that Japanese philosophy was heavily influenced by German thought from the Meiji Restoration (1868) and Japanese intellectuals found that German thought, particularly from the German Romantic thinkers onward, was relevant to their concerns. Germany was a new nation that struggled to achieve unity and recognition from the powers of Western Europe. The dominant Western interpretation of Enlightenment rationality put Japan in a position of intellectual inferiority but aspects of the German tradition presented an alternative with which to resist Western imperialism.

It is essential to state clearly from the outset that what connects these thinkers is not that they are wrong or that their ideas are fatally flawed. Nietzsche, Heidegger and the Kyoto School have made important and valuable contributions to world political thought. At the same time, some of their key concepts are open to abuse. It is not enough to say that they did not intend for their ideas to be used in this way, that they regretted that they were caught up in fascism and ultra-nationalism, or even that they attempted to resist, subtly, the misuse of their ideas. There is no denying that there are aspects to their thought that were complicit with fascism and ultra-nationalism. The point here is to examine why this was the case and how much this undermines the validity of their ideas.

It is also essential here that we contrast the anti-Enlightenment lineage to fascism and ultra-nationalism with the other sources of extremist thought, such as Nichiren Buddhism and Wang Yangming in Japan, and anti-Semitism, racialism and mysticism in the West. This does not mean that the original sources were intended to be used in this way. It is a matter of whether or not they can be easily used for nefarious purposes. For example, the works of some thinkers invite wider and malicious interpretation, such as Georges Sorel's (1847–1922) *Reflections on Violence* (1906), in which he opposed science and parliamentary socialism in order to pursue "Class War" through general strikes. No doubt this approach was intended as a better way to achieve socialist revolution but Sorel's ideas, particularly on the moral transformative power of violence, were used by fascists to justify their own brutality. Some are less straightforward, such as the ideas of Henri-Louis Bergson (1859–1941), whose concepts and advocacy of "intuitionism" were adopted by Mussolini and Nazi thinkers despite the fact he was Jewish and opposed fascism. Intuitionism is also linked to the ideas of Wang Yangming and the Kyoto School with similar issues raised in regard to the support they provided for fascism.

There are a range of thinkers and movements that have been called "fascist" but for the purposes of this book, the focus is on the relationship between philosophy and forms of ultra-nationalism and fascism in Japan and Europe. This means we must ignore similar forms of what is generically called "fascism" in China and other nations.[1] This is partly due to a lack of research material and texts but also because there were no major thinkers to emerge from these movements comparable to those in Japan and Europe. For similar reasons I have omitted a discussion of Francisco Franco (1892–1975) and *Acción Española* in Spain, right-wing movements in the Middle East,[2] as well as António de Oliveira Salazar (1889–1970) in Portugal, including the associated theory of *Lusotropicalism*, which was influential in both Iberia and Latin America.[3]

---

[1] In the case of China, this would include at the very least Liu Jianqun (劉健羣 1903–1972) and the Blue Shirts Society (藍衣社). See Maria Hsia Chang (1979) "'Fascism' and Modern China," *The China Quarterly*, 79: 553–567; Maria Hsia Chang (1985) *The Chinese Blue Shirt Society: Fascism and Developmental Nationalism*, Institute of East Asian Studies [and] Center for Chinese Studies, University of California, Berkeley; Frederic Wakeman Jr. (1997) "A Revisionist View of the Nanjing Decade: Confucian Fascism," *The China Quarterly*, 20: 395–432; Dooeum Chung (2000) *Elitist Fascism: Chiang Kaishek's Blueshirts in 1930's China*, Aldershot: Ashgate; and Anthony James Gregor (2000) *A Place in the Sun: Marxism and Fascism in China's Long Revolution*, Boulder, CO: Westview Press. In the case of Latin America, the focus would be on Falangism in Latin America, including Julio Meinvielle (1905–1973) and Bolivia's Óscar Únzaga (1916–1959).

[2] See Stefan Wild (1985) "National Socialism in the Arab near East between 1933 and 1939," *Die Welt des Islams*, 25(1/4): 126–173.

[3] Though not a right-wing theory, Lusotropicalism, created by Gilberto Freyre (1900–1987), was influential in both Iberia and Latin America and was adopted by Salazar, and is mentioned here only in connection with the discussion of Nietzsche that follows. See

NIETZSCHE AS A NATURAL STARTING POINT

German romanticism could have been used as the starting point for this chapter but it is best to first consider Friedrich Nietzsche (1844–1900), who raises similar issues to those implicated in the main thinkers in this chapter. Nietzsche has been famously associated with Nazism and has only relatively recently been rehabilitated as a political thinker, initially by Walter Kauffman but more recently by Ansell-Pearson and others.[4] We need to look at why he has been associated with the Nazis, and how his case is both related to and contrasts with other thinkers, such as Heidegger and the members of the Kyoto School, who similarly have been accused of involvement with Nazism, Fascism and ultra-nationalism.

Nietzsche argued that modern science and philosophy have destroyed conventional notions of truth and morality. This leads to nihilism as society tries to ignore what is effectively the "death of god" by setting up pious lies and focusing instead on material distractions. Nietzsche wanted to find a way to confront this nihilism. He envisions the emergence of Supermen (*Übermensch*) who will go beyond the constraints of conventional morality and law. They will overcome nihilistic complacency by exercising "will to power" to create new art, new relationships and make new discoveries. Such individuals act as if they had to live their life in an endless cycle (eternal return) so that they would do the most to make it a spectacle that is worth seeing again and again. That is, not a boring normal safe life but one full of adventure and conquest as well as tragedy and even suffering if it makes for greater achievements and drama. This is Nietzsche's solution to the drift in social norms in modern society toward mediocrity and hypocrisy. For these reasons Nietzsche opposed democracy because it pandered to the masses while giving them the illusion of choice and objected to socialism as protecting the mediocre. At the same time, his re-evaluation of all values opened the possibility for greater freedom for those who seized the opportunity.

Nietzsche collapsed into a semi-comatose state in Turin in 1889 and died in 1900 at the age of 55. It was his sister Elizabeth who fostered the connection between Nietzsche and the Nazis. This is despite the fact that Nietzsche disapproved of her marriage to a rabid anti-Semite with whom she had gone to Paraguay to set up an anti-Semitic colony. When her husband died soon after arriving in South America, Elizabeth returned to

---

Jeroen Dewulf (2014) "New Man in the Tropics: The Nietzschean Roots of Gilberto Freyre's Multiracial Identity Concept," *Luso-Brazilian Review*, 51(1): 93–111.

[4] Keith Ansell-Pearson (1994) *An Introduction to Nietzsche as a Political Thinker: The Perfect Nihilist*, Cambridge: Cambridge University Press.

Germany and took control of Nietzsche's care, especially after the death of their mother. Upon Nietzsche's death, she allowed collections of his unpublished notes to be released in a highly edited form that promoted the ideas she approved of. She also went through his papers and may have altered or destroyed letters and documents which she did not agree with or showed her and her family in a bad light. She kept control of Nietzsche's works and personal artefacts as a kind of shrine and played a role in encouraging the adoption of Nietzsche by the Nazis. Many of Nietzsche's ideas, such as the superman, master race and others, were easily distorted to fit into the Nazi ideological framework. Of course, this required that one ignored or dismissed his anti-German sentiments and positive statements about the Jews but it is difficult to ignore the fact that there is considerable material in the corpus of Nietzsche's work that is open to a right-wing interpretation. He viewed the ordinary mass of humanity as the herd, which implied that they were no better than livestock and expendable. He seems to have meant to encourage creative souls not to be held back by others in a quest for greatness but his dismissal of the value of the average person is savage. Many of his views could be interpreted as racist or misogynistic. It is true that Nietzsche's use of the term "master race" is not racial because it depends on the "will to power" which transcends race in the conventional sense. At the same time, Nietzsche does use racial terminology loosely in some of his writing as is common in the late nineteenth century. One must acknowledge feminist readings of Nietzsche as persuasive, particularly given his close friendships with women intellectuals of the time such as Lou Salomé (1861–1937) and Malwida von Meysenbug (1816–1903), but also note that not all of his statements about women can be easily interpreted as positive.

As with other authors, the issue is one of interpretation. In fact, Nietzsche himself viewed everything as open to interpretation: "Against that positivism which stops before phenomena, saying 'there are only facts,' I should say: no, it is precisely facts that do not exist, only interpretations. . ."[5] This suggests that there is no privileged reading of a text. In this book we have generally accepted that knowing the author's background, beliefs and historical context helps us to better understand the meaning of the texts but it does not enable us to find the "true" and definitive meaning. In fact, one could argue that once a sentence is outwardly expressed by the author, it is always subject to the interpretations of the readers or listeners. Yet if all texts are open to interpretation, does that mean that the ideas they contain can be used as one pleases? If not, what are the limits and why?

---

[5] Friedrich Nietzsche; Walter Kaufmann trans./ed. (1954) *The Portable Nietzsche*, New York, NY: Viking Press: 458.

Nietzsche seems to have known he would be misinterpreted and was well aware that his statements were inflammatory. For example, he declared "One day there will be associated with my name the recollection of something frightful . . . I am not a man, I am dynamite."[6] The question in the case of Nietzsche is should he (or any author) be held responsible for the subsequent use of ideas, especially ideas with great potential for abuse? Is there a philosophical equivalent to the prohibition on shouting "fire" in a crowded theatre that limits free speech in even the most liberal society?

Nietzsche is an interesting political thinker in this context. There are parallels in Carlyle but Nietzsche is much more philosophical and psychological. Nietzsche initially had more of an impact on artists than on political thought but was also an important influence on Max Weber (1864–1920) and Sigmund Freud (1856–1939). It might be contentious to suggest that any of these figures are political thinkers and one could argue that they all devalue politics: Nietzsche by dismissing the masses and giving free reign to self-actualizing individuals; Weber for his emphasis on authority and the inevitability of rational-bureaucratic authority; and Freud for viewing politics in terms of pathology rather than as a positive force in society. Nonetheless, the legacy of Nietzsche is also clear in the work of the Kyoto School and Martin Heidegger, to which we must now turn.

THE KYOTO SCHOOL

Similar issues are raised in the context of the Kyoto School, which was influenced in many ways by Nietzsche and the German philosophical tradition from which he arose. Japanese universities were organized on German models and study of the German language was the basis of education in Western science and thought, including history, law and philosophy. Elite students in the selective Imperial universities, particularly the universities of Tokyo and Kyoto, were trained in the German language and German thought. It is in this context that the Kyoto School is central to understanding pre-war Japanese philosophical thought.

The Kyoto School begins effectively with Nishida Kitarō (西田幾多郎 1870–1945). Nishida was born into a wealthy family but his father's business went bankrupt, and even though he was able to attend the top university in Japan, Tokyo Imperial University, his status was close to that of someone merely auditing courses. After graduation, he became a school teacher in his native Ishikawa prefecture, far from Tokyo, and this is when

---

[6] Friedrich Nietzsche; R.J. Hollingdale trans./ed. (1977) *The Nietzsche Reader*, Harmondsworth: Penguin Books.

he began to write philosophical papers, working toward his most famous work *An Inquiry into the Good* (*Zen no kenkyū* 善の研究) published in 1911.[7] This is based on his Buddhist studies which were influenced by a high school classmate, D.T. Suzuki (鈴木大拙貞太郎 1870–1966) who incidentally helped to introduce Zen Buddhism to the West through his English language books. Nishida, for his part, had a wide knowledge of both Eastern and Western science and philosophy, which informed his writing and led him far beyond Suzuki. Nishida's *An Inquiry into the Good* was well-received among philosophers and he obtained a post at Kyoto Imperial University in 1910, promoted to Professor of Philosophy in 1914, and for the next 18 years was responsible for the training of an entire generation of Japanese philosophers, including the key members of what came to be called the Kyoto School of Japanese philosophy.

Nishida begins with a form of phenomenology in his notion of "pure experience" (*junsui keikken* 純粋經驗), in which he argues that we experience things before we begin to reflect on, think about and try to make sense of them. He was influenced by the work of William James, Ernst Mach and others but his approach was rooted in the Zen Buddhist concept of *mu no kyōchi* (無の境地), literally "position of nothingness" or putting oneself in a state of mind and bodily activity of nothingness, and breaking down boundaries in an attempt to dissolve one's attachments, not just to things but to preconceived categories including the notion of one's self, in order to achieve enlightenment in a way that is much less focused on the sovereign individual of Western phenomenology. Nishida's later work extended this approach to add the key concept of *basho* (場所), which is translated as "place," but is more a logical starting point that attempts to overcome the subject–object distinction.[8] There is a hierarchy of concreteness among concepts at the basis of judgment, which Nishida terms a logic or order of topoi or places (*basho*). For example, judging something as beautiful or pleasing or good requires a standpoint (*basho*) from which a more detailed judgment of the character of things can be made. Things that we cannot easily differentiate in such a judgment scheme come from a place of "absolute nothingness" (*zettai mu* 絕對無). Absolute nothingness is Nishida's answer to Nietzschean nihilism in a way that simultaneously embraces and attempts to transcend negative nihilism. Nishida's absolute nothingness is closer to the Taoist idea of the *tao* as the unfathomable source of all. In

---

[7] Nishida Kitarō; Masao Abe and Christopher Ives trans. (1992) *An Inquiry into the Good*, New Haven, CT: Yale University Press.
[8] Nishida Kitarō; John W.M. Krummel and Shigenori Nagatomo trans. (2012) "Basho" in John W. M. Krummel and Shigenori Nagatomo eds, *Place and Dialectic: Two Essays by Nishida Kitarō*, Oxford: Oxford University Press: 49–102.

this it shares the concept of the "supreme ultimate" of Zhu Xi thought as the source of all reality wherein the contradictions have been resolved but latently await re-emergence. It is a source one can tap into for the ultimate good. This Taoist and neo-Confucian influence makes sense given that Zen Buddhism is meant to be the key influence on Nishida and Zen Buddhism incorporates Taoist influences as does neo-Confucianism.

The relevance of this type of thought to Buddhism might be questioned, however.[9] Indeed, one might argue that this is not emptiness in the Buddhist sense because Nishida's conceptualization is stated in a way that is too extreme and initially does not seem to follow the middle path. Yet, in the sense the emptiness is space for things to happen, it shares some of the possibilities of the Buddhist concept of emptiness. As noted before, emptiness (*sūnyatā*) is due to dependent origination in which the web of a larger chain of events that creates the self and all reality is essentially empty at any given point in time. Absolute nothingness follows this as a dialectic between being and non-being. It opens the possibility of transcending the particular and universal, which is, for the Kyoto School, the special culture milieu of Japan and the universalism of the West. Absolute nothingness allows all oppositions to exist and negates them at the same time. It is in this dialectal sense that absolute nothingness is used. After retirement in the early 1930s, Nishida became more interested in human relations, particularly the role of culture and nation. For Nishida, the nation must use the dialectical space of nothingness to realize itself.

Nishida trained an entire generation of Japanese philosophers who dominated philosophical faculties in Japan in the pre-war period. His closest followers were the Big Four of the Kyoto School (*Kyoto Gakuha Yontenō* 京都學派四天王), namely, Kōyama Iwao (高山岩男 1905–1993), Suzuki Shigetaka (鈴木成高 1907–1988), Kōsaka Saaki (高坂正顕 1900–1969) and Nishitani Keiji (西谷啓治 1900–1990). Even prominent philosophers such as Tanabe Hajime (田邊元 1885–1962), who deviated from Nishida's approach, had still been heavily influenced by him. Tanabe originally studied under Nishida but also studied in Germany under Husserl, Heidegger, and Oskar Becker during the years 1922–1923. Tanabe seemed to be particularly concerned with the danger of nihilism as identified by Nietzsche and in response he created the notion of a "Logic of Species." Tanabe viewed the nothingness of Nishida and his student Nishitani as intuitionism. In contrast, Tanabe saw nothingness as historically and prac-

---

[9] Matteo Cestari (2010) "Between Emptiness and Absolute Nothingness: Reflections on Negation in Nishida and Buddhism" in James Heisig and Rein Raud eds, *Frontiers of Japanese Philosophy, vol. 7: Classical Japanese Philosophy*, Nagoya: Nanzan Institute of Religion and Culture: 327.

tically situated, which allowed Tanabe to apply Nishida's idea of "absolute nothingness" to political situations. Nothingness exists in time and not as the eternal now. Following from this, Tanabe felt people should act rather than just contemplate because ethics can only be truly tested and realized in action. He was critical of the monism in the Western philosophical tradition from neo-Platonists to Hegel, which suggested that contemplation of the good alone is adequate.[10]

Another thinker associated with Kyoto University and Nishida, but not strictly considered part of the Kyoto School, was Watsuji Tetsurō (和辻哲郎 1889–1960), who initially published works on Nietzsche and Kierkegaard, and traveled to Germany to study under Heidegger. Watsuji returned to Japan and became the professor of ethics at Kyoto University, a post he held from 1934 until 1949. Watsuji's most important philosophical works are associated with ethics, particularly his *Ningen no Gaku toshite Rinigaku* (人間の學としての倫理學) or "Ethics as the Study of Humans," where he develops the concept of *Aidagara* (間柄) or between-ness.[11] Watsuji felt that Heidegger's questioning of being still reflected a Western pre-occupation with the individual because although we are existentially thrown into a world not of our own making, we are in the world with others. Heidegger's view of the relationship of being to others seems to be one of alienation and too focused on individual being so Watsuji wanted to emphasize the importance of being with others in the world and how human beings relate to each other. This work became the basis for his three volume *Ethics* (Rinrigaku 倫理學 1937, 1942, 1949).[12]

THE CASE OF HEIDEGGER

Martin Heidegger (1889–1976) has already been mentioned in the context of the Kyoto School and he plays an important role in understanding contemporary world political philosophy. Heidegger clearly had an

---

[10] James Fredericks (1990) "Philosophy as Metanoetics," in Taitetsu Unno and James W. Heisig eds, *The Religious Philosophy of Tanabe Hajime: The Metanoetic Imperative*, Fremont, CA: Asian Humanities Press: 59–60.

[11] 和辻哲郎 Watsuji Tetsurō (1934) 人間の學としての倫理學 (Ningen no Gaku toshite Rinigaku), 東京: 岩波書店 (Tokyo: Iwanami Shoten). This title is difficult to translate precisely because Watsuji is basing his theory of *Aidagara* (間柄) on a play on the word for human beings in Japanese and Chinese, *ningen* (人間), which he takes into its component parts as *nin* (人) meaning "person" and *gen* (間) meaning "between," thus the concept of human beings in the Chinese characters means, literally, "between people" and this leads Watsuji to see ethics as relating to the "between-ness" of people.

[12] Watsuji Tetsurō; Yamamoto Seisaku and Robert E. Carter trans. (1996) *Watsuji Tetsurō's Rinrigaku: Ethics in Japan*, Albany, NY: State University of New York Press.

impact on the development of modern Japanese philosophy though the argument has also been made that Heidegger himself was influenced by Japanese students, who, as we have seen, often visited Germany and worked with him and other philosophers.[13] The parallels between aspects of Heidegger's thought and East Asian ideas are striking but, as noted in previous chapters, similarity alone cannot prove that there was a direct influence. Study of the genesis of Heidegger's most important early work *Being and Time* (Sein und Zeit, 1927) suggests that the origins lie more in Western thought, particularly phenomenology and theology.[14] Heidegger was a student of Husserl who used phenomenological and hermeneutic techniques to question the most basic principles of human existence to get at the deep structures of our thoughts and understanding. Whereas Husserl believed that such an approach could allow us to logically analyze our understanding of the world, Heidegger argued that there are limits of our understanding, particularly the language we use in relation to grasping phenomena in the consciousness, so that we can only engage in an interpretative, or hermeneutic, approach to our own existence. This conclusion has profound political implications even if these are not immediately apparent.

Heidegger's *Being and Time* is an attempt at recovery of our lost sense of being or "is"-ness to focus on the being of human life as lived by each individual.[15] He uses the word *Dasein*, "being there," which in early Heidegger is the only way we know being. He goes on to look at how we are "Being-in-the-world." For example, there is "Ready-to-hand," where one is so absorbed in a routine practical activity that one is in a state of forgetfulness, such as a skilled craftsperson using a tool. In this case, tools and the skills to use them are part of a network of other entities which give it meaning in the context in which one is operating and one only notices a tool or context when things are not going smoothly, such as when a tool breaks or the skill cannot be applied to the material. The problem is that most philosophy focuses on what Heidegger calls "Present-at-hand," where we make something an object of contemplation as in scientific or reflective analysis, but this is not the totality of being. This also applies to our relation with others or "Being-with-others." One is "thrown" (*Geworfenheit*) into a world that is not of one's making, this is the legacy of the past, with which we must all deal. Yet, we are also prone to "Fallenness" (*Verfallen*) or going along with the crowd, the Them, that constant state of living in

---

[13] Richard May; Graham Parks trans. (1989) *Heidegger's Hidden Sources: East Asian Influences on His Work*, London: Routledge.

[14] Theodore Kisiel (1995) *The Genesis of Heidegger's Being and Time*, Berkeley, CA: University of California Press.

[15] Martin Heidegger; John Macquarrie and Edward Robinson trans. (1962) *Being and Time*, Oxford: Basil Blackwell.

the present moment, which is always tempting and easy to follow. However, Heidegger implies that one also has "projective possibility," potential to go beyond fallenness, to do something greater in the future than the averageness of everyday mass society would lead. To do so, one must engage "Time" and "Care," which includes awareness of one's mortality and temporal situation. This "Time" is not analytical time but time as lived by *Dasein*. Heidegger's aim is to be "authentic," that is, to find unity of all aspects of *Dasein*'s being in knowledge of being toward death, which means turning away from the everyday world and the Them. Said another way, to be "inauthentic" is to take up the temptations of the everyday world and the Them. This closes off *Dasein*'s possibilities.

The controversy over Heidegger stems from his involvement with Hitler's Third Reich, the debate over which was reignited by the work of Victor Farias.[16] Heidegger spoke in support of the Nazi Party and there is some evidence that he viewed Hitler, at least initially, as an authentic political leader who could lead Germany to greatness.[17] Despite working closely with Jewish colleagues and students over many years, Heidegger did little if anything to fight the persecution of Jews in academia. In fact, Heidegger's enthusiasm for the Nazis may explain why he was made the Rector of his University, becoming a Nazi Party member in the process. It is true that he resigned as Rector relatively quickly and appeared to have been viewed subsequently with suspicion by the Nazi Party but he was considered tainted enough by the Nazi regime to be purged during the Allied Occupation after World War II, and most damaging of all, he refused to apologize publicly or fully explain his involvement with the Nazis during the remainder of his long life.

The possible link between Heidegger's philosophy and his involvement with the Nazis can be found in a seminar on Hegel's *Philosophy of Right*, focused on an analysis of that work of political thought, which he gave in the academic year 1933–1934 when he had just become Rector and before he appears to have become disillusioned with the Nazis.[18] The evidence is

---

[16] Victor Farias (1989) *Heidegger and Nazism*, Philadelphia, PA: Temple University Press; Arnold I. Davidson (1989) "Questions Concerning Heidegger: Opening the Debate," *Critical Inquiry*, 15(2): 407–426; Gunther Neske and Emil Kettering eds, Lisa Harries trans. (1990) *Martin Heidegger and National Socialism. Questions and Answers*, New York, NY: Paragon House; and Richard Wolin (1991) *The Heidegger Controversy: A Critical Reader*, New York, NY: Columbia University Press.

[17] This raises the important question of how one would know if and when a *dasein* was "authentic" as pointed out by Michael Gillespie (1987) "Martin Heidegger" in L. Strauss and J. Cropsey eds, *History of Political Philosophy*, Chicago, IL: University of Chicago Press: 904.

[18] Emmanuel Faye; Michael B. Smith trans. (2009) *Heidegger: The Introduction of Nazism into Philosophy in Light of the Unpublished Seminars of 1933–1935*, New Haven, CT: Yale University Press.

based on Heidegger's very cryptic notes and the notes taken by students who participated in the seminar so there is much scope for interpretation.[19] Nonetheless, it is clear that Heidegger's reading and critique of Hegel provides clues as to how he saw the ideal state in relation to his hermeneutics of being. Hegel believes that submission to the state is done willingly by a people as necessary to create the order and stability that makes freedom possible, and it is through patriotism that a people accept the possible need to make the supreme sacrifice of their lives for the nation. For Heidegger, however, it is not freedom that is at issue but the very "being" (*dasein*) of individuals, that is, their place in existence. *Dasein* is found in the *volk*, not through patriotism but political indoctrination so the masses can accept the need to obey the leader (*führerprinzip*) who will give them meaning as an expression of the *volk*, ultimately in a total state or *volikish* state.[20] The meaning of *volk* here does not seem to be racial in Heidegger's initial formulation but the fact that it and other terms, such as the leader, were very similar to the terminology of Nazi ideology was probably not coincidental.

THE CASE OF THE KYOTO SCHOOL

Just as with Heidegger, the problem of the apparent collaboration of the Kyoto School with ultra-nationalist ideology and the military-led governments of pre-war and wartime Japan raises similar if slightly different issues. Imperialism and the domination of European thought seems to have inspired Nishida to draw on the intellectual resources of Japan to make a claim for the importance of Japanese philosophy. Japanese thinking was contrasted with universal thinking. Nishida and his followers seemed to have accepted some Western claims to universal knowledge, but since Nishida and others believed that this form of universalism was peculiar to the West, they felt they had no choice but to create an alternative rooted in Japanese culture. The logic is that all individuals are embedded in their culture so it is a natural starting point for understanding. This approach was based on two assumptions. One is that modern Western thought is so tainted with Western roots that it has no claim at all to be universal and the other is that there was a purely *Japanese* alternative. It is true that Western thought itself was a product of historical circumstances so not universal (even if it claims to be) but this is not to deny that some

---

[19] Martin Heidegger; Andrew J. Mitchell trans. Peter Trawny, Marcia Cavalcante Schuback and Michael Marder eds (2014) *On Hegel's Philosophy of Right: The 1934–35 Seminar and Interpretive Essays*, London: Bloomsbury.
[20] Heidegger; Mitchell trans. (2014) *On Hegel's Philosophy of Right*: 25–27 and 181–195.

of the concepts and puzzles raised have resonance and relevance to others more widely around the globe. Japanese thought too, then as now, is highly interpenetrated with non-Japanese ideas (East Asian, Western, and so on). Even if one ignores the same mistake as the *Kokugaku* movement made in assuming that one can isolate a distinctive form of Japanese thought separate from all past influence from non-Japanese ideas that shaped Japanese thought over time, the diversity of thought within what is called Japanese thought means that the Kyoto School itself was simply picking and choosing ideas that constituted what was Japanese. Some of the choices the individual thinkers made were influenced by personal idiosyncrasies and historical context, which means that the logic behind the Kyoto School definitions of what is Japanese was not much different than the choices made by ultra-nationalists.

The Kyoto School approach was more cosmopolitan to be sure but just as flawed as ultra-nationalists in identifying Japan as a special case. The alternative is where the ideas and systems of thought are judged on their merits in open intellectual exchange, as they are today, without the need to insist on an idealized and nationalistic notion of Japanese roots and context for their validity. There is no doubt most in the Kyoto School had nothing but disdain for ultra-nationalists but the differences were one of degree rather than kind because the Kyoto School was, like most Japanese in the period, for the lack of better words, extremely nationalistic. While Nishida's nationalism was often subtle and nuanced, it inspired others who interpreted it in a much more aggressive ultra-nationalist sense.[21] Nishida and some of his immediate followers may have on occasion tried to steer others away from an ultra-nationalist interpretation, there is no evidence that they directly opposed such an interpretation. Worse, they provided much support to those who used it in a nationalistic way. Indeed, the Kyoto School which developed under Nishida's guidance was widely implicated in extremist arguments. This is clear in the work of the "big four" Kyoto School thinkers. Of the four, Nishitani's ideas in relation to Japanese ultra-nationalism have been relatively well researched but the other three tend to be overlooked in studies of the complicity of the Kyoto School during the war. However, it is exactly the breadth of the involvement of the School and the depth of their commitment to ideas very similar to those underpinning extreme nationalism that becomes clear with a wider view of who was involved and how.

One source of concern is Kyoto School members' participation in two wartime conferences. One was organized by the journal *Chūō Kōron*

---

[21] Yoko Arisaka (1997) "Beyond East and West: Nishida's universalism and postcolonial critique," *The Review of Politics*, 59(3): 541–560.

(中央公論) in December 1941 on the "World-Historical Standpoint and Japan" (世界史的立場と日本), which included participants from the Kyoto School though not exclusively. Articles based on the dialogue in this conference were published in three separate wartime issues of *Chūō Kōron*, including the January 1942 issue on the "World-Historical Standpoint and Japan," the April 1942 issue on the "Ethics and Historicity of the Greater East Asian Co-prosperity Sphere" and the January 1943 issue on the "Philosophy of Total War" (*Sōryokusen no Tetsugaku* 総力戰の哲學). Finally, an edited version was published in a book. Even though *Chūō Kōron* was subsequently shut down by the wartime government, it is unlikely that it was because this and similar material was a challenge to the war effort even if it did not present the objectives of the war in exactly the way that the government wanted. The second conference was held in 1942, called the "Symposium on Overcoming Modernity" (*Kindai Chōkoku Zadankai* 近代超克座談会) and is much more focused on the philosophy of the Kyoto School in the wartime context. There is no denying that this symposium raises important philosophical issues about the nature of modernity and the role of Western dominance, but it also defends directly and indirectly, the logic of Japanese nationalism and imperialism in the period. The torturous logic used by defenders of the innocence of the Kyoto School participants in these conferences to explain away what was said is itself telling of the extent to which the evidence is damaging to the reputation of the Kyoto School.[22] It is possible that the Kyoto School participants were misled or quoted out of context or even edited to make their views more nationalistic than they might have been originally but there is no doubt they argued similar things in other publications over which they had considerably more editorial control.

There are several books solely authored by Kyoto School members that use the same logic as was the problem in the two symposiums and adopt the same terminology as ultra-nationalists. These include Kōyama Iwao's *Research into the Study of Cultural Topology* (Bunka Ruigatagaku Kenkyū 文化類型學研究) in 1941 and the *Philosophy of World History* (Sekai Shi no Tetsugaku 世界史の哲學) in 1942, Kōsaka Saaki's *The Philosophy of Race/Ethnicity* (Minzoku no Tetsugaku 民族の哲學) in 1942 and *An Outline of World Philosophy* (Rekishi Tetsugaku Josetsu 歴史哲學序説) in 1943, Suzuki Shigetaka's *The Concept of a Historic Nation* (Rekishiteki Kokka no Rinen 歴史的国家の理念) in 1941 and Nishitani

---

[22] James W. Heisig and John C. Maraldo eds (1995) *Rude Awakenings: Zen, the Kyoto School, & the Question of Nationalism*, Honolulu, HI: University of Hawaii Press; and David Williams (2005) *Defending Japan's Pacific War: The Kyoto School Philosophers and Post-White Power*, London: RoutledgeCurzon.

Keiji's *World-view and State-view* (Sekai Kan to Kokka Kan 世界観と国家観) in 1941. It does not matter if this perspective of the philosophy of world history running through all these works was attacked by even more extreme nationalists because it explained Japan's mission in terms of history and philosophy rather than the divine will of the emperor. This "world historical philosophy" still provided Japanese intellectuals and a wider reading public a sense that there was a deep philosophical justification for Japan's unique mission in world history and supported the idea that Japanese foreign policy and war aims were completely legitimate. This missionary zeal for Japanese superiority, or a sort of Japanese manifest destiny, was completely in step with expansive militaristic ultra-nationalism in Japan at the time. The most damning evidence is the direct involvement of those associated with the Kyoto School. Nishida himself was persuaded by the wartime government to write a speech on Japan's ideals to lead Asia out of Western domination and some of his ideas were used in support of the "Great East Asian Co-prosperity Sphere" (*Dai Tōa Kyōeiken* 大東亞共榮圈), a concept which itself has been coined by Miki Kiyoshi (三木清 1897–1945), another thinker closely associated with the Kyoto School. This concept was subsequently made into concrete policy by the Japanese wartime regime and used to ruthlessly exploit the areas of East Asia that they conquered.

Philosophical implications of Kyoto School complicity are clearest in those thinkers, unlike Nishida and Miki, who survived the war and tried to come to terms with the criticisms that they faced. This is clearest in the case of Hajime Tanabe whose *The Logic of Species and the World Schema* (*Shu no Ronri to Sekai Zushiki* 種の論理と世界図式) of 1935 contains much that was in tune with extreme nationalism in pre-war Japan.[23] Tanabe uses the word *shu* (種), which originally meant "seed" (*tane*) and is used more generically to mean "kind" as in kind of or type of a thing. It is also paired with other compounds (as is normal in East Asian languages) to form *jinshu* (人種) to mean "race" and *shuzoku* (種族) to mean "ethnicity." *Shu* has been generally translated in the context of Tanabe's work as "species," though some such as Heisig try to avoid any negative implications by translating *shu* as "the specific."[24] Nonetheless, in explaining his logic of species, Tanabe makes it clear that he is using the term as "race" though it may still be in the looser sense of a cultural concept akin to nation or folk

---

[23] A partial translation can be found in Tanabe Hajime; David Dilworth and Taira Sato (1969) "The Logic of The Species as Dialectics," *Monumenta Nipponica*, 24(3): 273–288.

[24] James W. Heisig (1995) "Tanabe's Logic of the Specific and the Spirit of Nationalism" in J. Heisig and J. Maraldo eds (1995) *Rude Awakenings*: 255–288 and James W. Heisig (2001) *The Philosophers of Nothingness: An Essay on the Kyoto School*, Honolulu, HI: University of Hawaii Press: 122.

(*volk*) as each nation or "species" provides the context in which individual lives and orientations are defined and pursued. He views *shu* as between humankind and the individual. He himself noted that his notion of *shu* is drawn from Hegel's concept of "objective spirit" as found in the customs, traditions and laws of a society. The individual stands in relation to this as the "subjective spirit" and beyond this is "absolute spirit," also called the "Divine Spirit" grounded in "absolute Nothingness" (*zettai mu*).[25] In his pre-war writing, this was intended to argue against individualism and subordinate the individual to the nation. Even if one accepts that the charge of "fascism" leveled at Tanabe was often crudely formulated[26] and that, in terms of behavior, Tanabe opposed, at a very low level, some of the excesses of ultra-nationalism in relation to those around him, the point is his "Logic" put emphasis on the nation and his other work on Japan's divine mission in a way that supported the logic of extreme nationalism.

In a post-war version of his Logic of Species, *The Dialectic of the Logic of Species* (*Shu no ronri no benshōhō* 種の論理の辯證法), Tanabe tries to explain that he meant to criticize individualism and, at the same time, warn against totalitarianism of the type that eventually prevailed in Japan.[27] Despite this, Tanabe himself appears to have regretted how his work was used for nationalistic purposes and that he failed to do anything to stop it. This is clear in his last major work, *Philosophy as Metanoetics* (*Zangedo to shite no tetsugaku* 懺悔道としての哲學), which he began writing toward the end of the war.[28] *Zange* (懺悔) means apology, confession, repentance but all founded on a sense of regret (*kuyami* 悔み). In it, Tanabe's critique for his failure and that of the Kyoto School as a whole is based on True Pure Land belief in "Other power" (*tariki* 他力) in the sense of humility before divine power. He criticizes Kant and Hegel for believing too much in the power of reason, but also Nishida for believing that the logic of *basho* would resolve the dialectic between individual experience and absolute nothingness. After the war, Tanabe supported social democracy as the best alternative of the time.[29] He was skeptical of democracy in principle, however, because, based on his reading of ancient Greek classical philosophy, it means only equality and does not necessarily provide for liberty. His

---

[25] Tanabe; Dilworth and Sato trans. (1969) "The Logic of The Species as Dialectics": 274.
[26] James W. Heisig (1995) "Tanabe's Logic of the Specific and the Spirit of Nationalism," *Rude Awakenings*: 256–268.
[27] 田邊元 (Tanabe Hajime) (1947) 種の論理の辯證法 (Shu no ronri no benshōhō) 大阪: 秋田屋 (Osaka: Akitaya).
[28] Tanabe Hajime; Takeuchi Yoshinori, Valdo Viglielmo and James W. Heisig trans. (1986) *Philosophy as Metanoetics*, Berkeley, CA: University of California Press.
[29] 田邊元 (Tanabe Hajime) (1946) 政治哲學の急務 (Seiji Tetsugaku no Kyūmu), 東京: 岩波書店), Tokyo: Iwanami Shoten.

view of liberty was still informed by Kant, Fichte and Hegel where it is seen as liberty in community with others. However, he believed that social democracy can serve Japan in the circumstances because it was based on *yūai* (友愛), which is normally translated as fraternity but Japanese *yūai* does not have the sexist connotation of fraternity (male siblings) as it is literally the combination of the characters for "friendship" and "love." For Tanabe, *yūai* comes from absolute nothingness.

The case of Watsuji Tetsurō raises similar issues. Watsuji wrote *Nihon Seishin Shi* (日本精神史) or "A History of the Japanese Spirit" in 1926 during the Taisho era in Japan, which was meant to be relatively liberal politically, but this book strongly hints at the superiority of the Japanese in terms of understanding of human nature and ethics. More famously he wrote *Sonnō Shisō to Sono Dentō* (尊皇思想とその傳統) or "Revere the Emperor Thought and its Tradition" in 1940, which justified emperor worship, emphasized the superiority of the Japanese and argued for the negation of self in subordination to the nation. This was clearly written in support of Japanese nationalism and played into the hands of ultra-nationalist and militarists. After the war, as with Tanabe, Watsuji may have regretted what he had written but again it reinforces the point that there was something in Kyoto School thought that was particularly susceptible to supporting nationalism or, at least, inhibited these individuals from doing anything meaningful to stop it from being used to promote or encourage extreme nationalism. It is true that some in the Kyoto School were critical of the direction that Japan was taking but they avoided openly fighting against the intellectual tide and only engaged in subtle criticism, and the efforts they did make were too little too late especially in light of their earlier contributions to infuse nationalism into the intellectual environment. Another approach might have been to keep a low profile and withdraw from public life, but they did not do that either. For most in the Kyoto School, there was certainly complicity with extreme nationalism if not outright enthusiasm.

OTHER SOURCES OF RIGHT-WING AND ULTRA-NATIONALIST IDEAS

If the philosophies of the Kyoto School and Heidegger contained little to steer those who held their beliefs from morally questionable involvements, the clearly identifiable philosophies of the extreme right and nationalism in the early and mid-twentieth century are even more problematic without a doubt. The problem is that the political thought of fascism, particularly the writings and ideas of the political leaders who represented the extreme right in Europe in the 1920s and 1930s, is largely derivative, rooted in earlier Romantic nationalism and nineteenth-century racialism. A few new ideas were put forth but there is nothing like a systematic and coherent political philosophy. Indeed, they seem to have selectively taken and reinterpreted ideas to fit their political ambitions. Again, this does not resolve the question of whether it is the ethical ambiguity of the philosophers or misuse of ideas by others which is more problematic.

It would be wrong to imply that the Kyoto School was entirely responsible for Japanese ultra-nationalism. The Meiji nation-building effort might be judged too successful by inculcating nationalism in Japan but less effective in promoting countervailing institutions and forces that could hold extremism in check. Even though party politics did develop after World War I in Japan during the period of so-called "Taisho Democracy," parties and politicians were corrupt and still limited in power by the Imperial Court. Most conservatives in pre-war Japan were party politicians, largely pragmatic, but there was a more extreme element which had a disproportionate influence. Indeed, one can easily point to many other organizations and thinkers that promoted extremist nationalist thought in the period that were more important than the Kyoto School. The two most notorious were the *Dai Nihon Kokusui Kai* (Greater Japan Patriotic Society 日本国粋会) and *Kokuhonsha* (State Basis Society 國本社). The role of the Japanese military in promoting ultra-nationalism included such groups and individuals as the *Sakurakai* (Cherry Blossom Society 桜会) organized by Hashimoto Kingorō (橋本欣五郎 1890–1957), not to mention the pan-Asianists such as Ōkawa Shūmei (大川周明 1886–1957). The Kyoto School were not worse than the others but in terms of their promotion of nationalism were more respected.

There was also the undercurrent of the extreme right in pre-war Japan that was not mainstream but certainly on the edges of the political elite and often worked with them. Two "traditional" forms of thought played a major role here. One was Wang Yangming (Ōyōmei) thought. This can be traced back to Saigo Takamori whose memory was used by Tōyama Mitsuru (頭山満 1855–1944) and his *Genyōsha* (玄洋社) to promote a right-wing and imperial version of Wang Yangming. Uchida Ryōhei (内田良平 1874–1937) and his *Kokuryūkai* (黒龍会) might also be placed in this category, because Uchida was a student of Toyama though probably Uchida was more influenced by *Shintō*/*Kokugaku* even if Wang Yangming and Shintōism were not incompatible despite older *Kokugaku* disdain for Chinese thought. The clearest example of Wang Yangming pseudo-"Fascism" was Nakano Seigo (中野正剛 1888–1943) who was originally a member of parliament with the main centrist opposition party but was increasingly radicalized and joined with others to promote revolutionary change in Japan. Nakano founded the Japanese Fascist organization called the *Tōhōkai* (東方会) or Eastern Society in 1936. He met with Mussolini (in 1937) and Hitler (in 1938), and his supporters wore armbands, shirts and symbols in imitation of the Nazis and Fascists. Nakano certainly emulated the Nazis and Fascists but largely as a populist and even then not a particularly successful one compared to Hitler and Mussolini.

The other "traditional" source of extreme Japanese nationalism was Nichiren Buddhism. Much of this can be traced back to Tanaka Chigaku (田中智學 1861–1939) who was a fiery ultra-nationalist Buddhist preacher. He influenced the former Nichiren priest and terrorist Inoue Nissho (井上日召 1887–1967) and his *Ketsumeidan* (血盟団) or "Blood Brotherhood," a small secret society that recruited young men who took an oath to assassinate national leaders they felt had undermined the nation (leading politicians) or exploited the people (major capitalists), based on the motto "One man, one death" (*ichinin, issatsu* 一人一殺), that is, each assassin was prepared to sacrifice their own life to take that of another, and on this basis, engaged in a campaign of assassination. Another Nichiren ultra-nationalist was Kita Ikki (北一輝 1883–1937) who was particularly influential with young army officers, through his advocacy of a form of national socialism, and was involved in the abortive military coup d'état of February 26, 1936, and was executed as one of the conspirators in 1937. Kita believed that the emperor must have absolute and supreme power but he advocated the abolition of the peerage system and still saw a role for a popularly elected parliament. Kita opposed existing laws restricting freedom of speech and press but also wanted to use the death penalty to execute anyone who opposed his revolutionary plans. Most radical of all were his ideas on the limitation of private property with any excess nationalized or redistributed. While he insisted that women should be free to work as equals with men, he still felt that they should be spared the burden of labor whenever possible and not used to replace men in labor except in a national emergency, and even though he believed that women should receive education equal to that of men, they should not be permitted to participate in politics. Most importantly, Kita insisted on the positive right to start war, that is, in addition to the right of self-defense, the state shall have the right to start a war on behalf of other nations and races unjustly oppressed by a third power, by which he meant wars for the independence of India, Chinese integrity, against all nations who occupy large colonies, and the right to seize Australia and Far Eastern Siberia for the development of the people of Asia.[30]

---

[30] Kita Ikki (1974) "General Outline of Measures for the Reorganization of Japan, 1923," in David John Lu ed., *Sources of Japanese History*, vol. 2, New York, NY: McGraw-Hill: 130–136.

The final Nichiren ultra-nationalist was Army General Ishiwara Kanji (石原莞爾 1893–1949), who together with General Itagaki Seishiro (板垣征四郎 1885–1948), effectively ran the Kwantung Army stationed in Manchuria as an independent military force. Ishiwara and Itagaki planned and carried out the seizure of Manchuria to obtain its resources and prepare for future wars. He actively promoted an East Asian League movement in preparation for what he believed would be a long-term war, a final war, with the United States. However, Ishiwara opposed the attempted military coup d'état led by Kita Ikki and young army officers because he was worried it would interfere with mobilization for war and because his focus was on East Asia as a whole and not just domestic politics as the soldier's revolt had been.[31] The power of Ishiwara's vision of final war was demonstrated in the Tokyo subway "Sarin" poison gas attack of March 1995 by members of the Aum Shinriyko sect in which 12 people died and many more were injured (though potentially the death toll could have been in the tens of thousands), because the Aum Sect was dedicated to a cataclysmic confrontation with the West drawn from Ishiwara's political prophesy that the final phase of a "Final World War"(最終戰爭) between Japan and America would occur around the year 2000. Ishiwara's apocalyptic vision came from his Nichiren Buddhism.

In contrast, European right-wing movements lacked much of a traditional ideological basis. For example, the Italian Fascist Benito Mussolini (1883–1945) was originally an Italian Socialist Party activist though unusually for a socialist, he believed that Nietzsche's ideas could be used to further the cause of socialism, particularly his critique of Christianity and will to power. Eventually, Mussolini began to advocate anti-egalitarianism and support for Nietzsche's idea of the *übermensch*. He was forced to quit the Italian Socialist Party when he came out in support of the war at the beginning of World War I. He decided to use socialist movement methods to organize a nationalist movement and rejected class as the basis for political change. Mussolini founded a new political movement, the "Fasci Rivoluzionari d'Azione Internazionalista" in 1914, who called themselves *Fascisti*. After violent clashes between his supporters and revolutionary socialists, Mussolini began to reinforce the notion of the necessity of political violence in his thought drawing on the work of Georges Sorel. Mussolini also read Plato's *The Republic*, which he felt shared ideas with fascism, such as rule by an elite, creation of a class of warriors, control of education and culture for the national interest, and opposition to democracy. Mussolini put forth a policy of pursuing *spazio vitale* (vital space), which was used to claim areas with ethnic Italians on the borders of

---

[31] Mark R. Peattie (1975) *Ishiwara Kanji and Japan's Confrontation with the West*, Princeton, NJ: Princeton University Press: 233–243.

Italy and ultimately to claim control of much of the Mediterranean based on ancient Roman control and superiority of the Italians over the Slavs and other people he considered to be less developed. This also justified his imperialism in Africa, starting with Ethiopia, due to his view that black people were inferior to whites.

Racism was also at the center of German Nazism. As with Mussolini, Adolf Hitler (1889–1945) in his autobiography, *Mein Kampf* (My Struggles) in two volumes (1925/1926) focused on the need for *Lebensraum* (living space) because, he argued, Germans were a dynamic and expanding people, they need to take land from those who had more than they could use or did not use it well. It is also related to his idea that the weak and sick should be destroyed to leave room for the strong and pure. He opposed parliamentary democracy as corrupt and its politicians as unprincipled opportunists only interested in power. Critical editions of *Mein Kampf* can provide some clues but all the sources of Hitler's philosophy can never be known with certainty and it is clear that he was not a political philosopher in any sense. He is merely mentioned here in the context of Heidegger and the Kyoto School by way of contrast and to put their complicity with dubious ideas and regimes in perspective. Overall Nazi ideas were drawn from a variety of sources including racialized ideas of *volk* as based on mystical and almost irrational bonds of alleged blood ties as developed in the work of Alfred Rosenberg (1893–1946), such as *Der Mythus des 20 Jahrhunderts* (1930), but there were also clearly influences from a variety of sources including the Austrian/German ultra-nationalist and occultist Guido von List (1848–1919), the French thinker Count Joseph Arthur de Gobineau (1816–1882), the anti-Semite composer Richard Wagner (1813–1883) and the British racialist Houston Stewart Chamberlain (1855–1927).

THE ALTERNATIVE POINTS OF CRITIQUE

The final perspective on the Kyoto School and Heidegger can be provided by contrast with thinkers in Japan, Germany and beyond who critiqued these thinkers and pointed at the time to the problems with their philosophies. For example, Heidegger needs to be contrasted with Ernest Cassirer (1874–1945). Cassirer and Heidegger publicly clashed in a debate in Davos in 1929, and the general consensus was that Heidegger came across as the deeper and more formidable philosopher.[32] Yet, Cassirer understood the failings of Heidegger's philosophy. In his *The Myth of the State*, Cassirer

---

[32] See, for example, Peter E. Gordon (2010) *Continental Divide: Heidegger, Cassirer, Davos*, Cambridge, MA: Harvard University Press.

pointed out that unlike early phenomenologists, Heidegger rejects notions of the truth and logic in philosophical thought as elusive because all that is possible is existential philosophy.[33] Heidegger seems to be arguing that no one, not even a philosopher,[34] can understand any more than the truth of one's own existence and this is itself bound by history. Cassirer perhaps exaggerates the pessimism and passivity induced by Heidegger's philosophy when he characterizes Heidegger as arguing that it is impossible to do anything with the historical conditions into which we are "thrown" (*Geworfenheit*) so that "we can only try to understand and interpret them, and cannot change them." Of course, this ignores the hope that Heidegger gives with the notion of resisting the "Them," though, as suggested above, this has its own dangers as Heidegger himself demonstrated. Cassirer's point was that Heidegger's philosophy renounced fundamental theoretical and ethical ideals so that an existential philosophy becomes a "pliable instrument" in the hands of political leaders and others who would use it for nefarious purposes.

The links of Cassirer and Heidegger with neo-Kantism are also instructive. Cassirer was a product of the Marburg School, which included such scholars as Hermann Cohen (1842–1918) and Paul Natorp (1854–1924), and emphasized epistemology and logic. Heidegger, on the other hand, was associated with Southwest (German) School (also known as the Baden School or Heidelberg School) of neo-Kantism, particularly with Heinrich Rickert (1863–1936), under whom Heidegger was an assistant and wrote his habilitation thesis. Heidegger's approach was very different from Rickert in some ways, given that Rickert believed that one must identify a hierarchy of values and emphasized those that transcended the needs of everyday life. Yet, Rickert also made a distinction between historical and scientific facts, and felt that philosophy must focus on the subjective standpoint for that is the only point of view from which the "meaning" of values makes sense, though this subject is not a real person but a concept, such as *dasein* as used by Heidegger.[35] As with Heidegger, Rickert also rejected metaphysics, and the two put less emphasis on epistemology (how we know what we know) and more on ontology (the question of what exists in the first place). Most importantly, Rickert and the Southwest School put emphasis on culture as the source of values. Culture for Heidegger meant the work of a poet such as Johann Hölderlin (1777–1843), who, in

---

[33] Ernst Cassirer (1946) *The Myth of the State*, New Haven, CT: Yale University Press: 292–293.
[34] Cassirer (1946) *The Myth of the State*: 293.
[35] Benjamin Crowe (2010) "Faith and Value: Heinrich Rickert's Theory of Religion," *Journal of the History of Ideas*, 71(4): 617–636.

Heidegger's view, linked together the German language, Germany and the purity of the *volk*. Even if one accepts the point that Heidegger took up the theme of Hölderlin in particular in the aftermath of his failed political involvements with the Nazis, it still reflects the deeper nationalistic basis for his existential politics.[36]

It is also useful to consider the contrast of the Kyoto School with Tosaka Jun (戸坂潤 1900–1945) in this context because he was also a student of Nishida. Tosaka was initially a physics student but became interested in philosophy, initially neo-Kantism, by trying to make sense of Kant's concept of space in the *Critique of Pure Reason*. This led Tosaka to a materialist perspective and he became a Marxist. This is not entirely surprising because neo-Kantism had strong links with socialism, including influences on Austro-Marxism and Eduard Bernstein.[37] Tosaka's analysis of Japanism (*Nippon or Nihon-shugi* 日本主義) was based on a class critique of how the military and intellectuals contributed to Japanist ideology. The English translation of his work alludes to his critique of "various contemporary scholars and theorists"[38] but this is laid out more clearly in one of the key chapters in his most famous work, *On Japan Ideology* (*Nihon Ideorogii Ron* 日本イデオロギー論),[39] which focuses specifically on the Kyoto School, particularly Nishida Kitarō and Watsuji Tetsurō. Tosaka was eventually imprisoned for his anti-Japanist views and died as a result. Perhaps sacrificing oneself for one's beliefs makes a thinker seem better but if it is a question of acting or not, then a philosophy that opposes wrongs is more likely to actively oppose those wrongs. This is not to argue that Marxism was better than the Kyoto School, but in the case of Tosaka it provided an ethical basis to critique the Kyoto School and its contribution of nationalism and to resist the trend toward nationalist-militarism when it was not easy to do so.

The Kyoto School and the pan-Asianists on the political right in Japan claimed that Japan was going to lead the liberation of Asia from Western domination. Collaboration occurred on a small scale in most countries though the case of India is most interesting in this regard. For example,

---

[36] Annemarie Gethmann-Siefert and Richard Taft (1989) "Heidegger and Hölderlin: The Over-Usage of 'Poets in an Impoverished Time'," *Research in Phenomenology*, 19(1): 59–88.

[37] See 波多野鼎 (Hatano Kanae) (1928) 新カント派社会主義 (Shinkantoha Shakaishugi) 東京: 日本評論社 (Tokyo: Nihon Hyōron Sha); and 横浜社会問題研究所編 (Yokohama Shakai and Mondai Kenkyujō eds) (1926) 新カント派の社会主義観 (Shinkantoha no Shakaishugi) 東京: 岩波書店 (Tokyo: Iwanami Shoten).

[38] Introduction John Person's translation of "The Fate of Japanism: From Fascism to Emperorism," in Ken C. Kawashima, Fabian Schaefer and Robert Stolz eds (2013) *Tosaka Jun: A Critical Reader*, Ithaca, NY: Cornell University Press: 59.

[39] Tosaka Jun; Kenn Nakata Steffensen trans. (2016) "Translation of Tosaka Jun's 'The Philosophy of the Kyoto School'," *Comparative and Continental Philosophy*, 8(1): 53–71.

Subhas Chandra Bose (सुभाषचन्द्र बोस 1897–1945), who had trained in law and other fields, had been leader of the Indian Congress Party but had to resign soon after. When World War II began, he joined with the Axis war effort, expressing admiration for the Nazis and Fascists, and actively worked with the Japanese fighting on the edge of Burma against the British. His efforts were not particularly effective but undermined British trust in Indian troops and the viability of an empire dependent on them, reinforced by the ambivalence of many Indians toward the British Empire after the fall of Singapore. Bose was inspired by the Darwinism of Spencer, Bergson's intuitionism and Hegel on the laws of progress but Bose believed that the spirit that drives us is "Love" that permeates and transcends all contradictions. That is, reality is "Spirit," in a Hegelian sense, working with a conscious purpose through time and space. However, it is impossible to know the "Absolute Truth". Bose believed that we can only aim at maximizing truth. He was the advocate for a strong centralized Indian state, based on the Congress Party (which would not wither away with independence), including state nationalization of all land and industry managed by a dictatorship. Bose died in a plane crash in 1945 in the Japanese colony of Taiwan after visiting Japan in support of the idea that the Japanese war effort was pan-Asianist.

The Indian poet and author Rabindranath Tagore (रवीन्द्रनाथ ठाकुर 1861–1941) frequently praised Japan, particularly how Japan had dealt with the threat of Western domination, but he was very critical of Japanese nationalism in contrast to Bose. Tagore argued that nationalism was undermining Japanese freedom and destroying the very distinctiveness of the Japanese that creating a strong Japanese nation was meant to protect:

> I have seen in Japan the voluntary submission of the whole people to the trimming of their minds and clipping of their freedom by their government, which through various educational agencies regulates their thoughts, manufactures their feelings, becomes suspiciously watchful when they show signs of inclining toward the spiritual, leading them through a narrow path not toward what is true but what is necessary for the complete welding of them into one uniform mass according to its own recipe. The people accept this all-pervading mental slavery with cheerfulness and pride because of their nervous desire to turn themselves into a machine of power, called the Nation, and emulate other machines in their collective worldliness.[40]

Note that this was written well before the militaristic 1930s. While not steeped in deep philosophical arguments, Tagore was also highly critical of the modern Western approach to civilization and demonstrates how the

---

[40] Rabindranath Tagore (1918) *Nationalism*, London: MacMillan and Co: 27.

concerns of the Kyoto School could have been expressed just as well, without the need to overemphasize the nation or sacrifice individual spiritual uplifting to collective uniformity. Tagore argued that human divisions were shallow and need not drive people apart.

The most important question in the cases of Heidegger and the Kyoto School is: did their philosophy play a role in their political actions? Those that seek to defend the Kyoto School and to a lesser degree Heidegger from the charge of complicity with ultra-nationalism and fascism do so in order to ensure that these thinkers' ideas and approaches continue to be viewed as interesting and important. The alternative, that they might be interesting and important despite the fact that they were complicit to a degree in working with extremist regimes, has been neglected. In fact, one can easily argue that the philosophies of both the Kyoto School and Heidegger are essentially amoral rather than immoral. The intuitive and liberating aspects of their work empowers but does not direct. As in the case of Nietzsche, they have potential to be misinterpreted and clearly played a role in providing ideological support for extremist regimes. It does not follow that the philosophies inherently and consistently tend to support dictatorship. They can have a value in other circumstances. However, it might also be argued that there is nothing intrinsic to these philosophies, such as clear moral boundaries, that would stop someone from using them for ends to which most would object.

One defense of the Kyoto School has questioned the assumption that nationalism was pernicious,[41] but the assumption that academia is prejudiced against nationalism is also a problem. Certainly, there is nothing wrong with nationalism in the sense that one shares a sense of place and culture with others, enjoys this sense of belonging and is even proud of where one lives and the culture in which one was raised or later adopted. National cultures, like all cultures, are complex with many subcultures that reinforce or play off what is perceived to be the mainstream. However, once a national culture is reified and made monolithic, and clear distinctions are made between us (who accept a standard definition of national culture) and them (that do not), then the problems begin to arise. The political right knows such tactics are effective and powerful so use this approach when they can.

This brings us to Carl Schmitt (1888–1985), who is an example of someone who is acknowledged as both seriously compromised by his political ties but also intellectually challenging and even useful. He was clearly and unapologetically involved with the Nazis and yet many, even those on the

---

[41] John C. Maraldo (1995) "Questioning Nationalism Then and Now: A Critical Approach to Zen and the Kyoto School" in J. Heisig and J. Maraldo eds, *Rude Awakenings*: 333.

political left, find his ideas valuable. His *The Concept of the Political* (Der Begriff des Politischen) of 1932 is a case in point.[42] Schmitt argues that to be political is to identify enemies and vanquish them. Liberals want to incorporate or tame their enemies but their enemies will constantly agitate to undermine them. This is because liberals do not like state power. Older forms of liberalism accepted that there must be a state but wanted to limit its power. More anarchistic or libertarian forms of liberalism reject the state entirely as a constraint on individual liberty. The political right and conservatives understand the necessity of state power and that the use of power is essential to political rule. For Schmitt, the unity of state and nation, which identifies enemies and excludes them, is essential to politics. Schmitt's anti-liberalism is popular with some on the left who believe that their opponents seek domination and that moderates and liberals ignore or obscure this fact. Schmitt's attack on political rationalism is also attractive for anti-foundationalists and postmodernists, much like the attractions of Nietzsche, Heidegger and the Kyoto School. Schmitt's argument in his *Political Theology* (*Politische Theologie*) of 1922 that modern political concepts are often secularized theology and that the modern attack on metaphysics obscures the underlying principles behind many modern political ideas, is also completely understandable based on the analysis in this book.[43] Therefore, one need not dismiss the potential contribution of Nietzsche, Heidegger, the Kyoto School or Schmitt but it is also legitimate to suggest that there are possible dangers with uncritical acceptance of their ideas and that one must question possible negative implications of their approaches to political thought.

CONCLUSION

We can see that this chapter is key to understanding the importance of the implicit cosmopolitanism underlying notions of equality among nations/races that was behind most of the metaphysics up until the nineteenth century. Of course, there were paternalistic distinctions between the civilized and barbarians, pagan and pious, but the underlying equality of all who had philosophical awareness was implicit until nineteenth-century imperialism and nationalism required racial and national distinctions to be made. Even within nations, Romantic political thought also demanded the

---

[42] Carl Schmitt; George Schwab trans. (2007) *Concept of the Political*, Chicago, IL: University of Chicago Press.
[43] Carl Schmitt; George Schwab trans. (2005) *Political Theology: Four Chapters on the Concept of Sovereignty*, Chicago, IL: University of Chicago Press.

subordination of the individual to the whole based on notions of nationality and race. The thinkers in this chapter take this development one step further by making the *volk* or *minzoku* in a loose nationalistic and racialist sense the metaphysical foundation for theory. It does not mean that all of the Kyoto School or Heidegger's ideas are wrong but intriguing ideas of nothingness and hermeneutic existentialism were easily used for nefarious purposes because they lack any moral metaphysical content or at least were not given one, in contrast to the Marxists and neo-Kantians, who for all their flaws, had a clearer sense of justice for all humans and sense of duty to fight the particularism of *minzoku*, *volk* and race. In this sense, metaphysics does matter.

15. Anti-colonialism and neo-liberalism (1920–1980)

This is one of two chapters on contemporary world political thought and one might question whether such recent forms of political thought can be considered part of the history of political thought at all. The history is very recent and some of the thinkers discussed are well within living memory so it may be difficult to adopt a historical perspective in the same way that we have approached ancient, medieval or even nineteenth-century thought. At the same time, contemporary thinkers and ideas create the context in which we think about the history of political thought. Inevitably texts are read in the context of the times and it means that certain issues are highlighted over others based on the interests of contemporary readers. Awareness of the context of reading is an important part of the history of political thought, particularly comparative political thought.

For most of the world, the struggle to achieve independence is the context in which political thought developed in the period after World War II. Indeed, a good deal of the research used in this book was initiated in the context of the search for the historical roots of new nations and independent people, usually part of the effort of the West trying to understand others but also part of attempts to build new historical identities. One might argue that "traditional" forms of thought have been undermined by modernity, especially science and technology. Resistance to Western dominance, however, has led to a search for alternatives. The initial approaches of newly independent nations were forms of socialism and what can only be called pan-regionalism (pan-Arabism, pan-Africanism, and so on). These were pursued in the context of anti-colonial struggles, both violent and non-violent, with political philosophies to justify the routes taken. Some of these methods might be seen as illiberal. Western thought, in contrast, tended toward new forms of liberalism, though neo-liberalism is usually used as a pejorative term to characterize recent developments in modern capitalism. In this chapter it is being used in a broader sense because post-war political thought that tries to fight for justice under neo-liberal economic conditions still relies on liberal assumptions. Rawls is as much a post-war liberal as Hayek. This does not eliminate the important distinctions between them but it helps to put them into global perspective.

VIOLENCE AND NON-VIOLENCE IN THE PHILOSOPHIES OF LIBERATION

Anti-colonialism in the twentieth century had a clear focus but the relative merits of peaceful versus violent movements for independence often vied for influence. Non-violence is most often associated with one of the most important thinkers of the twentieth century, Mohandas Gandhi ((मोहनदास करमचन्द गांधी 1869–1948), who played an important role in the struggle for the independence of India from British colonial rule. His political thought contains an incisive critique of modern Western civilization but he is not opposed to the West or its heritage. Indeed, his thought contains many Western influences such as Socrates, Rousseau, Thoreau, Carlyle and Tolstoy. However, he believes that modern Western civilization is based on mistaken foundations. Bhikhu Parekh has expressed this aspect of his political thought most succinctly.[1] He points out that Gandhi argued that the West has a particular body-centered view of the world that focused on keeping the individual separate from others so that it can only maintain its identity independently of others as separate bodies, which leads to a self-centered ego that wants to keep others at a distance to preserve the illusion of independence. The body is also related to consumerism because of the aim to satisfy the senses through material wants and desires but by their very nature these desires cannot be satisfied. Boredom with the old and fascination with the new will mean a never-ending search for new and more exciting material experiences and objects. This is how he explains Western consumerism (selfishness and multiplicity of wants) and greed (desire for expansion and increasing profit). However, Gandhi believed that this process dehumanizes us and is anti-human in the holistic sense. It perverts the human psyche and leads it to violence to seize what one can. Finally, wisdom is devalued unless it is practical knowledge to gain power and wealth to control nature and other human beings.

Gandhi's solution to this problem for India was based on traditional ideas though he gave them a new twist. *Swadeshi* (चुतेचि) or "self-sufficiency" had been an ideal behind the Indian independence movement since the nineteenth century but Gandhi uses it in the broader sense of an ethical community that is well-knit and ordered based on a strong shared spirit – the context in which one can live one's life fully in all senses, not just materially. Similarly, *satyagraha* (सत्याग्रह) or "truth force" had the power to challenge British colonial power but also to instill independence of mind and courage to act to do the right thing. Finally, *ahimsa* (अहिंसा), an

---

[1] Bhikhu Parekh (1989) *Gandhi's Political Philosophy: A Critical Examination*, London: Macmillian: 21–22.

ancient term denoting non-violence, was bolstered by Gandhi's view that it meant not just non-resistance or no harm to others but also willingness to sacrifice without anger toward one's enemy. Gandhi is more forgiving because he believed in power that originates outside of the human that can empower political change in oneself and one's enemies. Overall, he advocates what is effectively a non-violent anarchistic communalism.[2]

Gandhi is the most well-known advocate of non-violent revolution but Mao Zedong (毛澤東 1893–1976) is perhaps one of the most notorious advocates of violent revolution. Gandhi's source of political change is spiritual but materialistic power is the basis for change according to Mao. Mao follows Lenin in that he saw imperialism as the problem and underdeveloped countries as central to world revolution. However, even more than Lenin (but similar to M.N. Roy at the Second International in 1920) Mao believed that the underdeveloped nations were more likely to play a key role in fomenting world revolution. Moreover, Mao argued that peasants could be the leading force (not just a force subordinate to the working-class as Marx and Lenin argued) so that revolution in the cities would come last and not first. In order to organize the peasantry as a revolutionary force, they need to be taught to use revolutionary violence. He is quoted as saying "political power comes out of the barrel of a gun" based on the idea that the people, particularly the peasants, were reluctant to fight based on years of oppression but that military power, directed by the Communist Party, could be shown to be the only way to fight Japanese imperialists and all the people's enemies.[3] Not only did Mao believe in brute material force as the source of power, his "On contradictions" argues that there is a continuing dialectic struggle (drawn from Hegel via Marx) between the masses and the elite that Mao believed continued beyond the revolution.[4] In particular, there was the need to deal with the contradictions between peasants and workers (such as his policy in the late 1950s of the "Great Leap Forward," a massive mechanical attempt at collectivization of agriculture to empower the peasantry), and to mobilize peasants and workers against the new class of communist intellectuals and bureaucrats (as in the Cultural Revolution of the late 1960s). He argued in favor of permanent revolution because enemies of the masses can always appear and need to be confronted at all stages. The masses and not the elite should be the source of authority.

Léopold Sédar Senghor (1906–2001) developed what he considered

---

[2] See Raghavan Iyer (1986) *The Moral and Political Writings of Mahatma Gandhi, Vol. 1: Civilization Politics and Religion*, Oxford: Clarendon Press: 399–400.

[3] "Problems on War and Strategy" on November 6, 1938 at the Sixth Plenary Session, Central Committee, Chinese Communist Party, in Mao Tse Tung (1967) *Selected Works of Mao Tse-tung*, Peking: Foreign Languages Press, vol. II: 224–225.

[4] Mao Tse Tung (1967) *Selected Works*, vol. I: 311–347.

African socialism as an indigenous alternative to Marxism, drawing heavily from négritude philosophy.[5] Négritude, literally "blackness," was originally a French literary movement in the 1930s with the ideological aim to combat French colonialism and racism by emphasizing the virtues of being black in order to counter negative images of blackness, including taking pride not just in one's color but also traditional African traditions and practices. Senghor was a central figure in popularizing the term as a celebration of African ideas. Négritude thought also had an influence on Frantz Fanon (1925–1961) who also viewed language as central to identity and political action. Fanon argued the language used by colonizers also does violence to the colonized so fighting colonization also means one needs to change discourse, including the discourse of everyday life.[6] It is not just a matter of ending colonial rule, the minds of those that have been colonized also need to be decolonized to remove categories and assumptions that oppress. Nonetheless, colonization is based on the repressive power of violence through the police and military, not simply through language, so resistance to colonialism must be violent because it is the only reply to the violence of colonization that the colonizer will understand. This approach was also supported to a degree by Nelson Mandela (1918–2013), who, in his speech to the court upon being sentenced, pointed out that all peaceful demands for political rights for Africans were met by violence and therefore this compelled him and others to also use violence to fight for their political rights.[7]

The political thought of the post-war period in the Americas also provides a contrast between violent and non-violent approaches to political justice. The idea that this is political thought is perhaps better recognized in the case of Latin America than in the United States. The key contrast here is between the revolutionary Marxism of "Che" Guevara and "Liberation Theology," and between the philosophy of non-violent resistance of Martin Luther King and the violent rhetoric of Malcolm X. Ernesto "Che" Guevara (1928–1967) was an Argentinian who trained as a medical doctor and sacrificed a potentially lucrative career to fight for social justice. He joined the Cuban revolutionary army in the late

---

[5] Léopold Sédar Senghor, "What is Negritude?" in Gideon-Cyrus M. Mutiso and S.W. Rohio eds (1975) *Readings in African Political Thought*, London: Heinemann Educational: 83–84.

[6] Frantz Fanon; Constance Farrington trans. (1963) *Wretched of the Earth*, New York, NY: Grove Press.

[7] Nelson Mandela, "Black Man in a White Court" in Mutiso and Rohio eds, *Readings in African Political Thought*: 121–26 and Nelson Mandela, "Address to Court before Sentencing" in J. Ayo Langley ed. (1979) *Ideologies of Liberation in Black Africa 1856–1970: Documents on Modern African Political Thought from Colonial Times to the Present*, London: Rex Collings: 664–681.

1950s and earned the respect of his comrades for a willingness to endure hardship and follow orders despite his education and privileged position. This attitude was reflected in his political thought, centered on equality and unity, with a philosophy of *"el Hombre Nuevo"* (the New Man), who was selfless and non-materialistic.[8] When he was given a position of authority over the economy after the formation of a Cuban revolutionary government, he attempted to implement a program of "moral incentives" based on his ideals but the policy caused an immediate and noticeable drop in productivity and an increase in absenteeism so had to be abandoned. He left Cuba and offered his revolutionary experience to African armed anti-colonial movements but was not accepted so he decided to attempt to build an insurrectionary army of his own in Bolivia, which had poverty and oppression of the type that he thought would enable him to be effective. However, he was not trusted by the locals and one told the Bolivian Special Forces of the location of Guevara's guerrilla camp in the jungle so he was quickly surrounded by nearly 2,000 soldiers, and after a fire-fight in which Guevara was wounded, he was taken prisoner and executed soon afterward.

The non-violent alternative to the Marxist revolutionary approach in Latin America was "Liberation Theology" (*Teología de la liberación*), based on a term created by the Peruvian Catholic priest Gustavo Gutiérrez (b. 1928) in his *A Theology of Liberation* but others also adopted a similar approach that sin was largely a result of an unjust social structure in Latin America rather than inherent in the character of the poor.[9] It was criticized by the Vatican as Marxist for focusing on capitalism and the state rather than individual moral deficiencies as a source of sin, and for implying that the Catholic Church was itself a source of oppression historically. Yet Gutiérrez's main emphasis was on the Biblical problem of human dignity and the recognition that the poor deserve respect as much as the successful and wealthy. No one is destined to be poor but it does require effort to think, pray and hope in such a way as to not let poverty overcome the individual. Most importantly, poverty is caused by injustice and the poor need to work to treat themselves and have others treat them with dignity in order to be helped to overcome the poverty that the poor did not create so should not be forced to shoulder the blame.

In the United States of America, the non-violent approach was adopted

---

[8] Che Guevara; John Gerassi trans. (1968) *Venceremos! The Speeches and Writings of Che Guevara*, New York, NY: Macmillan Company.

[9] Gustavo Gutiérrez (1973) *A Theology of Liberation: History, Politics, and Salvation*, Maryknoll, NY: Orbis Books.

by Martin Luther King (1929–1968) who was a Christian minister. The main emphasis of his sermons and books was on the Christian gospels, including the ideas of Jesus from the Sermon on the Mount such as turning the other cheek in response to violence, the virtues of the meek, loving one's neighbors as one loves oneself and loving one's enemies and praying for them.[10] King's Christianity also provided a sense of mission to do God's will and act without fear despite the dangers to which his views and actions might expose him. At the same time, it is clear that the example of Mahatma Gandhi in India was also important. King visited India in 1959 to study non-violent resistance with the support of the Quaker group the American Friends Service Committee. King was also influenced by Leo Tolstoy and Henry David Thoreau among others. King's involvement with the Civil Rights movement in the late 1950s and 1960s was considered critical to legal changes that improved the status of African Americans in the United States.

Some at the time, in contrast, felt that non-violent methods were not effective and brought about only superficial or painfully slow progress. For example Malcolm X (1925–1965), a member of the organization the Nation of Islam from 1952 to 1964, claimed the Civil Rights movement's strategy of non-violence foolishly put black lives at risk and collaborated with the white establishment. Malcolm X believed that the only hope for the black population was to adopt armed self-defense to protect themselves.[11] He wanted a complete separation of whites and blacks, including a separate country for blacks within the United States, until the black population could return to Africa. Malcolm X and the Nation of Islam (led by Elijah Muhammad) claimed that black people were the original humans as humanity originated in Africa and therefore were superior to whites. Malcolm X eventually left the Nation of Islam and became a Sunni Muslim changing his name to El-Hajj Malik El-Shabazz (الحاج مالك الشباز). After this point, his views softened and he put more emphasis on international aspects of race under the influence of African thinkers such as Nkrumah and Nasser. Nonetheless, the debate over the choice between non-violent and violent strategies for political and social change continued in the United States and elsewhere.

---

[10] Books written by King include Martin Luther King Jr. (1958) *Stride Toward Freedom: The Montgomery Story*, New York, NY: Harper; Martin Luther King Jr. (1963) *Strength To Love*, New York, NY: Harper & Row; and King, Martin Luther Jr. (1964) *Why We Can't Wait*, New York, NY: Signet.

[11] Malcolm X and Alex Haley (1966) *The Autobiography of Malcolm X*, London: Hutchinson.

REGIONALISM, SOCIALISM AND AUTONOMY

Initially in the immediate aftermath of World War II in 1945 struggles against Western domination appeared to be straightforward. There was a general consensus outside the West on decolonization and self-determination with an emphasis on regional cooperation and socialism. It was agreed that the boundaries created by the colonial powers were often arbitrary or at least intended to serve colonial interests, but there was also a sense that existing borders needed to be retained in the absence of a clear alternative. The preferred options were forms of regionalism, such as pan-Africanism and pan-Arabism, in which older borders would become obsolete. Socialism in the newly independent states was not Western electoral socialism or even Soviet communism because it incorporated indigenous ideas of community and collective action, and was intended to overcome the disadvantages of capitalism as viewed by those that had suffered the most at the bottom of the world capitalist market hierarchy. Often this focused on self-sufficiency, though when this failed, it was a recipe for isolation and even dictatorship.

It is true that some political leaders emphasized the need for national states and not transnational community. Muhammad Ali Jinnah (محمد علی جناح, b. 1876 –d. 1948) is considered the father of Pakistan because he worked tirelessly to demand a separate Muslim state as part of the decolonization of India. Jinnah believed that Muslims and Hindus would not be able to work together in a united India because they had differences that could not be solved through parliamentary institutions. Only separate national states would provide the counter-balance to allow the co-existence of both communities, including for minorities in India and Pakistan. He argued that establishing peaceful co-existence would take years, just as the conflict between Protestants and Catholics in Europe took centuries to resolve. In this case, national independence rather than unity was seen to be the solution to political problems.

Similarly Kim Il Sung (金日成 1912–1994) in North Korea put forth a policy of *juche* (主體) by emphasizing the importance of Korean history to stimulate national pride and steel the masses to revolutionary struggle. North Korea was precariously balanced between China and the Soviet Union, and dependence on one or the other powerful neighbor held the danger of a loss of autonomy. At the same time, *juche* thought is also aimed at criticizing internal dissension and party official factionalism and the temptations of foreign ideas and wealth.[12] Unity was reinforced by

---

[12] See Kim Il Sung (1975) *On Juche in Our Revolution*, 2 volumes, Pyongyang: Foreign Languages Publishing House.

emphasizing the external threat. In contrast, with the thought of Hồ Chí Minh (胡志明 1890–1969) one finds a focus on unity through sensitivity to objective conditions. For example, when initial land reform efforts encountered stiff resistance because it was carried out bureaucratically by party cadres based on quotas, it alienated many smallholders. When Ho Chi Minh was put in charge, he did not apologize or attack others for their failings, he noted that alliances with poor and middling peasants had not been handled well and appealed for unity in the face of the struggles ahead, including the need to unite the nation. The point was that unity was essential for the Viet Minh because they could not afford to fight among themselves.[13]

Even though communist parties were formed in Arab nations early in the history of the communist movement (as noted in Chapter 13), communism never had the same attraction as in East Asia. Instead, pan-Arabism and moderate forms of socialism were more popular. Pan-Arabism began partly as a literary movement, for example, the work of Jurji Zaydan (جورجي زيدان b. 1861–d. 1914) fostered a sense of Arab identity through his novels and histories. However, the main pan-Arabist thinker was clearly Michel Aflaq (ميشيل عفلق b. 1910–d. 1989) whose influential thought can be found in his *The Battle for One Destiny* (Ma'rakat al-Masir al-Wahid معركة المصير الواحد) of 1958 based on various writings and editorial pieces. More important was his *In the Path of the Resurrection* (Fi Sabil al-Ba'ath في سبيل البعث) which set out his pan-Arab nationalist ideology, and can be summarized by the Arab Socialist Ba'ath Party slogan "Unity, liberty, socialism." The term *"ba'ath"* (بعث) literally means resurrection/rebirth. Ba'ath parties were established throughout the Arab world in order to create the political basis for Arab unity. Pan-Arabism would lead to the revitalization of the Arab people and liberate them from the control of colonial powers. In order to do this, the Arab people must be unified into one Arab Nation. Liberty was to be allowed in terms of thought and expression but was not possible in terms of governing power because a revolutionary movement needed to be led by a vanguard party, the Ba'ath Party, that would have to maintain a monopoly on political rule until complete unity was achieved through the elimination of factionalism, sectarianism and regionalism. Arab socialism was to be based on traditional Arab practices, particularly those that began with Muhammad and early Islam, including hospitality and public welfare, but also emphasized fostering strong and independent individuals. Yet,

---

[13] Hồ Chí Minh; Bernard B. Fall ed. (1984) *Ho Chi Minh on Revolution and War, Selected Writings 1920–1966*, Boulder, CO: Westview Press and Hồ Chí Minh; Jack Woddis ed. (1969) *Ho Chi Minh: Selected Articles and Speeches, 1920–1967*, London: Lawrence & Wishart.

there was also a clear sense in which Arab socialism was defined as Arab nationalism with the argument that the formation of an Arab nation would create the conditions under which the exploitation of the Arab masses could be eliminated.[14] One might be surprised to see little mention of Islam in this context. Even though religion was important, the focus of political thought during this period in the Arab world was on Arab identity and not religious identity with only a few exceptions. Aflaq was himself from a Christian background but viewed Islam as a revolutionary movement and that the original Arab ethos was transmitted by Islam so must continue to be respected. This also meant that secularism was not the aim in Arab nations.[15] Aflaq argued that Islam had a long tradition of toleration of other religions that could be the basis of the Arab nation and he was opposed to mixing Islam with the state so that all should have religious liberty in spiritual matters. That is, all religions in the Arab nation would be equally important even if the legacy of Islam for Arabs must be respected. At the same time, he claimed to be opposed to both atheism and any form of religious fundamentalism.

This trend in support of pan-Arab thought was also typified by Nasser and Gaddafi, two political leaders who have a weaker claim to be political thinkers on the level of others in this book but they did articulate a form of political thought and personify the fate of pan-Arabism and Arab socialism. Gamal Abdel Nasser Hussein (جمال عبد الناصر حسين, b. 1918–1970) was a key exponent of pan-Arabism and his sympathizers were located throughout the Arab world. Nasser advocated national consolidation prior to a loose regional confederation with the individual Ba'ath parties taking a leading role.[16] However, relations between Nasser and the leaders of Arab states were fraught with tension, particularly between Nasser and King Hussein of Jordan, but also in relation to the political leaders of Lebanon, Syria, Saudi Arabia and Iraq. These divisions were acerbated by attempts by the United States and Britain to undermine Nasser because they viewed him as a threat to their interests in the region. The US and UK supported the conservative King Saud who feared Nasserism was a threat to the monarchy. In response, Nasser nationalized British and French companies in Egypt and sought to cooperate with the Soviet Union. Nasser's political legacy was mixed, however, as he had come to power as

---

[14] Shahrough Akhavi (1975) "Egypt's Socialism and Marxist Thought: Some Preliminary Observations on Social Theory and Metaphysics," *Comparative Studies in Society and History*, 17(2): 191.

[15] See also Aflaq Michel (1977) *Choice of Texts from the Ba'th Party Founder's Thought*, Firenze: Cooperativa Officine grafiche.

[16] Kemal H. Karpat ed. (1982) *Political and Social Thought in the Contemporary Middle East*, 2nd edn, New York, NY: Praeger: 239–240.

a result of a military coup d'état and maintained power by authoritarian means so when he died suddenly of a heart attack in 1970, he remained a pan-Arabist icon but did not have any real subsequent impact in terms of political thought.

One pan-Arabist leader who lived longer was Muammar Gaddafi (معمر القذافي) c. 1942–2011). Gaddafi had been influenced by Nasser but produced his own political thought in the form of his *The Green Book*, eventually expanded to three volumes.[17] Gaddafi initially wanted to combine pan-Arab nationalism and "Islamic socialism" or *al-Jamahiriyah* (الجماهيرية), as opposed to atheist communism or materialistic capitalism. As the Arab world shifted to more emphasis on Islam after the 1970s, Gaddafi emphasized his traditional Sunni Muslim upbringing and argued that he was a conduit of Allah's will.[18]

A commitment of pan-Africanism, socialism and indigenous forms of political rule after independence were shared by all the major political thinkers in post-colonial Africa up until the 1970s. These thinkers also tended to be political leaders and the first presidents of newly independent nations. Haile Selassie I (1892–1975) is slightly different in that he had been a reformist ruler of an independent Ethiopia before World War II and the decolonization of Africa but he had been forced into exile when Fascist Italy invaded the country in 1937. After recovering independence, he advocated African unity as essential to the independence of African states, including those areas seeking freedom from colonial rule.[19] All African political leaders after World War II supported some form of pan-African philosophy but Haile Selassie was emblematic of the cause.

Even when the end of colonial rule was achieved, there was still a need to resist external control and promote socialism and democracy based on native African traditions. Kwame Nkrumah (1909–1972), the leader of Ghana after independence from Britain, warned that neo-colonialism was a danger after African countries were decolonized due to continued domination economically and geo-politically by the former colonial powers or

---

[17] Muammar Qaddafi [Gaddafi] (1976) *The Green Book, Part 1: The Solution of the Problem of Democracy, "The Authority of the People"*, London Brian & O'Keefe; Muammar. Qaddafi [Gaddafi] (1977) *The Green Book, Part 2: The Solution of the Economic Problem*, London: Martin Brian & O'Keefe and Muammar Qaddafi [Gaddafi] (1982) *The Green Book, Part 3: The Social Basis of the Third Universal Theory*, London: Brian & O'Keefe.

[18] Ronald Bruce St John (1983) "The Ideology of Muammar al-Qadhdhafi: Theory and Practice," *International Journal of Middle East Studies*, 15(4): 471–490.

[19] Haile Selassie I, "Towards African Unity" in J. Ayo Langley ed. (1979) *Ideologies of Liberation in Black Africa 1856–1970: Documents on Modern African Political Thought from Colonial Times to the Present*, London: Rex Collings: 328–340.

the other emerging powers, particularly the United States.[20] Former colonial and US economic investment and trading relationships, in particular, were a barrier to true African independence and development. Nkrumah was also a pan-Africanist and a socialist, as with other political leaders and thinkers in this period, and his socialism was derived more from African practices than from Western ideologies of socialism or communism because it was based primarily on egalitarianism and community.[21] Julius Nyerere's (1922–1999) African socialism is a case in point. His philosophy of *Ujamaa*, from the Swahili for "large family," was intended to stress the cooperative and mutually supportive nature of the new Tanzanian political economic system over which he presided. He sought to nationalize industry and develop indigenous collectivized industries to meet local needs. Pride in national self-reliance was to replace pride in tribes with the promotion of Swahili as a national language.[22] Similarly, Jomo Kenyatta (c. 1891–1978) spoke about the traditional *Gikuyu* system of rule, which was more widely consultative and based on notions of mutual support in order to reform the Kenyan economy.[23] Kenneth David Kaunda (b. 1924), the leader of post-independent Zambia advocated an "African Humanism" as the basis for his socialism.[24]

All these political leaders also insisted on maintaining a one-party state. Ahmed Sékou Touré (1922–1982), the first president of Guinea, articulated the reasons for this approach in his essay on "National Democracy," in which he argued that it did not matter if there was only one-party state so long as the members of the party were equal and the party was open to all of society. For him a one-party political system was crucial to maintaining unity against those forces that would undermine the newly independent state.[25] In the end, all of these leaders were forced from power after their one-party systems of rule deteriorated to dictatorship and their

---

[20] Kwame Nkrumah (1966) *Neo-colonialism: The Last Stage of Imperialism*, New York, NY: International Publishers.

[21] Kwame Nkrumah in J. Ayo Langley ed. (1979) *Ideologies of Liberation in Black Africa 1856–1970*: 617–638.

[22] Julius Nyerere in "The Gikuyu system of Government" in Mutiso and Rohio eds (1975) *Readings in African Political Thought*: 19–24 and "The *Gikuyu* system of government" in J. Ayo Langley ed. (1979) *Ideologies of Liberation in Black Africa 1856–1970*: 136–146.

[23] Jomo Kenyatta "Ujamaa – The Basis of African Socialism" in Mutiso and Rohio eds (1975) *Readings in African Political Thought*: 546–554, and "Ujamaa is Tanzanian Socialism!" in J. Ayo Langley ed. (1979) *Ideologies of Liberation in Black Africa 1856–1970*: 512–545.

[24] Kenneth Kaunda "Humanism in Zambia and a guide to its implementation" in J. Ayo Langley ed. (1979) *Ideologies of Liberation in Black Africa 1856–1970*: 555–571.

[25] Sekou Touré "National Democracy" in Mutiso and Rohio eds (1975) *Readings in African Political Thought*: 484–500 and "The Political Leader Considered as the Representative of a Culture" in J. Ayo Langley ed. (1979) *Ideologies of Liberation in Black Africa 1856–1970*: 601–616.

socialist economic policies failed due to external economic forces, internal corruption and other problems.

THE LOGIC OF NEO-LIBERALISM AND ANALYTICAL PHILOSOPHY

The outstanding political thought in the West in this period, particularly that with long-term influence, can be found in Britain and the United States. In contrast to the rest of the world (including the African American community within the United States itself) in which the role of violence, the need for unity and the egalitarianism of socialism were all important, the emphasis was on achieving justice through economic markets or rational and legal methods. Indeed, neo-liberal thinkers and business ideologies were developed in opposition to what they saw as the dominant state-led forms of management of the economy in the immediate post-war period, such as Keynesianism and what came to be called neo-corporatism, as well as the ideals of socialism and communism widely advocated around the world. Within the United States, the growing strength of the state was soon challenged by a strong strain of libertarianism. This libertarianism has left- and right-wing tendencies but the right-wing version fueled the emergence of neo-liberalism and neo-conservatism as political ideologies and in political thought. It might seem that academic political thought developed independently of the dominant political thought of Western elites and it can be argued that academic political philosophers and normative political analysts sought to critique and counter tendencies in neo-liberalism and neo-realism. The problem is that academic Anglo-Saxon political thought in the late twentieth century shared many of the reductionist and analytical assumptions of more conservative forms of thought, such as that of Karl Popper and Friedrich Hayek.

Friedrich Hayek (1899–1992) wrote *Road to Serfdom* toward the end of World War II (1944), as a polemic against socialism, even democratically elected socialism, which he viewed as an inevitable path to totalitarianism.[26] In the UK at the time Hayek was writing, the wartime state was heavily involved in industry and society, and the growing popularity of socialism, including the Labor Party in the wartime government, indicated a trend toward post-war socialist policies of the nationalization of most of industry (particularly steel, coal, railways, power generation and other utilities) and

---

[26] Friedrich Hayek (1944) *Road to Serfdom*, Chicago, IL: University of Chicago Press.

the creation of the National Health Service. Hayek believed that the danger to liberty was real and pressing even if the Allies won the war. Fascism was an obvious form of totalitarianism but he felt the democratic socialist version was also dangerous. By the time Hayek wrote his *Constitution of Liberty* (1960), he recognized the danger of socialism had largely passed but wanted to demonstrate the need for a maximum of personal liberty to create wealth.[27] He argued that civilization is a fragile achievement that has created the conditions of liberty under which wealth creation has become possible. People must be free to do the work they want, and acquire property and dispose of it as they see fit. Liberty is justified in both Kantian terms (a person should not be seen as a means, whereas socialist regimes merely see individuals as part of a plan or a means to an end) and also in J.S. Mill's argument that all choices are potentially bad but it is better if people are free to make their mistakes because it will create more opportunity to discover what works and what does not. He favored fostering many different forms of organization independent of the state, including both businesses and charities, but believed government involvement in society and the economy was always problematic and should be limited to as little as possible. He does not reject government coercion completely but it must not be arbitrary and must be predictable, such as fixed taxes or compulsory military service, and must be equally applied and limited to the bare minimum necessary to secure order. He still fears that democracy might lead to governments which want to redistribute and protect people by restricting personal liberty especially in economic activity. There is a need to defend markets from interference because they are based on and expressions of personal liberty.

The assumptions of neo-liberalism are partly drawn from protestant driven Social Darwinism directly or indirectly from Herbert Spencer but there is also a strong influence from logical positivism, drawn from those associated with the Vienna Circle or influenced by it. Karl Popper (1902–1994) was a key figure in this respect. Even though Hayek and Popper were never members of the Circle, they shared its methodological individualism. Popper attacked the holism and historicism of thinkers such as Hegel and Marx, and even Plato as the basis for totalitarianism. Like Hayek, Popper opposed social engineering by the state. These views or similar ones had an enormous impact on the political economy including that expressed by more popular theorists such as economist Milton Friedman (1912–2006). In his *Capitalism and Freedom* Friedman argues

---

[27] Friedrich A. Hayek (1960) *The Constitution of Liberty*, Chicago, IL: University of Chicago Press.

for economic freedom as a precondition for political freedom.[28] More importantly he was an influential professor at the University of Chicago where he taught a generation of economists and business students, including many from outside the United States.

Overseas students of US economics or business departments then went back to their country where they became deeply entrenched in the ruling elites, as in the Berkeley Mafia in Indonesia or Friedman's own students, the Chicago Boys, in Pinochet's Chile. The Berkeley Mafia and Chicago Boys are the most notorious examples but others, imbued with the same assumptions, dominated the International Monetary Fund (and similar regional and national institutions), economics departments and business schools as well as top management consultancies everywhere. In Japan, for example, the Matsushita Institute of Government and Management (*Matsushita Seikei Juku* 松下政経塾) promotes similar types of values and has been very politically active. Indeed, this form of political economic thought is ubiquitous throughout the globe, including in recent decades in India, China, Africa, Latin America and other areas where the immediate post-colonial consensus was fundamentally opposed to it, and is also influential in the former communist states of Eastern Europe. In this sense, Anglo-American political philosophy became the dominant form of political thought among economic and political elites around the world.

Post-war social science, particularly political science, shared many of the epistemological and ontological assumptions of neo-liberal thought as manifest in thinkers such as Hayek, Popper and Friedman. For this reason, political science departments, particularly in the United States, tended to dismiss political thought as archaic and only interesting as a quaint historical artefact. If it was taken seriously, contemporary political thought was seen as ideology or beliefs which had to be separated from the facts in order for scientific analysis to be undertaken. Political ideas or "values" were simply preferences and were not relevant to theory. The most extreme form of this approach has been rational choice which has been a major force in "political science" but even more completely dominates economics and related fields. Even seemingly "objective" academic theory has reflected US neo-liberal preoccupations and beliefs. For example, theories of social capital are based on neo-Tocquevillean assumptions about group behavior taken from a reading of US history and developed with a conservative bias focused on the fostering of non-state self-help groups.

After World War II the expansion in higher education in the United States led to the growing dominance of the social sciences in academic

---

[28] Milton Friedman (1962) *Capitalism and Freedom*, Chicago, IL: University of Chicago Press.

discourse. It was not until the 1970s that political philosophy, particularly analytical political philosophy, began to have something of a revival, though once again this was only possible because it shared the logical positivist assumptions of neo-liberalism. The resurrection of political thought in Anglo-Saxon countries can be traced to the legal-analytical approach of H.L.A. Hart (1907–1992) but the key figure was John Rawls, against whom thinkers such as Robert Nozick (1938–2002) developed competing theories though crucially based on similar assumptions about how political philosophy should be pursued. The attempt was to build a logical theory of rights and justice without much consideration of history or metaphysics, and when it was considered, it was only Western history and metaphysics, based on such thinkers as John Locke and Immanuel Kant. This new political philosophy shared the liberal and logical positivist foundations of the status quo despite showing more concern for justice.

John Rawls (1921–2002) and his *A Theory of Justice*[29] was particularly significant as a herald for the revival of post-war political philosophy. It allowed values to be discussed again, not as objective empirical data on the views of others, but as normative arguments that could be logically formulated and examined to test the rigor of the logic with which they were constructed. Rawl focuses on "justice" because he argues that "Justice is the first virtue of social institutions..."[30] In order for it to be real justice, it must be fair and stable. The rules must be clear to everyone and the outcomes acceptable to all. He then attempted to set forth set principles upon which a theory of justice might be constructed. He started with two procedural principles. The first is the "original position," which is a thought experiment where one assumes that one is free and equal with others with whom we agree on and commit to principles of social and political justice. This is the social contract or original contract in the form of the thought experiment. The second procedural principle is the "veil of ignorance," that is, one must decide the rules without knowing one's position in society because if one can possibly end up as a more disadvantaged member of society then one would presumably organize rules to be beneficial to all rather than just an elite few. Next Rawls assumed two basic principles of justice. First is liberty: each person has the right to have the most extensive basic liberty compatible with the liberty of others. Second is equality so that social and economic positions are to be (a) to everyone's advantage and (b) open to all. Controversially, he defines the second principle to mean that the weakest must be helped the most but the problem is that some, particularly the wealthiest and most advantaged

---

[29] John Rawls (1971) *A Theory of Justice*, Cambridge, MA: Belknap.
[30] Rawls (1971) *A Theory of Justice*: 3.

in a society, might be worse off as a result, because, he argues that social and economic inequalities are to be arranged to the "greatest benefit to the least-advantaged" members of society.[31] In doing so, Rawls provides a logical justification for some form of social democratic or redistributive or opportunity equalizing politics – a center-left position with hints of British and US experience.

In contrast, Robert Nozick (1938–2002) critiques Rawls using the same type of analytical logic but based on different assumptions, and reaches radically different conclusions. In *Anarchy, State, and Utopia*, Nozick argues that inequalities in the distribution of wealth created by a free exchange should not be made a problem because, as Kant argued, each person must be treated as an individual and not as a means to another end, such as a fairer society.[32] Nozick's view was that property rights are non-negotiable as a key aspect of one's personal liberty so that external compulsion to surrender one's wealth for redistribution is illegitimate. This was an attack on John Rawls' second principle of justice of *A Theory of Justice*. Therefore, we can see that assumptions about normative values still creep into analytical political philosophy even if they are articulated and constrained by seemingly objective rules.

Analytical political philosophers accept that there will be these differences but argue that analytical philosophy makes it necessary to set out one's premises clearly. In the end, however, if how values are interpreted and applied helps to determine the outcome, then it is more important to discuss the underlying basis of the values from the beginning rather than examining the logical consequences of these values, which can be structured to produce a predetermined conclusion. The analytical approach gives the impression of being rigorous and logical but crucially depends on the assumptions used at the outset. This is particularly relevant to a world history of political thought where, as we have seen, there is a huge diversity of assumptions and ideas of what constitutes human ethics and appropriate human relations. This point is reinforced by the work of Susan Moller Okin (1946–2004), who wanted to retain the logic of the Rawlsian system but modify it to take into account other value systems, such as that of feminists.[33] Since the important preconditions are assumed away or ignored by analytical political philosophy, the approach is largely limited to the Western academic community and a fairly narrow group within that.

---

[31] Rawls (1971) *A Theory of Justice*: 266.
[32] Robert Nozick (1974) *Anarchy, State, and Utopia*, New York, NY: Basic Books.
[33] Susan Moller Okin (1989) *Justice, Gender and the Family*, New York, NY: Basic Books.

CONCLUSION

The modern period of political thought is characterized by the denial or obscuring of metaphysical foundations. Metaphysics is still there, however, lurking below the surface if one looks. The notions that violence is necessary or that only non-violence preserves human dignity are based on assumptions about values and the theoretical dynamics of everyday violence rather that on empirical facts. Pan-Arabism and pan-Africanism relied on calls to organize and unite based on a race or language or region for reasons that are only valid if one believes in underlying principles that are not always explicitly articulated. The virtues of unfettered capitalism and markets are based on Western assumptions about human nature that go back to the Reformation, Adam Smith and Herbert Spencer that should not be seen as purely logical or scientific. One need only contrast these assumptions with Gandhi's critique of Western consumerism to see that a different set of principles can make a considerable difference. Similarly, the logic of analytical philosophy only works when there is agreement on fundamental premises, which is unrealistic in truly diverse society, not to mention globally. Metaphysics suggests a cosmology of forces beyond empirical fact that work in support of one's logical arguments. Yet, their very presence is what makes hope possible and can give one the strength to persevere in pursuing a just cause defying all logic. The problem was that after the 1970s, philosophical foundations were challenged more directly, further undermining the types of metaphysics upon which political thought depends, as we see in the next chapter.

16. Shifting foundations and return to origins (1980–2015)

This chapter is about thought after the apparent failure of both liberal modernity and left socialist secular revolution. Postmodern thinkers and movements challenge accepted approaches to understanding the world but find it difficult to explain the alternatives. Those with a clear approach seem to search for roots in the past, though are indelibly modern. The period covered in this chapter is very recent (so hardly history at all) and means any overview will necessarily be incomplete and will focus primarily on the major thinkers who at the time of writing appeared to have an influence with global significance.

This chapter will argue that these thinkers and approaches are a product of the crises of modernity, then highlight the implications for political thought and forms of resistance based on political thought. Just as the decline of the polis and small states or republics transformed political thought in the context of empires, there has been an attempt to find meaning and cohesion in the face of the atomization of modernity, perceived moral decline and destruction of the certainties underpinning the order of things. Postmodernism, for lack of a better term, in the West originally tended to ignore non-Western political ideas or deal with them problematically. However, postmodernism also has a relationship with political identity and even fundamentalism because the nihilism and relativism in modernism helps fuel the search of origins, fundamentals or attempts to build new identities. The focus here is mainly on Michel Foucault and Jacques Derrida because they raise potential ethical and methodological issues directly related to the analysis of political thought, and yet, as with most postmodernist thinkers, their legacy is ambiguous.

With the failure of socialism and pan-regionalism, and the relentless march of globalization legitimated by neo-liberal and other Western political thought, it is not surprising that there has been a reaction throughout the world. This reaction is primarily focused on a return to origins or a return to fundamentals. It is pursuit of what is perceived to be a pure original source of ancient truth to provide sure guidance and allegiance. Debates over immigration, racial discrimination, second languages, and separatist movements all suggest a distinctive political thought striving for purity in identity as a political reaction and as part of a search for political cohesion and community. The logic of genocide in Yugoslavia, Rwanda and elsewhere is the ultimate expression of this tendency. Yet the political thought underpinning these movements is itself an expression of modernity with a tendency toward absolutist categories and universalist principles even when expressed within the confines of localities or nation-states.

This chapter first examines the roots of postmodernism and feminism as an outgrowth of this movement, then highlights fundamentalist and related movements as recent phenomenon against the backdrop of the first two. Finally, the metaphysical implications of these positions must be discussed. One might argue that the destruction of foundations and the deconstruction or reconstruction of identities also leaves open the door to justifying the construction of fundamentalist, nationalist and racialist identity politics. In fact, postmodernism and feminism is complicit with neo-liberalism to accelerate change and perpetuates the domination of Western ideas. At the same time, the alternatives, rooted in a revival of the past, have limitations too. The lack of a positive metaphysics has led to stalemate.

CONTINENTAL PHILOSOPHY AND THE RISE OF POSTMODERNISM/POST-STRUCTURALISM

The juxtaposition of "continental" with "Anglo-Saxon" thought is well established but it must be remembered that they are both Western and cannot escape the assumptions of Western modernity even if the former would seem to be struggling against it. Any discussion of continental political thought should go back to Heidegger or at least his hermeneutics, and, by contrast and extension, to existentialism. Another strong trend in continental political thought was post-war Marxism, including the Frankfurt School and Critical Theory. In the past, thinkers associated with the Frankfurt School such as Theodor W. Adorno (1903–1969) and Herbert Marcuse (1898–1979) would have been considered essential to any overview of contemporary continental philosophy but these thinkers are no longer widely viewed as important. The attempts of Marcuse to forge a philosophy combining Marx and Freud was a failure though it probably helped to bring about the emergence of post-structuralist works of political economy such as *Anti-Oedipus: Capitalism and Schizophrenia* (*Capitalisme et schizophrénie: L'anti-Œdipe*, 1972) by Gilles Deleuze (1925–1995) and Félix Guattari and *Libidinal Economy* (*Économie Libidinale*, 1974) by Jean-François Lyotard (1924–1998). Thus, the Frankfurt School was surprisingly short-lived but was influential in its time. It is a historical phenomenon now, which is why it should be part of a history of world political thought.

One thinker associated with the Frankfurt School who maintained an influence longer than the rest is Jurgen Habermas (b. 1929). Habermas shares many of the influences operating in the Frankfurt School but can also be viewed as distinct from that school of thinkers in many ways. His main work has focused on the idea that communication is possible, not because there is a rational structure to the universe that makes it possible but instead because there is logic to communication between human beings that enables a degree of understanding. It is through communication that we can arrive at a more just, humane and egalitarian society. Even though his *Theory of Communicative Action* (1981) was critical of modernity, he was generally optimistic regarding the ability of communication in the public sphere to be engineered to promote the positive potential of modernity as promised in Enlightenment rationality.[1]

In contrast, post-structuralists, such as Michel Foucault (1926–1984), tend to be more skeptical of Enlightenment inspired reason. Foucault was influenced by both Nietzschean hermeneutics and post-war French Marxism to question the consequences and meaning of modernity. Foucault's archaeology of how individuals have been made into subjects and normalized reveals the ways in which knowledge and power have a subtle but profound role in modern society. His notion of "governmentality" exposes how power controls individuals beyond the formal power of the state. He has had an influence in many attempts to analyze the consequences of power and ideas across the world, including post-colonialism and feminism. Historians have been critical of the historical validity of his work, but it remains highly suggestive and poignant nonetheless. The notion of a perverse impact of Enlightenment reason against human beings is a powerful idea, though as we have seen this idea existed in the West at least since Rousseau and was one impulse of Romantic political thought. Therefore, it is not surprising that Foucault's two major "theoretical" works, *The Order of Things* in 1966 (original title in French was "*Les Mots et les choses*" or "Words and Things") and *The Archaeology of Knowledge* in 1971, show the imprint of Nietzsche, who also embodied Romantic reaction to a large degree. Foucault in particular follows Nietzsche's *Genealogy of Morals*, but suggests that it is more like archaeology with layers of attitude and practice being peeled away as one looks through old manuals and accounts of past practices. Moreover, since

---

[1] Jürgen Habermas; Thomas Burger and Frederick Lawrence trans. (1989) *The Structural Transformation of the Public Sphere: An Inquiry into a Category of Bourgeois Society*, Cambridge: Polity.

not everything is preserved in writing, especially the views of those who are the object of these institutions, careful reading and reconstruction are necessary to hear all relevant voices.

Foucault's three major "historical" works are *Madness and Civilization: A History of Insanity in the Age of Reason* (Folie et Déraison: Histoire de la folie à l'âge classique) in 1964 (with an earlier longer version in 1961), *Discipline and Punish* (1977) and *The History of Sexuality* in three volumes (1978, 1984) which demonstrate the ways in which modern society has not only led to the classification and manipulation of people but also internalized the process within institutions and the individual. No one actually fits the "norm" so the process of compulsion, sense of failure and reinforcement is endless. For example, in *Madness and Civilization*, Foucault shows that modern society tends to confine and psychologically intervene with those who are classified as "insane" to "cure" them, but in the past such individuals were not incarcerated or forced to change so were effectively left alone, particularly if they were not a danger to society. The modern idea of madness is a way of labeling "difficult" people in order to control them. Often the poor and beggars were also classified as mentally ill and so confined and forced to reform their behavior to meet societal norms. The same happened to middle-class women trapped in bad marriages who were labelled "hysterical" and confined to mental institutions. Similarly, *Discipline and Punish* explains how punishment was against the body in the past (lashings, and so on), but in modern society, there is an attempt to control the mind of the prisoner to "reform" them. Such an approach also extends to society at large as architectural design and other means of improving efficiency in the management of prisons, schools, armies, and businesses, all use subtle means to punish and discipline us to make us conform to the "norm." The emphasis is on training, examination, sorting of individuals by ability both justifies how we are treated by organizations and also inculcates a sense in us of perpetual failure to make the grade and the need to do better. Human beings are made subject (classified and controlled) through marks and grades in school and university, credit ratings, job evaluations, and so on.

For Foucault, Enlightenment reason, by trying to standardize and regularize us, has a dehumanizing effect. It may make things more efficient – which benefits some groups – but it is damaging to others. Finally, in *The History of Sexuality*, he shows how modern society, especially since Victorian times, has tried to define acceptable sexual behavior and practice. The categories of perverts, deviants, healthy practice, and so on were created to define normal and abnormal. Since each individual is a composite of differing feelings and tendencies, it led to an internalization of conflict in the self where the state penetrated the most powerful and primal urges we all have and used guilt and fear of deviancy to control us. In his *The History of Sexuality* on "Bio-Power" he even suggests that our basic biological urges are manipulated to regulate and control the life of populations. It is true that the source and control of power is not always clear in Foucault. A key concept is discourse but discourse often seems to be autonomous of state power in Foucault, though Rabinow claims that Foucault was only bracketing off discourse to see how far he could analyze it separate from the institutions in which it is embedded and the social practices which carry it.[2] The words one uses to identify one's place in the world and the place of others has meaning for social and political order. This has consequences for politics in terms of the exclusion of some or the advantages of others.

The political implications of Foucault's work are unclear. He participated in French disturbances of 1968, but was not led (as were some) to embrace the Communist Party, though he may have flirted with Maoism. French society at the time was highly politicized and for a philosopher not to be politically engaged was unusual and certainly an omission that had to be explained. Foucault's rejection of the organized left was especially important for the opening it gave to former Marxists not only after the Soviet invasion of Czechoslovakia but especially after the fall of communism. He himself seemed to have engaged in the politics of resistance on a small-scale, for example through involvement with movements to protect the rights of mental patients and prisoners.

Jacques Derrida (1930–2004) and his concept of deconstruction furthered critical analysis through what has been called radical hermeneutics. The problem is Derrida and many of his followers are often not explicit in their aims, perhaps out of a desire to avoid grand theories and narratives with their pretentions to timelessness and universality, which we have seen were particularly prominent in the systems of thought created by nineteenth-century thinkers. Derrida is most famous for his notion of deconstruction of texts. Moreover, he suggested a broad notion of "the text" so that all language, spoken and written, is a text to be deconstructed. Deconstruction itself is difficult to define precisely because it can involve a number of strategies and tactics. Some focus on binary oppositions, for example, to point out how we cannot often pin down exact opposites that we use in everyday life, such as heterosexual and homosexual, because they are not unalloyed opposites or there is an interrelationship between the two seeming oppositions. Another tactic is the use of neologisms or newly created words. It is one way in which Derrida in all his works demonstrates the

---

[2] Paul Rabinow "Introduction" in Michel Foucault; Paul Rabinow ed. (1984) *The Foucault Reader*, New York, NY: Pantheon Books: 9–10.

inability of language to cover all possibilities. In theory one could create a whole new vocabulary, of politics, metaphysics and so on to cover unsayable and imaginary ideas in order to bring them to life. Potentially this new vocabulary would be just as "real" as the old vocabulary. For example, "utopia" and "dystopia" were created words and opened radical alternative possibilities to contrast with present developments and fears or hopes of future trends. Any list of deconstructionist tactics is not (and never can be) exhaustive because the apparent certainties created by language can be undermined in a myriad of ways.

Perhaps most significant for the study of political thought are the tactics Derrida used to reveal the hidden trace behind a narrative or argument. For example, one might ask what are God-given or natural rights? Who or what is this god? Why and how has god given them to us? What is nature? How can nature bestow rights? Sometimes the trace is even more hidden and takes considerable reading between the lines to reveal. One example that Derrida uses is the American "Declaration of Independence," which he shows as an attempt to invoke a timeless transcendental being to legitimate political actions.[3] One can take these words at face value as a self-enacting statement of liberal-democratic faith, as most Americans do, but it is the same sort of foundation-less and grandiose hypocrisy which is behind any coup d'état or revolution – not all of which are seen as legitimate. Derrida's main aim was deflation of the grand pretentions of the author and he used it against many major philosophers to dispute or undermine their claims to the truth. One cannot ignore the fact that it was somewhat effective. At the same time, one must recognize the limits of deconstruction and radical hermeneutics. Some texts have more of a reserve of potential readings than others, though all texts have possible readings which range from the obvious to the absurd. It might sound tautological but if a text can be read plausibly a certain way, then that is one of the possibilities inherent in the text.

This points us to the ethical ambiguity in postmodernism and continental philosophy. It is a strategy of critique but it is often accused of denying foundations, including those that allow one to uphold institutions and practices such as democracy and equality. Derrida's own work hints at

---

[3] Jacques Derrida (2002) "Declarations of Independence," in *Negotiations: Interventions and Interviews, 1971–2001*, Stanford, CA: Stanford University Press: 46–54 but the translation of this text first appeared in *Caucus for a New Political Science* 15 (1986): 7–15; See also Bonnie Honig (1991) "Declarations of Independence: Arendt and Derrida on the Problem of Founding a Republic," *The American Political Science Review*, 85(1): 97–113; and Jacques De Ville (2008) "Sovereignty Without Sovereignty: Derrida's Declarations of Independence," *Law and Critique*, 19: 87–114.

tolerance, openness and freedom but since he recognizes the limits of how these concepts might be interpreted and used, he never explicitly endorses them. The closest he gets to saying something decisive is in his discussion of the "democracy of the future" in *Rogues: Two Essays*.[4] Derrida, even at his most transparent, takes his reader slowly and torturously through the ideas of others. He delights in paradoxes and seeks out those *aphoria* inherent in the problem before him, much in the tradition of Socrates. In *Rogues*, however, Derrida finally seems to be guiding his less adept readers through his work to lay out his political philosophy. He starts with the concept of *khōra* (χώρα) by adapting Plato's usage as a location of the "third kind" (*triton genos* τρίτον γένος), a space that is pre-existing and eternal in which both the idea of something and the thing itself can come to exist.[5] Heidegger used the word in the sense of "clearing" (*lichtung*) where "being" is "disclosed" (*erschlossenheit*) from the ancient Greek idea of the truth of philosophy as a process of disclosure or *aletheia* (ἀλήθεια). *Khōra* is essential to Derrida's politics as a place "between the logic of exclusion and that of participation."[6] From this, Derrida argues for "democracy to come" as the *khōra* of the political, that is, space to make democracy possible.[7] For Derrida, democracy is not straightforward because sometimes one must be undemocratic to preserve democracy. He refers to this as the autoimmune and uses the example of Algeria where democracy had to be suspended so Islamic militants could not gain power to destroy democracy. From this, he derives a "double injunction," that to support democracy one must be inclusive and speak to all the community[8] but a few must also keep the secret that democracy cannot be entrusted to everyone.[9] He claims his concept of "democracy to come" is a "weapon aimed at the enemies of democracy" because it points to the promise of democracy rather than satisfaction with any existing political arrangement and could extend beyond the nation-state itself.[10] He also insists that "democracy to come" is not democracy alone but democracy with justice as he argued in his *Specters*

---

[4] Jacques Derrida; Pascale-Anne Brault and Michael Naas trans. (2005) *Rogues: Two Essays on Reason*, Stanford, CA: Stanford University Press.
[5] Jacques Derrida; David Wood, John P. Leavey, Jr., and Ian McLeod trans. (1995) *On the Name*, Stanford, CA: Stanford University Press: 89. See also Derrida; Brault and Naas trans. (2005) *Rogues*: xiv–xv.
[6] Derrida; Wood, Leavey and McLeod trans. (1995) *On the Name*: 89. The similarity between Heidegger's and Nishida's *basho* has been noted by John W.M. Krummel (2016) "Chōra in Heidegger and Nishida," *Studia Phaenomenologica*, 16: 489–518.
[7] Derrida; Brault and Naas trans. (2005) *Rogues*: 82.
[8] In this translation, it gives "community" for (*koinē* κοινή) but in fact it means "common" as in shared.
[9] Derrida; Wood, Leavey Jr. and McLeod (1995) *On the Name*: 83–84.
[10] Derrida; Wood, Leavey Jr. and McLeod (1995) *On the Name*: 86–88.

of Marx.[11] Finally, drawing on his *Politics of Friendship*[12] he points out that it is problematic what to call a democracy since in fact it is usually an aristocracy, in the original sense of "government of the best," that has the approval of the many, the *demos*. This is the somewhat unsatisfying final culmination of Derrida's political thought. However, it is not surprising that this political thought is so underdeveloped and tentative because Derrida's approach is more useful for critique – exposing and pulling apart – than for building a sound conclusion.

For this reason, many post-structuralists can come across as amoral and even nihilistic in their views about the inevitable tendencies of modernity and the fate of individuals in the process. In reality, scholars who rely on postmodern or post-structuralist theorizing, tend to be "progressive," feminist, and radical in their political views but are often unwilling to subject to scrutiny the metaphysical assumptions that led them to their political position in the first place. Moreover, rather than challenging or resisting modernity, post-structuralism advances modernity further based on the relentless use of rationality (either to build or undermine foundations of philosophy), identification of subtle forms of control independent of state power but compatible with it (the market versus knowledge/power), and most importantly cultural relativism and a rejection of tradition. In fact, postmodernism is so ethically ambiguous that deconstruction can be used by advertising agencies to produce commercials to sell products or services more effectively and Foucault's governmentality can and has been used with the ultimate aim of enabling a business to motivate its workers or the state to manage its population more effectively by exploiting the logic of his theories.

On the positive side, continental political philosophy, including the work of Foucault and Derrida, has played a crucial role in the development of modern feminism. This could be defined to include the work of Simone de Beauvoir (1908–1986) such as *The Second Sex* (1949), though she was an existentialist and not a post-structuralist. It was not until the 1960s that feminist political thought developed rapidly when the work of a number of feminists, drawing on the continental approaches, raised important issues in gender and rethinking of historical perspectives. This is not to ignore early works but there is a noticeable increase in feminist political works, mainly by US writers, starting with *The Feminine Mystique* (1963) by Betty Friedan (1921–2006). The year 1970 was particularly remarkable for the publication of *The Dialectic of Sex: The Case for Feminist Revolution*

---

[11] Jacques Derrida; Peggy Kamuf trans. (1994) *Specters of Marx, the State of the Debt, the Work of Mourning, & the New International*, London: Routledge: 169.

[12] Jacques Derrida; George Collins trans. (2005) *The Politics of Friendship*, London: Verso Books: 95.

by Shulamith Firestone (1945–2012), *Sexual Politics* by Kate Millett (1934–2017), *Sisterhood is Powerful* by Robin Morgan (b. 1941), and *The Female Eunuch* by Germaine Greer (b. 1939). All these contributions opened up a critique of how power relations in the private realm of the household or family on both the social and psychological level could be used to control and oppress women and others. Important contributions were also made in this period by French psychoanalytic feminists Luce Irigaray (b. 1930) and Julia Kristeva (b. 1941), who even questioned the extent to which feminist politics requires the category "woman."

It is in this context that Judith Butler's *Gender Trouble: Feminism and the Subversion of Identity* (1990) is seen as a key work in "feminist" or, at least, "gendered" political thought.[13] She questioned the coherence of the categories of gender and sexuality by showing that clear tendencies between the sexes are largely culturally constructed and reinforced by repeated stylized bodily acts. Once these become the norm, they form a seemingly ontological "core" of gender. Butler took the notion of performative speech acts from the philosopher J.L. Austin (1911–1960) and demonstrated how gender, sex and sexuality, are essentially performative in that the statements about gender are not strictly true or false because they merely are a way of flagging up that one identifies oneself with that gender. Following from Foucault, she made it clear that the gendered, sexed, sexualized subject is formed through "regulative discourses" that are negotiated and internalized by individuals and form part of their identity. Such work supported questioning of what are "natural" gender roles and how truth claims about biological sex are also constructed through gendered assumptions about masculinity and femininity.

In this context, it was hoped that feminism would usher in a different type of politics.[14] One problem was that even though this critique provided the basis for empowering individuals to re-evaluate their subjective position and potentially take action, it was too individualistic and isolated in that it tended to overlook the need to emphasize solidarity and collective action to build the basis for society and political change.[15] A further problem was the question of who was to join with whom. Liberal and radical feminists, not to mention gender activists, had different approaches and agendas, and there was still the question of what it meant to be a "woman," for example, as the basis for joining together.

---

[13] Judith Butler (1990) *Gender Trouble: Feminism and the Subversion of Identity*, New York, NY: Routledge.

[14] Mary Dietz (2003) "Current Controversies in Feminist Theory," *Annual Review of Political Science*, 6: 399–431.

[15] Sharon Krause (2011) "Contested Questions, Current Trajectories: Feminism in Political Theory Today," *Politics & Gender*, 7(1): 105–111.

The final problem is that feminist political theory shared with postmodernism a heavy reliance on Western cultural and philosophical assumptions. Even within the context of the West, bell hooks (b. 1952) in *Ain't I a Woman?* (1981) argued feminism initially was written by and for middle- and upper-class white women whose backgrounds and experiences are very different from poor and minority women in the US, not to mention outside the West.[16] A key criticism of Western feminism is that it effectively sets up its own norms so that practices outside the West are often usually found wanting by definition.[17] It is very easy to find women outside the West who challenge purely Western notions of feminism such as Yamashita Etsuko[18] (山下悦子, b. 1955), Sarojini Sahoo[19] (ସରୋଜିନୀ ସାହୁ b. 1956), Aisha Abd al-Rahman (عائشة عبد الرحمن; b. 1913–1998) under pen name Bint al-Shati,[20] and Fatema Mernissi (فاطمة مرنيسي; b. 1940–2015). Mernissi's work in particular was very early in its concern that the dynamics of relationships between men and women in Islam required special consideration and that it was not appropriate to impose Western feminist concepts on the possibility of an Islamic feminism[21] though her approach is not without controversy.[22] Regardless of any possible criticism of these alternative feminisms or approaches to the status of women, it is clear that Western feminist thought has not effectively engaged with the world outside the West. Even the very terms of the debate in the academic literature, particularly the terms "First world" feminism and "Third world" feminism

---

[16] bell hooks (1981) *Ain't I a Woman? Black Women and Feminism*, London: Pluto Press: 121–122, 145–158.

[17] Chandra Talpade Mohanty (2003) "'Under Western Eyes' Revisited: Feminist Solidarity through Anticapitalist Struggles," *Signs: Journal of Women in Culture and Society*, 28(2): 499–535.

[18] 山下悦子 (Yamashita Etsuko) (1988) 日本女性解放思想の起源: ポストフェミニズム試論(Nihon josei kaihō shisō no kigen: Posuto feminizumu shiron), 東京: 海鳴社 (Tokyo: Kaimeisha), though one should note that Yamashita is on the conservative end of the feminist movement in Japan and not at all representative of the mainstream, see Ayako Kano (2011) "Backlash, Fight Back, and Backpedaling: Responses to State Feminism in Contemporary Japan," *International Journal of Asian Studies*, 8(1): 41–62, particularly page 51 forward.

[19] Sarojini Sahoo (2015) "Femininity and the Feminine Mystique," *Journal of East and West Thought*, 4(5): 67–76.

[20] Bint al-Shati'; Matti Moosa and D. Nicholas Ranson trans. (1971) *The Wives of the Prophet*, Lahore: Sh. Muhammad Ashraf. But also see Ruth Roded (2006) "Bint al-Shati's Wives of the Prophet: Feminist or Feminine?" *British Journal of Middle Eastern Studies*, 33(1): 51–66.

[21] Fatema Mernissi (1975) *Beyond the Veil: Male–Female Dynamics in a Muslim Society*, Cambridge, MA: Schenkman and Fatema Mernissi; Mary Jo Lakeland trans. (1991) *The Veil and the Male Elite: A Feminist Interpretation of Women's Rights in Islam*, New York, NY: Basic Books.

[22] Raja Rhouni ed. (2009) *Secular and Islamic Feminist Critiques in the Work of Fatima Mernissi*, Leiden: Brill.

are at best archaic but arguably seriously flawed even if drawn (usually unconsciously) from Mao Zedong's controversial three worlds schema. The "First" world, refers, presumably, to the US and Europe, but even though places like Japan and Singapore are as, if not more economically developed, they are excluded from the definition of "First" world, presumably because they are viewed as "backward" in some cultural sense. It also might be pointed out that countries in the so-called Third world, including Islamic states, have had female political leaders as head of state, something that the more "advanced" US has still not been able to achieve. Clearly, feminist political thought could benefit from being further explored in world historical perspective.

The key postmodern thinkers have also shared the general Western inability to engage the non-West effectively.[23] Foucault and Derrida, for example, tended to focus primarily on Western authors and texts with only a few relatively minor exceptions and never with the depth of knowledge and engagement they applied to Western thinkers and texts. The argument might be made that they did not have enough expertise to engage with texts and practices outside of the Western canon with which they were most familiar, which is fair enough. For example, Derrida is clearly on unfamiliar ground when he suggests the absence of Aristotle's *Politics* in the Islamic philosophic tradition as symptomatic of hostility to democracy. It ignores the fact that Aristotle's *Politics* was unknown in Europe until relatively late and the dominance of neo-Platonism in the Arabic philosophical tradition caused Aristotle to be interpreted in limited ways.[24] Worse, it implies a hostility to democracy as almost inherent in Islam, which is misleading at best. Similar issues were raised when Foucault commented on the Iranian revolution by seeming to praise it as resistance to Westernized modernity and his position was attacked by others as naïve and even harmful, particularly in his blindness to the implications for gender equality.[25] At the same time, Foucault was probably correct that contemporary forms of Islam were a product of modernity and were being mobilized as a basis for resistance to modernity.[26] The fact is that postmodernists such as Derrida

---

[23] Ian Almond (2007) *The New Orientalists: Postmodern Representations of Islam from Foucault to Baudrillard*, London: I.B. Tauris: 22–64.

[24] Derrida; Brault and Naas trans. (2005) *Rogues*: 31–32.

[25] Janet Afary and Kevin Anderson (2005) *Foucault and the Iranian Revolution: Gender and the Seductions of Islamism*, Chicago, IL: University of Chicago Press.

[26] Robbie Duschinsky (2006) "'The First Great Insurrection against Global Systems' – Foucault's Writings on the Iranian Revolution," *European Journal of Social Theory*, 9(4): 548; See also Alain Beaulieu (2010) "Towards a Liberal Utopia: The Connection between Foucault's Reporting on the Iranian Revolution and the Ethical Turn," *Philosophy and Social Criticism*, 36(7): 801–818; and Emad El-Din Aysha (2006) "Foucault's Iran and Islamic

and Foucault have been limited in that they are biased toward the West and this has an impact on how one might interpret their ideas and approaches.

FUNDAMENTALISM AND POLITICAL RELIGION

It is in this context that we must look at so-called fundamentalism, particularly Islamic fundamentalism. It is associated with a body of literature that constitutes an important segment of world political thought in this period so should not be ignored. Moreover, it is related to the problems of modernity and feminism raised by modern Western thinkers, though the connections are not transparent. First of all, we must address the term "fundamentalism," which is so pejorative and frequently abused in contemporary discourse that it is not a very helpful label. It tends to be applied primarily to religious movements, especially religious ideals that place religious principle over pragmatism or modernity (science, markets, and so on) but the degree to which they do so is often a matter of interpretation because most of these movements are themselves very much a product of as well as a reaction to modernity. Even if they often emphasize particular aspects of what are argued to be older or more traditional beliefs, they are based on logic and metaphysics that is very modern. Often what is being called "fundamentalism" is actually just highly politicized modernized religion. What appears to be a return to the past is actually a modern political response by relatively modernized and alienated members of society.[27]

Given the emphasis on Islam in recent years, it is easy to forget that the most political and influential fundamentalist movements have been Christian, particularly conservative Presbyterians starting with the Princeton Theological Seminary in the late nineteenth century and Baptist preachers in the early twentieth century based on a literal interpretation of the Bible. The Christian establishment was a strong supporter of conservative orthodoxy throughout the twentieth century. It became more organized as a major force in American politics in the late 1970s, most notably Jerry Falwell and his Moral Majority movement, in reaction to a perceived decline in traditional moral standards and the failure of the "born again" Christian presidency of Jimmy Carter. Similar groups and individuals soon became deeply involved in Republican Party politics, and

---

Identity Politics Beyond Civilization Clashes, External and Internal," *International Studies Perspectives*, 7: 377–394.

[27] Nikki R. Keddie (1998) "The New Religious Politics: Where, When, and Why Do Fundamentalisms Appear?" *Comparative Studies in Society and History*, 40(4): 696–723.

played a role in the successes of the party since the 1990s. It is difficult to identify a coherent ideology, however, or a representative body of political thought by one individual or group of individuals. Yet, there is no doubt that evangelistic protestant missionaries have had an influence on US politics and also influenced the rise of Christian fundamentalism in Latin America and Africa.

Other forms of political religion are even more amorphous. Jewish fundamentalism could be traced to groups like the Jewish Defense League or religious Zionism or Ashkenazi or Sephardic Haredi Judaism. It is a political force, particularly in Israel, but a minority group which, once again, does not have a coherent and prominent ideological or theoretical strain. The same can be said about Hindu fundamentalism. It is based on a variety of traditional beliefs but cannot be said to be coherent ideology represented by a prominent thinker. It feeds on traditional anti-Muslim and caste sentiment to politically mobilize Hindus. The Ayodhya dispute (in Hindi: अयोध्या विवाद, and in Urdu: وواد ایودهیا) is one dramatic manifestation of the movement where the Babri Mosque in Uttar Pradesh was claimed to have been built on a site traditionally regarded as the birthplace of the Hindu deity Rama so was attacked and demolished by Hindu activists. One would also be hard-pressed to identify Buddhist fundamentalisms because once again they constitute a modern manifestation of old ideas. The key feature is the political and often nationalistic bent of the movements. Nichiren Buddhism, as we have seen in pre-war Japan, had this tendency and it is not surprising that Nichiren is behind the major political groups in post-war Japan, such as *Sokagakkai* (創価学会), which organized its own political party, the *Kōmeitō* (公明党), that has participated in government, and *Risshō Kōsei Kai* (立正佼成会), which attempted to organize politically in the early post-war period but abandoned the attempt relatively soon after. In Burma/Myanmar, the 969 Movement, which appears to have taken advantage of anti-Muslim sentiment, is religious in the sense that the three digits is based on a numerological interpretation of the three Gems of the Buddhist (Buddha, Dharma and sangha) with each digit characterizing a list of attributes for each. Other political religious groups from other religions also exist but, once again, the primary issue, from the point of view of this book, is that these groups are rarely identified as possessing a clear and coherent system of thought, thinker or text at the level that one could consider as political thought.

It is in this context that one might ask why Islam seems to have produced the most thinkers and texts in the second half of the twentieth century that constitute a body of political thought? First of all, we need to consider the fact that political Islam has gained increasing attention, both politically and academically, in the West, and though this interest in Islam is not always directly related to political events, after each dramatic event involving Islam in a political sense, Islam is pushed higher up the political and academic agenda. It is also likely that as a revealed religion and one that has not taken the Protestant separation of church and state approach, it is particularly challenging for Western liberal democracies and academics who want to separate normative values or religion from political analysis. Differences between conventional interpretations of Islam and Western thought on gender issues only makes the context more fraught with difficulties. This is the hermeneutic context, not only of the discussion below but also of all treatment of Islamic political thought in this book.

We must also consider the nature of Islam itself. Islam demands a close relationship between belief and the daily activities of its followers, and that when politicized, can be interpreted as demanding one take action to rectify wrongs. In this context, a strategy of literalist reading against the demands of modernity highlights the political dimension in the context of the all-encompassing nature of Islamic belief. However, there is a danger in viewing Islam as a monolithic set of beliefs, which it is not, as we have seen. It is divided by philosophical, theological, national and sectarian differences. It is important to keep in mind these differences and how beliefs have developed over time. For example, initial attempts at formulating a "political Islam" were primarily based on Sunni beliefs, such as the work of Muhammad Iqbal (محمد اقبال) b. 1877–d. 1938) in his *The Reconstruction of Religious Thought in Islam* (الإسلام في الديني الفكر تجديد) in 1930[28] and Mohammed Asad (محمد أسد) b. 1900–d. 1992) and his *Principles of State and Government in Islam* (1961)[29] written in English, in the context of the formation of the state of Pakistan and in reaction to Western pressures on Islam. Here we will focus primarily on Egyptian and Pakistani forms of political Sunni Islam and political Shi'a Islam in Iran, though this discussion can do no more than highlight a few major thinkers.

It is easiest to begin a review of Sunni political thought with school teacher Hassan al-Banna (حسن البنا) b. 1906–d. 1949) who created the Muslim Brotherhood (الإخوان المسلمون) in Egypt in 1928. Originally it started as an educational movement to encourage the unity of Islam in personal, social and political life. Al-Banna himself believed that the political ideal for a Muslim must be a universal Caliphate but he was willing to engage with parliamentary democracy to build support and promote its ideas. He questioned the value of aspects of modernity but recognized useful

---

[28] Muhammad Iqbal (2013) *The Reconstruction of Religious Thought in Islam*, Stanford, CA: Stanford University Press.
[29] Mohammed Asad (1980) *Principles of State and Government in Islam*, Kuala Lumpur: Islamic Book Trust.

advances in science and technology, and separated this from Western materialism, of which he was highly critical. The Muslim Brotherhood became a mass organization and grew primarily in urban areas. Al-Banna did not advocate the use of violence to achieve his political aims because he believed that people could be persuaded to accept an Islamic state, though he was willing to condone violent self-defense if a follower was under physical attack. The Muslim Brotherhood's most notable thinker, however, was Sayyid Qutb (سيد قطب 1906–1966). Qutb's book *Milestones* (*Ma'alim fi al-Tariq* معالم في الطريق) in 1964 was a powerful critique of Western culture in contrast to the virtues of Islam.[30] He believed that the entire world was steeped in *jahiliyyah* (جاهلية) or pre-Islamic ignorance because Islam had become corrupted by ancient Greek, Roman, Persian, Christian, Jewish, and modern ideas ranging from philosophy and theology to everyday life. His shift to an emphasis on Islam appears to have occurred as the result of a visit to the United States between 1948 and 1950 where he witnessed widespread racism and sexual promiscuity but the politicization of his approach to Islam can be traced to the injustice and brutality he and other members of the Muslim Brotherhood were subjected to by the secular regime of Nasser. The notion of *jahiliyyah* was directed by him against secularists and fellow Muslims who promoted or acquiesced in what appeared to him to be the Westernization of Egypt by those who were ignorant of the true value of Islam. In order to fight Western corruption, Qutb believed that all of mankind could benefit from the spiritual values of Islam. In order to achieve this goal, he believed that Muslims must take a relatively uncompromising stance toward secularization. His program for action is somewhat vague, no doubt because much of his writing on politics was composed in prison and he had to choose his words carefully so as to not provide evidence of anti-government activity, but it also means that the scope for interpretation of his work is great. Qutb discusses themes in Islamic thought, including *jahiliyyah* and *jihad*, but infuses them with more sense of urgency and revolutionary potential. He insisted that anyone who opposed the Islamization of the state was an apostate and unbeliever, and was much more evangelical in his promotion of Islam through *jihad*, which for him includes aggressive action and not just defensive. He was imprisoned by the Egyptian government allegedly for plotting the assassination of Nasser and was executed in 1966. Even so, Qubt's work remained a strong influence and Muslim Brotherhood involvement in politics continued with the movement and Qubt's thought spreading to many countries in the Middle East and beyond.

---

[30] Sayyid Qutb (2005) *Milestones*, SIME (Studies in Islam and the Middle East) Journal, e-publishing.

We might also consider the work of A'bul A'la Maududi (ابو الاعلی مودودی b. 1903–d. 1979).[31] He advocated Islam as a "middle way" between capitalism and socialism or, as he put it in more extreme terms, between fascism and communism. He rejected any attempt at "modernizing" Islamic law or *shari'a* by a renewal of the concept of *ijtihad*, or reason. He advocated a literalist view of *shari'a* which he viewed as timeless and unchanging. In order to achieve a society governed by *shari'a* it was essential to wrest power from unbelievers and corrupt men to give it to the religiously righteous. He wanted an elected president and elected assembly but only to pass laws not already covered in *shari'a* and to enforce *shari'a*, and in contrast to the Muslim Brotherhood, Maududi proposed the organization of the moral and intellectual elite. Although he did not initially favor a separate state for Muslims during the decolonialization of India and was opposed to Pakistani nationalism, because he thought that there was a danger that nationalism would eclipse Islam, he was also worried that an independent India would lead the majority Hindus to oppress and destroy Islam. In order to protect Islamic interests, therefore, in 1941 he founded *Jamaat-e-Islami* (جماعتِ اسلامی), a political organization aimed at providing a political role for Islam by advocating a Muslim state based on Islamic law and philosophy in all areas of life. This state would be based on the entire Muslim community, not just the *ulama* (Islamic scholars). Maududi was initially in conflict with the secular leaders of Pakistan when it was formed but he and his organization were co-opted by General Muhammad Zia-ul-Haq (محمد ضیاء الحق 1924–1988) who adopted the policy of "Shariazation," after which members of *Jamaat-e-Islami* and its sympathizers were given jobs in the judiciary and civil service.

Maududi believed that since Islam means obedience to divine law, then nature and the laws of physics are Muslim in the sense that they follow what Allah mandates. Only humans and *jinn* are endowed with free will, so a Muslim chooses to follow divine law whereas a non-Muslim does not and, therefore, rejects divine law. To obey divine law means to have absolute obedience to God as revealed by the prophet Muhammad so a true Muslim must follow the strict demands of Islam. Moreover, Islam is comprehensive of the world, that everything in the life of a Muslim is touched by Islam, which includes politics, economics, science, and culture. Culture includes how one interacts with others, including how to dress and speak. True Islam needs to be protected from other cultures that would

---

[31] The focus of the discussion here is Sayyid A'bul A'la Maududi; Khurshid Ahmad trans./ed. (1955) *The Islamic Law and Constitution*, Lahore: Islamic Publications; and Sayyid A'bul A'la Maududi; Khurram Murad trans. (1960) *Towards Understanding Islam*, Lahore: Islamic Publications.

divert Muslims from the divine law. At the same time, Maududi relied on traditional views, particularly in relation to women, who were meant to manage the household, bring up children and provide comfort to their husband. He believed that women must be segregated and veiled if going into public including face and hands, and he was strongly opposed to the involvement of women in politics, though he did suggest that an all-female representative assembly might advise the government on women but have no power of its own. He continues to have an influence, particularly in Pakistan but his views have been eclipsed in some ways by the emergence of even more radical Islamist groups.

The views of Al-Banna and even Qutb and Maududi were relatively moderate by today's standards. It was individuals such as Muhammad abd-al-Salam Faraj (محمد عبد السلام فرج b. 1954–d. 1982), another Egyptian who took Qutb's ideas further by taking the notion of an inner spiritual *jihad* as the obligation of all Muslims and insisted on the role of violent *jihad* in radical Islam with his pamphlet *The Neglected Obligation* (Al-Farida Alghayiba الفريضة الغائبة).[32] He formed the group *Al-Jihad* (الجهاد) and was executed in 1982 for his role in the assassination of Egyptian president Anwar Sadat. It is this generation of Islamic political thinkers who have taken Islamic thought in a much more extreme direction in a way that is unprecedented despite their attempts to use earlier literature to support their views.

Political Shi'a thinkers are primarily but not exclusively Iranian. The most well-known is Ali Shariati (الله خميني b. 1933–d. 1977) who was a self-proclaimed revolutionary Islamic socialist.[33] He studied in Paris and read Sartre but was primarily influenced by Franz Fanon and Che Guevara. This led him to denounce imperialism, capitalism and consumer culture that threatened to engulf the world. He argued that only Islamic humanism could save the oppressed in general and the people of Iran in particular. Unlike Sunni fundamentalists, he respected the role of *ijtihad* as independent reasoning to modernize Islam – calling it permanent revolution. He advocated more rights for women, for example, but through the institutions of a modernized Islamic state. His approach was a combination of Islamic and Marxist critique of Western society, which was popular among radical youth in post-war Iran. In contrast, Ruhollah Khomeini (خم يعتى الله روح b. 1902–d. 1989) was much more focused purely on Islam and advocated

---

[32] Mohammad 'Abdus Salam Faraj; Abu Umamah trans. (2000) *Jihaad: The Absent Obligation*, Birmingham: Maktabah Al Ansaar.
[33] Ali Shari'ati; Hamid Algar trans. (1979) *On the Sociology of Islam*, Berkeley, CA: Mizan Press; Ali Shari'ati; R. Campbell trans. (1980) *Marxism and Other Western Fallacies*, Berkeley, CA: Mizan Press.

Velayat-e faqih (ولایت فقیه) or "Islamic Government," which was the name of a book based on a series of lectures he gave in 1970. The subtitle of this book was "Mandate of the Jurist" and it advocated rule by the right type of people or even person, which fits with the Shi'ite Imam tradition and the *ulama* tradition in Islam in general, those who are particularly pious, educated and wise, accepted by the people to judge cases in *shari'a* law. Unlike most traditional Shi'a believers, who avoided politics, he argued that Islam required a believer to be political. In fact, he saw attempts to depoliticize Islam or impose secular government as a Western plot to weaken Islamic countries. The main problems facing Iran was economic imperialism as the main problem and the Shah as the tool of its oppression so he opposed the Shah's modernization of Iran and wanted a strict *shari'a* state instead. Finally, there is Muhammad Hussein Fadl-Allāh (محمد حسين فضل الله; 1935–2010). Born in Iraq into a Lebanese family, he studied Islam in Iraq before moving to Lebanon in 1952; he was a prolific and relatively popular writer. He supported Khomeini's revolution in Iran but did not think it was suited to the situation in Lebanon and his relatively liberal views on women also set him apart from Iranian political Shi'a.

REVIVALS OF MODERNIZED TRADITIONAL EAST ASIAN POLITICAL THOUGHT

This period has also seen attempts at revival of traditional thought as adapted to the modern era. This was particularly prominent in East Asia. One example was the "Asian Values" debate, particularly the views put forward by Lee Kuan Yew (李光耀 1923–2015) and Mahathir ibn Mohamad (محضير بن محمد b. 1925), the political leaders of Singapore and Malaysia respectively in the 1980s, who were keen to respond to criticisms that their regimes were economically dynamic but not open liberal democracies. In doing so, they drew upon authoritarian, hierarchical and collectivist ideas from a variety of traditions, including the East Asian, especially in the case of Lee, and Islam in the case of Mahathir Mohamad. Mahathir also linked up with the Japanese right-wing nationalist Ishihara Shintarō (石原慎太郎 b. 1932) to argue the case for "Asian Values" as superior to that of the West. The most striking effort at the resurrection of traditional thought is the "New Confucianism" (*Xīn Rújiā* 新儒家). The movement is usually traced back to early twentieth-century Republican China as a counter movement to the New Culture Movement of the 1920s. However, when the Chinese Communist Party (CCP) took over mainland China, most of the thinkers fled to Taiwan, Hong Kong or the United States. The CCP heavily suppressed Literati thought and associated traditions, especially under Mao during the Cultural Revolution. However, in recent years even in the People's Republic of China there has been a gradual revival of New Confucianism. It tends to be rooted in the contribution of the Song learning (neo-Confucian school) but is not rigidly tied to it. Research in Literati thought at Chinese universities is encouraged and the Chinese government has gone so far as to call its vehicles to promote Chinese studies overseas "Confucius Institutes." In theory, the CCP is still officially communist so the New Confucianism is not the official ideology of the state as it was prior to 1911 but often research into Literati thought is promoted as part of Chinese nationalism and to form the basis for a Chinese identity to overcome the dangers of socio-economic, ethnic and regional divisions.[34]

The New Confucianism is commonly divided into generations. The first generation (1921–1949) was the reaction to the anti-Confucianism of the May 4 movement. The key figure in this generation was Xiong Shili (熊十力 1885–1968), initially a Buddhist and then a Wang Yangming neo-Confucian. He was heavily influenced by Buddhism and incorporates it into his Confucian theory but emphasizes the positive aspects of Confucianism over Buddhism. He argued that Confucianism does not ignore selfish attachment, death and the nature of being, so in that sense it is similar to Buddhism, but the practice of ritual (*li* 理) and attainment of *ren* (仁) is meant to develop "fundamental goodness" rather than a rejection of this world.[35] Another key figure in the first generation was Feng Youlan (馮友蘭 1895–1990) who adopted a stance closer to Zhu Xi to compare Chinese philosophy to Western philosophy in order to tease out useful concepts in Chinese thought, while recognizing the limitations of both.[36] It was the second generation (1950–1979) that fled to Taiwan, Hong Kong, and the United States after the formation of the People's Republic of China, and included: Tang Junyi (唐君毅 1909–1978), Mou Zongsan (牟宗三 1909–1995), and Xu Fuguan (徐復觀 1902/3–1982),[37] all students of Xiong Shili. Mou Zongsan was the most prominent of this group. Mou's metaphysics is

---

[34] Jesús Solé-Farràs (2013) *New Confucianism in Twenty-First Century China: The Construction of a Discourse*, London: Routledge.

[35] Yu-Kwan Ng (2003) "Xiong Shili's Metaphysical Theory About the Non-Separability of Substance and Function," in John Makeham (ed.), *New Confucianism: A Critical Examination*, New York: Palgrave Macmillan: 235; See also Wei-ming Tu (1976) "Hsiung Shih-li's Quest for Authentic Existence," in Charlotte Furth (ed.), *The Limits of Change: Essays on Conservative Alternatives in Republican China*, Cambridge, MA: Harvard University Press.

[36] Yu-lan Fung; Derk Bodde trans. (1952) *History of Chinese Philosophy*, 2 volumes, Princeton, NJ: Princeton University Press.

[37] See Su-San Lee (1999) "Xu Fuguan and New Confucianism in Taiwan (1949–1969): A Cultural History of the Exile Generation," PhD dissertation, Brown University.

similar to Xiong's but he extends his theories on mind and reality more directly to comparative philosophy.[38] Mou claims universality exists in all philosophical truths even if they are expressed in diverse ways. It is true that different systems of thought exist in different cultures but, in essence, they aim at the same types of philosophical truth. Beyond the facts of history, the fundamental characteristics of humans are the same in all places and times. Many in the current (Third) generation of New Confucianism are students of Mou Zongsan. The most prominent in this generation is Tu Weiming (杜維明 b. 1940).[39] This generation is seeking to promote Confucianism abroad, initially through scholars such as William Theodore De Bary (1919–2017) but also through other means such as Boston Confucianism. This generation is more willing to engage in practical issues of globalization and diversity but there is still a general reluctance to engage directly in political theory, even though there is a strong Wang Yangming influence on this group.

Finally, there is the revival of the study of Literati thought in mainland China.[40] This includes thinkers such as Deng Xiaojun (邓小军 b. 1951) who examined Western political thought and explored how Literati ideas might be used in support of democracy. It also includes Jiang Qing (蒋庆 b. 1953) who created the concept of "political Confucianism" out of Wang Yangming thought which he prefers to "mind Confucianism" or the School of the Mind, associated with Wang Yangming thought, but although he claims to make it political, it is more about reviving aspects of Literati thought that contribute stable political order and not the egalitarianism of the Ming dynasty Wang Yangming school. He is critical of New Confucianism from the 1920s for its entanglement with Western liberalism. He also believes that rejection of earlier forms of Confucianism led to the communist revolution and culminated in the chaos of the Cultural Revolution so the only way to rebuild Chinese political society on a stable

---

[38] Mou Zongsan; Esther C. Su trans. (2015) *Nineteen Lectures on Chinese Philosophy: A Brief Outline of Chinese Philosophy and the Issues It Entails*, San Jose, CA: Foundation for the Study of Chinese Philosophy and Culture; See also N. Serina Chan (2011) *The Thought of Mou Zongsan*, Leiden: Brill; and Sébastien Billioud (2011) *Thinking Through Confucian Modernity: A Study of Mou Zongsan's Moral Metaphysics*, Leiden: Brill.

[39] Weiming Tu (2008) "Rooted in Humanity, Extended to Heaven: The 'Anthropocosmic' Vision in Confucian Thought," *Harvard Divinity Bulletin*, 36(2), 58–68; Weiming Tu (2009) "Confucian Humanism as a Spiritual Resource for Global Ethics," *Peace and Conflict Studies*, 16(1), 1–8; Weiming Tu (2012) "A Spiritual Turn in Philosophy: Rethinking the Global Significance of Confucian Humanism," *Journal of Philosophical Research*, 37, 389–401; Weiming Tu (2014) "The Context of Dialogue: Globalization and Diversity," in Molefi Kete Asante, Yoshitaka Miike and Jing Yin (eds), *The Global Intercultural Communication Reader*, 2nd edn, New York, NY: Routledge: 496–514.

[40] A good overview of mainland thinkers can be found in David Elstein (2014) *Democracy in Contemporary Confucian Philosophy*, London: Routledge: 123–196.

foundation is to root it in the older Literati traditions.[41] Jiang argues that Literati thought is more focused on virtue than Western liberalism, because he sees liberalism as weighed down with an obsession over political rights. Finally there is Bai Tongdong (白彤東 b. 1970) who favors a form of Literati style meritocracy over one-person one-vote democracy because democracy tends to anti-intellectual and anti-elite populism that does not always produce good government. In fact, he argues that a political system that undermines rather than embraces expertise, as in many Western democracies, is not necessarily better than one in which experts and the most capable are valued and utilized effectively.[42]

One should also acknowledge those Western scholars who have made similar attempts to explain how Literati thought might be relevant for modern readers.[43] As we have seen in this book, the ideas of East Asia can be intriguing and thought provoking. However, some Western thinkers appear to be accepting the instrumental usage of Literati thought relatively uncritically.[44] Without a better understanding of the history of these ideas, and how they have been used, any abstract and universalized rendering of key concepts will be limited. Even worse, there is a danger that this thought will be used as part of nationalistic pride and "soft power" based on the geographical location of where it originated rather than the intrinsic value of the ideas.

CONCLUSION

Those thinkers that challenge conventional metaphysical foundations have serious problems. One is that their work has hidden metaphysical foundations that are not acknowledged. It is impossible to escape entirely the language and cultural assumptions in which one is thinking and writing. They seem to go some way toward acknowledging this problem but not the residual metaphysical assumptions that inform their own choices of what to defend and what to attack. Another problem is that the postmodernist aversion to new comprehensive systems of political thought and associated

---

[41] Jiang Qing; Edmund Ryden trans., Daniel Bell and Ruiping Fan eds (2016) *A Confucian Constitutional Order: How China's Ancient Past Can Shape its Political Future*, Princeton, NJ: Princeton University Press.

[42] Elstein (2014) *Democracy in Contemporary Confucian Philosophy*: 169–170.

[43] For example, David Hall and Roger Ames (1987) *Thinking Through Confucius*, Albany, NY: The State University of New York Press.

[44] Daniel A. Bell (2006) *Beyond Liberal Democracy: Political Thinking for an East Asian Context*, Princeton, NJ: Princeton University Press and Daniel A. Bell (2008) *China's New Confucianism: Politics and Everyday Life in a Changing Society*, Princeton, NJ: Princeton University Press.

metaphysics might merely assure the continued domination of Western varieties of stark modernity. It means that the main forms of resistance to modernity are fundamentalism and reactionary populism. That is, without obvious foundations, many still try to find something to hold onto. Forms of fundamentalism or attempts to return to traditional values (even if radically redefined) are attractive. Yet, despite the potential misuse of traditional ideas, we should not be distracted from engaging different forms of world political thought, including an examination of their historical development, in order to challenge existing dominant assumptions and inspire new ways of thinking.

Bibliography

PRIMARY SOURCES

The English translation only is usually cited in this book but in most cases the text in the original language has also been consulted. Those citations not in English are used because there is no English translation currently available.

The translator's name is given with the original author because in any translation, the translator is effectively the co-author. Where the original author is unclear or multiple authors are translated, the work is listed under the translator's name or, where there are multiple translators, the editor's name.

Afghānī, Sayyid Jamāl ad-Dīn al-; Nikki R. Keddie trans. (1983). *An Islamic Response to Imperialism: Political and Religious Writings of Sayyid Jamāl ad-Dīn "al-Afghānī"*. Berkeley, CA: University of California Press.
Aflaq, Michel. (1977). *Choice of Texts from the Ba'th Party Founder's Thought*. Firenze: Cooperativa Officine grafiche.
Alighieri, Dante; Aurelia Henry trans. (1904). *The De Monarchia of Dante Alighieri*. Boston, MA: Houghton, Mifflin and Co.
Alighieri, Dante; Prue Shaw trans. (1996). *Dante: Monarchy*. Cambridge: Cambridge University Press.
Aquinas, Thomas; Fathers of the English Dominican Province trans. (1920). *The Summa Theologiæ of St. Thomas Aquinas*, Online edition by Kevin Knight at New Advent: http://www.newadvent.org/summa/2094.htm (accessed November 23, 2017).
Aquinas, Thomas. (1955–1957). *Summa Contra Gentiles*. New York: Hanover House. Online edition by Joseph Kenny: http://www.dhspriory.org/thomas/english/ContraGentiles.htm (accessed November 23, 2017).
Aristophanes; Alan Sommerstein trans. (1973). *Aristophanes: Lysistrata, The Acharnians, The Clouds*. Harmondsworth: Penguin Classics.
Aristotle; Benjamin Jowett trans. (1908). *Aristotle's Politics*. Oxford: Clarendon Press.
Aristotle; David Ross trans. (1925). *The Nicomachean Ethics*. Oxford: Oxford University Press.

Aristotle; Earnest Barker trans. (1958). *The Politics of Aristotle*. Oxford: Oxford University Press.
Asad, Mohammed. (1980). *Principles of State and Government in Islam*. Kuala Lumpur: Islamic Book Trust.
Astell, Mary; Patricia Springborg ed. (1996). *Political Writings*. Cambridge: Cambridge University Press.
Augustine, Saint; John Healey trans. and Ernest Rhys ed. (1945). *City of God*. London: J.M. Dent.
Bakunin, Mikhail; Marshall Shatz trans. (1990). *Statism and Anarchy*. Cambridge: Cambridge University Press.
Ballou, Adin. (1854). *Practical Christian Socialism: A Conversational Exposition of the True System of Human Society*. Hopewell, MA: The author.
Barani, Ziauddin; Mohammed Habib and Afsar U.S. Khan trans. (1961). *The Political Theory of the Delhi Sultanate including a translation of Ziauddin Barani's Fatawa-i Jahandari, circa, 1358–9 AD*. Allahabad: Kitab Mahal: 1–116.
Barani, Ziauddin; H.M. Elliot trans. and John Dowson ed. (1871). "Tarikh-i Firoz Shahi," in *The History of Indian, by its Own Historians: The Muhammadan Period*, vol. III. London: Teubner and Co: 93–269.
Baylor, Michael G. trans./ed. (1991). *The Radical Reformation*. Cambridge: Cambridge University Press.
Beiser, Frederick C. trans./ed. (1996). *The Early Political Writings of the German Romantics*. Cambridge: Cambridge University Press.
Bell, Daniel A. (2006). *Beyond Liberal Democracy: Political Thinking for an East Asian Context*. Princeton, NJ: Princeton University Press.
Bell, Daniel A. (2008). *China's New Confucianism: Politics and Everyday Life in a Changing Society*. Princeton, NJ: Princeton University Press.
Bell, Susan Groag and Karen M. Offen eds. (1983). *Women, the Family, and Freedom: The Debate in Documents*. Stanford, CA: Stanford University Press.
Bernstein, Edward; Edith C. Harvey trans. (1911). *Evolutionary Socialism: A Criticism and Affirmation*. New York, NY: B.W. Huebsch.
Bodichon, Barbara Leigh Smith. (1866). *Reasons for the Enfranchisement of Women*. London: Chambers of the Social Science Association.
Bolívar, Simón; Gerald E Fitzgerald trans. (1971). *The Political Thought of Bolívar: Selected Writings*. The Hague: Martinus Nijhoff.
Brutus, Stephanus Junius; George Garnett trans. (2003). *Vindiciae, contra tyrannos: Or, Concerning the Legitimate Power of a Prince over the People, and of the People over a Prince*. Cambridge: Cambridge University Press.
Butler, Judith. (1990). *Gender Trouble: Feminism and the Subversion of Identity*. New York, NY: Routledge.

Cassirer, Ernst. (1946). *The Myth of the State*. New Haven, CT: Yale University Press.
Chaadayev, Peter Yakovlevich; Mary-Barbara Zeldin trans. (1969). *Peter Yakovlevich Chaadayev: Philosophical Letters & Apology of a Madman*. Knoxville, TN: University of Tennessee Press.
Chan, Wing-Tsit. (1963). *A Sourcebook in Chinese Philosophy*. Princeton, NJ: Princeton University Press.
Chen Qing-lan (陳清瀾); Chen Jian (陳建), Zhang Bo-xing (張伯行) and Zuo, Zong-tang (左宗棠) eds. (1968). *Chen Qing-lan Xiansheng Xuebu Tongbian* (陳清瀾先生學蔀通辯) 12 volumes (卷). Taipei: Yi wen yin shu guan (臺北: 藝文印書館).
Chinese Text Project: http://ctext.org/.
Chuō Kōron eds (中央公論). (1941). 世界史的立場と日本 (Sekai Shiteki Tachiba to Nihon). Tokyo: Chuō Kōron Sha (東京: 中央公論社).
Cicero, Marcus Tullius; Niall Rudd trans. (1998). *The Republic and The Laws*. Oxford: Oxford University Press.
Cicero, Marcus Tullius; James E.G. Zetzel trans. (1999). *On the Commonwealth and On the Laws*. Cambridge: Cambridge University Press.
Comte, Auguste; Gertrud Lenzer ed. (1975). *Auguste Comte and Positivism: The Essential Writings*. New York: Harper.
Confucius; Arthur Waley trans. (1938). *Analects*. New York: Vintage Books.
Confucius; D.C. Lau trans. (1998). *The Analects*. Harmondsworth: Penguin.
Confucius; B. Brooks and T. Brooks trans./eds. (1998). *The Original Analects: Sayings of Confucius and His Successors*. New York, NY: Columbia University Press.
Crawford, W.S. (1901). *Synesius: The Hellene*. London: Rivingtons.
Cusa, Nicholas of; Paul E. Sigmund. (1996). *Nicholas of Cusa: The Catholic Concordance*. Cambridge: Cambridge University Press.
Dante, see Alighieri, Dante.
Darke, Hubert trans. (2002). *The Book of Government, or, Rules for Kings: The Siyar al-Muluk, or, Siyasat-nama of Nizam al-Mulk*, 3rd edn. Surrey: Curzon Press.
De Bary, William Theodore, Irene Bloom and Joseph Adler. (1999). *Sources of Chinese Tradition, Volume 1: From Earliest Times to 1600*, 2nd edn. New York, NY: Columbia University Press.
De Bary, William Theodore and Richard Lufrano eds. (2000). *Sources of Chinese Tradition, Volume 2: From 1600 Through the Twentieth Century*, 2nd edn. New York: Columbia University Press.
De Bary, William Theodore, Donald Keene, George Tanabe and Paul Varley eds. (2001). *Sources of Japanese Tradition, Volume 1: From Earliest Times to 1600*, 2nd edn. New York, NY: Columbia University Press.
De Bary, William Theodore, Carol Gluck, and Arthur Tiedemann eds.

(2005). *Sources of Japanese Tradition, Volume 2: 1600–2000*, 2nd edn. New York, NY: Columbia University Press.
De Bary, William Theodore ed. (2008). *Sources of East Asian Tradition, Volume 1: Premodern Asia*. New York, NY: Columbia University Press.
De Bary, William Theodore ed. (2008). *Sources of East Asian Tradition, Volume 2: The Modern Period*. New York, NY: Columbia University Press.
Derrida, Jacques; Peggy Kamuf trans. (1994). *Specters of Marx, the State of the Debt, the Work of Mourning, & the New International*. London: Routledge.
Derrida, Jacques; David Wood, John P. Leavey, Jr., and Ian McLeod trans. (1995). *On the Name*. Stanford, CA: Stanford University Press.
Derrida, Jacques; George Collins trans. (2005). *The Politics of Friendship*. London: Verso Books.
Derrida, Jacques; Pascale-Anne Brault and Michael Naas trans. (2005). *Rogues: Two Essays on Reason*. Stanford, CA: Stanford University Press.
Diogenes; Robin Hard trans. (2012). *Sayings and Anecdotes: With Other Popular Moralists*. Oxford: Oxford University Press.
Dobbin, Robert F. (2012). *The Cynic Philosophers: From Diogenes to Julian*. London: Penguin Classics.
Douglass, Frederick. (1855). *My Bondage and My Freedom*. New York: Miller, Orton & Mulligan.
Dutton, George; Jayne Werner and John K. Whitmore eds. (2012). *Sources of Vietnamese Tradition*. New York, NY: Columbia University Press.
Eisai. (2004). "Promote Zen to Protect this Kingdom's Rulers," in Donald Lopez trans. *Buddhist Scriptures*. Harmondsworth: Penguin Books.
Emerson, Ralph Waldo; Joel Myerson, Ronald Bosco eds. (2010). *The Later Lectures of Ralph Waldo Emerson, 1843–1871*, vol. 2. Cambridge, MA: Harvard University Press.
Engels, Friedrich; Earnest Untermann trans. (1902). *The Origin of the Family, Private Property and the State*. Chicago, IL: Charles H. Kerr and Co.
Engels, Friedrich. (1908). *Socialism, Utopian and Scientific*. Chicago, IL: Charles H. Kerr.
Engels, Friedrich; Emile Burns trans. (1947). *Herr Eugen Dühring's Revolution in Science (anti-Dühring)*. Moscow: Progress Publishers.
Fanon, Frantz; Constance Farrington trans. (1963). *Wretched of the Earth*. New York, NY: Grove Press.
Fārābī, Al-; Richard Walzer trans. (1985). *Al-farabi on the Perfect State: Abū Naṣr Al-Fārābī's Mabādi' Ārā' Ahl Al Madīna Al-fāḍila*. Oxford: Clarendon.
Fārābī, Al-; Muhsin Mahdi trans. (2001). *Alfarabi: The Philosophy of Plato and Aristotle*, revised edn. Ithaca, NY: Cornell University Press.

Faraj, Mohammad 'Abdus Salam; Abu Umamah trans. (2000). *The Absent Obligation*. Birmingham: Maktabah Al Ansaar.

Feng, Youlan (Yu-lan Fung); Derk Bodde trans. (1952). *History of Chinese Philosophy*, 2 volumes. Princeton, NJ: Princeton University Press.

Flores Magón, Ricardo; David Poole trans. (1977). *Land and Liberty: Anarchist Influences in the Mexican Revolution*. Sanday: Cienfuegos Press.

Foucault, Michel; Richard Howard trans. (1965). *Madness and Civilization: A History of Insanity in the Age of Reason*. New York: Pantheon Books.

Foucault, Michel; A.M. Sheridan Smith trans. (1972). *The Archeology of Knowledge*. New York, NY: Pantheon Books.

Foucault, Michel; Alan Sheridan trans. (1973). *The Order of Things: An Archaeology of the Human Sciences*. New York, NY: Vintage Books.

Foucault, Michel; Alan Sheridan trans. (1977). *Discipline and Punish: The Birth of the Prison*. New York, NY: Random House.

Foucault, Michel; Paul Rabinow ed. (1984). *The Foucault Reader*. New York, NY: Pantheon Books.

Foucault, Michel; Robert Hurley trans. (1990). *The History of Sexuality, Vol 1: Introduction*. Harmondsworth: Penguin.

Foucault, Michel; Robert Hurley trans. (1990). *The History of Sexuality, Vol. 3: The Care of the Self*. Harmondsworth: Penguin.

Foucault, Michel; Robert Hurley trans. (1992). *The History of Sexuality, Vol. 2: The Use of Pleasure*. Harmondsworth: Penguin.

Fourier, Charles; Ian Patterson trans. (1996). *Fourier: "The Theory of the Four Movements"*. Cambridge: Cambridge University Press.

Friedman, Milton. (1962). *Capitalism and Freedom*. Chicago, IL: University of Chicago Press.

Fung, Yu-lan, see Feng Youlan.

Gaddafi (Qaddafi), Muammar. (1976). *The Green Book, Part 1: The Solution of the Problem of Democracy, "The Authority of the People"*. London: Brian & O'Keefe.

Gaddafi (Qaddafi), Muammar. (1977). *The Green Book, Part 2: The Solution of the Economic Problem*. London: Martin Brian and O'Keefe.

Gaddafi (Qaddafi), Muammar. (1982). *The Green Book, Part 3: The Social Basis of the Third Universal Theory*. London: Brian & O'Keefe.

Gandhi, Monhandas; Raghavan Iyer trans. (1986). *The Moral and Political Writings of Mahatma Gandhi, Vol. 1: Civilization Politics and Religion*. Oxford: Clarendon Press.

Ge Hong (Ko Hung); Jay Sailey trans. (1978). *The Master who Embraces Simplicity: A Study of the Philosopher Ko Hung, AD 283–343*. San Francisco, CA: Chinese Materials Center.

Ge Hong (葛洪); Honda Wataru trans. (本田済訳). (1990). *Baopuzi naihen* gaihen, 3 volumes (『抱朴子 内篇・外篇』全 3 巻). Tokyo: Heibon Sha (東京：平凡社).

Ghazzali, Al-; Fazal ul Karim trans. (1993). *Revival of Religious Learnings: Imam Al-Ghazzali's Ihya Ulum-id-Din*, 3 volumes. Karachi: Daral Ishaat.

Gihwa; Charles Muller trans. (2005). "Exposition of the Correct" (Hyeonjeong Non). http://www.hm.tyg.jp/~acmuller/jeong-gihwa/hyeonjeongnon.html (no longer accessible).

Gobineau, Arthur de; Michael Denis Biddiss trans. (1970). *Gobineau: Selected Political Writings*. London: Cape.

Gramsci, Antonio. (2000). *The Modern Prince and Other Writings*. New York, NY: International Publishers.

Gramsci, Antonio; Joseph A. Buttigieg and Antonio Callari trans. (2011). *Prison Notebooks*, 3 volumes. New York, NY: Columbia University Press.

Guevara, Ernesto "Che"; John Gerassi trans. (1968). *Venceremos! The Speeches and Writings of Che Guevara*. New York, NY: Macmillan Company.

Gutiérrez, Gustavo. (1973). *A Theology of Liberation: History, Politics, and Salvation*. Maryknoll, NY: Orbis Books.

Habermas, Jürgen; Thomas Burger and Frederick Lawrence trans. (1989). *The Structural Transformation of the Public Sphere: An Inquiry into a Category of Bourgeois Society*. Cambridge: Polity.

Hakeda, Yoshito S. (1972). *Kūkai and His Major Works*. New York, NY: Columbia University Press.

Hamilton, Alexander, James Madison and John Jay. (1961). *The Federalist; or, The New Constitution*. London: Dent.

Hay, Stephen ed. (1988). *Sources of Indian Tradition*, vol. 2, 2nd edn. New York, NY: Columbia University Press.

Hayek, Friedrich A. (1944). *Road to Serfdom*. Chicago, IL: University of Chicago Press.

Hayek, Friedrich A. (1960). *The Constitution of Liberty*. Chicago, IL: University of Chicago Press.

Hayford, Joseph Casely. (1970). *Gold Coast Native Institutions; With Thoughts upon a Healthy Imperial Policy for the Gold Coast and Ashanti*. London: Frank Cass.

He Yan (何晏); Zhongxin Zhuo (卓忠信) ed. (1969). *Lunyu He-shi jijie* with the Commentary by Zhu Xi [朱熹] (論語何氏集解). Taipei: Jiaxin Shuini Gongsi Wenhua Jijinhui (臺北：嘉新水泥公司文華基金會).

Hegel, Georg Wilhelm; Arnold V. Miller and John Niemeyer Findlay trans. (1977). *Phenomenology of Spirit*. Oxford: Clarendon Press.

Hegel, Georg Wilhelm Friedrich; Thomas Malcolm Knox trans. (1967). *Hegel's Philosophy of Right*. London: Oxford University Press.

Heidegger, Martin; John Macquarrie and Edward Robinson trans. (1962). *Being and Time*. Oxford: Basil Blackwell.
Heidegger, Martin; Andrew J. Mitchell trans. Peter Trawny, Marcia Cavalcante Schuback and Michael Marder eds. (2014). *On Hegel's Philosophy of Right: The 1934–35 Seminar and Interpretive Essays*. London: Bloomsbury.
Hemachandra; R.C.C. Fynes trans. (1998). *The Lives of the Jain Elders*. Oxford: Oxford University Press.
Hendrischke, Barbara. (2015). *The Scripture on Great Peace: The Taiping jing and the Beginnings of Daoism*. Berkeley, CA: University of California Press.
Hồ Chí Minh; Jack Woddis ed. (1969). *Ho Chi Minh: Selected Articles and Speeches, 1920–1967*. London: Lawrence & Wishart.
Hồ Chí Minh; Bernard B. Fall ed. (1984). *Ho Chi Minh on Revolution and War, Selected Writings 1920–1966*. Boulder, CO: Westview Press.
Hobbes, Thomas. (1651). *Leviathan, or the Matter, Forme, & Power of a Common-wealth Ecclesiasticall and Civill*. London: Andrew Crooke, at the Green Dragon in St. Pauls Church-yard.
hooks, bell. (1981). *Ain't I a Woman? Black Women and Feminism*. London: Pluto Press.
Hopfl, Harro M. trans./ed. (1991). *Luther and Calvin on Secular Authority*. Cambridge: Cambridge University Press.
Horner, I.B. trans. (1954–1959). *The Book of Middle Length Sayings (Majjhima Nikaya)*, 3 volumes. Bristol: Pali Text Society.
Horton, J.A.B. (1868). *West African Countries and Peoples*. London: W.J. Johnson.
Hughes, E.R. (1942). *Chinese Philosophy in the Classical Times*. New York, NY: E.P. Dutton.
Hume, David; L.A. Selby-Bigge ed. (1896). *A Treatise of Human Nature*. Oxford: Clarendon Press.
Hume, David; Fredrick Watkins ed. (1951). *Hume: Theory of Politics*. Edinburgh: Nelson.
Inagaki, Hisao trans. (2017). *Larger Sutra on Amida Buddha (Daimuryojukyo, or Larger Sukhavativyuha Sutra)*. http://web.mit.edu/stclair/www/larger.html (accessed June 28, 2017).
Iqbal, Muhammad. (2013). *The Reconstruction of Religious Thought in Islam*. Stanford, CA: Stanford University Press.
Itō Noe (伊藤野枝). (1996). *Itō Noe Zenshū*, 2 volumes. (伊藤野枝全集 第 2 巻). Tokyo: Gakugei Shorin (東京：學藝書林).
Ivanhoe, Philip J. trans. (2009). *Readings from the Lu-Wang School of Neo-Confucianism*. Indianapolis, IN: Hackett Publishing.

Jefferson, Thomas; Terence Ball ed. (1999). *Jefferson: Political Writings*. Cambridge: Cambridge University Press.

Jefferson, Thomas; Thomas Jefferson collection, Library of Congress. (n.d.). http://www.loc.gov/exhibits/jefferson/105.html (accessed November 23, 2017).

Jefferson, Thomas; National Archives. (n.d.). https://founders.archives.gov/?q=%20Author%3A%22Jefferson%2C%20Thomas%22&s=1111211111&r=1 (accessed November 23, 2017).

Jeong Dojeon; Charles Muller trans. (2005). "Array of Critiques against Buddhism" (Bulssi Japbyeon). http://www.hm.tyg.jp/~acmuller/jeong-gihwa/hyeonjeongnon.html (no longer accessible).

Jiang Qing; Edmund Ryden trans. and Daniel Bell and Ruiping Fan eds. (2016). *A Confucian Constitutional Order: How China's Ancient Past Can Shape its Political Future*. Princeton, NJ: Princeton University Press.

Johnson, Wallace trans. (1979). *The Tang Code, Volume One: General Principles*. Princeton, NJ: Princeton University Press.

Kaneko Fumiko; Jean Inglis trans. (1991). *The Prison Memoirs of a Japanese Woman*. Armonk, NY: M.E. Sharpe.

Kangle, R.P. trans. and ed. (1960, 1963, 1965). *The Kautiliya Arthasastra*, 3 volumes. Bombay: University of Bombay Press.

Kant, Immanuel; Thomas K. Abbott trans. (1879). *A Theory of Ethics*. London: Longman, Green.

Kant, Immanuel; Mary Gregor trans. (1996). *The Metaphysics of Morals*. Cambridge: Cambridge University Press.

Karant-Nunn, Susan C. and Merry E. Wiesner-Hanks eds. (2003). *Luther on Women: A Sourcebook*. Cambridge: Cambridge University Press.

Karpat, Kemal H. ed. (1982). *Political and Social Thought in the Contemporary Middle East*, 2nd edn. New York, NY: Praeger.

Khaldûn, ibn; Franz Rosenthal trans. (1958). *The Muqaddimah: An Introduction to History* (Bollingen Series, XLIII), 3 volumes. New York, NY: Pantheon Books.

Khan, Mirza Yusef; A.A. Seyed-Gohrab and S. McGlinn trans. (2010). *One Word – Yak Kaleme: 19th Century Persian Treatise Introducing Western Codified Law*. Amsterdam: University of Amsterdam Press.

Kim Il Sung. (1975). *On Juche in Our Revolution*, 2 volumes. Pyongyang: Foreign Languages Publishing House.

Kindī, Al; Alfred L. Ivry trans. (1974). *Al-Kindī's Metaphysics*. Albany, NY: State University of New York Press.

King, Martin Luther Jr. (1958). *Stride Toward Freedom: The Montgomery Story*. New York, NY: Harper.

King, Martin Luther, Jr. (1963). *Strength To Love*. New York, NY: Harper & Row.

King, Martin Luther Jr. (1964). *Why We Can't Wait*. New York, NY: Signet.

Kita Ikki. (1974). "General Outline of Measures for the Reorganization of Japan, 1923," in David John Lu ed., *Sources of Japanese History*, vol. 2. New York, NY: McGraw-Hill: 130–136.

Kitabatake Chikafusa; H. Paul Varley trans. (1980). *A Chronicle of Gods and Sovereigns: Jinnō Shōtōki of Kitabatake Chikafusa*. New York, NY: Columbia University Press.

Knox, John (1790). *The History of the Reformation in Scotland and Other Works*. Edinburgh: H. Inglis.

Kōsaka Saaki (高坂正顕). (1942). *Minzoku no Tetsugaku* (民族の哲學). Tokyo: Iwanami Shoten (東京：岩波書店).

Kōsaka Saaki (高坂正顕). (1943). *Rekishi Tetsugaku Josetsu* (歷史哲學序說). Tokyo: Iwanami Shoten (東京：岩波書店).

Kōtoku Shūsui (幸徳秋水); Kamisaki Kiyoshi trans. (神崎清訳). (2014). *Heiminshugi* (平民主義). Tokyo: Chūō Kōron Sha (東京：中央公論社).

Kōtoku Shūsui; Robert Thomas Tierney trans. (2015). *Monster of the Twentieth Century: Kōtoku Shūsui and Japan's First Anti-Imperialist Movement*. Berkeley, CA: University of California Press.

Kouyaté, S. ed. (1998). "La charte de Kurukan Fuga," http://www.frabenin.org/IMG/pdf/kurukan_fuga.pdf (accessed May 20, 2017).

Kōyama Iwao (高山岩男). (1941). *Bunka Ruigatagaku Kenkyū* (文化類型學研究). Tokyo: Kōbundō (東京：弘文堂書房).

Kōyama Iwao (高山岩男). (1942). *Sekai Shi no Tetsugaku* (世界史の哲學). Tokyo: Iwanami Shoten (東京：岩波書店).

Kropotkin, Peter. (1907). *The Conquest of Bread*. New York, NY: G.P. Putnam.

Kropotkin, Peter. (1972). *Mutual Aid: A Factor of Evolution*. New York, NY: New York University Press.

Laërtius, Diogenes; Robert Drew Hicks trans. (1925). *Lives of the Eminent Philosophers*, 2 volumes. London: William Heinemann.

Langley, J. Ayo ed. (1979). *Ideologies of Liberation in Black Africa 1856–1970: Documents on Modern African Political Thought from Colonial Times to the Present*. London: Rex Collings.

Lao tzu (Laozi). Arthur Waley trans. (1934). *The Way and Its Power: A Study of the Tao tê Ching and its Place in Chinese Thought*. London: G. Allen & Unwin.

Laozi, D., C. Lau trans. (1963). *Lao Tzu: Tao Te Ching*. Harmondsworth: Penguin.

Legge, James trans. (c.1920). *The Four Books* (華英四書). Shanghai: The Chinese Book Company.

Lenin, Vladimir I. (1970). *Imperialism, The Highest Stage of Capitalism: A Popular Outline*. Peking: Foreign Languages Press.

Lerner, Ralph and Muhsin Mahdi eds. (1963). *Medieval Political Philosophy: A Sourcebook*. Ithaca, NY: Cornell University Press.

Li Zhi (李贄); Masui Tsuneo trans. (増井経夫訳). (1969). *Funsho: Meidai Itan no Sho* (焚書—明代異端の書). Tokyo: Heibon Sha (東京：平凡社).

Locke, John. (1759). *The Works of John Locke esq*. 3 volumes. London: D. Browne, C. Hitch and L. Hawes, J. Shuckburgh, A. Millar, J. Beecroft, John Rivington, James Rivington and J. Fletcher, J. Ward, R. Baldwin, J. Richardson, S. Crowder, P. Davey and B. Law, T. Longman, E. Dilly, R. Withy, T. Payne, and M. Cooper.

Long, A.A. and D.N. Sedley trans./ed. (1987). *The Hellenistic Philosophers*, 2 volumes. Cambridge: Cambridge University Press.

Lu Xun; William A. Lyell trans. (1990). *Diary of a Madman and Other Stories*. Honolulu, HI: University of Hawaii Press.

Luxemburg, Rosa. (1971). *Selected Political Writings of Rosa Luxemburg*. New York, NY: Monthly Review Press.

Machiavelli, Niccolò; Ninian Hill Thomson trans. (1883). *Discourses on the First Decade of Titus Livius*. London: Kegan Paul, Trench and Co.

Machiavelli, Niccolò; William K. Marriot trans. (1908). *The Prince*. London: J.M. Dent.

Machiavelli, Niccolò; Robert Adams trans. (1977). *The Prince*. New York, NY: Norton.

Major, John S., Sarah Queen, Andrew Meyer and Harold Roth. (2010). *The Huainanzi: A Guide to the Theory and Practice of Government in Early Han China, by Liu An, King of Huainan*. New York: Columbia University Press.

Mao Tse Tung (Mao Zedong). (1967). *Selected Works of Mao Tse-tung*, 5 volumes. Peking: Foreign Languages Press.

Marsilius of Padua, see Padua, Marsilius of.

Marx, Karl; N.I. Stone trans. (1904). *A Contribution to the Critique of Political Economy*. Chicago, IL: Charles H. Kerr.

Marx, Karl; Daniel De Leon trans. (1907). *The Eighteenth Brumaire of Louis Napoleon*. Chicago, IL: Charles H. Kerr.

Marx, Karl. (1970). "Critique of the Gotha Program," in *Marx/Engels Selected Works*, vol. 3. Moscow: Progress Publishers: 13–30.

Maududi, Sayyid A'bul A'la; Khurshid Ahmad trans./ed. (1955). *The Islamic Law and Constitution*. Lahore: Islamic Publications.

Maududi, Sayyid A'bul A'la; Khurram Murad trans. (1960). *Towards Understanding Islam*. Lahore: Islamic Publications.

Mazzini, Joseph. (1907). *The Duties of Man and Other Essays*. London: J.M. Dent and Sons.

McRae, John R. trans. (2000). *The Platform Sutra of the Sixth Patriarch*. Berkeley, CA: Numata Center for Buddhist Translation and Research.

Menczer, Bela. (1962). *Catholic Political Thought 1789–1848*. Notre Dame, IN: University of Notre Dame Press: 59–76.
Mengzi (Mencius); D.C. Lau trans. (1970). *Mencius*. Harmondsworth: Penguin.
Mengzi (Mencius); Bryan W. Van Norden trans. (2008). *Mengzi: With Selections from Traditional Commentaries*. Cambridge, MA: Hackett Publishing Company.
Mernissi, Fatema. (1975). *Beyond the Veil: Male–Female Dynamics in a Muslim Society*. Cambridge, MA: Schenkman.
Mernissi, Fatema; Mary Jo Lakeland trans. (1991). *The Veil and the Male Elite: A Feminist Interpretation of Women's Right in Islam*. New York, NY: Basic Books.
Meynard, Thierry S.J. trans./ed. (2011). *Confucius Sinarum Philosophus (1687): The First Translation of the Confucian Classics*. Roma: Institutum Historicum Societatis Iesu.
Mill, James. (1825). *Essays on Government, Jurisprudence, Liberty of the Press and the Law of Nations*. London: J. Innes.
Mill, John Stuart and Harriet Hardy Taylor Mill; Alice S. Rossi ed. (1970). *Essays on Sex Equality by John Stuart Mill and Harriet Hardy Taylor Mill*. Chicago, IL: University of Chicago Press.
Mill, John Stuart. (1859/2001). *On Liberty*. Kitchener, Ontario: Batoche Books Limited.
Mo Di; Ian Johnston trans. (2010). *The Mozi: A Complete Translation*. New York, NY: Columbia University Press.
Montague, Lady Mary Wortley. (1764). *Letters: Written During Her Travels in Europe, Asia and Africa to Persons of Distinction, Men of Letters, etc. in Different Parts of Europe*. London: T. Becket and P. A. De Hondt.
Montesquieu; Melvin Richter trans. (1977). *The Political Theory of Montesquieu*. Cambridge: Cambridge University Press.
Morgan, Evan. (1933). *Tao – The Great Luminant: Essays from Huai Nan Tzu. With Introductory Articles, Notes, Analyses*. Shanghai: Kelly and Walsh.
Motoori Norinaga; John S. Brownlee trans. (1988). "The Jeweled Comb-Box: Motoori Norinaga's Tamakushige," *Monumenta Nipponica*, 43(1): 35–44.
Motoori Norinaga; Ann Wehmeyer trans. (1997). *Kojiki-den: Book 1*. Ithaca, NY: Cornell University Press.
Mou Zongsan; Esther C. Su trans. (2015). *Nineteen Lectures on Chinese Philosophy: A Brief Outline of Chinese Philosophy and the Issues It Entails*. San Jose, CA: Foundation for the Study of Chinese Philosophy and Culture.

Mutiso, Gideon-Cyrus M. and S.W. Rohio eds. (1975). *Readings in African Political Thought*. London: Heinemann Educational.

Najita, Tetsuo trans./ed. (1998). *Tokugawa Political Writings*. Cambridge: Cambridge University Press.

Niane, D.T. (2006). *Sundiata – An Epic of Old Mali*, 2nd edn. Harlow: Longman-Pearson.

Nicholas of Cusa, see Cusa, Nicholas of.

Nietzsche, Friedrich; Walter Kaufmann trans./ed. (1954). *The Portable Nietzsche*. New York, NY: Viking Press.

Nietzsche, Friedrich; R.J. Hollingdale trans./ed. (1977). *The Nietzsche Reader*. Harmondsworth: Penguin Books.

Nikam, N.A. and Richard McKeon trans./ed. (1959). *The Edicts of Asoka*. Chicago, IL: University of Chicago Press.

Nishida Kitarō; Masao Abe and Christopher Ives trans. (1992). *An Inquiry into the Good*. New Haven, CT: Yale University Press.

Nishida Kitarō; John W.M. Krummel and Shigenori Nagatomo trans. (2012). "Basho," in John W.M. Krummel and Shigenori Nagatomo eds, *Place and Dialectic: Two Essays by Nishida Kitarō*. Oxford: Oxford University Press: 49–102.

Nishitani Keiji (西谷啓治). (1943). *Sekai Kan to Kokka Kan* (世界観と国家観). Tokyo: Kōbundō (東京：弘文堂書房).

Nkrumah, Kwame. (1966). *Neo-colonialism: The Last Stage of Imperialism*. New York, NY: International Publishers.

Nozick, Robert. (1974). *Anarchy, State, and Utopia*. New York, NY: Basic Books.

Ockham, William of; John Kilcullen trans. and Arthur S. McGrade ed. (1992). *William of Ockham: A Short Discourse on Tyrannical Government*. Cambridge: Cambridge University Press.

Ockham, William of; John Kilcullen trans. and Arthur S. McGrade ed. (1995). *William of Ockham: "A Letter to the Friars Minor" and Other Writings*. Cambridge: Cambridge University Press.

O'Flaherty, Wendy Doniger trans. (1991). *Laws of Manu*. Harmondsworth: Penguin.

Ogyū Sorai; Lidin, Olof G trans. (1970). *Ogyū Sorai: Distinguishing the Way (Bendō)*. Tokyo: Sophia University Press.

Ogyū Sorai; Olof G. Lidin trans. (1999). *Discourse on Government (Seidan)*. Wiesbaden: Harrassowitz Verlag.

Ogyū Sorai; John A. Tucker trans. (2006). *Ogyū Sorai's Philosophical Masterworks: The Bendô and Benmei*. Honolulu, HI: University of Hawaii Press.

Okin, Susan Moller. (1989). *Justice, Gender and the Family*. New York, NY: Basic Books.

Olivelle, Patrick trans. (2008). *Upanisads*. Oxford: Oxford University Press.
Ōshiō Heihachirō (大塩平八郎); Yoshida Kōhei trans. (吉田公平訳). (1998). *Senshindō*, 2 volumes (洗心洞箚記 上下). Tokyo: Tachibana Publishing (東京: たちばな出版).
Ōsugi Sakae; Byron K. Marshall trans. (1992). *The Autobiography of Osugi Sakae*. Berkeley, CA: University of California Press.
Ōsugi Sakae (大杉栄). (1996). *Ōsugi Sakae Hyōron Shū* (大杉栄評論集). Tokyo: Iwanami Shoten (東京: 岩波書店).
Osugi Sakae; Michael Schauerte trans. (2014). *My Escapes from Japan*. Tokyo: Doyosha.
Owen, Robert; V.A.C. Gatrell ed. (1969). *A New View of Society and Report to the County of Lanark*. Harmondsworth: Penguin.
Padua, Marsilius of; Annabel Brett trans. (2005). *Marsilius of Padua: The Defender of the Peace*. Cambridge: Cambridge University Press.
Paul, Diana Y. and John R. McRae trans. (2004). *The Sutra of Queen Srimala of the Lion's Roar: The Vimalakirti Sutra*. Honolulu, HI: University of Hawaii Press.
Pizan, Christine de; Kate Langdon Forhan trans./ed. (1994). *The Book of the Body Politic*. Cambridge: Cambridge University Press.
Plato; Benjamin Jowett trans. (1892). *The Dialogues of Plato*, 5 volumes, 3rd edn. Oxford: Oxford University Press.
Plotinus; A.H. Armstrong trans. (1966). *Plotinus*, vol. I, 2nd edn. Cambridge: Harvard University Press.
Proudhon, Pierre-Joseph. (1863). *Du principe fédératif et de la nécessité de reconstituer le parti de la revolution*. Paris: E. Dentu.
Proudhon, Pierre-Joseph. (1876). *Works of P.J. Proudhon, Vol. 1: "What is Property?"* Princeton, NJ: Benjamin R. Tucker.
Qaddafi, Muammar, see Gaddafi, Muammar.
Quesnay, François (1888). *Œuvres économiques et philosophiques de F. Quesnay, fondateur du système physiocratique*. Paris: Peelman and Co.
Quesnay, François; Lewis A. Maverick trans. (1946). *China: A Model for Europe*. San Antonio, TX: Paul Anderson.
Qutb, Sayyid. (2005). *Milestones*. SIME (Studies in Islam and the Middle East) Journal, e-publishing.
Rawls, John. (1971). *A Theory of Justice*. Cambridge, MA: Belknap.
Reiss, H.S. trans. (1955). *The Political Thought of the German Romantics: 1793–1815*. Oxford: Basil Blackwell.
Rennyo; Ann T. Rogers and Minor L. Rogers trans. (1996). *Rennyo Shōnin Ofumi: The Letters of Rennyo*. Berkeley, CA: Numata Center for Buddhist Translation and Research.
Rhys Davids, T.W. trans. (1881). *Buddhist Suttas*. Oxford: Oxford University Press.

Rhys Davids, T.W. and Hermann Oldenberg trans. (1881). *Vinaya Texts*, 3 volumes. Oxford: Clarendon Press.

Rhys Davids, Caroline R. and F.L. Woodward trans. (1950–1965). *The Book of the Kindred Sayings (Sanyutta Nikaya)*, 5 volumes. Bristol: Pali Text Society.

Rousseau, Jean-Jacques; Donald A. Cress trans./ed. (2011). *Jean-Jacques Rousseau: The Basic Political Writings*, 2nd edn. Indianapolis, IN: Hackett Publishing.

Roy, Manabendra Nath (M.N.). (1987–1988). *Selected Works of M.N. Roy*, 2 volumes. Oxford: Oxford University Press.

Roy, Raja Rammohun; Jogendra Chunder ed. (1901). *The English Works of Raja Rammohun Roy*, 3 volumes. Calcutta: S. Roy.

Rushd, ibn; Ralph Lerner trans. (2005). *Averroes on Plato's Republic*. Ithaca, NY: Cornell University Press.

Sahoo, Sarojini. (2015). "Femininity and the Feminine Mystique," *Journal of East and West Thought*, 4(5): 67–76.

Saichō (Dengyō Daishi); Shōshin Ichishima ed. (2013). *The First Mahāyāna Precepts Platform at Mt. Hiei*. Tokyo: Tendai Buddhist Sect Overseas Charitable Foundation. http://www.tendai.or.jp/english/image/pdf/english_pamphlet.pdf (accessed June 27, 2017).

Saint-Simon, Claude-Henri de. (1817). *L'industrie ou Discussions politiques, morales et philosophique*. Tome 2. Paris: Bureau d'Administration.

Saint-Simon, Claude-Henri de. (1823). *Catechisme des industriels*. Paris: de Sétier.

Samguk Yusa (三國遺事). http://www.buddhist-canon.com/history/T49N2039.htm (accessed November 23, 2017).

Samguk Sagi (三國史記). http://ctext.org/wiki.pl?if=en&res=777507 (accessed November 23, 2017).

Schmitt, Carl; George Schwab trans. (2005). *Political Theology: Four Chapters on the Concept of Sovereignty*. Chicago, IL: University of Chicago Press.

Schmitt, Carl; George Schwab trans. (2007). *Concept of the Political*. Chicago, IL; University of Chicago Press.

Shari'ati, Ali; Hamid Algar trans. (1979). *On the Sociology of Islam*. Berkeley, CA: Mizan Press.

Shari'ati, Ali; R. Campbell trans. (1980). *Marxism and Other Western Fallacies*. Berkeley, CA: Mizan Press.

Shati', Bint al; Matti Moosa and D. Nicholas Ranson trans. (1971). *The Wives of the Prophet*. Lahore: Sh. Muhammad Ashraf.

Shaw, George Bernard. (1900). *Fabianism and the Empire*. London: Grant Richards.

Shenzi, Eirik Lang Harris trans. (2016). *The Shenzi Fragments: A Philosophical Analysis and Translation*. New York, NY: Columbia University Press.

Shenzi, M. Thompson ed. (1979). *The Shen Tzu Fragments.* Oxford: Oxford University.
Sieyès, Abbé Emmanuel Joseph. (1987). "What is the Third Estate?" in Keith M. Baker ed., *Readings in Western Civilization, Volume 7: The Old Regime and the French Revolution.* Chicago, IL: University of Chicago Press: Chapter 14.
Smith, Adam. (1945). *An Inquiry Into the Nature and Causes of the Wealth of Nations.* Woodstock Ontario: Devoted Publishing.
Somadeva; Oscar Botto trans. (1962). *Il Nitivakyamrta di Somadeva Suri.* Torino: Universita di Torino, Faculta di Lettere e Filosofia, Fodanzione Parini-Chirio.
Spencer, Herbert. (1868). *Social Statics, or, The Conditions Essential to Human Happiness Specified, and the First of Them Developed.* London: Williams and Norgate.
Spencer, Herbert. (1894). *The Principles of Biology,* 2 volumes. London: Williams and Norgate.
Spencer, Herbert. (1969). *The Man versus the State with Four Essays on Politics and Society.* Harmondsworth: Penguin Books.
Spivak, Gayatri Chakravorty. (1988). "Can The Subaltern Speak?" in Cary Nelson and Lawrence Grossberg eds, *Marxism and the Interpretation of Culture.* Basingstoke: Macmillan: 271–313.
Stirner, Max; Steven Tracy Byington trans. and David Leopold ed. (1995). *Stirner: The Ego and its Own.* Cambridge: Cambridge University Press.
Sun Yat-sen; Frank W. Price trans. (1927). *San min chu i, The Three Principles of the People.* Shanghai: China Committee, Institute of Pacific Relations.
Sutta Central: Early Buddhist texts, translations, and parallels: https://suttacentral.net/ (accessed November 23, 2017).
Suzuki Shigetaka (鈴木成高). (1941). *Rekishiteki Kokka no Rinen* (歷史的国家の理念). Tokyo: Kōbundō (東京：弘文堂書房).
Tagore, Rabindranath. (1918). *Nationalism.* London: MacMillan and Co.
Tahtawi, Rafi' Rifa'a Al; Daniel L. Newman trans. (2002). *An Imam in Paris: Al-Tahtawi's Visit to France (1826–31).* London: Saqi Books.
Tanabe Hajime (田邊元). (1946). *Seiji Tetsugaku no Kyūmu* (政治哲學の急務). Tokyo: Iwanami Shoten (東京：岩波書店).
Tanabe Hajime (田邊元). (1947). *Shu no Ronri no Benshōhō* (種の論理の辯證法). Osaka: Akitaya (大阪：秋田屋).
Tanabe Hajime; David Dilworth and Taira Sato trans. (1969). "The Logic of The Species as Dialectics," *Monumenta Nipponica,* 24(3): 273–288.
Tanabe Hajime; Takeuchi Yoshinori, Valdo Viglielmo and James W. Heisig trans. (1986). *Philosophy as Metanoetics.* Berkeley, CA: University of California Press.

Taymiyyah, ibn; Umar Farrukh trans. (2006). *The Political Shariyah on Reforming the Ruler and the Ruled.* Dijon: Dar ul Fiqh.

Thompson, William, Anna Wheeler, Richard Taylor and John Stuart Mill. (1825). *Appeal of one Half of the Human Race, Women, against the Pretensions of the other Half, Men.* London: Longman, Hurst, Rees, Orme, Brown and Green, and Wheatley and Adlard.

Tolstoy, Leo; Leo Wiener trans./ed. (1904). *The Complete Works of Count Tolstoy.* Boston: D. Estes and Company.

Tosaka Jun; Ken C. Kawashima, Fabian Schaefer, Robert Stolz eds. (2013). *Tosaka Jun: A Critical Reader.* Ithaca, NY: Cornell University Press.

Tosaka Jun; Kenn Nakata Steffensen trans. (2016). "Translation of Tosaka Jun's 'The Philosophy of the Kyoto School'," *Comparative and Continental Philosophy*, 8(1): 53–71.

Trotsky, Leon; R.T.C. trans. (1964). *The Essential Trotsky.* London: Unwin Books.

Trotsky, Leon; George Breitman. (1969–1975). *Writings of Leon Trotsky*, 14 volumes. New York, NY: Pathfinder Press.

Tu, Weiming. (2008). "Rooted in Humanity, Extended to Heaven: The 'Anthropocosmic' Vision in Confucian Thought," *Harvard Divinity Bulletin*, 36(2), 58–68.

Tu, Weiming. (2009). "Confucian Humanism as a Spiritual Resource for Global Ethics," *Peace and Conflict Studies*, 16(1), 1–8.

Tu, Weiming. (2012). "A Spiritual Turn in Philosophy: Rethinking the Global Significance of Confucian Humanism," *Journal of Philosophical Research*, 37, 389–401.

Tu, Weiming. (2014). "The Context of Dialogue: Globalization and Diversity," in Molefi Kete Asante, Yoshitaka Miike and Jing Yin eds., *The Global Intercultural Communication Reader*, 2nd edn. New York, NY: Routledge: 496–514.

Vasubandhu; Leo M. Pruden trans. from French translation of Louis de La Vallée Poussin. (1988). *Abhidhramakośabhāsyam*, vol. 2. Berkeley, CA: Asian Humanities Press.

Vico, Giambattista; Thomas G. Bergin and Max H. Fisch trans. (1968). *The New Science of Giambattista Vico: Revised Translation of the Third Edition (1744).* Ithaca, NY: Cornell University Press.

Voltaire; Jacqueline Marchand ed. (1962). *Essai sur les moeurs et l'esprit des nations.* Paris: Editions Sociales.

Vyasa; Kisari Mohan Ganguli trans. (1883–1896). *The Mahabharata.* Calcutta: Bharata Press.

Vyasa; James L. Fitzgerald trans. (2004). *The Mahabharata*, vol. 7. Chicago, IL: University of Chicago Press.

Waley, Arthur trans. (1946). *Book of Songs*. London: George Allen & Unwin.
Wali-Allah, Shah; Al-Ghazzali, Muhammad. (2008). *The Socio-Political Thought of Shah Wali Allah*. New Delhi: Adam Publishers & Distributors.
Wang Bi; Richard John Lynn trans. (1994). *The Classic of Changes: A New Translation of the I Ching as Interpreted by Wang Bi*. New York, NY: Columbia University Press.
Wang Bi; Richard John Lynn trans. (1999). *The Classic of the Way and Virtue: A New Translation of the Tao-te Ching of Laozi as Interpreted by Wang Bi*. New York, NY: Columbia University Press.
Wang, Robin R. ed. (2003). *Images of Women in Chinese Thought and Culture: Writings from the Pre-Qin Period through the Song Dynasty*. Indianapolis, IN: Hackett Publishing Company.
Waterfield, Robin trans. (2009). *The First Philosophers: The Presocratics and Sophists*. Oxford: Oxford University Press.
Watson, Burton trans. (1963). *Basic Writings of Mo Tzu, Hsün Tzu and Han Fei Tzu*. New York, NY: Columbia University Press.
Watsuji Tetsurō (和辻哲郎). (1934). *Ningen no Gaku toshite Rinigaku* (人間の學としての倫理學). Tokyo: Iwanami Shoten (東京：岩波書店).
Watsuji Tetsurō; Yamamoto Seisaku and Robert E. Carter trans. (1996). *Watsuji Tetsurō's Rinrigaku: Ethics in Japan*. Albany, NY: State University of New York Press.
Wayman, Alex and Hideko Wayman trans. (1974). *The Lion's Roar of Queen Srīmālā*. New York, NY: Columbia University Press.
William of Ockham, see Ockham, William of.
Winstanley, Gerrard; Christopher Hill ed. (1973). *Law of Freedom and Other Writings*. Harmondsworth: Penguin Books.
Wootton, David ed. (2003). *The Essential Federalist and Anti-Federalist Papers*. Indianapolis, IN: Hackett Publishing Company.
X, Malcolm and Alex Haley. (1966). *The Autobiography of Malcolm X*. London: Hutchinson.
Xunzi; Eric L. Hutton trans. (2014). *Xunzi: The Complete Text*. Princeton, NJ: Princeton University Press.
Xunzi; John Knoblock trans. (1988–1994). *Xunzi: A Translation and Study of the Complete Works*. 3 volumes. Stanford, CA: Stanford University Press.
Yamashita Etsuko (山下悦子). (1988). *Nihon josei kaihō shisō no kigen: Posuto feminizumu shiron* (日本女性解放思想の起源：ポストフェミニズム試論). Tokyo: Kaimeisha (東京：海鳴社).
Yampolsky, Philip B. trans. (1967). *The Platform Sutra of the Sixth Patriarch*. New York, NY: Columbia University Press.
Zhuangzi; Burton Watson trans. (1968). *The Complete Works of Chuang Tzŭ*. New York, NY: Columbia University Press.

Zhuangzi; A.C. Graham trans. (1981). *Chuang-tzŭ: The Seven Inner Chapters and Other Writings from the Book Chuang-tzŭ*. London: Allen & Unwin.
Zhuangzi; Feng Youlan (Yu-lan) trans. (2016). *Chuang Tzŭ: A New Selected Translation with an Exposition of the Philosophy of Kuo Hsiang (Guo Xiang)*. Heidelberg: Springer.

SECONDARY SOURCES

Abbott, Nabia. (1942). "Women and the State in Early Islam," *Journal of Near Eastern Studies*, 1(1): 106–126.
Adelman, Jeremy. (2007). "Between Order and Liberty: Juan Bautista Alberdi and the Intellectual Origins of Argentine Constitutionalism," *Latin American Research Review*, 42(2): 86–110.
Afary, Janet and Kevin Anderson. (2005). *Foucault and the Iranian Revolution: Gender and the Seductions of Islamism*. Chicago, IL: University of Chicago Press.
Akhavi, Shahrough. (1975). "Egypt's Socialism and Marxist Thought Some Preliminary Observations on Social Theory and Metaphysics," *Comparative Studies in Society and History*, 17(2): 190–211.
Allen, William B. (2009). *Rethinking Uncle Tom: The Political Thought of Harriet Beecher Stowe*. New York: Rowman & Littlefield.
Almond, Ian. (2007). *The New Orientalists: Postmodern Representations of Islam from Foucault to Baudrillard*. London: I.B. Tauris.
Alzate, Elissa B. (2014). "From Individual to Citizen: Enhancing the Bonds of Citizenship Through Religion in Locke's Political Theory," *Polity*, 46(2): 211–232.
Ames, Roger T. (1983). *The Art of Rulership: A Study in Ancient Chinese Political Thought*. Honolulu, HI: University of Hawaii Press.
Amstutz, Galen. (1998). "Shin Buddhism and Protestant Analogies with Christianity in the West," *Comparative Studies in Society and History*, 40(4): 724–747.
Analayo. (2011). "Brahmā's Invitation the Ariyapariyesana-sutta and its Madhyama-agama Parallel," *Journal of the Oxford Centre for Buddhist Studies*, 1: 12–38.
Ansell-Pearson, Keith. (1994). *An Introduction to Nietzsche as a Political Thinker: The Perfect Nihilist*. Cambridge: Cambridge University Press.
Arisaka, Yoko. (1997). "Beyond East and West: Nishida's Universalism and Postcolonial Critique," *The Review of Politics*, 59(3): 541–560.
Arjomand, Said Amir. (1994). "'Abd Allah ibn al-Muqaffa' and the 'Abbasid Revolution'," *Iranian Studies*, 27(1/4): 9–36.

Aysha, Emad El-Din. (2006). "Foucault's Iran and Islamic Identity Politics Beyond Civilization Clashes, External and Internal," *International Studies Perspectives*, 7: 377–394.
Baldry, H.C. (1959). "Zeno's Ideal State," *The Journal of Hellenic Studies*, 79: 3–15.
Bareau, André. (1955). *Les premiers conciles bouddhiques*. Paris: Presses Universitaires de France.
Barnes, Archie, Don Starr, and Graham Ormerod. (2009). *Du's Handbook of Classical Chinese Grammar*. London: Alcuin Press.
Barnes, Gina L. (2014). "A Hypothesis for Early Kofun Rulership," *Japan Review*, 27: 3–29.
Baron, Hans. (1955). *The Crisis of the Early Italian Renaissance: Civic Humanism and Republican Liberty in an Age of Classicism and Tyranny*. Princeton, NJ: Princeton University Press.
Bates, Jonathan. (2008). *The Genius of Shakespeare*. London: Picador.
Beaulieu, Alain. (2010). "Towards a Liberal Utopia: The Connection between Foucault's Reporting on the Iranian Revolution and the Ethical Turn," *Philosophy and Social Criticism*, 36(7): 801–818.
Bellah, Robert and Hans Joas. (2012). *The Axial Age and Its Consequences*. Cambridge, MA: Harvard University Press.
Bender, Ross. (1979). "The Hachiman Cult and the Dokyo Incident," *Monumenta Nipponica*, 34(2): 125–153.
Bentwich, Norman. (1910). *Philo-Judaeus of Alexandria*. Philadelphia, PA: The Jewish Publication Society of America.
Best, Jr., Edward E. (1970). "Cicero, Livy and Educated Roman Women," *The Classical Journal*, 65(5): 199–204.
Bevir, Mark. (1992). "The Errors of Linguistic Contextualism," *History and Theory*, 31(3): 276–298.
Bhopal, Abida Sultaan of. (1980). "The Begums of Bhopal," *History Today*, 30: 30–35.
Billioud, Sébastien. (2011). *Thinking Through Confucian Modernity: A Study of Mou Zongsan's Moral Metaphysics*. Leiden: Brill.
Black, Anthony. (2008). "The 'Axial Age': What was it and what does it signify," *The Review of Politics*, 70(1): 23–39.
Blanchette, I. and K. Dunbar. (2000). "How Analogies are Generated: The Roles of Structural versus Superficial Similarity," *Memory and Cognition*, 28(1): 108–124.
Bluhm, William T., Neil Wintfeld and Stuart H. Teger. (1980). "Locke's Idea of God: Rational Truth or Political Myth?" *The Journal of Politics*, 42(2): 414–438.
Bodart-Bailey, Beatrice. (1993). "The Persecution of Confucianism in Early Tokugawa Japan," *Monumenta Nipponica*, 48(3): 293–314.

Boesche, Roger. (1990). "Fearing Monarchs and Merchants: Montesquieu's Two Theories of Despotism," *The Western Political Quarterly*, 43(4): 741–761.

Bourdieu, P. and L.J.D. Wacquant eds. (1992). *An Invitation to Reflexive Sociology*. Cambridge: Polity Press.

Brubaker, Stanley C. (2012). "Coming into One's Own: John Locke's Theory of Property, God, and Politics," *The Review of Politics*, 74: 207–232.

Bruce St John, Ronald. (1983). "The Ideology of Muammar al-Qadhdhafi: Theory and Practice," *International Journal of Middle East Studies*, 15(4): 471–490.

Bruni, Leonardo. (1996). "Oration on the Death of Nanni Strozzi (1428)," in P. Viti ed., *Opere Letterarie e Politiche*, Torino: Utet: 703–749.

Burson, Jeffrey D. (2015). "Unlikely Tales of Fo and Ignatius Rethinking the Radical Enlightenment," *French Historical Studies*, 38(3): 391–420.

Burtt, Edwin A. (1925). *The Metaphysical Foundations of Modern Physical Science: A Historical and Critical Essay*. London: Kegan Paul, Trench, Trubner.

Callanan, Keegan. (2014). "Liberal Constitutionalism and Political Particularism in Montesquieu's 'The Spirit of the Laws'," *Political Research Quarterly*, 67(3): 589–602.

Cestari, Matteo. (2010). "Between Emptiness and Absolute Nothingness: Reflections on Negation in Nishida and Buddhism," in James Heisig and Rein Raud eds, *Frontiers of Japanese Philosophy, Vol. 7: Classical Japanese Philosophy*. Nagoya: Nanzan Institute of Religion and Culture: 320–346.

Chan, N. Serina. (2011). *The Thought of Mou Zongsan*. Leiden: Brill.

Chan, Wing-tsit. (1979). "Introduction," in Ariane Rump trans., *Commentary on the Lao Tzu by Wang Pi*. Honolulu, HI: University of Hawaii Press.

Chandra, Bipan. (1987). *India's Struggle for Independence*. New Delhi: Penguin Books.

Chatterjee, Indrani. (2016). "Women Monastic Commerce and Coverture in Eastern India Circa 1600–1800," *Modern Asian Studies*, 50(1): 175–216.

Chattopadhyaya, Debiprasad. (1968). *Lōkayata: A Study in Ancient Indian Materialism*. New Delhi: People's Publishing House.

Chen, Jinhua. (2003). "More than a Philosopher: Fazang (643–712) as a Politician and Miracle Worker," *History of Religions*, 42(4): 320–358.

Chroust, Anton-Hermann. (1965). "The Ideal Polity of the Early Stoics: Zeno's 'Republic'," *The Review of Politics*, 27(2): 173–183.

Clarke, Michelle Tolman. (2005). "On the Woman Question in Machiavelli," *The Review of Politics*, 67(2): 229–255.

Colish, Marcia L. (1978). "Cicero's De Officiis and Machiavelli's Prince," *The Sixteenth Century Journal*, 9(4): 80–93.

Collier, David and James E. Mahon, Jr. (1993). "'Conceptual Stretching' Revisited: Adapting Categories in Comparative Analysis," *The American Political Science Review*, 87(4): 845–855.
Conway, Christopher. (2015). "Gender Iconoclasm in Echeverria's La cautiva and the Captivity Paintings of Juan Manuel Blanes," *Decimononica*, 12(1): 116–133.
Conze, Edward. (1963). "Buddhist Philosophy and Its European Parallels," *Philosophy East and West*, 13(1): 9–23.
Conze, Edward. (1963). "Spurious Parallels to Buddhist Philosophy," *Philosophy East and West*, 13(2): 105–115.
Cook, Daniel J. (2015). "Leibniz, China, and the Problem of Pagan Wisdom," *Philosophy East and West*, 65(3): 936–947.
Cornell, Laurel L. (1990). "Peasant Women and Divorce in Preindustrial Japan," *Signs*, 15(4): 710–732.
Cousins, Lance. (2013). "The Early Development of Buddhist Language and Literature in India," *Journal of the Oxford Centre for Buddhist Studies*, 5: 89–135.
Creel, Herrlee G. (1974). *Shen Pu-Hai: A Chinese Political Philosopher of the Fourth Century BC*. Chicago, IL: University of Chicago Press.
Crone, Patricia. (1987). "Did al-Ghazali Write Mirror for Princes? The Authorship of the Nasihat al Mulūk," *Jerusalem Studies in Arabic and Islam*, 9: 167–191.
Crowe, Benjamin. (2010). "Faith and Value: Heinrich Rickert's Theory of Religion," *Journal of the History of Ideas*, 71(4): 617–636.
Cua, A.S. (1982). *The Unity of Knowledge and Action: A Study of Wang Yang Ming's Moral Psychology*. Honolulu, HI: University of Hawaii Press.
Dalal, Urvashi. (2015). "Femininity, State and Cultural Space in Eighteenth Century India," *The Medieval History Journal*, 18(1): 120–165.
Davidson, Donald. (2001). *Inquiries into Truth and Interpretation*. Oxford: Oxford University Press.
Davies, Catherine. (2005). "Colonial Dependence and Sexual Difference: Reading for Gender in the Writing of Simón Bolívar (1783–1830)," *Feminist Review*, 79: 5–19.
De Ville, Jacques. (2008). "Sovereignty without Sovereignty: Derrida's Declarations of Independence," *Law and Critique*, 19: 87–114.
Detlefsen, Karen. (2012). "Margaret Cavendish and Thomas Hobbes on Freedom, Education, and Women," in Nancy J. Hirschmann and Joanne H. Wright eds, *Feminist Interpretations of Thomas Hobbes*. University Park, PA: Pennsylvania State University Press: 149–168.
Deuchler, Martina. (1995). *The Confucian Transformation of Korea*. Cambridge, MA: Harvard University Press.

Dietz, Mary. (2003). "Current Controversies in Feminist Theory," *Annual Review of Political Science*, 6: 399–431.

Dimberg, Ronald G. (1974). *The Sage and Society: The Life and Thought of Ho Hsin-yin*. Honolulu, HI: University of Hawaii Press.

Ding, John Zijiang. (2011). "Self-Transformation and Moral Universalism: A Comparison of Wang Yangming and Schleiermacher," *Journal of East-West Thought*, 1(1): 79–104.

Dirlik, Arif. (1985). "The New Culture Movement Revisited: Anarchism and the Idea of Social Revolution in New Culture Thinking," *Modern China*, 11(3): 251–300.

Douglass, E. Jane Dempsey. (1984). "Christian Freedom: What Calvin Learned at the School of Women," *Church History*, 53(2): 155–173.

Drury, Shadia B. (1985). "The Esoteric Philosophy of Leo Strauss," *Political Theory*, 13(3): 315–337.

Duschinsky, Robbie. (2006). "'The First Great Insurrection against Global Systems' – Foucault's Writings on the Iranian Revolution," *European Journal of Social Theory*, 9(4): 547–558.

Eisenstadt, Shmuel N. (2000). "Multiple Modernities," *Daedalus*, 129(1): 1–29.

Elshakry, Marwa. (2010). "When Science Became Western: Historiographical Reflections," *Isis*, 101(1): 98–109.

Elstein, David. (2014). *Democracy in Contemporary Confucian Philosophy*. London: Routledge.

Engel, David M. (2003). "Women's Role in the Home and the State: Stoic Theory Reconsidered," *Harvard Studies in Classical Philology*, 101: 267–288.

Faye, Emmanuel; Michael B. Smith trans. (2009). *Heidegger: The Introduction of Nazism into Philosophy in Light of the Unpublished Seminars of 1933–1935*. New Haven, CT: Yale University Press.

Federman, Asaf. (2009). "Literal Means and Hidden Meanings: A New Analysis of Skillful Means," *Philosophy East and West*, 59(2): 125–41.

Finocchiaro, Maurice A. (1981). "Fallacies and the Evaluation of Reasoning," *American Philosophical Quarterly*, 18(1): 13–22.

Firro, Tarikk. (2013). "The Political Context of Early Wahhabi Discourse of Takfir," *Middle Eastern Studies*, 49(5): 770–789.

Fitzpatrick, Matthew P. (2008). *Liberal Imperialism in Germany: Expansionism and Nationalism, 1848–1884*. Oxford: Berghahn Books.

Frazer, Michael. (2006). "Esotericism Ancient and Modern Strauss versus Straussianism on Political-Philosophical Writing," *Political Theory*, 34(1): 33–61.

Fredericks, James. (1990). "Philosophy as Metanoetics," in Taitetsu Unno and James W. Heisig eds, *The Religious Philosophy of Tanabe Hajime:*

The Metanoetic Imperative. Fremont, CA: Asian Humanities Press: 59–60.

Fukuda Shigeru. (1995). "On the Position of Nie Shuangjiang (聶雙江) and Luo Nian'an (羅念庵) in the Wang-yangming School (陽明學派)," *Journal of the Bulletin of the Sinological Society of Japan*, 47: 133–148.

Fung, Yu-Lan; Derk Bodde trans./ed. (1948). *A Short History of Chinese Philosophy*. New York: Free Press.

Fung, Yu-Lan; Derk Bodde trans./ed. (1983). *History of Chinese Philosophy, Volume 2: The Period of Classical Learning from the Second Century BC to the Twentieth Century AD*. Princeton, NJ: Princeton University Press.

Gadamer, Hans-Georg. (1989). *Truth and Method*, 2nd edn. London: Sheed and Ward.

Gethmann-Siefert, Annemarie and Richard Taft. (1989). "Heidegger and Hölderlin: The Over-Usage of 'Poets in an Impoverished Time'," *Research in Phenomenology*, 19(1): 59–88.

Ghoshal, U.N. (1959). *A History of Indian Political Ideas: The Ancient Period and the Period of Transition to the Middle Ages*. Madras: Oxford University Press.

Giles, James. (1993). "The No-Self Theory: Hume, Buddhism, and Personal Identity," *Philosophy East and West*, 43(2): 175–200.

Gillespie, Michael. (1987). "Martin Heidegger," in L. Strauss and J. Cropsey eds, *History of Political Philosophy*. Chicago, IL: University of Chicago Press: 904.

Glucklich, Ariel. (1988). "The Royal Scepter ('Daṇḍa') as Legal Punishment and Sacred Symbol," *History of Religions*, 28(2): 97–122.

Goldin, Paul R. (2005). *After Confucius: Studies in Early Chinese Philosophy*. Honolulu, HI: University of Hawaii Press.

Goldman, Robert. (1977). *Gods, Priests and Warriors: The Bhrgus of the Mahabharata*. New York, NY: Columbia University Press.

Goldstone, Robert L. (1994). "The Role of Similarity in Categorization," *Cognition*, 52(2): 125–157.

Gombrich, Richard. (1996). *How Buddhism Began: The Conditioned Genesis of the Early Teachings*. London: The Athlone Press.

Gopnik, Alison. (2015). "How an 18th-Century Philosopher Helped Solve My Midlife Crisis: David Hume, the Buddha, and a search for the Eastern roots of the Western Enlightenment," *The Atlantic*, https://www.theatlantic.com/magazine/archive/2015/10/how-david-hume-helped-me-solve-my-midlife-crisis/403195/ (accessed May 22, 2017).

Gordon, Peter E. (2010). *Continental Divide: Heidegger, Cassirer, Davos*. Cambridge, MA: Harvard University Press.

Graham, A.C. (1986). *Studies in Chinese Philosophy and Philosophical Literature*. Singapore: Institute of East Asian Philosophies.

Ha Ki-Rak. (1986). *A History of Korean Anarchist Movement*. Taegu: Anarchist Publishing Company.

Habib, S. Irfan and Dhruv Raina. (1989). "Copernicus, Colombus, Colonialism and the Role of Science in Nineteenth Century India," *Social Scientist*, 17(3/4): 51–66.

Hale, Charles A. (1965). "Jose Maria Luis Mora and the Structure of Mexican Liberalism," *The Hispanic American Historical Review*, 45(2): 196–227.

Hammersley, Rachel. (2013). "Rethinking the Political Thought of James Harrington: Royalism, Republicanism and Democracy," *History of European Ideas*, 39(3): 354–370.

Hankins, James. (2009). "A Mirror for Statesmen: Leonardo Bruni's History of the Florentine People." Unpublished paper, Harvard University. https://dash.harvard.edu/bitstream/handle/1/2958221/BruniHistoryHJ.pdf?sequence=4 (accessed May 20, 2017).

Harootunian, Harry D. (1988). *Things Seen and Unseen: Discourse and Ideology in Tokugawa Nativism*. Chicago, IL: University of Chicago Press.

Hatano Kanae (波多野鼎). (1928). *Shinkantoha Shakaishugi* (新カント派社会主義). Tokyo: Nihon Hyōron Sha (東京：日本評論社).

Heisig, James W. and John C. Maraldo eds. (1995). *Rude Awakenings: Zen, the Kyoto School, and the Question of Nationalism*. Honolulu, HI: University of Hawaii Press.

Heisig, James W. (2001). *The Philosophers of Nothingness: An Essay on the Kyoto School*. Honolulu, HI: University of Hawaii Press.

Herling, B.L. (2006). *The German Gītā: Hermeneutics and Discipline in the German Reception of Indian Thought, 1778–1831*. New York: Routledge.

Hewitt, Nancy A. (1986). "Feminist Friends: Agrarian Quakers and the Emergence of Woman's Rights in America," *Feminist Studies*, 12(1): 27–49.

Hiltebeitel, Alf. (2001). *Rethinking the Mahābhārata: A Reader's Guide to the Education of the Dharma King*. Chicago, IL: The University of Chicago Press.

Hirschman, Albert O. (1970). "The Search for Paradigms as a Hindrance to Understanding," *World Politics*, 22(3): 329–343.

Ho, Norman P. (2010). "'Stare Decisis' in Han China: Dong Zhongshu, the Chunqiu and the Systematization of Law," *Tufts Historical Review*, 3(1): 153–169.

Hobby, Elaine. (1999). "Winstanley, Women and the Family," *Prose Studies*, 22(2): 61–72.

Hollyday, F.B.M. (1970). *Bismarck*. New York: Prentice Hall.

Honig, Bonnie. (1991). "Declarations of Independence: Arendt and Derrida on the Problem of Founding a Republic," *The American Political Science Review*, 85(1): 97–113.

Hooper, W. (1917). "Cicero's Religious Beliefs," *The Classical Journal*, 13(2): 88–95.

Hosseini, Hamid. (1998). "Seeking the Roots of Adam Smith's Division of Labor in Medieval Persia," *History of Political Economy*, 30(4): 653–681.

Hourani, Albert. (1962). *Arabic Thought in a Liberal Age, 1798–1939*. Oxford: Oxford University Press.

Howland, Douglas. (2001). "Translating Liberty in 18th Century Japan," *Journal of the History of Ideas*, 62(1): 161–181.

Hsiao, Kung-chuan; Frederick W. Mote trans. (1979). *History of Chinese Political Thought, Volume 1: From the Beginnings to the Sixth Century AD*. Princeton, NJ: Princeton University Press.

Hwang, Dongyoun. (2016). *Anarchism in Korea: Independence, Transnationalism, and the Question of National Development, 1919–1984*. Albany, NY: State University of New York Press.

Ige, S. (2003). "Rhetoric and the Feminine Character: Cicero's portrayal of Sassia, Clodia and Fulvia," *Akroterion*, 48: 45–57.

Israel, Jonathan. (2007). "Admiration of China and Classical Chinese Thought in the Radical Enlightenment (1685–1740)," *Taiwan Journal of East Asian Studies*, 4(1): 1–25.

Itsuki Hiroyuki (五木寛之). (1994). *Rennyo: Seizoku Guyū no Ningenzō* (蓮如—聖俗具有の人間像). Tokyo: Iwanami Shoten (東京：岩波書店).

Jackson, H.J. (1993). "Coleridge's Women, or Girls, Girls, Girls Are Made To Love," *Studies in Romanticism*, 32(4): 577–600.

Jacobson, N.P. (1969). "The Possibility of Oriental Influence in Hume's Philosophy," *Philosophy East and West*, 19(1): 17–37.

James, C.L.R. (1980). *The Black Jacobins: Toussaint L'Ouverture and the San Domingo Revolution*. London: Allison & Busby.

Jaspers, Karl. (1953). *The Origin and Goal of History*. New Haven, NJ: Yale University Press.

Jordan, Sara and Cary J. Nederman. (2004). "Between Sartori and Skinner: Methodological Problems in the Study of Comparative Political Thought," Annual Meeting of the American Political Science Association (APSA), Chicago, IL.

Jorrin, Miguel and John D. Martz. (1971). *Latin American Political Thought and Ideology*. Chapel Hill, NC: University of North Carolina Press.

Kano, Ayako. (2011). "Backlash, Fight Back, and Backpedaling: Responses to State Feminism in Contemporary Japan," *International Journal of Asian Studies*, 8(1): 41–62.

Keddie, Nikki R. (1998). "The New Religious Politics: Where, When, and

Why Do Fundamentalisms Appear?" *Comparative Studies in Society and History*, 40(4): 696–723.
Kim, Hodong. (2004). *Holy War in China: The Muslim Rebellion and State in Chinese Central Asia, 1864–1877*. Stanford, CA: Stanford University Press.
Kim, Hung-gyu. (2012). "The Rhetoric of Royal Power in Korean. Inscriptions from the Fifth to Seventh Centuries," *Cross Currents: East Asian History and Culture Review*, 2, https://cross-currents.berkeley.edu/sites/default/files/e-journal/articles/final_kim.pdf (accessed November 23, 2017).
Kornicki, P.F., Mara Patessio and G. Rowley. (2010). *The Female as Subject: Reading and Writing in Early Modern Japan*. Ann Arbor, MI: Michigan Monograph Series in Japanese Studies No. 70, Center for Japanese Studies, University of Michigan.
Krause, Sharon. (2011). "Contested Questions, Current Trajectories: Feminism in Political Theory Today," *Politics & Gender*, 7(1): 105–111.
Lai, Yuen Ting. (1985). "The Linking of Spinoza to Chinese Thought by Bayle and Malebranche," *Journal of the History of Philosophy*, 23(2): 151–178.
Lambert, Yves. (1999). "Religion in Modernity as a New Axial Age: Secularization or New Religious Forms?" *Sociology of Religion*, 60(3): 303–333.
Lamotte, Étienne. (1958). *Histoire du bouddhisme indien: Des origines à l'ère Saka*. Louvain: Publications universitaires, Institut orientaliste.
Larrère, Catherine. (2011). "Jean-Jacques Rousseau on Women and Citizenship," *History of European Ideas*, 37(2): 218–222.
Lee, Bae-yong. (2008). *Women in Korean History*. Seoul: Ewha Woman's University Press.
Lee, Ki-Baik; Edward W. Wagner trans. (1988). *A New History of Korea*. Cambridge, MA: Harvard University Press.
Lee, Su-San. (1999). "Xu fuguan and New Confucianism in Taiwan (1949–1969): A Cultural History of the Exile Generation," PhD dissertation, Brown University.
Li, Wai-Yee. (1999). "Heroic Transformations: Women and National Trauma in Early Qing Literature," *Harvard Journal of Asiatic Studies*, 59(2): 363–443.
Likhitpreechakul, Paisarn. (2012). "Decoding Two 'Miracles' of the Buddha," *Journal of the Oxford Centre for Buddhist Studies*, 2: 209–222.
Manning, C.E. (1973). "Seneca and the Stoics on the Equality of the Sexes," *Mnemosyne*, 26(2): 170–177.
Maraldo, John C. (1995). "Questioning Nationalism Then and Now: A Critical Approach to Zen and the Kyoto School," in J. Heisig and J. Maraldo eds: *Zen, the Kyoto School, and the Question of Nationalism*. Honolulu, HI: University of Hawaii Press: 333.

Martin, Richard C. and Woodward, Mark R. (1997). *Defenders of Reason in Islam: Mu'tazilism from Medieval School to Modern Symbol*. Oxford: Oneworld Publishers.

Matsumura Naoko; Maya Hara trans. (2006). "Rennyo and the Salvation of Women," in Mark L. Blum and Shin'ya Yasutomi eds, *Rennyo and the Roots of Modern Japanese Buddhism*. Oxford: Oxford University Press: 59–71.

McCadden, Joseph J. (1964). "The New York-to-Cuba Axis of Father Varela," *The Americas*, 20(4): 376–392.

McDermott, James P. (2003). *Development in the Early Buddhist Concept of Kamma/Karma*. New Delhi: Munshiram Manoharlal.

McGrath, Alister. (1987). *The Intellectual Origins of the European Reformation*. Oxford: Basil Blackwell.

McHahon, Keith. (2013). "Women Rulers in Imperial China," *Nan Nü*, 15(2): 179–218.

McMullin, Neil Francis. (1977). "Oda Nobunaga and the Buddhist institutions," PhD dissertation, Vancouver, BC: University of British Columbia.

McNair, Amy. (2007). *Donors of Longmen: Faith Politics and Patronage in Medieval Chinese Buddhism*. Honolulu, HI: University of Hawaii Press.

Melchert, Christopher. (2006). *Ahmad ibn Hanbal*. Oxford: One World.

Melzer, Arthur M. (2014). *Philosophy Between the Lines: The Lost History of Esoteric Writing*. Chicago, IL: University of Chicago Press.

Mitchell, Joshua. (1990). "John Locke and the Theological Foundation of Liberal Toleration: A Christian Dialectic of History," *The Review of Politics*, 52(1): 64–83.

Mohanty, Chandra Talpade. (2003). "'Under Western Eyes' Revisited: Feminist Solidarity through Anticapitalist Struggles," *Signs: Journal of Women in Culture and Society*, 28(2): 499–535.

Morefield, Jeanne. (2004). *Covenants without Swords: Idealist Liberalism and the Spirit of Empire*. Princeton, NJ: Princeton University Press.

Morelli, Henriette M. (2005). "An Incarnated Word: A Revisionary Reading of 'The Insurrection of Women' in Thomas Carlyle's *The French Revolution*," *Women's Studies*, 34(7): 533–550.

Mori Noriko (森紀子). (1977). "He Xinyin Ron—Meikyō Itsudatsu no Kōzu" (可心隱論」―名教逸脱の構図), *Shirin* (史林), 60(5): 650–689.

Mungello, David E. (1980). "Malebranche and Chinese Philosophy," *Journal of the History of Ideas*, 41(4): 551–578.

Murray, Pamela S. (2001). "'Loca' or 'Libertadora'? Manuela Sáenz in the Eyes of History and Historians, 1900–c. 1990," *Journal of Latin American Studies*, 33(2): 291–310.

Mus, Paul. (1964). "Thousand-Armed Kannon A Mystery or a Problem,"

Journal of Indian and Buddhist Studies (印度學佛教學研究), 12(1): 470–438 (pagination is backwards in the original).

Najmabadi, Afsaneh. (2006). "Gender and Secularism of Modernity: How Can a Muslim Woman Be French?" *Feminist Studies*, 32(2): 239–255.

Nakamura, Hajime. (1969). *A History of the Development of Japanese Thought From AD 592 to 1868*. Tokyo: Kokusai Bunka Shinkokai.

Nattier, Janice J. and Prebish, Charles S. (1977). "Mahāsāṃghika Origins: The Beginnings of Buddhist Sectarianism," *History of Religions*, 16(3): 237–272.

Nawas, John Abdallah. (2015). *Al-Ma'mūn, the Inquisition, and the Quest for Caliphal Authority*. Atlanta, GA: Lockwood Press.

Needham, Joseph. (1956). *Science and Civilisation in China, Volume 2: History of Scientific Thought*. Cambridge: Cambridge University Press.

Needham, Joseph. (1986). *Science and Civilization in China*: vol. 4, part 3. Taipei: Caves Books.

Netton, Ian Richard. (1998). "Al-Farabi, Abu Nasr," in Edward Craig and Oliver Leaman eds, *Routledge Encyclopedia of Philosophy*, vol. 3. London: Routledge.

Ng, Yu-Kwan. (2003). "Xiong Shili's Metaphysical Theory About the Non-Separability of Substance and Function," in John Makeham ed., *New Confucianism: A Critical Examination*. New York: Palgrave Macmillan: 219–251.

Nivison, David S. and Van Norden, Bryan W. (1996). *The Ways of Confucianism: Investigations in Chinese Philosophy*. La Salle, IL: Open Court.

O'Meara, Dominic. (2003). *Platonopolis: Platonic Political Philosophy in Late Antiquity*. Oxford: Clarendon Press.

Okada Takehiko. (1973). "The Chu Hsi and Wang Yang-ming Schools at the End of the Ming and Tokugawa Periods," *Philosophy East and West*, 23(1/2): 139–162.

Okada Takehiko (岡田武彦). (2004). *Ōyōmei to Meisue no Jugaku* (王陽明と明末の儒学). Tokyo: Meitoku Shuppan Sha (東京: 明徳出版社).

Orzech, Charles D. (1989). "Puns on the Humane King," *Journal of the American Oriental Society*, 109(1): 17–24.

Pankhurst, Richard. (1957). *The Saint Simonians, Mill and Carlyle: A Preface to Modern Thought*. London: Sidgwick & Jackson.

Parekh, Bhikhu. (1989). *Gandhi's Political Philosophy: A Critical Examination*. London: Macmillian.

Parel, Anthony. (1992). "The Comparative Study of Political Philosophy," in Anthony J. Parel and Ronald C. Keith eds, *Comparative Political Philosophy: Studies Under the Upas Tree*. Lanham, MD: Lexington Books: 11–28.

Parker, Kim Ian. (1996). "John Locke and the Enlightenment Metanarrative: A Biblical Corrective to a Reasoned World," *Scottish Journal of Theology*, 49: 57–73.
Peattie, Mark R. (1975). *Ishiwara Kanji and Japan's Confrontation with the West*. Princeton, NJ: Princeton University Press.
Perlmann, Moshe. (1964). "Review of The Book of Government or Rules for Kings; The Siyāsat-nāma or Siyar al-Mulūk of Niẓām Al-Mulk by Hubert Darke," *Journal of the American Oriental Society*, 84(4): 422.
Pines, Yuri. (2002). *Foundations of Confucian Thought: Intellectual Life in the Chunqiu Period (722–453 BCE)*. Honolulu, HI: University of Hawaii Press.
Pitkin, Hanna Fenichel. (1999). *Fortune is a Woman: Gender and Politics in the Thought of Niccolo Machiavelli*, 2nd edn. Chicago, IL: University of Chicago Press.
Pittau, Joseph. (1969). *Political Thought in Early Meiji Japan, 1868–1889*. Cambridge, MA: Harvard University Press.
Pocock, J.G.A. (1971). *Politics, Language and Time: Essays on Political Thought and History*. Chicago, IL: University of Chicago Press.
Potter, Mary. (1986). "Gender Equality and Gender Hierarchy in Calvin's Theology," *Signs: Journal of Women in Culture and Society*, 11(4): 725–773.
Pulzer, Peter. (1997). *Germany 1870–1945: Politics, State Formation, and War*. Oxford: Oxford University Press.
Racine, Karen. (2012). "For Glory and Bolívar: The Remarkable Life of Manuela Sáenz," *Journal of Latin American Studies*, 44(1): 184–186.
Ramelli, Ilaria. (2009). "Origen, Patristic Philosophy, and Christian Platonism. Re-Thinking the Christianisation of Hellenism," *Vigiliae Christianae*, 63: 217–263.
Ranum, Orest. (1969). "Personality and Politics in the *Persian Letters*," *Political Science Quarterly*, 84(4): 606–627.
Reihman, Gregory M. (2013). "Malebranche and Chinese Philosophy: A Reconsideration," *British Journal for the History of Philosophy*, 21(2): 262–280.
Rentmeester, Casey. (2014). "Leibniz and Huayan Buddhism: Monads as Modified Li?" *Lyceum*, 13(1): 36–57.
Rhouni, Raja ed. (2009). *Secular and Islamic Feminist Critiques in the Work of Fatima Mernissi*. Leiden: Brill.
Robin, Corey. (2000). "Reflections on Fear: Montesquieu in Retrieval," *The American Political Science Review*, 94(2): 347–360.
Roded, Ruth. (2006). "Bint al-Shati's Wives of the Prophet: Feminist or Feminine?" *British Journal of Middle Eastern Studies*, 33(1): 51–66.
Roover, Jakob De and S.N. Balagangadhara. (2008). "John Locke, Christian

Liberty, and the Predicament of Liberal Toleration," *Political Theory*, 36(4): 523–549.
Rorty, Richard. (1989). "Review of Larson and Deutsch (1988). Interpreting Across Boundaries New Essays in Comparative Philosophy," *Philosophy East and West*, 39(3): 332–337.
Rosen, Stanley. (2003). *Hermeneutics as Politics*, 2nd edn. New Haven, CT: Yale University Press.
Ross, Brian H. (1989). "Distinguishing Types of Superficial Similarities," *Journal of Experimental Psychology: Learning, Memory, and Cognition*, 15(3): 456–468.
Roussillon, Alain. (2001). "'Ce qu'ils nomment 'Liberté'. . .' Rifāʿa al-Ṭahṭāwī, ou l'invention (avortée) d'une modernité politique ottoman," *Arabica*, 48(2): 143–185.
Russell, Gül A. (1993). "The Impact of the Philosophus Autodidactus: Pocockes, John Locke, And The Society of Friends," in Gül A. Russell ed., *The "Arabick" Interest of the Natural Philosophers in Seventeenth-Century*. Leiden: Brill.
Sanft, Charles. (2010–2011). "*Chunqiu jueyu* Reconsidered On the Legal Interest in Subjective States and the Privilege of Hiding Family Members' Crimes as Developments from Earlier Practice," *Early China*, 33/34: 141–169.
Sartori, Giovanni. (1970). "Concept Misformation in Comparative Politics," *American Political Science Review*, 64(4): 1033–1053.
Satō Hirō (佐藤弘夫). (2010). *Nihon Chūsei no Kokka to Bukkyō* (日本中世の国家と仏教). Tokyo: Yoshikawa Kō Bunkan (東京：吉川弘文館).
Saxonhouse, Arlene W. (1985). *Women in the History of Political Thought: Ancient Greece to Machiavelli*. New York: Praeger.
Scalapino, Robert A. and George T. Yu. (1961). *The Chinese Anarchist Movement*. Berkeley, CA: University of California, Berkeley, Center for Chinese Studies.
Schopen, Gregory. (1997). *Bones, Stones, and Buddhist Monks: Collected Papers on the Archaeology, Epigraphy, and Texts of Monastic Buddhism in India*. Honolulu, HI: University of Hawaii Press.
Schott, Jeremy M. (2003). "Founding Platonopolis: The Platonic Politeia in Eusebius, Porphyry, and Iamblichus," *Journal of Early Christian Studies*, 11(4): 501–531.
Schroeder, Susan. (1994). "Father José María Luis Mora, Liberalism, and the British and Foreign Bible Society in Nineteenth-Century Mexico," *The Americas*, 50(3): 377–397.
Sekiguchi, Sumiko. (2010). "Confucian Morals and the Making of a 'Good Wife and Wise Mother': From 'Between Husband and Wife there

is Distinction' to 'As Husbands and Wives be Harmonious,'" *Social Science Japan Journal*, 13(1): 95–113.
Sharma, J. P. (1968). *Republics in Ancient India, c. 1500–c. 500 BC.* Leiden: E.J. Brill.
Sheehan, James. (1978). *German Liberalism in the Nineteenth Century.* Chicago, IL: University of Chicago Press.
Sheppard, Anne. (2013). "Proclus' Place in the Reception of Plato's Republic," in Anne Sheppard ed., *Ancient Approaches to Plato's Republic*. London: Institute of Classical Studies: 107–115.
Shimokawa Ryōko (下川玲子). (2001). *Kitabatake no Jugaku* (北畠親房の儒学). Tokyo: Perikan Sha (東京：ぺりかん社).
Siegel, Paul N. (1950). "Milton and the Humanist Attitude Toward Women," *Journal of the History of Ideas*, 11(1): 42–53.
Siemes, Johannes. (1969). *Hermann Roesler: The Making of Meiji State.* Tokyo: Charles E. Tuttle Co.
Sigmund, Paul E. (2005). "Jeremy Waldron and the Religious Turn in Locke Scholarship," *Review of Politics*, 67(3): 407–418.
Skinner, Quentin. (1969). "Meaning and Understanding in the History of Ideas," *History and Theory*, 8(1): 3–53.
Skinner, Quentin. (1998). *Liberty before Liberalism*. Cambridge: Cambridge University Press.
Slomp, Gabriella. (1994). "Hobbes and the Equality of Women," *Political Studies*, 42(3): 441–452.
Solé-Farràs, Jesús. (2013). *New Confucianism in Twenty-First Century China: The Construction of a Discourse.* London: Routledge.
Staiano-Daniels, Lucia. (2006). "Illuminated Darkness: Hegel's Brief and Unexpected Elevation of Indian Thought in 'On the Episode of the Mahabharata known by the name Bhagavad-Gita by Wilhelm von Humboldt'," *The Owl of Minerva*, 43(1/2): 75–99.
Stern, Gertrude H. (1940). "Muhammad's Bond with the Women," *Bulletin of the School of Oriental and African Studies*, 10(1): 185–197.
Stoetzer, O. Carlos. (1998). *Karl Christian Friedrich Krause and his Influence in the Hispanic World*. Köln: Böhlau.
Strauss, Leo. (1952). *Persecution and the Art of Writing*. New York: The Free Press.
Sutton, Nick. (1997). "Aśoka and Yudhisthira: A Historical Setting for the Ideological Tensions of the Mahābhārata?", *Religion*, 27(4): 333–341.
Takahashi Tomio (高橋富雄). (1990). *Tokuichi and Saichō – Moo Hitotsu no Seitō Bukkyō* (「徳一と最澄」 – もう一つの正統仏教). Tokyo: Chūō Kōron Sha (東京: 中央公論社).
Takeuchi Yoshio [武内義雄]. (1939). *Rongo no Kenkyū* (論語之研究). Tokyo: Iwanami Shoten (東京: 岩波書店).

Takii Kazuhiro (瀧井一博). (2010). "Itō Hirobumi wa Nihon no Bisumaruku ka?" (伊藤博文は日本のビスマルクか), *Yūroppa Kenkyū* (ユーロパ研究), 9: 203–210.

Tampiah, S.J. (1977). *World Conqueror and World Renouncer: A Study of Buddhism and Polity in Thailand against a Historical Background.* Cambridge: Cambridge University Press.

T'ang, Chun-i. (1973). "The Criticisms of Wang Yang-ming's Teachings as Raised by his Contemporaries," *Philosophy East and West*, 23: 163–186.

Tartaglia, James. (2014). "Rorty's Thesis of the Cultural Specificity of Philosophy," *Philosophy East and West*, 64(4): 1017–1038.

Tate, J.W. (2013). "Dividing Locke from God: The Limits of Theology in Locke's Political Philosophy," *Philosophy and Social Criticism*, 39(2): 133–164.

Taylor, Rodney Leon and Howard Yuen Fung Choy. (2005). *The Illustrated Encyclopedia of Confucianism: N–Z*. New York, NY: Rosen Publishing.

Tenenbaum, Susan. (1973). "Montesquieu and Mme. de Stael: The Woman as a Factor in Political Analysis," *Political Theory*, 1(1): 92–103.

Tenenbaum, Susan. (1982). "Woman through the Prism of Political Thought," *Polity*, 15(1): 90–102.

Thapar, Romila. (1960). "Aśoka and Buddhism," *Past and Present*, 18(1): 43–51.

Thapar, Romila. (1990). *A History of India, Volume 1: Early India from the Origins to AD 1300*. Harmondsworth: Penguin.

Van Hensbroek, Peter Boele. (1999). *Political Discourses in African Thought: 1860 to the Present*. Westport, CN: Greenwood Press.

Vander Waerdt, Paul A. (1994). "Zeno's Republic and the Origins of Natural Law," in Paul A. Vender Waerdt ed., *The Socratic Movement*. Ithaca, NY: Cornell University Press: Chapter 11.

Vasalou, Sophia. (2008). *Moral Agents and their Deserts the Character of Mu'tazilite Ethics*. Princeton, NJ: Princeton University Press.

Vlastos, Gregory. (1991). *Socrates, Ironist and Moral Philosopher*. Ithaca, NY: Cornell University Press.

Voegelin, Eric. (1990). "Equivalences of Experience and Symbolization in History," in Ellis Sandoz ed., *The Collected Works of Eric Voegelin, Vol. 12: Published Essays, 1966–1985*. Baton Rouge: Louisiana State University Press: 115–133.

Vuylsteke, R.R. (1982). "The Political Philosophy of Tung Chung-shu (179–104 BC): A Critical Exposition," PhD dissertation. Honolulu, HI: University of Hawaii.

Waldron, Jeremy. (2002). *God, Locke, and Equality: Christian Foundations of John Locke's Political Thought*. Cambridge: Cambridge University Press.

Walser, Joseph. (2005). *Nāgārjuna in Context: Mahāyāna Buddhism and Early Indian Culture*. New York, NY: Columbia University Press.

Walthall, Anne. (1991). "The Life Cycle of Farm Women in Tokugawa Japan," in Gail Lee Bernstein ed., *Recreating Japanese Women, 1600–1945*. Berkeley, CA: University of California Press: 42–70.

Wang, Robin R. (2005). "Dong Zhongshu's Transformation of 'Yin-Yang' Theory and Contesting of Gender Identity," *Philosophy East and West*, 55(2): 209–231.

Wang, Youru. (2017). *Historical Dictionary of Chan Buddhism*. Lanham, MD: Rowman and Littlefield Publishers.

Watsuji Tetsurō (和辻哲郎). (1927). *Genshi Bukkyō no Jissen Tetsugaku* (原始佛教の實踐哲學). Tokyo: Iwanami Shoten (東京：岩波書店).

Weed, Laura E. (2002). "Kant's Noumenon and Sunyata," *Asian Philosophy*, 12(2): 77–95.

Weinstein, Stanley. (1987). *Buddhism Under the Tang*. Cambridge: Cambridge University Press.

Weiss, Penny A. (1987). "Rousseau, Antifeminism, and Woman's Nature," *Political Theory*, 15(1): 81–98.

Williams, David. (2005). *Defending Japan's Pacific War: The Kyoto School Philosophers and Post-White Power*. London: RoutledgeCurzon.

Wolpert, Stanley. (1962). *Tilak and Gokhale: Revolution and Reform in the Making of Modem India*. Berkeley, CA: University of California Press.

Wong, Young-tsu. (2003). "Discovery or Invention: Modern Interpretations of Zhang Xuecheng," *Historiography East and West*, 1(2): 178–203.

Wood, Ellen Meiksins and Neal Wood. (1978). *Class Ideology and Ancient Political Theory: Socrates, Plato, and. Aristotle in Social Context*. Oxford: Basil Blackwell.

Wood, Neal. (1967). "Machiavelli's Concept of Virtù Reconsidered," *Political Studies*, 15(2): 159–172.

Yampolski, Philip. (2003). "Zen. A Historical Sketch," in Takeuchi Yoshinori ed., *Buddhist Spirituality: Later China, Korea, Japan and the Modern World*. Delhi: Motilal Banarsidass: 3–23.

Yokohama Shakai Mondai Kenkyujō eds. (横浜社会問題研究所編). (1926). *Shinkantoha no Shakaishugi* (新カント派の社会主義観). Tokyo: Iwanami Shoten (東京：岩波書店).

Young, Homer H. (1956). "The Founding Fathers on the Education of Women," *Rice Institute Pamphlet, Rice University Studies*, 43(1): 48–63.

Yu Mingguang. (2002). "Xunzi's Philosophy and the School of Huang Lao: On the Renewal and Development of Early Confucianism," *Contemporary Chinese Thought*, 34(1): 37–60.

Zastoupil, Lynn. (1994). *John Stuart Mill and India*. Stanford, CA: Stanford University Press.

Zhang Zhao-wei. (2009). "Wan Ting-yan's Yi-ology Based on Mind/Heartology," *Studies of Zhouyi and Ancient Chinese Philosophy* 3. http://211.86.56.178:8080/english0/periodical/200903.asp#8 (accessed April 10, 2017).

Glossary of concepts

For East Asian terminology, the *pinyin* reading is given first as well as the Wade-Giles system of Romanization for reference (the latter is used in many older academic sources so useful for further research). Often the Japanese, Korean and Vietnamese reading is also given. Both systems of Korean transliteration are given here. The characters used are the classical ones before the national simplifications made in the late twentieth century. Reconstruction of a more accurate contemporary pronunciation is not used but is possible. Long vowels are given for Japanese terms. Most Chinese terms are given with tonal marks where known. Tonal marks are often omitted in the book but given here for reference.

For Arabic terminology, the *International Journal for Middle Eastern Studies* (*IJMES*) transliteration is mainly used though not always consistently. Where often used variations exist, there is an attempt to list these as well. I have used an apostrophe to transliterate the letter "ayn" (ع) in the middle of words but omitted it otherwise. Note that the prefix *al-* (ا) is ignored and the entry is put alphabetically with the word after *al-*. Persian and other south Asian terms are also listed where relevant in Arabic or Arabic variant scripts.

For Indian terms, the most common reading is given. Where variations exist, these are listed as well. Pali is used for early Buddhist terms though it is likely that an Ardha-Magadhi type language was in fact used for which we do not have the script. Pali is often transliterated into Western alphabet but Sanskrit works as well if not better. Where there is a Sanskrit translation of a term from later Buddhist literature, then this is given as well. However, it is fully recognized that it is anachronistic to use Sanskrit for the time of Buddha and his successors even if it is the closest equivalent in this context. Often the East Asian equivalents are also given for Buddhist terms relevant to thought in East Asia.

For ancient Greek and Latin, transliteration methodology is relatively set so variations are rare but noted where relevant.

ABBREVIATIONS

ch. = Chinese (*pinyin*)
jp. = Japanese

kr. = Korean (*revised Romanization*)
m.r. = McCune–Reischauer system of transliterating Korean
pa. = Pali
pe. = Persian
sk. = Sanskrit
vt. = Vietnamese
w.g. = Wade-Giles system of transliterating classical Chinese

Abolitionism: The movement to abolish slavery.
Absolute: Quasi-deistic concept in Hegel thought where it constitutes the holistic notion of the totality of human progress (*World Spirit*) as both the process itself on a practical level and the dynamics of the process on a theoretical level.
Absolute nothingness, see *zettai mu*.
Adiaforía (ἀδιαφορία): Indifference.
Āgama (आगम), ch. ahánjīng (阿含經): Originally, word for "collection" or "group" but used for the collection of the sayings of the Buddha translated into classical Chinese.
Agathos (ἀγαθός): Goodness, virtue.
Ahimsa (अहिंसा): Literally, "no injury" or "no harm" but usually denoting a philosophy of non-violence.
Aidagara (間柄): Watsuji Tetsurō's concept of "between-ness" used to stress the interconnection between human beings; based on the characters for human (ningen 人間) in Japanese which is based on the characters for person (人) and between (間).
Ājīvakas (आजीवक): Ascetic sect founded by Makkhali Gosala, believing in fatalism.
Akunin shōki (悪人正機): Shinran's view that those who are evil should not be ignored because such persons are particularly in need of Buddha's compassion.
Akutō (悪黨): Literally, "bad gang" or "bad party", but meaning organized groups of commoners in medieval Japan, organized for economic or other purposes, outside of official status systems.
Ālayavijñāna (आलयविज्ञान): Store consciousness, where the seeds (*bīja*) of other forms of consciousness are deposited.
Aletheia (ἀλήθεια): The idea of the truth as a process of disclosure or unconcealing to bring into view something that is hidden.
Allāh (الله): The Arabic word for the God of the Abrahamic religions (Judaism, Christianity and Islam).
Amor fati: Literally, to "love one's fate" or to accept the role that fate has assigned; generally associated with the thought of Friedrich Nietzsche who implied that one should challenge oneself to do great things but

accept one's fate regardless of whether or not it entails failure, tragedy, farce or damnation.

Anabaptist: Christian sect that believes that only baptism and conscious acceptance of Christianity as an adult makes one a true Christian; literally, re-baptism from the classical Greek "anabaptismos" (ἀναβαπτισμός).

Anaideia (Αναιδεια): Shamelessness, imprudent.

Analects (論語) ch. *Lúnyǔ*: Ancient text believed to record the sayings of Confucius and his followers.

Analytical philosophy: The approach to philosophy that relies on clear, logical steps in setting out arguments based on precisely defined concepts and procedures.

Anarchism: Opposition to the state and related forms of authority in the belief that all such authority is inevitably oppressive.

Anicca, Pāli (अनिच्चा) sk. anitya (अनित्य) or (無常) ch. wúcháng; jp. mujō; kr. musang; vt. Vô thường: Literally, impermanence; in Buddhism, the notion that everything decays and disappears so excessive attachment to things and people will only bring suffering (*dukkha*).

Apokatastasis (ἀποκατάστασις), also transliterated as apokatastasis: The reconstitution, restitution, or restoration to the original or primordial condition, including of souls to the One in neo-Platonism.

Aporia (ἀπορεία): Challenging puzzles and profound doubts.

Apotreptikos (ἀποτρεπτικός): Inner voice.

Aql (عقل): Used by Al-Farabi to translate the term for mind (from Greek *nous* in neo-Platonism).

Aql al-faal (عقل فعال): The active intellect or creative mind as the highest and most important form of the mind.

Arête (ἀρετή): Excellence.

Arhat (अर्हत्) Chinese characters for the sound (阿羅漢): Literally, "one who is worthy" or who has achieved or is working to achieve nirvana through discipline and ascetic practices; in Theravāda Buddhism, arhats are perfect beings and are a goal achievable by some humans but in Mahāyāna Buddhism, arhats are advanced on the path to enlightenment yet imperfect so short of full Buddhahood.

Ārya (आर्य): "Noble" in ancient Aryan literature.

Asabiyya (عصبيّة), sometimes transliterated as *asabiyyah*: Often translated as "social cohesion", but also as "group solidarity", "tribal spirit" or "esprit de corps".

Asceticism: Denial of involvement with the world, both physically and socially, particularly pleasurable aspects, to train the mind and body for spiritual goals; see *Askesis*.

Asharite (الأشعرية): Early "traditionalists" who used philosophical arguments to defend conservative practices and oppose the introduction of classical philosophy into Islamic thought.

Asian values: Arguments made in the 1980s and 1990s to explain the success of economic development in East Asian countries; suggested that some traditional Asian values were more conducive to stable and moral economic development than Western values.

Áskesis (ἄσκησις): Literally, "exercise" or "training", but the basis for ascetic practices.

Ātman (आत्मन्): Self.

Augustus: "Venerated".

Autárkeia (αὐτάρκεια): Self-sufficiency.

Authenticity (Eigentlichkeit): Used by Heidegger as the condition of living one's life with concern for one's potential but also one's mortality, as against going along with the monotony of everyday life; from "eigentlich", meaning truly or properly.

Avatamsaka, see *Mahāvaipulya Buddhāvataṃsaka Sūtra*.

Azuchi Disputation (Azuchi Shuron 安土宗論): Debate between the Nichiren and True Pure Land representatives in 1579 ordered by Oda Nobunaga to settle the frequent disputes between the two sects.

Ba'ath (بعث): Literally, "resurrection/rebirth" in Arabic: name of the pan-Arab movement and component political parties in the Middle East.

Badawa (بداوة): Nomadic life.

Baohuanghui (保皇會): Literally, "Protect the Emperor Society"; formed in Victoria, Canada in 1899 by Kang Youwei and Liang Qichao to promote constitutional monarchy and peaceful reform.

Baopuzi (抱朴子): Usually translated as "The Master who Embraces Simplicity"; a book by *Ge Hong*.

Basho (場所): Literally, "place", but also translated as "topoi" based on a reference to use of the idea in Plato. It is a relativistic position created by Nishida Kitarō to suggest a hierarchy of concepts used to make judgments that is beyond the simple subject–object distinction.

Bayt al-Hikma (بيت الحكمة): Literally, "House of Wisdom"; institute for philosophical studies founded by Harun Al-Rashid.

Běntǐ (本體) w.g. pen-t'i: noumenon, often translated as "original substance" or sometimes "ontological substance".

Beopseong (法性), m.r. *Pŏpsŏng*: Literally "Dharma Nature"; early Buddhist school unique to Korea.

Berkeley Mafia: Term for the group of US educated Indonesia economists who worked for the military government in Indonesia after the military coup d'état in 1965.

Bhajanaloka (भजनलोक): The "receptacle world"; the totality of good/

evil actions based on seeds of karma or bīja out of which arises the "outside" world as we experience it.

Bhikkhu (pali), sk. bhikṣu (भिक्षु) ch. bǐqiū, jp. biku, kr. bigu, vt. tỉ-khâu (比丘): Literally "beggar" but meaning a fully ordained male Buddhist monk.

Bhikkhuni (pa.), sk. bhikṣuṇī (भिक्षुणी), ch. bǐqiūní, jp. bikuni, kr. biguni (比丘尼) also jp. ama (尼): Fully ordained female Buddhist nun. See *Bhikkhu*.

Bīja (बीज): Literally, seed or seeds; the way in which karma is stored in store or storehouse consciousness.

Bio-power: Term created by Michel Foucault to describe how the modern state and society controls large numbers of individuals through restrictions on their bodily movement and actions, including use of rules to implant views on how one should use or not use one's own body.

Bodhicitta (बोधिचित्त) ch. putixin; jp. bodaishin (菩提心): A form of awakening in a Buddha that leads them to have a compassionate desire to seek enlightenment for all sentient beings.

Bodhisattva (बोधिसत्त्व) pa. bodhisatta (बोधिसत्त), ch. púsà, jp. bosatsu, kr. bosal, vt. bồ tát (菩薩): One who has reached Bodhicitta; originally refers to the Buddha in his previous lives, but the highest goal of practitioners in Mahāyāna Buddhism.

Bodhisattva Precepts (菩薩戒) ch. púsà jiè, jp. bosatsukai: Moral rules in Mahāyāna Buddhism to guide those on the path to becoming a Bodhisattva; it includes 10 major precepts (*shi zhong jie* 十重戒) for Bodhisattvas and 48 minor precepts for those on the bodhisattva path.

Boston Confucianism: Group of New Confucian scholars associated with Harvard, Boston and other universities in the Boston area.

Bourgeoisie: The wealthy elite class of major investors, property owners, merchants and business owners and managers in Marxist thought.

Brahmā (ब्रह्मा): Ancient Indian god who created the universe.

Brahmajala Sūtra (梵網經) ch. Fànwǎng jīng, jp. Bonmōkyō: Literally "Brahmā Net" Sūtra; key Mahāyāna Sutra.

Brahman (ब्रह्मन्): In Indian thought, the highest universal principle or unified concept of ultimate reality.

Brahmin (ब्राह्मण): Religious or scholarly caste.

Buddha-nature in practice (行佛性) ch. háng Fó xìng, jp. gyō-Busshō: The actual practical obstacles to Buddhahood in a person.

Buddha-nature in principle (理佛性) ch. lǐ Fó xìng, jp. ri-Busshō: The idea that anyone can become a Buddha.

Buddhānusmṛti (बुद्धानुस्मृति): Literally, "mindfulness of the Buddha"; keeping the Buddha and his teachings in mind at all times.

Buddhist state (佛國) ch. Fó guo, jp. Bukkoku, kr. Bulguk: State in which Buddhism is widely practiced or adopted by the state.

Bulssi Japbyeon (佛氏雜辨): Attack on Buddhism by the *neo-Confucian Jeong Dojeon*; translated as "Array of Critiques against Buddhism."

Bushi (武士): Literally, "warrior official" originally appointed by the Japanese Imperial Court for military and policing roles but evolved into a caste of warriors in medieval and Tokugawa Japan. See also *Samurai*.

Cai (才): The "capabilities" of an individual including all talents, intellectual capacity, physical abilities, emotional stability and moral sense.

Cakkavatti (Pali; Sanskrit – cakravartin चक्रवर्तिन्): Literally, wheel mover, also cakravartiraajan (चक्रवर्तिराजन्), literally, wheel turner monarch, meaning emperor over all other kings, often translated as "universal monarch".

Caliph (خليفة) more accurately transliterated as *khalīfah*: Literally, "deputy" but meaning effectively Muhammad's successor in terms of carrying on his legacy as a political ruler and chief administrator.

Cārvāka (चार्वाक): School of materialist thought, originally referred to as the Lokāyata.

Catholic Church: The institutionalized Christian Church in the Western Roman Empire and Western Europe until the Reformation; the term "Catholic" from *katholikismos* (καθολικισμός), meaning "universal doctrine".

Caudillo: "Strongman" in Latin America, denoting illegitimate power and influence.

Chán (禅禪) based on the Chinese *chan-na* transliteration of the Sanskrit term *dhyāna* (ध्यान) meaning "meditation": Meditation based *sect* (宗) of Buddhism; called *Seon* in Korea, *Thiền* in Vietnam and *Zen* in Japan.

Chán fǎ (禪法): Literally, method of meditation, used in both Buddhism and neo-Confucianism.

Chicago Boys: Group of Chilean economists in the 1970s and 1980s, trained at the Department of Economics of the University of Chicago, who worked for various Latin American governments, including the dictatorship in Chile established in 1993.

Chūn Qiū (春秋): Historical record of the state of Lu in the *Chūnqiū Shídài*; also known as the *Lín Jīng* (麟經). Literally, "Spring and Autumn" but refers to a terse historical record of the Spring and Autumn period of the *Zhou* dynasty, often translated as Spring and Autumn Annals, which has been the subject of numerous ancient commentaries.

Chūnqiū Fánlù (春秋繁露) w.g. Ch'unch'iu Fanlou: Key text by the Han Literati Dong Zhongshu, translated as "Luxuriant Dew of the Spring and Autumn Annals"; also translated as "Pearls of the Spring and Autumn Annals".

Chūnqiū Shídài (春秋時代): Literally, "Spring and Autumnal period" of the *Zhou* dynasty (771–476 BC).

Civil rights movement: Movement in the United States to end racial segregation and discrimination laws in the 1950s and 1960s.

Code of Laws (律令) ch. *lüling*; jp. *ritsuryō*; kr. *ryul ryeong*, vt. *luật lệnh*: Literati inspired system of laws.

Commonwealth: From "common weal" or common well-being, which was meant to signify the common interests of the members or population of a state as opposed to the interests of a small group (oligarchy or aristocracy) or one individual (monarchy); originally used as an English translation of Latin *res publica*, or literally, "things public", which became the basis for the word *republic*.

Conceptual stretching: The process by which a concept created for one case is also used to cover another case but in doing so the meaning of the original context is stretched to accommodate differences in the different cases being covered.

Confucianism, see *ru* below.

Cooperatives: Organizations jointly controlled by members to produce goods or services for mutual benefit of the members.

Critical Theory (Kritische Theorie): First used by the Frankfurt School in the sense of social and political theory that aimed at taking a critical stance toward existing society and institutions in order to change them rather than just study them objectively; more widely defined as social and political theory that questions sources of social domination and political oppression.

Cynics (κυνισμός): Followers of ancient Greek philosophy based on living a virtuous life in accordance with nature and not necessarily following normal social conventions.

Daigaku jiken (大逆事件): Literally "great reversal incident" but usually translated as the High Treason Incident; a plot to assassinate the emperor of Japan in 1910 that was used by the Japanese government to round up and execute anarchists.

Daimon (δαίμων): Spirit.

Daimyō (大名): Powerful local lords in the Warring States and Tokugawa Shōgunate periods in Japan.

Danda (दण्ड): Literally, "rod" or "stick", meaning punishment, power to punish, which is indicative of the sovereign power of the ruler.

Dandaniti (दण्डनीति): Policy or skills for wielding sovereign power as a ruler.

Dasein: Literally "being there" but often translated as "presence" or "existence"; used by Heidegger to question the place of humans in the world and often used by him as the generic category of human existence.

Datsuaron (脱亞論): Fukuzawa Yūkichi's argument that Japan should "leave Asia" intellectually and seek its future in line with the West.

Dé (德): Moral force, sometimes translated as virtue.

Deconstruction: The method created by Jacques Derrida to take the apparent structure and clarity of a *text* to demonstrate its weaker assumptions and foundations.

Delian league (Συμμαχία της Δήλου) 478–404 BC: An alliance of Greek states led by Athens originally formed to fight Persia but the navy created by the league became the basis of Athenian power and the league members subordinated to Athenian power and policy.

Democracy: From ancient Greek *dēmokratía* (δημοκρατία), literally strength of the *demos* (δημος) or "masses" or "mob", but usually referring to popular forms of rule; in modern states, this is usually based on some form of representative institutions but also historically based on popular rule by a demagogue (δημαγωγός) usurping and operating outside of institutional structures.

Dharma (धर्म) ch. fǎ, jp. hō (法): Law or morality or righteousness; used in a wider sense of the way in which the universe works and according to the way it should work. Used with significant variations in both Hinduism and Buddhism.

Dharmakāya (धर्मकाय): Literally, "dharma-body" or "truth body" of a Buddha, which is beyond normal human conception and part of the higher law of the universal that the Buddha taught.

Dharmasastra (धर्मशास्त्र): Literally, text of law, but generally a set of rules for behavior that are considered as appropriate to the role of different groups in society.

Dictatorship of the proletariat: Concept created by Karl Marx that workers, as the majority and the class historically suited to the task, would have to reform political institutions for the benefit of society after a socialist revolution and guard against attempts from the bourgeoisie to thwart reform.

Differences within similarities: No matter how similar two concepts might appear, it is important to highlight the important differences in how different concepts are created, defined, used and so on, in order to avoid accepting superficial similarities when the differences are in reality profound.

Digambara (दिगम्बर): Literally, "sky clad" or those Jain ascetics who wear no clothes.

Diggers: A group of radical protestants who sought to occupy unused land of the wealth for the benefit of all, particularly the poor; "diggers" because they literally dug up and cultivated land; some of this group also known as True *Levellers*.

Dīgha Nikāya: Collection of long discourses of the Buddha; largely the same as the Dīrgha Āgama (Cháng Ahánjīng 長阿含經) in East Asian Buddhism.

Direct action: The notion that concrete actions to challenge unjust laws or authority must be used to achieve one's political goals because discussion and persuasion alone is not enough to bring about change.

Discourse: Any system of linguistic and symbolic communication, including informal conversation, that creates a complex web of meaning in which individuals make sense of their world and their place in it.

Dissenting sect: Christian sect, usually Protestant that did not conform to the practices of the state Church; primarily used in the English and British political context.

Djeli, see *Griot*.

Doctrinal school (教): Used for schools of East Asian Buddhism that tend to be text-based and have a monastic focus as opposed to *Sects* (see entry).

Doctrine of the mean (中庸) ch. Zhongyong: One of the Four Books of neo-Confucianism; based on a chapter taken from the *Liji*.

Dong lin xue (東林學) w.g. Tung lin: Literally, East Grove School, usually given as Dong Lin School; founded in the Song dynasty, played a role in supporting Zhu Xi School of Principle orthodoxy in the Ming dynasty.

Dukkha (Pali दुक्ख; Sanskrit duḥkha दुःख); 苦 ch. *kŭ*; jp. *ku*; kr. *ko*; vt. *khổ*: Literally, unsatisfactory, uneasy, uncomfortable, but usually meaning or translated as "suffering".

Edo school (江戶學): The urbane and artistic school of *Kokugaku*.

Egalitarianism: The view that all people are of equal worth as human beings and should be respected equally.

Egoism: Early anarchist philosophy developed by Max Stirner who suggested that one should reject all ideologies, religions, causes and political systems in order to live one's life as one wants in cooperation with others who are similarly free from the control of others.

Eidos (εἶδος): Form, theory of forms/ideas.

Elenchus (ἔλεγχος): Enquiry based on keen scrutiny.

Encyclopédie (1751–1772), full name is "Dictionnaire raisonné des sciences, des arts et des métiers": General encyclopedia published in France intended to produce a secular depository of knowledge as an alternative to religious knowledge propagated by the Catholic Church.

Encyclopedistes: Writers who contributed to the Encyclopédie.

Enlightenment: A movement to give priority to reason and rationality over convention, superstition, dogma and tradition in organizing society and politics, which is usually narrowly applied to the thought of eighteenth-century Europe.

Erschlossenheit: Heidegger uses the word to indicate "disclosure" or exposure to examination from the ancient Greek idea of the truth of philosophy as a process of disclosure or *aletheia* (ἀλήθεια).

Eternal return (Ewige Wiederkunft): An ancient notion, now mostly associated with Friedrich Nietzsche, of the repetition of an infinite loop of the same events over and over again, though Nietzsche is often interpreted as meaning that one should live one's life as if one had to live it over and over again in order to maximize the dramatic and heroic as if one was to make one's life worth living again and again; also translated as "eternal recurrence".

Ethos (ἦθος): Ethical norms.

Eudaimonia (εὐδαιμονία): Literally, "eu" meaning "good" and "*daimōn*" spirit, meaning well-being, but often translated as "happiness".

Evidential approach, see *Kǎozhèng*.

Fǎ (法): Literally, "standards", but often translated as "law", later used as the Buddhist concept of dharma.

Fabian Society: British socialist organization founded in 1884 to promote gradual reform of society rather than dramatic violent revolutionary change.

Fǎ-jiā (法家): Often translated as "Legalism" but also sometimes as "Realism", as in realist in political matters rather than an idealist or moralist.

Fallenness, see *Verfallen*.

Falsafa (فلسفة): Literally, "philosophy" but used in Islamic societies to designate intellectual subjects derived from classical Greek and Roman thought as well as non-religious work on mathematics and physics in addition to philosophy in the narrow sense.

Fascism: Most narrowly, is the name of the political movement created by Mussolini in 1914, the "Fasci Rivoluzionari d'Azione Internazionalista", who called themselves Fascisti or Fascists, after the ancient Roman symbol for power; from the Latin "fascis" or bundle of rods, symbolizing unity in strength but also the rods of authority and punishment; often used as a general term for state interventionist racist nationalism.

Fatwa-i-jahandari (فتاوى جهان داري): Book of political theory by Ziauddin Barani.

Feminism: Belief that women should be respected as much as men.

Final dharma age, ch. Mò fǎ, jp. Mappō (末法): Millennialist concept of "degenerate" latter days of Buddhist dharma believed to begin 2,000 years after Sakyamuni to last for "10,000 years" during which the world

is in chaos and the teachings of the Buddha alone are inadequate to attain enlightenment.
Final world war, see *Saishūsensō*.
Fiqh (فقه): Jurisprudence or legal thought in Islam.
Five Bushel Sect (*Wudou mi dao* 五斗米道): Early Taoist quasi-religious political movement.
Five cardinal Literati virtues, see *Wǔ cháng*.
Five classics, see *Wǔjīng*.
Five elements (五行) ch. *Wǔxíng*: Literally, "five goings", best translated as "Five Phases".
Flower Garland, ch. huáyán, jp. kegon, kr. hwaeom (華嚴): Sutra and related School of Thought based on *Avatamsaka Sutra* (see entry).
Four books (四書) ch. *Sìshū*: Four ancient texts central to the curriculum of neo-Confucianism, namely, the *Analects*, the *Mencius*, the *Great Learning* and the *Doctrine of the Mean*.
Four Heavenly Kings (Caturmahārāja चतुर्महाराज), ch. Sìdà tiānwáng, jp. Shidai tennō, kr. Sadae cheonwang, vt. Tứdai thiênvương (四大天王): Four divine Buddhist Kings who protect Buddhists and Buddhist states from harm with the four kings representing the four directions they oversee.
Frankfurt School: Loose school of thought associated with the Frankfurt-based Institute for Social Research based on various combinations of academic Hegelian Marxism, sociology, psychoanalysis and existentialism.
Fukko Shintō (復古神道): Literally, "revive old *Shintō*"; a movement to recover an older allegedly more pure form of *Shintō* believed to have existed before Japanese contact with Literati civilization.
Fundamentalism: An attempt to grasp a purer form of a movement, idea or religion by using a literal interpretation that is seen as more suited to the original form of the movement, idea or religion, and thus more correct and worthy.

Gana-rajya (गणराज्य): Literally, "equal kingship" or "equal government", meaning government of equals.
Gana-sangha (गणसङ्घ): Literally, "equal assembly", meaning assembly of equals.
Gbara: Representative assembly set out in the *Kouroukan Fougan*.
General will, see *volonté générale*.
Genyōsha (玄洋社): Literally, Dark Ocean Society; pan-Asianist and ultra-nationalist group in Japan begun in the late Meiji period.
Geworfenheit: Literally, "thrown" but used by Heidegger to indicate the fact that everyone enters (is thrown into) an already existing world over which we have had no influence so must cope with as it is.

Gewu (格物): Neo-Confucian concept, often translated as the "investigation of things", meaning that the principle (*li*) inherent in phenomena can be best understood by examining the principle as manifest in things themselves.

Gikuyu: Kenya's president Kenyatta identified this system of rule based on traditional African consultative and cooperative relationships in and between tribes.

Golden Light Sūtra (Suvarṇaprabhāsa Sūtra सुवर्ण प्रभास उत्तम सूत्र), ch. Jīn guāng míng jīng, jp. Konkōmyō kyō (金光明經), full name is the "Sovereign King of Sutras, the Sublime Golden Light" (Suvarṇaprabhāsottamasūtrendrarājaḥ सुवर्णप्रभासोत्तमसूत्रेन्द्रराज): Buddhist texts that offer protection to rulers.

Golpum System (骨品制度): Literally, "bone quality" system; system of status regulation in the Silla dynasty with the two top level termed "bone" (*gol* 骨) ranks, "sacred bone" (*seonggol* 聖骨) for that part of the Kim royal family of pure royal blood and "true bone" (*jingol* 眞骨) for the rest of the royal family, mainly the Park and Seok branch families with "Head Ranks" (*dupum* 頭品) for other aristocratic families and then, below them, commoners.

Gōng yang zhuàn (公羊傳) w.g. Kung-yang: Commentary on the *Chunqiu* by *Gongyang*.

Governmentality: The processes by which governments manipulate and control individuals through subtle processes in order to make them easier to govern.

Gozan (五山) system: Literally, "five mountains" based on the Zen temples established with support of the Kamakura Shōgunate, starting with three monasteries in Kyoto and two in Kamakura but eventually increasing to five monasteries in each city.

Great learning (大學) ch. Dàxué: One of the Four Books of neo-Confucianism; based on a chapter taken from the *Liji*.

Great Tang code (唐律): Legal code of Tang dynasty first published in 624.

Griots: West African storytellers and sometimes advisors to kings. Also referred to as *djeli*, *jeliw*, *jeli*, *jali*, *guewel* and *iggawen* (from to sing, *iggiw*) in different areas and languages of West Africa.

Gui-ji (歸寂): The Quietist or Tranquility School or right-wing of Wang Yangming thought.

Guksa (國師), also *Kuksa*: *State Preceptor* in Korea.

Guliang zhuàn (穀梁傳) w.g. Ku-liang: Commentary on the *Chūnqiū* by Guliang.

Guómíndǎng (國民黨), w.g. Kuomintang, or officially the Zhōngguó Guómíndǎng (中國國民黨): Chinese Nationalist Party.

Gusan (九山) system: Literally, "nine mountains" system established by

Seon temples in the late Goryeo period, usually with the cooperation of a local militarized aristocracy.

Hadara (حضارة): Civilized life or urbanism.

Hadith (حديث): Literally, "reports" but referring to collections of sayings attributed to Muhammad or his key followers.

Hajj (حج): Pilgrimage to Mecca required of all Muslims once in a lifetime if physically and financially possible.

Han (藩): A domain of territory held by a lord during the Warring States and Tokugawa Shōgunate periods in Japan.

Hàn (漢): Dynasty that ruled continental East Asia from 206 BC to 220 AD; also used as a term for those who were completely assimilated into Literati society and culture of the major East Asian dynasties so that they have no other ethnic affiliation (such as Zhuang, Miao, Uyghur, Tibetan, Manchu, Korean and so on), usually comprising a majority of the population in continental East Asia outside Tibet, Mongolia, Indochina and the Korean peninsula.

Ḥayy ibn Yaqdhān (حي بن يقظان): Literally, "Alive, son of Awake", Latin title: Philosophus Autodidactus, literally, "self-taught philosopher"; English title: "The Improvement of Human Reason: Exhibited in the Life of Hai Ebn Yokdhan."

Henosis (ἕνωσις): Literally, "oneness"; the goal of *theurgy* (see entry).

Hermeneutics: Simply, interpretation, but usually with the broader meaning of strategies of interpretation.

High treason incident, see *Daigaku Jiken*.

Hikmah (حكمة): wisdom.

Hirata school (平田學): A highly nationalist and religious form of *Kokugaku* founded by the Hirata Atsutane.

Historicism: The idea that historical context is important to understanding a concept or text; it ranges from "weak historicism" where the historical context is taken into account in interpretation to "strong historicism" where it is argued that only those who lived in the original historical context can truly understand the concept or text.

Hồng-Đức thiện chính thư (鴻德善政書): Good Book of Government of the Hong Duc Era.

Hósios (ὅσιος): Pious, hallowed, holy.

Hossō (法相宗): The Japanese term for the Yogācāra sect of Buddhism.

Huáyán Jinshīzi zhāng (華嚴金師子章): "On the Golden Lion" Fazang's essay on Flower Garland (Huáyán) philosophy presented to the court of Empress Wu.

Huguenots: French *Protestants*.

Hun (魂) tamashi (jp.): Soul.

Hungu faction (勳舊派): Powerful former officials who became owners of large tracts of land and dominated the Court in early Joseon Korea.

Hurriyya (حُرِّيَّة): Concept of personal political liberty in Arabic.

Hyeonjeong non (顯正論) or "Exposition of the Correct" by the Korean monk Gihwa.

Hyeonjeong non (顯正論): Defense of Buddhism by Gihwa, a Seon Buddhist monk, in response to neo-Confucian attacks; translated as "Exposition of the Correct".

Hyle (ὕλη): Matter, considered passive and inert in Stoic metaphysics.

Hwajaeng (和諍): Literally, "harmonization of conflict".

Hwarang (花郎): Elite trained group of young people in the Silla dynasty.

Icchantika (इच्छन्तिक) ch. yīchǎntí, jp. issendai, kr. ilcheonje (一闡提): Person so deluded or flawed that they lack Buddha nature and are incapable of achieving enlightenment.

Iddah, al (العدة): Literally "the counting" or an appropriate period of time to elapse between divorce and remarriage to avoid confusion over the paternity of children.

Ihya Ulum al-Din (إحياء علوم الدين), also Ihya'u Ulumiddin: Translated as "The Revival of the Religious Sciences" by Al-Ghazali.

Ijtihād (اجتهاد): Literally, "effort" meaning effort to make sense or interpret based on reasoning or mental faculties in general rather than relying solely on tradition.

Ikki (一揆): Revolt but usually applied to peasant uprisings or commoner riots.

Ikkō ikki (一向一揆): Literally, "one way revolt", reflecting the single-mindedness of True Pure Land believers when they engaged in revolt against authority.

Imām (إمام): In Sunni Islam, the term is applied widely to religious leaders in a community, such as those leading prayers in a mosque, but in Shi'a Islam it is a more exclusive term reserved for only very special religious leaders, chosen by God and near divine perfection.

Immortals, see *Shenxian*.

Imperialism: Extension of the power of a state over another state or territory to control it, mainly for the benefit of the stronger state.

Individualism: Places the most value on the individual over the collective values of the state, society, religion or group, particularly where there is a conflict between the individual and collective.

Integration: In hermeneutics, the notion that the first step in understanding a concept or text must be to interpret it so that it makes sense; ideas or texts must be integrated into one's thought processes as interesting or useful before it can be looked at more extensively to gain an understanding of other possible interpretations.

Invisible hand: The notion that free trade and competition results in the best outcomes because a hidden force seems to create a just balance as if guided by an invisible hand.

Irtifāqāt (ارتفاقات): Literally "support" or "easements" to enable aspects of civilization but used by Shāh Walīullāh to denote stages in the development of civilization.

Irresolvable dialectic: The notion that two similar concepts should be contrasted to explore what is different and what is similar but the differences should never be dismissed and resolved by positing a "core" universal concept that explains both because the tension between the differences despite similarities is important to respecting both concepts.

Jahiliyyah (جاهلية), also ǧāhiliyyah or jāhilīyah: Literally, "ignorance" but originally used to denote pre-Islamic ignorance or a state of ignorance of Islam; often used to imply that an individual or society has lost its understanding of Islam.

Jamahiriyah, al- (الجماهيرية) or al-Ǧamāhīriyyat: A form of Islamic socialism advocated by Muammar Gadaffi.

Jātaka tales (जातक): Literally, "birth history" or stories of the Buddha in his previous lives in both human and animal form.

Jeonghyesa (定慧社): Translated as the "Samadhi and Prajñā society"; group created by the Goryeo Seon Buddhism monk Jinul to establish a community of practitioners who were more lofty-minded and disciplined than in existing sects.

Jesuits, more accurately, the Society of Jesus (Societas Iesu): Highly disciplined Catholic evangelical organization which traveled widely from its creation in the sixteenth century to study the language and thought of different civilizations in order to spread Catholicism.

Jian'ai (兼愛): Literally, "inclusive care" but often translated as universal love or impartial care.

Jihād (جهاد): Literally, "striving" or "struggle"; originally, armed struggle against unbelievers, but also often interpreted as struggle to better oneself spiritually or raise the moral standard of the community; used in both senses in the *Quran*.

Jīng-shìh (經世), w.g. ching-shi: Usually translated as "statecraft"; a term used by late Qing dynasty reformers who advocated a focus on practical, concrete matters rather than the neo-Confucian ideal.

Jìngzuò (靜坐): Practice of quiet sitting; not just Buddhist meditation because used in some approaches to neo-Confucianism.

Jinn, al- (الجن), also given as djinn or genies with the singular form as jinni, djinni, or genie (الجني): Spirits mentioned in the Quran and other Islamic texts; similar to the ancient Greek *daimon*.

Jinnō shōtōki (神皇正統): Literally, Legitimate Succession of Gods and Sovereigns written by *Kitabatake Chikafusa* in 1339 to support the claims of the Emperor Go-Daigo to assume power.

Jiriki (自力): Literally, "self-power", the term given by Shinran to delusional efforts to reach enlightenment on one's own or by conventional means.

Jisha bugyō (寺社奉行): An official position in domains in Japan, most systematically in the Tokugawa period, of, literally, the "Magistrate of temples/shrines" who oversaw the land-holdings, construction of buildings, training of monks and registration of parishioners of local Buddhist temples and Shinto shrines; called the *Shūmon bugyō* (宗門奉行) or "Magistrate of Religion" in some domains.

Jitō (地頭): Literally, "land heads", usually translated as "land stewards", who were appointed to manage local manors and land holdings in theory owned by Court officers but often controlled by provincial governors and the Shōgun.

Juche (主體): North Korean political concept of self-reliance based on the rejection of reliance on external powers; the term in East Asian thought also used to denote objectivity.

Junsui keikken (純粋經驗): Literally, "pure experience" but related to phenomenological notion of approaching reality with no preconceptions.

Jūnzǐ (君子): Literally, child of a sovereign, that is, a prince, but meaning and translated as "gentleman" or "superior man"; sometimes also translated as "noble man", but not in terms of status, only behavior.

Jǔrén (挙人): Civil service examination process.

Jūshichi Jō Kenpō (十七条憲法): Literally, "Seventeen Article Constitution"; associated with Prince Shōtoku and the use of Literati political ideas to organize government in early ancient Japan.

Kabane (姓): Ancient Japanese system of Imperial Court ranks for major clan representatives or *uji* based on a relationship either to the Imperial family or specific deities.

Kagathos (κἀγαθός): Good, brave, noble.

Kairos (καιρός): Appropriate action for the circumstances.

Kalam (كلام), shortened name of Ilm al-Kalām (علم الكلام): Literally "science of discourse", with kalām meaning "word" but refers to Islamic scholastic theologians who attempt to reconcile Islam and philosophy; also sometimes referred to as speculative reasoning.

Kalos (καλός): Good, beautiful.

Kǎojùxué (考証學): Translated as "evidential learning"; approach to Literati thought developed in late Ming and early Qing dynasties in

Glossary of concepts 445

reaction to the intuitionism of Wang Yangming school by focusing on the meaning of texts rather than the heart/mind.

Karma (कर्म): Literally works, deeds, actions but used in Hinduism and later Buddhism to indicate how the fruits of one's past actions influence one's future lives after reincarnation.

Katanagari(刀狩): Nationwide sword-hunt conducted by Toyotomi Hideyoshi in late sixteenth-century Japan that effectively disarmed the peasantry leaving only a small elite of *bushi* retainers in possession of swords.

Kathekon (καθῆκον): "Appropriate behavior," "suitable actions," or "action in keeping with nature," or "proper function." Translated by Cicero as officium or duty and by Seneca as convenentia.

Kenchi (検地): Nationwide cadastral survey conducted in 1595 by Toyotomi Hideyoshi to assess the productive capacity of the land as the basis of a system of taxation and official income.

Khedive (خديو) Khediww in Arabic, from the original Turkish, sometimes transliterated as Hidiv: Viceroy or local ruler in the Ottoman Empire first used by Mohammed Ali Pasha to declare his autonomy from the Ottoman Caliph.

Khōra (χώρα): Originally meant the area outside an ancient Greek *polis* urbanized area but still part of the city's territory; used by Plato and Derrida to indicate a space in which both the idea of something and the thing itself can come to exist.

Kingdom of ends (Reich der zwecke): Concept of Immanuel Kant used to indicate the ideal constitutional and legal arrangements by which all members of the society are viewed as ends in themselves, and not as the means to an end by other members of society or the state.

Kitab ārā ahl al-madīna al-fāḍila (كتاب آراء أهل المدينة الفاضلة): Literally, "Book of the essential features of the opinions of the citizens of the best state" by Al Farabi; usually translated as "The Perfect State" or "The Virtuous State."

Kitāb a'sshifah (كتاب الشفاء): Literally, "Book of Healing" of which Book X of ibn Sina's *Metaphysics*; translated into Latin as *Sufficientia*.

Kitāb as-Sittah, al- (الكتب الستة): Literally "the six books" or the six hadith collections, the order of authenticity which varies between different schools of interpretation or doctrine.

Kitāb Ḥujjat Allāh al-Bālighah (كتاب حجة الله البالهة) more correctly transliterated as *Kitāb Ḥujjat Allāh al-Bāli3ah*: "The Book of the Conclusive Argument from God"; Shāh Walīullāh's political theory.

Kitāb l-ibar (كتاب العبر): Literally "Book of Lessons" by ibn Khaldun; full title is "Book of Lessons, Record of Beginnings and Events in the History of the Arabs and Berbers and their Powerful Contemporaries" or "Kitāb l-ibar wa Diwānu l-Mubtada wa l-Habar f ī tarikhi l-arab wa l-Barbar wa man Āsarahum min Dawī Ash-Sha'n l-Akbār" in Arabic.

Kogaku (古學): Literally, "ancient learning" in Japanese but usually denoting study of ancient texts prior to the Han dynasty rather than later interpretation from later dynasties, particularly the Song dynasty.

Kojiki (古事記): Literally, "Records of Ancient Matters"; early mainly mythological account of Japanese history, particularly the lineage of the Japanese Imperial family.

Kokki (国記): Literally, "Record of Countries"; now lost record of the numerous small clan-based kingdoms that made up prehistoric and early ancient Japan.

Kokugaku (國學): Literally, "national studies"; often translated as "nativist" but focused on Japanese literature and poetry initially and subsequently a nationalist literary movement against Literati and Buddhist thought, both of which were viewed as foreign in origin.

Kokuhonsha (國本社): Right-wing nationalist organization in pre-war Japan organized by mainstream conservative politicians but also included others from the military, business and the peerage; translated as "State Basis Society" but meaning that the state must be rooted in core principles of Imperial legitimacy and power.

Kokujin (國人): Local powerbrokers, often the de facto major landowners, in Warring States Japan.

Kokuryūkai (黒龍会): Japanese right-wing ultra-nationalist organization named after the Amur River name in Chinese with characters meaning "Black Dragon"; literally "Black Dragon Society".

Kokushi (國師): *State Preceptor* in Japan.

Kokutai (國体): Often translated as "national essence" but mystical and inseparable union of the state and Japanese culture, including a leading role for the Japanese emperor, as defined by *Kokugaku* nationalists.

Kōmeitō (公明党): Literally, "Public Enlightenment Party"; the political party sponsored by the lay Buddhist organization Sokagakkai; sometimes translated as "Clean Government Party" due to the adoption of the name by the party from a government initiative to stamp out corruption in early post-war politics.

Kouroukan fougan, also transliterated as Kurukan fuga: Constitution of the Mali Empire created after the battle of Krina in 1235.

Kshatravidya (क्षत्रविद्या): The science or wisdom to be a ruler.

Kshatriya (क्षत्रिय): Derived from the word kshatra (क्षत्र) or, literally, "those who rule, have authority"; warrior caste.

Kufr (كفر): Unbelief, that is, not believing in God, particularly Allah.

Kung-fu (功夫): Moral effort.

Kurukan fuga, see *Kouroukan fougan*.

Laissez-faire: Literally, French for "let do" but used in the sense of allowing markets to operate freely with minimal or no regulation or intervention because they will be more effective and efficient in such circumstances.

Lebensraum: Literally, "living space"; see *Spazio vitale*.

Levellers: A movement in the English Civil War period that advocated equality, religious tolerance and popular involvement in politics and government.

Lǐ (理): Often translated as "principle" as in the principles that govern the universe, but indicating the ideal form of things, relationships, etc.; also used in the sense of "truth" by Chan Buddhists.

Lǐ (禮): Ritual but includes both formal and informal aspects, with meaningful social, political and other consequences (see *performative*); also translated as propriety.

Li (里): Ancient East Asian measure of distance, approximately half a kilometer.

Lǐ jì (禮記): Translated as the Book of Rites or Record of Rites or Classic of Rites; one of the *Five Classics* based on fragmentary information of ancient rituals, etiquette and related practices. As part of the *Six Classics* or *Five Classics*, the *Liji* can also include the Rites of *Zhou* (*Zhou li* 周禮) and the Book of Etiquette and Rites (*Yi li* 儀禮).

Liángzhī (良知): Literally, knowledge of the good but generally implied that it is inherent knowledge of the good.

Liberales: Movement that fought against the Spanish monarchies of Ferdinand VII and his daughter Isabella II which followed the end of the French occupation of Spain after the Napoleonic Wars; the first political group to use the label "liberal".

Liberalism: A philosophy of political and legal equality, and freedom of the individual to act within a framework of the minimal law necessary to defend social order.

Liberation theology (Teología de la liberación): Christian theology focused on concern for the oppressed originating with Catholic thinkers in Latin America who wanted to put forward a moral response to poverty and inequality.

Lichtung: Heidegger used the word in the sense of "clearing" or opening where "being" is "disclosed" (*erschlossenheit*).

Lín jīng (麟經), see *Chūn Qiū*.

Linguistic contextualism: The idea that the meaning of words is context sensitive so that a better understanding of the meaning of concepts can be gained by greater understanding of the language from which the concept arose and was originally embedded.

Literati, see *Ru*.

Liùjīng (六經): *Six classics* of ancient East Asia, namely the *Shi Jing*, the *Shu Jing*, the *Li Ji*, the *Yijing*, the *Chunqui*, and the Book of Music (*Yuejing* 樂經), the last of which no longer exists. Sometimes referred to as the *Five Classics* if excluding the Book of Music.

Liùyì (六藝): Literally the "six arts" or six areas of knowledge and skill required for the educated individual in ancient East Asia.

Liùzhèng (六正): Translated as "Six Ways of Government Service" or Six Good [Forms of] Conduct; set of six forms of ritual behavior to be exercised by ministers toward the ruler.

Logical positivism: The philosophical position that knowledge is only possible if it is verified by empirical observation; rejects all forms of metaphysical speculation.

Logos (λόγος): Literally "I say" but seen as plea, reason, grounding, reasoned argument, also translated as word, particularly in a Christian context; basis for the modern word, "logic".

Lokāyata, see *Cārvāka*.

Lotus sutra, see *Saddharmapuṇḍarīka Sūtra*.

Lusotropicalism: The theory that the Portuguese were more effective in their colonization efforts due to their mixed racial and cultural heritage that made them more humane, friendly, and adaptable to other climates and cultures.

Madınah, al- (المدينة): Literally, "city" but usually used in the sense of a state or political regime based on ancient Greek political thought associated with the concept of *polis*.

Madınah al-dallah, al- (المدينة الضلالة) or al-dalalah: The erring city but can also mean going-astray, straying or misguided city.

Madinah al-fadila, al- (المدينة الفاضلة): The virtuous city.

Madınah al-fasiqah, al- (المدينة الفاسقة): The wicked city but can also mean immoral, debauched, dissolute or evildoing city.

Madınah al-jahilah, al- (لمدينة الجاهلية) or al-jahiliyah: The ignorant city.

Madınah al-mubaddilah, al- (المدينة المبدلة): The misguided city but can also mean mixed up, turncoat or renegade city.

Madrasa (مدرسة): Arab school, both religious and secular types, and not limited to any particular religion in many cases.

Magistrate: An individual holding an official position in government, often with discretionary powers in terms of the interpretation and execution of the law.

Mahajanapadas (महाजनपद): The sixteen "states" of Ancient India, though these were more quasi-tribal units and not countries in a modern sense with *maha*, literally "great", and *janapada*, literally "foothold of a tribe".

Mahārāja (महाराज): Great king, also given as *maharajah*.

Mahāsāṃghika (महासांघिक), ch. Dàzhòng Bù, jp. Daishubu (大衆部): Literally, the "greater mass", i.e., the majority often given as "The Great Sangha". Early Indian Buddhist group in favor of no change to Sangha rules or *vinaya*.

Mahāvaipulya Buddhāvataṃsaka sūtra (महावैपुल्यबुद्धावतंसकसूत्र), ch. Dàfāngguǎng Fóhuáyán Jīng, jp. Daihōkō Butsu-kegon Kyō, kr. Daebanggwang Bul-hwa-eom Gyeong, vt. Đại Phương Quảng Phật Hoa Nghiêm kinh, (大方廣佛華嚴經); often shortened to *Āvataṃsaka Sūtra* (अवतंसक-सूत्र), ch. Huáyán Ing, jp. Kegon kyō, kr. Hwa-eom Gyeong, vt. Hoa Nghiêm kinh (華嚴經): Literally, "Great Vaipulya Sutra of the Buddha's Flower Garland", where *vaipulya* (वैपुल्य) means "spacious"; key text in the Flower Garland School of early East Asian Buddhism.

Māhāyāna (महायान) ch. dàchéng, jp. daijō, kr. dae-seung, vt. đại thừa (大乘): Literally, "Great Vehicle"; form of Buddhism that relies less on individual ascetic discipline and more on help from super mundane beings on the path to enlightenment; dominant form of Buddhism in East Asia.

Majjhima Nikāya: Middle-length Discourses of the Buddha; largely the same as the Madhyama Āgama (Zhōng Āhán 中阿含經) of East Asian Buddhism.

Mamluk (مملوك): Slaves taken from their parents when very young and trained under strict religious and military education to become Muslim soldiers and officials.

Mandinka, also Mandenka, Mandinko, Mandingo, Manding or Malinke: A West African ethnic group.

Manicheanism: Belief in cosmological dualism between evil forces inherent in material being and the good inherent in spiritual being; advocates asceticism to purify the soul and attain spiritual goodness.

Mansa: Title of the ruler of Mali Empire; based on the Mandinka language word for leader, sultan, king or emperor.

Manusmṛti (मनुस्मृति) or Laws of Manu.

Maripgan (麻立干) m.r. Maripkan: Title given to rulers in Korea prior to the introduction of Literati government titles; similar to nomadic ruler titles, such as the Mongol term "khan", that is, more of an extended clan leader than head of government.

Matsushita Institute of Government and Management (Matsushita Seikei Juku 松下政経塾): Established in 1979 by the founder of Panasonic corporation, Matsushita Kōnosuke (松下幸之助, 1894–1989), to promote business management solutions to political and economic issues.

Meiji restoration (明治維新): Overthrow of the Tokugawa Shōgunate and rise to power of a reformist modernizing elite in 1868.

Mein kampf: Autobiography of Adolf Hitler published in two volumes in 1925 and 1926; literally, "my struggles".

Mencius (孟子) ch. Mèngzĭ: The text believed to contain the words of Mencius, an early Literati thinker.

Metaphysics: Used in the narrow sense of any theory that is based on dynamics that are not empirically verifiable.

Mihna (محنة), also transliterated as miḥnah: Literally, "trial" or "testing" but referring to an inquisition by Caliph al-Mamun in support of Mu'tazila interpretation of Islam.

Mikkyō (密教): Literally, "secret teachings" for the Shingon form of esoteric Buddhism in Japan.

Minponshugi (民本主義): Literally, the "people as the basis"-ism; a form of constitutional monarchial democracy, advocated by Yoshino Sakuzō, based on "the people" but not popular sovereignty.

Mito school (水戸學): Loose grouping of historians and thinkers in the Mito domain in Tokugawa Japan with some association with the *Kokugaku* movement.

Mu, see *Wu*.

Mu no kyōchi (無の境地): Literally, "position of nothingness" or a state of mind and bodily activity of nothingness to break down boundaries to dissolve attachments.

Muslim brotherhood (الإخوان المسلمون): Founded by Hassan al-Banna in Egypt in 1928.

Mutazila (المعتزلة): Islamic theologians who used reason to support their theological arguments.

Namo amitābhāya (नमोऽमिताभाय) in classical Chinese 南無阿彌陀佛, pronounced in ch. Nāmó Ēmítuófó, jp. Namu Amida Butsu, kr. Namu Amita Bul, vt. Nammo Azida Fut: Literally, "Homage or Devotion to the Buddha of the Infinite Light"; an invocation of the phrase is central to Pure Land Buddhism.

Nation of Islam: Movement formed in 1930 to raise the political and social status of African Americans through a distinctive philosophy based on Islamic religious principles.

Neglected Obligation, The (الفريضة الغائبة), transliterated as Al-Farida al-gha'iba or Alfarida alghayiba; Literally, the "Absent Obligation", the latter word particularly in the sense of religious duty, so could also be translated as "The Neglected Duty"; title of the book by the Jihadist Muhammad abd-al-Salam Faraj.

Négritude: From "blackness" in French, which was originally a pejorative term similar to "nigger" in English, but adopted by Francophone writers of African ancestry, particularly in the 1930s, to emphasize the virtues and positive aspects of being black.

Nembutsu, see *Niàn fó*.

Neo-Confucianism: A concept imported from the West (hence no Chinese characters) based on a mistranslation using the term Confucianism, and usually given in East Asia as Song Learning (宋學), Song-Ming Principle School (宋明理學) or School of the Way (道學), the last not to be confused with Taoism.

Neo-Conservativism: Loose category of politicians, academics and others, centered around former US leftists and those influenced by them, who promoted an aggressive form of free market liberalism and assertive US interventionist foreign policy since the 1970s.

Neo-Liberalism: Movement to reduce size and power of the state by privatization and deregulation in support of free markets and free trade, and opposed to state-mandated social welfare programs and income redistribution.

Neo-Tocquevillean: Often used as a slightly pejorative term for the theoretical approach, often used in US academic circles, that suggests the basis for stable democracy is found in widespread citizen involvement in intermediate social organizations and clubs (between family and the state) based on the work of Alex de Tocqueville; such an approach tends to oppose state involvement in dealing with social problems, such as poverty, in favor of voluntary private organizations, such as churches, charities and so on.

New Confucianism, see *Xīn Rújiā*.

New Culture Movement, see *Xīn wénhuà yùndòng*.

New texts (今文經學) Jīnwén Jīng xué; w.g. Chinwen Ching Hsueh): Refers to early Han dynasty versions of Chinese Warring States period texts written in characters standardized by the Qin dynasty; new texts were not too much different from the old text but reflect the evolution of Literati thought since the Qin which saw Confucius as a much more mystical figure promoting Sage learning. This fit with the approach of Dong Zongshu and the Song neo-Confucianists. See also, *Old texts*.

New Woman Association, see *Shin Fujin Kyōkai*.

Nichiren shōshū (日蓮正宗): Literally, "Orthodox School of Nichiren" Buddhism; lineage of this sect is from only one of Nichiren's disciples.

Nichiren shū (日蓮宗): The Nichiren sect of Buddhism is a federation of temples organized by all the original disciples of Nichiren except one (see *Nichiren Shōshū*).

Niệm phật, see *Niàn fó*.

Niàn fó (念佛) jp. *nembutsu*, kr. *yeombul*, vt. *niệm Phật*: Literally, "mindful-

452 *A world history of political thought*

ness of the Buddha" from the sk. *buddhānusmṛti* (बुद्धानुस्मृति) or pa. *buddhānussati*; simple verbal formula to call on *Buddha* for rebirth in Pure Land.

Nihilism: Literally, belief in nothing; rejection of all organized belief systems.

Nihon Shoki (日本書紀): One of the earliest historical records of Japan, based on older history and documents, with some degree of historical detail.

Nippon-shugi (日本主義): Literally, "Japanism" or the notion that Japan should be the center of all things; also given as Nihon-shugi but the use of pronunciation "Nippon" implies a more nationalist tone.

Nirmāṇakāya (निर्मानकाय): Literally, "transformation body", meaning physical manifestation of Buddha in our physical world.

Niti (नीति): Used to indicate prudence, moral code, management, conduct, guidance, policy but used in the sense of (legal) right, political wisdom, prudent counsel, correct conduct.

Nitivakyamrtam (नीतिवाक्यामृत): Literally, the "Nectar of the Science of Polity", with Niti as political wisdom (see above) and vākya (वाक्य) indicating discourse or talks and amrta (अमृत) as the ambrosia or nectar of immorality, such as that drunk by gods.

Nomos physis (Νόμος φύσις): Literally laws or norms of nature, but used as the basis of the theory of natural law.

Normative: A philosophical approach that focuses on standards or norms of behavior that ought to be adopted; often contrasted with empirical as in study of actual behavior rather than the ideal or most desirable behavior.

Nous (νοῦς or νόος): The mind (Aristotle) or Intellect (neo-Platonism).

Nuevo Hombre, el: Literally, "the New Man"; Che Guevarra's belief that socialism could foster the emergence of a selfless and non-materialistic individual who was motivated by doing one's best for the sake of society rather than for personal economic rewards.

Nyamakala: Families or clans who had the monopoly on certain trades in a guild system in the Mali Empire.

Nyonin shōki (女人正機): Rennyo's view that women have a special need for Buddhist compassion.

Ogyo yangjong (五教兩宗): Goryeo divisions of Buddhism with the five text-based doctrinal schools (*Vinaya* or Gyeyul, Flower Garland or Hwaeom, the Three Treatises or Samnon, Nirvana or Yeolban, and Beopseong) and two meditation-based sects (Cheontae and Seon).

Ōhō butsuhō izon (王法佛法依存): Interdependence between the royal and Buddhist realms.

Old texts (古文經學) Gǔwén Jīng xué; w.g. Kuwen Ching Hsueh: Refers to pre-Qin discovered during the Han dynasty, written in archaic characters and supposedly produced before the burning of the books in the Qin dynasty, as opposed to the "New Texts"; a few "Old Texts" were forgeries but key "Old Text" versions were used in later philological criticism of Han and Song dynasty reinterpretation of key Literati texts. See also, *New texts*.

One, the (τὸ ἕν): The ultimate unity of all things in neo-Platonism.

Ōnin Rebellion (応仁の亂): Between 1467–1477 a local dispute between two local lords escalated into a national struggle for power that undermined the Ashikaga Shōgunate and marks the beginning of the Japanese Warring States period (1467–1600).

Original position: Concept of John Rawls as part of a *thought experiment* used to replace the notion of a state nature by having one think out the consequences of one's position in political society when one does not know where one fits in political society; see also *Veil of ignorance*.

Padshah Begum (پادشاه بیگم): Special honorific designation of the most revered female of the Mughal Empire.

Pali Canon: Collection of the sayings of the Buddha written in the Pali language, a language that is likely close to the original in which the Buddha spoke to his followers.

Parrhēsia (παρρησία): Literally "all" (πᾶν) and "utterance, speech" (ῥῆσις) meaning "to speak everything", that is, freedom to speak one's mind, to speak candidly.

Paticcasamuppada (प्रतीत्यसमुत्पाद), pa. *pratītyasamutpāda* (पटिच्चसमुप्पाद): Dependent origination or the notion that all things in the world are the product of a complex chain of cause and effect.

Peloponnesian war (Πελοποννησιακός Πόλεμος) 431–404 BC: War fought between ancient Greek city-state of Athens and its *de facto* empire in the Delian League against the Peloponnesian League led by the ancient monarchy of Sparta.

People: Refers to the human population of a state or to a larger ethnic, religious or other identity group to which a large population belongs; often seen as needing control or seen as the basis of support or rule, including popular or even democratic rule.

Performative: The notion that making some types of statements perform meaningful acts in themselves, such as oaths or marriage vows, with legal, social or political consequences.

Permanent revolution: The idea that the revolutionary class must pursue its aims regardless of claims of other groups in society.

Phenomenology: The philosophical approach to engaging the world with the absolute minimum of conscious preconceptions in order to make sense of how one perceives and engages the world.

Philology: Study of the historical origins of language as used in key texts.

Phronēsis (φρόνησις): Practical wisdom (versus theoretical wisdom); wisdom acquired by experience with real world problems.

Physei doulos (φύσει δοῦλος): Slaves by nature who, according to Aristotle, are incapable of ruling themselves so must be under the control of others.

Physiocrats: Literally, "government by nature" in Greek; early school of political economy which emphasized productive labor as the source of wealth, particularly that derived from the land in rural areas which was considered more natural than the wealth in cities from exchange and speculation.

Physis (φύσις): Nature.

Pneuma (πεῦμα): Literally, wind, but also given as vital breath, breath, spirit and used in Stoic cosmology for the property of the universe that allowed things to be manifest.

Polis (πολις): Literally, "city" in ancient Greece but often used as a term for government, state or political regime in classical Greece, Roman and Islamic political thought.

Political animal (πολιτικό ζώο): Used by Aristotle and later thinkers to argue that human beings can only be viewed as part of a political community and not merely as individuals.

Politikos (πολιτικός): Ancient Greek terms used by Plato and Aristotle to indicate an individual with the skills to participate in ruling a state.

Ponos (πονος): Work.

Pŏpsŏng, see *Beopseong* (法性): "Dharma Nature" School; Buddhist school unique to Korea.

Positivism: The notion that everything in the world, including social and political relations, can be explained by observable natural phenomenon that operate in a law-like pattern.

Post-colonialism: The attempt to study people on their own terms while recognizing that, in the post-colonial condition, words and associated ideas have been created and imposed by political systems that have historically and culturally oppressed so that authentic articulation and use of ideas is limited; actual life experience can exceed and alter existing meanings of concepts, leading to new ways of understanding and sites of resistance for authentic expression outside of colonial categories.

Postmodernism: Generic popular term for rejection of modern science and social science; the term usually includes or is substituted for *post-structuralism*.

Post-structuralism: The approach that rejects the positivist view that the

world can be explained by objective analysis of clear and permanent structures.
Prajñā (प्रज्ञ) pa. paññā; ch. zhì, jp. chi, kr. ji (智): "Wisdom" or "knowledge", thought more in the sense of discerning knowledge or insight.
Princeps: "First citizen."
Principle of charity: The philosophical approach that one should try to make the best case for statements or ideas by interpreting in the most favorable way that makes the most sense.
Proletariat: The working class in Marxism but originally meaning the property-less class who earn their living through exchanging their labor for a wage.
Propaganda of the deed: The notion that dramatic acts can serve to promote a cause, particularly associated with nineteenth-century *anarchism* and the thought of *"Hans" Most*.
Protestant: Form of Christianity that began with the reform movement against corruption in the Catholic Church in the reformation.
Providentia: Translated in English as "providence" from pro- "ahead" and videre "to see" but meaning the future as it will unfold, by implication in a natural and just way; Originally a stoic term but later strongly associated with Christian notions of divine providence as set by God.
Psyche (ψυχή): Soul.
Pudgalavāda (पुद्गलवाद पुद्गल), ch. bǔtèjiāluó lùnzhě, jp. futogara ronsha (補特伽羅論者): Literally, "theory of person", meaning the "personalist" school of Buddhism that argued that the idea of a pudgala or "person" is required to make sense of karma and rebirth.
Pure Land (浄土) ch. Jìngtǔ, jp. Jōdo, kr. Jeongto, vt. Tịnh Độ: Buddhist realm in which sentient beings can achieve Enlightenment more easily.

Qì (氣): Literally, spark, but used as the concept of all that is empirically manifest in the universe; more than materialism because it includes electro-magnetic forces and even psychology.
Qīng tán (清談): Literally, "pure conversation", but meaning wide ranging discussion unconstrained by formality, which was popular in the period after the end of the Han dynasty and associated with *Xuánxué* thought.
Qiyas (قياس): Deductive analogy or reasoning in Islamic jurisprudence to supplement the Quran and hadith where there is no clear precedent.
Quakers: Christian protestant group that rejected formal priesthood and sought to implement ideals of piety and radical egalitarianism in everyday acts; formally known as the Religious Society of Friends.
Quran, al- (القرآن), also koran: Literally, "the recitation"; key text in Islam in which it is viewed as revelation from God (*Allāh*).

Racism: The ideology and belief that there are specific identifiable races with clear differences between them and that some are superior to others.

Raghuvamsha (रघुवंश): Poem by Kalidasa.

Raja (राजा) from Sanskrit *rājan* (राजन्): King or kingly.

Rajadharma (राजधर्म): Royal duties or the kingly way.

Rajavritta (राजावृत्तिल्व): True/correct behavior of kings such as truth and compassion.

Ran (亂): Violent incident or series of incidents.

Rangaku (蘭學): Literally, "Dutch Studies" for Western knowledge from the fact that most Western literature was imported from Holland and written in Dutch during the early Tokugawa period; "Ran" from Japanese for *oran* (和蘭) or *oranda* (和蘭陀) from Japanese pronunciation of "Holland", "gaku" for "studies" or "learning".

Rashidun caliphs (اَلْخُلَفَاءُ الرَّاشِدُونَ) most accurately transliterated as *al-Khilāfah ar-Rāshidah*: Literally, "rightly guided caliphs," specifically the first five caliphs, namely Abū Bakr (c. 573–634), Umar (583–644), Uthman (576–656), Ali (601–661), Hasan ibn Ali (624–670).

Recht: Often translated as "law" or "jurisprudence" but also meaning true, just or right.

Reconstruction: The attempt to recover the original or true meaning of the text by using the evidence of the life of the author and the historical context in which the author wrote in order to reconstruct the original or true meaning.

Reflexivity: The process of questioning one's background, interests and pre-conceptions toward the subject one is studying in order to be sensitive to how these might distort one's understanding of the subject and even cause harm to others by how the subject is studied, analyzed and discussed.

Reform Act of 1832: British electoral reform aimed at ensuring more equal representation and enfranchised nearly twice as many individuals but stopped well short of universal suffrage, even for men.

Reign of Terror, or simply "The Terror" (la Terreur): Period of a large number of politically motivated executions from 1793 to 1794 during the French Revolution.

Reikon (霊魂): Literally, spirits and demons; ancient spiritual forces with great powers.

Religion: Primarily a Western concept, the use of which one must take care in applying to non-Western societies; but, loosely conceived, is a widely held set of beliefs based on faith in divine forces with a set of practices (lay behavior and liturgy) supporting these beliefs, often administered by formal organizations established to promote these beliefs.

Religion of humanity: Secularized religious system created by Auguste Comte as a modern substitute for conventional religion.

Ren (仁): The moral concept of "good", emphasized by Confucius and later Literati, sometimes translated as benevolence, humanness or goodness.

Republican: Form of government that involves institutions involving rule by large numbers of individuals rather than rule by a single individual, such as a monarch or dictator.

Revisionism: Often used to describe attempts to soften earlier more militant forms of socialism, such as that advocated by Karl Marx, by revising the methods by which society will be changed to avoid reliance on violent revolution.

Revive China Society or Xīngzhōnghuì (興中會), w.g. Hsing Chung Hui: Late Qing dynasty revolutionary group led by Sun Yat-sen.

Risshō kōsei kai (立正佼成会): A new religion of Japan that broke from the Nichiren Shū Buddhist organization to form an independent sect.

Roman Catholic Church, see *Catholic Church*.

Romanticism: Emphasis on strong aesthetic and emotional experience over rationality and abstract idealism.

Rōnin (浪人): Often translated as "masterless samurai", that is, of Japanese elite warrior training and sociopolitical status, but not employed by a lord or domain. Literally, "flowing person" with "flow" from strongly flowing water or waves.

Ru (儒): Literati, that is, literate in classical literature. Often mistakenly translated as Confucian but does often indicate a particular interest in and respect for the literature associated with Confucius and his various followers.

Rūpakāya (रूपकय) ch. sèshēn, jp. iromi (色身): Literally, "outward appearance or color body", meaning the physical body of the Buddha.

Saddharmapuṇḍarīka sūtra (सद्धर्मपुण्डरीक सूत्र), ch. Miàofǎ Liánhuá jīng, jp. Myōhō Renge kyō, kr. Myobeop Yeonhwa gyeong, vt. Diệu pháp Liên hoa kinh (妙法蓮華經), often shortened to ch. Fǎhuá jīng, jp. Hokke-kyō, kr. Beophwa gyeong, vt. Pháp hoa kinh (法華經) or "Lotus Sutra": Literally, "Lotus Blossom of the Fine Dharma Sūtra"; key text in East Asian Buddhism.

Sage, see *Shèngrén*.

Sahwa (士禍): Violent purges of officials in early Joseon Korea.

Saishūsensō (最終戰争): Nichiren thinker Ishiwara Kanji's concept of "Final World War" in which Japan and the United States would be engaged in a protracted and destructive war for global dominance that Japan would win.

Salafism (سلفية): Derived from the Arabic term "salaf" (سلف) meaning "predecessors" from "al-salaf al-ṣāliḥ" (السلف الصالح) or "pious predecessors"; often defined as the first three generations of followers of Muhammad with the implication that they better understood the true meaning of Muhammad's teaching due to the close historical proximity to him and his immediate followers, but sometimes used pejoratively to criticize those who adopt a narrow and ultra-conservative interpretation of Islam.

Samadhi (समाधि): State of meditative consciousness.

Sambhogakāya (सम्भोगकाय): Literally, "enjoyment-body", meaning the manifestation of a Buddha in different realms associated with that Buddha, such as the *Pure Land*.

Samguk Sagi (三國史記): Literally "Historical Account of the Three Kingdoms"; a relatively factual account of the Three Kingdoms period in Korean history.

Samguk Yusa (三國遺事): Literally "Memorabilia of the Three Kingdoms"; an account of the Three Kingdoms period in Korean history incorporating myths as well as some potentially factual information.

Saṃmitīya (संमितीया), ch. zhèngliàng bù, jp. shōryōbu (正量部): Popular Indian Buddhist sect in first millennium AD.

Samrat (सम्राज्): King of kings or overlord.

Samurai (侍): Literally, "retainers", who originally were servants of the Imperial Court but evolved into a military class in Japan. See also, *Bushi*.

Saṃyutta Nikāya: Connected or Kindred Discourses of the Buddha; largely the same as the Saṃyukta Āgama (Zá Ahánjīng 雜阿含經) in East Asian Buddhism.

Sanankunya (also sanankou[n]ya, sinankun, senenkun, senankuyaa): West African practice where one should or may treat another or each other as if cousins or close family members with whom familiar jokes or humorous insults are exchanged. Often translated as "joking relationship" or "cousinage."

Sangha (सङ्घ) in Pali; sk. samgha (संघ): Literally "assembly" (see entry for *gana-sangha*) but subsequently used to mean Buddhist community of monks, both in small communities and the theoretical community of all Buddhist monks.

Sangō shiiki (三教指帰): Translated as "Principles of the Three Teachings" by Kūkai published in 798.

Sangyō kisho (三經義疏): Commentaries on three key Buddhist sūtras attributed to Prince Shōtoku: the "Lotus Blossom of the Fine Dharma Sūtra" (*Myōhō Renge Kyō* 妙法蓮華經), the "Vimalakīrti Sūtra" (*Yuima Kyō* 維摩經) and the "Śrīmālādevī Sūtra" (*Shōman kyō* 勝鬘經).

Sānjiao (三教) jp. sankyō, kr. samjiào: Literally, the "three teachings" i.e., Literati, Taoism and Buddhism.

Sankin kotai (参勤交代): System of "alternative attendance" where the lords of all domains in Tokugawa Japan had to spend part of the year in residence in the capital, Edo.

Sānmínzhǔyì (三民主義): Usually translated as the "Three principles of the people" created by Sun Yat-sen to promote revolution in Qing dynasty and guide the future development of the Republic of China; the three principles were mínzú (民族) or "nationalism", mínquán (民權) or "people's rights", and mínshēng (民生) "people's life".

Sānshī (三師) jp. sanshi: Translated as the "Three Scholarly Occupations" but more correctly as the "Three Excellencies" indicating the three top civil service positions in the Literati court system, namely the Grand Preceptor (太師), also called the Grand Master, Grand Tutor (太傅) and Grand Protector (太保).

Sarim faction (士林派): Literati-official of Joseon Korea in favor of a strict interpretation of *neo-Confucianism* applied to governing the nation.

Sarvāstivāda (सर्वास्तिवाद) in Sanskrit, pa. sabbatthivāda, ch. shuōyīqiēyǒu-bù, jp. setsuissai bu (説一切有部): Literally, "all exists theory". Early school of Buddhist thought that argued that all dharmas – past, present and future, and everywhere – exist simultaneously, which denies any reality to an individual "self" fixed in a particular place and time.

Satyagraha (सत्याग्रह): Literally, "truth insistence" or a force for truth by which one can instill independence of mind and courage to act to do the right thing.

Scholasticism: Use of established religious and metaphysical dogma to analyze problems.

Scientific socialism: Term created by *Karl Marx* to distinguish his theories of social development leading to socialism from earlier *utopian socialism*.

Sect (宗) ch. Zōng, jp. Shu, kr. Jong, vt. Tông: Used for schools of East Asian Buddhism as distinguished from *doctrinal schools* (教); a sect has more of a liturgy than doctrinal schools.

Sengoku (戰國): Japan in the Warring States period between 1467 and 1600.

Senshindō (洗心洞): Literally, Clean or Pure Heart Grotto; the name of the school set up by Ōshio Heihachirō.

Senshindō sakki (洗心洞箚記): Book based on lectures by *Ōshio Heihachirō*, a late Tokugawa Ōyōmei thinker and police official who led an uprising in Osaka in 1837. For meaning of *Senshindō* (洗心洞), see entry above.

Seon, see *Chán*.

Sesok-ogye (世俗五戒): Literally, "Five Commandments for Secular Life" written by *Won Gwang* and used by the *Hwarang*.

Seven Sages of the bamboo grove, see *Zhúlín qīxián*.

Seventeen article constitution, see *Jūshichi jō kenpō*.
Shamen bu jingwangzhe lun (沙門不敬王者論): Translated as "A Monk Does Not Bow Down Before A King" written by Hui-Yüan in 404.
Shari'a (شريعة): Islamic legal tradition.
She (射): Archery, one of the Ancient East Asian "six arts" (liùyì).
Shèn (神) jp. *kami* or *shin*, kr. *sin*: God, spirit, usually associated with animist beliefs but also applicable to humans and heavenly beings; as in Western languages, the term "spirit" can also have a psychological meaning as well.
Shèngrén (聖人): Literally "holy person" but usually translated as "sage" in the context of Literati thought with the meaning of extraordinarily wise in Literati thought and goal of later Literati personal and professional cultivation; mentioned by Confucius in relation to the model of early emperors who combined effective rule with moral authority.
Shènmíng (神明): Literally spiritual light or perhaps enlightenment but usually translated as "intelligence."
Shènqì (神器): Literally, sacred instrument.
Shènwáng (聖王), see *Shèngrén*.
Shènxiān (神仙): Literally, spirit hermit; also translated as "Immortal".
Shì (勢): Circumstantial advantage, power, or authority in early Taoist-Legalist thought.
Shījīng (詩經): Translated the Book of Poetry or Book of Songs or Classic of Poetry; one of the *Five Classics* based on a collection of ancient poetry and songs.
Shin Fujin Kyōkai (新婦人協会): Literally, "New Woman Association" was formed by Ichikawa Fusae and Hiratsuka Raicho in 1919 to agitate for the involvement of women in politics in Japan.
Shingon (真言): Literally "True Word"; sect of Buddhism in Japan based on esoteric Vajrayana Buddhism.
Shinron (新論): Literally, "New Theses"; a work by Aizawa Seishisai aimed at strengthening the state through popular forms of national unity.
Shintō (神道): Literally, "way of the gods"; animistic polytheistic belief system in Japan.
Shítǐ (實體): "Actual forms".
Shíwén (實文): "Actual writings".
Shíxíng (實行): "Actual activities".
Shíyòng (實用): "Actual use".
Shōgun (将軍): Japanese military leaders who ruled Japan, nominally under appointment by the Imperial Court but mainly based on feudary ties with military allies.
Shramana (श्रमण), also given as sramanas: Ascetic wanders.
Shravakas (श्रावक) ch. shēngwén, jp. shōmon (聲聞): Literally, "one who

proclaims and hears" or a stage in ascetic sects such as Jainist or Buddhist beyond lay follower but not fully enlightened.

Shū (書): Calligraphy, one of the Ancient East Asian "six arts" (*liùyì*).

Shū (數): Mathematics, one of the Ancient East Asian "six arts" (*liùyì*).

Shudra (शूद्र): Caste of servants, menial workers.

Shugo (守護): Literally, "protector", usually translated as "governor" or "constable", were appointed to manage one or more provinces of Japan in the interests of Court officials, though often they served the interests of a Shōgun or themselves.

Shū Jīng (書經): Translated as the Book of Documents or Classic of History; one of the Five Classics based on ancient documents and records of events; also given as *Shangshu* (尚書).

Siddha (सिद्ध): Literally "one who is accomplished" also translated as "great thinker" or "sage", referring to both physical and spiritual perfection or enlightenment leading to supernatural power.

Siddharaja (सिद्धराज): Enlightened king.

Sitātapatrā (सितातपत्रोष्णीष) ch. Báisǎngài fúdǐng; jp. Byakusangai Butchō (白傘蓋佛頂): Literally, "White Parasol Buddha Top" or a deification of the wisdom springing from the topknot on the head of Gautama Buddha in the form of a Vajrayana Buddhist goddess who protects against supernatural danger and is associated with nonviolent cakravartin (universal monarch) rule.

Six arts, see *Liùyì*.

Six classics, see *Liùjīng*.

Six Ways of Government Service, see *Liùzhèng*.

Siyar al-muluk (سيرالملوك), *Siyasat-nama* (سياست نامه) in Persian: Literally, the "conduct of kings"; title of book attributed to Nizam al-Mulk, but not likely written by him with the title usually translated as "Rules for Kings" or "Book of Government".

Siyāsat al-madina (سياست المدينه): Farsi (Persian) term for ruling the state (literally, the "politics or political affairs of the city").

Skandhas (Sanskrit: स्कन्ध) or khandhas (Pāli): Literally "heaps, aggregates, groups" of sensations, perceptions (space, time, etc.) and consciousness that make up our understanding of human existence.

Social Darwinism: Application of Darwin's theory of evolution to dynamics within human society to suggest that certain individuals or groups, including races and nationality, are more fit to survive physically, morally and economically, so that the superior individuals and groups (races) must be permitted to flourish and the weaker to disappear.

Socialism in one country (Социализм в отдельно взятой стране) or, sotsializm v odnoy otdelno vzyatoy strane: Policy of Stalin aimed at building socialism in the Soviet Union after it became apparent that earlier predictions that the Soviet revolution would lead to worldwide revolution did not come to fruition.

Soft power: The power to persuade through cultural and philosophical ideas rather than through military or economic coercion.

Sokagakkai (創価学会): Literally, "Creative Values Study Group"; Buddhist lay organization, which has broken away from the Nichiren Shōshū Buddhist sect; politically involved in Japan and active in promoting Buddhism internationally.

Sokushin jōbutsu (即身成佛) ch. jíshēnchéngfó: Japanese term for concept of realization of Buddhahood with one's existing body, which suggested that anyone can attain Buddhahood without the need for reincarnation into a high type of being first.

Sonnō jōi (尊皇攘夷), literally, "Revere the Emperor, Expel the Barbarian": Key slogan of the Loyalist movement and led for calls for the emperor to replace the Tokugawa shōgun as the leader of Japan as the basis of national renewal to fight the threat of Western encroachment.

Sophists (σοφιστής): Teachers of rhetoric, debate and public speaking; sometimes used pejoratively to indicate those who are not interested in the truth and only interested in persuading others and winning an argument.

Sophos kagathos (σοφός κἀγαθός): Beauty of knowledge.

Spazio vitale: Literally, "vital space" but the idea that a group of people, such as a nation, require adequate or additional space because they are superior or dynamic so require land more than others who are considered inferior, often aided by colonial and imperialist policies of annexation and emigration.

Spirit (Geistes): Used in Hegel's philosophy where it is often translated as mind or spirit or mind/spirit, it contrasts with *xin* as heart/mind in that "geistes" is more general and applied to groups of people or periods in history, whereas *xin* is related to an individual.

Śrīmālādevī Siṃhanāda sūtra (श्रीमालादेवीसिंहनादसूत्र) ch. Shengmanshizihou yicheng dafangbian fangguangjing, jp. Shōman shishiku ichijō daihōben hōkōgyō (勝鬘師子吼一乘大方便方廣經): Literally, the "Lion's Roar of Queen Śrīmālā", an early Mahāyāna Buddhist text in which Queen Śrīmālā teaches that there is a form of consciousness in each being with the potential to attain liberation from the defilements of attachment to this world.

Statecraft, see *jīng-shìh*.

State preceptor (國師) kr. Guksa or Kuksa, jp. Kokushi: The top monk or monks appointed by the Imperial Court to oversee the *sangha* of the state.

Sthaviravāda (स्थविरवाद; 上座部): Literally "those seated higher", often given as "Sect of The Elders", early Buddhist group of senior monks who favored additions to the *sangha* rules or *vinaya*.

Stoics (Στωικισμός): Literally, those who gathered in the colonnades (*stoa*) of the ancient Athenian agora market, but indicating the school of thought beginning with Zeno, which was very influential in Hellenic and Roman political thought.

Store consciousness, see *Ālayavijñāna*.

Sufism, see *Taṣawwuf*.

Sundiata epic, also spelled Son-Jara or Sundjata: Semi-historical account of the story of Sundiata Keita and his creation of the Mali Empire.

Sunnah (سنة): Literally, "way" or path but used in Islamic to designate a path and manner of living based on the teachings of the prophet Muhammad.

Śūnyatā (शून्यता) Pa. suññatā, ch. kōng, jp. kū (空): Emptiness.

Suppression of Buddhism (崇儒廢佛), ch. chóngrú fèifó, jp. sūju-haibutsu, kr. sungyu pyebul: Literally, "promote Literati ("Confucianism") abolish Buddha (Buddhism), also sungyu ôkpul (崇儒抑佛) "promote Confucianism, reject Buddhism" in Korean; the policy of the suppression of Buddhism and promotion of Literati (neo-Confucian) thought in Joseon Korea and Tokugawa Japan.

Survival of the fittest: The phrase created by Herbert Spencer and later adopted by Charles Darwin to describe those members of a species who were best adapted for survival but often associated with Social Darwinism.

Śvētāmbara (श्वेतांबर) or śvētapaṭa (श्वेतपट): Literally, "white-clad" Jainist ascetics who wear white robes.

Swadeshi (चुतेचि) Hindi word: Literally, "self-sufficiency"; used to suggest basis for being independent, economically and politically.

Syndicalism: Management of society through union and industrial organization based on democratic control by workers.

Taeguksa (大國統): Literally, Great State Controller or Overseer; title given to *Silla* monk *Jajang* who was put in charge of the *Silla sangha*.

Taehak (太學): Ancient Korean institution of higher education teaching *Literati* thought.

Taika (大化): Literally, "great change"; the system of reforms to Japanese Imperial government starting in 645, which led to full Literati style governmental and legal system.

Tàijí (太極) w.g. T'ai chi: Literally, the "great pole" or "great polarity" but often translated as the "supreme ultimate".

Tàijí túshuō (太極圖說): Translated as "Explanation of the Diagram of Highest Motion" by Zhou Dunyi which became a key text in the development of neo-Confucianism.

Taika (大化): Literally, "great change"; the system of reforms to Japanese Imperial government starting in 645, which led to full Literati style governmental and legal system.

Taishō Democracy (大正デモクラシー): Period in modern Japanese history under the Taishō emperor (大正天皇, 1879–1926, r. 1912–1926) considered to be relatively liberal, during the period from the appointment of the first non-aristocratic prime minister in 1918 to the passage of the law for elections under universal manhood suffrage in 1925.

Tàixū (太虛) w.g. T'ai hsü, jp. Taikyo: Literally, "great vacuity" or "great void" but used to indicate the nothingness from which things emerge; has also been translated as "aether", a term that was used in nineteenth-century physics to indicate an unseen substance that was posited to exist in between physical things in order to transmit light and non-physical forces.

Tàizhōu school (泰州學派): Ming dynasty school of Wang Yangming thought included a range of participants from all levels of Ming society.

Takfir (تكفير): Verbal excommunication by declaring another Muslim as an "unbeliever" in Islam.

Tanamannyonya: The concept of "blood pacts" in Mali society based on shared family relations; these ties can cut across rather than reinforce other cleavages such as tribe, ethnicity, regionalism, and so on.

Táng lǜ shūyì (唐律疏議): Commentary on Great Tang Code added to the Code in 653.

Tanzimat (تنظيمات): Literally, "Reorganization"; an ambitious program of reform decreed by Ottoman Sultan and Caliph *Mahmud II*.

Tào (道): Literally the path or road but usually meaning the Way, as in the way things go. Also given as *Dào* but here the Wade-Giles has become acceptable as the preferred reading for many scholars.

Tarikh-i-firuz shahi (تاريخ فيروز شاهي): Historical work of Ziauddin Barani.

Tariki (他力): Literally, "other-power", or the notion of Shinran that the power of a force greater than ourselves or humans in general is required to achieve enlightenment.

Taṣawwuf (تصوف): Islamic mysticism; translated into English as Sufism.

Tawḥīd (توحيد): Literally, "to unify" or the idea that God is a single unique indivisible entity; also transliterated as tawheed and touheed or tevhid.

Telos (τέλος): The ends, aims.

Temple of literature (文廟) Vt. *Văn Miếu*: Center of education in Literati teachings in Dai Viet.

Tendai, see *Tiāntai*.

Tendō (天道): Literally, way of heaven but used in Japan in part as a substitute for the "mandate of heaven" (*tiānmíng* 天命).

Tenebrae: Literally, "darkness" in Latin; used by Petrarch and then by subsequent European Renaissance thinkers to characterize intellectual life in Europe after the end of the classical period of Greek and Roman learning after the fall of Rome in the fifth century; original of the term "Dark Ages" for this period.

Tenmei (天命): The will of heaven in Japanese thought but without the connotation of *tiānmíng* in East Asian thought (despite using the same characters).

Tenmon (天文) also given as Tenbun: Regnal era years 1532–1555 of the Emperor Go-Nara.

Tenmon hokke no ran (天文法華の亂): Translated as Temmon Hokke Rebellion or Tenmon Lotus Uprising, *hokke* referring to the "Lotus Sutra" favored by Nichiren believers who were at the center of the uprising in Kyoto in 1536, and *ran* (亂) for large-scale often violent incident.

Tenmon hōnan (天文法難): Literally, difficulty of the dharma in the Tenmon era but usually translated as the Tenmon Persecution by *Nichiren* followers.

Tennoki (天皇記): Literally, "Record of the Emperors"; now lost record of the Japanese Imperial lineage.

Terauke seido (寺請制度): Literally, "temple receiving system" or Tokugawa period system of registration with a Buddhist temple, though some individuals were permitted to register with a Shinto Shrine instead. Also called the *danka* (檀家) or *jidan* (寺檀) system, *dan* referring to the Buddhist altar, and *ka* to the family and *ji* to the temple.

Text: The object of *deconstruction*, which includes not only written texts but speech, images and other forms of communication that can be "read" in some sense.

Theravāda: Major school of Buddhism, descended from an early schism in the Buddhist sangha as the Sect of the Elders (Sthaviravāda) with more emphasis on monastic discipline and attainment of the status as an enlightened *arhat* through human effort; developed as a distinct school in Sri Lanka from which it spread to Southeast Asia to become the predominant form of Buddhism in South Asia.

Theurgy (θεουργία): Literally, "divine-working" or specific practices to return to the neo-Platonist ideal of the One.

Thiền, see *Chán*.

Third World: A term usually associated with Mao Zedong, in which the capitalist countries led by the United States were the First World, the communist bloc led by the Soviet Union was the Second World, and the economically developing nations were the Third World, possibly led by the People's Republic of China.

Thought experiment: Thinking through the consequences of a set of arrangements based on a priori rules that constrain the choices one can plausibly conjecture as alternatives.

Three teachings, see *Sānjiào*.

Three principles of the people, see *Sān mín zhǔyì*.

Thrown or *throwness*, see *Geworfenheit*.

Tiān (天) w.g. *tien*: Literally, "heaven" but used as a key concept in East Asian political thought as it is the source of power and change; can be used a non-anthropomorphic version of God or, better, the collective power of the universe based on an equilibrium of some kind.

Tiān Gōng (天公): Heavenly Master, see *Yù Huáng*.

Tiānmìng (天命): Literally, heaven's orders, but translated as the "mandate of heaven", that is, the series of man-made and natural events that leads to the collapse of one dynasty and justifies the rise of another.

Tiānshī (天師): Heavenly or Celestial Teacher or Master; usually associated with top leader role in Taoism.

Tiāntai (天台) w.g. Tientai, jp. Tendai, kr. Cheontae, vt. Thiênthai: Early sect of East Asian Buddhism with a liturgy for lay practitioners, which increased the popularity of Buddhism mainly among the aristocracy initially.

Tōhōkai (東方会): Literally, Eastern Society; a quasi-fascist organization set up by Nakano Seigo to foster his political ambitions.

Tongzhi restoration (同治中興), c.1860–1874: Attempt by pragmatic political leaders to bolster the Qing dynasty.

Transcendental: A philosophical method of overcoming or finding a way around normal limits on empirical and logical understanding.

Transcendentalism: Movement in the United States in the 1820s and 1830s that rejected conventional piety and also materialist intellectualism in order to embrace sophisticated biblical hermeneutics and transcendental philosophy of Kant together with what were believed to be similar forms of thought from India and East Asia.

True Pure Land (浄土真宗) jp. Jōdo Shinshū: Pure Land sect in Kamakura Japan established by Shinran.

Übermensch: Literally, "overman" but usually translated as "superman"; the goal set by Friedrich Nietzsche for man to strive to overcome himself and become something greater by going beyond the existing constraints of conventional social constraints to create new art, new relationships, make new discoveries and so on.

Uisa (義士): Literally, "righteous officials" but used to designate those Seon Buddhist monks who engaged in resistance against the Japanese invasion of Joseon in the sixteenth century.

Ujamaa, literally, extended or large "family" in Swahili: Coined by Tanzanian President Nyerere as the ideal of a cooperative and mutually supportive economic philosophy.

Uji (氏): Major clan lineages of ancient Japan.

Ulama (علماء), also given as *ulema*: Roughly, legal scholars or sometimes called jurists, though not always in official judicial positions; often used as binding arbitrators in questions of *shari'a* law.

Ummah (أمة): Literally, community in the sense of a community sharing beliefs or other attributes that transcends nation, ethnicity, etc. to refer specifically to the community of Muslims.

Umran, al- (العمران): Literally, constructions, developments, populating, used by ibn Khaldūn to indicate types of human society.

Upanisads (उपनिषत्): Late collection of essays included in the corpus of Vedic literature that contain key philosophical concepts in early Indian thought.

Upasaka (उपासक): Lay followers of an ascetic sect such as Buddhism or Jainism.

Upasakadyayana (उपासकाध्ययन): Instructions written by Somadeva for Jainist lay followers or *upasaka* explaining *shravakas*.

Upāya-kaushalya (उपाय कौशल्य): Based on words upāya (उपाय), "expedient method", particularly to teach, with kaushalya (कौशल्य) "cleverness", but usually translated as "skill in means" by which stories and analogies are used to teach Buddhist ideas, even if in a slightly inaccurate way of portraying the detail of concepts or theories, as a first step to understanding; heuristic method.

Utilitarianism: The philosophy that moral and political ideas must be judged on utility, that is, how useful they are for society as a whole, rather than on consistency with tradition or abstract metaphysical principles.

Utopian socialism: Term created by *Frederick Engels* to distinguish Marxist *scientific socialism* from early socialist theories that, he believed, relied on unrealistic assumptions.

Vaishnavism: The power of the god Vishnu through avatars.

Vaishya (वैश्य): Caste of craft workers and traders in the India caste system.

Vajrayana (बज्रयान), ch. Jīngāngshèn, jp. Kongōjō (金剛乘): Translated variously as "Thunderbolt Vehicle" or "Diamond Vehicle"; tantric Buddhism with esoteric teachings and practices, particularly in Tibetan Buddhism and Shingon Buddhism in Japan.

Varna (वर्ण): Literally "color", term used to denote caste in ancient India.

Vāsana (वासना): Literally "perfuming" from adhivāsana (अधिवासन), which means to invest an image with divine power or to perfume or purify, which is the process by which seeds of karma or *bīja* are activated in the world.

Vatsīputrīya (वात्सीपुत्रीय) ch. dúzĭ bù, jp. tokushibu (犢子部): Early Indian Buddhist sect.

Vedic (वेदा): Pertaining to the Vedas or ancient epic Aryan poetry and the literature that developed surrounding these texts.

Veil of ignorance: The philosophical thought experiment technique of John Rawls in which one is required to make rules for an ideal society without knowing one's own position in society, with the assumption that one will be compelled to make arrangements as fair and equitable as possible out of fear of ending up as one of the most disadvantaged members of society.

Velayat-e faqih (ولایت فقیه): Persian language book on Islamic government by Ruhollah Khomeini published in 1970; translated as "Governance of the Jurist" but also called "Islamic Government" (حکومت اسلامی, Hokumat-i eslami).

Verfallen: Literally, "forfeit", "lapse" or "decay", but usually translated as "fallenness" in the context of Heidegger's philosophy in which it is a state of going along with the crowd in terms of everyday mundaneness.

Vibhajjavāda (pa.) sk. Vibhajyavāda (विभज्जवा), ch. fēnbiéshuō-bù, jp. funbetsusetsu bu (分別說部): Literally, doctrine of analysis.

Victorian: During the reign of Queen Victoria (1819–1901), the Queen of the United Kingdom (r. 1837–1901), particularly the latter half of her reign.

Việt Điện u linh tập (粵甸幽靈集, also 越甸幽靈集 with the first two characters a different transliteration of the name Dai Viet into classical Chinese): Collection of Stories on Spirits of the Departed in the Viet Realm compiled by Lý Tế Xuyên.

Vijñapti-mātra (विज्ञप्तिमात्र): Literally, "reports of everything" but usually translated as "mere representation of consciousness".

Vimalakīrti nirdeśa sūtra (विमलकीर्तिनिर्देशसूत्र), also "Vimalakīrti Sūtra", ch. Wéimó jīng, jp. Yuima Kyō (維摩經): Literally, the "Advice of Vimalakīrti" with Vimalakīrti a lay Buddhist who teaches nondualism, *śūnyatā* and the role of silence.

Vinaya (विनय) ch. lü, jp. ritsu, kr. yul, vt. luật (律): Literally meaning "leading out", often translated as "discipline", meaning the rules governing Buddhist monastic communities; the classical Chinese character can also mean simply "law".

Virtû: Skill, including criminal skill, suggested by Machiavelli as key to the successful ruler.

Volk: German word, original meaning the people but acquired an increasingly mystical sense of ethnic bonds based on blood and cultural ties as developed by German Romantics and the Nazis.

Volonté générale: Usually translated as "general will"; in the context of

Rousseau's political thought it sets out the long-term "public interest" of all of society rather than the will of the majority at any given time.

Wahhabism (الوهابية): From the surname of Muhammad ibn Abd al-Wahhab whose ultraconservative interpretation of Islam was adopted by the House of Saud that has ruled Saudi Arabia since the eighteenth century; usually used as a pejorative term for ultraconservative interpretations of Islam along the lines of al-Wahhab and his successors.

Waka (和歌): Classical Japanese poetry written in Japanese, usually composed by educated Japanese who would have normally written in classical Chinese which was the lingua franca of the educated in East Asia until the twentieth century.

Wāli (والي), also Vali: Governor of a large administrative area in the Ottoman Empire.

Wényánwén (文言文): Classical literary form of the Literati.

Wénzìyù (文字獄): Literary persecution.

Will to power (Wille zur Macht): Key concept of Friedrich Nietzsche that he believed both described the key force in humans and could be the basis for enabling humans to strive for their full potential.

World spirit: In Hegel, this is the manifestation of the unfolding of the Absolute through history.

Wu (無): Usually translated as "nothingness".

Wǔ cháng (五常): Five constant or cardinal Literati virtues, namely benevolence (rén 仁), righteousness (yì 義), propriety (lǐ 禮), wisdom (zhì 智) and fidelity or trust (xìn 信).

Wǔ jīng (五經): Five ancient texts predating Confucius and considered foundational to ancient East Asian Literati thought, namely the *Shi Jing*, the *Shu Jing*, the *Li Ji*, the *Yi Jing* and the *Chunqiu*.

Wu jün wu chen (無君無臣) Wade-Giles *wu chun wu chhen*: No rulers, no officials.

Wǔ shan Shicha (五山十刹) System: Literally, "Five Mountain Ten Monastery" system was developed in the Southern Song dynasty in which Chan temples adopted a form of bureaucracy aligned with the state.

Wúwéi (無爲): Literally no action, but often means action through non-action.

Xiānrén (仙人) w.g. Hsien Jen: Hermit but usually implying some spiritual inclination, especially associated with Taoism.

Xiànchéng (現成): The Realization or Actualization School or left-wing of Wang Yangming thought.

Xiào (孝) jp. kō: Usually translated as "filial piety" but often popularly referred to as "respect for elders"; often expressed in exaggerated forms in traditional literature in East Asia.

Xiăorén (小者): Small or petty individual.

Xīn (心) w.g. *hsin,* jp. shin or kokoro: Literally "heart" but, as in the Western sense, it is also used to mean the mind or feelings.

Xīn rújiā (新儒家): "New Confucianism" of the twentieth century, not to be confused with *neo-Confucianism*.

Xīn wénhuà yùndòng (新文化運動): Literally, the New Culture Movement; starting in World War I and continuing into the 1920s, this movement attacked traditional Literati culture and instead advocated Western ideas.

Xìng (性) w.g. *hsing*: Nature or underlying character, often used in East Asia to denote and discuss human nature.

Xiūzhèng (修証): The Cultivation or Enlightenment School, or moderate school of Wang Yangming thought.

Xuántóng (玄同) w.g. *hsuan thung*: Mysterious equality or mysterious sameness.

Xuánxué (玄學) w.g. *hsüan-hsüeh*: Variously translated as the Dark, Mysterious or Illusory Learning; School of Literati thought that flourished after the end of the Han dynasty.

Yángwù (洋務), literally, "Western works": Late Qing dynasty reform initiative to adopt Western military technology and practices to strengthen the Chinese state.

Yek Kalameh (یک کلمه): Literally "One Word" in Persian; Mirza Yusef Khan's book that attempts to reconcile constitutional law with the Islamic practice of *shari'a* law.

Yí (儀): Ceremony.

Yì (義): Morality in the sense of right and wrong, often translated as "righteousness" or "rightness".

Yì (意): Will as in volition.

Yìjing (易經): Translated as the "Book of Changes" or "Classic of Changes"; one of the *Five Classics* based on records of divination for the Imperial Court from the early *Zhou* dynasty, so also given as the *Zhōuyì* (周易).

Yin-Yang (陰陽): Opposite but also complementary pairs of attributes, such as dark/light, weak/strong, female/male and so on, though with some aspects of the opposite attribute contained in each attribute; name of the school of thought based on complementary opposites that developed in Warring States period China and became integrated into later Literati and Taoist thought.

Yogācāra (योगचर) ch. Yúqiexíng, jp. Yugagyō, kr. Yugahaeng, vt. Du-già Hành (瑜伽行): Buddhist school of thought that focuses on the world as it is experienced rather than concerning itself with ontology;

translations of the East Asian term for the school (唯識 or ch. Wéishí, jp. Yushiki, kr. Yusig, vt. Duy Thức) as "consciousness only" is somewhat misleading as reality is not necessarily denied.

Yù (禦): Charioteering, one of the Ancient East Asian "six arts" (*liùyì*).

Yuè (樂): Music, one of the Ancient East Asian "six arts" (*liùyì*).

Zen, see *Chán*.

Zettai mu (絶対無): Literally, "absolute nothingness". Key concept in Kyoto School philosophy.

Zhàn Guó (戰國): Warring States period in ancient East Asia from c. 475 to 221 BC.

Zhēnguàn zhèngyào (貞觀政要): Record of the policies and philosophy of rule of the *Tang* dynasty *Taizong* emperor and his advisors.

Zhēnguān zhī zhì (貞觀之治): Literally, the "Reign of Zhenguan"; period of stable government under the *Tang* Emperor *Taizong*.

Zhi xing heyi (知行合一): Thought and action as one.

Zhōng (忠) jp. chū: Loyalty.

Zhòngchén (重臣): Top advisors of an East Asian emperor, king or other ruler.

Zhōu (周): Ancient East Asian dynasty from c. 1046–256 BC, usually split into the Western Zhou (1046–771 BC), when the dynasty was firmly in control, and the Eastern Zhou (770–255 BC), when actual power was increasing held de facto by independent states.

Zhoū yì (周易): Ancient text for divination originating primarily from the early Zhou dynasty, often translated as the "Classic of Changes" or "Book of Changes"; also given as *Yijing*.

Zhúlín qīxián (竹林七賢): Literally, "Seven wise of the Bamboo Grove" but translated as "Seven Sages of the Bamboo Grove" or "Seven Worthies of the Bamboo Grove"; a group of Western Jin period thinkers who advocated escapism and critiqued Literati thought.

Zìqiiáng (自強): Literally, self-strengthening, late Qing dynasty reform initiative.

Zìrán (自然): Literally, "self as is", meaning natural or naturally; sometimes given as "self-so".

Zīzhì tōngjiàn (資治通鑒): Often translated as "Comprehensive mirror to aid in government"; manual for politics and administration written by Sima Guang.

Zoku (族): Often translated as "species" but the concept is used by Tanabe Hajime in a way that is not the same as the Japanese word for "species", which is *shuzoku* (種族), and closer to the Japanese word for nation or *volk*, which is *minzoku* (民族), with more nationalist connotations and interpreted as such in Japan prior to the end of World War II.

Zoroastrianism: Belief in a Ahura Mazda, a transcendent and powerful being who incorporates cosmological dualism of order and chaos in permanent conflict; it rejects the asceticism and material/spiritual dualism of *Manichaeism*, however.

Glossary of names

This index includes full names and alternative names for the individuals mentioned in this book. Honorific titles are often omitted when not part of the conventional name by which the individual was known at the time. This is particularly important with Muslim names, particular the names of revered individuals, but also true in East Asia, India and the West, including titles of saints, royalty, and so on. No disrespect is intended or should be inferred.

East Asian names are given with the surname first and then first or given name, as has always been standard practice in East Asia. For Chinese names, the pinyin reading is given first and Wade-Giles system of Romanization for reference (many older sources use it so it is useful to know to access older material on these thinkers). Traditional Chinese characters are used for all names as used at the time. Korean names also are given in traditional Chinese characters as used at the time they were active. For Korean names alternative spellings using McCune–Reischauer are also noted. Most East Asian thinkers have multiple names. Only one is usually used in the text but the alternatives, where relevant, are listed here. East Asian names are given with surname first as the normal practice. In addition, many later Literati scholar-officials have, in addition to their birth name, pen names or pseudonyms (*hào* 號), "style" or "courtesy" names, or sobriquet (*zi* 字) given to them in childhood or adulthood by teachers or others. Birth names are used in the text but other names, where known, are given here because they are sometimes used in primary and secondary sources. Standard titles (*jué* 爵) and posthumous names (*shì* 謚 or *shìhào* 謚號) are often used for East Asian royalty, particularly monarchs whose names characterize their rule as determined after their death, which is the one normally used in English. Long vowels are given for Japanese words except those commonly used in English. Accents and other pronunciation marks are given for Chinese, Korean and Vietnamese names and words wherever possible.

For Arabic names, the most common reading is given. Where variations exist, these are listed as well. For Persian and non-Indian South Asian individuals, local script names are also often given unless the individual is better known by their Arabic name.

For Indian names, the most common reading is given. Where variations exist, these are listed as well, particularly transliteration of Buddhist names into East Asian languages.

For ancient Greek and Latin, the transliteration style is relatively set so variations are rare but full name information, usually including birthplace information, is often needed to distinguish between individuals with the same or similar names.

Spanish and Portuguese names often have maternal and paternal surnames included but generally are given under their paternal name unless better known by another.

Prefixes to surnames, patronymics/matronymics or place names that identify an individual, such as "de", "von", of (ó), ibn (ابن) or al- (ال), are ignored when listing the name alphabetically.

ABBREVIATIONS

b. = born
BC = Before the Common Era (i.e., Western calendar)
c. = circa
d. = died
fl. = floruit
r. = reign dates or dates as ruler
m.r. = McCune–Reischauer
w.g. = Wade-Giles
ch. = Mandarin (pinyin)
jp. = Japanese
kr. = Korean
pa. = Pali
vt. = Vietnamese

Abbasid Caliphate (الخلافة العباسية) c.750–1258: Third Islamic Caliphate.
'Abduh, Muhammad' (محمد عبده) b.1849–d.1905: Egyptian Islamic jurist and liberal reformer.
Abe Isoo (安部磯雄) 1865–1949: Early Japanese Christian socialist.
Abī Ṭālib, ali ibn (علي ابن أبي طالب) b. 601–d. 661: Cousin and son-in-law of Muhammad; Caliph from 656 to 661; Shi'a Imam 632–661.
Acharya, Mandayam Parthasarathi Tirumal 1887–1951: Former Indian Communist Party leader who left the party to promote anarchism.
Adams, John 1735–1826: American statesman who favored relatively centralized federalist government.
Adorno, Theodor W. 1903–1969, born Theodor Ludwig Wiesengrund:

Sociologist, philosopher and composer associated with the Frankfurt School.

Afghani, Sayyid Jamal-al-Din al- (سيد جمال الدين افغاني) b. 1839–d. 1897: Islamic political activist and modernizer.

Aflaq, Michel (ميشيل عفلق) b. 1910–d. 1989: Key pan-Arabist leader and thinker.

Agrippina, Julia 15–59, also Agrippina Minor or Agrippina the Younger, and Augusta Agrippina: Mother of Emperor Nero.

Aizawa Seishisai (会沢正志斎) 1781–1863, birth name Aizawa Yasushi (会沢安): *Kokugaku* thinker based in Mito domain.

Alberdi, Juan Bautista 1810–1884: Latin American liberal constitutional thinker.

Alcibiades (Ἀλκιβιάδης) 450–404 BC, full name is Alcibiades, son of Cleinias, from the deme of Scambonidae (Alkibiádēs Kleiníou Skambōnídēs, Ἀλκιβιάδης Κλεινίου Σκαμβωνίδης): Ancient Greek politician, friend of Socrates and name of two dialogues by Plato.

Alexander I 1777–1825, full name is Aleksandr Pavlovich (Александр Павлови), literally, Alexander, son of Paul: Russian Tzar.

Alexander the Great (Ἀλέξανδρος ὁ Μέγας) 356–323 BC, short name of Alexander III of Macedon: Founded a short-lived empire from 330 to 323 BC.

Alfaro, Eloy 1842–1912, full name is José Eloy Alfaro Delgado: President of Ecuador 1895–1901 and 1906–1911; leader of Liberal revolution against pro-Catholic conservative President Gabriel Garcia Moreno.

ʿAlī, Ḥasan ibn (علي ابن الحسن) b. 624–d. 670, full name is Al-Ḥasan ibn ʿAlī ibn Abī Ṭālib (أبي ابن علي ابن الحسن طالب طالب): Son of *Ali ibn Abī Ṭālib* and his successor as Caliph but forced to abdicate a little over half a year later.

Alvarez, Agustin 1857–1914, full name is Agustin E. Alvarez Suárez: Argentinian liberal positivist sociologist and educator who also served as an army brigadier general.

Amaterasu (天照): Japanese Sun goddess who is considered the ancestral goddess of the Japanese Imperial family.

Amin, Qasim (قاسم أمين) b.1863–d.1908: Arab women's rights advocate.

Amitābha (अमिताभ or 阿彌陀佛), also given as Amitāyus or ch. Āmítuó Fó, w.g. Amit'uo Fo, jp. Amida Butsu, kr. Amita Bul, vt. Adiđà Phật: Celestial Buddha in Mahāyāna Buddhism, who exists in a Pure Land in another world but has the power to help people in ours and other worlds.

An Hyang (安珦) 1243–1306, pen name was Hoeheon (晦軒): Korean Literati-scholar who introduced neo-Confucianism formally into Gyoreo Korea.

An Lushan (安禄山) 703–757: Ethnic Turk who was a top commander of T'ang imperial army and led a revolt against the Emperor Xuanzong.

Anaximander (Ἀναξίμανδρος) 610–546 BC: Presocratic.

Antisthenes (Ἀντισθένης) 445–365 BC: follower of Socrates and early cynic philosopher.

Antoun, Farah (فرح انطون) b.1874–d.1922, also spelled Farah Antun: Early Arab Christian socialist.

Aquinas, Thomas 1225–1274, or Tommaso d'Aquino in his native Italian: Key medieval Catholic thinker and later Saint.

Aristotle (Ἀριστοτέλης) 384–322 BC: Ancient Greek philosopher who wrote on a wide variety of topics and considered a key thinker in both Western and Islamic philosophy; Islamic scholars often refer to Aristotle as the "First Teacher" or *al-mu'allim al-awwal* (المعلم الأول).

Arrian (Ἀρριανός) c. 86–c. 146, literally, Arrianos, his full name is Lucius Flavius Arrianus, possibly Lucius Flavius Arrianus Xenophon, more specifically Arrian of Nicomedia: Follower of *Epictetus* who wrote down the lectures and thought of *Epictetus*.

Asclepius (Ἀσκληπιός): Ancient Greek god of medicine.

Ashoka (अशोक), see *Maurya, Ashoka*.

Astell, Mary 1666–1731: British political thinker.

Augustine, Saint 354–430, full name is Aurelius Augustinus Hipponensis, best known as Saint Augustine of Hippo: Late Roman Christian Bishop who wrote *The City of God*.

Aurangzeb (أورنكزيب) b.1618–d.1707: Mughal emperor.

Austin, J.L. 1911–1960, full name is John Langshaw Austin: British philosopher of language.

Azuchi–Momoyama period (安土桃山時代) 1568–1600: The final years of the Japanese Warring States period from the entry of Oda Nobunaga's forces into Kyoto until the establishment of the Tokugawa Shōgunate.

Baekje (百濟): Korean state during Three Kingdoms period from 18 BC to 660.

Bai, Mamola 1715–1795: A female member of the Rajput community of ruling families who acted as regent and effectively ruled Bhopal for nearly 50 years.

Bai Tongdong (白彤東) b. 1970: Chinese professor of philosophy.

Bakunin, Mikhail (Михаил Бакунин) 1814–1876, shortened name of Mikhail Alexandrovich Bakunin (Михаил Александрович Бакунин): Early anarchist thinker.

Ballou, Adin 1803–1890: Key theorist of the Christian socialist movement.

Bambara, also Bamana or Banmana: A Mandé people related to the people who formed the Mali Empire but the Bambara caused the final collapse of the Mali Empire as they grew as an independent power.

Banna, Hassan al- (حسن البنا) b.1906–d.1949: Founder of the Muslim Brotherhood in Egypt.

Bao Jingyan (鮑敬言), w.g. Pao Ching-yen: Early Chinese thinker considered first anarchist.

Barani, Ziauddin (ضياء الدين بَرَني) b.1285–d.1357: In the Tughlaq dynasty of the Dehli Sultanate is simply pious but not as extreme in his views. His political theory is found in his book *Fatwa-i-Jahandari* (فتاوى جهان داري).

Barreda, Gabino 1820–1881: Mexican medical doctor, educator and Comtean positivist philosopher.

Barreto, Luis Pereira 1840–1923: Brazilian medical; doctor, scientist and Comtean positivist philosopher.

Bayle, Pierre 1647–1706: French philosopher known for his work on skepticism and religious tolerance.

Beauvoir, Simone de 1908–1986, full name is Simone Lucie Ernestine Marie Bertrand de Beauvoir: French writer, philosopher and feminist.

Bellamy, Edward 1850–1898: Author and Christian socialist.

Bellamy, Francis 1855–1931: Baptist minister, author of the United States' Pledge of Allegiance, and Christian socialist.

Bello, Andrés 1781–1865, full name is Andrés de Jesús María y José Bello López: Venezuelan reform leader, poet and scholar.

Bentham, Jeremy 1748–1832: English political theorist, legal and social reformer; most closely associated with utilitarianism.

Beomnang (法朗) 632–646: Monk who brought Seon (Zen) Buddhism to Korea during the Silla dynasty.

Beop (法) ?–600, r. 599–600, m.r. Pŏp: King of Baekje; named after the "dharma" as a particularly pious Buddhist ruler.

Beopheung (法興) 514–540, m.r. Pŏphŭng: King of the Silla dynasty; literally "propagator of the dharma".

Bergson, Henri-Louis 1859–1941: French philosopher.

Berkman, Alexander 1870–1936: Russian émigré to the US who played a key role in spreading anarchist ideas.

Bernstein, Eduard 1850–1932: Socialist politician who advocated "evolutionary socialism", sometimes called "revisionist socialism".

Bey, Ahmed (باي أحمد) c. 1784–1850, full name is Ahmed Bey ben Mohamed Sherif: Last Ottoman ruler of Tunisia and Algiers r. 1826–1848.

Bidam (毗曇) ?–647: Silla aristocracy and leader of a revolt against Queen Seondeok.

Bimbisara (बिम्बिसारो) c. 558–c. 491 BC, also called Srenika: King, ruler of Magadha (मगध).

Bismarck, Otto von 1815–1898, short name for Otto Eduard Leopold Fürst von Bismarck-Schönhausen, Prince of Bismarck: Minister President in control of Prussian government from 1862 to 1890.

Blackstone, William 1723–1780: English jurist and politician; most well-known for his book *Commentaries on the Laws of England* on the principles of the common law tradition in England.

Blyden, Edward Wilmot 1832–1912: African writer, educator and diplomat.

Bo Qin (伯禽) r. c. 1042–c. 997 BC: The eldest son of the Duke of Zhou who founded the Zhou dynasty, established the state of Lu (魯).

Bodin, Jean 1530–1596: French legal and political philosopher.

Bolívar, Simón 1783–1830, full name is Simón José Antonio de la Santísima Trinidad Bolívar y Palacios: Revolutionary who led the liberation of much of Latin America from Spanish colonial control.

Bonald, Louis Gabriel Ambroise de 1754–1840: French anti-revolutionary thinker and politician.

Bose, Subhas Chandra (सुभाषचन्द्र बोस) 1897–1945: Former leader of the Indian Congress Party sympathetic to Axis powers in World War II.

Bou (普雨) 1515–1565: Joseon monk who taught a form of Pure Land Seon and had royal patrons.

Bruni, Leonardo 1370–1444, also Leonardo Aretino: Italian renaissance humanist, political writer and historian.

Buddha (बुद्ध): Literally, "the enlightened one". Many Buddhas exist but often refers to the historical figure of "Gautama Siddhārtha" (see entry below).

Bulguksa (佛國寺): Literally, Buddhist State Temple, built in 528 during the early Silla Kingdom.

Burke, Edmund 1729–1797: British parliamentarian, philosopher and political theorist.

Burrus, Sextus Afranius 1–62: Prefect of the Praetorian Guard and, together with Seneca, advisor to Nero.

Butler, Judith b. 1956: Philosopher and gender theorist.

Calvin, John 1509–1564: Early Protestant leader and thinker.

Carlyle, Thomas 1795–1881: Scottish historian, satirist and essayist.

Carrel, Alexis 1873–1944: French Nobel prize-winning scientist who advocated eugenics and sympathized with the pro-Nazi Vichy government.

Cassirer, Ernest 1874–1945: Neo-Kantian philosopher who engaged Heidegger in the so-called Davos Disputation in 1929.

Chaadayev, Petr Yakovlevich (Пётр Яковлевич Чаадаев) 1794–1856, sometimes first name as Peter or Pyotr: Russian philosopher and critic of Russian backwardness.
Chamberlain, Houston Stewart 1855–1927: British racialist thinker.
Chanakya (चाणक्य) 370–283 BC, also spelled Chankya: Advisor to Chandragupta Maurya, founder of the Mauryan Empire, who may have written the *Arthasastra* under the pen name Kautilya.
Chaulukya (चालुक्य): Dynasty in the Gujarat area of India between 940 and 1244.
Chen Qing-lan (陳清瀾) 1497–1567: Ming dynasty Literati critical of Wang Yangming thought.
Chinul, see *Jinul*.
Chong Chedu (鄭齊斗) 1649–1736, m.r. Cheng Chatoo also by pen name Hagok (霞谷) courtesy name 字は士仰.
Chrysippus of Soli (Χρύσιππος ὁ Σολεύς) 280–207 BC: Early Stoic thinker.
Chulalongkorn 1853–1910: English name of the Siamese king Phra Bat Somdet Phra Poraminthra Maha Chulalongkorn Phra Chunla Chom Klao Chao Yu Hua (พระบาทสมเด็จพระปรมินทรมหาจุฬาลงกรณ์ พระจุลจอมเกล้าเจ้าอยู่หัว), who reigned from 1868 to 1910.
Cicero (Kikerōn, Κικέρων) 106–43 BC, full name is Marcus Tullius Cicero: Roman orator, politician and philosopher.
Clemens, Titus Flavius c. 150–c. 215, also known as Clement of Alexandria (Κλήμης ὁ Ἀλεξανδρεύς): Early Church Fathers relatively sympathetic to philosophy.
Cleyre, Voltairine de 1866–1912: Early US anarchist and feminist.
Cohen, Hermann 1842–1918: One of the founders of the Marburg School of neo-Kantianism.
Coleridge, Samuel Taylor 1772–1834: English poet and philosopher.
Comte, Auguste 1798–1857, full name is Isidore Auguste Marie François Xavier Comte: French sociologist and philosopher; associated with the concepts of positivism, progress and sociology.
Condorcet, Marquis de 1743–1794, full name Marie Jean Antoine Nicolas de Caritat, also known as Nicolas de Condorcet: Mathematician and political thinker.
Confucius (孔子) c. 551–c. 449 BC, Original name was Kong Qiu (孔丘 Kǒng Qiū), Courtesy name was Zhongni (仲尼 Zhòngní), in East Asia, he is referred to as Kongzi (孔子), literally "Master Kong" but "Confucius" is the Latinization of Kong Fuzi (孔夫子), "Grand Master Kong", which is "K'ung Fu-tzu" in Wade-Giles.
Constant, Benjamin 1767–1830, full name is Henri-Benjamin Constant de Rebecque: French reformer; first self-identified "liberal".
Constant, Benjamin, of Brazil 1836–1891, full name is Benjamin Constant

Botelho de Magalhães: Military officer and founder of the Comtean positivist movement in Brazil.

Crates of Thebes (Κράτης ὁ Θηβαῖος) c. 365–c. 285 BC: Early Cynic philosopher and teacher of Zeno of Citium.

Crito (Κρίτων) c. 469–4 BC, friend of Socrates and name of dialogue featuring him by Plato. Specifically, Crito of Alopece (Kríton Alōpekēthen, Κρίτων Ἀλωπεκῆθεν).

Dai Nihon Kokusui Kai (大日本国粋会): Formed in 1919 after World War I in Japan by right-wing mainstream politicians and business leaders to combat the rise of the left, particularly the left-wing workers movement; translated as "Greater Japan Patriotic Society".

Dai Zhen (戴震) 1724–1777, w.g. Tai Chen: Qing thinker critical of neo-Confucianism.

Dao An (道安) 314–385: Very early Buddhist monk and teacher of Huiyuan.

Daosheng (道生) c. 360–434, w.g. Tao Sheng: Created some of the philosophical basis for Chan Buddhism; disciple of the Indian Buddhist text translator Kumarajiva.

Daoxin (道信) 580–651, w.g. Tao-hsin, j. Dōshin: Fourth Chan (Zen) Buddhist patriarch.

Dazai Shundai (太宰春台) 1680–1747, also Dazai Shuntai, pen names were Jun (純) and Shishien (紫芝園), courtesy name, Norio (徳夫), but he was also called Yauenmon (弥右衛門): Relatively radical student of Ōgyu Sorai.

De Bary, William Theodore 1919–2017: Professor of China and East Asian culture at Columbia University.

Debs, Eugene Victor "Gene" 1855–1926: American labor union organizer and Socialist Party candidate.

Deleuze, Gilles 1925–1995: French post-structuralist philosopher.

Delhi Sultanate (سلطنة دلهی) c.1206–1526: Islamic kingdom in India.

Democritus (Δημόκριτος) 460–370 BC: Presocratic "atomist".

Deng Xiaojun (邓小军) b. 1951: Chinese professor of literature and advocate of revival of political Literati thought.

Derrida, Jacques 1930–2004: French philosopher and literary critic best known for creating methods of "deconstruction".

Diderot, Denis 1713–1784: French philosopher and writer; most well-known as the chief editor and a key contributor to the *Encyclopédie, ou dictionnaire raisonné des sciences, des arts et des métiers* aimed at creating a repository of secular knowledge.

Diogenes of Sinope (Διογένης ὁ Σινωπεύς): A key founder of cynic philosophy.

Disraeli, Benjamin 1804–1881, also known as the 1st Earl of Beaconsfield: British prime minister, Conservative Party leader, and reformer.
Diyaf, Ahmad ibn Abi 1874–1804 (أحمد بن أبي الضياف): Ottoman reformer.
Dōgen (道元) 1200–1253: Early Japanese Zen teacher.
Dong Zhongshu (董仲舒) 179–104 BC, w.g. Tung Chung-shu: Influential Literati scholar who institutionalized Literati thought and practice in the Han dynasty.
Dōrim (道琳): Buddhist monk who undermined King Gaero of the Silla dynasty.
Douglass, Frederick 1818–1895, born Frederick Augustus Washington Bailey: Abolitionist, writer and statesman.
Dōui (道義) d. 825: Monk who helped to spread Seon Buddhism in Silla dynasty.
Du Ruhui (杜如晦) 585–630: Government minister and advisor to Tang dynasty Emperor Taizong.
Dushun (杜順) fl. c. 600: Founded Flower Garland School in early Tang dynasty.

Eastern Jin (晉朝): Dynasty in East Asia from 265 to 420.
Echeverria, Esteban 1805–1851: Latin American writer opposed to dictatorship.
Eisai (栄西) 1141–1215: Early Japanese Zen teacher.
Emerson, Ralph Waldo 1803–1882: Essayist, poet and leader of the transcendentalist movement in the United States.
Enfantin, Barthélemy Prosper 1796–1864: Key disciple of Henri de Saint Simeon who spread Saint Simeon's ideas after this death.
Engels, Friedrich 1820–1895: Business man, social researcher and radical socialist theorist.
Enryakuji (延暦寺): Tendai sect temple complex on Kyoto's eastern Mt. Hieizan, founded in 788 during the early Heian period by Saichō.
Epictetus (Ἐπίκτητος) 55–135: Roman Stoic philosopher.

Fadl-Allāh, Muhammad Hussein (محمد حسين فضل الله), b.1935–d.2010: Shi'a thinker based in Lebanon.
Fang Qiao (房誚) 579–648, also known from his courtesy name Xuanling (玄齡): Government minister and advisor to Tang dynasty Emperor Taizong.
Farabi, al- (الفارابي) c. 872–c. 951, full name is Abū Naṣr Muḥammad ibn Muḥammad al Fārābī (ابو نصر محمد بن محمد الفارابي): Early Islamic philosopher and most important philosopher in Islam after Aristotle; known in medieval Western Europe as Alpharabius.
Faraj, Muhammad abd-al-Salam (محمد عبد السلام فرج), b.1954–d.1982:

Founder of the organization *Jihad* in Egypt and author of *Jihad: The Neglected Obligation*.

Fazang (法藏) 643–712: Flower Garland School monk who worked in support of Empress Wu Zetian.

Feng Guifen (馮桂芬) 1809–1874, w.g. Feng Kuei-fen: Late Qing dynasty reformer advocating *statecraft*.

Feng Youlan (馮友蘭) 1895–1990, better known in English as w.g. Fung Yu-lan: Modern Chinese philosopher.

Ferdinand VII 1784–1833: King of Spain ruled 1808 and 1813–1833; viewed as a reactionary ruler who lost most of Spain's Latin American colonies.

Fichte, Johann Gottlieb 1762–1814: German philosopher and early German nationalist.

Ficino, Marsilio 1433–1499: Italian renaissance neo-Platonist translator.

Firestone, Shulamith 1945–2012: Radical feminist author and activist.

Flores Magón, Ricardo 1874–1922, full name is Cipriano Ricardo Flores Magón: Mexican anarchist active in both Mexico and the United States.

Former Qin (前秦) 351–394: One of the Sixteen Kingdoms.

Foucault, Michel 1926–1984, full name is Paul-Michel Foucault: French philosopher and social theorist.

Fourier, Charles 1772–1837, full name is François Marie Charles Fourier: Early *utopian socialist*.

Franco, Francisco 1892–1975, full name is Francisco Franco Bahamonde: Spanish General who ruled as a dictator from 1939 to 1975.

Freud, Sigmund 1856–1939: Austrian neurologist and founder of psychoanalysis.

Freyre, Gilberto 1900–1987: Brazilian sociologist and creator of the concept of lusotropicalism.

Friedan, Betty 1921–2006: Writer, activist and feminist.

Friedman, Milton 1912–2006: Free market economist.

Fujiwara Seika (藤原惺窩) 1561–1619: Buddhist monk who taught neo-Confucian thought to *Tokugawa Ieyasu*.

Fukuzawa Yukichi (福澤諭吉) 1835–1901: Japanese author, translator, educator and journalist.

Fula, also Fulani: A mixed North African and Muslim people.

Fulo, Empire of the Great 1490–1776, also known as the Denanke Kingdom or Denianke Kingdom created by the armed migration of Fula nomads.

Furnivall, Frederick James 1825–1910: Co-creator of the Oxford English Dictionary and Christian socialist.

Gaddafi, Muammar (معمر قذافي) c. 1942–2011, full name is Muammar Muhammad Abu Minyar al-Gaddafi (معمر محمد أبو منيار القذافي), also known as Colonel Gaddafi, with many variations on spelling of surname including Kadafi, Qaddafi, Qadhafi and Gathafi: Leader of Libya from 1969 to 2011.

Gaero (蓋鹵)?–475, r. 455–475, m.r. Kaero: Silla dynasty King.

Gallienus c. 218–268: Roman Emperor; full name is Publius Licinius Egnatius Gallienus Augustus.

Gan Zhongke (甘忠可) fl. late first century BC: Han dynasty official; author of *Tiānguān lì Bāoyuán Tàipíng jīng* (天官歷包元太平經).

Gandhara: An ancient Indo-Aryan kingdom which was located in what is now northern Pakistan, but was heavily influenced through conquests by Alexander the Great and the subsequent arrival of Buddhism to produce a hybrid Indo-Hellenic Buddhist culture.

Gandhi, Mohandas Karamchand (मोहनदास करमचन्द गांधी) 1869–1948: Indian independence movement leader who advocated strategy of non-violence; often given the title Mahātmā (महात्मा), literally "great soul" but normally translated as "high-souled" or "venerable".

Gang Hang (姜沆) 1567–1618, m.r. Kang Hang: Joseon neo-Confucian Literati, captured by the Japanese during their invasion of Korea who played a role in transmitting neo-Confucianism to Japan.

Gaozi (告子) c. 420–350 BC, w.g. Kao-tzu: Honorific name "Master Gao" for Gao Buhai (告不害).

Gautama Siddhārtha (सिद्धार्थ गौतम) c. 563–c. 483 BC or c. 480–c. 400 BC: Original name of the Buddha (see entry).

Ge Hong (葛洪) 283–343, w.g. Ko Hung: Former Jin dynasty official and author of the Baopuzi (抱朴子) or "The Master who Embraces Simplicity".

George, Henry 1839–1897: American quasi-socialist political economist.

Ghazali, Al (الغزالي) b. 1058–d. 1111, full name is Abū Ḥāmid Muḥammad ibn Muḥammad al-Ghazālī (أبو حامد محمد بن محمد الغزالي): Prominent Islamic scholar and administrator; known in medieval Western Europe as Algazelus or Algazel.

Gihwa (己和) 1376–1433, pen names Hamheo (涵虛) and Teuktong or Deuktong (得通): Wrote a defense of Buddhism, *Hyeonjeong non*.

Gladstone, William Ewart 1809–1898: British prime minister, Liberal Party leader and reformer.

Gobineau, Joseph Arthur Comte de 1816–1882: Early racist thinker.

Go-Daigo (後醍醐) 1288–1339: Emperor of Japan who attempted to restore Imperial Court power.

Goguryeo (高句麗): Korean state in Three Kingdoms period from 37 BC–668.

Gokhale, Gopal Krishna (गोपाल कृष्ण गोखले) 1866–1915: Indian independence leader and politician.

Goldman, Emma 1869–1940: Russian émigré to the US who spread anarchist ideas.

Go-Nara (後奈良) 1495–1557: Emperor of Japan.

Gong Zizhen (龔自珍) 1792–1841, w.g. Kung Tzu-chen: Late Qing dynasty reformer.

Gongyang Gao (公羊高): Native of the state Qi and student of Confucius' follower Zixia; wrote an important commentary on the *Chunqiu*.

Gosala, Makkhali b. c. 484: Advocate of asceticism in ancient India.

Gouze, Marie 1748–1793, pen name Marie-Olympe de Gouges: French feminist writer.

Greer, Germaine b. 1939: Writer and commentator.

Grimké, Angelina 1805–1879: Abolitionist and women's rights activist.

Grimké, Sarah 1792–1873: Abolitionist and women's rights activist.

Gu Yanwu (顧炎武) 1613–1682, also known as Gu Tinglin (顧亭林): Ming dynasty philologist.

Guattari, Pierre-Félix 1930–1992: French post-structuralist psychotherapist, philosopher and semiologist.

Guevarra, Ernesto "Che" 1928–1967, full name is Ernesto Rafael Guevara de la Serna, also known simply as Che: Latin American Marxist revolutionary.

Guicciardini, Francesco 1483–1540: Italian renaissance historian and political writer.

Guo Xiang (郭象) d. 312, w.g. Kuo Hsian: *Xuanxue* scholar and editor/commentator on the text of the *Zhuangizi*.

Gutiérrez Merino, Gustavo b. 1928, often simply Gustavo Gutiérrez: Peruvian theologian and Dominican priest.

Gwalleuk (觀勒) fl. late sixth/early seventh century, m.r. Kwallŭk: Baejke monk who transmitted Buddhism to Japan in 602.

Gwanggaeto the Great (廣開土太王) r. 391–412, m.r. Kwanggaet'o-taewang: King of *Goguryeo*.

Gwon Geun (權近) 1352–1409, m.r. Kwŏn Kŭn, pen name Yangchon (陽村): Late Gyoreo Literati-scholar who used neo-Confucianism to oppose the state.

Gyeomik (謙益) also given as Kyomik: Baekje Buddhist monk.

Gyoki (行基) 668–749: Name of Japanese Buddhist monk particularly working to serve commoners through charitable work when Buddhism was limited to the aristocracy.

Gyoreo (高麗) 918–1392, m.r. Koryŏ: Korean dynasty.

Gyunyeo (均如) 923–973: Goryeo monk who helped to reconcile the doctrinal differences between Hwaeom (Flower Garland School Buddhism) and Seon (Zen/Chan).

Habermas, Jurgen b. 1929: German sociologist and philosopher associated with the Frankfurt School.
Haeinsa (海印寺): Established in 802 during the later Silla Kingdom; repository of the Eighty Thousand Tripitaka Koreana.
Hamilton, Alexander 1757–1804: American statesman; co-editor and author of *The Federalist Papers*.
Han (漢): East Asian dynasty from 206 BC to 220 AD.
Han Fei (韓非) c. 280–233 BC: Author of the *Han Feizi* (韓非子); Prince of the state of Han (韓).
Hanbal, Ahmad ibn (احمد بن حنبل), b. 780–d. 855, full name is Aḥmad bin Muḥammad bin Ḥanbal Abū ʿAbd Allāh al-Shaybānī (احمد بن محمد بن حنبل ابو عبد الله الشيباني): Early conservative Islamic jurist and theologian.
Hanshan Deqing (憨山德清) 1546–1623: Ming dynasty monk who spread Pure Land and Chan *nianfo*.
Harrington, James 1611–1677: English constitutionalist, often argued to be a republican theorist.
Hart, H.L.A. 1907–1992, full name is Herbert Lionel Adolphus Hart: Legal philosopher.
Hashimoto Kingorō (橋本欣五郎) 1890–1957: Right-wing Japanese Army officer involved in military plots to overthrow the civilian government in Japan; one of the founders of the *Sakurakai*.
Hatta Shūzō (八太舟三) 1886–1934: Early Japanese anarchist.
Hayek, Friedrich 1899–1992: Free market economist and political writer.
Hayford, Joseph Casely 1866–1930, full name is Joseph Ephraim Casely Hayford, also known as Ekra-Agiman: Ghanaian lawyer, journalist and politician.
He Bo (河伯): Literally, Lord of the river. Ancient Chinese river god.
He Xinyin (何心隱) 1517–1579, w.g. Ho Hsin-yin: Student of Wang Xinzhai's *Taizhou School*.
He Yan (何晏) 195–249: One of the founders of *Xuanxue* school along with Wang Bi.
He Zhen (何震) 1884–c. 1920: Early Chinese anarchist and feminist based in Tokyo.
Hegel, Georg Wilhelm Friedrich 1770–1831: German philosopher.
Heian (平安): Period of Imperial rule in Japan from 794 to 1185.
Heidegger, Martin 1889–1976: German philosopher.
Hemachandra, Acharya (अथवा हेमचन्द्रसूरि) 1089–1172: Jainist monk and important writer in the development of Sanskrit literature.
Heraclitus of Ephesus (Ἡράκλειτος ὁ Ἐφέσιος) 535–475 BC: Presocratic.
Himiko (卑弥呼): Ancient Japanese Queen who ruled as a Shamanness.

Hipparchia of Maroneia (Ἱππαρχία ἡ Μαρωνεῖτις) fl. c. 325 BC: Ancient Greek Cynic philosopher.

Hirata Atsutane (平田篤胤) 1776–1843: Founder of the Hirata School of *Kokugaku*.

Hiratsuka Raicho (平塚らいてう) 1886–1971: Early Japanese women's rights advocate.

Hồ Chí Minh (胡志明) 1890–1969: Leader of the communist revolution in North Korea.

Hōjō Masako (北条政子) 1156–1225: A Japanese political leader who was married to Minamoto no Yoritomo, the first Kamakura shōgun.

Hölderlin, Johann Christian Friedrich 1770–1843: German idealist poet.

Holkar, Maharani Ahilya Bai (महाराणी अहिल्या बाई होळकर) 1725–1795: Maratha Queen of the Malwa kingdom.

Hōnen (法然) 1133–1212: Monk who established the Japanese Jōdo (Pure Land) sect in Japan.

Honganji (本願寺) also given as Hongwanji: Literally, "Temple of the Primal Vow"; used as the term to denote the largest school of True Land (Jōdo Shinshū) Buddhism in Japan but also the name of individual temples in the sect, including temple built in 1321 on the site of Shinran's tomb.

Hongwu (洪武) 1328–1398: First emperor of the Ming dynasty; see also *Zhu Yuanzhang*.

hooks, bell b. 1952, pen name of Gloria Jean Watkins: Author, feminist and social activist; note that use of lower case for name is intentional.

Horton, James Africanus Beale 1835–1883: Soldier, entrepreneur, banker, physician and writer.

Hōryūji (法隆寺): First and oldest temple in Japan commissioned by Prince Shōtoku and completed in 607.

Huan, Duke (魯桓公) 711–694 BC: Duke of the state of Lu in the Zhou dynasty.

Huang-di (黄帝): Literally, "Yellow Emperor".

Huang Zong-xi (黄宗羲) 1610–1695, w.g. Huang Tsunghsi courtesy name Taichong (太冲): Late Ming and early Qing dynasty Wang Yangming thinker.

Hughes, Thomas 1822–1896: Author and Christian Socialist.

Huineng (惠能) 638–713: Sixth patriarch of Chan Buddhism.

Huisi (慧思) 515–577: Third patriarch of *Tiāntai* Buddhism.

Huiyüan (慧遠) 334–416: Buddhism monk active in the Eastern Jin dynasty.

Hujwiri, Al- (الهجویری) c. 1000–1076: Early Sufist thinker.

Hume, David 1711–1776: Scottish philosopher.

Hus, Jan c. 1369–1415: Lecturer in Prague and early Catholic Church reform advocate.

Hwangyongsa (皇龍寺): Literally, Imperial Dragon temple, completed in early 644 during the Silla Kingdom to pray for protection of the nation.

Hyŏn'gwang (玄光): Baekje Buddhist monk who studied in Jin dynasty under Huisi (慧思); King Wideok used his knowledge to promote Buddhism.

Hypatia (Ὑπατία) c. 350/370–415: Head of the neo-Platonic school in Alexandria.

Iamblichus (Ἰάμβλιχος) c. 245–c. 325, also known as Iamblichus Chalcidensis, or Iamblichus of Apamea: Neo-Platonist who developed *Theurgy* to train individuals to attain higher levels towards the "One" through the "Soul" and "Intellect".

Ichadon (異次頓) 501–527, also known as Geochadon (居次頓) and by courtesy names such as Yeomdo (厭道): Buddhist convert in Silla who allowed himself to be martyred to promote Buddhism.

Ichikawa Fusae (市川房枝) 1893–1981: Early Japanese women's right advocate.

Inoue Kowashi (井上毅) 1843–1895: Japanese bureaucrat and politician who put forward radical constitution reform ideas.

Inoue Nissho (井上日召) 1887–1967: Former Nichiren Buddhist priest and leader of the terrorist group Ketsumeidan (血盟団) or Blood Brotherhood.

Irigaray, Luce b. 1930: Feminist, linguist and cultural theorist.

Isabella II 1830–1904: Queen of Spain, r. 1833–1868, opposed by the reactionary Carlists who opposed a female monarch.

Ishihara Shintarō (石原慎太郎) b. 1932: Japanese novelist and politician.

Ishiwara Kanji (石原莞爾) 1893–1949: Japanese Army General and Nichiren political thinker.

Itagaki Seishiro (板垣征四郎) 1885–1948: Japanese Army General who worked with Ishiwara Kanji; executed as a war criminal after Tokyo War Crimes Trials.

Itō Hirobumi (伊藤博文) 1841–1909: Japanese political leader who oversaw writing of the Meiji Constitution and served as the first Prime Minister under the new system.

Itō Jinsai (伊藤仁斎) 1627–1705: Japanese Literati philosopher and teacher.

Itō Noe (伊藤野枝) 1895–1923: Early Japanese feminist anarchist.

Jade Emperor, see *Yù Huáng*.

Jajang (慈藏) 590–658, m.r. Chajang: Silla monk appointed to give more order to the Silla *sangha*.

Jay, John 1745–1829: American statesman; co-editor and author of *The Federalist Papers*.

Jayasiṃha (जयसिंह) r. c. 1092–1141: King in the Chaulukya (चालुक्य) dynasty in Gujarat.

Jefferson, Thomas 1743–1826: American revolutionary and statesman who helped to author the Amercian "Declaration of Independence".

Jeong Dojeon (鄭道傳) 1324–1398, m.r. Chong Tojon, pen name Sambong (三峰): Literati-scholar and official who helped to propagate neo-Confucianism to bring down the Gyoreo dynasty; served as an official in the subsequent Joseon dynasty.

Jiang Qing (蔣庆) b. 1953: Academic critic of New Confucianism; advocate of political or constitutional forms of Confucianism.

Jindeok (眞德) ?–654, r. 647–654, m.r. Chindŏk: Second queen to rule Silla; last ruler of Silla from "sacred bone" rank.

Jinheung (眞興) 526–576, r. 540–576, m.r. Chinhŭng: King of Silla dynasty.

Jinmu Tennō (神武天皇): Mythical first emperor of Japan.

Jinnah, Muhammad Ali (محمد على جناح) b. 1876–d.1948: Politician and independence leader who is considered the "Father of Pakistan".

Jinul (知訥) 1158–1210, m.r. *Chinul*: Korean Goryeo dynasty Seon sect monk.

Jo Gwangjo (趙光祖) 1482–1519: Top Literati official in the reign of King Jungjon in Joseon Korea who brought the Sarim Faction into power.

Joseon (朝鮮) 1392–1919, also Chosŏn, Choson, Chosun: Korean dynasty; also referred to as the Yi (李) dynasty after the family name of the founder, *Yi Seonggye*.

Jufukuji (寿福寺): First Zen temple in Kamakura sponsored by Hōjō Masako after the death of her husband in 1199.

Julian 331–363, full name is Flavius Claudius Iulianus Augustus, Φλάβιος Κλαύδιος Ἰουλιανὸς Αὔγουστος: Roman Emperor.

Jungjong (中宗) 1488–1544, r. 1506–1544: King of Joseon Korea who brought *Sarim faction* into power at Court.

Kada Azumamaro (荷田春満) 1669–1736: Advocate of Fukko Shintō and initiator of the Kokugaku movement.

Kagawa Toyohiko (賀川豊彦) 1888–1960: Christian reformer who advocated unionism and cooperatives as an alternative to capitalism.

Kamakura Shōgunate (鎌倉幕府) 1185–1333: First period of Shōgunal rule in Japan.

Kamichika Ichiko (神近市子) 1888–1981: Early Japanese radical feminist.

Kammu (桓武) 737–806, r. 781–806: Japanese emperor who moved capital from Nara to Kyoto and inaugurated the Heian period.

Glossary of names

Kamo Mabuchi (賀茂真淵) 1697–1769: Follower of *Kada Azumamaro* and influential teacher of *Kokugaku*.
Kaneko Fumiko (金子文子) 1903–1926: Early Japanese feminist anarchist.
Kaneko Kentarō (金子堅太郎) 1853–1942: Japanese politician and diplomat; served initially as secretary to Itō Hirobumi.
Kang Youwei (康有為) 1858–1927, w.g. K'ang Yu-wei: Late Qing and Chinese Republican scholar, political thinker and reformer.
Kangxi, Emperor (康熙帝) 1654–1722: Early Qing dynasty emperor.
Kanishka the Great (कनिष्क) 127–163: Emperor of Kushan.
Kanno Sugako (管野須賀子) 1881–1911: Early Japanese anarchist.
Katayama Sen (片山潜) 1860–1933: Former Christian and socialist turned Marxist-Leninist who helped to found the Japanese Communist Party.
Katayama Tetsu (片山哲) 1887–1978: Christian, lawyer and union rights advocate in pre-war Japan and early post-war Japanese prime minister as the leader of the Japanese Socialist Party.
Katō Chikage (加藤千蔭) 1735–1808: Leading figure in the *Kokugaku* movement as part of the Edo School of *Kokugaku*; worked closely with *Motoori Norinaga* with whom he was a fellow student of Kamo Mabuchi.
Katō Hiroyuki (加藤弘之) 1836–1916: Japanese academic and politician; expert on political constitutions.
Katsu Kaishu (勝海舟) 1823–1899: Late Tokugawa period reformer and founder of modern Japanese navy in Meiji period.
Kaunda, Kenneth David b. 1924: Socialist former leader of Zambia.
Kautilya (कौटिल्य): Author of *Arthasastra*, see *Chanakya*.
Keita, Dankaran Toumani, or Tuman: First son of Naré Maghann Konaté.
Keita, Sundiata 1217–c. 1255: Legendary founder of the Mali Empire.
Keita, Uli I 1225–1270: Only son of Sundiata Keita; reigned as Mansa of Mali Empire from 1255 to 1270.
Kenyatta, Jomo c. 1891–1978: President of Kenya.
Khaldūn, ibn (ابن خلدون) b. 1332–d. 1406, full name is Abū Zayd 'Abd ar-Raḥmān ibn Muḥammad ibn Khaldūn al-Ḥaḍramī (أبو زيد عبد الرحمن بن محمد بن خلدون الحضرمي): Muslim government official, jurist, historian and sociologist.
Khan, Malkom (ملکم خان) b. 1833–d. 1908: Persian constitutional reformer.
Khan, Mirza Yusef (میرزا یوسف خان) d. 1895, full name is Mirza Yusef Khan Mostashar od-Dowle (میرزا یوسف خان مستشارالدوله): Persian constitutional reformer.
Khan, Syed Ahmad bin Muttaqi 1817–1898 (سر سید احمد خان): India administrator and reformer.
Khayzuran bint Atta, al- (الخیزران بنت عطاء) d. 789: A former slave from

Yemen; played an important political role in the governments of her husband, the Caliph Al-Mahdi, and her sons, Caliphs Al-Hadi and Harun al-Rashid.

Khomeini, Ruhollah (خم يعتى الله روح) b.1902–d.1989: Iranian Shi'a political leader who argued for an Islamic theocratic state.

Kim Il Sung (金日成) 1912–1994: Founder of the People's Republic of Korea (North Korea).

Kim Jwajin (金佐鎭) 1889–1930, m.r. Chwa-chin, pen name Baegya (白冶) m.r. Paegya: Korean anarchist who established the army and cooperative anarchist councils in Manchuria to fight the Japanese colonial authorities in Korea.

Kindī, al (الكندي) c. 801–873, full name is Abu Yūsuf Ya'qūb ibn 'Isḥāq aṣ-Ṣabbāḥ al-Kindī (أبو يوسف يعقوب بن إسحاق الصبّاح الكندي): Early Islamic philosopher; known in medieval Western Europe as Alkindus.

Kingsley, Charles 1819–1875: Author and Christian socialist.

Kita Ikki (北一輝) 1883–1937: Japanese imperial socialist, ultra-nationalist writer and activist.

Kitabatake Chikafusa (北畠親房) 1293–1354: Author of the Jinnō Shōtōki, and advisor to Emperor Go-Daigo of Japan.

Knox, John c. 1514–1572: Key figure in the Calvinist movement in Scotland.

Konaté, Naré Maghann, also called Maghan Kon Fatta or Maghan the Handsome: Mandinka king and father of Sundiata Keita in the Sundiata Epic.

Kōsaka Saaki (高坂正顕) 1900–1969: One of the Kyoto School "Big Four".

Kōtoku Shūsui (幸徳秋水) 1871–1911: Early Japanese anarchist and anti-imperialist.

Kōyama Iwao (高山岩男) 1905–1993: One of the Kyoto School "Big Four".

Krause, Karl Christian Friedrich 1781–1832: German philosopher who combined mysticism with a commitment to liberty; influential in Spain and Latin America for his rationalism and liberalism arising out of a Christian romanticism.

Kristeva, Julia (Юлия Кръстева) b. 1941: Philosopher, psychoanalyst, literary critic and feminist.

Kropotkin, Peter (Пётр Кропоткин) 1842–1921, shortened and Westernized version of name Pyotr or Petr Alexeyevich Kropotkin (Пётр Алексеевич Кропоткин): Russian aristocrat and key early anarchist thinker.

Kūkai (空海) 774–835: Heian Buddhism monk who founded Shingon sect in Japan after acquiring mastery of esoteric Buddhism in China.

Kumarpal (कुमारपाल) 1143–1173: King in the Chaulukya dynasty; patron to Hemachandra.

Glossary of names

Kumazawa Banzan (熊沢蕃山) 1619–1691: Key Wang Yangming thinker in the early Tokugawa Shōgunate.

L'Ouverture, Toussaint 1743–1803, full name is François-Dominique Toussaint L'Ouverture or Louverture: Former slave who led revolt in Haiti in 1791.

Lastarria, José Victorino 1817–1888: Chilean positivist liberal thinker, academic and diplomat.

Le (黎) 1428–1527: Vietnamese dynasty influenced by neo-Confucianism. Sometimes referred to as the Later Le dynasty due to an earlier shorter dynasty of the same name. After 1527, a period of warlordism began and the dynasty existed in name only until 1789.

Le Thanh Tong (黎聖宗) 1442–1497: Key emperor of the (later) Le dynasty considered to be an especially successful ruler.

Lee Kuan Yew (李光耀) 1923–2013: Founding statesman of Singapore; prime minister from 1959 to 1990.

Lee Yo (李瑤) 1536–1584: Rare example of Joseon Literati critical of orthodox *neo-Confucianism* and praised Wang Yangming.

Leibniz, Gottfried Wilhelm (von) 1646–1716: German philosopher.

Lenin, Vladimir (Владимир Ленин) 1870–1924: Russian revolutionary.

Leucippus (Λεύκιππος) fl. 5th cent. BC: Presocratic "atomist".

Li Dazhao (李大釗) 1888–1927, w.g. Li Ta-Chao: Co-founder of the CCP, though originally a Kropotkin influenced communist anarchist.

Li Gong (李塨) 1659–1733, courtesy name Li Gangzhu 李剛主, 号 pen name Shugu 恕谷: Pragmatic and critical Literati thinker of the early Qing dynasty.

Li Shizeng (李石曾) 1881–1973: Early Chinese anarchist based in Paris who later became a nationalist and anti-communist.

Li Ssu (李斯) c. 280–208 BC: Early *Fǎ-jiā*, student of *Xunzi*.

Li Zhi (李贄) 1527–1602, pen name was Li Zhou-wu (李卓吾) w.g. Li Cho-wu: One of the most radical of Wang Xin-zhai students from the Taizhou School.

Liang Qichao (梁啟超) 1873–1929: Chinese scholar, journalist, and reformer.

Limantour, José Yves 1854–1935, full name is José Yves Limantour y Marquet: Mexican financier who also served as Minister of Finance from 1893 to 1911; family wealth based on land holding obtained when liberal anti-clerical laws led to the sale of church land.

List, Guido von 1848–1919: Austrian/German ultra-nationalist and occultist.

Liu An (劉安) d. 122 BC: Prince of the Han dynasty and associated with the composition of the *Huinanzi*.

Liu Jianqun (劉健羣) 1903–1972: Chinese Nationalist (Guómíndǎng) official, sometimes credited with formation of the Blue Shirts Society (藍衣社), a quasi-fascist organization; one of the key ideologists in support of the Blue Shirts Society.

Liu Shifu (劉師復) 1884–1915: Early Chinese anarchist based in Tokyo.

Liu Shipei (劉師培) 1884–1919: Early Chinese anarchist based in Tokyo; husband of *He Zhen*.

Locke, John 1632–1704: English philosopher and political theorist.

Longmen Stone Statue Grotto (龍門石窟): Complex of numerous massive Buddhist stone statues added from the Northern Wei dynasty and especially in the Tang dynasty, including from the Empress Wu as a Vairocana Buddha.

Lu Jiuyuan (陸象山) 1139–1193: Founder of the School of the Mind or Heart, one form of neo-Confucianism; friend and opponent of Zhu Xi.

Lü Liuliang (呂留良) 1629–1683: Literati scholar-official in the late Ming dynasty who refused to serve in the Qing dynasty.

Lu Xun (魯迅) 1881–1936, w.g. Lu Hsün, original name Zhou Shuren (周樹人) but born Zhou Zhangshou (周樟壽): Key novelist and short story writer in the Chinese New Culture movement.

Luo Nian'an (羅念菴) 1504–1564, w.g. Lo Nien An, also 羅洪先 Luó Hóng Xiā, w.g. Lo Hung-hsein, courtesy name 達夫，pen name 念菴.

Luo Qinshun (羅欽順) 1465–1547 aka Lo Cheng-an aka Lo, Ch'in-shun aka Luo, Zheng'an: Ming dynasty Literati critical of Wang Yangming.

Luo Rufang (羅汝芳) 1515–1588, also known as Luo Jin-xi 羅近溪 w.g Lo Chin-hsi: Follower of Wang Yangming.

Luther, Martin 1483–1546: Former Catholic monk-scholar credited with initiating the Protestant Reformation in Europe.

Luxemburg, Rosa 1871–1919: Marxist revolutionary who was a naturalized German of Polish-Jewish descent.

Lý Tế Xuyên (李濟川) fl. 1400: Compiled the *Collection of Stories on Spirits of the Departed in the Viet Realm* (Việt Điện U Linh Tập).

Lý Thánh (李聖) 1023–1072: Emperor in the Lý dynasty of Dai Viet.

Lyotard, Jean-François 1925–1998: French philosopher and literary theorist.

Lysander (Λύσανδρος) d. 395: Ancient Spartan general.

Machiavelli, Niccolò 1469–1527, full name was Niccolò di Bernardo dei Machiavelli: Italian renaissance advisor, diplomat, historian and political thinker.

Madison, James 1751–1836: American statesman; co-editor and author of *The Federalist Papers* and of the United States Constitution.

Mahavira c. 540–468 BC: Founder of Jainism; also known as Vardhamāna.

Mahmud II (محمود ثانى) b.1785–d.1839: Ottoman Sultan and Caliph.
Maistre, Joseph-Marie Comte de 1753–1821: French aristocrat and conservative thinker.
Maitreya (मैत्रेय) ch. Mílè Púsà, jp. Miroku Bosatsu, kr. Mireuk Bosal, vt. Di-lặc Bồ-tát (彌勒菩薩): Next Buddha to come to our universe.
Malcolm X, see *X, Malcolm*.
Malebranche, Nicolas 1638–1715: French priest and philosopher who attempted to reconcile Catholicism and rationalism.
Mandela, Nelson Rolihlahla 1918–2013: Anti-apartheid activist, revolutionist and president of South Africa.
Mao Zedong (毛澤東) 1893–1976, w.g. Mao Tse Tung, simplified Chinese characters are 毛泽东: Chinese revolutionary leader.
Marananta (摩羅難陀), Marananta is Korean pronunciation, original is possibly Mālānanda: Indian monk from Gandhara who transmitted Buddhism to Baekje from Eastern Jin in 384.
Marcuse, Herbert 1898–1979: Sociologist associated with the Frankfurt School.
Marx, Karl 1818–1883: Revolutionary socialist thinker who advocated *scientific socialism*.
Maududi, A'bul A'la (ابو الاعلى مودودى) b.1903–d.1979 with surname also given as Maudoodi or Mawdudi and first name also added as Sayed or Sayyid: Key Pakistani Muslim thinker.
Maurice, Frederick Denison 1805–1872: Christian socialist leader and author of *The Kingdom of Christ* (1838).
Maurya, Ashoka (अशोक मौर्य) d. 232 BC, r. c. 268–232 BC, also given as *Asoka*: Ruler of the Mauryan Empire.
Maurya, Chandragupta (चन्द्रगुप्त मौर्य) 340–298 BC: Founder of the Mauryan Empire.
Mazzini, Giuseppe 1805–1872: Republican thinker and leader in the Italian unification movement.
Meinvielle, Julio 1905–1973: Argentine priest and ultra-conservative political writer.
Mencius (孟子) 372–289 BC: Latinized honorific name "Master Meng".
Mendes, Raimundo Texeira 1855–1927: Key promoter of Comte's Positivist philosophy and Religion of Humanity in Brazil.
Mernissi, Fatema (فاطمة مرنيسي) 1940–2015, sometimes Fatima Mernissi: Islamic feminist.
Meysenbug, Malwida von 1816–1903: European republican intellectual.
Mill, Harriet Taylor 1807–1858, born Harriet Hardy: English political philosopher and women's rights advocate.
Mill, James 1773–1836, birth name was James Milne: Historian and political economist.

Mill, John Stuart 1820–1903: English political philosopher.

Millett, Kate 1934–2017, full name is Katherine Murray Millett: Feminist writer, activist and artist.

Milton, John 1608–1674: English poet and early Republican thinker.

Minamoto no Yoritomo (源頼朝) 1147–1199: First Shōgun of the Kamakura Shōgunate.

Mirabeau, Marquis de 1715–1789, full name is Victor de Riqueti, Marquis de Mirabeau.

Mirandola, Giovanni Pico della 1463–1494: Italian renaissance neo-Platonist translator.

Mohamad, Mahathir bin (محضير بن محمد) b. 1925: Prime minister of Malaysia from 1981–2003.

Mongkut 1804–1868: English name of the Siamese King Phra Bat Somdet Phra Poramenthra Maha Mongkut Phra Chom Klao Chao Yu Hua (พระบาทสมเด็จพระปรเมนทรมหามงกุฎ พระจอมเกล้าเจ้าอยู่หัว), who reigned from 1851 to 1868.

Montagu, Mary Wortley 1689–1762: English aristocrat and letter writer who published the letters of her travels in Europe and the Ottoman Empire.

Montesquieu 1689–1755 The short name of Charles-Louis de Secondat, Baron de La Brède et de Montesquieu.

Mora, José Maria Luis 1794–1850: Mexican Catholic priest and reformer.

Moreno, Gabriel García 1860–1875, full name was Gabriel Gregorio Fernando José María García y Moreno y Morán de Buitrón: Conservative president of Ecuador.

Morgan, Robin b. 1941: Actor, poet, writer and feminist activist.

Morris, William 1834–1896: Self-professed Marxist and leader of the Arts and Crafts movement.

Mosse, Albert 1846–1925: German judge and legal scholar who served as an advisor on constitutional and legal affairs to the Meiji government in Japan.

Mossi: African people who emerged as a powerful force in the thirteenth century in West Africa based on a powerful cavalry.

Most, Johann Joseph "Hans" 1846–1906: German émigré to United States who spread anarchist theory, particularly his idea of "propaganda of the deed."

Motoori Norinaga (本居宣長) 1730–1801: Most influential exponent of *Kokugaku*.

Mou Zongsan (牟宗三) 1909–1995: Key figure of the second generation of New Confucianism movement of the twentieth century.

Mozi (墨子) c. 470–391 BC: Literally "Master Mo", the honorific name of Mo Di (墨翟).

Glossary of names

Mu (武) 580–641: King of Baekje r. 600–641.

Muhak (無學) 1327–1405: Last Korean State Preceptor at the end of the Goryeo dynasty.

Muhammad (محمد) c. 570–632: Called "the prophet"; the founder of Islam.

Munjeong (文定) 1502–1565: Queen of Joseon dynasty who favored Buddhism.

Muqaffaʿ, ibn al- (ابن المقفع) d. c. 756, full name is Abū Muhammad ʿAbd Allāh Rūzbih ibn Dādūya (ابو محمد عبدالله روزبه ابن دادويه): Persian translator, convert to Islam and advisor to the Umayyad and Abbasid Caliphates.

Murasaki Shikibu (紫式部) c. 973–1014: Heian period female novelist.

Murata Harumi (村田春海) 1746–1811: Teacher and leader of the Edo School of Kokugaku.

Muromachi Shōgunate (室町幕府) 1338–1573, also called the Ashikaga (足利) Shōgunate: Period of feudal warrior rule in Japan.

Muryeong (武寧) 462–523: King of Baekje r. 501–523.

Musa 1280–1337, r. 1312–1337, full name is Musa Keita I: Mansa of the Mali Empire; famous for his extreme wealth based on control of gold trade.

Mūsā, Salāmah (سلامه موسى) b.1887–d.1958, also spelled Salama Moussa: Early Arab Christian socialist.

Muso Soseki (夢窓疎石) 1275–1351: First Zen National Preceptor in Japan.

Mussolini, Benito Amilcare Andrea 1883–1945: Founder of Italian Fascist movement and party; Prime Minister of Italy (1922–1945).

Myeongjon (明宗) 1534–1567, r. 1545–1567: King of Joseon Korea who favored Buddhism.

Nakano Seigo (中野正剛) 1888–1943: Japanese politician and journalist who founded the Japanese fascist organization Tōhōkai (東方会) or Eastern Society.

Nāgārjuna (नागार्जुन) c. 150–250, ch. Lóngshù, jp. Ryūju (龍樹): Early Indian Buddhist philosopher.

Nakae Chōmin (中江兆民) 1847–1901, pen name of Nakae Tokusuke (中江 篤助): Japanese journalist and political theorist.

Nakae Toju (中江藤樹) 1608–1648: Father of Wang Yangming thought in Japan.

Nam Yeongkyung (南彦經) 1528–1594: Rare example of Joseon Literati critical of orthodox neo-Confucianism and praised Wang Yangming.

Nanda (नंदा) 345–321 BC: Indian dynasty.

Nanda, Mahapadma (महापद्म नंदा), 450–362 BC: Founder of the Nanda dynasty.

Naoroji, Dadabhai (दादाभाई नौरोजी) 1825–1917: Founder of the East India Association in 1867 was to counter the racialist propaganda in England.

Nasser Hussein, Gamal Abdel (جمال عبد الناصر حسين) b. 1918–d.1970, better known as simply Nasser: Egyptian president and pan-Arabist.

Natorp, Paul Gerhard 1854–1924: One of the founders of the Marburg school of neo-Kantianism.

Nguyên Thánh Thiên Cảm (元聖天感) d. 1287: Queen in the Trần dynasty; wife of King Trần Thanh Tong, and mother of King Trần Nhân Tông and Trần Hung Daō.

Nichiren (日連) 1222–1282: Japanese monk who founded the Nichiren Buddhist sect based on *nembutsu* belief in the "Lotus Sutra".

Nie Shuang Jiang (聶雙江) 1487–1563, w.g. Nieh Shuang Chiang, also Nie Bao (聶豹): Figure in the so-called Tranquility School of Wang Yangming.

Nietzsche, Friedrich Wilhelm 1844–1900: German philologist and writer.

Nishida Kitarō (西田幾多郎) 1870–1945: Japanese philosopher; founder of the *Kyoto School.*

Nishitani Keiji (西谷啓治) 1900–1990: One of the Kyoto School "Big Four".

Nizam Al-Mulk (نظام الملک) 1018–1092, also known as Abu Ali Al Hassan Al Tusi: Persian scholar who became a vizier in the Seljuq Empire.

Nkrumah, Kwame 1909–1972: President of Ghana.

Northern and Southern Dynasties (南北朝): A series of East Asian dynasties split between north and south from 420 to 589 including such states as the Northern Wei and Northern Zhou.

Northern Wei (北魏): Dynasty in East Asia from 446 to 452.

Northern Zhou (北周): Dynasty in East Asia from 557 to 581.

Novalis 1772–1801, the pen name of Georg Philipp Friedrich Freiherr von Hardenberg: Early German Romantic movement thinker.

Nozick, Robert 1938–2002: Philosopher and political theorist.

Nulji (訥祇) r. 417–458, m.r. Nulchi: Maripgan of Silla.

Nyerere, Julius 1922–1999: President of Tanzania.

Oda Nobunaga (織田信長) 1534–1582: First of three "unifiers" of Japan at the end of the Warring States period; known for his ruthless use of violence.

Ogyū Sorai (荻生徂徠) 1666–1728: Tokugawa Shōgunate Literati official and ancient learning scholar.

Ōkawa Shūmei (大川周明) 1886–1957: Pan-Asianist and Japanese right-wing political activist.

Okin, Susan Moller 1946–2004: Feminist analytical political philosopher.

Origen (Ὠριγένης) 184/185–253/254, also known as Origen Adamantius

Glossary of names

(Ὠριγένης Ἀδαμάντιος): Early Church Father who was sympathetic to neo-Platonism but his ideas were rejected as too close to that philosophy.

Ōshio Heihachirō (大塩平八) 1793–1837: Police official and Japanese Ōyōmei thinker, who led a revolt in Osaka in the late Tokugawa period.

Ōsugi Sakae (大杉栄) 1885–1923: Early Japanese anarchist.

Ottoman Empire (عثمانيه عليه دولت) c. 1299–1923: Turkish Islamic state that for much of its existence dominated the Eastern Mediterranean, southeastern Europe, the Middle East and large parts of North Africa.

Ouyang Xiu (欧陽修) 1007–1072: Historian and epigraphical expert who sought to readvocate a return to original readings of ancient texts.

Owen, Robert 1771–1858: Early utopian socialist who advocated cooperative communities.

Ōyōmei: Japanese pronunciation of Wang Yangming.

Paine, Thomas 1737–1809: English born revolutionary, mainly active as a naturalized citizen in the United States of America.

Panaetius (Παναίτιος) c.185–c.109 BC: Stoic thinker.

Park Yeol (朴烈) 1902–1974: Korean anarchist.

Parmenides of Elea (Παρμενίδης ὁ Ἐλεάτης) 510–440 BC: Presocratic.

Pasha, Mohammed Ali (محمد علي باشا) b. 1769–d. 1849: Albanian commander in the Ottoman army; later governor (wāli والي) and then Khedive of Egypt and Sudan.

Pedro II 1825–1891: Last emperor and monarch of Brazil.

Peralta, José 1855–1937, full name is José Peralta Serrano: Advisor to Ecuadoran President *Eloy Alfaro* and a Kraussian romantic liberal reformer.

Petrarch 1304–1374: Anglicized name of Francesco Petrarca.

Philo of Alexandria (Φίλων ὁ Ἀλεξανδρεύς) c. 25 BC–c. 50: Jewish thinker who attempted to reconcile Judaism with classical learning, particularly Greek philosophy.

Pizan, Christine de 1364–1431: Author who is said to be the first feminist as a result of key ideas in her book, *The Book of the City of Ladies* (*Le Livre de la Cité des Dames*, c. 1405).

Plato (Πλάτων) c. 427–c. 347 BC: Ancient Greek philosopher, student of Socrates.

Plotinus (Πλωτῖνος) 205–270: Founder of neo-Platonism.

Popper, Karl Raimund 1902–1994: Philosopher of science.

Porphyry (Πορφύριος, c. 234–c. 305 AD) also Porphyry of Tyre: Student of Plotinus who edited Plotinus' Enneads, which include a biography of Plotinus by Porphyry.

Prasenjit (प्रसेनजित्) fl. 6 BC, also pa. Pasenadi: King, ruler of Kosala.

Proclus (Πρόκλος) 412–485, also called the Proclus Lycaeus (Πρόκλος ο

Λύκιος) or Proclus the Successor (Próklos ho Diádokhos Πρόκλος ὁ Διάδοχος).

Proudhon, Pierre-Joseph 1809–1865: First self-declared "anarchist" who argued that "property is theft".

Pythagoras of Samos (Πυθαγόρας ὁ Σάμιος) c. 570–c. 495 BC: Presocratic.

Qin (秦) w.g. Ch'in: Early Chinese state that formed the basis of the dynasty, 221–206 BC that unified China after the Warring States period; origin of the term "China".

Qin Shi Huang (秦始皇): Literally, the "first emperor of the Qin dynasty". He was born Ying Zheng (嬴政) or Zhao Zheng (趙政), a prince of the state of Qin (秦) but became the emperor who re-unified the states of China after the long and slow collapse of the Zhou dynasty.

Qing (清) w.g. Ch'ing: Dynasty founded by Manchu ethnic group in North China that ruled much of continental East Asia from 1644 to 1912.

Queen Mother of the West, see Xiwangmu.

Quesnay, Francois 1694–1774: French economist and medical doctor; leading Physiocrat.

Quốc Học Viện (國學院): National Educational Academy was established in 1253 to teach a neo-Confucian curriculum in Dai Viet.

Quốc Tử Giám (國子監): The first national university in Dai Viet established in 1070; translated as "Imperial Academy".

Qushayri, al- (القشيري) b. 986: Early Sufist thinker.

Qutb al-Dīn Aibak (قطب الدين أيبك) b. 1150–d. 1210, also spelt Qutb ud-Dīn Aibak or Qutub ud-Din Aybak: Founder of the Turkic *Mamluk* dynasty in Delhi.

Qutb, Sayyid (سيد قطب) b. 1906–d. 1966, also given as Kotb: Member of the Egyptian Muslim Brotherhood and key modern Islamic political theorist.

Rahman, Aisha Abd al- (عائشة عبد الرحمن) b. 1913–d. 1998: Writer on women in Islam under pen name Bint al-Shati.

Ramirez, Ignacio 1818–1879: Mexican liberal romantic positivist agitator, exiled from Mexico but eventually serving as a cabinet member of the Mexican Supreme Court judge; famous for his atheism.

Ranade, Mahadev Govind (महादेवगोविन्द रानडे) 1842–1901: Indian social reformer and independence activist.

Rashid, Harun al (هَارُون الرَشيد) b. 763/766–d. 809, r. 786–809: Fifth Abbasid Caliph.

Rawls, John Bordley 1921–2002: Moral and political philosopher.

Rennyo (連如) 1415–1499: Key True Pure Land leader of the Warring States period in Japan.

Rickert, Heinrich John 1863–1936: One of the founders of the Baden or Southwest school of neo-Kantianism; teacher of Martin Heidegger.

Rodrigues, Olinde 1795–1851, shortened name of Benjamin Olinde Rodrigues: Banker who became key disciple of Henri de Saint Simeon and spread Saint Simeon's ideas after his death.

Rosas, Juan Manuel de 1793–1877: Argentine dictator.

Rosenberg, Alfred Ernst 1893–1946: Nazi ideologist.

Rousseau, Jean Jacques 1712–1778: Citizen of Geneva; controversial essayist, novelist and political thinker.

Roy, Manabendra Nath (মানবেন্দ্রনাথ রায়) 1887–1954: Former Indian Communist Party leader who left the party to pursue his own version of radical socialism.

Roy, Rammohan (রাজা রামমোহন রায়) 1772–1833: Early Indian liberal Hindu reformer. An alternative transliteration is Ram Mohan Roy.

Rujing (如净) 1163–1228, w.g. Ju-ching: Chan Buddhist teacher of the Japanese Zen Buddhist teacher Dōgen.

Rushd, ibn (ابن رشد) b. 1126–d. 1198: Islamic philosopher; known in medieval Western Europe as Averroes.

Ruskin, John 1819–1900: Popular British writer/essayist and Christian socialist.

Sabi (泗沘) 538–660: Key time period in the Korean Baekje kingdom.

Sáenz, Doña Manuela 1797–1856, full name is Doña Manuela Sáenz y Aizpuru: Latin American revolutionary who worked with and had a relationship with Simon Bolivar.

Sahoo, Sarojini (ସରୋଜିନୀ ସାହୁ), b. 1956: Indian feminist writer.

Saichō (最澄) 767–822: Japanese monk who established Chinese T'ien-t'ai sect in Japan.

Saigō Takamori (西郷隆盛) 1828–1877: Japanese politician and Wang Yangming thinker.

Saint-Simon, Henri de 1760–1825, shortened name of Claude-Henri de Rouvroy, Comte (count) de Saint-Simon: Early utopian socialist thinker.

Sakamoto Ryoma (坂本竜馬) 1835–1867: Late Tokugawa reformer.

Sakuma Shōzan (佐久間象山) 1811–1864: Late Tokugawa political reformer.

Salazar, António de Oliveira 1889–1970: Portuguese economist and politician; prime minister and effective dictator of Portugal from 1932 to 1968.

Salomé, Lou 1861–1937, born Louise von Salomé, name also given as Lou Andreas-Salomé after marriage to linguistics scholar Friedrich Carl Andreas in 1887: Influential writer and early psychoanalyst.

Sarmiento, Domingo Faustino 1811–1888: President of Argentina, writer and political thinker.
Savarkar, Vinayak Damodar (विनायक दामोदर सावरकर) 1883–1966: Indian pro-independence activist, lawyer, and writer.
Sayyid, Ahmed Lutfi al- (أحمد لطفي السيد) b. 1872–d. 1963: Egyptian intellectual and anti-colonial activist.
Schlegel, Friedrich 1772–1829, full name is Karl Wilhelm Friedrich Schlegel, after 1814, von Schlegel: Key German Romantic.
Schmidt, Johann Kaspar 1806–1856, better known as *Max Stirner* (pen name): Advocated egoism as an early form of anarchism.
Schmitt, Carl 1888–1985: German jurist and political thinker.
Scipio Aemilianus 185–129 BC: Roman politician; full name is Publius Cornelius Scipio Aemilianus Africanus Numantinus, but also known as Scipio Africanus Minor or Scipio Africanus the Younger.
Sejo (世祖) 1417–1468, r. 1455–1468: Seventh king of Joseon dynasty.
Sejong (世宗) 1397–1450, r. 1418–1450, birth name Yi Do (李祹), childhood name or sobriquet Wonjung (元正): Fourth king of Joseon dynasty.
Selassie, Haile 1892–1975: King of Ethiopia; first head of the Organization for African Unity.
Seneca c. 4 BC–65 AD: Advisor to Emperor Nero; full name is Lucius Annaeus Seneca, also known as Seneca the Younger.
Senghor, Léopold Sédar 1906–2001: First president of Senegal (1960–1980) who helped to politicize and spread the concept of *négritude*.
Seondeok (善德) ?–647, r. 632–647, m.r. Sŏndŏk: First queen of Silla to be made ruler.
Seong (聖) ?–554, r. 523–554, m.r. Sŏng: King of Baekje.
Shang Yang (商鞅) 390–338 BC: Also Lord Shang; early Legalist; Legalist text associated with him but probably not written by him.
Shantaō (善導) 613–681: Tang dynasty monk who was the effective founder of Pure Land Buddhism.
Shariati, Ali (شريعتی علی) b. 1877–d. 1933: Iranian Islamic revolutionary.
Shen Buhai (申不害) w.g. Shen Pu-Hai: prime minister from 351 BC to his death in 337 BC, author of the *Shenzi* (申子), literally Master Shen.
Shen Dao (慎到) c. 350–c. 275 BC: Author of *Shenzi* (慎子), key work of Legalist theory.
Shenxiu (神秀) ?–706: Leader of the Northern school of Chan Buddhism after the split with the Southern school.
Shinran (親鸞) 1173–1263: Former monk who established the True Pure Land (Jōdo Shinshū) sect in Kamakura Japan.
Shōheikō (昌平黌): Official school for Literati studies in Tokugawa Japan; named after the birthplace of Confucius, Changping (昌平), rendered

Glossary of names

as Shōhei in Japanese. It was closed after the Meiji Restoration and is now called Yushima Seidō (湯島聖堂).

Shōmu (聖武) 701–756: Emperor of Japan who strongly favored Buddhism.

Shōtoku, Prince (聖徳太子) 572–622: Prince appointed by Empress Suiko to carry out political reforms including the introduction of Buddhism to Japan.

Shùn (順) 115–144, r. 125–144: Emperor of Han dynasty.

Shundao (順道), also given as Sundo: Monk sent by Former Qin to transmit Buddhism to *Goguryeo* in 372.

Sidney, Algernon 1623–1683: Early English constitutional monarchist.

Sierra, Justo 1848–1912, full name is Justo Sierra Méndez: Mexican writer, historian and political advocate of Comtean positivism and liberalism.

Sieyès, Emmanuel Joseph 1748–1836, also Abbé Sieyès: French Roman Catholic clergyman and political thinker.

Silla (新羅): Korean state during Three Kingdoms period 57 BC–668 AD, then sole state on Korean peninsula between 668 and 935.

Sima Guang (司馬光) 1019–1086: Northern Song period Literati scholar and official.

Sina, ibn (ابن سينا) b. 980–d. 1032: Islamic philosopher; known in medieval Western Europe as Avicenna.

Sinhaeng (神行) 704–779: Monk who popularized Seon Buddhism in Silla dynasty.

Smith, Adam 1723–1790: Scottish philosopher and economist.

Socrates (Σωκράτης) 469–399 BC: Foundational thinker in ancient Greek political thought.

Somadeva (सोमदेव) fl. 959–966: Author of the *Nitivakyamrtam* and *Upasakadyayana*, key Jainist texts.

Sombre, Joanna Nobilis c. 1753–1836, popularly known as Begum Samru (बेगम समरू) birth name Farzana Zeb un-Nissa: Led mercenary army of Europeans and Indians of her husband after his death to rise to become the ruler of the Principality of Sardhana in India.

Song (宋) 960–1279: East Asian dynasty split between the Northern Song (北宋), 960–1127 and Southern Song (南宋), 1127–1279.

Songgwangsa (松広寺): Located at Mt. Jogye (曹溪山); founded by Jinul as an outgrowth of his *Jeonghyesa* movement.

Songhai Empire 1464–1591, also Songhay: At one time a dominant state in the Western Sahel.

Sorel, Georges 1847–1922: Revolutionary socialist advocate of violent action.

Sosurim (小獸林) ?–384, r. 371–384: King of Goguryeo.

Spinoza, Baruch de 1632–1677, born Benedito de Espinosa, published in Latin as Benedictus de Spinoza: Dutch rationalist philosopher of Sheperdic Jewish/Portuguese origin.

Śrīmālā (श्रीमाला) ch. Shèngmán, jp. Shōman, vt. Thǎngman (勝鬘): Indian Buddhist queen and central figure in sutra named after her.

Staël, Germaine de 1766–1817, full name is Anne Louise Germaine de Staël: Influential French socialite and writer.

Stalin, Joseph (Иосиф Сталин) 1878–1953, more accurately Iosif Stalin: Russian revolutionary and dictator.

Stein, Lorenz von 1815–1890: German professor of political administration, economics and sociology who advised the Meiji government in Japan on constitutional matter.

Stirner, Max 1806–1856, pen name of Johann Kaspar Schmidt: Advocated "egoism", which can be viewed as an early form of anarchism.

Stowe, Harriet Elisabeth Beecher 1811–1896: Author of *Uncle Tom's Cabin*, which had a great impact on the fight against slavery in the United States.

Stuart, Mary 1542–1587: Better known as Mary, Queen of Scots; reigned over Scotland from 1542 to 1567.

Sui (随): Dynasty in East Asia from 581 to 618.

Suiko (推古) 554–628, r. 593–628: Empress of Japan; appointed Prince Shōtoku to carry out reforms including the introduction of Buddhism to Japan.

Suleyman 1341–1360: *Mansa* of the Mali Empire.

Sun Yat-sen (孫逸仙) 1866–1925: Chinese revolutionary leader.

Sundo (順道) fl. fourth century, ch. Shundao: Early Korean monk.

Suzuki, Daisetz Teitaro (鈴木大拙貞太郎) 1870–1966: Japanese Buddhist who popularized knowledge of Buddhism through books written in English. Suzuki's name is usually given in Western order with surname last. His middle name, Teitaro, was his first name at birth, and Daisetzu his pen name.

Suzuki Shigetaka (鈴木成高) 1907–1988: One of the Kyoto School "Big Four".

Synesius (Συνέσιος) c. 373–c. 414: Neo-Platonist; student of Hyptia, and Bishop of a Ptolemais in the late Roman Empire.

Tagore, Rabindranath (रवीन्द्रनाथ ठाकुर) 1861–1941: Indian poet and philosopher.

Tahtawi, Rafi' Rifa'a al- (رفاعة رافع الطهطاوي) b. 1801–d. 1973: Egyptian Muslim translator and travel writer.

Taizong (太宗) 626–649, w.g. T'ai-Tsung: Emperor in the Tang dynasty.

Takano no Niigasa (高野新笠) c. 720–790: Mother of Japanese Emperor Kammu.

Tanabe Hajime (田邊元) 1885–1962: Japanese philosopher critical of Nishida and other members of the Kyoto School but still strongly associated with that School.

Tanaka Chigaku (田中智學) 1861–1939: Japanese ultra-nationalist Nichiren Buddhist preacher.

Tang (唐): East Asian dynasty 618–907.

Tang Junyi (唐君毅) 1909–1978: Second generation New Confucian.

Thompson, William 1775–1833: Irish social reformer and philosopher.

Thoreau, Henry David 1817–1862: American naturalist, travel writer and essayist.

Tilak, Bal Gangadhar (लोकमान्य टिळक) 1856–1920, born Keshav Gangadhar Tilak: Indian nationalist, social reformer, teacher and lawyer.

Timur (تیمور) 1336–1405: Turco-Mongol convert to Islam who established a major empire in the Middle East; known as Tamerlane in the West.

Timurid 1370–1507: Dynasty founded by Timur.

Tissa, Devanampiya 250 BC–210 BC: Early Sri Lankan king who accepted Buddhism.

Tocqueville, Alexis de 1805–1859, full name is Alexis Charles Henri Clérel, Viscount de Tocqueville: French diplomat, political analyst and historian; best known for his first-hand account of early democratic society in the United States of America.

Tokugawa Ieyasu (德川家康) 1542–1616: Last of three "unifiers" of Japan at the end of the Warring States period; founded Tokugawa Shōgunate.

Tokugawa Mitsukuni (德川光圀) 1628–1701: Daimyo of the Mito domain in Tokugawa Japan who commissioned a major history of Japan.

Tokugawa Nariaki (德川斉昭) 1800–1860: Daimyo of the Mito domain in Tokugawa Japan who aligned the Mito School of scholars with the Kokugaku movement.

Tokugawa Shōgunate (德川幕府): Dynasty that effectively ruled Japan from 1615 to 1868.

Tokuichi (德一) 760–783: Hossō monk who opposed Saichō initiative to give the Tendai sect more influence in the Imperial Court through changes in the training and ordination of monks.

Tolstoy, Leo (Лео Толстой) 1828–1910, shortened name of Count Lev Nikolayevich Tolstoy (Лев Николаевич Толстой): Russian aristocrat, Christian socialist and novelist.

Tongdosa (通度寺): Buddhist temple established in 646 during the reign of Queen Seondeok of Silla and containing relics of the historical Buddha brought by Jajang from the Tang Empire.

Tosaka Jun (戸坂潤) 1900–1945: Japanese Marxist materialist and technologist political thinker.

Touré, Ahmed Sékou 1922–1982: First president of independent Guinea.

Tōyama Mitsuru (頭山満) 1855–1944: Japanese right-wing thinker and organizer. Founded the Genyōsha (玄洋社).

Toyotomi Hideyoshi (豊臣秀吉) 1536–1598: Second of the "unifiers" of Japan at the end of the Warring States period; invaded Korean peninsula with aim of conquering Ming dynasty.

Trần (陳): Dynasty that ruled Đại Việt from 1225 to 1400.

Trần Hưng Đaō (陳興道) 1228–1300: Supreme Commander of Đại Việt forces that repelled Mongol invasions during the Trần dynasty.

Trần Minh Tông (陳明宗) 1300–1357, birth name Trần Mạnh (陳奣): Emperor of Tran dynasty in Dai Viet.

Trần Nhân Tông (陳仁宗) 1258–1308: Third King of the Trần dynasty.

Trần Thanh Tong (陳聖宗) 1240–1290: Second King of the Trần dynasty.

Trotsky, Leon (Лев Троцкий) 1879–1940, born Lev Davidovich Bronstein: Russian revolutionary.

Truong Hán Siêu (張漢超) ?–1354: Neo-Confucian official in Dai Viet who wanted to introduce neo-Confucian reforms.

Tu Weiming (杜維明) b. 1940: New Confucian philosopher.

Tuareg, also Twareg or Touareg: North African Berber people or tribe.

Tudor: Dynasty that ruled England from 1485 to 1603.

Tudor, Elizabeth 1533–1603: Better known as Elizabeth I of England; r. 1558–1603.

Tuệ Trung Thượng Sĩ (慧中上士) 1230–1291: Birth name Trần Tung (陳嵩), prince in the *Tran* dynasty, general and then Thien monk.

Tufayl, ibn (ابن طفيل) d. 1185, also known as ibn Tufail, Aben Tofail or Ebn Tophail: Muslim court official philosopher and novelist best known for writing the philosophical novel, *Hayy ibn Yaqdhan*.

Tughlaq 1414–1320 (تغلق): Turko-Muslim dynasty of the Dehli Sultanate.

Tughlaq, Firuz Shah (فيروز شاه تغلق) b. 1309–d. 1388, r. 1351–1388: Sultan in the Tughlaq dynasty of the Sultanate of Delhi.

Tunisi, Khayr al-Din al (خير الدين التونسي) 1820–1890, sometimes referred to as Hayreddin Pasha: Late Ottoman Empire politician and reformer.

Uchida Ryōhei (内田良平) 1874–1937: Japanese right-wing thinker and organizer. Founded the Kokuryūkai (黒龍会).

Uicheon (義天) 1055–c. 1101: Buddhist monk who established Cheontae sect in Goryeo.

Umayyad Caliphate (الخلافة الأموية) from 661 to 750: Early Islamic dynasty.

Únzaga, Óscar 1916–1959, full name is Óscar Únzaga de la Vega: Bolivia nationalist and socialist political activist.

Vairocana (वैरोचन), phonetically in classical Chinese as 毘盧遮那, but literal meaning also used in classical Chinese as *guāngmíng biànzhào*

(光明遍照): Literally, "bright, shining illuminating light" associated with the sun, but used as the name of a Buddha viewed as the embodiment of the concept of Emptiness.

Varela, Félix 1788–1853, full name is Félix Varela y Morales: Cuban Catholic priest and liberal reformer.

Varona, Enrique José 1849–1933: Cuban writer and philosopher who originally promoted Comtean positivism but later was influenced by Herbert Spencer and then Friedrich Nietzsche.

Vasubandhu (वसुबन्द) fl. fourth century: Early Indian Buddhist philosopher.

Vico, Giambattista 1668–1744: Neapolitan writer, jurist and historian.

Vimalakīrti (विमल कीर्ति), ch. Wei-mo, jp. Yuima, kr. Yuma (維摩): Literally, vimala (विमल) "stainless, undefiled" and kīrti (कीर्ति) "fame, glory, reputation": Supposedly a wealthy follower of the Buddha; the central figure in the "Vimalakirti Sutra".

Wagner, Richard 1813–1883: German composer and anti-Semite.

Wahhab, Muhammad ibn Abd-al (محمد بن عبد الوهاب) b. 1703–d. 1792.

Walīullāh, Shāh (الله ولي شاه) b. 1703–d. 1762, also given as Wali-Allah of Delhi: Indian Islamic political thinker who advocated tolerance between the different forms of Islam and developed a theory of human development.

Wan Simo (萬思默) fl. early seventeenth century, w.g. Wan Ssu-mo, also called Wan Ting-yan (萬廷言): Wang Yangming follower of the Tranquility School.

Wang Bi (王弼) 226–249, w.g. Wang Pi: Early theorist in the *Xuanxue* school.

Wang Fuzhi (王夫之) 1619–1692, w.g. Wang Fu-chih, courtesy name Ernong (而農), pseudonym Chuanshan (船山).

Wang Gui (王珪) 571–639: Government minister and advisor to Tang Emperor Taizong.

Wang Longxi (王龍溪) 1498–1583, or 王竜谿, w.g. Wang Lung-hsi, given name Ji (幾) w.g. Chi, courtesy name Ruzhong (汝中): Direct student of Wang Yangming in the Realization School.

Wang Xinhai (王心齋) 1483–1541, w.g. Wang Hsin-chai also known by given name 王艮 Wang Ken or w.g. Gen., courtesy name (字) was Ruzhi (汝止), posthumously called Xin-zhai (心齋): Key successor to Wang Yangming.

Wang Yangming (王陽明), given name Wang Shouren 王守仁, courtesy name Bo'an (伯安): Ming neo-Confucian thinker of the "heart and mind" school.

Watsuji Tetsurō (和辻哲郎) 1889–1960: Japanese philosopher associated with the Kyoto School.

Webb, Beatrice 1858–1943, shortened name of Martha Beatrice Webb, Baroness Passfield, maiden name Potter: Co-founder of the Fabian Society.

Webb, Sidney 1859–1947, shortened name of Sidney James Webb, 1st Baron Passfield: Co-founder of the Fabian Society.

Weber, Max 1864–1920: German sociologist.

Wèi Yuán (魏源) 1794–1857, born Wei Yuanda (魏遠達), courtesy names Moshen (默深) and Hanshi (漢士): Late Qing reformer advocating *statecraft*.

Wei Zheng (魏徵) 580–643: Government minister and advisor to Tang Emperor Taizong.

Wen (文) 581–604: First emperor of Sui dynasty.

Wen, Marquis of Wei (魏文侯), r. 445–396 BC, birth name Wei Si (魏斯): Ruler of the major state of Wei in the Zhou dynasty Warring States period.

Western Jin (西晉) 265–316.

Wideok (威德) 525–598, r. 554–598, m.r. Widŏk: King of Baekje.

Winstanley, Gerrard 1609–1676: Radical thinker in the period of the English Civil War and Commonwealth periods.

Wollstonecraft, Mary 1759–1797: Advocate of women's rights.

Won Gwang (圓光) 541–c. 630 m.r. Won Kwang: Silla dynasty monk who wrote "Five Commandments for Secular Life" (Sesok-ogye 世俗五戒); also known by title Won Gwang Beop Sa (圓光法士) or Teacher of the Dharma.

Wonhyo (元曉) 617–686: Silla monk of the Flower Garland School.

Wu (武帝) r. 141 BC–87 BC: Emperor of Han dynasty.

Wu Jing (吳兢) 670–749, w.g. Wu Ching: Court historian of the Tang dynasty who compiled the *Zhenguan Zhengyao*.

Wu Zetian (武則天) 684–705: Only Empress (female ruler) in Chinese history.

Wu Zhihui (吳稚暉) 1865–1953: Early Chinese anarchist; later became nationalist and anticommunist.

Wycliffe, John c. 1320–1384: Oxford University lecturer and early Catholic Church reform advocate.

X, Malcolm 1925–1965, born Malcolm Little but used X to eliminate his slave owner patronymic and later changed his name to El-Hajj Malik El-Shabazz (الشباز مالك الحاج): African-American Islamic black rights activist.

Xenophanes of Colophon (Ξενοφάνης ὁ Κολοφώνιος) 570–470 BC: Presocratic.

Xenophon (Ξενοφῶν) c. 430–354 BC: Student of Socrates; mercenary soldier.

Xi Kang (嵇康) 223–262, w.g. Ji Kang, Courtesy name, Shuye (叔夜): Taoist philosopher who was one of the Seven Sages of the Bamboo Grove.

Xianbei (鮮卑): Nomadic tribe in Northeast Asia existing from about 3 BC to 6 AD.

Xiang Xiu (向秀) c. 223–c. 275: One of the Seven Sages of the Bamboo Grove.

Ximen Bao (西門豹): Student of *Zixia*, rationalist and successful politician in the state of Wei.

Xiong Shili (熊十力) 1885–1968, w.g. Hsuing Shih-li: First generation *New Confucian*.

Xiwangmu (西王母): Literally, Queen Mother of the West, the Queen of the Immortals.

Xu Fuguan (徐復觀) 1902/3–1982: Second generation New Confucian, student of *Xiong Shili*.

Xuanzong (唐玄宗) 712–756, w.g. Hsuan-tsung: Emperor of the Tang dynasty.

Xunzi (荀子) 298–c. 235 BC w.g. Hsun tzu; literally "Master Xun" for the individual named Xun Kuang (荀況): Follower of Confucius who emphasized ritual, training and meritocracy.

Yamaga Sokō (山鹿素行) 1622–1685: Initiator of the Ancient Learning approach in Japan.

Yamashita Etsuko (山下悦子) b. 1955: Japanese academic and writer on women's issues in Japan.

Yan Yuan (顏元) 1635–1704, courtesy name Yan Hunran (顏渾然) or Yan Yizhi (顏易直).

Yang (煬) 604–617: Second and last emperor of Sui dynasty.

Yang Jian (楊堅) 541–604, w.g. Yang Chien: Founder of the Sui dynasty; referred to as Emperor *Wen*.

Yang Yuhuan (楊玉環) 719–756, often called Yang Guifei (楊貴妃), literally, imperial consort Yang: Highest ranking imperial consort of T'ang Emperor Xuanzong and implicated in a revolt against him.

Yang Zhu (楊朱) 440–360 BC: Proto-Taoist thinker criticized by Mencius.

Yeonsan (燕山君) 1476–1506, r. 1494–1506: King of Joseson Korea but considered so cruel and debauched that he was not given a posthumous royal title as monarch so simply referred to as Prince Yeonsan as if he never was king.

Yi Hwang (李滉) 1501–1570, most common pen name was Toegye (退溪) and courtesy name was Gyeongho (景浩): Neo-Confucian scholar in the Joseon period focused on principle (理) and author of *The Ten Diagrams on Sage Learning* (聖學十圖), a book popular throughout East Asia.

Yi I (李珥) 1536–1584: Neo-Confucian scholar in the Joseon period focused on material-force (氣).

Yi Saek (李穡) 1328–1396, pen name Mokeun (牧隱): Teacher of neo-Confucianism in the late Gyoreo dynasty whose students encouraged the overthrow of the dynasty.

Yi Seonggye (李成桂) 1335–1408: Founder of the Joseon dynasty in Korea.

Yin, Duke (隱公) 722–712 BC, birth name Xigu (息姑): Duke of the state of *Lu* under the Zhou dynasty.

Yokoi Shōnan (横井小楠) 1809–1869: Late Tokugawa and early Meiji political reformer.

Yomei (用明) r. 585–587: Emperor of Japan; father of Prince Shōtoku.

Yongzheng (雍正) 1678–1735: Fifth *Qing* dynasty emperor.

Yoshida Shōin (吉田松陰) 1830–1859: Late Tokugawa Japan educator and Wang Yangming political activist.

Yoshino Sakuzō (吉野作造) 1878–1933: Japanese political theorist.

Youzi (有子), courtesy name Zi Ruo (子若), You Ruo (有若) given name: Literally "Master You"; a late student of Confucius, and possibly not taught directly by him, only by one of his students.

Youyang Nanye (歐陽南野) 1496–1554, w.g. Ouyang Nan-ye, also Youyang Chongyi (歐陽崇一): Key student of Wang Yangming.

Yù Dì (玉帝), see *Yù Huáng*.

Yù Huáng (玉皇), also Yù Dì (玉帝): The Jade Emperor is the ruler of Heaven and all realms below heaven including mortals.

Yudhishthira (युधिष्ठिर): Fictional prince and later king who is the central character in the Mahabharata. Literally, "the one who is steady in war", from the words, *yuddha* (युद्ध) meaning "war", and *sthira* (स्थिर) meaning "steady".

Zapata, Emiliano 1879–1919, shortened name of Emiliano Zapata Salazar: Leader in the Mexican Revolution; agrarian movement *Zapatismo* named after him.

Zaydan, Jurji (جورجي زيدان) b.1861–d.1914: Arab novelist and historian who encouraged pan-Arab sentiment.

Zeenat-un-Nissa (زينة النساء) b.1643–d.1721, also Zinat-un-Nissa: Literally, "Jewel among Women"; second daughter of Mughal Emperor Aurangzeb; given the title *Padshah Begum*.

Zeng Guofan (曾國藩) 1811–1871, w.g. Tseng Kuo-fan: Late Qing dynasty neo-Confucian reformer.

Zeno of Citium (Ζήνων ὁ Κιτιεύς) c. 334–c. 262 BC: Founder of the Stoic school of classical thought.

Zhang Heng (張衡) w.g. Chang Heng: Son of Zhang Ling, leader of the Five Bushel Sect.

Zhang Ling (張陵) w.g. Chang Ling, also known as Zhang Tao Ling (張道陵): Founder of the Five Bushel Sect.

Zhang Lu (張魯) w.g. Chang Lu: Grandson of Zhang Ling, leader of the Five Bushel Sect.

Zhang Renjie (張人傑) 1877–1950: Early Chinese anarchist based in Paris; later became a nationalist and anticommunist.

Zhang Xuecheng (章學诚) 1738–1801, w.g. Chang Hsüeh-ch'eng: Qing dynasty historian and philosopher.

Zhaung Zi (莊子) 369–286 BC, w.g. Chuang Tzu, honorific name of Zhuang Zhou (莊周), w.g. Chuang Chou: Early Taoist thinker.

Zheng Zi (曾子): Honorific name of Zeng Shen or Zeng Can (曾參), courtesy name Ziyu (子輿), a late student of Confucius.

Zhou Dunyi (周敦頤) 1017–1073, w.g. Chou Tun-yi: Song dynasty philosopher who created the cosmological basis for neo-Confucianism.

Zhu Xi (朱熹) 1130–1200: The crowning figure in Song dynasty learning, often called neo-Confucianism.

Zhu Yuanzhang (朱元璋) 1328–1398, w.g. Chu Yuan-chang: Founder of the Ming dynasty; became Emperor *Hongwu*, first Ming emperor.

Zia-ul-Haq, Muhammad (محمد ضياء الحق) b. 1924–d. 1988: Pakistani General and President of Pakistan (1978–1988).

Zigong (子貢), courtesy name of Duanmu Ci (端木賜): Student of Confucius.

Zixia (子夏) c. 507–c. 420 BC, w.g. Tzu-hsia, courtesy name of Bu Shang (卜商) w.g. Pu Shang: Student of Confucius who was the most immediately influential as a teacher.

Zizi (子思) c. 481–402 BC: Grandson of Confucius; teacher of Mencius.

Index

Abbasid Caliphate 132–3, 138, 474
Abduh, Muhammad 298–9, 474
Abe Isoo 322–3, 474
Abī Tālib, Ali ibn 131, 474
abolitionism 293, 430
Absolute 288, 430, 469
absolute nothingness *see* zettai mu
Acharya, Mandayam Parthasarathi Tirumal 326, 474
Adams, John 257, 474
adiaforía (ἀδιαφορία) 72, 430
Adorno, Theodor W. 374, 474–5
advisor 60, 64, 76, 84, 87, 95, 103, 124, 132, 136, 145, 150, 176, 180, 183, 187, 191, 194, 215, 224, 236, 272, 440, 471, 478–9, 481, 490, 492, 494, 495, 497, 500, 505–6 *see also* official
Afghani, Sayyid Jamal-al-Din al- 298, 475
Aflaq, Michel 363–4, 475
Agama (आगम) 45, 430
agathos (ἀγαθός) 37, 430 *see also* good
Agrippina, Julia 87, 475
ahimsa (अहिंसा) 357–8, 430
aidagara (間柄) 337, 430
Aizawa Seishisai 274, 460, 475
Ājīvakas 31, 430
akunin shōki (悪人正機) 226, 430
akutō (悪黨) 194–5, 206, 430
ālayavijñāna (आलयविज्ञान) 108, 430
Alberdi, Juan Bautista 278, 475
Alcibiades 29–30, 475
aletheia (ἀλήθεια) 379, 430, 438
Alexander I 277, 475
Alexander the Great 60–61, 67–8, 73–6, 242, 475
Alfaro, Eloy 307, 475
Alī, Hasan ibn 131, 475
Allah 173–4, 243, 365, 388, 430, 446, 455
Alvarez, Agustin 307, 475

Amaterasu 111, 183, 269, 475
Amida Buddha *see* Amitābha Buddha
Amin, Qasim 292, 475
Amitābha Buddha 109, 135, 167–70, 173, 204, 226, 430, 452, 475
amor fati 431
An Hyang 176, 475
An Lushan 140, 476
Anabaptist 212–13, 431
anaideia (αναιδεια) 72, 431
Analects 29, 34–5, 40–41, 43–6, 51–4, 60, 69, 95, 112, 129, 135, 236–7, 431, 439
analytical philosophy 367–72, 431
anarchism 17, 72, 115, 310, 316–20, 326–8, 354, 358, 431
Anaximander 36, 476
anicca (अनिच्चा) 33, 431
anti-colonialism 356–72 *see also* colonialism
Antisthenes 56, 71–2, 476
Antoun, Farah 322, 476
apokatastasis (ἀποκατάστασις) 118, 431
aporia (ἀπορεία) 37, 431
apotreptikos (ἀποτρεπτικός) 431
aql (عقل) 137–8, 430
aql al-faal (عقل فعال) 138, 431
Aquinas, Thomas 149, 154–5, 164–7, 172–4, 476
arête (ἀρετή) 36, 67, 71, 431
arhat (अरहत्) 92–3, 431, 465
aristocrats and aristocracy 38, 40, 70, 85, 125–8, 130, 134–5, 139–44, 146, 158–60, 162, 168, 171, 178, 197, 205, 213–14, 225, 246, 250, 260–61, 288, 298, 380, 435, 440, 441, 464, 466, 477, 484, 490, 493, 494, 503 *see also* oligarchy
Aristotle 18, 37, 51, 58–63, 67, 70–71, 74, 116–17, 132, 136–7, 154–5,

511

165–7, 171–4, 192, 219–20, 225, 250, 299, 383, 476
Arrian 87, 476
ārya (आर्य) 31, 431
asabiyya (عصبيّة) 192, 431
asceticism 152–3, 431, 449
Asclepius 44, 476
Asharite 138, 431–2
Ashoka *see* Maurya, Ashoka
Asian Values 390, 432
áskesis (ἄσκησις) 72, 432
assembly 27, 36, 191, 195, 278, 388–9, 439, 458
Astell, Mary 251, 293, 476
ātman (आत्मन्) 31, 33, 92, 107, 432
Augustine, Saint 103, 118–20, 122, 153, 155, 476
Augustus 81, 432
Aurangzeb 252, 476
Austin, J.L. 381, 476
autárkeia (αὐτάρκεια) 71, 432
authenticity 339, 432
Avatamsaka Sūtra *see* Mahāvaipulya Buddhāvatamsaka Sūtra
Azuchi Disputation 207, 432
Azuchi–Momoyama period 227, 476

ba'ath (بعث) 363–4, 432
badawa (بداوة) 192, 432
Baekje 101, 127–8, 476
Bai, Mamola 252, 476
Bai Tongdong 393, 476
Bakunin, Mikhail 316–18, 476
Ballou, Adin 321, 476
Bambara 177, 477
Banna, Hassan al- 386–8, 450, 477
Bao Jingyan 115, 477
Baohuanghui 303, 432
Baopuzi 115, 432, 483
Barani, Ziauddin 175, 178, 180, 186, 477
Barreda, Gabino 308, 477
Barreto, Luis Pereira 308, 477
basho (場所) 335, 344, 432
Bayle, Pierre 246, 477
Bayt at-Hikma 132, 432
Beauvoir, Simone de 380, 477
Bellamy, Edward 321, 477
Bellamy, Francis 321, 477
Bello, Andrés 275–6, 278, 307, 477

Bentham, Jeremy 248, 270, 275, 278, 313, 477
běntǐ (本體) 217, 432
Beomnang 136, 477
Beop 127, 477
Beopheung 125, 477
Beopseong 432
Bergson, Henri-Louis 331, 352, 477
Berkeley Mafia 369, 432
Berkman, Alexander 317, 477
Bernstein, Eduard 320–21, 477
Bey, Ahmed 272, 477
bhajanaloka (भजनलोक) 108, 432–3
bhikkhu 433
bhikkhuni 90, 433
Bidam 144, 477
bīja (बीज)108, 430, 433, 467
Bimbisara 26, 28, 478
bio-power (biopouvoir) 377, 433
Bismark, Otto von 306, 320, 478
Blackstone, William 248, 478
Blyden, Edward Wilmot 295–6, 478
Bo Qin 28, 478
bodhicitta (बोधिचित्त) 91, 433
bodhisattva (बोधिसत्त्व) 91, 108, 118, 142, 145, 168, 433
Bodhisattva Precepts 142, 433
Bodin, Jean 219–20, 478
Bolivar, Simón 260–61, 280, 478
Bonald, Louis Gabriel Ambroise de 263, 478
Bose, Subhas Chandra 352, 478
Boston Confucianism 433, 492
Bou 184, 478
bourgeoisie 324, 433, 436
Brahmā 142, 433
Brahmajala Sūtra 142, 433
Brahman 82, 433
Brahmin 26, 31–2, 38–9, 61, 83, 104–5, 107, 433
British East India Company 270
Bruni, Leonardo 180–81, 197, 478
Buddha (as concept or particular manifestation) 25–33, 38–45, 48–50, 59–60, 63, 68–9, 90–91, 100, 106, 108–9, 126, 129–30, 134, 139, 142, 145, 160–61, 167–8, 170, 179, 204, 230, 385, 429, 430, 433, 436, 439, 443, 449–50, 452, 453, 457, 458, 461, 475, 478, 492, 493, 503, 505

Buddha, the (historical person) vi, 25–33, 38–45, 48–50, 59–60, 63, 68–9, 90–91, 100, 106, 108–9, 129–30, 134, 139, 145, 161, 167, 179, 230, 247, 385, 429, 430, 433, 436, 439, 443, 449, 452, 453, 457, 458, 461, 478, 483, 503, 505; for the historical Buddha before enlightenment *see* Gautama Siddhārtha
Buddhahood 92, 108, 135, 142, 156, 221, 431, 433, 462
Buddha nature 135, 142, 160, 433, 442
buddhānusmṛti (बुद्धानुस्मृति) 167, 433, 452
Buddhist state 134, 439
Bulguksa 126, 478
Bulssi Japbyeon 183, 434
bureaucracy 38, 82, 146, 158, 183, 204, 208, 223, 232, 276, 285, 334, 358, 363, 469, 487 *see also* advisor, civil service, official
Burke, Edmund 262–3, 297, 306, 478
Burrus, Sextus Afranius 87, 478
bushi (武士) 189–90, 205, 434 *see also* samurai
Butler, Judith 381, 478

cai (才) 112, 434
cakkavatti 51, 59–60, 64, 68, 108, 434
Caliph 131–3, 138, 147, 152, 271, 434
Calvin, John 213–14, 227–8, 259, 478
Carlyle, Thomas 265–6, 282, 334, 357, 478
Carrel, Alexis 478
Cārvāka 31, 434
Cassirer, Ernest 349–50, 478
Catholic Church 187–8, 193, 212–13, 227, 229, 263, 279, 289, 306, 360, 434, 437
caudillo 260, 307–8, 434
Chaadayev, Petr Yakovlevich 277, 479
Chamberlain, Houston Stewart 349, 479
Chan 135–6, 155–6, 158–63, 165, 167, 173, 179, 184, 208–9, 221–2, 434
Chán fa 434
Chanakya 75, 479
charity 1, 15–18, 105, 119, 139, 172, 455

Chaulukya 150, 479
Chen Qing-lan 218, 479
Chicago Boys 369, 434
Chong Chedu 218, 479
Christian Reformation 212–14
Christian socialism 320–23
Chrysippus of Soli 86, 96, 479
Chulalongkorn 304, 479
Chun Qiu 34, 51, 79, 84, 140, 156, 434
Chūnqiū Fánlù 79, 434
Chūnqiū Shídài 434
Cicero 80–81, 85–6, 89–91, 96–7, 166, 180, 479
citizen 9, 26, 30, 35–8, 40, 42–3, 58, 63, 66, 68, 81, 89, 193, 197–8, 257–61, 265, 276, 278, 279, 282, 289, 295
Civil Rights movement 361, 435
civil service 164, 231, 234, 270, 273, 288, 444, 459 *see also* advisor, bureaucracy, official
civilization vii, viii, 3–6, 11, 14–15, 17, 25–6, 47, 58–9, 68, 73–5, 88–9, 91, 98–9, 115, 121–2, 124–5, 148–9, 164, 177, 181, 192–3, 230, 242, 255, 281, 283–7, 289–91, 293–4, 296, 298, 301, 305, 315, 352, 357–8, 368, 375–6, 384, 439, 443
class 38–40, 42, 54, 61, 63, 81, 89–90, 138, 162, 182–3, 205, 209, 224, 251, 260, 269, 275–6, 306–7, 310, 312, 315–16, 321–2, 324, 331, 348, 351, 358, 376, 382, 433, 436, 453, 455, 458
class bias 38–42, 61–3
Clemens, Titus Flavius 118, 479
Cleyre, Voltarine de 317, 479
Code of Laws 101, 435
Cohen, Hermann 350, 479
Coleridge, Samuel Taylor 265, 282, 479
colony and colonialization viii, 36, 60, 190, 213, 239, 256–8, 260–62, 280, 285, 296–8, 304–5, 307, 318–19, 321, 332, 347, 352, 356–69, 388, 448, 454, 462, 478, 482, 490, 500 *see also* imperialism
commonwealth 97, 214, 219, 229, 256–7, 435
communism 225, 287, 312, 314–17, 319–20, 324–9, 358, 362–3, 365–7, 369, 377, 388, 390–92
community 15, 37, 39, 44, 50, 61, 63,

69, 81–2, 85, 88–90, 99–100, 102, 112, 122, 131, 134, 139, 151, 160, 179, 182, 196, 204–6, 213, 219, 224, 226, 239–42, 252, 256, 259, 269–70, 313–14, 345, 357, 362, 367, 371, 374, 379, 388, 442–3, 454, 458, 467
Comte, Auguste 287–90, 292, 294, 298–9, 307–8, 479
conceptual stretching 11, 435
Condorcet, Marquis de 279, 479
Confucianism 25–6, 28–9, 33–5, 38–46, 48, 51–3, 59–60, 70–71, 77, 79–80, 95, 112, 135, 156–7, 167, 174, 179, 216, 223, 233, 235–6, 246, 248, 266, 286–7, 391–2 *see also* Literati, Ru
Confucius 6, 25, 26, 28–9, 33–5, 38–46, 48, 51–7, 59–62, 65, 70–71, 77, 79–80, 94–5, 112, 129, 135, 157, 167, 179, 233, 235, 236, 246, 248, 287, 391, 393, 431, 451, 457, 460, 469, 479, 484, 500, 507–9
Constant, Benjamin 276, 479
Constant, Benjamin, of Brazil 308, 479–80
cooperatives 316–17, 319, 321, 323, 435
cosmology 17, 20, 44, 63–8, 73, 91–7, 105, 118, 156, 174, 268, 372, 454
Crates of Thebes 58, 480
critical theory 374, 435
Crito 44, 480
Cynics 56, 58–61, 63, 67–8, 70–72, 84–5, 435

Dai Nihon Kokusai Kai 346, 480
Dai Zhen 234, 480
Daigaku Jiken 318, 435
daimon (δαίμων) 43, 72, 435
Daimyō 206–8, 227, 269, 310, 435
danda (दण्ड) 77, 83, 105, 435
dandaniti (दण्डनीति) 105, 435
Dao An 480
Daosheng 135, 480
Daoxin 136, 480
"dark learning" metaphysics 109–16 *see also* Xuánxué
Darwin, Charles 291, 461, 463
Dasein 338–40, 350, 435
datsuaron (脱亞論) 301, 436
Dazai Shundai 237, 480
dé (德) 35, 45, 437 *see also* moral force

De Bary, William Theodore 392, 480
Debs, Eugene Victor "Gene" 480
deconstruction 374, 377–8, 380, 436
Deleuze, Gilles 374, 480
Delhi Sultanate 178, 180, 186, 480
Delian League 29, 436, 453
democracy 18, 28, 30, 40, 62, 137, 238, 249, 257–8, 260–61, 265–6, 275–6, 287–8, 290–92, 302–4, 325–7, 332, 344–6, 348–9, 365–6, 368, 378–80, 383, 386, 392–3, 436
Democritus 36, 480
demos (δημος) 40, 85, 380 436 *see also* masses
Deng Xiaojun 392, 480
Derrida, Jacques 373, 377–80, 383–4, 480
dependent arising/origination 32–3, 39, 106–7, 336, 453 *see also* paticcasamuppada
dhamma 5, 64, 82–3, 88, 91 *see also* dharma
dharma (धर्म) 4–5, 31, 44, 64, 75, 82, 105–6, 108, 127, 136, 160–61, 165, 167–8, 203, 249, 385, 436 *see also* dhamma
dharmakaya (धर्मकाय) 108–9, 145, 436
Dharmasastra 82–3, 106, 150, 436
dialectic 1, 9, 13, 240, 289, 314, 335–6, 343–4, 358, 380, 443
dictatorship of the proletariat (diktatur des proletariats) 315, 436
Diderot, Denis 259, 480
differences within similarities 10–13, 436
Digambara 150, 436
Diggers 225, 228, 436
Dīgha Nikāya 49, 436–7
Diogenes of Sinope 56, 61, 67–8, 72, 480
direct action 317–18, 437
discourse 80, 87, 115, 181, 220, 243, 269, 359, 370, 377, 381, 384, 437
Disraeli, Benjamin 306, 481
dissenting sect 219, 228, 437
Diyaf, Ahmad ibn Ali 271, 297, 481
divine 43, 53, 87, 96–7, 99, 103–7, 116–18, 120, 131, 155, 165–6, 173–4, 181, 188, 213, 219–20, 222, 240, 243, 247, 259, 262, 343–4, 388–9, 456, 465

djeli 191, 437, 440
doctrinal school 135, 159–60, 437, 452, 459
Doctrine of the Mean 157, 236, 437, 439
Dōgen 160, 162, 221, 481
Dong lin xue 218, 437
Dong Zhongshu 79–80, 94, 481
Dōrim 127, 481
Douglass, Frederick 293, 481
Dōui 136, 481
Du Ruhui 481
dukkha (दुक्ख) 33, 431, 437
Dushun 134, 481
duty 43, 64, 66, 67, 87–8, 96, 103, 106, 114, 186, 192, 194, 249–50, 355, 445, 450

Eastern Jin 100, 127, 481
Echeverria, Esteban 278, 481
Edo School 269, 437, 489, 495
egalitarianism 89, 144, 222, 229, 348, 366–7, 392, 437
egoism 317, 437, 500, 502
eidos (εἶδος) 58, 66, 437
Eisai 160–62, 481
elenchus (ἔλεγχος) 37, 437
elite and elitism 25–6, 31, 34, 36, 38, 40–42, 47, 61–3, 81, 84, 88–91, 97, 98, 102, 109, 115, 117, 119, 125, 130, 136, 139, 149, 160, 167–8, 171, 183–4, 195, 199, 207, 231, 245, 251, 254, 257, 266, 269, 270, 276, 278, 298, 301–2, 308, 313, 322, 344, 346, 348, 358, 367, 369, 370, 382, 388, 393, 433, 449, 457
Elizabeth I 228, 504
Emerson, Ralph Waldo 266, 281, 481
emperor 74, 77, 84, 87–9, 92–3, 100, 102, 109–11, 118, 123–4, 128, 139–41, 143, 145, 155, 162–3, 167, 176, 181–2, 185, 187, 189, 192, 208, 210–11, 231, 233, 252, 268–9, 274, 300, 303, 318, 322, 343, 345, 347, 351, 432, 434–5, 444, 446, 449, 460, 462, 464–5, 471, 475–6, 481, 483–4, 486, 488–92, 497–8, 500–502, 504–9 see also empress, king, ruler
empress 93, 128, 145–6, 226, 441, 482, 492, 501–2, 506 see also queen, ruler

emptiness 9, 106–7, 109, 336, 414, 463, 505 see also śūnyatā
Encyclopédie 259, 437
Encyclopedistes 259, 437
Enfantin, Barthélemy Prosper 313, 481
Engels, Friedrich 312, 314–15, 328, 481
enlightenment 33, 39, 41, 91–2, 100, 108, 113, 136, 142, 156, 160, 162–4, 167–9, 173, 224, 335, 431
Enlightenment, The (historical period) 149, 217, 229–57, 260, 264, 273, 275–6, 282, 288–9, 292, 309, 330, 375, 437–8
Enryakuji 141, 205–6, 481
Epictetus 87–8, 481
equality 38–42
erschlossenheit 379, 438, 447
eternal return 332, 438
ethics 1, 8–10, 15–18, 20, 25–6, 36–7, 42–3, 61–2, 67–8, 70, 75–6, 79, 81–8, 105–6, 115, 122, 139, 142, 149, 151, 154, 156, 189–94, 216, 243, 249–50, 291, 298, 337, 342, 345–6, 350–51, 357, 371, 373, 378–80, 383, 392, 438 see also virtue
ethos (ἦθος) 36, 438
eudaimonia (εὐδαιμονία) 37, 58, 67, 71, 137, 438
evil 37, 55, 64, 69, 87, 103, 105–6, 108, 119–20, 137, 150, 164, 166, 169, 174, 184, 187, 221, 226, 262, 305, 311

fa (法) 55, 77, 80, 438
Fă-jiā (法家) 51, 54–7, 68–70, 77, 79, 80, 81, 84, 93–4, 95, 206, 438, 491
Fabian Society 321, 438, 506
Fadl-Allāh, Muhammad Hussein 390, 481
fallenness see Verfallen
falsafa (فلسفة) 149, 152–4, 438
Fang Qiao 124–5, 481
Farabi, al- 8, 120, 134, 136–8, 147–8, 153, 171, 173, 192, 481
Faraj, Muhammad abd-al-Salam 389–90, 481–2
fascism 303, 329–55, 365, 368, 388, 438
fate 61, 71, 96, 431
Fatwa-i-Jahandari 180, 186, 438, 477
Fazang 145–6, 482

feminism 40, 198, 228, 285, 292–3, 313, 317–20, 333, 371, 374–5, 380–84, 438
Feng Guifen 273, 482
Feng Youlan 391, 482
Ferdinand VII 277, 482
Fichte, Johann Gottlieb 264, 345, 482
Ficino, Marsilio 193, 482
filial piety 41–6, 51–4, 84, 89, 124, 126, 164, 174, 212, 216, 469
final dharma age (末法) 167, 438–9
Final World War *see* Saishūsensō
fiqh (فقه) 133, 439
Firestone, Shulamith 381, 482
Five Bushel Sect 110, 439, 508–9
Five Cardinal Literati Virtues *see* wǔ cháng
Five Classics 185, 439, 447–8, 460–61, 470 *see also* wǔ jīng
Five Elements 95, 156, 439
Flores Magón, Ricardo 317–18, 482
Flower Garland 101, 109, 134–6, 143, 145–6, 159–60, 182, 439, 441, 449
Former Qin 101, 482
fortune 84, 160, 188–9
Foucault, Michel 373, 375–7, 380–81, 383–4, 482
Four Books 185, 236, 437, 439 *see also individual texts* Analects, Doctrine of the Mean, Great Learning, Mencius
Four Heavenly Kings 130, 139, 439
Fourier, Charles 312–13, 328, 482
Franco, Francisco 331, 482
Frankfurt School 374–5, 435, 439
Freud, Sigmund 334, 374, 482
Freyre, Gilberto 331–2, 482
Friedan, Betty 380–81, 482
Friedman, Milton 368–9, 482
Fujiwara Seika 215, 482
Fukko Shintō 267, 439
Fukuzawa Yukichi 300–302, 482
Fula 482
Fulo, Empire of the Great 177, 482
fundamentalism 138, 185–6, 238, 244, 364, 373–4, 384–90, 394, 439
Furnivall, Frederick James 321, 482

Gaddafi, Muammar 364–5, 482–3
Gaero 127–8, 483
Gallienus 102, 483
Gan Zhongke 109, 483

gana-rajya (गणराज्य) 27, 439
gana-sangha (गणसङ्घ) 27, 439, 458
Gandhara 92, 483
Gandhi, Monhandas Karamchand 357–8, 361, 372, 483
Gang Hang 215, 483
Gaozi 70–71, 483
Gautama Siddhārtha 25, 30, 167, 483
Gbara 191, 195, 439
Ge Hong 115, 483
gender 20, 40–42, 61–3, 68, 90, 94, 96, 227, 254, 280, 282, 291–6, 317–18, 380–81, 383, 386, 398, 478 *see also* women
general will *see* volonté générale
Genyōsha 346, 439, 504
George, Henry 327, 483
Geworfenheit 338, 350, 439
gewu (格物) 157, 235, 440
Ghazali, Al 152–4, 172–3, 483
Gihwa 183–4, 483
gikuyu 366, 440
Gladstone, William Ewart 306, 483
Gobineau, Joseph Arthur Comte de 294, 349, 483
Go-Daigo 176, 181–3, 194, 444, 483
Goguryeo 101–2, 125, 127, 483
Gokhale, Gopal Krishna 297, 483
Golden Light Sūtra 366, 440
Goldman, Emma 317, 484
golpum system (骨品制度) 125, 440
Go-Nara 465, 484
Gong Zizhen 273, 484
Gongyang Gao 484
Gongyang Zhuàn 51, 79, 140–41, 440
good and goodness 25, 31, 34, 35, 37, 40, 43, 46, 54–5, 58–9, 62, 64, 68–9, 82, 86–7, 89, 100, 103, 106, 108, 116, 118, 128, 130, 137, 144, 150–51, 166, 173, 187, 189, 211, 217, 221–2, 234, 248–9, 259, 262, 311, 335–7, 391 *see also* agathos, liángzhi, ren
Gosala, Makkhali 31, 430, 484
Gouze, Marie 279, 484
governmentality 375, 380, 440
gozan (五山) 160, 162, 215, 440
Great Learning 52, 94, 235–6, 439–40
Great Tang Code 124, 440, 464
Greer, Germaine 381, 484
Gregory the Great, Pope 122

Index

Grimké, Angelina 293, 484
Grimké, Sarah 293, 484
griots 175, 180, 191, 440
Gu Yanwu 231–2, 484
Guattari, Pierre-Félix 374, 484
Guevara, Ernesto "Che" 359–60, 389, 484
Guicciardini, Francesco 181, 484
Gui-ji 217, 440
Guksa (國師) 159–60, 162, 184, 440, 462 *see also* State Preceptor
Guliang zhuàn 140–41, 440
Guo Xiang 113–15, 484
Guómindang 440
Gusan (九山) 158, 440–41
Gutiérrez Merino, Gustavo 360, 484
Gwalleuk 128, 484
Gwanggaeto the Great 102, 484
Gwon Geun 176–7, 484
Gyeomik 127, 484
Gyoki 139, 484
Gyoreo 181, 484
Gyunyeo 136, 159, 484

Habermas, Jurgen 375, 485
hadara (حضارة) 192, 440
hadith (حديث) 131–3, 153, 441, 445, 455
Haeinsa temple 159, 485
hajj (حج) 177, 441
Hamilton, Alexander 258, 485
han (藩) 215, 441
Han dynasty 73–4, 79–80, 83–4, 93, 98, 101, 109–11, 115, 125, 130, 179, 232, 485
Han Fei 56–7, 77–9, 94–5, 485
Hanbal, Ahmad ibn 138, 485
Hanshan Deqing 208, 485
harmony 35-6, 53, 71, 84, 86, 96, 113, 118, 127, 129, 134, 148, 159, 188, 213, 232, 259, 264, 442
Harrington, James 225, 485
Hart, H.L.A. 370, 485
Hashimoto Kingorō 346, 485
Hatta Shūzō 319, 485
Hayek, Friedrich 356, 367–9, 485
Hayford, Joseph Casely 304–5, 485
Hayy ibn Yaqzan 244, 441, 504
He Bo 60, 485
He Xinyin 222, 485
He Yan 111–13, 485

He Zhen 320, 485
heaven 34, 49, 61, 62, 69, 71, 84, 89, 95, 106, 110–11, 112, 115, 124, 144–5, 156, 164, 166, 173, 186, 207, 213, 216, 221–2, 234, 310–11, 322, 464–6, 508 *see also* tiān
Hegel, Georg Wilhelm Friedrich 287–9, 303, 314–15, 337, 339–40, 344–5, 352, 358, 368, 485
Heian period 141, 143, 160, 485
Heidegger, Martin 69, 330, 332, 334, 336–40, 345, 349–51, 353–5, 374, 379, 485
Hemachandra, Acharya 150–51, 485
henosis (ἕνωσις) 117, 441
Heraclitus of Ephesus 36, 485
heredity and hereditary 38, 55, 62, 125, 132, 215, 224, 226, 261, 300
hermeneutics 6, 8, 19, 84, 231, 237, 256, 267, 338, 340, 355, 374–5, 377–8, 386, 441
hierarchy and hierarchical 26, 38, 40, 54, 61–2, 88–9, 96, 110, 117, 124, 129, 171, 174, 181, 195, 213, 227, 232, 236, 280, 287, 335, 262, 390
High Treason Incident *see* Daigaku Jiken
hikmah (حكمة) 241, 441
Himiko 111, 485
Hipparchia of Maroneia 63, 486
Hirata Atsutane 268–9, 486
Hirata School 269, 441
Hiratsuka Raicho 292, 460, 486
historicism 1, 13–15, 230–38, 255, 368, 441
history, role of 179–81
Hitler, Adolf 339, 347, 349, 449
Hô Chin Minh 363, 486
Hōjō Masako 161, 486
Hölderlin, Johann Christian Friedrich 350–51, 486
Holkar, Maharani Ahilya Bai 252, 486
Hombre el Nuevo 360, 451
Hōnen 168–70, 173, 226, 486
Hong Duc thien chinh thu 185, 441
Honganji 204–5, 486
Hongwu 486
hooks, bell 382, 486
Horton, James Africanus Beale 296, 486

Hōryūji 129, 486
hósios (ὅσιος) 43, 441
Hossō 141–3, 441
Huan, Duke 29, 93, 486
Huang Zong-xi 231, 486
Huang-di 93, 486
Huáyán jinshīzi zhāng 146, 441
Hughes, Thomas 321, 486
Huguenots 214, 441 *see also* Protestants
Huineng 135–6, 486
Huisi 127, 486
Huiyüan 100, 486
Hujwiri, Al- 153, 486
human nature 68–72
Hume, David 246–8, 266, 346, 487
hun (魂) 441 *see also* spirit
Hungu faction 190, 442
hurriyya (حُرِّيَّة) 271, 442
Hus, Jan 188, 212, 487
hwajaeng (和諍) 134, 442
Hwangyongsa 126, 487
Hwarang 126, 442
Hyeonjeong non 184, 442
hyle (ὕλη) 96, 442
Hyŏn'gwang 127, 487
Hypatia 102, 487

Iamblichus 117–18, 487
icchantika (इच्छन्तकि) 108, 135, 142, 442
Ichadon 125, 487
Ichikawa Fusae 292, 487
iddah, al (العدة) 253, 442
Ihya Ulum al-Din 153, 172, 442
ijtihād (اجتهاد) 132, 388–9, 442
ikki (一揆) 206, 442
ikkō ikki (一向一揆) 206–7, 442
imām (إمام) 131–2, 166, 242–3, 271, 390, 442
Immortals *see* shenxian
imperial decline 99–103
imperialism 255–6, 282–309, 312, 318, 321, 324, 329–30, 340, 349, 354, 358, 366, 389–90, 442 *see also* colony and colonialism
individualism 67, 203, 266, 318, 344, 368, 381, 442
Inoue Kowashi 302, 487
Inoue Nissho 347, 487

integration 16, 43, 84, 122–48, 182, 442–3
invisible hand 247, 443
Irigaray, Luce 381, 487
irresolvable dialectic 13, 443
irtifāqāt (ارتفاقات) 241–2, 253, 443
Isabella II 277, 447, 487
Ishihara Shintarō 390, 487
Ishiwara Kanji 348, 487
Islamic political thought 151–5
Itagaki Seishiro 302, 348, 487
Itō Hirobumi 301, 487
Itō Jinsai 235–6, 487
Itō Noe 319, 487

Jade Emporor *see* Yù Huáng
jahiliyyah (جاهلية) 387, 443
Jajang 126, 488
Jamahiriyah, al- 365, 443
Jâtaka Tales 82, 443
Jay, John 258, 488
Jayasimha 150–51, 488
Jefferson, Thomas 257–8, 280, 488
Jeong Dojeon 177, 183–4, 190, 195, 488
Jeonghyesa 160, 443, 501
Jesuits 247, 263, 443
jian'ai (兼愛) 54, 443
Jiang Qing 392–3, 488
jihād (جهاد) 133, 186, 238, 243, 387, 389, 443, 450, 482
Jindeok 144, 488
jīng-shì (經世) 273–4, 443
jìngzuò (靜坐) 217, 443
Jinheung 125, 488
Jinmu Tennō 269, 488
jinn, al- (الجن) 388, 443–4 *see also* spirit
Jinnah, Muhammad Ali 362, 488
Jinno Shotoki 179, 181–2, 444, 490
Jinul 160, 184, 443, 488
jiriki (自力) 169, 444
Jisha bugyō 216, 444
Jitō 189, 444
Jo Gwangjo 190, 488
Joseon dynasty 177, 183–5, 190, 195, 214, 216, 218, 229, 235, 488
juche (主体) 362, 444
Jufukuji 161, 488
Julian 118, 488
Jungjong 190, 488

junsui keikken (純粋経験) 335, 444
jūnzǐ (君子) 4, 39–40, 444
jurén (挙人) 234, 444
Jūshichi Jō Kenpō 129, 444

kabane (姓) 129, 444
Kada Azumamaro 267, 488
kagathos (κἀγαθός) 35, 66, 444
Kagawa Toyohiko 323, 488
kairos (καιρός) 117, 444
kalam (كلام) 138, 444
kalos (καλός) 35, 444
Kamakura Shōgunate 160–62, 168, 170–71, 176, 189, 204, 488
kami (神) 205, 460
Kamichika Ichiko 319, 488
Kammu 128, 140–41, 169, 489
Kamo Mabuchi 267, 269, 489
Kaneko Fumiko 319, 489
Kaneko Kentarō 301, 489
Kang Youwei 287, 292, 294, 303–4, 489
Kangxi, Emperer 231, 489
Kanishka the Great 92, 489
Kanno Sugako 318, 489
Kant, Immanuel 248–50, 254–5, 264, 266, 319, 344–5, 350, 370–71
kaojùxué (考証学) 234, 444–5
karma (करम) 32–3, 45, 92, 108, 433, 445
katanagari (刀狩) 207, 445
Katayama Sen 323, 325, 489
Katayama Tetsu 323, 489
kathekon (検地) 70, 445
Katō Chikage 269, 489
Katō Hiroyuki 301, 303, 489
Katsu Kaishu 300, 489
Kaunda, Kenneth David 366, 489
Kautilya 75, 489
Keita, Dankaran Toumani 191, 489
Keita, Sundiata 179–80, 191, 195, 463, 489
Keita, Uli I 192, 489
kenchi (検地) 207, 445
Kenyatta, Jomo 366, 489
Khaldūn, Ibn 175, 178–81, 187, 189, 192, 195–6, 248, 255, 271, 298, 489
Khan, Kublai 163
Khan, Malkom 272, 489
Khan, Mirza Yusef 272–3, 489

Khan, Syed Ahmad bin Muttaqi 270, 286, 489
Khayzuran bint Atta, al- 147, 489–90
Khedive 271, 445
Khomeini, Ruhollah 389, 490
khōra (χώρα) 379, 445
Kim Il Sung 362–3, 490
Kim Jwajin 319, 490
Kindī, Al 132–3, 490
king 4, 26–8, 41, 51, 59–61, 64–6, 71, 73, 75–7, 80, 82–3, 85, 89–90, 99–101, 103–6, 108, 114, 117, 125, 127–8, 130, 139, 150–52, 155, 158–61, 163, 167, 176–7, 184–7, 189–92, 197, 203, 219–20, 225, 237, 240, 252, 258, 264–5, 304, 308, 321, 364, 434, 439–40, 446, 448, 449, 456, 458, 460, 468, 471, 476–88, 490, 493–7, 499–501, 503–4, 505, 507–8 *see also* emperor, mansa, maripgan, monarch, queen, ruler
King, Martin Luther 359–61
kingdom of ends (reich der zwecke) 249, 264, 445
Kingsley, Charles 321, 490
Kita Ikki 347–8, 490
Kitab al-shifa 151, 445
Kitab ara al-madina al-fadila 445
Kitab as-Sittah 131, 445
Kitab Hujjat Allah al-Balighah 241, 243, 445
Kitabatake Chikafusa 175–6, 179, 181–3, 189, 194, 490
knowledge 32, 37, 45, 53, 63, 66–9, 115, 116, 118, 120, 133, 136, 156, 166, 168, 210–12, 217, 220, 221, 223, 234, 242, 244, 248, 261, 266, 267, 271, 272, 273, 279, 300, 311, 325, 335, 339, 340, 357, 375, 380, 383, 437, 447–8, 455–6, 462, 480 *see also* wisdom
Knox, John 228, 490
kogaku (古学) 235, 445–6
Kojiki 129, 179, 446
Kokki 129, 446
Kokugaku 266–9, 274, 281, 299, 341, 346, 437, 441, 446
Kokuhonsha 346, 446
kokujin (国人) 205, 446
Kokuryukai 346, 446, 504

Kokushi 162, 446, 462 *see* State Preceptor
kokutai (國体) 274, 446
Kōmeitō 385, 446
Konaté, Naré Maghann 190–91, 490
Kōsaka Saaki 336, 342, 490
Kotoku Shusui 318, 323, 490
Kouroukan Fougan 180, 191, 195, 439, 446
Kōyama Iwao 336, 342, 490
Krause, Karl Christian Friedrich 307, 490
Kristeva, Julia 381, 490
Kropotkin, Peter 316–18, 328, 490
kshatravidya (क्षत्रविद्य) 103, 446
Kshatriya 27, 31–2, 73, 104–5, 446
kufr (كفر) 133, 446
Kūkai 143–4, 490
Kumarpal 151, 490
Kumazawa Banzan 223–4, 491
kung-fu (功夫) 217, 446
Kurukan Fuga *see* Kouroukan Fougan

laissez-faire 79, 247, 446–7
Lastarria, José Victorino 307, 491
law 18, 44, 55, 64, 67, 72, 73, 77–8, 81–6, 89, 93, 96–8, 100–101, 105, 109, 117–19, 122–5, 129–33, 140, 152, 165–7, 174, 184, 186–7, 191–2, 195–8, 203, 213, 219–20, 224–5, 237, 239–40, 242, 245, 247–50, 252, 254, 271–3, 275, 278–9, 281, 288, 300, 305, 315, 317, 326, 332, 334, 344, 347, 352, 388–90, 435–8, 447–9, 452, 456, 464, 467–8, 470, 474, 478, 491
Le dynasty 185, 491
Le Thanh Tong 185, 491
Lebensraum 349, 447 *see also* Spazio vitale
Legalists 74, 77–8, 102, 124–6, 141, 190, 460, 500 *see also* Fǎjiā
Lee Kuan Yew 390, 491
Lee Yo 218, 49
Leibniz, Gottfried Wilhelm 246, 491
Lenin, Vladimir 323–6, 358, 491
Leucippus 36, 491
Levellers 225, 229, 436, 447
li (里) 110, 447
li (理) 113, 135, 156–7, 164–5, 209–11, 213, 230, 232, 234–5, 391, 447

li (禮) 5, 34–5, 45, 156–7, 164, 233, 447
Li Dazhao 328, 491
Li Gong 233–4, 491
Li Shizeng 320, 491
Li Ssu 56, 77, 491
Li Zhi 222–3, 226, 491
Liang Qichao 303, 491
liángzhi (致良知) 211, 217, 447 *see also* good
Liberales 276–7, 447
liberalism 263, 273–9, 284–309, 317, 327, 354, 392–3, 447
Liberation Theory 359–60, 447
lichtung 379, 447
Liji 437, 440, 447
Limantour, José Yves 308, 491
Lin Jīng *see* Chun Qiu
linguistic contextualism 6, 447
List, Guido von 349, 491
Literati 9, 51, 61, 65, 70, 77–80, 84, 88–9, 93–6, 98–102, 110–15, 123–9, 134–5, 138, 140–41, 143–4, 146, 148–9, 155–9, 162–4, 167, 173, 176, 179, 182–5, 189–90, 195, 204, 207–10, 214–16, 230–35, 237, 245–6, 248, 250, 267–9, 273, 286–7, 302, 304, 326–7, 390–3, 447 *see also* Confucianism, Ru
Liu An 93–4, 491
Liu Jianqun 331, 492
Liu Shifu 320, 492
Liu Shipei 320, 492
liùyi (六藝) 233, 448
liùzhèng (六正) 126, 448
Locke, John 18, 68, 229, 231, 238–44, 254–5, 370, 492
logical positivism 368, 370, 448
logos (λόγος) 36, 96, 448
Lokāyata *see* Cārvākā
Longmen Stone Statue Grotto 145, 492
Lotus Sutra 127, 135, 142, 144, 170, 173, 448, 457
L'Ouverture, Toussaint 260, 491
Lu Jiuyuan 165, 209, 211, 492
Lü Liuliang 233, 492
Lu Xun 328, 492
Luo Nian'an 217, 492
Luo Qinshun 218, 492

Luo Rufang 222, 492
Lusotropicalism 331, 448
Luther, Martin 212–13, 227, 492
Luxemburg, Rose 324–5, 492
Lý Tê Xuyên 179, 468, 492
Lý Thánh 162, 492
Lyotard, Jean-François 374, 492
Lysander 30, 492

Machiavelli, Niccolò 40, 76, 80, 175, 178, 180–81, 188–9, 193–4, 197–9, 206, 225, 492
madinah, al- (المدينة) 137, 448
Madison, James 258, 492
madrasa (مدرسة) 152, 448
magistrate 55, 133, 211, 214, 216, 261, 310, 444, 448
Mahajanapadas 26, 448
maharaja (महाराज) 27, 448
Mahāsāmghika 50, 69, 91–3, 109, 448–9
Mahāvaipulya Buddhāvatamsaka Sūtra 134, 449
Mahavira 31, 492
Māhāyāna 63–4, 91–2, 109, 141–2, 144–5, 449
Mahmud II 271, 493
Maistre, Joseph-Marie Comte de 262–3, 493
Maitreya Buddha 126, 135, 145, 168, 493
Majjhima Nikāya 49, 449
Malcolm X see X, Malcolm
Malebranche, Nicolas 246, 493
Mali Empire 177, 179, 191, 195, 446, 449, 452, 463, 477, 489, 495, 502
Mamluk 177–8, 186, 272, 449
mandate of heaven 62, 84, 89, 111, 145, 183, 216, 311, 464, 466 see also tiānmíng
Mandela, Nelson Rolihlahla 359, 493
Mandinka 190–91, 449
Manicheanism 119, 449
mansa 177, 191–2, 449 see also king
Manusmrti 82–3, 449
Mao Zedong 358, 377, 383, 391, 493
Marananta 127, 493
Marcuse, Herbert 374, 493
maripgan 125, 449 see also king, emperor

Marx, Karl 314–16, 320–21, 324, 327–8, 358, 368, 374, 493
Marxism 3, 16–17, 314–16, 321, 323–8, 351, 355, 359–60, 374–5, 377, 389
Mary Queen of Scots 228, 502
Matsushita Institute of Government and Management 369, 449
masses 20, 40, 98, 124, 139, 144, 153, 167, 169, 171, 174, 184, 194, 196, 203, 222, 294, 327, 332, 334, 340, 358, 362, 364, 436 see also demos
Maududi, Sayyid A'bul A'la 388–9, 493
Maurice, Frederick Denison 321, 493
Maurya, Ashoka 76, 493
Maurya, Chandragupta 74–6, 493
Mazzini, Giuseppe 307, 493
Meiji 300–302, 330, 346, 449
Meiji Restoration 300, 330, 449
Mein Kampf 349, 449
Meinvielle, Julio 331, 493
Mencius (person and text) 52–5, 57, 60–62, 66, 70–71, 80, 93–4, 157, 166–7, 211, 234, 236, 248, 311, 493, Mencius (text only) 450
Mendes, Raimundo Texeira 308, 493
merit and meritocracy 38–9, 54–5, 61–2, 79, 89, 129, 224, 236, 393, 507
Mernissi, Fatema 382, 493
metaphysics 1, 8–10, 20, 31, 42–4, 63, 78, 89, 91–121, 132, 134–8, 149, 154, 156–7, 164–7, 172, 174, 181, 189, 220, 229–31, 235, 244, 249–50, 266, 286–8, 350, 354–5, 370, 372, 374, 378, 380, 384, 391–4, 450
Meysenbug, Malwida von 333, 493
mihna (محنة) 138, 450
mikkyō (密教) 143, 450
Mill, Harriet Taylor 292, 493
Mill, James 275–6, 278, 281, 284, 493
Mill, John Stuart 17, 284, 289–90, 292, 294, 297, 299, 313, 368, 494
Millett, Kate 381, 494
Milton, John 225–6, 228, 494
Minamoto no Yoritomo 161, 494
Minponshugi 303, 450
minzoku (民族) 342, 355, 471 see also nation, volk
Mirabeau, Marquis de 247, 494
Mirandola, Giovanni Pico della 193, 494

Mito School 269, 450
Mohamad, Mahathir bin 390, 494
monarch and monarchy 26, 30, 32, 38–9, 59–61, 64–5, 77, 83, 85, 101, 126–7, 132, 136, 145, 159, 161, 166, 178, 182, 187, 190, 199, 203, 213–14, 225–6, 239, 245, 249–50, 257, 262, 265, 271, 276–7, 288, 303–4, 308, 364, 432, 434–5, 447, 450, 453, 457, 461, 473, 487, 497, 501 see also emperor, empress, king, queen, ruler
Mongkut 304, 494
Montagu, Mary Wortley 253–4, 494
Montesquieu 245, 254, 258, 280, 326, 494
Mora, José Maria Luis 278, 293–4, 494
moral force 42, 53, 55–6, 69, 89, 437 see also dé
morals and morality 8–9, 15, 25, 31, 38, 42, 44, 46, 65, 69–71, 73, 75–6, 80–81, 84–8, 89, 95, 96–7, 99, 104–5, 107, 112, 119, 124, 131, 137, 139, 142, 155, 161, 165, 166, 188–9, 194, 209, 212, 216–17, 227, 232–3, 235, 241, 246–51, 254, 265, 268–9, 273–4, 279–80, 286, 288, 291, 298–9, 310, 312, 315, 322, 323, 331, 332, 345, 353, 355, 358, 360, 373, 375, 380, 384, 388, 392, 432, 433, 434, 436, 438, 443, 446, 447, 448, 452, 457, 460, 461, 467, 470, 498
Moreno, Gabriel Garcia 263, 307, 494
Morgan, Robin 381, 494
Morris, William 321, 494
Mosse, Albert 301, 494
Mossi 177, 494
Most, Johann Joseph "Hans" 317, 494
Motoori Norinaga 267–9, 281, 494
Mou Zongsan 391–2, 494
Mozi 53–4, 61, 68, 70, 222, 494
Mu 128, 495
mu (無) 335-336, 344 see also wu
mu no kyōchi (無の境地) 335, 450
Muhak 184, 495
Muhammad 131–2, 137–8, 147, 171, 177, 388, 495
Munjeong 184, 495
Muqaffa, Ibn al- 132, 495
Murasaki Shikibu 281, 495
Murata Harumi 269, 495

Muromachi Shōgunate 176, 495
Muryeong 128, 495
Musa 177, 495
Mūsā, Salāmah 322, 495
Muslim Brotherhood 386–8, 450, 477
Muso Soseki 162, 495
Mussolini, Benito 331, 347–9, 495
Mutazilite 133, 138, 450
Myeongjon 184, 495

Nakano Seigo 346, 495
Nāgārjuna 106–7, 135, 495
Nakae Chōmin 302–3, 495
Nakae Toju 223–4, 495
Nam Yeongkyung 218, 495
Namo Amitābhāya 167, 450
Nanda, Mahapadma 73–4, 495
Nanda dynasty 73–5, 495
Naoroji, Dadabhai 295, 297, 496
Nasser Hussein, Gamal Abdel 361, 364–5, 387, 496
nation and nationalism 144, 170, 175, 178, 182, 262–4, 268–9, 274, 277, 283, 289, 299–300, 303, 305–7, 309, 320, 326–7, 330–55, 362–6, 374, 385–6, 388, 390–91, 393 see also minzoku, volk
Nation of Islam 361, 389, 450
Natorp, Paul Gerhard 350, 496
Nazism 331–3, 339–40, 347–53, 385
Neglected Obligation 389, 450
négritude 359, 450
nembutsu (念佛) 169–71, 204, 450, 496 see also niàn fó
neo-Confucianism 149, 155, 157–8, 162, 166, 171, 173–7, 181–5, 190, 194, 208–16, 218, 221–3, 226–7, 229–35, 250, 267, 273–4, 336, 391, 451
neo-conservativism 367, 451
neo-liberalism 356–72, 374, 451
neo-Platonism 98–9, 102–3, 116–20, 132, 137, 147–8, 152–4, 173–4, 193, 220, 244, 266, 337, 383
neo-Tocquevillean 369, 451
New Confucianism 390–92, 451 see also Xīn Rújiā
New Culture Movement 292, 327–8, 390 see also Xin Wénhuà Yùndòng

New Texts 111, 287, 451 *see also* Old Texts
New Woman Association *see* Shin Fujin Kyōkai
Nguyên Thánh Thiên Cám 163, 496
niàn fó (念佛) 167, 452 *see also* nembutsu, yeombul, niêm phât
Nichiren 170–71, 173, 182, 204, 206–7, 229, 331, 347–8, 385, 496
Nichiren sect 170–71, 173, 182, 204, 206–7, 229, 331, 347–8, 385, 451
Nie Shuang Jiang 217, 496
niêm phât 167, 451 *see also* niàn fó
Nietzsche, Friedrich Wilhelm 15, 328, 330–37, 348, 353–4, 375, 496
nihilism 107, 183, 302, 332, 335–6, 373, 380, 452
Nihon Shoki 129, 452
Nippon-shugi 351, 452
Nirmānakāya 108, 452
Nishida Kitarō 334–7, 340–41, 343–4, 351, 496
Nishitani Keiji 336, 341–3, 496
niti (नीति) 150, 452
Nitivakyamrtam 150, 452
Nizam Al-Mulk 152–4, 172, 496
Nkrumah, Kwame 361, 365–6, 496
nomos physis (Νόμος φύσις) 72, 452
non-violence 357–61
normative 247, 367, 370–71, 386, 452
Northern and Southern Dynasties 111, 123, 496
Northern Wei 123, 496
Northern Zhou 101, 123, 496
nous (νοῦς) 117, 137, 430, 452
Novalis 264–5, 496
Nozick, Robert 370–71, 496
Nulji 125, 496
nyamakala 191, 452
Nyerere, Julius 366, 496
nyonin shōki (女人正機) 226, 452

Oda Nobunaga 206–7, 496
office and official 26, 28, 38, 55, 62, 74, 76, 78, 81–2, 84, 86–9, 95–6, 100, 114–15, 123, 125, 128–9, 133, 136, 140–44, 153–6, 159, 162, 164, 170, 177–8, 180–81, 183, 185, 187, 189–90, 196, 207–10, 214–15, 217, 222, 224, 231–3, 235, 259, 274, 286, 296–8, 301, 308, 310–11, 326–7, 362, 391, 434, 442, 444–5, 448–9, 457, 459, 461, 466–7, 469, 473, 483, 488–9, 492, 496–7, 501, 502, 504 *see also* advisor, bureaucracy, civil service
Ogyo yangjong (五教兩宗) 160, 452
Ogyū Sorai 235–7, 496
ōhō butsuhō izon (王法佛法依存) 203, 452
Ōkawa Shūmei 346, 496
Okin, Susan Moller 371, 496
Old Texts 111, 287, 452–3 *see also* New Texts
oligarchy 29–30, 62, 85, 190, 239, 435 *see also* aristocracy
One, the (τὸ ἕν) 116–18, 120, 171, 431, 453
Onin Rebellion 204–5, 453
Origen 118, 496–7
original position 370, 453 *see also* veil of ignorance
Ōshio Heihachirō 310–12, 328, 497
Osugi Sakae 318–19, 497
Ottoman Empire 178, 239, 253–4, 256, 271–2, 297–8, 497
Ouyang Xiu 156, 497
Owen, Robert 312–13, 328, 497
Ōyōmei 223, 299–300, 302–3, 346, 497

Padshah Begum 252, 453
Paine, Thomas 257, 497
Pali Canon 45, 64, 82, 453
Panaetius 86, 89, 497
Park Yeol 319, 497
Parmenides of Elea 36, 497
parrhesia (παρρησία) 71, 453
Pasha, Mohammed Ali 271, 445, 497
paticcasamuppada (प्रतीत्यसमुत्पाद) 32, 453 *see also* dependent origination/arising
peace and peaceful 29, 35, 76–7, 93, 104–5, 109, 115, 119–20, 124, 162, 170, 177, 184, 187–8, 204, 209, 220, 222, 321, 327, 357, 359, 362
Pedro II 308, 497
Peloponnesian War 26, 29, 453
people, 39, 53, 61–2, 73, 78–9, 86, 88–9, 94–5, 110, 113, 115–16, 130, 139, 156, 165–6, 168–71, 175, 183, 191,

194, 197–8, 205–6, 211, 213, 216, 221–6, 240–42, 258–64, 268, 271–2, 275, 278, 285, 291, 296, 302–3, 305, 309, 311–12, 314, 322, 326–7, 340, 347, 358, 390, 450; definition of 453 *see also* demos, masses, popular
Peralta, José 307, 497
performative 381, 447, 453
permanent revolution 324, 358, 389, 453
Petrarch 180, 193, 465, 497
petty 35, 40–41, 470 *see also* xiǎorén
phenomenology 335, 338, 453–4
Philo of Alexandria 118, 497
philology 231–2, 267, 275–6, 454
phronēsis (φρόνησις) 58, 67, 238, 454
physei doulos (φύσει δοῦλος) 62, 454
physiocrats 247, 454
physis (φύσις) 96, 454
piety 8, 37, 43, 65, 71, 147, 186–7, 455
Pizan, Christine de 198, 497
Plato 18, 40–41, 45–6, 48, 51, 58–60, 62–3, 66–8, 70–71, 85, 90, 116–18, 132–3, 147, 154, 171, 192–3, 348, 368, 379
Plotinus 102, 116–17, 138, 153, 193, 497
pneuma (πεῦμα) 96, 454
polis (πόλις) 87, 117, 373, 445, 448, 454
political animal 67, 454
political power 17, 59, 63, 66–9, 75, 98, 127, 132–3, 144, 146, 168, 171, 175, 181, 188, 207, 272, 275, 312, 326
politikos (πολιτικός) 4, 454
ponos (πονος) 72, 454
poor (poverty) 39–40, 64–5, 86, 88, 184, 195, 220, 224, 246, 257, 308, 310–11, 314, 319, 322, 360, 363, 376, 382, 436
Popper, Karl Raimund 367–9, 497
Pŏpsŏng *see* Beopseong
popular 30, 33, 62, 68, 85, 98, 103, 107, 109, 111, 119, 123, 133, 136, 138, 139, 149, 153, 157, 162, 167–8, 173, 181, 184, 188, 194, 197, 199, 203, 205, 208, 212–14, 218, 221–6, 229, 257, 261, 267, 269, 274, 290, 302, 306, 320, 321, 347, 359, 363, 367, 436, 447, 450, 453 *see also* demos, masses, people

Porphyry 116–17, 497
positivism 298, 307–8, 333, 368, 370, 448, 454
post-colonialism 365, 369, 375, 454
postmodernism 354, 373–84, 454
post-structuralism 374–84, 454–5
pragmatic and pragmatism, 58, 60, 67, 76, 218, 235, 240, 273, 300, 327, 346, 384, 466
prajñā (प्रज्ञ) 33, 143, 160, 443, 455
Prasenjit 26, 28, 497
Princeps 81, 455
principle 36, 44, 75, 82, 96, 113–14, 116, 143, 154, 155, 157–8, 164–6, 180, 209–12, 218, 220, 222, 224, 230, 232–5, 237, 248, 265, 267, 272, 281, 290, 298–9, 306, 322, 326, 338, 370–72, 386, 433, 437, 440, 446, 447, 451, 507 *see also* li (理)
principle of charity 1, 15–18, 455
Proclus 118, 497–8
proletariat 315–16, 321, 323–4, 436, 455
propaganda of the deed 317, 455
property 39, 140, 194–5, 214, 219, 238–40, 247, 249, 254, 257, 278, 315–16, 347, 368, 371, 398, 433, 454–5, 498
Protestants 213–14, 219, 227, 229, 240, 259, 279, 289, 293, 362, 368, 385–6, 455
Proudhon, Pierre-Joseph 316, 498
providence 85, 87, 96, 103, 119, 166, 181, 188, 455
providentia 96, 103, 455 *see also* providence
psyche (ψυχή) 117, 357, 455
Pudgalavāda 92, 107, 455
punishment 54, 56, 60, 65, 68, 77–8, 80, 83–4, 105–6, 124, 129, 184, 186, 192, 239, 310, 325, 376 *see also* danda
Pure Land 108, 135, 140, 167–70, 173, 184, 208, 226, 455
Pythagoras of Samos 36, 58, 498

qi (氣) 112–13, 157, 164–6, 209–10, 218, 232, 234, 455
Qi state 29, 51
Qin dynasty 73–5, 451, 498
Qin Shi Huang 498

Qing dynasty 209, 226–7, 231, 303, 318, 327, 443, 498
qīng tán (清談) 114, 455
qiyas (قياس) 133, 455
Quakers 213, 224, 228–9, 455
queen 41, 89, 102, 144–6, 163, 184, 228, 252, 277, 462, 468, 477, 485–8, 495–6, 500, 502–3 *see also* empress, king, ruler
Queen Mother of the West *see* Xiwangmu
Quesnay, Francois 247–8, 498
Quôc Hoc Vien 185, 498
Quôc Tír Giám 162, 498
Quran 131–2, 147, 153, 443, 455
Qushayri, Al- 153, 498
Qutb, Sayyid 387, 389, 498
Qutb al-Dīn Aibak 498

race 284–5, 291–6, 305, 333, 342–3, 347, 354–5, 361, 372, 461
racism 285, 293–4, 296, 309, 317, 333, 349, 355, 359, 389, 438, 456
Raghuvamsha 456
Rahman, Aisha Abd al- 382, 498
raja (राजा) 27, 105, 456
rajadharma (राजधर्म) 105, 456
rajavritta (राजावृत्तित्व) 104, 456
Ramirez, Ignacio 308, 498
ran (亂) 456
Ranade, Mahadev Govind 296, 498
Rangaku 266–7, 456
Rashid, Harun al 132, 147, 498
Rashidan caliphs 131, 456
Rawls, John Bordley 356, 370–71, 498
realism 75–81
recht 249, 456
reconstruction 15–16, 179, 374, 376, 386
reflexivity 15–18, 456
Reform Act of 1832 275, 456
Reformation 212–14
regionalism 362–7
Reign of Terror *see* Terror, the
reikon (霊魂) 268, 456
reincarnation 31, 33, 45, 49
religion 2, 9–10, 12, 16–17, 42–5, 63, 96–148, 151–2, 154, 165, 181, 186–9, 196, 199, 203, 214, 216, 219–20, 225–6, 229–30, 240, 242, 259, 263, 265, 268, 279, 285–90, 299, 312–13, 323, 364, 384–90, 456
Religion of Humanity 288, 290, 308, 457
ren (仁) 5, 35, 45, 70, 79, 114, 164, 234, 287, 391, 457 *see also* good
Renaissance 181–9
Rennyo 204–6, 226–8, 498
republicanism 26–8, 32, 38–9, 50, 59, 81, 85, 194, 197, 214, 224–5, 228–9, 256–7, 271, 292, 307–8, 384, 390, 457
revisionism 320–23, 325, 457
Revive China Society 303, 327, 457
Rickert, Heinrich John 350, 499
Risshō Kōsei Kai 385, 457
ritual 5, 18, 25, 28–9, 32, 34–5, 43–4, 46, 53–4, 62, 69, 71, 89, 95–6, 98, 110–11, 114, 118, 127, 140, 143–4, 159–61, 171, 177, 187, 192, 218, 233, 267, 273, 311, 391, 447
Rodrigues, Olinde 313, 499
Roman Catholic Church *see* Catholic Church
romanticism 256–83, 289, 303, 307, 332, 457
rōnin (浪人) 223, 235, 457
Rosas, Juan Manuel de 278, 499
Rosenberg, Alfred Ernst 349, 499
Rousseau, Jean Jacques 17, 68, 258–60, 263, 266, 282, 298, 357, 375, 499
Roy, Manabendra Nath 325–6, 358, 499
Roy, Raja Rammohan 270, 280, 286, 499
Ru (儒) 51–2, 54–6, 60–61, 65, 69–70, 111 *see also* Confucianism; Literati
Rujing 162, 499
ruler viii, 8–9, 17, 27–8, 35, 37, 42, 51, 53, 56, 59–69, 73–4, 76–84, 86, 88–9, 94–5, 98, 100, 103, 105–6, 108–11, 115, 119, 123–5, 130–31, 133, 135–8, 144–7, 151–2, 155–6, 161–2, 164–7, 174–5, 182, 185–7, 189–92, 194, 196, 208, 214, 216, 225, 228, 233, 236, 239, 241–3, 250–52, 258, 260, 270–73, 279, 288, 298, 365, 434–5, 440, 445–6, 448, 449, 468–9, 471, 474, 477–8, 482, 488, 491, 493, 497, 500–501, 506, 508 *see also* emperor, empress, king, queen, monarch

rūpakāya (रूपकय) 109, 457
Rushd, ibn 136, 154, 171, 174, 192, 499
Ruskin, John 321, 499

Sabi 127, 499
Saddharmapundarīka Sūtra *see* Lotus Sutra
Sáenz, Doña Manuela 280, 499
Sage 42, 59, 66, 71, 78, 89, 112–14, 156, 166–7, 287, 311, 457 *see also* shèngrén
Sahoo, Sarojini 382, 499
sahwa (士禍) 190, 457
Saichō 141–3, 499
Saigō Takamori 302–3, 346, 499
Saint-Simon, Henri de 312–13, 328, 499
Saishūsensō 348, 457
Sakamoto Ryoma 300, 499
Sakuma Shōzan 274, 499
Salafism 458
Salazar, Antónion de Oliveira 331, 499
Salomé, Lou 333, 499
samadhi (समाधी) 160, 443, 458
sambhogakāya (सम्भोगकाय) 108–9, 458
Samguk Sagi 128, 458
Samguk Yusa 126, 128, 458
Sammitīya 92, 458
samrat (समराज्) 75, 458
samurai (侍) 161, 207, 215, 223–4, 227, 235, 251, 269, 300, 302, 310, 322, 458 *see also* bushi
Samyutta Nikāya 41, 458
San Gyō Kisho 130, 458
sanankunya 191, 458
sangha (सङ्घ) 27–8, 39, 48, 50–51, 82, 91–3, 126, 129–30, 160–62, 184, 385, 458
Sangō shiiki 143, 458
sānjiao (三教) 184, 222, 458
sankin kotai (参勤交代) 224, 459
Sanmínzhuyì 326, 459
Sānshī 126, 459
Sarim Faction 190, 459, 488
Sarmiento, Domingo Faustino 278, 282, 500
Sarvāstivāda 92, 107–9, 459
satyagraha (सत्याग्रह) 357, 459
Savarkar, Vinayak Damodar 307, 500
Sayyid, Ahmed Lutfi al- 299, 500

Schlegel, Friedrich 265, 500
Schmidt, Johann Kaspar 317, 500
Schmitt, Carl 353–4, 500
scholasticism 230–31, 278–9, 459
science 285–91
scientific socialism 314–16, 459, 467
Scipio Aemilianus 87, 500
sect 107, 110, 134–5, 140–45, 150, 157, 159–63, 167–73, 179, 184, 204–5, 207, 213, 219, 228–9, 268–71, 286, 313, 348, 363, 386, 459
Sejo 190, 500
Sejong 190, 500
Selassie, Haile 365, 500
Seneca 87, 500
Senghor, Léopold Sédar 358–9, 500
sengoku 203–8, 459 *see also* Warring States period
Senshindō 310–11, 459
Senshindō Sakki 311, 459
Seon 135–6, 158–60, 167–8, 184, 441–3, 452, 459, 466, 477–8, 481, 484, 488, 501 *see also* Chán
Seondeok 144, 500
Seong 127–8, 500
Sesok-ogye 126, 459
Seven Sages of the Bamboo Grove *see* zhúlín qīxián
Seventeen Article Constitution *see* Jūshichi Jō Kenpō
sex and sexuality 41, 68, 76, 119, 172–3, 223, 227, 253–4, 281, 313, 316, 322, 376–7, 381, 387
Shamen bu jingwangzhe lun 100, 460
Shang Yang 54–5, 57, 74, 77, 500
Shantaō 167, 500
Shari'a 131, 186, 242, 273, 388–90, 460
Shariati, Alo 389, 500
she (射) 233, 460
shèn (神) 110, 113, 460 *see also* spirit, kami, daemon, jinn
Shen Buhai 55, 500
Shen Dao 55, 57, 69, 500
shèngrén (聖人) 112, 460 *see also* Sage
shènming (神明) 113, 460
shènqi (神器) 113, 460
shènxian 110–11, 460
Shenxiu 136, 500
shì (勢) 55, 460
Shījīng 33–4, 460

Shin Fujin Kyōkai 292, 460
Shingon 135, 140–41, 143, 160–61, 168, 171, 204, 460
Shinran 169–70, 173, 204–5, 226–7, 430, 444, 500
Shinron 274, 460
Shintō 128, 171, 205, 235, 267–8, 346, 460 *see also* kami
shíti (實體) 233, 460
shíwén (實文) 233, 460
shíxíng (實行) 233, 460
shíyòng (實用) 233, 460
Shōgun 161, 207, 236, 274, 444, 460
Shōheikō 215, 500–501
Shōmu 139, 146, 501
Shōtoku, Prince 128–30, 146, 170, 501
shramana (श्रमण) 31, 82, 460
shravakas (श्रावक) 150, 460–61
shù (術) 55
shū (書) 233, 461
shù (數) 233, 461
Shū Jīng 461
Shudra 32, 73, 461
shugo 189, 461
Shùn 109, 167, 501
Shundao 101, 501
Siddha 461
Siddharaja 150, 461
Sidney, Algernon 226, 501
Sierra, Justo 308, 501
Sieyès, Emmanuel Joseph 260, 501
Silla dynasty 101, 125–8, 134, 136, 144, 158, 168, 501
Sima Guang 155, 471, 501
Sina, ibn 136, 151–3, 173, 501
Sinhaeng 136, 501
Sitātapatrā 161, 461
Six Arts *see* liùyi
Six Classics *see* liùjing
Six Ways of Government Service *see* liùzhèng
Siyar al-Muluk 152, 172, 461
Siyasat al-madina 241, 461
skandhas (स्कन्ध) 92, 107, 461
skill 34, 36–7, 44, 55–6, 63–4, 69–70, 105, 119, 150, 173, 189, 192, 194, 252–3, 261, 272, 289, 338, 435, 448, 454, 467–8
Smith, Adam 247–8, 372, 501

Social Darwinism 291, 294, 301, 303, 309, 352, 368, 461
socialism in one country 324, 461–2
Socrates 25–6, 29–30, 35–8, 40–46, 48, 56, 58–9, 62–3, 67, 69, 357, 379, 501
soft power 393, 462
Sokagakkai 385, 446, 462
sokushin jōbutsu (即身成佛) 142, 462
Somadeva 150, 501
Sombre, Joanna Nobilis 252, 501
Song dynasty 155, 158, 160, 162–4, 182, 232, 501
Songgwangsa 160, 501
Songhai Empire 177, 501
sonnō jōi (尊皇攘夷) 274, 462
Sophists 36–7, 40, 58–9, 462
sophos kagathos (σοφός κἀγαθός) 66, 462
Sorel, Georges 331, 348, 501
Sosurim 101, 501
soul 66, 87, 96, 99, 103, 106, 116–19, 137–8, 150, 152, 154, 166, 171, 174, 209, 230, 259, 311, 431 *see also* hun, psyche
spazio vitale 348, 462
Spinoza, Baruch de 345–6, 501–2
spirit and spiritual 16, 31, 39, 43, 62, 72, 94, 97, 99, 102, 106, 110, 112–13, 118, 120, 122, 132, 134, 139, 153, 158, 162, 166, 173, 179, 188, 192, 206, 222, 224, 226, 236, 240–41, 243, 245, 253, 258, 265–8, 272, 274, 286–8, 344–5, 352–3, 357–8, 364, 387, 389, 392, 430, 431, 435, 438, 443, 444, 449, 454, 456, 460, 461, 462, 468, 469, 472, 492 *see also* daemon, jinn, kami, shen
Srīmālā 146, 502
Srīmālādevī Simhanāda sūtra 146, 462
Staël, Germaine de 280, 502
Stalin, Joseph 324–6, 502
State Preceptor 159–60, 162, 184, 440, 462 *see also* Guksa, Kokushi
statecraft 82, 273–4 *see also* jīng-shì
Stein, Lorenz von 301, 502
Sthaviravāda 50, 69, 91–2, 462–3
Stirner, Max 317, 502
Stoics 58–9, 63, 70, 84–90, 96, 98, 116, 463
store consciousness *see* alayavijñāna

Stowe, Harriet Elisabeth Beecher 293, 502
Stuart, Mary *see* Mary Queen of Scots
suffrage 281, 292–3, 456, 464
Sufism *see* Tasawwuf
Sui dynasty 129, 502
Suiko 128, 146, 501–2
Suleyman 177, 502
Sun Yat-sen 303, 326, 459, 502
Sundiata epic 179–80, 190–92, 463
Sundo *see* Shundao
Sunnah (سنة) 138, 463
sūnyatā (शून्यता) 106, 336, 463 *see also* emptiness
suppression of Buddhism 123, 181, 463
survival of the fittest 291, 463
Suzuki, Daisetz Teitaro 335–6, 502
Suzuki Shigetaka 336, 342, 502
Svētāmbara 150, 463
swadeshi (चुतेची) 357, 463
syndicalism 316–20, 463
Synesius 102–3, 502

Taeguksa 126, 463
taehak (太學) 101, 463
Tagore, Rabindranath 352–3, 502
Tahtawi, Rafi' Rifa'a al- 5, 271, 276, 299, 502
tàijí (太極) 156, 463
Tàijí túshuo (太極圖說) 156, 463
Taika 129, 463–4 Taishō Democracy 292, 345–6, 464
tàixū (太虛) 157, 311, 464
Tàizhōu School 222, 464
Taizong 124–5, 502
Takano no Niigasa 128, 502
takfir (تكفير) 243–4, 464
Tanabe Hajime 336–7, 343–5, 503
Tanaka Chigaku 347, 503
tanamannyonya 191–2, 464
Tang dynasty 124, 126, 128, 130, 134–5, 140, 143, 156, 158, 160, 163, 168, 503
Tang Junyi 391, 503
Tang lu shuyi 124, 464
Tanzimat 271, 464
tào (道) 34, 44, 54, 65, 69–70, 79, 94, 99, 110, 112–13, 116, 335–6, 464
Taoism 9, 15, 17, 34, 51, 53–7, 59, 61, 65–71, 77–80, 89, 93–5, 98–9, 109–12, 115, 117, 124, 129, 135, 139–40, 143, 145, 156–7, 173, 184, 194, 210, 222, 247–8, 267–8, 286–7, 320, 335–6, 464
Tarikh-i-Firuz Shahi 180, 464
tariki (他力) 169–70, 344, 464
Tasawwuf 153, 464
tawhīd (توحيد) 243, 464
taxes 56, 162, 209, 242, 247, 257, 310, 312, 368
telos (τέλος) 58, 67, 85, 464
Temple of Literature 162, 464
Tendai *see* Tiāntai
tendō (天道) 207, 216, 464
tenebrae 180, 465
tenmei (天命) 216, 311, 465
Tenmon 206, 465
Tenmon hokke no ran 206, 465
Tenmon hōnan 206, 465
Tennoki 129, 465
terauke seido (寺請制度) 216, 465
Terror, the 260, 262, 276
text 377, 465
textual criticism 44–6, 231–8
Theravāda 92–3, 431, 465
theurgy (θεουργία) 117–8, 441, 465, 487
Thiên 135, 158, 163, 167, 173, 465 *see also* Chán
Third World 382–3, 465
Thompson, William 281, 503
Thoreau, Henry David 266, 357, 361, 503
thought experiment 370, 453, 465–6
Three Principles of the People *see* Sanmínzhuyì
Three Scholarly Occupations 126, 459
Three Teachings *see* sānjiao
thrown/throwness *see* Geworfenheit
tiān (天) 34, 466 *see also* heaven
Tiān Gōng 111, 466
tiānming (天命) 216, 465, 466 *see also* mandate of heaven
tiānshī (天師) 110, 466
Tiāntai 108, 135, 159–61, 168, 466
Tilak, Bal Gangadhar 297, 503
Timur 178, 503
Timurid dynasty 178, 503
Tissa, Devanampiya 90, 503
Tocqueville, Alexis de 290, 503

Tōhōkai 347, 466
Tokugawa Ieyasu 207, 215, 503
Tokugawa Mitsukuni 269, 503
Tokugawa Nariaki 269, 503
Tokugawa Shōgunate 207–8, 214–16, 223–4, 226–7, 229, 236, 251, 266, 269, 274, 281, 300, 311, 503
Tokuichi 141–2, 503
tolerance 231, 238–44, 291, 379, 447, 477
Tolstoy, Leo 298–9, 322, 357, 361, 503
Tongdosa 126, 503
Tongzhi Restoration 303, 466
Tosaka, Jun 351, 503
Touré, Ahmed Sékou 366, 503
Tōyama Mitsuru] 346, 504
Toyotomi Hideyoshi 207, 215, 445, 504
Trân dynasty 163, 185, 504
Trân Hung Daō 163, 504
Trân Ming Tông 185, 504
Trân Nhân Tông 163, 504
Trân Thanh Tong 163, 504
transcendental 109, 249, 266, 378, 466
transcendentalism 266, 466
Trotsky, Leon 324–5, 328, 504
True Pure Land 170, 173, 181, 204–7, 226, 229, 344, 466
Truong Hán Siêu 185, 504
Tu Weiming 392, 504
Tuareg 177, 504
Tudor, Elizabeth *see* Elizabeth I
Tudor dynasty 219, 228, 504
Tuê Trung Thuong Sĩ 163, 504
Tufayl, Ibn 244–5, 504
Tughlaq, Firuz Shah 180, 504
Tughlaq dynasty 178, 186, 504
Tunisi, Khayr al-Din Al 272, 298, 504

übermensch 332, 348, 466
Uchida Ryōhei 346, 504
Uicheon 160, 504
uisa (義士) 184–5, 466
Ujamaa 366, 466–7
uji (氏) 128–9, 444, 467
ulama (علماء) 133, 153, 272, 297–8, 388, 390, 467
ultra-nationalism 329–55 *see also* nationalism
Umayyad Caliphate 131–2, 504
ummah (أمة) 131, 467

umran, al- (العمران) 192, 467
unity 28, 36–7, 74, 84, 96, 113, 116, 134, 159, 171, 188, 218–19, 257, 262, 276, 287, 292, 303, 306, 308, 326, 330, 339, 354, 360, 362–3, 265–7, 386, 438, 453, 460
universal suffrage 281, 292–3, 456, 464
Únzaga, Óscar 331, 504
Upanisads 9, 31, 467
upasaka (उपास क) 150, 467
Upasakadyayana 150, 467, 501
upaya-kaushalya (उपाय कौशल्य) 63, 467
utilitarianism 248, 275–8, 467, 477
utopian socialism 312–4, 459, 467

Vairocana Buddha 109, 139, 145, 492, 504–5
Vaishnavism 31, 99, 467
Vaishya 32, 61, 467
Vajrayana 467
Varela, Félix 279, 281, 505
varna (वर्ण) 31–2, 50, 467
Varona, Enrique José 307, 505
vāsana (वास ना) 108, 467
Vasubandhu 107–8, 135, 505
Vatsīputrīya 92, 468
vedic (वेदा) 26–7, 31–3, 45, 83, 95, 103, 468
veil of ignorance 370, 468
Velayat-e faqih 390, 468
verfallen 338–9, 468
Vibhajjavāda 92–3, 468
Vico, Giambattista 237, 255, 505
Victorian 290, 376, 432, 468
Viêt Diên U Linh Tâp 179, 468
vijñapti-matra (वज्ञिअपर्ति मात्र) 107, 468
Vimalakīrti 130, 144, 505
Vimalakīrti Sutra 130, 144, 468
vinaya (व नय) 39, 50, 69, 91, 127, 135, 449, 468
violence 31, 43, 65, 68, 80, 80, 104–5, 119, 150, 205, 225, 244, 258, 278, 306, 316, 331, 348, 357–61, 367, 372, 387, 430, 483, 496
virtû 194, 468
virtue 16, 35, 37, 42, 44, 54, 56, 67, 69, 93, 100, 111–12, 120, 126, 137, 164, 182–3, 185, 194, 220, 241, 248, 251,

257, 259, 261, 359, 372, 387, 393, 430, 437, 439, 450, 469 *see also* ethics
volk 340, 343–4, 349, 351, 355, 468, 471 *see also* minzoku, nation
volonté générale 259–60, 468–9

Wagner, Richard 349, 505
Wahhab, Muhammad ibn Abd-al 243–4, 505
Wahhabism (الوهابية) 243–4, 469
waka (和歌) 215, 267, 469
wāli (والي) 271, 469, 497
Walīullāh, Shah 231, 238, 241–4, 253, 255, 443, 505
Wan Simo 217, 505
Wang Bi 111–13, 164, 505
Wang Fuzhi 231–2, 505
Wang Gui 125, 505
Wang Longxi 221–2, 505
Wang Xinzhai 221–2, 505
Wang Yangming 203, 209–12, 215–18, 221–4, 226, 229, 231, 250, 268, 299–300, 310, 331, 346, 391–2, 505
Warring States period 55–6, 62, 70, 74, 79, 95, 109, 112, 203–8, 214, 216, 459
warrior backgrounds 25–30
Watsuji Tetsurō 337, 345, 351, 505
wealth and wealthy 27, 30, 38, 40, 49, 62, 64, 67, 75–7, 79, 86, 88, 124, 137, 140, 142, 163, 178, 192, 223, 225, 236, 237, 259, 261, 289, 308, 310–11, 313–14, 334, 357, 360, 362, 368, 370–71
Webb, Beatrice 321, 506
Webb, Sidney 321, 506
Weber, Max 334, 506
Wèi Yuán 273, 506
Wei Zheng 124–5, 506
Wen 93, 123, 506
Wen, Marquis of Wei 60, 506
wényánwén (文言文) 327, 469
wénziyù (文字獄) 469
Western Jin 471, 506
Wideok 127, 487, 506
will to power (der Wille zur Macht) 332–3, 348, 469
Winstanley, Gerard 225, 228–9, 506
wisdom 33, 37, 58, 67, 100, 103, 130, 132, 143, 161, 164, 182, 238, 241, 246, 254, 357, 432, 441, 446, 452, 454, 455, 461, 469 *see also* knowledge, prajñā, phronēsis
Wollstonecraft, Mary 279, 293, 506
women 20, 27, 30, 36–42, 53, 61–3, 81, 88–91, 95, 104, 126, 144–7, 167–75, 194–8, 205, 207, 222, 226–8, 231, 243, 251–6, 279–83, 285, 292–3, 301, 313, 315–18, 327, 333, 347, 376, 381–2, 389–90, 438, 452, 460, 475, 484, 486–7, 498, 506–8 *see also* feminism, gender
Won Gwang 126, 459, 506
Wonhyo 134, 159, 506
World spirit (Weltgeist) 288, 430, 469
wu 112–13 *see also* mu, wu wei
Wu 93, 506
wu (無) 469
wǔ cháng (五常) 126, 164, 469
wǔ jīng (五經) 469, 506
Wu Jing 124
wu jūn wu chen (無君無臣) 115, 469
wǔ shan shicha (五山十刹) 158, 469
wu wei (無為) 65–6, 70, 89, 117, 247, 469
Wu Yantong 163
Wu Zetian 145, 226, 482, 492, 506
Wu Zhihui 320, 506
wuji (無極) 156
Wycliffe, John 188, 212, 506

X, Malcolm 359, 361, 506
Xenophanes of Colophon 36, 506
Xenophon 46, 61, 506
Xi Kang 114–15, 507
xiān rén (仙人) 110, 469
Xianbei 507
Xiànchéng 217, 221, 469
Xiang Xiu 114, 507
xiào (孝) *see* filial piety
xiǎorén (小者) 40, 470 *see also* petty
Ximen Bao 57, 60, 507
xīn (心) 209, 217, 462, 470
Xīn Rújiā (新儒家) 390, 470
Xin Wénhuà Yùndòng 292, 327–8, 390, 470
xing (性) 55, 70, 84, 112
Xiong Shili 391–2, 507
Xiūzhèng 217, 470
Xiwangmu 111, 507
Xu Fuguan 391, 507

xuántóng (玄同) 115–16, 470
Xuánxué 111–14, 156, 164, 470 see also "dark learning"
Xuanzong 139–40, 476, 507
Xunzi 55–7, 62, 70–71, 77, 93–4, 507

Yamaga Sokō 235, 507
Yamashita Etsuko 382, 507
Yan Yuan 233, 507
Yang 123, 507
Yang Jian 123, 507
Yang Yuhuan 140, 507
Yang Zhu 53, 507
Yángwù 274, 470
Yek Kalameh 272, 470
Yeombul (念佛) 167, 184, 452
Yeonsan 190, 507
yí (儀) 34, 470
yì (義) 34, 71, 79, 114, 159, 164, 234, 311, 469, 470
yì (意) 217, 470
Yi Hwang 190, 218, 507
Yi I 190, 508
Yi Saek 176, 183, 508
Yi Seonggye 184, 508
Yijing 111–12, 156–7, 470
Yin, Duke 29, 508
Yin-Yang 79, 89–90, 93, 129, 470
Yogacara 107–8, 135, 141, 143, 470–71
Yokoi Shōnan 274, 508
Yomei 128, 508
Yongzheng 233, 508
Yoshida Shōin 300, 508
Yoshino Sakuzō 303, 350, 508
You Zi 52–4, 508
Youyang Nanye 217, 508
yù (禦) 233, 471
Yù Dì see Yù Huáng
Yù Huáng 110–11, 508
Yudhishthira 104–6, 508
yuè (樂) 233, 471

Zapata, Emiliano 318, 508
Zaydan, Jurji 363, 508
Zeenat-un-Nissa 252, 508
Zen 160–62, 181, 204, 214–15, 221, 335–6, 342, 353, 434, 440, 471, 481, 488, 495, 499 see also Chán
Zeng Guofan 273–4, 508
Zeno of Citium 58, 70, 84, 90, 463, 508
zettai mu (絕對無) 335–7, 344–5, 471
Zhàn Guó see Warring States period
Zhang Heng 110, 508
Zhang Ling 110, 509
Zhang Lu 110, 509
Zhang Renjie 320, 509
Zhang Xuexcheng 234, 509
Zhaung Zi 53–4, 509
Zheng Zi 52–3, 509
Zhenguàn Zhèngyào 124, 471
Zhenguàn Zhi Zhì 124, 471
zhi xing heyi (知行合一) 211, 471
zhōng (忠) 216, 471
zhòng chén (重臣) 124, 471
Zhōu 28–9, 33–5, 52, 54, 69, 74, 101, 123, 233, 471
Zhou Dunyi 156–7, 164, 463, 509
Zhouyi 217, 471
Zhu Xi 17, 149, 162, 164–7, 174, 176, 183, 209–11, 215, 217–18, 223, 232–5, 336, 391, 509
Zhu Yuanzhang 208, 509
Zhúlín qixián 114, 471
Ziauddin Barani 178, 180, 186, 509
Zia-ul-Haq, Muhammad 388, 509
Zigong 51, 60, 509
ziqiáng (自強) 274, 471
zirán (自然) 113–4, 471
Zixia 51, 57, 60, 70, 79, 509
Zizhi tongjian 155, 471
Zizi 157, 509
zoku (族) 471
Zoroastrianism 132, 472